Seventh Edition

LEGAL TERMINOLOGY

Kent D. Kauffman, J.D.
Member of the Indiana Bar
Associate Professor of Business Law,
Purdue University Fort Wayne, Fort Wayne, Indiana

Gordon W. Brown, J.D.
Member of the Massachusetts and Federal Bars
Professor Emeritus,
North Shore Community College, Danvers, Massachusetts

330 Hudson Street, NY NY 10013

Vice President, Portfolio Management: Andrew Gilfillan
Portfolio Manager: Gary Bauer
Editorial Assistant: Lynda Cramer
Field Marketing Manager: Bob Nisbet
Product Marketing Manager: Heather Taylor
Director, Digital Studio and Content Production: Brian Hyland
Managing Producer: Jennifer Sargunar
Content Producer: Rinki Kaur
Manager, Rights Management: Johanna Burke
Operations Specialist: Deidra Smith
Creative Digital Lead: Mary Siener

Managing Producer, Digital Studio: Autumn Benson
Content Producer, Digital Studio: Maura Barclay
Full-Service Project Manager: Ranjith Rajaram
Full-Service Project Management and Composition: Integra
 Software Services Pvt. Ltd.
Cover Designer: Studio Montage
Cover Art (or Cover Photo): Alexander Kirch/Shutterstock
Printer/Binder: LSC Communications, Inc.
Cover Printer: Phoenix Color/Hagerstown
Text Font: Times LT Pro 10/12

Library of Congress Cataloging-in-Publication Data

Names: Brown, Gordon W., 1928- author. | Kauffman, Kent D., author.
Title: Legal terminology / Kent D. Kauffman, J.D., member of the Indiana Bar, Associate Professor of
  Business Law, Purdue University Fort Wayne, Fort Wayne, Indiana; Gordon W. Brown, J.D., Member of
  the Massachusetts and Federal bars, Professor Emeritus, North Shore Community College, Danvers, Massachusetts.
Description: Seventh edition. | Upper Saddle River, N.J. : Pearson, [2019] | Includes index.
Identifiers: LCCN 2017029102 | ISBN 9780134849225 | ISBN 0134849221
Subjects: LCSH: Law—United States—Terminology. | LCGFT: Textbooks.
Classification: LCC KF156 .B725 2019 | DDC 349.7301/4—dc23
  LC record available at https://lccn.loc.gov/

2017029102

15 2025

ISBN 10:   0-13-484922-1
ISBN 13: 978-0-13484922-5

This is dedicated to my wife, Karen, and my son, Reagan. Karen, your radiant spirit refreshes me every day, and without your encouragement I would never have the privilege to have my name on this book's cover. Reagan, no earthly honor could ever make me more proud and no adventure could be more rewarding than being your father.

Kent D. Kauffman

For the 30 years that I taught full time at North Shore Community College, practiced law part time, and wrote textbooks such as this, I have many people to thank. Among them are talented people in the fields of education, publishing, and law. The ones who bore the burden of my efforts, however, are my wife, Jane, for her never-ending support and encouragement, and my children, Steven, Matthew, Deborah, Jennifer, Timothy, and David. They grew to be outstanding people even without my being with them during many of their growing-up activities because of my strong work ethic. It is to these wonderful family members that this book is dedicated with many thanks and much love.

Gordon W. Brown

CONTENTS

PREFACE

Legal Terminology, Seventh Edition has been revised to improve accuracy and currency. This text is designed to develop your understanding of legal terms in concert with their usage in the legal field. Emphasis is placed on learning terms in context through the study of law itself and on using legal terminology in many different ways, rather than relying on rote memorization of terms. The short easy-to-understand chapters are written in a lively manner to hold your attention and engage your interest in the law.

NEW TO THIS EDITION

- Major revisions and updates to the primary legal authority or legal doctrines presented in every chapter.
- "Learning Objectives" are now included and begin each chapter.
- More legal citations added to existing statutes and case law throughout the text.
- New chapter on the Uniform Commercial Code.
- New "Terms in Action" added throughout the chapters.
- New "Web Wise" features throughout the chapters.
- New material on e-Contracts and cyber law.
- New additions to the Glossary, including over 20 new terms with definitions.
- Updated Instructor's Materials, including a new test bank.

INSTRUCTOR SUPPLEMENTS

Instructor's Manual with Test Bank. Includes content outlines for classroom discussion, teaching suggestions, and answers to selected end-of-chapter questions from the text. This also contains a Word document version of the test bank.

TestGen. This computerized test generation system gives you maximum flexibility in creating and administering tests on paper, electronically, or online. It provides state-of-the-art features for viewing and editing test bank questions, dragging a selected question into a test you are creating, and printing sleek, formatted tests in a variety of layouts. Select test items from test banks included with TestGen for quick test creation, or write your own questions from scratch. TestGen's random generator provides the option to display different text or calculated number values each time questions are used.

PowerPoint Presentations. Our presentations are clear and straightforward. Photos, illustrations, charts, and tables from the book are included in the presentations when applicable.

To access supplementary materials online, instructors need to request an instructor access code. Go to **www.pearsonhighered.com/irc**, where you can register for an instructor access code. Within 48 hours after registering, you will receive a confirming e-mail, including an instructor access code. Once you have received your code, go to the site and log on for full instructions on downloading the materials you wish to use.

ALTERNATE VERSIONS

eBooks. This text is also available in multiple eBook formats. These are an exciting new choice for students looking to save money. As an alternative to purchasing the printed textbook, students can purchase an electronic version of the same content. With an eTextbook, students can search the text, make notes online, print out reading assignments that incorporate lecture notes, and bookmark important passages for later review. For more information, visit your favorite online eBook reseller or visit www.mypearsonstore.com.

ACKNOWLEDGMENTS

Special thanks to the following reviewers who provided excellent technical and practical suggestions for improvement and readability for the new edition:

Christy Powers, *St. Petersburg College*

Carol Rosborough, *Houston Community College*

Trinette Zarran, *Miami Dade College*

We would also like to express our gratitude to the reviewers of the previous edition:
Brian Craig, Globe University/Minnesota School of Business; Cathy Underwood, Pulaski Technical College; Pam Cummings, Minnesota State Community and Technical College; Leslie Ratliff, Griffin Technical College; Paula Witt, Houston Community College; Linda Cupick, Daytona Beach Community College; Jody L. Cooper, Blackhawk Technical College; and Claudine Dulaney, International Institute of the Americas.

We would also like to thank the following survey respondents who helped us to refine the coverage of the textbook:

Joseph Kline, *South Plains College*

Barry Puett, *State College of Florida, Manatee-Sarasota*

Linda Wenn, *Central Community College*

Susan Balman, *Butler Community College*

Jerrold Fleisher, *Suny Rockland Community College*

Cathy Carruthers, *Lewis & Clark Community College*

Glenda Hanson, *Renton Technical College*

Teresa Harbacheck, *College of Western Idaho*

Gwendolyn Pope, *J. F. Drake State Technical College*

Sabrina Swann, *Central Georgia Technical College*

Diana Yohe, *Bristol Community College*

William Yenna, *Kingsborough Community College*

Jody Cooper, *Blackhawk Technical College*

Joyce Zweedyk, *Kalamazoo Valley Community College*

Bob Loomis, *Spokane Community College*

Larena Grieshaber, *Independence Community College*

Karin Kelley, *Bates Technical College*

Sharolyn Sayers, *Milwaukee Area Technical College*

Kim Phifer-Starks, *Mississippi Gulf Coast Community College*

Thea Hosselrode, *Allegany College of Maryland*

Georganne Copeland, *Centralia College*

Marilyn Wudarcki, *North Idaho College*

Betty Lambert, *Des Moines Area Community College*

Sonya Rambo, *West Kentucky Community & Technical College*

Toni Clough, *Umpqua Community College*

Gloria Bailey, *Atlantic Technical Center*

Crystal Sullivan, *Umpqua Community College*

Elizabeth Snodgrass, *Mountain Empire Community College*

Crystal Price, *Alvin Community College*

Douglas Rogers, *Jefferson State Community College*

Carolyn Sharpe, *Cleveland Community College*

Mary Balmages, *Cerritos College*

Amy Wilson, *Zane State College*

Lori Asante, *Cincinnati State Technical and Community College*

Maxine Boggy, *Atlantic Technical Center*

Marissa Wawrzyniak, *Brevard Community College*

Our hope is that this book will provide to instructors a clear roadmap for navigating the courses for which this book is used, and to the students a treasure chest of terms and principles that will assist you throughout your legal courses and into your careers.

ABOUT THE AUTHORS

Kent D. Kauffman is Associate Professor of Business Law at Purdue University Fort Wayne (formerly called Indiana University Purdue University-Fort Wayne), in Fort Wayne, Indiana. He is licensed to practice law in Indiana and is certified as a mediator in Indiana. He is a summa cum laude graduate of Temple University and a graduate of The Dickinson School of Law of the Pennsylvania State University. For 15 years, Professor Kauffman was the Chair of the Paralegal Studies Department at Ivy Tech Community College in Fort Wayne, Indiana.

Professor Kauffman is the author of various academic journal articles and other books, including *Legal Ethics*, in its third edition and published by Delmar Cengage Learning. He is a multiple recipient of Who's Who in American Education® and Who's Who in American Law®. Professor Kauffman is the recipient of various teaching awards, including being inducted into the Indiana University Faculty Academy on Excellence in Teaching (FACET), as well as being awarded on multiple occasions as Professor of the Year by Delta Sigma Pi, his university's co-educational business fraternity.

Gordon W. Brown, is a Professor Emeritus of North Shore Community College, Danvers, Massachusetts, where he taught for 30 years. He also taught for two years at Pepperell High School, Pepperell, Massachusetts, and for six years at Endicott College in Beverly, Massachusetts.

In addition to writing the first five editions of this book, Professor Brown is the author of the first three editions of *Administration of Wills, Trusts, and Estates* published by Delmar Cengage Learning. Over a 30-year period, he co-authored eight editions of *Understanding Business & Personal Law* and seven editions of *Business Law with UCC Applications*, published by McGraw-Hill.

In 1998, Professor Brown was awarded the Outstanding Educator Award from his alma mater, Salem State University. He received his law degree from Suffolk University and practiced law part time while teaching full time. He is a retired member of the Massachusetts and federal Bars.

Terms Used in Practice and Procedure

Inga Ivanova/Shutterstock

Whether you work as a court reporter, an office technician, a paralegal, or a business executive, knowledge of the procedures involved in taking a case to court is important. Indeed, people outside of the legal field also have an interest in court procedure, stemming either from their own personal experiences or from reading about trials and watching them in movies and on television. After differentiating between the federal and state court systems, Chapter 1 examines the subject of selecting the court, including the matters of jurisdiction and venue. This chapter also explores alternative dispute resolution mechanisms available for those who wish to settle disputes outside the traditional court system of litigation. Chapter 2 explains criminal trial procedure, beginning with the arrest, preliminary hearing, indictment, and arraignment, followed by sentencing and defendants' rights. Chapter 3 discusses civil trial procedure including court selection, pleadings, service of process, and attachments. Chapter 4 explains defensive pleadings including the demurrer, five commonly used motions, the defendant's answer, the counterclaim, the cross-claim, and the cross-complaint. Methods of discovery, including interrogatories, and depositions, are examined in Chapter 5. The process of impaneling the jury, including the examination and challenging of jurors, is explained in Chapter 6, and the steps in a trial are outlined in Chapter 7. Finally, Chapter 8 discusses how legal ethics rules affect the professional behavior of lawyers and their nonlawyer employees.

1

Court Systems and Jurisdiction

ANTE INTERROGATORY

(literally means "the before question" and is a sneak preview of the chapter)

The power of a court to review a lower court's decision is called (A) original jurisdiction, (B) in rem jurisdiction, (C) exclusive jurisdiction, or (D) appellate jurisdiction.

LEARNING OBJECTIVES

LO 1: Describe the federal court system

LO 2: Explain when the U.S. supreme court takes cases for review

LO 3: Distinguish the three types of courts in the state court system

LO 4: Define jurisdiction and categorize the types of jurisdiction

LO 5: Contrast an in personam action from an in rem action

LO 6: Explain how jurisdiction is different from venue

LO 7: Compare and contrast negotiation, mediation and arbitration

KEY TERMS

admiralty

alternative dispute resolution (ADR)

appeal

appellate courts

appellate jurisdiction

arbitration

arbitrator

arbitrator's award

binding arbitration

caucus

cert. den.

change of venue

circuits

code

compulsory arbitration

conciliation

conciliator

concurrent jurisdiction

court

courts of appeal

diversity of citizenship

exclusive jurisdiction

federal district courts

federal question

forum non conveniens

in personam action

in personam jurisdiction

in rem action	nonbinding arbitration
jurisdiction	ordinance
justice	original jurisdiction
local action	plenary jurisdiction
long-arm statutes	quasi in rem action
mandatory arbitration	res
maritime	statute
mediation	transitory action
mediator	venue
mini-trial	writ of certiorari
negotiation	

WEBSITES FOR PRONUNCIATION HELP

http://dictionary.cambridge.org/us/pronunciation/english/audio

https://www.howtopronounce.com

A **court** is a body of government organized to administer justice. There are two court systems in the United States—the federal court system and the state court systems.

FEDERAL COURTS

The federal court system, established by Article III of the U.S. Constitution, includes the U.S. district courts, the U.S. courts of appeals, and the U.S. Supreme Court. Those courts hear cases that raise a **federal question**—a matter that involves the U.S. Constitution, acts of Congress, or treason. Federal courts also decide cases that involve **diversity of citizenship**—a term used to describe cases between persons from different states, between citizens of the United States and a foreign government, and between citizens of the United States and citizens of a foreign country. Diversity cases must exceed the sum of $75,000. In addition, federal courts hear bankruptcy cases, patent and copyright cases, and **admiralty** or **maritime** cases—those pertaining to the sea.

U.S. District Courts

There are 94 U.S. district courts in the federal court system and they are the trial courts. Each state and federal territory (Puerto Rico, for example) and the District of Columbia have at least one U.S. district court within its boundary. These courts are also called **federal district courts**, and there are both civil and criminal district courts.

> **Sources of Law**
>
> There are five principal sources of law in the United States:
>
> 1. Federal and state constitutions
> 2. English common law
> 3. Federal and state **statutes** (and **ordinances**, which are laws passed by local or municipal legislative bodies)
> 4. Court decisions (when made by appellate courts, they are also called "common law," but not "English common law")
> 5. Administrative regulations
>
> The federal government and many state governments consolidate, or otherwise codify, their statutes, administrative regulations, and other laws into a systematic collection called a **code**. The

(Continued)

> United States Code (the U.S.C.) and the California Civil Code are examples. Legislative codes, like the U.S.C., are similar in structure to administrative codes, like the Code of Federal Regulations (the C.F.R.), but their sources are different. Legislative codes are created by legislatures, while administrative codes are created by administrative agencies, sometimes called bureaucracies.

U.S. Courts of Appeals

The United States is divided into 13 judicial **circuits**. Eleven of the federal circuits are regional and numbered. There is also a D.C. Circuit for the District of Columbia, and a circuit for specialized federal cases, like patent cases, called the Federal Circuit. With exception for the Federal Circuit, which only has a court of appeals and whose jurisdiction is based on subject matter rather than geography, each circuit has at least one U.S. district court and its corresponding circuit court of appeals. U.S. circuit courts of appeals decide cases that have been appealed from their respective federal district courts. A group of three judges decides most cases that are appealed to a Federal Circuit of appeals court. For example, the 7th Circuit hears federal cases from a total of seven districts in Illinois, Indiana and Wisconsin, and the 7th Circuit Court of Appeals is located in Chicago, IL.

> **Word Wise**
> *Different Meanings for "Court"*
>
> The court officer announced, "The court is now in session!" Used in this way, the term "court" means a body, including judge and jury, organized to administer justice. Lawyers are officers of the court.
> "May it please the court" is a sentence often used by lawyers when addressing a judge. The term "court" as used here means "judge."
> "I'll see you in court," the attorney said to her fellow attorney. Here, the term "court" probably refers to the courthouse building.

U.S. Supreme Court

The U.S. Supreme Court is the highest court in the land. It hears appeals from both the U.S. courts of appeals and also from the highest state courts when those cases involve federal law or issues of national significance. Coming from the Latin word *supremus* (the last), the term *supreme* means "superior to all other things."

In the U.S. Supreme Court, appeals are heard when four out of the nine **justices** (the title given to the highest appellate court judges) believe that the case is important enough to be heard. When it agrees to hear a case on appeal, the U.S. Supreme Court issues a **writ of certiorari**, an order from a higher court to a lower court to deliver its records to the higher court for review. When the Court decides not to hear an appeal, as it does with most cases, the Court denies issuing the writ of certiorari by writing the abbreviation "**cert. den.**" on the court record. Generally, the Supreme Court grants certiorari to 70–80 cases each year from over 7,000 petitions.

TERMS IN ACTION

The **U.S. Supreme Court** has nine **justices**, who have their job for life. As of 2016, each justice earns $249,300 per year, but the Chief Justice earns $260,700. President Washington nominated the judges for the first Supreme Court, which had six justices. Because the Constitution doesn't state how many justices the Supreme Court should comprise, the number is determined by Congress. The first Congress chose six (one chief justice and five associate justices) as part of the Judiciary Act of 1789, which also established three **circuit courts** and 13 **district courts**.

One of the Supreme Court's early cases, *Chisholm v. Georgia*, concluded in 1793 that the individual states were within its **jurisdiction** and could be sued in a federal court. From 1789 until 1869, Congress increased the size of the Court to seven justices, then nine, and even ten. But in the Judiciary Act of 1869, Congress set the number of justices at nine, where it has remained.

Source: judiciary.senate.gov; supremecourt.gov

STATE COURTS

Each state in the United States—and the District of Columbia—has its own court structure that is separate from the executive and legislative branches of state government. Like federal courts, state courts are divided into three broad categories—trial courts, intermediate appellate courts, and supreme courts.

State Trial Courts

State trial courts have general authority to hear cases involving activity that occurred in a particular state. Called superior courts, circuit courts, or courts of common pleas, they are typically arranged so there is one in each county. Major civil and criminal cases, both jury and non-jury, are tried in these county courts.

In addition, somewhat lesser courts with limited jurisdiction (authority), including district, or municipal, courts; juvenile courts; traffic courts; housing courts; and probate courts, are located throughout each county. Each county also has special courts that handle such matters as adoption, divorce, and the settlement of estates.

State Intermediate Appellate Courts

Following a court's decision, either party may file an **appeal**—that is, a request to a higher court to review the decision of the lower court that tried the case. Courts that review the decisions of lower courts are called **courts of appeal** or **appellate courts**. Many states have intermediate appellate courts where appeals must be taken and heard by a three-judge panel before deemed being eligible to go to the state's supreme court.

State Supreme Court

Each state has a court of last resort—a state supreme court. Parties aggrieved by lower state court decisions may appeal to their state's supreme court, whose decision is usually final. Petitions for certiorari from state supreme court decisions may be made to the U.S. Supreme Court but, as earlier stated, those petitions for an appeal are granted only when a federal or U.S. constitutional question is raised. State supreme courts also regulate the practice of law and oversee the administration of the justice system in their states.

JURISDICTION AND VENUE

Jurisdiction is the power or authority that a court has to hear a particular case. Such power is given to the court either by the federal or a state constitution or by a federal or state statute. If, by chance, a court without jurisdiction should hear a particular case and make a decision, the party who lost the case would certainly win an appeal on the grounds the decision is void because of lack of jurisdiction.

Some courts have **original jurisdiction** over certain cases, meaning that they have the power to hear the case originally—when it first goes to court. Other courts have **appellate jurisdiction**, which means that they have the power to hear a case when it is appealed—that is, when an aggrieved party is petitioning an appellate court to review the decision of a lower court. When only one court has the power to hear a particular case, to the exclusion of all other courts, the court is said to have **exclusive jurisdiction**. When two or more courts have the power to hear a case, they have **concurrent jurisdiction**. A court with concurrent jurisdiction has the right, under a doctrine called **forum non conveniens**, to refuse to hear a case if it believes that justice would be better served if the trial were held in a different court. Some courts have exclusive original jurisdiction or exclusive appellate jurisdiction over particular cases. Similarly, some courts have concurrent original jurisdiction or concurrent appellate jurisdiction over certain cases.

Word Wise
To Speak

"Dic," "dict," and "dit," whether used as prefixes or suffixes, mean "to say" or "to speak," as in these words:

> verdict
>
> jurisdiction
>
> edict
>
> indictment
>
> dictation
>
> dictator
>
> contradict

When considering the question of jurisdiction, one of the first points that must be determined is whether the case is an in rem, quasi in rem, or in personam action.

In Rem Action

An **in rem action** is a lawsuit that is directed against property rather than against a particular person. The action usually concerns title to real property and, if so, is called a **local action**. It seeks to settle some questions about the property, and the court's decision affects everyone in the world, not merely the parties in the case. For a court to have jurisdiction over an action in rem, the property (called the **res**) must be located in the state (and, usually, in the county) where the court sits. In addition, some kind of notice must be given to people who may have an interest in the proceeding.

Quasi in Rem Action

If a defendant owns real property in one state and lives in another, the court where the real property is located has jurisdiction over the property only, but not over the person. If suit is brought in that court and the out-of-state defendant does not appear, the plaintiff's recovery will be limited to an amount up to the value of the property in question located in that state. Such a lawsuit is called a **quasi in rem action**. In such a case, the court has jurisdiction over the defendant's property, but not over the defendant's person; therefore, the most the defendant can lose is the out-of-state real property. Usually, when this type of jurisdiction prevails, the dispute the court is asked to settle has nothing to do with title to the property.

In Personam Action

In an **in personam action** (personal action), the plaintiff must select a court that has jurisdiction over not only the subject matter, but also over the parties involved in the case. **In personam jurisdiction** (personal jurisdiction) means jurisdiction over the person. A court automatically has personal jurisdiction over the plaintiff because the plaintiff has submitted to the court's jurisdiction by filing a complaint in that court. In contrast, a court has jurisdiction over a defendant only if the defendant lives in the jurisdiction, has a business in the jurisdiction, or engages in legally significant behaviors, such as driving in the jurisdiction. An exception is that state courts will obtain personam jurisdiction over anyone who is served by process while inside the state's boundaries. Service of process is explained in Chapter 2.

Not every would-be defendant resides in the jurisdiction where a plaintiff would file suit. So, how would a court have personal jurisdiction over the defendant? Some so-called **long-arm statutes** allow one state court to reach out (with its long arm) to obtain personal jurisdiction over a person in another state if that person does much business in the state where the court is located, or performs other significant actions in that state. For example, a person from Indiana driving a vehicle in North Carolina can be sued in North Carolina over allegations related to his or her driving in that state. The term **plenary jurisdiction** refers to the situation in which a court has complete jurisdiction over the plaintiff, the defendant, and the subject matter of a lawsuit.

An action that does not concern land is called a **transitory action** and may be brought in more than one place as long as the court in which it is heard has proper jurisdiction.

Venue

The place where the trial is held is called the **venue**. Each state has established rules of venue for the purpose of providing convenient places for trials. Such rules state exactly where particular actions may be brought. If the plaintiff's attorney begins an action in a court of improper venue, the defendant's attorney may have the case transferred or dismissed by filing a motion for that purpose or by raising that issue in the defendant's answer (a document discussed in Chapter 18). If the defendant's attorney does not raise the question of improper venue, the court may hear the case as long as it has jurisdiction. The difference between venue and jurisdiction is that jurisdiction relates to the power of the court to hear a case, whereas venue relates to the geographic location where the action should be tried.

Sometimes, for the sake of justice, one of the parties will ask the court to change the place of the trial. The court, in some cases, has the power to order a change of venue. A **change of venue** is the removal of a suit begun in one county or district and the replacement of it to another county or district for trial. Pretrial publicity is often a reason for a defendant to seek a change in venue. In those instances, the defendant will argue in a pretrial motion that, because of negative media coverage, the defendant will be unable to be tried by an impartial jury unless the trial is moved elsewhere.

TERMS IN ACTION

Near the finish line of the Boston Marathon on April 15, 2013, two bombs made out of pressure cookers exploded 12 seconds apart, killing three and injuring over 250 others. A few days later, the FBI announced that two Chechen brothers, Dzhokhar and Tamerian Tsarnov, were the primary suspects. After killing an MIT police officer and carjacking an SUV, the brothers eluded police until Dzhokhar was captured on April 19. However, before Dshokhar was captured, the brothers killed a Boston police officer in a shootout that included Tamerian dying when Dzhokhar ran him over in the stolen SUV while fleeing. Upon Dzhokhar's subsequent capture, some U.S. Senators thought that he should be treated as an enemy combatant for his terroristic acts, rather than a criminal, but eventually 30 criminal charges were brought against him in the **U.S. District Court** for the District of Massachusetts. Tsarnov's public defenders sought a **change of venue** for the upcoming trial, arguing he couldn't receive a fair trial in Boston, in light of the nature of the charges and the accompanying overwhelming publicity. The prosecutors responded that the publicity, which included a cover on "Rolling Stone" magazine and various articles on Tsarnov's normally American upbringing, had the effect of humanizing, rather than demonizing him. The district judge refused to grant the change of venue and the trial took place in Boston in the spring of 2015. Tsarnov was convicted of all 30 charges on April 8, 2015 and sentenced to death on June 24.

Sources: bostonglobe.com, latimes.com, politico.com, weeklystandard.com

ALTERNATIVE DISPUTE RESOLUTION

In civil cases, rather than take their disputes to court, some people prefer to use quicker, less complicated, and less expensive methods to resolve disputes. The distinct and alternative processes for settling legal disputes by means other than litigation are known collectively as **alternative dispute resolution (ADR)**. The various forms of alternative dispute resolution include negotiation, mediation, arbitration, and mini-trials.

Negotiation

Negotiation is a two-party process by which each side, without the help of a neutral third party, attempts to conclude its dispute by bargaining with the other until one side agrees to the other side's offer of settlement. One doesn't have to be represented by an attorney in a negotiation; but, often those involved in legal disputes being negotiated do have legal representation. Negotiated settlements are evidenced by a written agreement (a contract), which frequently requires the terms of the negotiated settlement to remain private.

Mediation

Mediation sometimes called **conciliation** is an informal process in which a neutral third person, called a **mediator (or conciliator)** listens to both sides and makes suggestions for reaching a solution. The mediator tries to persuade the parties to compromise and settle their differences. Often, the mediation takes place in stages; both sides meet together with the mediator and then break into private sessions called caucuses. In a **caucus**, the mediator uses his or her listening skills and the ability to ask probing questions in an attempt to learn what the interests are behind each side's demands. From that point on, the mediator seeks small gains from each side and works to try to bring the disputing parties together so that a mutually acceptable agreement (the settlement) can be reached. Although the mediator is not empowered to make the parties settle, the mediator has authority over the mediation process.

Arbitration

In contrast, **arbitration** is a method of settling disputes in which a neutral third party, called an **arbitrator** makes a decision after hearing the arguments on both sides. Arbitration takes place when parties contractually agree to resolve their dispute according to a predetermined arbitration process. Although arbitration is quicker and cheaper than a trial, parties can still agree to engage in a limited form of discovery and gather evidence in preparation for the arbitration hearing. At the hearing, documents can be submitted to the arbitrator or arbitration panel and witnesses can be called to testify. If the parties agree in advance to **binding arbitration**, the decision of the arbitrator or arbitration panel will be final and must be followed. The arbitrator's decision must be in writing and is commonly known as the **arbitrator's award**, regardless of which side the arbitrator rules in favor of. One of the serious consequences of binding arbitration is that the right to appeal a binding arbitration decision is nearly impossible to secure.

If, instead, the parties agree to **nonbinding arbitration** the arbitrator's decision is simply a recommendation and need not be complied with. Arbitration that is required by agreement or by law is called **compulsory** or **mandatory arbitration**.

Mini-trial

An increasingly popular method of settling disputes is an informal trial, sometimes referred to as a **mini-trial** run by a private organization established for the purpose of settling disputes out of court. Retired judges and lawyers are often used to hear the disputes, and the parties agree to be bound by the decision.

Reviewing What You Learned

After studying the chapter, write the answers to each of the following questions:

1. What types of cases are heard by federal courts?

____

____

____

____

2. Under what circumstances may an appeal be made from a state supreme court to the U.S. Supreme Court? _______________

____

____

3. What types of cases do U.S. courts of appeals decide?

____

____

____

____

4. For a court to have jurisdiction over an in rem action, where must the property be located?

____

____

____

5. If a defendant owns real property in one state and lives in another, which court has jurisdiction in an in rem action?

____

____

____

6. In a situation such as that described in question 5, if suit is brought against the defendant in the state where the property is located and the out-of-state defendant does not appear, to what will the plaintiff's recovery be limited?

____

____

____

7. To bring a lawsuit against a person and hold that person personally liable, what kind of action must be brought?

____

____

____

8. If the plaintiff's attorney begins an action in a court of improper venue, what may the defendant's attorney do?

____

____

____

9. What is the difference between jurisdiction and venue?

____

____

____

10. What is the difference between mediation and arbitration?

____

____

____

11. Explain what negotiation is and how it is settled.

____

____

____

12. How is mediation done and what is a caucus?

13. Explain what binding arbitration is.

____

____

____

Understanding Legal Concepts

Indicate whether each statement is true or false. Then, change the italicized word or phrase of each false statement to make it true.

ANSWERS

_____ **1.** Cases heard by the U.S. courts of appeals are decided by *three* judges.

_____ **2.** The U.S. Supreme Court hears appeals when *five* out of the nine justices believe that the case is important enough to be heard.

_____ **3.** If, by chance, a court should hear a particular case and make a decision without having *jurisdiction*, the decision would be meaningless.

_____ **4.** Some courts have *exclusive original jurisdiction* or exclusive appellate jurisdiction over particular cases.

_____ **5.** Courts *never* have concurrent original jurisdiction over cases.

_____ **6.** An action in rem is a lawsuit that is directed against *a particular person.*

_____ **7.** For a court to have jurisdiction over an *in rem action,* the property must be located in the state (and, usually, in the county) where the court lies.

_____ **8.** If a defendant owns real property in one state and lives in another, the court with jurisdiction where the real property is located has jurisdiction over the *person* and not the *property*.

_____ **9.** When parties *negotiate*, there is no neutral third party involved.

_____ **10.** When parties agree in advance to *binding* arbitration, the decision of the arbitrator must be followed.

Checking Terminology (Part A)

From the list of legal terms that follows, select the one that matches each definition.

ANSWERS

a. Admiralty

b. appellate courts

c. appellate jurisdiction

d. arbitrator's award

e. caucus

f. cert. den.

g. circuits

h. concurrent jurisdiction

i. court

j. courts of appeal

k. diversity of citizenship

l. exclusive jurisdiction

m. federal question

n. federal district courts

o. formus non conveniens

p. in personam action

q. in rem action

r. justice

s. local action

t. maritime

u. negotiation

v. original jurisdiction

w. plenary jurisdiction

x. quasi in rem action

y. transitory action

z. writ of certiorari

_____ **1.** The power of two or more courts to hear a particular case.

_____ **2.** The power to hear a case when it first goes to court.

_____ **3.** A lawsuit that is directed against property rather than against a particular person.

_____ **4.** The right of a court to refuse to hear a case if it believes that justice would be better served if the trial were held in a different court.

_____ **5.** A lawsuit that can be brought in only one place.

_____ **6.** Courts that hear most federal cases when they originally go to court, before there is an appeal.

_____ **7.** A lawsuit in which the court has jurisdiction over the defendant's property, but not over the defendant's person.

_____ **8.** A lawsuit that may be brought in more than one place as long as the court in which it is heard has proper jurisdiction.

_____ **9.** A matter that involves the U.S. Constitution, acts of Congress, or treason.

_____ **10.** Pertaining to the sea. (Select two answers.)

_____ **11.** Name given to the division of U.S. district courts.

_____ **12.** Title given to an appellate court judge.

_____ **13.** An order from a higher court to a lower court to deliver its records to the higher court for review.

_____ **14.** Possible basis of federal jurisdiction for parties who live in different states.

_____ **15.** The power of one court only to hear a particular case, to the exclusion of all other courts.

_____ **16.** A lawsuit in which the court has jurisdiction over the person.

_____ **17.** The power to hear a case when it is appealed.

_____ **18.** Courts that review the decision of lower courts. (Select two answers.)

_____ **19.** Final, written decision in binding arbitration.

_____ **20.** Private session with a mediator.

_____ **21.** Complete jurisdiction.

Checking Terminology (Part B)

ANSWERS

a. alternative dispute resolution
b. appeal
c. arbitration
d. arbitrator
e. binding arbitration
f. change of venue
g. code
h. compulsory arbitration
i. conciliation
j. conciliator
k. in personam jurisdiction
l. jurisdiction
m. long-arm statutes
n. mandatory arbitration
o. mediation
p. mediator
q. mini-trial
r. negotiation
s. nonbinding arbitration
t. res
u. statute
v. venue

____ 1. Arbitration that is required by agreement or by law. (Select two answers.)
____ 2. Arbitration in which the decision of the arbitrator will prevail and must be followed.
____ 3. An informal process in which a neutral third party listens to both sides and makes suggestions for reaching a solution. (Select two answers.)
____ 4. The removal of a suit begun in one county or district and replacement of it to another county or district for trial.
____ 5. The power or authority that a court has to hear a case.
____ 6. The property; the thing.
____ 7. Statutes that allow one state to exercise personal jurisdiction over a person in another state.
____ 8. An informal trial run by a private organization established for the purpose of settling disputes out of court.
____ 9. A term that means to settle disputes by a method other than litigation.
____ 10. A method of settling disputes by which a neutral third party makes a decision after hearing the arguments on both sides.
____ 11. A neutral third person in an arbitration who listens to both sides and makes a decision with regard to the dispute.
____ 12. Arbitration in which the arbitrator's decision is simply a recommendation and need not be complied with.
____ 13. A systematic collection of statutes, administrative regulations, and other laws.
____ 14. The place where a trial is held.
____ 15. A request to a higher court to review the decision of a lower court.
____ 16. A law passed by a legislature.
____ 17. A neutral third person in a conciliation session who listens to both sides and who makes suggestions for reaching a solution. (Select two answers.)
____ 18. Two-party process of bargaining until one side agrees to an offer of settlement from the other side.
____ 19. Jurisdiction over the person.

Using Legal Language

Read the following story and fill in the blank lines with legal terms taken from the list of terms at the beginning of this chapter:

To settle a dispute by means other than litigation over who owned the lot next to her, Susan tried to get Conrad to participate in a(n) ________________________ resolution. Conrad wanted to use ________________________, because he didn't want anyone else involved. Susan wanted to use ________________________ (also called ________________________)—an informal process in which a neutral third person listens to both sides and makes suggestions for reaching a solution. This case was not one involving a defendant who owned land in one state and lived in another; therefore, it was not a(n) ________________________ action. The ________________________ for the trial was Salem because the disputed land was located there, and the court in that city had ________________________ over the case. Because the case involved title to land, the trial had to be held in the county where the ________________________ was located, and because the suit was directed against property, it was a(n) ________________________ action, not a(n) ________________________ action. The suit was a(n) ________________________ action rather than a(n) ________________________ action, because it could be brought only in one place. In addition, because the Salem court was the only one that had the power to hear the case, it had ________________________ rather than ________________________. Owing to the fact that the case was being tried for the first time, the court had ________________________, not ________________________.

Criminal Trial Procedure

ANTE INTERROGATORY

*A formal written charge of a crime made by a grand jury is called
(A) an arraignment, (B) a criminal complaint, (C) a citation,
(D) an indictment.*

LEARNING OBJECTIVES

LO 1: Explain what probable cause is and its relation to an arrest

LO 2: Explain the miranda warnings

LO 3: Explain the purpose of a preliminary hearing

LO 4: Contrast an information from an indictment

LO 5: Explain the process and purpose of an arraignment

LO 6: Explain what reasonable doubt is

LO 7: Contrast the types of sentences

LO 8: Categorize the constitutional rights criminal defendants have

LO 9: Distinguish a bifurcated trial from a severance of action

KEY TERMS

action
arraignment
arrest
arrest warrant
bail
beyond a reasonable doubt
bifurcated trial
citation
commutation of sentence
concurrent sentences
consecutive sentences
convict
crime
criminal complaint
cumulative sentences
defendant
extradition

fact finder
grand jury
guilty
inadmissible
indictment
information
intent
malefactor
mandatory sentence
minimum sentence
Miranda warnings
nolo contendere
pardon
parole
parole board
parole commission
parolee
personal recognizance

plaintiff	rules of criminal procedure
plea bargaining	search warrant
preliminary hearing	seizure
probable cause	sentence
probable cause hearing	severance of actions
prosecute	suspended sentence
prosecution	victim's impact statement
reasonable doubt	

WEBSITES FOR PRONUNCIATION HELP

http://dictionary.cambridge.org/us/pronunciation/english/audio

https://www.howtopronounce.com

The process of taking a criminal case to court is governed by rules that have been adopted by federal and state governments. The federal **rules of criminal procedure** govern criminal actions brought in federal courts. These rules are available on the Internet. Individual states have also adopted rules of procedure that must be followed when bringing criminal actions in those states. These rules are not "statutes" even though they are often located in a statutory code. Rules of court (like rules of criminal procedure and rules of evidence) are generally created by the U.S. Supreme Court for federal rules, and state supreme courts for state rules. Statutes are created by legislatures.

A **crime** is an offense against the public at large. It is a wrong against all of society, not merely against the individual victim. For that reason, the **plaintiff**—that is, the one who **prosecutes** (brings the action)—in a criminal case is always the federal, state, or local government, which has the burden of proving its case. The one against whom the action is brought is known as the **defendant**. A person found guilty of a crime is known as a **malefactor** or **convict**.

ARREST

A criminal **action** (lawsuit or court proceeding), known as a **prosecution**, begins with the issuance of an **arrest warrant**, which is a written order of the court commanding law enforcement officers to arrest a person and bring him or her before the court. To **arrest** means to deprive a person of his or her liberty by being taken into custody. Suspects can be arrested without a warrant when there is **probable cause**—a reasonable belief based on the facts known at the time—that an offense has been committed. Police searches of an arrested person or his or her property must be based on a valid search warrant or permissible exception such as a search of a person immediately after the arrest. All **seizures** of evidence of criminality must be based on a valid search warrant or on a permissible exception. For example, if police arrest a person and, for the sake of the safety of the police, search that person's clothing and find a weapon, the police may seize that weapon without a warrant.

Miranda Warnings*

When arrested, via a procedure called the Miranda warning, suspects must be told, before being questioned, that they have the following constitutional rights:

1. They have the right to remain silent.
2. Any statements made by them may be used against them to gain conviction.
3. They have the right to consult with a lawyer and to have a lawyer present during questioning.
4. A lawyer will be provided without cost for indigent defendants.

Any statements made by the accused that were obtained in violation of this rule are **inadmissible** (cannot be received as evidence in court).

Miranda v. Arizona, 384 U.S. 436 (1966).

A process known as **extradition** permits the return of fugitives to the state where they are accused of having committed a crime. The governor of the state to which a fugitive has fled makes the order of extradition.

For minor offenses such as traffic violations, a citation is issued instead of an arrest warrant. A **citation** is a written order by a police officer (or by a judge) commanding a person to appear in court for a particular purpose.

PRELIMINARY HEARING

After the arrest, a **criminal complaint** (a written statement of the essential facts making up the offense charged) is drafted by the arresting authorities. Next, the suspect is brought before the court for a **preliminary hearing**, also called a **probable cause hearing**, which is a hearing before a judge to determine whether there is sufficient evidence to believe that the person has committed a crime. If the court finds probable cause, the defendant is either kept in jail or released on **bail** (money or property left with the court to ensure that the person will return to stand trial) or on **personal recognizance** (a personal obligation to return to stand trial).

INDICTMENT

In misdemeanor cases, a date is set for a trial. In felony cases, formal charges must be brought either by an **indictment** (a formal written charge of a crime made by a grand jury) or, if waived in some states, by **information** (a formal written charge of a crime made by a public official, such as the prosecutor, rather than by a grand jury). A **grand jury** is a jury consisting of between 5 and 23 persons at the state level, and between 16 and 23 people in the federal system, who listen to evidence presented by the prosecutor and decide whether or not the evidence is sufficient to charge someone with the commission of a crime.

ARRAIGNMENT

Following the indictment or information, the person charged with the crime must face **arraignment**, which is the act of calling a prisoner before the court to answer the indictment or information. The charge is read to the person, and he or she is asked to plead "**guilty**" (a plea of admission to having committed the crime), "**not guilty,**" or, when permitted, "**nolo contendere**" (a plea in which the defendant neither admits nor denies the charges). If the person pleads guilty or nolo contendere, he or she is sentenced by the court. Sometimes, the prosecution and defense will work out a mutually satisfactory disposition of the case through a process known as **plea bargaining**. In a plea bargain, the defendant often will plead guilty to a lesser offense in exchange for a lighter sentence. Any such arrangement must be approved by the court. A date is set for a trial when a person pleads not guilty.

REASONABLE DOUBT

To convict someone of a crime, the prosecution must prove its case to the fact finder beyond a reasonable doubt. **Beyond a reasonable doubt** means that the **fact finder** (the jury, or the judge in a nonjury trial) is fully persuaded that the accused has committed the crime with the required criminal **intent**, which is the necessary mental state that precedes the criminal act. Beyond a reasonable doubt does not require absolute certainty, but if there is a **reasonable doubt**—that is, a real doubt based on reason and common sense—the accused must be acquitted.

◼ TERMS IN ACTION

St. Paul-Minneapolis, police officer Kara Breci was patrolling a high-crime area in November 2008, when she spotted a car in a White Castle restaurant parking lot with two men in the car and a third man, with no food, getting into the back seat. Believing that she was watching a drug deal in action, she and her partner approached the car, and after one quick question, one of the occupants confessed to having "weed." The police ordered them to exit the car. One of the men, Frank Irving Wiggins, was wearing low-slung pants that dropped when he got out of the car after he put his hands in the air. Officer Breci immediately grabbed the pants' waistband to pull them up, and in so doing she found a handgun. Convicted **beyond a reasonable doubt** of illegal weapons possession, Wiggins appealed on the ground that the search of his pants was unconstitutional because the officer had no **search warrant**. But the Minnesota Court of Appeals upheld the conviction, concluding that Officer Breci's hiking up of Wiggins's pants didn't constitute a search at all, but was reasonably done to protect her safety and also to prevent Wiggins from any unnecessary embarrassment.

Source: abajournal.com; *State v. Wiggins*, 788 N.W.2d 509 (Minn. App. 2010)

Web Wise

- For overviews of criminal and civil procedure, go to the Legal Information Institute (LII) at **www.law.cornell.edu**. Click on Wex legal dictionary/encyclopedia under the "Learn more" box; then type "civil procedure" or "criminal procedure" in the search box.
- In addition to the website just mentioned, the federal procedural rules can be found at **www.findlaw.com**. At that site, type "Federal Resources" in the search box. Then type "Rules of Civil Procedure" or "Rules of Criminal Procedure" in the box to search again.
- Find out about *Internet jurisdiction* by going to **www.findlaw.com** and keying in "internet jurisdiction" in the search box.
- Learn about the federal court system (for Chapter 1) by going to **www.uscourts.gov** and then about the federal rules of criminal procedure by clicking on the "Rules and Policies" tab on the right side of the top of the website.

SENTENCING

When the defendant is found guilty in a criminal case, the judgment of the court imposing punishment is called a **sentence**. At the time of sentencing, most states allow victims to make impact statements. A **victim's impact statement** is a statement to the court, at the time of sentencing, relating the impact that the crime had on the victim or on the victim's family. Depending on state law, impact statements are made before or after sentencing and are often preserved for use at a later time by a **parole board** or **parole commission** (a group of people authorized to grant parole). For example, the Texas Board of Pardons and Paroles considers victim impact statements prior to voting on inmates' applications. **Parole** is a conditional release from prison, allowing the **parolee** (person placed on parole) to serve the remainder of a sentence outside of prison under specific terms.

When two or more sentences are imposed on a defendant, to be served one after the other, they are called **consecutive** or **cumulative sentences**. If they are to be served at the same time, they are called **concurrent sentences**. A **suspended sentence** is one given formally, but not actually served. Suspended sentences are sometimes given to first-time defendants and tied to certain conditions, such as completing community service, entering (and completing) a substance abuse program, or simply staying out of trouble. A **mandatory sentence** is a fixed sentence that must be imposed, with no room for discretion. A **minimum sentence** refers to the shortest amount of time that a prisoner must serve before being released or placed on parole.

The President of the United States in federal cases and state governors in state cases have the power to change sentences, making them less severe. Such a change is known as a **commutation of sentence**. A **pardon**, on the other hand, is a setting aside of punishment altogether by a government official, without the exoneration of guilt.

> ## ▌ TERMS IN ACTION
>
> Perhaps you never wondered what was the longest single prison **sentence** ever given in America. In case you did, you can stop. In 1981, a jury in Alabama sentenced triple-murderer Dudley Wayne Kyzer to two **consecutive life sentences** and 10,000 years. Kyzer was convicted in 1976 of murdering his wife, mother-in-law, and a college student, and was sentenced to death. But his death sentence was overturned, and Kyzer was resentenced. At that hearing, the prosecuting attorney who originally won the conviction and death penalty asked for (and got) two consecutive life sentences and an additional 10,000 years. Even the *Guinness Book of World Records* once declared it the longest prison sentence. It has since listed a 30,000 year sentence for a child rapist as the longest, but Kyzer's 10,000 years begins after serving *two life sentences*. Alabama law allows inmates to apply for **parole** after 10 years, but Kyzer has been denied repeatedly, as recent as 2016, at the age of 74.
>
> Source: tuscaloosanews.com; associatedcontent.com; guinnessworldrecords.com

DEFENDANTS' RIGHTS

In addition to certain rights that they are informed of when arrested (see the **Miranda Warnings** box in Chapter 1), defendants in criminal cases have the following rights:

1. The right to be free from any unreasonable search and seizure. (U.S. Constitution, Fourth Amendment)
2. The right to a speedy trial. (U.S. Constitution, Sixth Amendment)
3. The right to plead not guilty. (inherent in the U.S. Constitution, the Bill of Rights)
4. The right to be represented by an attorney. (U.S. Constitution, Sixth Amendment)
5. The right to a court-appointed attorney if the defendant cannot afford one. (*Gideon v. Wainwright*, 372 U.S. 335 (1963))
6. The right to summon witnesses and require their attendance. (U.S. Constitution, Sixth Amendment)
7. The right to confront and cross-examine witnesses. (U.S. Constitution, Sixth Amendment)
8. The right to be presumed innocent until proven guilty, by a judge or jury, beyond a reasonable doubt. (*Taylor v. Kentucky*, 436 U.S. 478 (1978))

TRIAL SEPARATION

Sometimes, trials are divided into separate parts. A **bifurcated trial** is a trial divided into two parts, providing separate evidence presentations and fact-findings for different issues in the same lawsuit. For example, in criminal cases, one portion may be held to determine the guilt or innocence of the defendant, followed by a separate hearing, if necessary, to determine sanity or punishment. In non-criminal personal-injury cases, separate proceedings sometimes are held on the questions of liability and damages.

A different kind of trial separation, called **severance of actions**, occurs when a court separates lawsuits or prosecutions involving multiple parties into separate, independent cases resulting in separate final judgments. Rule 14 of the Federal Rules of Criminal Procedure grants federal judges broad discretion to grant a severance of action.

Reviewing What You Learned

After studying the chapter, write the answers to each of the following questions:

1. Who brings the action in a criminal case?

____

____

____

2. When does a criminal action begin?

____

____

____

3. What happens to the defendant if the court finds probable cause that he or she committed a crime?

____

____

____

4. How many people serve on a grand jury and what is the jury's function?

____

____

____

5. How does an indictment differ from an arraignment?

____

____

____

6. What must occur if the judge or jury finds that there is a reasonable doubt that the defendant committed the crime?

____

____

____

7. When arrested, what must a suspect be told before being questioned?

____

____

____

8. For what reason do you believe that victims' impact statements are often preserved for later use by a parole board?

____

____

____

9. How does a commutation of a sentence differ from a pardon?

____

____

____

10. What is the difference between a bifurcated trial and a severance of action?

____

____

____

Understanding Legal Concepts

Indicate whether each statement is true or false. Then, change the italicized word or phrase of each false statement to make it true.

ANSWERS

_____ **1.** A crime is an offense against *the individual victim alone*. It *is not* a wrong against all of society.

_____ **2.** The one who brings an action in a criminal case is *usually* the federal, state, or local government.

_____ **3.** A grand jury is a jury consisting of *not more than* 23 people.

_____ **4.** An indictment is a formal written charge of a crime made by a *grand jury*.

_____ **5.** Nolo contendere is a plea in which the *plaintiff* neither admits nor denies the charges.

____ **6.** To convict someone of a crime, the prosecution must prove *beyond a reasonable doubt* that the defendant committed the crime.

____ **7.** A *pardon* is a conditional release from prison allowing the person to serve the remainder of a sentence outside of prison under specific terms.

____ **8.** A *suspended* sentence is a sentence given formally, but not actually served.

____ **9.** Two or more sentences imposed on a defendant to be served at the same time are *consecutive* sentences.

____ **10.** A *severance of action* is a trial that is divided into two parts, providing separate hearings for different issues in the same lawsuit.

Checking Terminology (Part A)

From the list of legal terms that follows, select the one that matches each definition.

ANSWERS

a. action
b. arraignment
c. arrest
d. arrest warrant
e. bail
f. beyond a reasonable doubt
g. bifurcated trial
h. citation
i. commutation of sentence
j. concurrent sentences
k. consecutive sentences
l. Convict
m. crime
n. criminal complaint
o. cumulative sentences
p. defendant
q. extradition
r. fact finder
s. grand jury
t. guilty
u. inadmissible
v. indictment
w. information
x. Intent

____ **1.** A written order by a judge or police officer commanding a person to appear in court for a particular purpose.

____ **2.** An offense against the public at large.

____ **3.** A person against whom a legal action is brought.

____ **4.** A lawsuit or court proceeding.

____ **5.** A written order of the court commanding law enforcement officers to arrest a person and to bring him or her before the court.

____ **6.** The act of calling a prisoner before the court to answer an indictment or information.

____ **7.** A written statement of the essential facts making up an offense charged in a criminal action.

____ **8.** Money or property left with the court to ensure that a person will return to stand trial.

____ **9.** The return of fugitives to the state where they are accused of having committed the crime.

____ **10.** A formal, written charge of a crime, made by a grand jury.

____ **11.** When the fact finder is fully persuaded that the accused has committed a crime.

____ **12.** The jury in a jury trial or the judge in a non-jury trial.

____ **13.** A trial that is divided into two parts, providing separate hearings for different issues in the same lawsuit.

____ **14.** Two or more sentences imposed on a defendant to be served one after the other. (Select two answers.)

____ **15.** The necessary mental state that precedes the criminal act.

____ **16.** A formal written charge of a crime made by a public official rather than by a grand jury.

____ **17.** Two or more sentences imposed on a defendant to be served at the same time.

____ **18.** The changing of a sentence to one that is less severe.

____ **19.** A person found guilty of a crime.

____ **20.** To deprive a person of his or her liberty.

Checking Terminology (Part B)

From the list of legal terms that follows, select the one that matches each definition.

ANSWERS

a. mandatory sentence
b. Malefactor
c. minimum sentence
d. Miranda warnings
e. nolo contendere
f. pardon
g. parole
h. parole board
i. parole commission

____ **1.** The judgment of the court imposing punishment when the defendant is found guilty in a criminal case.

____ **2.** A person placed on parole.

____ **3.** Reasonable grounds for belief that an offense has been committed.

____ **4.** The party by whom criminal proceedings are started or conducted; the state.

____ **5.** A plea in which the defendant neither admits nor denies the charges.

____ **6.** A hearing before a judge to determine whether there is sufficient evidence to believe that the person has committed a crime. (Select two answers.)

____ **7.** A fixed sentence that must be imposed, with no room for discretion.

j. parolee	____ **8.** A personal obligation by a person to return to stand trial.
k. personal recognizance	____ **9.** The shortest amount of time that a prisoner must serve before being released or placed on parole.
l. plea bargaining	
m. preliminary hearing	____ **10.** A group of people authorized to grant parole. (Select two answers.)
n. probable cause	____ **11.** A setting aside of punishment altogether, by a government official.
o. probable cause hearing	____ **12.** A statement to the court, at the time of sentencing, relative to the impact that the crime had on the victim or on the victim's family.
p. prosecute	
q. prosecution	____ **13.** A sentence that is given formally, but not actually served.
r. reasonable doubt	____ **14.** A conditional release from prison allowing the person to serve the remainder of a sentence outside of prison under specific terms.
s. rendition	
t. rules of criminal procedure	____ **15.** Regulations that govern the proceedings in criminal cases.
u. seizure	____ **16.** The working out of a mutually satisfactory disposition of a case by the prosecution and by the defense.
v. sentence	
w. severance of actions	____ **17.** The separation of lawsuits or prosecutions involving multiple parties into separate, independent cases, resulting in separate final judgments.
x. suspended sentence	
y. victims' impact statements	____ **18.** Taking Property upon the production of a search warrant.
	____ **19.** Taking Property upon the production of a search warrant.
	____ **20.** Doubt based on reason.

Using Legal Language

Read the following story and fill in the blank lines with legal terms taken from the list of terms at the beginning of this chapter:

Alphonse, high on drugs and carrying a handgun, broke into Krista's apartment one evening, unaware that Krista and her dog Lilly were present. Lilly lunged at the surprised Alphonse, causing him to shoot himself in the foot. Krista disarmed the bleeding Alphonse and called 911. When the police arrived, Alphonse was placed under ______________________; that is, deprived of his liberty. He was also told about his rights, called ____________________. The next morning, Alphonse went before the court for a(n) ____________________ hearing, which is also called a(n) ____________________ hearing. The judge set a high ____________________ to ensure Alphonse's return to stand trial. The district attorney presented the case to a(n) ____________________ jury, which issued a(n) ____________________ —a formal written charge of a crime. This was followed by a court appearance called a(n) ____ at which Alphonse pleaded ____________________, denying that he had committed the crime. The trial that followed was governed by regulations known as ____________________. The state brought the action, that is, ____________________, against Alphonse, who was the ____________________. To find Alphonse guilty, the jury, that is, the ____________________, was required to find beyond ____________________ that Alphonse committed the crime. At the time of sentencing, Krista was able to give a(n) ____________________ pointing out the effect the crime had on her life. Alphonse was given a(n) ____________________ sentence—one that is fixed, with no room for discretion.

Civil Trial Procedure

ANTE INTERROGATORY

A formal notice to the defendant that a lawsuit has begun and that the defendant must file an answer within the number of days set by state law is a (A) complaint, (B) declaration, (C) summons, (D) verification.

LEARNING OBJECTIVES

LO 1: Explain the basics of how a lawsuit begins, including if and when a plaintiff has a case to file

LO 2: Define a pleading and explain what a complaint consists of

LO 3: Explain service of process and what a defendant needs to do to avoid a default judgment

LO 4: Categorize the steps needed for a plaintiff to obtain an attachment

LO 5: Contrast a trustee process/garnishment with an attachment

LO 6: Explain and apply the common burden of proof in a civil case

LO 7: Define the writ of execution

LO 8: Define a summary proceedings

KEY TERMS

ad damnum	defendant
affiant	deponent
affidavit	docket
allege	docket number
allegation	Doe defendants
answer	encumbrance
attachment	ex parte
aver	garnishee
averments	garnishment
cause of action	gravamen
civil action	justiciable
class action	legal issues
complaint	lien
constructive service	lis pendens
counterclaim	litigant
declaration	litigation
default judgment	personal service
	petition

plaintiff	summary proceeding
pleadings	summons
preponderance of evidence	trial docket
process	trial list
process server	trustee
pro se	trustee process
ripeness doctrine	verification
rules of civil procedure	writ
service of process	writ of attachment
standing to sue	writ of execution
statute of limitations	writ of garnishment
substituted service	

WEBSITES FOR PRONUNCIATION HELP

http://dictionary.cambridge.org/us/pronunciation/english/audio

https://www.howtopronounce.com

A **civil action**—that is, a lawsuit other than a criminal one—comes about when two or more people become involved in a dispute they are unable to settle by themselves. One of them seeks to have a third party, the court, resolve the dispute for them. To do this, a court action known as **litigation** (a suit at law) must be brought. The parties to a lawsuit are called **litigants**. The person who brings the suit is called the **plaintiff**. The person against whom the suit is brought is called the **defendant**. A **class action** is a lawsuit brought, with the court's approval, by one or more persons on behalf of a very large group of people who have the same interest in the matter.

Under the **ripeness doctrine**, a court will not hear a case unless there is an actual, present controversy for the court to decide. Judges will not decide cases that are hypothetical or speculative. To be brought to court, potential cases must be **justiciable**—appropriate for court assessment.

The federal **rules of civil procedure** govern civil cases brought in federal courts. These rules can be found on the Internet (**https://www.law.cornell.edu/rules/frcp**). For example, Rule 23 federal rule of civil procedure governs class actions brought in federal court. Individual states also have adopted rules of civil procedure that apply to cases brought in their state courts.

BEGINNING A CIVIL ACTION

To begin a civil lawsuit, the plaintiff usually makes an appointment with an attorney and tells the attorney the facts of the dispute as he or she understands them. The attorney, after listening to the client's version of the facts, determines the **legal issues** (questions of law) that are involved in the case. The attorney then tells the client about the law as it applies to the legal issues and gives the client an opinion as to how successful a lawsuit might be. The client, with the advice of the attorney, then decides whether or not to bring the lawsuit. A plaintiff may file a lawsuit without an attorney's help, by representing himself or herself, which is known as appearing **pro se**. While it may inadvisable, plaintiffs and defendants have the right to be pro se in any legal proceeding.

An important consideration for the attorney is whether the client has standing to sue. **Standing to sue** means that a party has a tangible, legally protected interest at stake in a lawsuit. For example, you could not bring suit against someone who breached your friend's contract, because you were not a party to that contract. You would not have "standing."

Another critical consideration is whether the applicable **statute of limitations** bars the lawsuit from being filed. Statutes of limitation set a time limit for how long plaintiffs can wait, after the plaintiff is aware of the action (or reasonably should be aware), to file a lawsuit. Time limits vary according to the kind of suit being filed, and are set by statutes. For example, in many jurisdictions the statute of limitations for personal injury lawsuits is two years and often the statute of limitations for lawsuits based on written contracts is six years.

If the client decides to bring suit, the attorney usually writes a letter to the defendant, saying that he or she represents the plaintiff and has been authorized to bring suit against the defendant. In the letter, the attorney often makes an attempt to settle the case out of court and gives the defendant a few days to answer the letter. If no settlement can be reached, the plaintiff's attorney will begin the lawsuit.

SELECTING THE COURT

The attorney's first task in bringing suit is to select the court in which to bring the action. In choosing a court, the attorney must determine which court has jurisdiction over both the person who is being sued and the subject matter of the case, as discussed in Chapter 1.

PLEADINGS

Civil suits are begun and defended at the outset by the use of papers known as pleadings. **Pleadings** are the written statements of claims and defenses used by the parties in the lawsuit. Pleadings serve the purpose of giving notice to all parties of the claims and defenses in the suit; in addition, pleadings narrow the issues for trial so that both parties and the court know the legal issues that must be decided.

To begin a civil suit, the plaintiff's attorney files a complaint with the clerk of the court, which is the plaintiff's first pleading. A **complaint** (called a **declaration** at common law) is a formal document containing a short and plain statement of the claim, indicating that the plaintiff is entitled to relief and containing a demand for the relief sought. The complaint sets forth the plaintiff's **cause of action**, which is the ground on which the suit is maintained. The essential basis, or gist, of the complaint is known as the **gravamen** of the lawsuit. The complaint contains **allegations** (also called **averments**), which are claims that the party making the complaint expects to prove. To **allege**, or to **aver**, means to make an allegation; to assert positively. The clause in the complaint stating the damages claimed by the plaintiff is called the **ad damnum**. In some states, a complaint must be accompanied by a verification signed by the plaintiff. A **verification** is a written statement made by the plaintiff, under oath, confirming the correctness, truth, or authenticity of a pleading. In some states, especially in courts of equity (see Chapter 7), civil suits are begun by the filing of a **petition**—a written application for a court order.

The lawsuit officially begins when the complaint or petition is filed with the court. The plaintiff's attorney either mails (registered or certified) or hand-delivers the complaint to the court, with the proper filing fee. The clerk of court keeps a record, called a **docket**, of cases that are filed and assigns a **docket number** to each case. The term **trial docket** or **trial list** refers to the calendar of cases that are ready for trial.

Due to the advance of technology, pleadings and other papers may be filed or served electronically, according to Rule 5 of the Federal Rules of Civil Procedure, provided that the local federal courts allow for electronic filing and that other parties consent to electronic service. States have similar allowances. Indiana Trial Rule 5(F) allows for the electronic filing of pleadings. To protect the privacy of litigants, Rule 5.2 of the Federal Rules of Civil Procedure requires that certain personal information (Social Security number or date of birth) be presented in a way that does not entirely disclose the information. For example, the last four numbers of a person's Social Security number only may be listed.

Once the complaint is filed with the court, the defendant is notified of the suit by a method known as process. **Process** is defined as the means of compelling the defendant in an action to appear in court.

The root "ver-" used in the term "verification" is from the Latin word for "truth," *veritas*. Other words with the same root are:

Word	Meaning
Verdict	Decision of the jury (see Chapter 20)
Verify	To prove to be true

Even that most familiar word, "very," which means "truly" or "really," comes from the root "ver-."

SERVICE OF PROCESS

A summons is used to notify the defendant of the lawsuit. A **summons** is a formal notice to the defendant that a lawsuit has begun and that the defendant either must file an answer within the number of days set by state law or lose the case by default. **Service of process** is the delivering of summonses or other legal documents to the people who are required to receive them. A summons is obtained from the court, filled out, and given, along with a copy of the complaint, to a **process server** (a person who carries out service of process). The process server delivers copies of the summons and the complaint to the defendant and then fills in the back of the summons indicating when and how service was made. The summons is then returned to the court.

The process server may serve process by delivering a copy of the summons and complaint to the defendant personally, which is known as **personal service**. Service that is not personal service is called **constructive service** when the summons and complaint are left at the defendant's last and usual place of abode and **substituted service** when they are delivered to the defendant's agent, mailed, or published in a newspaper. If the defendant is a corporation, process may be served on an officer of the corporation, on a registered agent of the corporation, or on the person in charge of the corporation's principal place of business. When the defendant's whereabouts are unknown, process may be served by publication in a newspaper. In some states, service may be made by mail. As stated earlier, the Federal Rules of Civil Procedure authorize electronic service, provided that there is written consent by the party to be served.

When names of defendants are unknown, summonses and complaints refer to people as **Doe defendants**, such as First Doe, Second Doe, John Doe, and Jane Doe.

TERMS IN ACTION

In the 2008 movie "Pineapple Express," Seth Rogan's character plays a **process server** who uses creative methods to get divorce papers or **civil complaints** served on defendants, including impersonating a doctor and serving a **summons** on a surgeon during an operation. That may not be too far from reality for those who sometimes have to use deception to find defendants, some of whom don't want to be found. Process servers might have to dodge menacing dogs while trying to find hiding homeowners who don't want to receive **service of process** on foreclosure actions, and they risk personal injury if they are attacked by angered recipients of subpoenas or legal documents. California and Washington State allow process servers to temporarily trespass in order to do their job. Whereas **substitute service** is allowed in all jurisdictions, nothing beats being able to say, "You've been served." Even Mark

(Continued)

Zuckerberg, the billionaire who created Facebook, heard those words when a process server got past security at a fancy ski resort in Idaho, where Zuckerberg was having lunch in 2010. One process server in Seattle was so unpopular for his menacing tactics that the *Seattle Times* wrote an article about him in 2010, recounting how he once pitched a tent outside a target's house and camped there until the guy came home. Service of process can even be deadly. In 2008, a process server in Colorado was murdered after personally serving an irate husband at the divorcing couple's home.

Source: seattletimes.com; businessinsider.com; thedenverchannel.com

The Answer

Upon receiving the summons, the defendant has a time limit to file an **answer**, which is the defendant's pleading. For example, in the federal system, a defendant generally has 21 days after being served the summons to file an answer; in New Jersey state court, an answer must be filed within 35 days of service of process. An answer is a written response to the plaintiff's complaint, filed with the court where the complaint was filed. An answer denies or admits the specific allegations in the complaint, or it may claim a lack of knowledge about the truthfulness of the complaint's allegations. A defendant's answer may also include a **counterclaim**—a suit filed against the plaintiff—which would then require the plaintiff's written response.

Default Judgment

When a defendant fails to file an answer or other pleading in response to a summons and complaint, he or she may lose the case by default. A **default judgment** is a court decision entered against a party who has failed to plead or defend a lawsuit.

Differences Between Criminal and Civil Actions

	Criminal Action	Civil Action
1. **Who brings the action?**	The government	The injured party
2. **What is the plaintiff's burden of proof?**	Prove guilt beyond a reasonable doubt	Prove liability by a preponderance of evidence
3. **What can be the result for a losing defendant?**	Prison, fine, or both; death; restitution	Pay money (damages) to the winning party; do or refrain from doing a particular act

ATTACHMENTS

At times, plaintiffs need the assurance that if they obtain a judgment against the defendant (that is, win the lawsuit), money will be available from the defendant to pay the amount of the judgment. This assurance is accomplished by attaching the defendant's property at the beginning of the action. An **attachment** is the act of taking a person's property and bringing it into the custody of the law so it may be applied toward the defendant's debt if the plaintiff wins the suit.

The method of obtaining an attachment varies somewhat from state to state. Under a typical state law, the plaintiff's attorney files a motion for attachment with the court at the same time the complaint is filed. The plaintiff's attorney must also file an affidavit signed by the plaintiff, stating facts that would warrant a judgment for the plaintiff. An **affidavit** is a written statement sworn to under oath, before a notary public, as being true to the affiant's own knowledge, information, and belief. An **affiant** (also called a **deponent**) is a person who signs an affidavit. The motion, affidavit, summons, and complaint, together with a notice of hearing, are sent to the process server, who serves them on the defendant. A hearing is then held by the court to determine whether or not to allow the attachment. The court may allow the attachment if it finds that a reasonable likelihood exists that the plaintiff will recover a judgment against the defendant for the amount of the attachment over and above any insurance coverage that the defendant has.

Ex Parte Hearing

Sometimes, the plaintiff's attorney wishes to attach the defendant's property, but does not want to notify the defendant in advance that an attachment is going to occur. In such cases, the plaintiff's attorney attends an ex parte session of the court. **Ex parte** means that the hearing is attended by one party only. The plaintiff's attorney asks the court to allow the attachment without notifying the defendant beforehand. The court may allow the attachment without notifying the defendant if it finds (1) that the defendant is not within its jurisdiction (but the defendant's property is, thereby giving it quasi in rem jurisdiction), or (2) that a danger exists that the defendant will conceal the property, sell it, or remove it from the state, or (3) that a danger exists that the defendant will damage or destroy the property.

Writ of Attachment

A **writ** is a written order of a court, returnable to the same, commanding the performance or nonperformance of an act. If the court allows an attachment, the judge signs a paper called a **writ of attachment**. This written order is to the sheriff, commanding the sheriff to attach the real or personal property of the defendant, up to an amount approved by the court.

When real property is attached, the writ of attachment or a notice of **lis pendens** (pending suit) is recorded at the registry of deeds in the county where the property is located. This procedure has the effect of putting a lien on the property until the lawsuit is completed. A **lien** (also called an **encumbrance**) is a claim that one person or entity has against the property of another. The claim attaches to the property until the lawsuit is completed. If the plaintiff obtains a judgment against the defendant, an officer of the court, such as a sheriff, can sell the property under the court's direction and obtain the money to satisfy the judgment.

If personal property is attached, the court officer may take possession of it, or in some circumstances place a keeper over it, or sell it immediately as in the case of perishable property. With variations from state to state, certain items are exempt from attachment, such as necessary wearing apparel, furniture and books up to a particular value, tools necessary to carry on a trade, and materials and stock up to a specified value. Other technical restrictions on the attachment of personal property exist.

Trustee Process and Garnishment

Sometimes, it is necessary to attach property of the defendant that is being held by another person. This is most commonly done to attach money that the defendant has in a bank account or wages or other money that has been earned by the defendant, but not yet paid.

The procedure for attaching the defendant's property that is in the hands of a third person is called **trustee process** in some states and **garnishment** in others. To begin trustee process, the plaintiff's attorney obtains a trustee process summons, or a **writ of garnishment** from the court, fills it out, and files it with the court, together with the complaint, a motion for approval of attachment on trustee process, and a supporting affidavit. The defendant is notified (unless the attachment is on an ex parte basis), and a hearing is held by the court to determine whether the trustee process attachment should be allowed. If it is allowed, the summons is sent to the process server, who serves it on the **trustee** or **garnishee** (the one holding the defendant's property). The summons orders the trustee to file, within a prescribed number of days after service, a disclosure under oath of the goods, effects, or credits, if any, of the defendant that are in the possession of the trustee at the time of service. In some states, trustee process cannot be used in actions for malicious prosecution, slander, libel, assault and battery, and specific recovery of goods. Certain other actions are also exempt from trustee process. With some exceptions, the plaintiff must file a bond with the court before trustee process can be used. The bond is for the purpose of paying the defendant's court costs and damages in the event that the attachment was wrongfully brought by the plaintiff.

> ### TERMS IN ACTION
>
> Although O.J. Simpson is scheduled for a 2017–2018 release from a Nevada prison for various convictions stemming from a 2008 Las Vegas robbery, he succeeded in winning his first criminal trial in 1994, known as "the trial of the century." Charged with the double murder of his ex-wife Nicole Brown Simpson and her friend Ron Goldman, Simpson was found not guilty after a nine-month-long nationally televised trial. But in 1997, Simpson was found liable in the civil, wrongful-death case, filed after the criminal case, and the jury awarded the Brown and Goldman families $33.5 million. After failing to pay the damages, the plaintiffs began the process of **attachment**. While Simpson's NFL pension was deemed to be exempt from **garnishment**, eventually much of his nonexempt property was sold at auction to help pay his judgment. Simpson's most famous personal property, his 1968 Heisman trophy, sold for $230,000. A grand piano at Simpson's home wasn't sold at auction, however, because a judge agreed with Simpson's lawyers that it was a gift made by Simpson and Nicole in 1984 to Simpson's mother, but was kept at his Brentwood mansion. In 1999, the State of California filed a tax **lien** against Simpson for well over $1,000,000.
>
> Source: accountingtoday.com; people.com; web.archive.org; usatoday.com; latimes.com

BURDEN OF PROOF

Recall that in criminal cases, the prosecution must *prove beyond a reasonable doubt* that the defendant committed the crime. In civil cases, the burden of proof is different. To win a civil case, the plaintiff must prove the case by a **preponderance of evidence**—evidence of the greatest weight. This degree of proof requires the judge or jury to believe that the evidence more likely than not favors the plaintiff. Preponderance of the evidence is not a quantitative standard. For example, one credible witness for the plaintiff may be sufficient for the preponderance standard, even over multiple, inauthentic witnesses or witnesses with poor memories testifying for the defendant.

ENFORCING THE JUDGMENT

If the losing party is ordered to pay money to the winning party and does not do so, the winning party must ask the court for a **writ of execution**. This process is used to enforce a judgment for the payment of money. The writ orders the sheriff to enforce the judgment.

SUMMARY PROCEEDINGS

Lengthy and complicated trials are expensive for the parties and the governmental agencies administering them. Whenever possible, it is beneficial to hold a trial quickly, in a simple manner. A **summary proceeding** is the name given to a short and simple trial, one that occurs without much or any traditional discovery process (which will be discussed in Chapter 5). Proceedings held in small-claims courts are examples of summary proceedings.

Reviewing What You Learned

After studying the chapter, write the answers to each of the following questions:

1. How does the plaintiff's attorney begin a civil suit?

2. What two purposes do pleadings serve?

3. How is the defendant notified that a lawsuit has been brought against him or her?

____

____

4. Describe three ways that process may be served on the defendant.

____

____

____

____

5. In what ways may process be served if the defendant is a corporation?

____

____

____

____

____

6. How can plaintiffs be assured that money will be available from defendants if the plaintiffs win a lawsuit?

____

____

____

____

7. Under a typical state law, what two documents must the plaintiff's attorney file with the court to obtain an attachment?

____

____

____

8. How is the defendant notified of the plaintiff's motion for attachment?

____

____

9. The court may allow an attachment if it finds what?

____

____

____

10. On what three occasions may the court allow an attachment without notifying the defendant beforehand?

____

____

____

11. What is done with the writ of attachment or notice of lis pendens when real property is attached?

____

____

____

____

12. What is a statute of limitations and why is it important?

____

____

____

____

Understanding Legal Concepts

Indicate whether each statement is true or false. Then, change the italicized word or phrase of each false statement to make it true.

ANSWERS

____ 1. To begin a lawsuit, the plaintiff's attorney files a *summons* with the clerk of the court.

____ 2. *Pleadings* help to narrow the issues for trial so that both parties and the court know what legal issues must be decided.

____ 3. A *complaint* is a formal notice to the defendant that a lawsuit has begun and that the defendant either must file an answer within the number of days set by state law or lose the case by default.

____ 4. To obtain an attachment, under a typical state law, the plaintiff's attorney files a motion for attachment with the court *at the same time that* the complaint is filed.

____ 5. An affiant is also known as a *deponent*.

____ 6. An ex parte session of the court is attended by *both parties* to the suit.

____ 7. A *writ of attachment* is a written order to the sheriff to attach the property of the defendant.

____ 8. When real property is attached, the writ of attachment is recorded at the *city or town hall* where the property is located.

____ 9. The procedure for attaching the defendant's property that is in the hands of a third person is called *a writ of encumbrance* in some states.

____ 10. A trustee process *summons* orders the trustee to file, within a prescribed number of days, a disclosure under oath of the goods, effects, or credits of the defendant that are in the possession of the trustee.

Checking Terminology (Part A)

From the list of legal terms that follows, select the one that matches each definition.

ANSWERS

a. ad damnum
b. affiant
c. affidavit
d. allegation
e. allege
f. answer
g. attachment
h. aver
i. cause of action
j. civil action
k. class action
l. complaint
m. constructive service
n. counterclaim
o. declaration
p. default judgment
q. defendant
r. deponent
s. docket
t. docket number
u. Doe defendants
v. encumbrance
w. ex parte
x. garnishment
y. gravamen
z. justiciable
aa. legal issues
bb. lien
cc. lis pendens

____ 1. A record of cases that are filed with the court.

____ 2. A formal document containing a short and plain statement of the claim, indicating that the plaintiff is entitled to relief and containing a demand for the relief sought. (Select two answers.)

____ 3. The act of taking a person's property and bringing it into the custody of the law so that it may be applied toward the defendant's debt if the plaintiff wins the case.

____ 4. A person who signs an affidavit. (Select two answers.)

____ 5. On one side only.

____ 6. A claim that one person or entity has against the property of another. (Select two answers.)

____ 7. A procedure for attaching the defendant's property that is in the hands of a third person.

____ 8. The ground on which a suit is maintained.

____ 9. A number assigned to each case by the clerk of court.

____ 10. A written statement sworn to under oath, before a notary public, as being true to the affiant's own knowledge, information, and belief.

____ 11. A type of service in which the summons and complaint are left at the defendant's last and usual place of abode.

____ 12. References to defendants whose names are unknown.

____ 13. The defendant's pleading in written response to the plaintiff's complaint.

____ 14. A court decision entered against a party who has failed to plead or defend a lawsuit.

____ 15. The essential basis or gist of a complaint filed in a lawsuit.

____ 16. Appropriate for court assessment.

____ 17. Questions of law to be decided by the court in a lawsuit.

____ 18. A pending suit.

____ 19. Claims that the party making it expects to prove.

____ 20. To make an allegation; to assert positively. (Select two answers.)

____ 21. defendant's suit filed against the plaintiff.

____ 22. person against whom a lawsuit is brought.

____ 23. The clause in the complaint stating the damages claimed by the plaintiff

Checking Terminology (Part B)

From the list of legal terms that follows, select the one that matches each definition.

ANSWERS

a. litigants
b. litigation
c. personal service
d. petition
e. litigant
f. plaintiff
g. pleadings
h. preponderance of evidence
i. process
j. process server
k. ripeness doctrine
l. rules of civil procedure
m. service of process
n. standing to sue
o. statute of limitations
p. substituted service
q. summary proceeding
r. summons
s. trial docket
t. trial list
u. trustee
v. trustee process
w. verification
x. writ
y. writ of attachment
z. writ of execution

_____ **1.** A written application for a court order.
_____ **2.** A party that has a tangible, legally protected interest at stake in a lawsuit.
_____ **3.** Parties to a lawsuit.
_____ **4.** Evidence of the greater weight.
_____ **5.** Regulations that govern the proceedings in civil cases.
_____ **6.** A suit at law.
_____ **7.** The principle under which the court will not hear a case unless there is an actual, present controversy for the court to decide.
_____ **8.** A short and simple trial.
_____ **9.** A written order to the sheriff, commanding the sheriff to enforce a judgment of the court.
_____ **10.** The written statements of claims and defenses used by the parties in the lawsuit.
_____ **11.** A formal notice to the defendant that a lawsuit has begun and that the defendant either must file an answer within the number of days set by state law or lose the case by default.
_____ **12.** The calendar of cases that are ready for trial. (Select two answers.)
_____ **13.** A written order to the sheriff commanding the sheriff to attach the real or personal property of the defendant.
_____ **14.** A person who holds legal title to property in trust for another.
_____ **15.** A written statement made under oath, confirming the correctness, truth, or authenticity of a pleading.
_____ **16.** The means of compelling the defendant in an action to appear in court.
_____ **17.** The delivering of summonses or other legal documents to the people who are required to receive them.
_____ **18.** Set time limit for how long plaintiffs can wait to file a lawsuit.
_____ **19.** The delivery of a copy of the summons and complaint to the defendant personally.
_____ **20.** A written order of a court, returnable to the same, commanding the performance or nonperformance of an act.
_____ **21.** A type of service in which the summons and complaint are delivered to the defendant's agent, mailed, or published in a newspaper.
_____ **22.** A person who carries out service of process.
_____ **23.** One who brings a lawsuit.

Using Legal Language

Read the following story and fill in the blank lines with legal terms taken from the list of terms at the beginning of this chapter:

After checking to see whether the client's case wasn't too old, but was still within ________________________________ ____________________, the attorney began the lawsuit by filing the ________________________, which is the plaintiff's first ____________________________, with the clerk of the court, who assigned a(n) ________________________________ to the case to identify it. The attorney then had the ________________________________ serve copies of the ________________________________ and complaint on the defendant, who was called a(n) ________________________ because of an unknown name. Because of the fact that ________________________________—that is, the means for compelling the defendant to appear in court—occurred by leaving the papers at the defendant's last and usual place of abode, it was not ________________________ service; instead, it was called ________________________________. The attorney

also filed a motion for a(n) ________________________________ at a(n) ________________________ session of the court to place a(n) ________________________________, which is also called a(n) ____________________________ on the defendant's real property, without the defendant being notified beforehand. Along with the motion, the attorney was required to file a(n) ________________________________, which was signed under oath by the client, who was called the________________________________ or ____________________________. The court allowed the attachment, and the ________________________________ was recorded at the Registry of Deeds. Because this did not involve the attachment of property in the hands of a third party, ________________________________, which is also called ________________________________, was not used. As case preparations for trial were concluding, it was placed on the docket.

4

Defensive Pleadings in Civil Trials

ANTE INTERROGATORY

A statement or claim that the party making it expects to prove is a(n)
(A) affirmative defense, (B) allegation, (C) demurrer, and (D) cross-complaint.

LEARNING OBJECTIVES

LO 1: Explain the purpose of a demurrer

LO 2: Define a motion and categorize some of the important defensive motions

LO 3: Compare and contrast a motion to dismiss without prejudice with a motion to dismiss with prejudice

LO 4: Compare and contrast a motion for judgment on the pleadings with a motion for summary judgment

LO 5: Explain what must be and what can be in the defendant's answer

LO 6: List common affirmative defenses

LO 7: Explain a counterclaim, including distinguishing a compulsory conterclaim from a permissive counterclaim

LO 8: Contrast a cross-claim from a counterclaim

KEY TERMS

affirmative defense

answer

confession and avoidance

counterclaim

cross-claim

cross-complaint

default judgment

demurrer

dismissal

dismissal with prejudice

dismissal without prejudice

misnomer

motion

motion for a more definite statement

motion for judgment on the pleadings

motion for recusal

motion for summary judgment

motion to dismiss

motion to strike

nonsuit

overrule

recuse

reply

summary judgment

sustain

WEBSITES FOR PRONUNCIATION HELP

http://dictionary.cambridge.org/us/pronunciation/english/audio
https://www.howtopronounce.com

After a civil action has begun and the summons and complaint have been served on the defendant, it is necessary for the defendant to file one or more defensive pleadings within a certain number of days from the date of service of the summons. The number of days within which this filing must be done varies from state to state. In Massachusetts, a defensive pleading must be filed within 20 days; in California, 30 days. If a defensive pleading is not filed within the mandated period, the defendant will lose the case by default unless the court sets aside the default judgment, for good cause, including "excusable neglect," or even fraud committed by the person who filed the suit.

DEMURRER

A defensive pleading used at common law and infrequently used in a few states is the demurrer. A **demurrer** is a pleading available to the defendant to attack the plaintiff's complaint by raising a point of law, such as the failure of the complaint to state a cause of action on which relief can be granted. In effect, a demurrer points out that even if the plaintiff's allegations are true, no cause of action exists. Some grounds for using a demurrer follow:

1. The complaint does not state facts sufficient to constitute a cause of action.
2. The court has no jurisdiction over the subject matter of the case.
3. The plaintiff has no legal capacity to sue.
4. Another action is pending between the same parties for the same cause.
5. A defect, or misjoinder of the parties, in the suit exists.

If the court **sustains** (supports) the demurrer, the case will end by a nonsuit unless the court allows the plaintiff to amend the complaint. A **nonsuit** is the termination of an action without adjudicating issues on the merits. If the demurrer is **overruled** (annulled, made void, or not sustained), the defendant is given a certain number of days to file an answer (to be discussed later).

The federal courts and many states have eliminated the demurrer as a formal type of answer, replacing it with one or more of the motions that will be discussed subsequently.

MOTIONS

A **motion** is a written or oral request made to a court for certain action to be taken. For example, when an attorney believes that the sitting judge is biased or prejudiced against a client, the attorney might make a **motion for recusal**. This is a request that the judge **recuse** (disqualify) himself or herself from the case because of the unfairness.

Motions are made for many different reasons and can be made by either party to a suit. Some of the important defensive motions follow:

1. motion to dismiss
2. motion for a more definite statement
3. motion to strike
4. motion for judgment on the pleadings
5. motion for summary judgment

Motion to Dismiss

In some cases, the plaintiff will do something that will give the defendant grounds to have the case dismissed. When this happens, the defendant may make a **motion to dismiss** the case. **Dismissal** is an order disposing of an action without trial of the issues. The motion must be made within a prescribed number of days after the defendant receives service of process.

After a motion to dismiss is filed with the court and sent to the opposing (plaintiff's) attorney, the attorney for the defendant marks up the motion to be heard by the court during one of its motion sessions. At this session, the attorneys for the parties argue their viewpoints as to the merits of the motion. The clients usually do not attend the motion session. The judge then makes a decision to either allow or deny the motion. If the motion to dismiss is allowed by an order for **dismissal without prejudice**, the plaintiff is allowed to correct the error and bring another action on the same claim. In contrast, if the order is a **dismissal with prejudice**, the plaintiff is barred from bringing another suit on the same claim. If the motion to dismiss is denied, the defendant is given a certain number of days to file an answer.

The defendant may make a motion to dismiss for any of the following reasons:

1. lack of jurisdiction over the subject matter of the case
2. lack of jurisdiction over the defendant personally
3. improper venue
4. insufficiency of process (such as a defective summons)
5. insufficiency of service of process (as when service of process is made on someone not authorized to accept service)
6. failure to state a claim on which relief can be granted
7. failure to join a necessary party
8. **misnomer** (mistake in the name) of a party
9. pendency of a prior action in a court of the same state

Motion for a More Definite Statement

If a pleading is so vague that the other party cannot properly respond to it, a **motion for a more definite statement** may be made. If the motion is allowed, the other party must file the more definite statement within a prescribed number of days (usually 10). The one who brought the motion then has 10 more days to answer the more definite statement. If the motion is denied, the answer must be filed within 10 days after notice of the court's denial.

Motion to Strike

A **motion to strike** may be used by either party to have stricken from any pleading any insufficient defense or any redundant, immaterial, impertinent, or scandalous matter.

Motion for Judgment on the Pleadings

A **motion for judgment on the pleadings** may be made by either the defendant or the plaintiff. It must be made only after both the plaintiff's complaint and the defendant's answer have been filed. The plaintiff might make the motion on the ground that the defendant's answer does not set forth a legally sufficient defense. The defendant might make the motion on the ground that the plaintiff's complaint does not state a claim on which relief can be granted.

TERMS IN ACTION

In 2009, a federal judge in Florida responded to a lawyer's **motion for dismissal** by denying it and writing in his order that the motion was "riddled with unprofessional grammatical and typographical errors that nearly render the entire motion incomprehensible." Reading the motion with a red pen in hand, U.S. District Judge Gregory Presnell marked it up as if it had been turned in for a grade, which in a way is true about all pleadings and motions submitted to courts. Included in the lawyer's motion were typographical errors, apostrophe errors, spacing errors, and the use of wrong words (e.g., "attended on" instead of "intended to"). The judge made a copy of the motion with his corrections on it, attached it to his **order denying the**

(Continued)

> **motion without prejudice**, and ordered the lawyer to show a copy of the red-inked motion to his client. Judge Presnell seems to be a stickler with a sense of humor, because he made news in 2006 when he ordered the lawyers in a case who couldn't even agree to the location of a deposition to play one game of "Rock, Paper, Scissors" in the presence of a paralegal, giving the winner the right to choose the deposition site.
>
> Source: abovethelaw.com; abajournal.com; blogs.wsj.com

Motion for Summary Judgment

A **motion for summary judgment** may be made when all of the papers filed in a case show there is no genuine issue of material fact and that the party making the motion will win the case as a matter of law. Designed to avoid an unnecessary trial, a **summary judgment** is an immediate decision by the trial judge, based on the documents filed by the parties, such as affidavits, depositions, and admissions.

Defendant's Answer

Unless the case is dismissed by the allowance of a motion to dismiss, the defendant must file a written **answer** within a prescribed number of days after service of process, and in many jurisdictions the time limit is 20 days. The defendant's answer must state in short and plain terms the defenses he or she wishes to assert. In addition, each of the claims made by the plaintiff must be admitted or denied. If the defendant is without knowledge or information sufficient to form a belief as to the truth of an allegation, he or she may so state, which has the effect of a denial. If an allegation is partly true and partly false, the defendant may admit part and deny part of the allegation. If the defendant fails to deny an allegation made in the plaintiff's complaint, it is automatically admitted.

Failure to file an answer will cause a **default judgment** to be entered. This judgment is entered on failure of a party to appear or plead at the proper time.

TERMS IN ACTION

A blind lawyer in Philadelphia who sued an escort for overbilling him on his credit card faced a **counterclaim** by the escort, who claimed that the lawyer inappropriately touched her; but both claims were **dismissed**. In 2008, attorney John F. Peoples filed a federal lawsuit against Ginger Dayle, alleging she overbilled him by at least $8,000 for what he later stated in a deposition were prostitution services at her apartment. Because Mr. Peoples is blind, Ms. Dayle entered the dollar amounts for him on the credit card charge receipts she gave him, which he signed. He also sued the credit card company used for the transactions, accusing it of breach of contract for not removing the overcharges. Upon being sued, the credit card company filed an **answer** and a **motion for summary judgment**. It claimed that, because illegal contracts are void and because prostitution is illegal in Pennsylvania, it couldn't be liable for breach of contract relating to those charges. Ms. Dayle filed an **answer** denying overbilling Peoples, and she filed a counterclaim. She alleged that she was teaching a personal exercise class to Peoples and that he sexually harassed her during one of their 25 sessions. The federal district judge agreed with the credit card company and granted it the order of **dismissal**. He then **dismissed without prejudice** Ms. Dayle's counterclaim so that she could file it in state court, because having dismissed the entire case, the judge lacked jurisdiction over her suit. Mr. Peoples then appealed the decision to the 3rd Circuit Court of Appeals, where he lost. He then sought the U.S. Supreme Court's review on the matter, but in 2011 it refused to take the case.

Source: abajournal.com; abovethelaw.com; *Peoples v. Discover Financial Services*, 209 WL 3030217 (unpublished)

Affirmative Defenses

Many times, the defendant will have done the act for which he or she is being sued, but will have some other reason that will stop the plaintiff from winning the case, which is called an **affirmative defense** (a **confession and avoidance** under the common law). The defendant admits the plaintiff's allegation, but introduces something new that constitutes a defense to it. When an affirmative defense is used in federal and in many state courts, it must be stated in the defendant's answer. If it is omitted from the answer, that particular defense is lost and cannot be used later.

The affirmative defenses are as follows:

accord and satisfaction	injury by fellow servant
arbitration and award	laches
assumption of risk	license
contributory negligence	payment
discharge in bankruptcy	release
duress	res judicata
estoppel	statute of frauds
failure of consideration	statute of limitations
fraud	waiver
illegality	

COUNTERCLAIM

If the defendant (after receiving the summons and complaint) wishes to bring a suit against the plaintiff, he or she will file a counterclaim. A **counterclaim** is a claim that the defendant has against the plaintiff. It is made a part of the defendant's answer. The counterclaim is *compulsory* if the defendant wishes to bring a claim that arises out of the same transaction or occurrence as that of the plaintiff's suit, the venue is correct, and the court has jurisdiction. If the defendant's counterclaim is not related to the event that caused the original suit, the counterclaim is *permissive*. For example, a neighbor could sue another for negligence, but the second neighbor could file a counterclaim for breach of contract, over an unpaid lawnmower. The plaintiff is required to file a reply to the defendant's counterclaim within a prescribed number of days after receiving the counterclaim. The **reply** is the legal name given to the answer to the counterclaim.

Word Wise
Compound Words

In addition to words made up of prefixes, suffixes, and roots, English has many words made by compounding—that is, joining two or more words already in usage to create a new word with a new meaning. The term "counterclaim," introduced in this chapter, is such a word. Almost any combination of the parts of speech may be used to create a compound word. The following methods are the most common: noun with adjective (heartsick, airtight); adjective with noun (blackberry, hothouse); preposition with noun (overhead, downfall); verb with adverb (dugout, kickoff).

CROSS-CLAIM

Sometimes, a suit will be brought against two defendants, and one of those defendants will wish to bring a claim against the other defendant. A claim brought by one defendant against another defendant in the same suit is called a **cross-claim**. The subject matter of the cross-claim must arise out of the same transaction or occurrence as that of the original suit. A cross-claim must be answered within a prescribed number of days after it is received.

CROSS-COMPLAINT

The State of California uses a pleading known as a **cross-complaint** in place of a counterclaim and a cross-claim. The California cross-complaint may be used to file a claim by a defendant against (1) another defendant, (2) a third party, and (3) the plaintiff in the same action.

> **Web Wise**
>
> Go to **www.quizlet.com** to create customized vocabulary flash cards, play study games, and find vocabulary for a variety of subjects.

Reviewing What You Learned

After studying the chapter, write the answers to each of the following questions:

1. What must the defendant do after he or she has been served with a summons and a complaint? What will happen if this is not done?

2. What is one ground for using a demurrer?

3. Who usually attends the hearing for the demurrer to be heard by the court?

4. Name four important defensive motions.

5. Who attends a motion session? What happens at such a session?

6. What must the defendant do if the motion to dismiss is denied?

7. List three grounds for a motion to dismiss.

8. What may the opposing party do if a pleading is so vague that the party cannot respond to it?

____

____

____

____

9. What may the opposing party do if a pleading contains an insufficient defense or any redundant, immaterial, impertinent, or scandalous matter?

____

____

____

____

10. On what ground might a plaintiff make a motion for judgment on the pleadings? On what ground might a defendant make such a motion?

____

____

____

11. What must the defendant's answer state?

____

____

____

12. What will be the result if the defendant fails to deny any allegation made in the plaintiff's complaint?

____

____

____

13. What will be the result if an affirmative defense is omitted from the defendant's answer?

____

14. List three affirmative defenses.

____

____

____

15. What may the defendant do if he or she wishes to bring a suit against the plaintiff? In what way is this related to the defendant's answer?

____

____

____

____

16. How must the plaintiff respond to a defendant's counterclaim?

____

____

____

17. Who are the parties to a cross-claim? Out of what must the subject matter of a cross-claim arise?

____

____

____

____

Understanding Legal Concepts

Indicate whether each statement is true or false. Then, change the italicized word or phrase of each false statement to make it true.

ANSWERS

_____ **1.** In many states, after an action has begun, it is necessary for the defendant to file one or more defensive pleadings within *20 days* from the date of service of the summons.

_____ **2.** If the court *sustains* a demurrer, the defendant is given a certain number of days to file an answer.

_____ **3.** A motion to dismiss *may be* allowed for failure to state a claim for which relief can be granted.

_____ **4.** A motion to dismiss may be allowed for *misnomer* of a party.

_____ **5.** A motion for judgment on the pleadings may be made by *the defendant only*.

_____ **6.** The plaintiff might make a motion for judgment on the pleadings on the ground that the *defendant's answer* does not set forth a legally sufficient defense.

_____ **7.** Unless the case is dismissed by the allowance of a motion to dismiss, the defendant must file a *written* answer within a prescribed number of days after service of process.

_____ **8.** If the defendant fails to deny an allegation made in the plaintiff's complaint, the allegation is *automatically admitted*.

_____ **9.** When an affirmative defense is used, the defendant *denies* the plaintiff's allegation.

_____ **10.** A *cross-claim* is a claim that the defendant brings against the plaintiff.

Checking Terminology

From the list of legal terms that follows, select the one that matches each definition.

ANSWERS

a. affirmative defense
b. answer
c. confession and avoidance
d. counterclaim
e. cross-claim
f. cross-complaint
g. default judgment
h. demurrer
i. dismissal
j. dismissal without prejudice
k. dismissal with prejudice
l. misnomer
m. motion
n. motion for a more definite statement
o. motion for judgment on the pleadings
p. motion for summary judgment
q. motion for recusal
r. motion to dismiss
s. motion to strike
t. nonsuit
u. overrule
v. recuse
w. reply
x. summary judgment
y. sustain

_____ **1.** Mistake in name.

_____ **2.** A dismissal in which the plaintiff is allowed to correct the error and to bring another action on the same claim.

_____ **3.** A claim that the defendant has against the plaintiff.

_____ **4.** To support.

_____ **5.** A motion made by the defendant, asking the court to dismiss the case.

_____ **6.** A claim brought by one defendant against another defendant in the same suit.

_____ **7.** The termination of an action that did not adjudicate issues on the merits.

_____ **8.** A defense that admits the plaintiff's allegations, but introduces another factor that avoids liability. (Select two answers.)

_____ **9.** A motion asking the court to order the other party to remove from a pleading any insufficient defense or any redundant, immaterial, impertinent, or scandalous matter.

_____ **10.** A motion by a party, when a pleading is vague, asking the court to order the other party to make a more definite statement.

_____ **11.** A pleading used in California by a defendant to file a claim against another defendant, a third party, and the plaintiff in the same action.

_____ **12.** The main pleading filed by the defendant in a lawsuit in response to the plaintiff's complaint.

_____ **13.** To annul, make void, or refuse to sustain.

_____ **14.** A dismissal in which the plaintiff is barred from bringing another action on the same claim.

_____ **15.** The plaintiff's answer to the defendant's counterclaim.

_____ **16.** A motion by either party for a judgment, in that party's favor, based solely on information contained in the pleadings.

_____ **17.** Disqualify.

_____ **18.** A judgment entered on failure of a party to appear or plead at the proper time.

_____ **19.** A written or oral request made to a court for certain action to be taken.

_____ **20.** A request that a judge disqualify himself or herself from a case because of bias or prejudice.

Sharpening Your Latin Skills

In the space provided, write the definition of each of the following legal terms, referring to the glossary when necessary:

ad damnum ___________________________________

lis pendens ___________________________________

ex parte ___________________________________

nolo contendere ___________________________________

in personam ___________________________________

quasi in rem ___________________________________

in rem ___________________________________

Using Legal Language

Read the following story and fill in the blank lines with legal terms taken from the list of terms at the beginning of this chapter:

After reading the allegations in the plaintiff's complaint and determining that they were not vague, the attorney for the defendant decided not to file a motion ___________________________________. Similarly, because the complaint contained nothing that was redundant, immaterial, impertinent, or scandalous, the attorney for the defendant did not file a(n) ___________________________________. The attorney did, however, file a motion ___________________________________ on the ground of ___________________________________ (mistake in name) of a party. A(n) ___________________________________ is an order disposing of an action without trial of the issues. When the defendant's motion was disallowed by the court, the defendant's attorney filed a(n) ___________________________________ within the prescribed time, which contained the ___________________________________ defense (called a(n) ___________________________________ under the common law) of the statute of frauds. Neither party filed a(n) ___________________________________, which may be filed only after the plaintiff's complaint and defendant's answer have been filed and which replaces the older ___________________________________. The defendant's attorney also filed a(n) ___________________________________ to bring a claim against the plaintiff, which arose out of the same transaction. In answer to this claim, the plaintiff filed a(n) ___________________________________. Because the case did not have two defendants, no ___________________________________ was filed.

Methods of Discovery

ANTE INTERROGATORY

An agreement between the parties involved in a suit (through their attorneys) regulating any matter relative to the proceedings is a(n) (A) deposition, (B) interrogatory, (C) subpoena, (D) stipulation.

LEARNING OBJECTIVES

LO 1: List the common methods of discovery

LO 2: Explain what an interrogatory is and on whom interrogatories may be served

LO 3: Compare and contrast depositions with interrogatories

LO 4: Differentiate the types of depositions

LO 5: Explain when depositions may be used in court proceedings

LO 6: Explain how a party to an action may obtain in discovery of documents and things

LO 7: Explain why a party would want to enter another party's property or seek a physical or medical examination of another party

LO 8: Summarize the response a party would make after the other party makes a request for an admission

KEY TERMS

bill of particulars
cross-questions
demand for bill of particulars
deponent
deposition
deposition on oral examination
deposition on written questions
discovery
discovery sanction
e-discovery
electronically stored information (ESI)
impeach
interrogatories
metadata

motion for order compelling discovery
notary public
party to a suit
perjury
recross-questions
redirect questions
safe harbor provision
stipulate
stipulation
subpoena
subpoena ad testificandum
subpoena duces tecum
verbatim
verification

WEBSITES FOR PRONUNCIATION HELP

http://dictionary.cambridge.org/us/pronunciation/english/audio
https://www.howtopronounce.com

In the past, it was considered good legal practice for one party to a lawsuit to give the other party as little information as possible about the case before the trial. Today, the opposite is true. In fact, Rule 26(b)(1) of the Federal Rules of Civil Procedure states in part, "Parties may obtain discovery regarding any nonprivileged matter that is relevant to a party's claim or defense and proportional to the needs of the case...." Attorneys will often enter into agreements, called stipulations, about different aspects of the case. A **stipulation** is an agreement between the parties involved in a suit (an action) regulating any matter relative to the proceedings. Attorneys may, for example, **stipulate** (agree) to extend the time for pleading, waive objections, admit certain facts, or continue the case to a later date.

Several methods, called methods of **discovery**, have been established that allow each party to obtain information from the other party and from witnesses about the case before going to trial. In this way, the real issues in the case are exposed early, and much less time is wasted. The most common methods of discovery follow:

1. Bill of particulars
2. Interrogatories
3. Depositions
4. Production of documents and things
5. Permission to enter on land
6. Physical and mental examinations
7. Requests for admission

BILL OF PARTICULARS

In some states, including California, the plaintiff is not required to set forth in the complaint the details of the amount due on a contract for the sale of goods. All that is required by the plaintiff is to set forth the total amount owed. If the defendant files a pleading, called a **demand for bill of particulars**, within a prescribed period (10 days after service of process in California), the plaintiff must deliver to the defendant details of the amount owed in the form of a bill of particulars. A **bill of particulars** is a written statement of the particulars of a complaint, showing the details of the amount owed. In California, the bill of particulars must include a **verification** if the complaint contains a verification. A verification is a written statement or declaration made under penalty of perjury, often placed at the end of a document (such as a pleading), that the underlying document is true.

INTERROGATORIES

After an action has begun, any **party to a suit** (any plaintiff and any defendant) may ask written questions of any other party to the suit. The written questions are called **interrogatories**. They may be served on any defendant, along with the summons and complaint or at a later time. They may be served on the plaintiff at any time after the action has begun. If not sent along with the summons and complaint, interrogatories are usually served by a copy being mailed to the opposing attorney, and the original copy is filed with the court. Rule 33 of the Federal Rules of Civil Procedure limits the number of interrogatories that may be served on a party to 25. Other states have similar limitations. In Massachusetts, up to 30 interrogatories may be served. Florida also limits interrogatories to 30, unless the court approves a motion for more, on the basis of good cause.

Interrogatories must be answered in writing, and signed by the client answering them under the penalties of **perjury**—that is, intentionally giving false testimony under oath. Each interrogatory must be answered separately and fully unless it is objected to, in which event the reasons for objection must be stated. The party interrogated has 30 or 45 days, depending on the jurisdiction, to file the answers to the interrogatories with the court and to mail a copy of the answers to the interrogating party. In California, interrogatories and answers to interrogatories are not filed with the court unless the court orders them to be filed.

Rules governing the failure of a party to answer interrogatories vary from state to state. For example, California law provides for the interrogating party to file a motion to compel interrogatories when necessary. Massachusetts law provides that if the party interrogated fails to file the answers within 45 days, the interrogating party may file an application for a request for final judgment (against the defendant) or a request for a dismissal (against the plaintiff), whichever is appropriate. The clerk of court will then notify all parties that a final judgment or a dismissal will be entered unless the answers are filed within 30 days. If 30 days elapse without an answer to the interrogatories being filed, the interrogator may reapply for a final judgment or a dismissal, and it will be allowed by the court if the answers are not, by then, on file.

DEPOSITIONS

An important method of discovery before the trial occurs is the **deposition**, which is the testimony of a witness given under oath, but not in open court. Unlike interrogatories, which may be served only on another party, depositions may be taken of any "person," according to Rules 30 and 31 of the Federal Rules of Civil Procedure. The witness who gives the testimony is known as a **deponent** (one who gives testimony under oath). Two principal types of depositions are (1) depositions on oral examination and (2) depositions of witnesses on written questions.

Depositions on Oral Examination

After an action begins, any party may take the testimony of any person, including a party, by **deposition on oral examination**. In this deposition, lawyers orally examine and cross-examine a witness. With a few exceptions, permission of the court is not required for this deposition. Witnesses may be compelled to attend by **subpoena**, sometimes called a **subpoena ad testificandum** (a court order commanding a person to appear and testify in a legal action).

A party desiring to take the deposition must give a prescribed number of days' written notice to every other party to the action. The notice must state the time and place for taking the deposition and the name and address of each person to be examined. A **subpoena duces tecum** is a court order commanding a person to appear and bring certain papers or other materials that are pertinent to the legal action. Accountants and record keepers are often subpoenaed this way. If a subpoena duces tecum is to be served on the person to be examined, the materials to be produced must be listed on the notice.

Depositions are taken before a person authorized to administer oaths, such as a **notary public**. Lawyers for each side examine and cross-examine the witnesses. The testimony is recorded by a court reporter or stenographer, either electronically or by traditional stenographic means. Usually, the stenographer is also a notary public and performs both functions of administering the oath and taking down the testimony. Instead of participating in the oral examination, parties may, if they wish, submit written questions to be answered by the witness under oath. The questions and answers are taken down **verbatim** (word for word) by the stenographer.

After the testimony is transcribed it is either read or shown to the witness whose testimony it is. Any changes that the witness desires to make are written on the deposition by the officer who administered the oath, with reasons given by the witness for the changes. The deposition is signed by the witness, or a reason is noted for the witness's failure to sign. It is then hand delivered to the court or mailed to the court by registered or certified mail, although some states, such as Missouri, no longer automatically require a deposition to be filed with the court.

Depositions of Witnesses on Written Questions

After an action begins, any party may take the testimony of any person, including a party, by **deposition on written questions**. In this type of deposition, lawyers examine and cross-examine a witness who has received in advance written questions to be answered. Witnesses may be compelled to attend, by subpoena. A party desiring to take such a deposition must serve the written questions on all parties to the action, together with the name and address of the person who is to answer them and the name and address of the officer before whom the deposition is to be taken. In some states, after the questions are served, a party may serve **cross-questions** (questions asked by a deponent in response to questions asked at a deposition) on any other party. The party receiving the cross-questions may serve **redirect questions** (further questions in response to cross-questions) on all other parties. In addition, after being served with redirect questions, a party may serve **recross-questions** (further questions asked in response to redirect questions) on all other parties.

The depositions of witnesses on written questions are handled by the stenographer and filed with the court in the same manner that depositions on oral examinations are handled, as explained earlier.

Use of Depositions in Court Proceedings

When the case goes to court, the depositions may be used to contradict or **impeach** (call into question or cast doubt on) any contrary testimony of a witness. According to Rule 32 of the Federal Rules of Civil Procedure, the deposition may also be used at the trial if the witness is dead; the witness is at a distance greater than 100 miles from the place of the trial; the witness is unable to testify because of age, sickness, infirmity, or imprisonment; or if other exceptional circumstances make it desirable that the deposition be used.

TERMS IN ACTION

In 1961, Marie Robertson gave a $35-million-dollar gift to Princeton University, which was set up as a foundation meant to support the Woodrow Wilson School of Public and International Affairs. In 2002, Mrs. Robertson's son and daughter sued Princeton, alleging mismanagement and fraud, and seeking to obtain control over the funds, which by then had grown to over $500 million. The lawsuit was the most expensive in Princeton's history, largely due to the extensive **discovery** in the case. By 2004, the plaintiffs had deposed close to 40 witnesses and were scheduled to depose 20 more. Thousands of **document examinations** took place in preparation of the depositions, some of which lasted many hours. One **deposition** of a former Princeton administrator who graduated from Princeton in 1940, took over six days, due in part to the **deponent's** age and health. The lawsuit eventually settled in 2008. Princeton ultimately retained control over the foundation, but part of the settlement included Princeton's paying to the plaintiffs over $40 million in legal costs incurred during the six-year litigation.

Source: dailyprincetonian.com; nj.com

PRODUCTION OF DOCUMENTS AND THINGS

Any party may serve on any other party a request for permission to inspect and copy documents (including writings, drawings, graphs, charts, photographs, and other data compilations) or to inspect and copy, test, or sample any tangible things.

The party on whom the request is made must serve a written response, within a prescribed number of days after the service of the request, stating the request will be permitted or that it is objected to, with reasons given for any objection. If an objection occurs, the party submitting the request may make a **motion for order compelling discovery**. After a hearing, the court may allow or disallow the motion.

E-DISCOVERY

Parties may also obtain discovery of electronic communications or other information stored electronically rather than on paper. This form of discovery, known as **e-discovery**, has grown dramatically as more and more data are exclusively created and stored electronically, such as e-mail, text messages, or other forms of social media like Facebook.com. This type of information is often referred to as ESI (**electronically stored information**).

In 2006, the Federal Rules of Civil Procedure were amended to reflect the growth of e-discovery. The changes included a definition of ESI and the acknowledgment that ESI is discoverable. When documents are created on a computer, another form of data is created "underneath" the document. This information is about the creation of the document or file, and is called **metadata**. For example, as this textbook was being written on word processing software, information on the documents was being invisibly stored, including the dates the files were accessed, whose computers were being used, and the various changes made to the files before they were saved as final drafts. Metadata are akin to an electronic fingerprint, and they are discoverable.

Discovery costs are always a concern in litigation, and e-discovery has raised new concerns over costs. Traditionally, a party pays the costs of responding to the other side's discovery requests, which is expensive in and of itself. But the costs of finding and retrieving all the thousands—and sometimes, millions—of electronic data can be exorbitant. Therefore, Rule 26 of the Federal Rules of Civil Procedure now allows a party who is asked to produce ESI to shift the costs of production to the requesting party, where the ESI being sought is not readily accessible. Additionally, Rule 37(f) was amended to create what is commonly referred to as a **safe harbor provision**, which protects a party from **discovery sanctions** (court-ordered penalties for failing to produce evidence) when a party cannot produce ESI because it was lost due to the routine good-faith operations of an electronic information system.

Web Wise

In the advent of e-discovery rules becoming more common, websites and web logs (blogs) have been created to inform the legal community about recent changes to e-discovery rules, or to provide cases dealing with e-discovery controversies. The following are a few websites and blogs that focus on e-discovery:

www.ediscoverylaw.com

www.electronicdiscoveryblog.com

www.allaboutediscovery.com

www.theediscoveryblog.com

TERMS IN ACTION

It can be confusing to know whether **electronic communications** are subject to **e-discovery** or instead are protected by a privilege against discovery. A California appellate court ruled in 2011 that an e-mail sent by a client to her lawyer was not protected by the attorney–client privilege, and was **discoverable** because the client sent the e-mail from her work e-mail account. In that case, the court found that the employee had no reasonable expectation of privacy in such an e-mail. But in 2010, the New Jersey Supreme Court reached a nearly opposite conclusion in a similar case. In both cases, the plaintiffs were suing their employers and both employees had sent e-mails to their personal attorneys. One difference between the two cases was that in the California case, the employee sent the personal e-mail through her work e-mail account, whereas in the New Jersey case, the employee sent her e-mail by way of her work computer, but through her personal, password-protected Gmail account, an e-mail service available on Google.com. And in 2016, a U.S. magistrate judge ruled that the broad scope of Rule 26 of the Federal Rules of Civil Procedure required two defendants who worked as doctors for a prison to search for and produce certain e-mails on their personal computers. The plaintiff, a transgender inmate in a county correctional facility, brought the federal suit alleging the defendants were dismissive of the plaintiff's medical condition and stopped her hormone therapy. The defendants argued their personal computer devices were not subject to discovery, but the judge ruled otherwise, in part because the defendants were being sued in their individual capacity, not their official capacity. Furthermore, the judge thought, to the extent any **electronically stored information** (ESI) showing bias against the plaintiff existed, it would make sense they would be sent on personal, rather than work, computers.

Source: wired.com; *Holmes v. Petrovich Development Co., LLC.*, 191 Cal.App.4th 1047 (2011); *Stengart v. Loving Care Agency, Inc.*, 990 A.2nd 651 (2010); *Sunderland v. Suffolk City*, No. CV 13-4838 (E.D.N.Y. June 14, 2016)

<table>
<tr><td colspan="3">Word Wise
Time Prefixes</td></tr>
<tr><td>Prefix</td><td>Meaning</td><td>Examples</td></tr>
<tr><td>re-</td><td>again</td><td>reapply, rediscover, reorganization, rebuttal, recross questions, redirect questions, republish</td></tr>
<tr><td>post-</td><td>after</td><td>postpone, postgraduate, postmortem</td></tr>
<tr><td>pre-</td><td>before</td><td>preadolescence, prearrange, predecease, premarital, premeditated, prenuptial</td></tr>
</table>

PERMISSION TO ENTER ON LAND

Any party may serve on any other party a request to permit entry on land or other property in the possession or control of the party on whom the request is served. The entry may be for the purpose of inspecting, measuring, surveying, photographing, testing, or sampling the property. The party to whom the request is made must respond in the manner described in the section titled "Production of Documents and Things."

PHYSICAL AND MENTAL EXAMINATIONS

When the mental or physical condition of a party is in controversy, the court in which the action is pending may order the party to submit to a physical or mental examination. The order may be made only on motion for good cause and after notice is given to the person to be examined.

REQUESTS FOR ADMISSION

A party may serve on any other party a written request for admission of the truth of any matter that is relevant to the case. The request may relate to statements, opinions of fact or law, or the genuineness of documents.

The party to whom the request is directed must file a written answer within a prescribed number of days after service of the request. The answer must state, under the penalties of perjury, (1) a denial of the matter; (2) a reason that the answering party cannot truthfully admit or deny the matter; or (3) an objection, with reasons, to the request. If such an answer is not filed, the matter is considered by the court to be admitted.

Reviewing What You Learned

After studying the chapter, write the answers to each of the following questions:

1. How do methods of discovery used in the past compare with those of today?

____

____

____

2. List seven common methods of discovery.

____

____

____

3. To whom may interrogatories be asked?

____

____

____

4. Who signs the answers to the interrogatories?

____

____

____

5. What are the differences between a deposition and an interrogatory?

____

____

____

6. Depositions are taken in front of whom? The testimony is taken down by whom?

____

____

____

7. What occurs after the testimony of a deposition is transcribed?

____

____

____

8. Describe the back-and-forth questioning procedure that occurs when a deposition on written questions occurs.

____

____

____

9. Under what circumstances may depositions be used in court?

____

____

____

10. How must a party who is requested to produce documents respond to such request?

____

____

____

11. For what purposes may a person request permission to enter on land of another?

____

____

____

12. Under what circumstances may the court order a party to submit to a physical or mental examination?

____

____

____

13. How must a party who is requested to admit a particular matter respond?

____

____

____

14. What types of information or data are part of the e-discovery world?

____

____

____

15. How have the discovery rules changed to accommodate e-discovery?

____

____

____

16. What are metadata and who creates them?

____

____

____

Understanding Legal Concepts

Indicate whether each statement is true or false. Then, change the italicized word or phrase of each false statement to make it true.

ANSWERS

_____ **1.** Attorneys *never* enter into agreements about different aspects of a case.

_____ **2.** After an action has begun, any *party to a suit* may ask written questions of any other party to a suit.

_____ **3.** Interrogatories must be answered in writing and signed by the *attorney* answering them, under the penalties of perjury.

_____ **4.** A deposition is the testimony of a witness given under oath *in* open court.

_____ **5.** For a subpoena duces tecum properly to be served on a person to be examined, the materials to be produced *must be* listed on the notice.

_____ **6.** When depositions are taken, lawyers for each side *examine and cross-examine* the witnesses.

_____ **7.** A deposition of a witness *must not be* used at a trial if the witness is dead.

_____ **8.** Any party may serve on *any other party* a request to permit entry on the other's land.

_____ **9.** The court may order a party to submit to a physical, *but not* a mental, examination.

_____ **10.** If a party to whom a request for admission is directed fails to answer, the matter is considered by the court to be *admitted*.

Checking Terminology

From the list of legal terms that follows, select the one that matches each definition.

ANSWERS

a. bill of particulars
b. cross-questions
c. demand for bill of particulars
d. deponent
e. deposition
f. deposition on oral examination
g. deposition on written questions
h. discovery
i. discovery sanction
j. e-discovery
k. electronically stored information (ESI)
l. impeach
m. interrogatories
n. metadata
o. motion for order compelling discovery
p. notary public
q. party to a suit
r. perjury
s. recross-questions
t. redirect questions
u. safe harbor provision
v. stipulate
w. stipulation
x. subpoena
y. subpoena ad testificandum
z. subpoena duces tecum
aa. verbatim

_____ **1.** A person or organization participating or having a direct interest in a legal proceeding.

_____ **2.** Methods that allow each party to obtain information from the other party and from witnesses about a case before going to court.

_____ **3.** A form of discovery, in a civil action, in which parties are given a series of written questions to be answered under oath.

_____ **4.** The testimony of a witness given under oath, but not in open court, and later reduced to writing.

_____ **5.** An order commanding a person to appear and testify in a legal action. (Select two answers.)

_____ **6.** An order commanding a person to appear and bring certain papers or other materials that are pertinent to a legal action.

_____ **7.** A person authorized to administer oaths, attest to and certify documents, take acknowledgments, and perform other official acts.

_____ **8.** The giving of false testimony under oath.

_____ **9.** One who gives testimony under oath.

_____ **10.** An agreement between the parties to an action regulating any matter relative to the proceedings.

_____ **11.** Call into question.

_____ **12.** Questions asked by a deponent concerning questions to be asked at a deposition.

_____ **13.** Further questions asked by a deponent in response to redirect questions.

_____ **14.** A deposition in which lawyers examine and cross-examine a witness who has received, in advance, written questions to be answered.

_____ **15.** A written statement of the particulars of a complaint, showing the details of the amount owed.

_____ **16.** Protection of a party from discovery sanctions when a party cannot produce ESI because it was lost due to routine operations.

_____ **17.** Court-ordered penalties for failing to produce evidence.

_____ **18.** A motion asking the court to order the other party to produce certain writings, photographs, or other requested items.

_____ **19.** Discovery of electronic communication stored electronically rather than on paper.

_____ **20.** To agree.

_____ **21.** Word for word.

_____ **22.** Electronic fingerprints, which are information about the creation of an electronic document or file.

Using Legal Language

Read the following story and fill in the blank lines with legal terms taken from the list of terms at the beginning of this chapter:

Before going to trial, attorney Mary Grey entered into an agreement, called a(n) _______________________, with the opposing side, admitting certain facts. She also used certain methods of _______________________ to obtain information from the other party and from witnesses about the case. She sent 30 questions, called _______________________, to be answered under oath by Conrad Allen, the defendant, who was a(n) _______________________ to the suit. She also sent a(n) _______________________, rather than a plain _______________________, to Leroy Henning, a witness, commanding him to bring with him certain payroll records of the defendant to a(n) _______________________, which is the testimony of a witness given under oath, but not in open court. Because written questions were submitted in advance to Leroy, the _______________________, this was known as a(n) _______________________. After receiving the questions, Leroy sent _______________________ to be answered by the plaintiff. The plaintiff, in turn, responded with further questions, called _______________________ to be answered by Leroy. The testimony was taken before a(n) _______________________, who was authorized to administer oaths, and written down _______________________— that is, word for word—by a stenographer. When the case goes to court, the questions and answers may be used to _______________________ —that is, call into question— Leroy's testimony. If Leroy gives false testimony, it is known as _______________________.

6

Pretrial Hearing and Jury Trial

ANTE INTERROGATORY

The examination of jurors by the court to see that they stand indifferent and have no biases against any of the parties is referred to as the (A) venire, (B) voir dire, (C) array, or (D) venue.

LEARNING OBJECTIVES

LO 1: Explain the purpose of a pretrial hearing and list what can be done in a pretrial hearing

LO 2: List what constitutional sources provide a right to a jury

LO 3: Summarize the process of selecting a jury, distinguishing the traditional method from the one day-one trial method

LO 4: Summarize the process of impaneling the jury, including how a foreperson is chosen

LO 5: Explain how jurors are examined in the voir dire process, including listing the five common reasons why a juror would be initially excused

LO 6: Contrast a challenge for cause from a peremptory challenge

KEY TERMS

alderpeople
alternate jurors
array
bench trial
challenge
challenge for cause
challenge to the array
foreperson
impaneled
indifferent
jurors
jury
jury panel
jury pool

jury waived trial
master
motion in limine
motion to quash the array
one day–one trial jury system
peremptory challenges
petit jury
pretrial (or pre-trial) hearing
selectpeople
talesmen
taleswomen
venire
voir dire
writ of venire facias

WEBSITES FOR PRONUNCIATION HELP

http://dictionary.cambridge.org/us/pronunciation/english/audio

https://www.howtopronounce.com

PRETRIAL HEARING

Before a trial is held, a **pretrial hearing** usually occurs. This hearing is designed to help the trial judge timely manage the case. Only the attorneys for each side are required to attend the hearing, but many attorneys like to bring their clients to have them available for questions that may arise. The attorneys appear before the judge to consider the possibility of doing any of the following:

1. simplify the issues to be resolved by the fact finder at trial
2. amend the pleadings
3. obtain admissions of fact
4. limit the number of expert witnesses
5. refer the case to a master[1]
6. settle the case
7. agree on damages
8. discuss other matters that may aid in the disposition of the action

Attorneys may make a variety of motions to the court during the pretrial hearing stage. A **motion in limine** is a pretrial motion asking the court to prohibit the introduction of prejudicial evidence by the other party. In Latin, limine means "at the threshold." A report of the pretrial hearing becomes a part of the record of the case.

RIGHT TO JURY TRIAL

Article III, Section 2, as well as the Sixth Amendment of the U.S. Constitution, grants the right to a trial by jury in all criminal cases, and the Seventh Amendment guarantees the right to a jury trial in any civil case involving more than $20, under the Federal Rules of Civil Procedure, any party may make a demand for a jury trial on the other party no later than 14 days after the service of the last pleading. In many states' civil procedure rules, parties have 10 days after the service of the last pleading to demand a jury trial. If a jury trial is not requested, a trial without a jury, called a **bench trial** (in some jurisdictions, a **jury waived trial**), will be held.

A **jury** (from the Latin *jurare*, meaning "to swear") is a group of people, called **jurors**, selected according to law and sworn to determine the facts in a case. The ordinary jury of 12 people used for the trial of a civil or criminal action is known as a **petit jury** to distinguish it from a grand jury, which issues indictments. It is not unusual in many jurisdictions that civil juries can have between 6 and 12 people. The system of selecting the jury varies from state to state. One system is described here.

Selecting the Venire

The **jury pool**, or large group of people from which juries are selected, is called the **jury panel** or the **venire**. Sometimes, it is referred to as the **array**. The selection of the venire has changed in recent years. Many jurisdictions have done away with the traditional method and replaced it with the "one day–one trial" system. Both methods are described here.

TRADITIONAL METHOD   Under the traditional method of selecting jurors, each city and town is required to prepare a list each year of everyone of good moral character who is eligible to serve on a jury. Each name on the list is placed on a separate ballot and kept in a ballot box by the city or town clerk. Before each sitting of the court (a sitting lasts one month), the clerk of

---

[1] A **master** is a lawyer appointed by the court to hear testimony in the case and to report back to the court his or her findings or conclusions.

court sends a **writ of venire facias** to each city and town within the court's jurisdiction. This writ orders the city or town to provide a designated number of jurors for the next sitting of the court. Jurors' names are then drawn from the ballot box by the mayor and alderpeople of a city and by the selectpeople of a town. **Alderpeople** are men and women elected to serve as members of the legislative body of a city. **Selectpeople** are men and women elected to serve as the chief administrative authority of a town. Jurors whose names are drawn by the cities and towns are summoned to appear before the court for jury duty for a month.

Historically, under this traditional method of selecting the venire, members of the clergy, lawyers, practicing physicians and surgeons, nurses, public school teachers, and certain other people are exempt from jury duty. However, many states have eliminated occupational exemptions for jury service. In some jurisdictions, persons of at least a certain age (65, 70, or even 75) can request to be exempt from jury service, and in a few jurisdictions, breastfeeding mothers can be excused from jury duty. The judge may exempt others from jury duty if it is best for the public interest or if such duty will impose an undue hardship on the person selected.

ONE DAY–ONE TRIAL METHOD   Another method of jury selection is coming into wider use. Called the **one day–one trial jury system**, it is designed to provide the courts with juries consisting of fair cross sections of the community and to reduce the burden of jury duty on certain classes of citizens.

The system varies from state to state. Under the Massachusetts system, which was the first state to implement the one-day-one trial method in 1979, a new group of jurors appears in the jury pool (venire) each day. Jurors who are not selected for a trial on that day are excused from further duty and cannot be called again for three years. Jurors who are selected for a trial serve only for that trial and no longer.

Under this system, there are generally no exemptions from jury duty. Every citizen 18 years old or older who can speak and understand the English language and is physically able must serve. Citizens 70 years old or older may choose not to serve. To be eligible to serve, persons must have been a resident or inhabitant for six months or more in the county in which they are summoned. Jurors are selected randomly by computer from an annual census list provided by the cities and towns. In the Massachusetts system, each juror, when summoned, is entitled to one postponement of up to one year from the date summoned. This postponement allows a juror to choose a more convenient date if the assigned date is not suitable. Each juror, when summoned, may request a transfer of courthouse location if the juror encounters a hardship in reporting to the assigned location.

Continuing the Massachusetts jury system example, jurors are only paid for their service after the third day of jury duty at a rate of $50 per day. Jurors who are employed must be compensated by their employers for the first three days of jury duty at their normal rate of pay.

IMPANELING THE JURY

On the day the jurors are summoned to court, the clerk of court places each juror's name on a ballot and puts it in a ballot box. When a case is ready for trial, the members of the venire are brought into open court. Twelve of their names are picked out of the ballot box, and those chosen

---

Word Wise
"People" Rather than "Men"

The use of "man" or "men" as a generic term was found to be obsolete in 1971 by both the National Council for Teachers of English and the *Oxford English Dictionary*. (But in 2014, the *Oxford English Dictionary* added "mansplain" to its list of words, defining it as a man explaining something—typically to a woman—in a condescending or patronizing way.) Use of the term "people" in this chapter, such as *alderpeople* and *selectpeople,* reflects this shift.

Alternatives to the generic terms "man" and "men" include person, people, human being(s), civilization, society, individual(s), somebody, someone, anyone, all of us, everyone, humankind, humanity, the public, citizen(s), worker(s), member(s), and women and men.

take seats in the jury box. In some states, if the case is expected to be lengthy, 14 or 16 jurors are **impaneled** (enrolled) to hear the case instead of 12, but before deliberations begin, the jury is reduced (by lot) to 12 members who decide the case. Those who are removed are retained as **alternate jurors** (additional jurors impaneled in case of sickness or removal of any of the 12 who are deliberating). In some states, alternate jurors are chosen separately from regular jurors at the beginning of the trial and designated as such. The plaintiff and defendant may stipulate that the jury shall consist of any number less than 12 if they wish to do so.

In some states, the judge chooses one of the members of the jury to be the **foreperson** (the presiding member of a jury who speaks for the group). In other states, the foreperson is elected by members of the jury. If, for whatever reasons, an insufficient number of jurors make up a jury, the judge has the power to send the sheriff out onto the street to obtain bystanders or people from the county at large to serve on the jury. Jurors who are chosen this way are called **talesmen** and **taleswomen**, although this term has seemingly become archaic. For example, 28 U.S.C §1866, a federal statute on jury selection, was amended in 1968 by replacing "talesman" with language on selecting jurors "at random."

EXAMINATION AND CHALLENGE OF JURORS

Members of the jury must stand indifferent—that is, they must have a neutral, or unbiased, opinion before the trial begins. To establish such indifference, the jurors are examined under oath. This examination is called the **voir dire,** an expression meaning "to speak the truth." In law in the Anglo–Norman language, however, it means "an oath to say what is true." During voir dire, the court attempts to determine whether any of the jurors

1. are related to either party or either attorney;
2. have any connection to the case;
3. have expressed or formed an opinion about it;
4. are aware of any bias or prejudice that they may have in the case; or
5. know of any reason that they do not stand indifferent.

Any juror who does not stand indifferent is replaced (by lot) by another juror from the venire.

An attorney from either side may **challenge** (call or put into question) any member of the jury and ask the court to have him or her removed from the jury. A **challenge to the array**, sometimes called a **motion to quash the array**, is a challenge to the entire jury because of some irregularity in the selection of the jury. If allowed by the court, the entire jury must step down and a

TERMS IN ACTION

In 1991, one of the late Massachusetts Senator Ted Kennedy's nephews, William Kennedy Smith, was accused of raping a woman late in the evening of Good Friday on the beach at the Kennedy family estate in Palm Beach, Florida. William Kennedy Smith is the son of Jean Kennedy Smith and is a medical doctor. William claimed that the sex was consensual and not rape, and the trial was broadcast on national television. The defense team, led by renowned lawyer Roy Black (whose clients range from pop star Justin Bieber to Palm Beach resident and radio talk show host Rush Limbaugh), used jury consultants before and during **voir dire** to help pick the six-member **jury.** Choosing the jury of four women and two men took almost four weeks. The defense succeeded in its **motion in limine** to exclude from the trial the testimony of three women whom the prosecution planned on calling to testify that William had sexually assaulted them also. After a 10-day trial, the jury **deliberated** for 77 minutes and returned a "not guilty" verdict on December 11, 1991. One of the **jurors**, Lisa Heller, later began dating Roy Black, and they were married in 1994.

Source: ABA Journal; washingtonpost.com; people.com

new jury is selected. **Challenges for cause** are challenges to individual jurors when it is believed that a juror cannot be fair or does not stand **indifferent**—that is, impartial, unbiased, and disinterested. No limit exists to the number of challenges for cause that may be made. **Peremptory challenges** are challenges for which no reason need be given. State law varies as to the number of peremptory challenges allowed. In Massachusetts, for example, a defendant in a criminal case where the punishment could be life imprisonment is allowed 12 peremptory challenges, and the prosecution is allowed as many peremptory challenges as the total number allowed for all defendants in the same case. In California, each side is allowed 20 peremptory challenges in cases involving the death penalty or life imprisonment, whereas in civil cases each party is allowed six peremptory challenges.

In 1986, the U.S. Supreme Court held, in *Batson v. Kentucky*, that peremptory challenges based on race are unconstitutional. Today, lawyers who argue that a peremptory challenge was granted for unlawfully discriminatory reasons are said to make a "Batson challenge."

TERMS IN ACTION

In 1986, the U.S. Supreme Court ruled, in *Batson v. Kentucky*, 476 U.S. 79, that it was unconstitutional to use **peremptory challenges** on four black members of the **jury venire**, because attempting to eliminate the possibility of having any black jurors in order to get an all-white jury was a form of racial discrimination. In 2008, the Court confirmed that doctrine in *Snyder v. Louisiana*, 552 U.S. 472. In that case, the prosecuting attorney in a death penalty case against a black defendant used a peremptory challenge on a black member of the venire, arguing in part that the juror appeared nervous and had too busy a schedule to serve. But the Supreme Court concluded that the trial judge erred in granting the peremptory challenge, because other white jurors weren't subject to the same nervousness analysis nor removed because of similarly busy schedules.

Source: oyez.org

Web Wise

Since anyone **can publish** anything **on the Web,** here are **5 W's** to ask whenever you consider the information you find there:

Who created the site?
- Does the author have suitable credentials?
- Is the "author" an organization or association?

What type of site is it?
- .edu = educational
- .com = commercial
- .org = organization
- .gov = government
- .net = network/utilities
- .mil = military
- .law = law firms (available as of 2015)

When was the site created or updated?
- Is the site being maintained, or has it been abandoned?

Where can you find more information?
- Are sources documented with footnotes or links?

(Continued)

> **Why** was this site created?
> To sell, entice?
> To inform, give facts and data?
> To persuade?
> To advocate a point of view?

Reviewing What You Learned

After studying the chapter, write the answers to each of the following questions:

1. Who may demand a jury trial?

____

____

____

2. What is the purpose of a pretrial hearing?

____

____

____

3. Under the traditional method of selecting a jury, who is exempt from jury duty? How long do jurors serve?

____

____

____

4. Under the one day–one trial system of jury selection, who is exempt from jury duty and how long do jurors serve?

____

____

____

5. Describe the method that is used to impanel a jury in a particular trial.

____

____

____

6. Under what circumstances may more than 12 jurors hear a case? How many jurors ultimately decide such a case?

____

____

____

7. In what two ways may jury forepersons be selected?

____

____

____

8. Under what circumstances may the judge send the sheriff out into the street to obtain jurors?

____

____

____

9. List two of the five reasons that would cause a juror not to stand indifferent.

____

____

____

10. How many challenges for cause may be made?

____

____

____

Understanding Legal Concepts

Indicate whether each statement is true or false. Then, change the italicized word or phrase of each false statement to make it true.

ANSWERS

_____ **1.** The ordinary jury of 12 people used for the trial of a civil or criminal action is known as a *petit* jury.

_____ **2.** A pretrial hearing is held for the purpose of *delaying the trial as much as possible.*

_____ **3.** When a writ of venire facias is sent to a city, the mayor and alderpeople *personally choose* the names of people for jury duty.

_____ **4.** Under the traditional method of selecting the venire, *members of the clergy and lawyers* are exempt from jury duty.

_____ **5.** Under the one day–one trial system of jury selection, practicing physicians and surgeons, nurses, and public school teachers *are exempt* from jury duty.

_____ **6.** Under the U.S. Constitution, peremptory challenges *may* be based on race.

_____ **7.** When a case is ready for trial, the names of 12 members of the venire are *picked out of a ballot box* to serve on the jury.

_____ **8.** If at least seven jurors have been chosen for a case, but not enough jurors are left on the venire to make up a complete jury, the judge *may* send the sheriff out onto the street and obtain bystanders to serve on the jury.

_____ **9.** Members of the jury *must* stand indifferent.

_____ **10.** A limit exists to the number of *challenges for cause* that may be made of prospective jurors.

Checking Terminology

From the list of legal terms that follows, select the one that matches each definition:

ANSWERS

a. alderpeople
b. alternate jurors
c. array
d. bench trial
e. capital criminal case
f. challenge
g. challenge for cause
h. challenge to the array
i. foreperson
j. impaneled
k. indifferent
l. jurors
m. jury
n. jury panel
o. jury pool
p. jury waived trial
q. master
r. motion in limine
s. motion to quash the array
t. one day–one trial jury system
u. peremptory challenge
v. petit jury
w. pretrial hearing
x. selectpeople
y. talesmen and taleswomen
z. venire
aa. voir dire
bb. writ of venire facias

_____ **1.** A case in which the death penalty may be inflicted.

_____ **2.** The presiding member of a jury who speaks for the group.

_____ **3.** Members of a jury.

_____ **4.** A challenge of a juror for which no reason need be given.

_____ **5.** A challenge to the entire jury because of some irregularity in the selection of the jury. (Select two answers.)

_____ **6.** Bystanders or people from the county at large chosen by the court to act as jurors when there are not enough people left on the venire.

_____ **7.** The large group of people from which a jury is selected for a trial. (Select four answers.)

_____ **8.** A system designed to provide the courts with juries consisting of fair cross sections of the community and to reduce the burden of jury duty on certain classes of citizens.

_____ **9.** Listed as members of the jury.

_____ **10.** People elected to serve as members of the legislative body of a city.

_____ **11.** A written order to cities and towns to provide a designated number of jurors for the next sitting of the court.

_____ **12.** A challenge of a juror made when it is believed that the juror does not stand indifferent.

_____ **13.** Impartial, unbiased, and disinterested.

_____ **14.** The ordinary jury of 6 or 12 people used for the trial of a civil or criminal action.

_____ **15.** Additional jurors impaneled in case of sickness or removal of any of the regular jurors who are deliberating.

_____ **16.** To speak the truth. The examination of jurors by the court to see that they stand indifferent.

_____ **17.** A trial without a jury. (Select two answers.)

_____ **18.** A group of people selected according to law and sworn to determine the facts in a case.

_____ **19.** A lawyer appointed by the court to hear testimony in a case and report back to the court his or her findings or conclusions.

_____ **20.** A pretrial motion asking the court to prohibit the introduction of prejudicial evidence by the other party.

Using Legal Language

Read the following story and fill in the blank lines with legal terms taken from the list of terms at the beginning of this chapter:

The plaintiff's attorney, Mary Grey, attended a(n) _________________________ before the judge, prior to the trial, in an attempt to speed up the trial. Mary wanted a jury trial instead of referring the case to a(n) _________________________ _________________________ that is, a lawyer appointed by the court to hear testimony. In addition, she did not want a(n) _________________________ _________________________ or a(n) _________________________, which is a trial without a jury. The clerk of court sent a(n) _________________________ to each city and town within the court's jurisdiction to obtain jurors for the next sitting of the court. When the trial began, jurors were selected by lot from the _________________________ (the jury pool), and after the _________________________ was held to be sure that they stood _________________________, 14 jurors were _________________________ to hear the case. The number included two _________________________ who would be used in case of sickness or removal of any of the regular jurors. No _________________________ for cause existed, but several _________________________ did, which required no reason to be given. The lawyers did not wish to stipulate to a lesser number of jurors, and no need to obtain _________________________ existed—that is, bystanders or people from the county at large selected to serve on the jury. This trial was not a(n) _________________________, because it did not involve the death penalty. A woman was chosen to be the _________________________, who would speak for the group.

Steps in a Trial

ANTE INTERROGATORY

The decision of a jury is called a (A) judgment, (B) judgment n.o.v.,
(C) decree, (D) verdict.

LEARNING OBJECTIVES

LO 1: Explain what the purpose of a plaintiff's opening statement is

LO 2: Identify the types of evidence that can be presented in the plaintiff's case in chief

LO 3: Explain the difference between evidence that is relevant and evidence that is admissible

LO 4: Explain the difference between direct examination and cross-examination

LO 5: Identify when and why a plaintiff would make a motion for a directed verdict

LO 6: Categorize the purpose of the defendant's opening statement and when it is made

LO 7: Contrast the parties' closing arguments with their opening statements

LO 8: Identify where jury verdicts must be unanimous, and under what conditions they could be non-unanimous

LO 9: Distinguish a judgment of the merits from a judgment on the pleadings and a judgment notwithstanding the verdict

LO 10: Identify what an appellate court's job is and what possible decisions it can make

KEY TERMS

adjudicating

adjudication

admissible evidence

affirm

appeal

appeal bond

appellant

appellee

case in chief

circumstantial evidence

closing argument

consent decree

court of equity

cross-examination

decree

defendant in error

deliberate

direct evidence

direct examination

DNA

DNA sample

documentary evidence	preliminary injunction
equity	prima facie case
exhibit	questions of fact
hearsay	questions of law
hung jury	real evidence
injunction	rebuttal
judgment	relevant evidence
judgment notwithstanding the verdict	remand
judgment n.o.v.	respondent
judgment on the merits	reverse
judgment on the pleadings	ripe for judgment
jury charge	sequester
leading questions	set aside
mistrial	summation
motion for a directed verdict	testimonial evidence
non obstante verdicto	vacate
opening statement	verdict
polling the jury	verdict contrary to law

WEBSITES FOR PRONUNCIATION HELP

http://dictionary.cambridge.org/us/pronunciation/english/audio

https://www.howtopronounce.com

Steps in a Jury Trial

The common steps in a jury trial are listed below and will be discussed throughout the chapter.

1. Plaintiff's opening statement
2. Plaintiff's case in chief
3. Defendant's opening statement
4. Defendant's case in chief
5. Requests for instructions to the jury
6. Final arguments (summation)
7. Instructions to the jury (jury charge)
8. Jury's verdict
9. Court's judgment or decree
10. Appeal
11. Execution, in civil cases
12. Sentencing, in criminal cases

PLAINTIFF'S OPENING STATEMENT

After the jury is impaneled, the plaintiff's attorney makes an **opening statement**. The attorney outlines the case by telling the jury (the judge, in a nonjury trial) what the plaintiff's evidence will prove. The opening statement must set forth a **prima facie case**—that is, the statement must be legally sufficient as proof of the case unless it is rebutted by contrary evidence.

PLAINTIFF'S CASE IN CHIEF

Next, the plaintiff's attorney puts in the **case in chief**—that is, she or he introduces evidence to prove the allegations that were made in the pleadings and in the opening statement. Evidence that is pertinent and proper to be considered in reaching a decision, according to specific rules, is known as **admissible evidence**. Evidence tending to prove or disprove an alleged fact is termed as **relevant evidence**. Not all relevant evidence is necessarily admissible. For instance, the rules of evidence on **hearsay** might prohibit the use of an out of court statement even though it, logically, is relevant. Hearsay is an out of court statement offered in court to prove the truth of the matter being asserted in court. For example, a witness could be prohibited from testifying as to what the witness heard someone else say about the underlying case. Hearsay is generally inadmissible because it can't be cross-examined for truthfulness, but there are over 20 exceptions to the hearsay rule. And other relevant evidence might be inadmissible because it unfairly prejudices the defendant.

Evidence is classified as testimonial, documentary, or real. **Testimonial evidence** consists of oral testimony of witnesses made under oath in open court. **Documentary evidence** consists of such evidence as written contracts, business records, correspondence, wills, and deeds. **Real evidence** consists of actual objects that have a bearing on the case, such as an item of clothing, a weapon found at the scene of the crime, a photograph, a chart, a model, fingerprints, or **DNA** (deoxyribonucleic acid)—the double strand of molecules which carries a cell's unique genetic code. A **DNA sample** is biological evidence of any nature that is utilized to conduct DNA analysis. Tangible items that are introduced as evidence are referred to as **exhibits**.

When a witness testifies as to something that he or she observed, such as "I saw that man shoot the gun," it is called **direct evidence** because the testimony directly relates to the fact in issue. (Did that man shoot the gun?) When the testimony or other evidence is offered to permit the trier of fact to draw a conclusion about the existence or nonexistence of a fact, it is called **circumstantial evidence**. Continuing the gunshot example, if a witness testifies that he saw the defendant take a gun into a room that had another person in it, the witness heard a shot and then saw the defendant leave the room carrying the gun, that would be circumstantial evidence that the defendant shot the person in the room.

To begin this phase of the trial, the plaintiff's attorney calls his or her first witness to the witness stand. The examination of one's own witness is called **direct examination**. The attorney must ask questions in such a way as to draw the information from the witness, in the witness's own words, without asking **leading questions** (questions that suggest to the witness the desired answer). When the plaintiff's attorney has no further questions, the witness may be questioned by the opposing attorney on **cross-examination**. Leading questions are allowed on cross-examination. An example of a leading question is, "You were in the bar that night, and drunk, weren't you?" The plaintiff's attorney may conduct a redirect examination on issues brought up in the cross-examination, which may be followed by a re-cross-examination by the defendant's attorney.

Word Wise
Around

The Latin root "circum" used in the term "circumstantial evidence" means "around." The distance around a circle is its circumference. Besides the concrete image and implied action, "circum" can also indicate the *idea* of "around." *Circumstantial evidence* relies on proving facts indirectly; it "goes around" evidence from which other facts are to be inferred.

After all the plaintiff's witnesses are examined in this way and all other evidence that the plaintiff has is introduced, the plaintiff's attorney rests the case. At this point, the defendant's attorney may make a **motion for a directed verdict**—that is, ask the court to find in favor of the defendant without giving the case to the jury. The motion will be allowed if the court finds that the evidence the plaintiff presented is insufficient as a matter of law to support a verdict in the plaintiff's favor.

DEFENDANT'S OPENING STATEMENT

Either after the plaintiff's attorney makes her or his opening statement, or after the plaintiff's attorney rests the case, the defendant's attorney makes an opening statement. He or she outlines the defendant's side of the case and tells the jury of the evidence that will be introduced to rebut or to contradict the plaintiff's evidence.

DEFENDANT'S CASE IN CHIEF

The defendant's attorney must introduce the evidence that is necessary to support the defensive claims that were made in the defendant's answer and in the opening statement. As before, one cannot ask leading questions of one's own witnesses.

After all the defendant's witnesses have been examined and cross-examined and any other evidence has been presented, the defendant's attorney rests the case. At this point, the plaintiff's attorney may present a **rebuttal** case—that is, introduce evidence that will cancel the effect of the evidence introduced by the other side. Either party may make a motion for a directed verdict at this time.

REQUESTS FOR INSTRUCTIONS TO JURY

At the close of the evidence, the attorneys may file written requests that the judge instruct the jury on the law as set forth in the requests. The judge must inform the attorneys of his or her decision on the requests before the attorneys give their final arguments to the jury.

CLOSING ARGUMENTS

At the close of the presentation of the evidence, each attorney argues his or her side of the case to the jury, or to the judge in a nonjury trial. The time length for closing arguments is left to the trial judge's discretion. In this **closing argument** or **summation** the attorneys summarize the evidence (and its significance) that has been introduced in their favor. Because the burden of proof rests with the prosecution in a criminal case and the plaintiff in civil case, those lawyers may choose to make rebuttal arguments after the defense's closing arguments.

▌ TERMS IN ACTION

Juror misbehavior can sometimes result in a declaration of a **mistrial**, or a **reversal** in an **appeal**, requiring a new trial. Recently, jurors have been caught using their Blackberries, iPhones, and Twitter accounts during trials. In a 2009 civil case from Arkansas, a juror tweeted eight times during the trial, including sending one tweet that read, "I just gave away TWELVE MILLION DOLLARS of someone else's money!" The defense made a motion for a new trial because of the seemingly biased tweet, but the trial judge denied the motion because the tweet was made after the jury's verdict. In 2011, a juror in a civil trial in Texas attempted to "friend" the defendant on Facebook. Not only was that juror removed from the case, but he was criminally charged with contempt of court. Sometimes, jurors don't misbehave, but they get sick. In 2007, former University of Notre Dame football coach Charlie Weiss sued two doctors and Massachusetts General Hospital for medical malpractice. One day during the trial, a juror passed out in the jury box. The two doctors immediately left the defendants' table and went to the aid of the juror, who was taken to the hospital. Weiss's attorney then sought and received a mistrial, arguing that the remaining jurors could have been tainted in favor of the defendants by seeing them offering volunteer medical assistance. Later that year, a second jury ruled in favor of the doctors.

Source: abajournalnews.com; law.com; dfw.cbslocal.com; boston.com

INSTRUCTIONS TO JURY

The jury must be told what the law is in that particular case. Not only are jurors not expected to know the law, but the trial judge is also responsible for all legal matters during the trial. Therefore after the closing arguments, the judge tells the jury the law that must be applied. This is called the **jury charge**. When it **deliberates**—considers the case slowly and carefully—the jury must apply the law and legal standards given to them to the facts in making its decision. In highly publicized cases, jurors are sometimes **sequestered**—that is, isolated, or set apart, from society in a hotel during the deliberation period to prevent them from being exposed to outside influences.

VERDICT

The decision of the jury is called the **verdict**. In a federal criminal trial, the jury must agree unanimously in order to reach a verdict, and in a federal civil trial, the verdict must be unanimous unless the parties agree otherwise. While it is natural to expect unanimous verdicts in criminal cases in state courts, they are not required constitutionally, and Louisiana and Oregon allow for guilty verdicts in non-capital criminal case where at least 10 out of 12 jurors vote to convict. If a jury cannot reach a verdict, a **mistrial** (an invalid trial of no consequence) is called, and a new trial may be held. In civil cases, not all verdicts must be unanimous, and supermajority verdicts (five-sixths of the members of the jury) are permitted in many states. Additionally, in some states, the plaintiff and the defendant may agree that a different majority of the jurors will be taken as the verdict. For example, in Indiana, civil juries consist of six jurors unless the parties agree to a lesser number, and the verdict must be unanimous unless the parties agree to a stated majority. When individual jurors are asked whether they agree with the verdict given by the jury foreperson, that is called **polling the jury**. A deadlocked jury is often referred to as a **hung jury**.

Web Wise

- For an overview of evidence, go to the Legal Information Institute (LII) at ***www.law.cornell.edu***. When there, click on Wex legal dictionary/encyclopedia in the Learn More box. Then in the search box type "evidence." In addition to the Federal Rules of Evidence, you will find federal and state cases on the subject.
- Look for practice and procedure information for your state by going to ***www.findlaw.com***. When there, type "jurisdiction" in the search box, then click the name of your state.
- For more information on the trial system in America, go to the American Bar Association's Public Education Resources web page: ***www.americanbar.org/groups/public_education/resources.html***. Once there, find the "Resources for the Public" tab and then the link titled "How Courts Work."

JUDGMENT OR DECREE

Following the jury's verdict, the court issues a **judgment**, also called an **adjudication**, which is the decision of a court of law. The judgment is the act of the trial court finally **adjudicating** (determining) the rights and liabilities of the parties. This determination is the court's decision in the case. A case is said to be **ripe for judgment** when it reaches the stage when everything has been completed except the court's decision. A **judgment on the merits** is a court decision based on the evidence and facts introduced. In contrast, a **judgment on the pleadings** will be rendered without hearing evidence if the court determines that it is clear from the pleadings that one party is entitled to win the case as a matter of law. Similarly, if the judge believes that the jury's verdict is incorrect as a matter of law (a **verdict contrary to law**), he or she may issue a **judgment notwithstanding**

the verdict also called a **judgment n.o.v.** (from the Latin **non obstante verdicto**), which is a judgment in favor of one party notwithstanding a verdict in favor of the other party.

The decision of a court of equity is called a **decree**. **Equity** means that which is just and fair. A **court of equity** is a court that administers justice according to the system of equity. It is able to grant relief to people when no adequate remedy is otherwise available. To illustrate, a court of law can usually do nothing more than award money to an injured party. In contrast, a court of equity can issue an **injunction**—that is, order someone to do or refrain from doing a particular act. Sometimes, a court of equity will issue a **preliminary injunction** before hearing the merits of a case in order to prevent injustice. A **consent decree** is a decree that is entered by consent of the parties, usually without an admission of guilt or wrongdoing. This type of decree cannot be appealed because the parties have agreed to it.

TERMS IN ACTION

A British nanny named Louise Woodward, living in Massachusetts, was convicted in 1997 of second-degree murder for the killing of an eight-month-old baby boy under her care. The evidence presented was that Woodward, hired to be the boy's au pair by his parents (both of whom were doctors), was careless and irresponsible and that she killed the infant in what is commonly called "shaken baby syndrome." But after her conviction, her defense attorneys—who included Barry Scheck, one of O.J. Simpson's attorneys from his 1994 double-murder trial acquittal—made a motion to the trial judge, asking that he set aside the conviction because it was a **verdict contrary to law**. The trial judge granted that motion and, in a rare instance of judicial discretion, replaced the second-degree murder conviction with an involuntary manslaughter conviction, which was **upheld** when the prosecution **appealed**. Ms. Woodward was released from jail, having been sentenced to the 279 days she already served in jail during the prosecution and she moved back to Britain.

Source: nytimes.com

APPEAL

A party not satisfied with the final judgment or legal ruling of a trial court may ask a higher court to reverse the decision. That request is made in an **appeal**, which is directed to an appellate court. Appellate courts resolve questions (or issues) of law, unlike trial courts, which resolve questions of fact. A party bringing an appeal is called an **appellant**. A party against whom an appeal is brought is called an **appellee**, a **respondent**, or a **defendant in error**. Only questions of law may be raised on appeal. **Questions of law** are questions relating to the application or interpretation of law. Such questions are not decided by a jury. **Questions of fact**—that is, questions about the activities that took place between the parties that caused them to go to court—are for the jury to decide and cannot be appealed unless the jury is plainly wrong as a matter of law. To be heard by an appellate court, an appeal must be filed within a prescribed period—typically 30 days from the entry of judgment.

When an appellate court takes a case and agrees with the lower court's decision, it will **affirm**—that is, approve—the decision. In contrast, when an appellate court disagrees with a lower court decision, it will **reverse** or **set aside**(make void) the decision, or it will **vacate** the judgment and **remand** (send back) the case to the lower court for further proceedings. A defendant who loses a civil trial (and therefore has a judgment to pay, as determined by the jury) posts an **appeal bond**, which is some dollar-amount of financial security posted to the court to guarantee the payment of the damages and the cost of an appeal if the defendant were to lose the appeal.

Reviewing What You Learned

After studying the chapter, write the answers to each of the following questions:

1. List the steps in the order that they occur in a jury trial.

2. What is one requirement of an opening statement?

3. Differentiate among testimonial evidence, documentary evidence, and real evidence.

4. Give an example for each of testimony that is (a) direct evidence and (b) circumstantial evidence.

5. Under what circumstances are leading questions allowed and not allowed?

6. Under what circumstances may a motion for a directed verdict be allowed?

7. Under what circumstances may the plaintiff's attorney introduce rebuttal evidence?

8. What is the difference between questions of law and questions of fact, and which may be raised on appeal?

9. To reach a verdict in a criminal case, how must the jury agree?

10. What decisions can an appellate court reach in an appeal?

Understanding Legal Concepts

Indicate whether each statement is true or false. Then, change the italicized word or phrase of each false statement to make it true.

ANSWERS

_____ **1.** In the *opening statement,* the attorney outlines the case by telling the jury what the evidence will prove.

_____ **2.** When a witness testifies as to something he or she observed, such as "I saw that man shoot the gun," it is called *circumstantial* evidence.

_____ **3.** Leading questions are allowed on *direct* examination.

_____ **4.** After the plaintiff's attorney rests the case, the defendant's attorney *makes an opening statement.*

_____ **5.** When final arguments are made, the plaintiff's attorney argues *first.*

_____ **6.** A jury never decides questions of *fact.*

_____ **7.** In a criminal case, the jury must agree unanimously to reach a *verdict.*

_____ **8.** Following the jury's verdict, the court issues a *judgment.*

_____ **9.** The decision of a court of equity is called a *decree.*

_____ **10.** Only questions of *fact* may be raised on appeal.

Checking Terminology (Part A)

From the list of legal terms that follows, select the one that matches each definition.

ANSWERS

a. adjudicating
b. adjudication
c. admissible evidence
d. affirm
e. appeal
f. appeal bond
g. appellant
h. appellee
i. case in chief
j. circumstantial evidence
k. consent decree
l. court of equity
m. cross-examination
n. decree
o. defendant in error
p. deliberate
q. direct evidence
r. direct examination
s. DNA
t. DNA sample
u. documentary evidence
v. equity
w. exhibit
x. hung jury
y. injunction
z. judgment
aa. judgment notwithstanding the verdict
bb. judgment n.o.v.
cc. judgment on the merits
dd. judgment on the pleadings
ee. respondent

_____ **1.** The examination of one's own witness.

_____ **2.** A bond often required as security to guarantee the cost of an appeal, especially in civil cases.

_____ **3.** Approve.

_____ **4.** A deadlocked jury; one that cannot agree.

_____ **5.** A tangible item that is introduced in evidence.

_____ **6.** Determining finally by a court.

_____ **7.** Evidence that directly relates to the fact in issue.

_____ **8.** A party bringing an appeal. (Select three answers.)

_____ **9.** A court decision based on the evidence and facts introduced.

_____ **10.** A party against whom an appeal is brought. (Select three answers.)

_____ **11.** A judgment rendered in favor of one party notwithstanding a verdict in favor of the other party. (Select two answers.)

_____ **12.** A court that administers justice according to the system of equity.

_____ **13.** A judgment rendered without hearing evidence if the court determines that it is clear from the pleadings that one party is entitled to win the case.

_____ **14.** That which is just and fair.

_____ **15.** Evidence that is pertinent and proper to be considered in reaching a decision, according to specific rules.

_____ **16.** The decision of a court of equity.

_____ **17.** Evidence that relates to some fact other than the fact in issue; indirect evidence.

_____ **18.** The decision of a court of law. (Select two answers.)

_____ **19.** Evidence consisting of such documents as written contracts, business records, correspondence, wills, and deeds.

_____ **20.** A court judgment.

_____ **21.** The examination of an opposing witness.

_____ **22.** A request to a higher court to review the decision of a lower court.

_____ **23.** The introduction of evidence to prove the allegations that were made in the pleadings and in the opening statement.

_____ **24.** An order of a court of equity to do or refrain from doing a particular act.

_____ **25.** The double strand of molecules that carries a cell's unique genetic code.

_____ **26.** Biological evidence of any nature that is utilized to conduct DNA analysis.

_____ **27.** A decree that is entered by consent of the parties.

_____ **28.** To consider slowly and carefully.

Checking Terminology (Part B)

From the list of legal terms that follows, select the one that matches each definition.

ANSWERS

a. closing argument
b. jury charge
c. leading questions
d. mistrial
e. motion for a directed verdict
f. non obstante verdicto
g. opening statement
h. polling the jury
i. preliminary injunction
j. prima facie case
k. questions of fact
l. questions of law
m. real evidence
n. rebuttal
o. relevant evidence
p. remand
q. reverse
r. ripe for judgment
s. sequester
t. set aside
u. summation
v. testimonial evidence
w. vacate
x. verdict
y. verdict contrary to law
z. tangible evidence

_____ 1. Send back.
_____ 2. In a jury trial, a motion asking the court to find in favor of the moving party as a matter of law, without having the case go to the jury.
_____ 3. Questions about the activities which took place between the parties that caused them to go to court.
_____ 4. Final statements by the attorneys, summarizing the evidence that has been introduced. (Select two answers.)
_____ 5. The decision of a jury.
_____ 6. Actual objects that have a bearing on the case, such as an item of clothing, a weapon found at the scene of a crime, a photograph, a chart, or a model.
_____ 7. Notwithstanding a verdict.
_____ 8. Instructions to a jury on matters of law.
_____ 9. Evidence tending to prove or disprove an alleged fact.
_____ 10. An attorney's outline, related to the jury, of anticipated proof.
_____ 11. Legally sufficient for proof unless rebutted or contradicted by other evidence.
_____ 12. A procedure in which individual jurors are asked whether they agree with the verdict given by the jury foreperson.
_____ 13. Questions that suggest to the witness the desired answer.
_____ 14. Oral testimony of witnesses made under oath in open court.
_____ 15. Questions relating to the application or interpretation of law.
_____ 16. An invalid trial of no legal consequence.
_____ 17. Make void. (Select two answers.)
_____ 18. The introduction of evidence that will destroy the effect of the evidence introduced by the other side.
_____ 19. An injunction issued by a court before hearing the merits of a case.
_____ 20. A verdict that is incorrect as a matter of law.
_____ 21. The stage of a trial when everything has been completed except the court's decision.
_____ 22. To isolate or set apart from society.

Sharpening Your Latin Skills

In the space provided, write the definition of each of the following legal terms, referring to the glossary when necessary.

certiorari _______________________________

non obstante verdicto _______________________________

prima facie _______________________________

subpoena _______________________________

subpoena ad testificandum _______________________________

subpoena duces tecum _______________________________

venire _______________________________

venire facias _______________________________

Using Legal Language

Read the following story and fill in the blank lines with legal terms taken from the list of terms at the beginning of this chapter.

The plaintiff's attorney, Mary Grey, was required to set forth a(n) _________________________ in her opening statement before the jury. Her evidence consisted of a photograph, which was _________________________; payroll records, which were _________________________; and oral statements of a witness, which were _________________________. On the stand, Mary's witness, Leroy Henning, said, "I am the payroll clerk, and these payroll records are true and correct." This was _________________________ evidence, not _________________________, and because she was examining her own witness, Mary's examination was called _________________________. Mary could not ask _________________________, which suggest to the witness the desired answer. The opposing attorney could do so, however, on _________________________. At the close of Mary's case, the opposing attorney made a(n) _________________________, asking the court to find in favor of his client. This request was denied, and the case went to the jury, whose decision is called a(n) _________________________. Following this decision, the court issued its _________________________, which is sometimes called a(n) _________________________ in a court of equity. Mary's client won the case, and the opposing attorney decided not to _________________________ to a higher court because only _________________________ may be raised at that time. Had he done so, his client would have been called the _________________________ and would have had to put up a(n) _________________________ as security.

Legal Ethics

ANTE INTERROGATORY

A lawyer's requirement to keep secret what she or he learns about the client is known as (A) the attorney–client privilege, (B) a frivolous claim, (C) the duty of lawyer–client confidentiality, (D) the duty of competence.

LEARNING OBJECTIVES

LO 1: Summarize the sources of legal ethics rules and identify the exams one might have to take in order to be licensed to practice law

LO 2: Explain the concepts of competence and truthfulness in a law practice setting

LO 3: Synthesize how the ethics rules on the unauthorized practice of law and a lawyer's duty of supervision impact what paralegals and legal assistants do

LO 4: Compare and contrast the duty of client confidentiality with the attorney–client privilege

LO 5: Summarize the ethics concept of a conflict of interest and provide an example of a prohibited conflict of interest

LO 6: Distinguish the common types of legal fees

LO 7: Explain the basic rules on lawyer advertising and solicitation

LO 8: Categorize some of the key ethics issues needing to be addressed due to the practice of law in a cyber world

LO 9: Summarize the process of attorney discipline, including identifying the types of attorney sanctions

KEY TERMS

American Bar Association (ABA)
attorney–client privilege
bar exam
Canons of Professional Ethics
comments
competent
confidential communication
conflict of interest
contingency fee
costs

diligence
disbarment
disciplinary commission
duty of confidentiality
ethics opinions
ex parte communication
flat fee
frivolous suits
grievance
guidelines
hourly billing

informed consent
legal assistant
legal ethics
legal fees
license suspension
Model Code of Professional
Responsibility
Model Rules of Professional Conduct
Multistate Bar Exam (MBE)

Multistate Performance Test (MPT)
nonbillables
paralegal
private reprimand
public reprimand
Rules
soliciting
Uniform Bar Exam (UBE)
waiver

WEBSITES FOR PRONUNCIATION HELP

http://dictionary.cambridge.org/us/pronunciation/english/audio

https://www.howtopronounce.com

Legal ethics was originally a tradition of do's and don't's informally applied in the legal profession. In 1887, Alabama became the first jurisdiction to adopt rules of legal ethics, and in 1908 the **American Bar Association (ABA)**, the largest voluntary bar association in America, created its first set of ethics rules, called the **Canons of Professional Ethics**. The ABA adopted the **Model Code of Professional Responsibility** in 1969, and then replaced it in 1983 with the **Model Rules of Professional Conduct**, which were updated in 2003 and revised in part, beginning in 2012, with a primary focus on ethics rules that relate to technology and global legal practice developments. The ABA Model Rules are formatted with mandatory **Rules**, followed by explanatory **Comments** designed to help the reader understand the focus of the rules. The ABA and their jurisdictional counterparts issue **ethics opinions**, which are formal answers (having a similarity in style to appellate court opinions) to questions about the interpretation or application of the ethics rules. It is important to note that, because ethics opinions come from bar associations and not courts, they do not have the force of law and are not equivalent to an operative ethics rule or court opinion interpreting an ethics rule.

Lawyers are licensed in the jurisdiction where they have passed the **bar exam**, which is usually a multi-day exam on that jurisdiction's common law, statutory law, and regulatory law. Applicants for law licensure in all states Except Maryland and Wisconsin must also pass a national ethics exam, called the Multistate Professional Responsibility Exam (MPRE), which is a multiple-choice exam covering knowledge of established ethics rules. Additionally, all states but Louisiana administer the **Multistate Bar Exam** (MBE), developed by the National Conference of Bar Examiners, and which is a 200-multiple choice exam covering seven subject areas. And some jurisdictions administer the **Multistate Performance Test** (MPT), also developed by the National Conference of Bar Examiners, and which is intended to evaluate an examinee's fundamental lawyering skills, rather than measuring substantive legal knowledge. Furthermore, some jurisdictions administer the **Uniform Bar Exam** (UBE), coordinated by the National Conference of Bar Examiners and which includes the MBE. The UBE uniformly tests knowledge and skills required to practice law and results in a portable score that can be transferred for admission to practice law in those jurisdictions that accept the UBE.

Lawyer conduct is regulated by the highest appellate court in a state, which adopts or creates a set of legal ethics rules and then investigates accusations of lawyer misconduct. Forty-nine

---

Web Wise

- For more information on the law licensure exams administered by the National Conference of Bar Examiner, including the MBE, MPT, and UBE, as well as the specific law licensure requirements of your jurisdiction, go to ***www.ncbex.org***.
- For more information on jurisdiction-specific requirements for law licensure, including what jurisdictions allow for bar reciprocity (transfer of one's license to another jurisdiction based on the type of bar exam initially taken), go to ***www.barreciprocity.com***.

states and the District of Columbia have adopted the ABA Model Rules as the operative lawyer conduct rules. California still uses its own set of legal ethics rules. Most states have also adopted **guidelines** for the use, by lawyers, of paralegals or legal assistants. These guidelines are directed to lawyers and address how to ethically use their employees in the support of clients' needs. The two largest paralegal and legal assistant organizations are the National Federation of Paralegal Associations (NFPA) and the National Association of Legal Assistants (NALA); both organizations have their own sets of ethics rules that apply to their members.

COMPETENCE AND TRUTHFULNESS

Lawyers have a mandatory duty to provide **competent** representation, according to Model Rule 1.1, which means that a lawyer may not take on a case or engage in litigation in which the area of the law or intricacy of the procedure involved is beyond the lawyer's knowledge base or skill. **Diligence** is an important component of competence, and Model Rule 1.3 requires the lawyer to act with reasonable diligence and promptness. Competence and diligence also involve keeping the client reasonably informed about the status of his or her matter, and responding to client requests for information.

Web Wise

- For information on the National Federation of Paralegal Associations, go to ***www.paralegals.org***
- For information on the National Association of Legal Assistants, go to ***www.nala.org***

Despite what the public may think about the general character of lawyers, truthfulness toward clients, the court, and even third parties is required by various ABA Model Rules. Part of being dishonest includes failing to disclose one's status as an attorney or paralegal, and engaging in **ex parte communication**. "Ex parte" literally means "by or for one party," but in the context of dishonest communication it refers to a lawyer involved in a case who communicates with the judge while the other party's lawyer is unaware of the communication. Lawyers are also prohibited from bringing **frivolous suits** or frivolous appeals. A lawsuit or appeal is "frivolous" if it is meant to harass someone, or if there is no basis in law or fact for bringing it.

TERMS IN ACTION

Abraham Lincoln was a lawyer when he wrote what is known as "Notes for a Law Lecture," which was found by his secretaries after his assassination in 1865. Although it isn't known that Lincoln ever presented it as a speech, "Notes for a Law Lecture" is thought to be from 1850. A little over 700 words long, this straight-as-an-arrow sermonette provides unique insight into Lincoln's view of what it meant to be a successful attorney. And with so much of Lincoln's writings and speeches, Lincoln got right to the point: "The leading rule for the lawyer, as for the man of every other calling, is **diligence**. Leave nothing for tomorrow which can be done today. Never let your correspondence fall behind. Whatever piece of business you have in hand, before stopping, do all the labor pertaining to it which can then be done." And realizing back then what many lawyers seem hesitant today to recommend, Lincoln wrote, "Discourage litigation. Persuade your neighbors to compromise whenever you can. Point out to them how the nominal winner is often a real loser—in **fees, expenses**, and waste of time. . . .There will still be business enough. Never stir up litigation. A worse man can scarcely be found than one who does this." Discussing his view on legal fees, Lincoln wrote, "The matter of fees is important, far beyond the mere question of bread and butter involved. An exorbitant fee should never be claimed." Lincoln's final paragraph is the most often cited portion and discusses his view on the need for honest lawyers. Part of that paragraph includes the following caution: "Let no young man choosing the law for a calling for a moment yield to the popular belief—resolve to be **honest** at all events; and if in your own judgment you cannot be an honest lawyer, resolve to be honest without being a lawyer."

Source: abrahamlincoln.org

THE UNAUTHORIZED PRACTICE OF LAW
AND THE DUTY OF SUPERVISION

ABA Model Rule 5.1 prohibits a lawyer from assisting a non-lawyer in the unauthorized practice of law, a concept that encompasses a variety of actions, including when a non-lawyer represents someone in court or gives legal advice. ABA Model Rule 5.3 governs a lawyer's supervision of his or her non-lawyer employees. Because paralegals and legal assistants are not licensed members of the bar, lawyers (as their employers) are held responsible for the ethical misconduct of their employees and for failing to adequately supervise them. Included in the requirement of supervision is ensuring that **paralegals** and **legal assistants** do not commit the unauthorized practice of law, which includes giving legal advice. Paralegals are those non-lawyer employees trained or educated to engage in substantive legal work under the supervision of their employing attorneys. Legal assistants are often synonymous with "paralegals," although some lawyers consider a legal assistant to be someone less trained or educated than a paralegal. Even when paralegals are allowed to engage in substantive legal work, they are not allowed to engage in the practice of law.

CONFIDENTIALITY

ABA Model Rule 1.6 requires a lawyer to protect his or her client information. This duty applies to statements made to the lawyer, documents given to the lawyer, as well as any other information the lawyer learns about the client, whatever its source. The **duty of confidentiality** applies to the lawyer's employees as well. Prospective clients are protected by Model Rule 1.18, which prohibits lawyers from using information that they learn from those whose cases they do not take. Exceptions to the duty of confidentiality include implied authorizations, which are necessary to meet the client's needs; disclosures that are intended to prevent the client from committing a serious or dangerous crime; or disclosures that a lawyer needs to make in order to defend against a charge made by the client against the lawyer.

The **attorney–client privilege** is related to the duty of confidentiality, but its concept comes from evidence law. It protects a lawyer from having to testify against his or her client, even when issued a subpoena. However, for the attorney–client privilege to apply, the attorney has to be asked to divulge a **confidential communication** (a conversation or writing that expresses personal or private information) that the client had with his or her attorney. For example, the client's location is a fact and not a confidential communication, and is generally not protected by the attorney–client privilege.

■ TERMS IN ACTION

Laurence Tribe, the famous constitutional law professor from Harvard, often used social media to express his opposition to President Trump during the 2016 presidential campaign. On one occasion, his tweeting became the source of the kind of controversy tailor-made for a law school class debate or exam question. In August 2016, Tribe responded to a tweet from Democratic consultant Bob Shrum, by tweeting "I have notes of when Trump phoned me for legal advice in 1996. I'm now figuring out whether our talk was privileged." Hours later, he tweeted that he was free to disclose the notes but decided against doing so. Soon after, some lawyers and legal scholars took to their own social media accounts to denounce Tribe for violating the **duty of confidentiality** owed to Trump. They argued that a "privilege" is a concept associated with the **attorney–client privilege** and is at stake when a lawyer is subpoenaed to disclose confidential client communication, whereas client confidentiality is an ethics issue and generally prohibits lawyer from voluntarily disclosing client information, which can include information not thought to be "privileged" in the evidentiary sense of the word. Professor Tribe indignantly responded to his critics that he had done nothing wrong, in that announcing Trump had called him didn't mean the call was a secret, and since Tribe believed others would have known about that call, then Tribe's disclosure that it had happened wasn't a private fact and nothing Trump should be ashamed of. The problem with that defense, Tribe's critics stated, was that the ethics rules, in particular Rule 1.6 of the **Model Rules of Professional Conduct**, don't give attorneys discretion to decide if disclosing client information would be embarrassing to the client. Instead, its focus includes whether the client gave **informed consent** to the release of the information. Furthermore, even if Trump didn't hire Tribe as his attorney in 1996, Model Rule 1.18 states that when one discusses a legal matter with a lawyer for the purposes of possibly hiring the lawyer, that person has the status of a "prospective client" and deserves the confidentiality protection of a "former client" as stated in Model Rule 1.9.

Sources: lawnewz.com; blogs.wsj.com; nationallawjournal.com; forbes.com; americanbar.org

CONFLICTS OF INTEREST

Lawyers and their employers are expected to avoid **conflicts of interest**. A conflict of interest is a situation in which the lawyer is torn between loyalty to two or more clients or loyalty between the client and the lawyer. For example, a lawyer's loyalty would be at issue if the lawyer, who is representing a wife in a divorce, were asked by the husband to represent him against the wife in a negligence lawsuit alleging that the husband slipped and fell in a restaurant owned by the wife. Model Rules 1.7–1.13 concern conflicts of interest, and those rules prohibit a lawyer from representing two clients against each other or one client against a former client, or from being involved romantically with a current client (unless the personal relationship predates the professional relationship).

One important conflict of interest rule prohibits a lawyer or paralegal from changing jobs and working at a law firm that has a client involved in a case against a party that was a client at the lawyer's or paralegal's former law firm. With most of the conflicts of interest rules, exceptions are made when the client whose interests are to be protected gives **informed consent** (acknowledged awareness of the likely consequences for taking a course of action) and waives the conflict of interest problem. **Waiver** is the voluntary relinquishment of a known privilege, or right.

LEGAL FEES

Lawyers are required to charge reasonable **legal fees** and **costs**. Reasonableness is discussed in Model Rule 1.5 and includes the lawyer's experience, the difficulty of the case, and the chance that the lawyer will be prevented from taking other similar cases, due to the conflict of interest rules. Unlike legal fees (which are the charges for the lawyer's time or efforts), costs are the expenses associated with a legal matter, such as filing fees.

Lawyers who engage in **hourly billing** may not charge two different clients for the same amount of time. Lawyers are allowed to bill separately for the use of their paralegals, provided that the client is aware and approves. Certain law firm costs, such as overhead expenses (rent, paperclips, utilities), are considered **nonbillables**, and the act of charging them is unreasonable. Some lawyers charge a **flat fee** for their work and don't bill for the hours involved. A flat fee is a sum-certain cost of the lawyer's services and is not based on the lawyer's hourly rate times the lawyer's billable hours.

When a lawyer charges a **contingency fee** (or called a contingent fee), that fee agreement must be in writing and signed by the client. Contingency fees are commonly charged for personal injury cases and other tort cases, and if the plaintiff wins, the contingency fee is calculated as a percentage of the plaintiff's awarded damages. Under Model Rule 1.5, contingency fees are not allowed to be charged in criminal cases and divorce cases. Model Rule 5.4 prohibits lawyers from sharing a percentage of their legal fees with their paralegals and legal assistants, although an exception in the rule is made for non-lawyer employers being part of an employer's retirement plan, even if the money going into the retirement plan comes from legal fees.

ADVERTISING AND SOLICITATION

ABA Model Rule 7.1 prohibits all lawyer communication about the lawyer's services from being misleading, whereas Model Rule 7.2 allows lawyers to advertise their services in print, on radio and television, and on the Internet. The ABA leaves to individual jurisdictions the decision to govern what may and may not be presented in an advertisement, and most jurisdictions do not allow lawyers to include their past successes in their advertisements. Some jurisdictions prohibit lawyers from using actors in their commercials.

Model Rule 7.3 prohibits a lawyer and his or her employees from **soliciting** a prospective client through live contact (including online contact), unless the prospective client is also a lawyer, or is a family member or close friend of the lawyer. When written solicitations (such as a letter sent by a lawyer to an accident victim, intended to ask that person to become the lawyer's client) are sent to prospective clients, lawyers are required to put "Advertising Material," on the envelope and solicitation documents.

LEGAL ETHICS IN A CYBER WORLD

The legal community has been playing catch-up with respect to the intersection of technology, social media and legal ethics. Part of the focus of the ABA's most recent effort to revise sections of the Model Rules of Professional Conduct includes responding to the questions raised by the ever-increasing use of the Internet to practice law. Some of the issues needing to be resolved include determining the following: how and when lawyers and law firms may ethically incorporate social media into their law practice; what content may be on a law firm's web site; whether a lawyer may write a blog that includes discussion of the lawyer's past or current cases; whether lawyers may use online referral services that funnel web users to the law firm websites; whether a lawyer may use an online coupon website to promote the lawyer's services; whether a lawyer may be part of a law practice-related website that allows users (such as former clients or other lawyers) to rate or endorse the lawyer; whether lawyers or their paralegals may use social media to investigate prospective jurors, witness in cases, or even opposing clients; whether lawyers may solicit the business of those who are the lawyer's Facebook "friends" or part of the lawyer's LinkedIn network, and whether lawyers may practice law exclusively on the Internet (having no physical office).

Answers to these types of questions often come in the form or ethics opinions and, eventually, changes to the ethics rules. For example, the ABA issued an ethics opinion in 2010, concluding that all lawyer website information was subject to the truthfulness requirements by then-existing ethics rules. In 2014, the ABA issued an ethics opinion that permitted lawyers to review the web presence of jurors or potential jurors, but prohibited contacting them through social media. Many jurisdictions have issues ethics opinions for their lawyers on similar matters, and some state and local bar associations have created guides for ethical use of social media.

ATTORNEY DISCIPLINE

The ABA does not regulate lawyers; the highest court in a given jurisdiction does. If a client believes that he or she has been subject to the lawyer's misconduct, the client can file a written accusation against the lawyer, called a **grievance**. The grievance is filed with that jurisdiction's **disciplinary commission**, which is empowered by its jurisdiction's supreme court to investigate the grievance and decide whether or not to bring ethics charges against the attorney. If a lawyer is found to have violated his or her jurisdiction's rules of professional conduct, a disciplinary sanction is given. Such sanctions range from a **private reprimand** (where the lawyer's name is not included with the official censure), to a **public reprimand**, to a short **license suspension** (involving the lawyer's automatically being allowed to practice law at the suspension's conclusion), to a longer suspension (under which the lawyer must apply for reinstatement to the practice of law at the suspension's conclusion), to even **disbarment**, which is permanent loss of a law license. However, some jurisdictions allow an attorney to apply for reinstatement to the practice of law after a multi-year disbarment term. For example, a disbarred Indiana attorney is permanently disbarred, whereas a disbarred Florida attorney who has not previously been disbarred may apply for reinstatement after five years.

Reviewing What You Learned

After studying the chapter, write the answers to each of the following questions:

1. List the current set of rules that the American Bar Association uses for legal ethics.

____

____

____

2. What do lawyers need to pass before they can practice law? Please explain.

____

____

3. What are the two mandatory duties lawyers have, according to Model Rules 1.1 and 1.3?

____

____

____

4. What does truthfulness (or the inverse) include, according to the ABA Model Rules?

____

____

____

5. Explain how a lawyer is responsible for his paralegal's conduct.

____

____

____

6. What are the exceptions to the duty of confidentiality?

____

____

____

____

7. What is the purpose of the attorney–client privilege?

____

____

____

____

8. What is the difference between a flat fee and a contingent (or contingency) fee?

____

____

____

____

9. What are some of the guidelines for advertising and soliciting?

____

____

____

____

10. List and explain the disciplinary sanctions that may be given to a lawyer.

____

____

____

____

Understanding Legal Concepts

Indicate whether each statement is true or false. Then change the italicized word or phrase of each false statement to make it true.

ANSWERS

______ 1. The *American Bar Association* regulates lawyer conduct.

______ 2. Most states have adopted *guidelines* for the lawyer's use of paralegals.

______ 3. A *frivolous suit* has no basis in law for bringing a claim or appeal.

______ 4. Paralegals are not allowed to engage in *substantive legal work.*

______ 5. Overhead expenses may be charged in *hourly billing.*

______ 6. *Flat fees* are commonly charged for personal injury and other tort.

______ 7. A client can file a written accusation against a lawyer, called a *reprimand.*

______ 8. Lawyers are required to put the words "advertising material" on *written solicitations.*

______ 9. *Private reprimand* is permanent loss of a law license.

Checking Terminology

From the list of legal terms that follows, select the one that matches each definition.

ANSWERS

a. attorney–client privilege
b. bar exam
c. Canons of Professional Ethics
d. comments
e. competent
f. confidential communication
g. conflict of interest
h. contingency fee
i. diligence
j. disbarment
k. disciplinary commission
l. duty of confidentiality
m. ex parte communication
n. flat fee
o. frivolous suit
p. grievance
q. informed consent
r. legal assistant/paralegal
s. legal ethics
t. legal fees
u. license suspension
v. Model Code of Professional Responsibility
w. Model Rules of Professional Conduct
x. nonbillables
y. paralegal
z. private reprimand
aa. public reprimand
bb. Rules
cc. soliciting

______ 1. Torn between loyalties to two or more clients.
______ 2. Originally, a list of do's and don't's for lawyers,
______ 3. Permanent loss of a law license.
______ 4. Lawyer's name is not on official censure.
______ 5. Protection from having to testify against one's clients.
______ 6. Not allowed to practice law for a short period.
______ 7. Sum-certain cost of lawyer's services; not per hour.
______ 8. Test on law and ethics for lawyer licensure.
______ 9. Act of seeking a specific client.
______ 10. Staying on top of a case with promptness.
______ 11. Charges for the lawyer's time or efforts.
______ 12. A lawyer has the knowledge base and skill to handle a legal issue.
______ 13. Knowledge of the likely consequences.
______ 14. Help for the reader to understand the focus of Rules.
______ 15. First set of ethics rules by ABA.
______ 16. Law firm costs that cannot be charged to clients.
______ 17. Mandatory format in the ABA Model Rules.
______ 18. Protecting client information.
______ 19. Nonlawyer trained to do substantive legal work.
______ 20. Ethics rules adopted in 1969 by the ABA.
______ 21. Meant to harass someone or having no basis in law.
______ 22. Payment in a percentage of plaintiff's damages.
______ 23. Nonlawyer trained less than a paralegal.
______ 24. Lawyer's name on official censure.
______ 25. Investigates grievances; brings ethics charges.
______ 26. Ethics rules adopted by ABA in 2003.
______ 27. Written accusation against a lawyer.
______ 28. Private client information shared with a lawyer.
______ 29. Unethical lawyer communication with a judge.

Using Legal Language

Read the following story and fill in the blank lines with legal terms taken from the list of terms at the beginning of this chapter.

After graduating from law school, Eve sought to be licensed to practice law. She sought a state that had _______________________, so she took the bar exam in a state that administered the _______________________, as well as the _______________________, both of which are created by the _______________________. She also took the _______________________, which tested her knowledge of established ethics rules, sometimes called _______________________ rules.

Once licensed to practice law, Eve is required to follow her state's professional responsibility rules, which for most states are based on the ABA's _______________________. They are formatted with mandatory _______________________, followed by explanatory _______________________. If Eve had a question about the ethics rules and their application, she can ask her bar association for an _______________________, to help guide her conduct.

While there are many aspects to ethical lawyering, Eve needs to make sure her representation is _______________________, which means she is capable of adequately handling the matter for which she is hired. To help her with her law practice, Eve hired a _______________________, who is not licensed to practice law but can do many substantive legal tasks, provided there is adequate lawyer supervision. Like Eve, those employees are required to follow the applicable ethics rules, including those that require the _______________________ of client information and communication. Eve needs to be careful to avoid _______________________, which would include representing one client to the disadvantage of another client.

As it concerns billing her clients, Eve could charge a _______________________ in certain cases, which is a percentage of the plaintiff's recovery. Eve needs to be careful when _______________________ business from prospective clients, because most of those activities are prohibited when directed toward a prospective client through live contact. If it is thought that Eve failed to follow her jurisdiction's ethics rules, a _______________________ can be filed against her. In the event, her jurisdiction's _______________________ successfully prosecutes the case, Eve could receive a sanction as light as a _______________________, or she could have her license _______________________ or she could even be _______________________.

Terms Used in Constitutional and Criminal Law

Comstock/Stockbyte/Getty Images

CHAPTER 9
Constitutional Law

CHAPTER 10
Crimes, Accomplices, and Defenses

CHAPTER 11
Crimes Against Property

CHAPTER 12
Crimes Against the Person and Human Habitation

CHAPTER 13
Homicide

CHAPTER 14
Crimes Against Morality and Drug Abuse

In our society, criminal law not only dominates the news, but also penetrates deeply into our culture by way of TV thrillers, violent movies, and suspense-filled mystery stories. And yet, the criminal law is bound by the limits set in the U.S. Constitution, so Part Two opens with an overview of the Constitution and a summary of its key parts. Then, Part Two discusses many of the crimes that we have heard about or have been exposed to since childhood. After defining a crime and explaining its components, Chapter 10 highlights the three broad classes of crimes and describes accomplices and criminal defenses. Chapter 11 explains the elements of crimes and discusses crimes against property, including larceny, embezzlement, bribery, extortion, coercion, receipt of stolen goods, and forgery. Chapter 12 explores crimes against the person, such as robbery, mayhem, assault, battery, and rape, in addition to crimes against human habitation—that is, burglary and arson. The subject of homicide is explained in Chapter 13. Crimes against morality, including adultery, fornication, bigamy, polygamy, incest, sodomy, miscegenation, abortion, pornography, and drug abuse are examined in Chapter 14.

Constitutional Law

ANTE INTERROGATORY

*The first 10 amendments in the U.S. Constitution are known as the
(A) Supremacy Clause, (B) judicial review doctrine, (C) Articles
of Confederation, (D) Bill of Rights.*

LEARNING OBJECTIVES

LO 1: Identify the Constitution's structure,
including distinguishing the articles
from the amendments

LO 2: Identify the branches of the federal
government, including the powers of
each branch.

LO 3: Explain how the system of checks
and balances operates in the federal
government

LO 4: Explain what an amendment is and
contrast the bill of rights with the
other amendments

KEY TERMS

amendments

Articles of Confederation

articles

bicameral

Bill of Rights

cabinet

checks and balances

clause

elastic power

executive branch

express powers

federalism

House of Representatives

judicial branch

judicial review

legislative branch

pocket veto

Senate

separation of powers

Supremacy Clause

treaties

U.S. Constitution

U.S. Supreme Court

veto

WEBSITES FOR PRONUNCIATION HELP

http://dictionary.cambridge.org/us/pronunciation/english/audio

https://www.howtopronounce.com

The **U.S. Constitution** is the first governing document in world history that creates representative democracy, expressly limits the powers of government, and grants specific rights to the people. But it was not the first foundational governing document in American history. The **Articles of Confederation** loosely governed the states from 1781 until the Constitution was ratified in 1789. Drafted and sent to the states for ratification in 1777, the Articles of Confederation allowed the Continental Congress to direct the Revolutionary War—through George Washington—and conduct European diplomacy, but it wasn't until 1781 that the final state, Maryland, ratified it. The Articles of Confederation lacked some elements that were put into the Constitution, including an executive branch, a judicial branch, a national army, and the power to tax.

THE CONSTITUTION'S STRUCTURE

At the Constitutional Convention in 1787, the framers decided to create a federal constitution that would provide for direct and indirect representation, and would have **separation of powers** by giving independent authority to each of the three branches of government. Those branches of government are the **legislative branch**, **executive branch**, and **judicial branch**. The Constitution consists of seven **articles**, which are the separate, original parts of the Constitution, and 27 **amendments**, which modify or invalidate earlier parts of the Constitution. The Constitution's structure provides for **federalism**, which allows state governments to retain their individual governing powers, even though the federal government is given broad powers. The Constitution's Seventh Article provides for the Constitution to become effective upon the ratification of it by nine states, which actually happened by 1788. But it wasn't until May 1790 that Rhode Island, the last of the 13 states, ratified the Constitution.

THE BRANCHES OF GOVERNMENT

Article I of the Constitution is directed to the establishment of the federal Congress. The federal legislature is **bicameral**, which means that there are two chambers, or houses of representation. The **House of Representatives** has 435 members. Members of the House of Representatives serve two-year terms, and while the number of representatives in the House is set at 435, the number of representatives for each state shifts based on the results of the federal census, which takes place every ten years. As of the 2010 federal census, the average number of people in a congressional district is 710,767. The **Senate** has 100 senators who serve six-year terms. Each state gets two senators. Article I gives the power to make laws to the Congress. Either chamber of Congress may begin a legislative bill, with the exception that taxing legislation must start in the House of Representatives. Congress's **express powers** are the specifically stated powers of Congress and are found in Article I, Section 8. Included in those powers are the power to declare war and the power to regulate interstate commerce. Congress also has the power to make all laws necessary and proper to carry out its express powers, sometimes called its **elastic power**.

Article II creates the executive branch, which is headed by the U.S. President. The president's responsibilities include carrying out the laws passed by the Congress, directing all federal military forces, and appointing all federal judges. The president also appoints the heads of the executive departments of the government, called the **cabinet**. The cabinet includes the Department of State, the Department of Defense, and the Department of the Treasury. The president also makes **treaties**, which are legally enforceable agreements with foreign governments.

Article III of the constitution creates the **U.S. Supreme Court**. Its jurisdiction is primarily appellate, but it also is given original jurisdiction over certain legal matters, such as if a state were to sue another state. Beyond being the highest court in the federal judicial system, the Supreme Court is the highest and most powerful court in the country because Article VI of the Constitution has a **clause** (a distinct part of a constitutional Section) known as the **Supremacy Clause**, which makes federal law preeminent when federal and state law conflict. And due to the doctrine of **judicial review**, the Supreme Court has the power to declare acts of Congress and acts of the executive branch unconstitutional. There are nine justices on the U.S. Supreme Court, who are entitled to serve on the court for life.

CHECKS AND BALANCES

In order to prevent one branch of government from becoming too dominant, the Constitution creates a system of **checks and balances**, which allows each branch to counteract the powers of the other branches. For instance, the president can **veto** a bill rather than signing it into law. Veto is Latin for "I forbid," and if the president strikes down a piece of legislation through a veto, or refuses to sign it (called a **pocket veto**), the Congress can override the veto with a two-thirds majority vote. The Senate can refuse to vote for the president's judicial or cabinet appointees. And the Supreme Court can declare federal legislation unconstitutional.

TERMS IN ACTION

The **veto** power is one of the presidential powers which demonstrates the **separation of powers** and the **checks and balances** inherent in the Constitution. Whether the president uses a traditional veto, directly striking down the legislation, or refuses to sign a bill, called a pocket veto, Congress can exercise its checks and balances power by overriding the veto, provided both houses again vote for passage of the bill by a two-thirds majority. In the history of the U.S. Constitution (as of this writing), there have been 2,573 vetoes and only 110 instances of vetoes being overridden. George Washington issued two vetoes, and both were overridden, whereas John Adams and Thomas Jefferson never vetoed any legislation. Neither did William Henry Harrison, but he served as president for only 32 days. He died from pneumonia and the folklore is that he caught it from giving America's longest inaugural address in very bad weather and without wearing an overcoat. Franklin Roosevelt (who was president from 1932 until his death in 1945) issued a total of 645 vetoes. Of these, 372 were regular vetoes and 263 were pocket vetoes. Only 9 were overridden. Barack Obama issued 12 vetoes, one of which was overridden: his 2016 veto of the legislation allowing the families of the September 11, 2001 terrorist attacks to sue Saudi Arabia for any role it may have played in the conspiracy. As of this writing, Donald Trump has issued no vetoes.

Source: senate.gov; history.com

AMENDMENTS

In order to make changes to the U.S. Constitution, as later generations would desire, Article V provides for a process to amend the Constitution. A total of 27 amendments have been passed, although the first 10 amendments, known as the **Bill of Rights**, were ratified simultaneously in 1791. The Bill of Rights provides specific freedoms to Americans, such as the First Amendment's guarantee of freedom of religion, freedom of speech, and freedom of press. The Bill of Rights also puts certain restrictions on the federal government, such as the Fourth Amendment's prohibition on warrantless searches, and the Eighth Amendment's prohibition on cruel and unusual punishment. Later amendments have made slavery illegal, granted equal protection to former slaves, granted women the right to vote, and reduced the voting age to 18. The Bill of Rights' freedoms originally protected Americans against the federal government. For instance, the First Amendment's freedom of speech guarantee was meant to prohibit the federal government from interfering or prohibiting one's protected speech rights. States and certainly private actors (employers, for example) were not impacted by the Bill of Rights. However, federal courts have applied most of the Bill of Rights protections to the states (and by extension, local governments), beginning in 1925, when the U.S. Supreme Court held that the freedom of speech clause applied to the states, in the case, *Gitlow v. New York*.

TERMS IN ACTION

Does the freedom of speech guarantee in the **Bill of Rights** include all speech? No. Not only are some categories of speech unprotected by the Constitution (slander, for instance), but also other categories of speech are illegal (extortion and bribery, for example). In 2011, the **U.S. Supreme Court** dealt with the question of whether the First Amendment protected the ranting of a small religious sect whose members are infamous for going to the funerals of soldiers and picketing with signs that say hateful things to the surviving family members. From Topeka, Kansas, family members belonging to what is known as the Westboro Baptist Church have gone to over 600 funerals of those who died serving the country in Afghanistan and Iraq. Carrying pickets that say things like, "God Hates Fags" and "Thank God for Dead Soldiers," the group also yells at the grieving family members, if given the chance. The family of Matthew Snyder, a marine who died in Iraq in 2006, was subject to the picketing at their son's funeral and sued the tiny fringe group for intentional infliction of emotional distress. The case reached the Supreme Court, who decided in an eight-to-one vote in March 2011 that the hateful speech was protected "public speech." Chief Justice John Roberts wrote in the majority decision that, despite the noxiousness of what was being said, the content was protected because the protesters were expressing their view that America was being divinely punished for its tolerance of homosexuality. That qualified the statements as commentary on a public matter. Justice Samuel Alito was the lone dissenter, and he wrote that the First Amendment doesn't protect people from brutalizing innocent victims like the Snyder family. In 2015, the court took a different view with respect to the confederate flag. In *Walker v. Texas Division, Sons of Confederate Veterans, Inc.*, the Supreme Court ruled in a five-to-four vote that Texas could deny the request of a specialty license plate with two confederate flags on it. The majority opinion, by Justice Stephen Breyer, determined that such a license plate—being issued by Texas—was government speech. So, Texas could reject it on the basis that it might offend others. The dissenting opinion, written by Justice Alito, argued that restricting license plate messages to that which might offend someone else was unconstitutional viewpoint discrimination.

Source: *Snyder v. Phelps, 562* U.S. 443 (2011); washingtonpost.com; *Walker v. Texas Division, Sons of Confederate Veterans, Inc.*, 576 U.S. __ (2015)

Constitution Wise

First Amendment Rights

free exercise clause	Guarantees to all persons the freedom to exercise (to worship, speak about, live out) one's religion.
establishment clause	Prohibits the government from establishing a state religion.
freedom of speech	Guarantees to all persons the right to speak, both orally and in writing.
freedom of the press	Guarantees to all persons the right to publish and circulate their ideas without government interference.

freedom of assembly	Guarantees to all persons the right to peaceably associate and assemble with others.
free exercise clause	Guarantees to all persons the right to freely practice their religion.

Protection for Criminal Defendants

right to trial by jury	Gives criminal defendants the right to a speedy and public jury trial (Sixth Amendment).
right to confront witnesses	Gives criminal defendants the right to confront witnesses against them (Sixth Amendment).
self-incriminating protection	Gives criminal defendants the right to refuse to testify against themselves (Fifth Amendment).
cruel and unusual punishment	Protects criminal defendants from being subject to excessive bail and cruel and unusual punishment (Eighth Amendment).
double jeopardy protection	Protects criminal defendants from being tried twice for the same offense (Fifth Amendment).

Other Meaningful Clauses

commerce clause	Gives Congress the power to regulate commerce with foreign nations and among the different states (Art. IV, § 1).
supremacy clause	Makes the U.S. Constitution and federal laws the supreme law of the land (Art. VI, § 1).
full faith and credit clause	Requires each state to recognize the laws and court decisions of every other state (Art. IV, § 1).
privileges and immunities clause	Requires states to give out-of-state citizens the same rights as they give their own citizens (Art. IV, § 2; Fourteenth Amendment).
equal protection clause	Requires that similarly situated persons receive similar treatment under the law (Fourteenth Amendment).
due process clause	Provides that no person shall be deprived of life, liberty, or property without fairness and justice (due process of law) (Fifth Amendment; Fourteenth Amendment).

Web Wise

- For an online look at the U.S. Constitution, including the Bill of Rights and all amendments, as well as sequential and subject indexes, go to **www.constitutionus.com**
- For information on the U.S. Supreme Court, including biographies of its justices, an online tour of the Supreme Court building, and summaries of all Supreme Court cases, including how the justices voted, as well as links to the cases in full, go to **www.oyez.org**

Reviewing What You Learned

After studying the chapter, write the answers to each of the following questions:

1. What are the differences between the U.S. Constitution and the Articles of Confederation?

2. How was the federal government given separation of powers by the Constitution?

3. What are the differences between articles and amendments?

4. What is federalism?

5. What does *bicameral* mean?

6. How many members of the House of Representatives are there, and what term length do they serve?

7. How many members of the Senate are there, and what term length do they serve?

8. What are some powers in Article I of the U.S. Constitution that Congress has the power to exercise?

9. What do the executive branch powers include in Article II of the U.S. Constitution?

10. Describe some of the powers of the U.S. Supreme Court listed in Article III of the Constitution.

11. What is the Supremacy Clause?

12. What does the doctrine of judicial review express?

13. What are checks and balances and how does each branch of government exercise them?

14. What does the Bill of Rights do? How do the Bill of Rights apply to the states?

Understanding Legal Concepts

Indicate whether each statement is true or false. Then, change the italicized word or phrase of each false statement to make it true.

ANSWERS

_____ 1. The *U.S. Constitution* was the first foundational governing document in American history.

_____ 2. Our federal constitution provides *national* representation.

_____ 3. *Articles* modify or invalidate earlier parts of the constitution.

_____ 4. *Federalism* allows state governments to retain their individual governing powers, even though the federal government is given broad powers.

_____ 5. The number of representatives in the *Senate* is based on each state's population.

_____ 6. Congress's *elastic powers* are the specifically stated powers of Congress and are found in Article 1, section 8.

_____ 7. The *executive branch* is headed by the U.S. President.

_____ 8. The jurisdiction of the *U.S. Supreme Court* is primarily appellate, but it also is given original jurisdiction over certain legal matters.

_____ 9. Latin for *treaties* is "I forbid."

_____ 10. The *pocket veto* puts certain restrictions on the federal government.

Checking Terminology

From the list of legal terms that follows, select the one that matches each definition.

ANSWERS

a. amendment
b. Articles of Confederation
c. articles
d. bicameral
e. Bill of Rights
f. cabinet
g. checks and balances
h. clause
i. elastic powers
j. executive branch
k. express powers
l. federalism
m. House of Representatives
n. judicial branch
o. judicial review
p. legislative branch
q. pocket veto
r. Senate
s. separation of powers
t. Supremacy Clause
u. treaties
v. U.S. Constitution
w. U.S. Supreme Court
x. veto

_____ 1. The first governing document in world history that created representative democracy.

_____ 2. Allows state governments to retain their individual governing powers; federal government is given broad powers.

_____ 3. Branch of government that makes laws.

_____ 4. Legally enforceable agreements with foreign countries.

_____ 5. Specifically stated powers of Congress.

_____ 6. Modifications to the body of the Constitution.

_____ 7. Highest court in the United States.

_____ 8. The U.S. Supreme Court heads this.

_____ 9. Based on each state's population.

_____ 10. Power to make laws in order to carry out express powers.

_____ 11. Smaller house of representation.

_____ 12. Loosely governed colonies and states until 1789.

_____ 13. The president's official refusal to sign a bill.

_____ 14. Independent authority to each branch of government.

_____ 15. Seven separate, original parts of the Constitution.

_____ 16. Makes federal law preeminent when federal and state law conflict.

_____ 17. Supreme Court's power to declare acts of Congress and the executive branch unconstitutional.

_____ 18. The U.S. President leads this.

_____ 19. The act of the president's striking down a piece of legislation.

_____ 20. A legislature consisting of two separate bodies.

_____ 21. A distinct part of a constitution section.

_____ 22. Allows each branch of government to counteract powers in another branch.

_____ 23. Heads of executive departments of government.

_____ 24. First 10 amendments to the U.S. Constitution.

Using Legal Language

Read the following story and fill in the blank lines with legal terms taken from the list of terms at the beginning of this chapter.

The _____________________ preceded the _____________________ as the foundational governing document. The Constitution took effect in 1789 after it was _____________________ by nine states. The Constitution consists of seven _____________________ and 27 _____________________, of which the first ten are known as the _____________________. The powers of Congress are found in _____________________; the powers of the Presidency are found in _____________________ and the powers of the Supreme Court are found in _____________________. The specific powers of Congress are known as its _____________________ powers, while the power of Congress to do what is necessary and proper are known as its **elastic** power. The power of the Supreme Court to declare acts of Congress and acts of the executive branch unconstitutional is known as _____________________. When federal law conflicts with state law, federal is controlling because of the Constitution's _____________________ Clause. The president's power to veto legislation, and Congress's power to override a veto are examples of _____________________.

Although originally directed toward the federal government, the _____________________ has since mostly been applied to the states. Two key First Amendment Rights include the _____________________ and the _____________________. Two key constitutional protections for criminal defendants include the _____________________ and the _____________________. Two other meaningful clauses in the main body of the Constitution include the _____________________ and the _____________________.

Crimes, Accomplices, and Defenses

ANTE INTERROGATORY

Being tried twice for the same offense is (A) entrapment, (B) petit treason, (C) double jeopardy, (D) ex post facto.

LEARNING OBJECTIVES

LO 1: Identify the two elements required to exist for most crimes to be committed

LO 2: Contrast crimes that are mala in se from crimes that are mala prohibita and provide examples of each

LO 3: Identify the three principal criminal categories

LO 4: Explain what constitutes treason under American law

LO 5: Summarize the concepts that distinguish felonies from misdemeanors

LO 6: Define a principal in the first degree and a principal in the second degree and provide examples of each

LO 7: Explain what an accessory before the fact is and what limits are placed on such an accessory's criminal liability

LO 8: Explain what an accessory after the fact is and what limits are placed on such an accessory's criminal liability

LO 9: Identify the key characteristics of common criminal defenses

LO 10: Identify key constitutional protections for criminal defendants

LO 11: Identify what cybercrimes are and what key federal statute exists to combat it

KEY TERMS

accessory after the fact

accessory before the fact

accomplice

actus reus

aiding and abetting

alibi

common law

computer fraud and abuse act

conspiracy

constructively

cybercrime

cyberlaw

defense

double jeopardy

entrapment

exclusionary rule

ex post facto

felony

fruit of the poisonous tree doctrine

good faith exception to the exclusionary rule	penal laws
high treason	petit treason
hot pursuit doctrine	plain view doctrine
illegal profiling	principal in the first degree
incarceration	principal in the second degree
intoxication	probable cause
insanity	prosecutor
mala in se	search warrant
mala prohibita	self-defense
mens rea	stop and frisk rule
misdemeanor	strict liability crime
model penal code	treason

WEBSITES FOR PRONUNCIATION HELP

http://dictionary.cambridge.org/us/pronunciation/english/audio

https://www.howtopronounce.com

A crime consists of either the voluntary commission or the voluntary omission of an act (known as **actus reus**), punishable by a fine, imprisonment, or both. No act is criminal unless it is both prohibited and penalized by the law of the place where it is committed. A crime is a "public wrong," in that it is an offense thought to be committed against society as a whole, even if the act has an individual victim. Hence, a public official, the **prosecutor**, pursues the legal case against the defendant. By contrast, a tort is a "private wrong." In addition, the English common law required the act to be committed with a particular state of mind known as **mens rea**, which means criminal intent. Laws that impose a penalty or punishment for a wrong against society are called **penal laws**. The U.S. Constitution prohibits Congress or any state from passing a law that is **ex post facto** (after the fact)—that is, one that holds a person criminally responsible for an act that was not a crime at the time of its commission. Similarly, the Fifth Amendment of the U.S. Constitution prevents people from being tried twice for the same offense, which is known as **double jeopardy**. For example, if a man is charged with burglary and the jury's verdict is not guilty, the prosecutor (the person, representing the jurisdiction where alleged crimes occur, who brings charges against those whom the police have arrested) cannot refile the charges, as if the first trial was a practice round. However, if the jury cannot reach a verdict, the judge can declare a "hung jury," which ends the trial. In this situation, the prosecutor would not violate the double jeopardy provision by seeking to retry the defendant.

Web Wise

- For an overview of criminal law and a link to your state criminal code, go to ***www.law .cornell.edu/wex/criminal_law***
- The website of the U.S. Department of Justice is located at ***www.justice.gov.***
- To read about computer crime go to the Department of Justice's webpage, which is ***www .cybercrime.gov.***

CRIMES MALA IN SE AND MALA PROHIBITA

Crimes are divided into two classes: those acts that are wrong in and of themselves, such as murder, rape, and robbery; and those that are not inherently wrong, but are criminal acts simply because they are prohibited by statute. The former are called crimes **mala in se** (wrongs in themselves) and require a wrongful or unlawful intent on the part of the perpetrator. The latter are called crimes **mala prohibita** (prohibited wrongs) and require no wrongful intent on the part of the perpetrator. All that is necessary is the doing of the act regardless of the intent of the actor. Under the **common law** used in England and the American Colonies before the American Revolution all crimes were mala in se. Common law is a term with multiple definitions, but a primary definition of it is judge-made law, which means appellate court decisions based on legal doctrines and traditions, rather than specific statutes. That can include English common law, as well as court cases after the American Revolution.

To illustrate a crime mala prohibita, a 1906 state statute made it a crime to transport intoxicating liquor within the state without a license. A truck driver in the employ of a common carrier (which was bound to accept all packages offered to it for transportation and which had no right to compel a shipper to disclose the package's contents) was convicted of violating the statute when he transported an unmarked sugar barrel filled with liquor. Nothing about the appearance of the barrel caused suspicion as to its contents, and the truck driver was ignorant of the fact that it contained intoxicating liquor. The appellate court upheld the conviction, saying that the only fact to be determined is whether the defendant did the act. The court held that knowledge of the wrongdoing or wrongful intent was immaterial in the case of a crime mala prohibita. The court said that the legislature has the power to prohibit certain acts regardless of moral purity or ignorance.

The type of mala prohibita crime discussed in the above example is also a **strict liability crime**, which is a crime that has no criminal intent (mens rea) requirement. Some acts are declared by statute to be crimes even though there is no corresponding criminal intent. Typically, strict liability crimes are created to protect the public from acts thought to be so dangerous as to be categorized as crimes, regardless of the intent of the actor. Speeding is an example of a strict liability and mala prohibita crime. There is nothing inherently evil about driving extremely fast, yet driving above the posted speed limit is illegal, and not realizing you were driving above the speed limit is irrelevant because your intent is irrelevant in such a violation.

PRINCIPAL CRIMINAL CATEGORIES

Crimes are divided into three principal groups: treason, felonies, and misdemeanors.

Treason

Under the common law of England, treason was divided into **high treason** (acts against the king) and **petit treason** (acts against one's master or lord). Such a division was never followed in America, however. Instead, **treason** is defined in the U.S. Constitution as levying war against the United States or giving aid and comfort to the nation's enemies. The charge of treason has been brought only a few dozen times in U.S. history. The first treason charge since the end of World War II era was brought in 2006 against Adam Gadahn, a California man who appeared in propaganda videos for Al Queda during the war on terrorism. At the time of the treason indictment, Gadahn's whereabouts were unknown, and in 2015 he was killed by a drone strike in Pakistan.

Felonies and Misdemeanors

A **felony** is a major crime, although its exact definition differs from state to state. It is defined in some states as "punishment by hard labor" and in others as "an infamous crime" or a crime subject to "infamous punishment." A **misdemeanor** conversely is a less serious crime than a felony. Many states distinguish between a felony and a misdemeanor by the length of **incarceration** (confinement) involved in the sentence. For example, in Massachusetts, "a crime punishable by death or imprisonment in the state prison is a felony. All other crimes are misdemeanors" (M.G.L. ch.274 §1). In that state, the minimum sentence in a state prison is two-and-one-half years. Many states have classified felonies and misdemeanors according to punishment by using a lettering or numbering system. A "class A felony," for example, would have a different punishment from a "class B felony." Murder, rape, armed robbery, and assault with a deadly weapon are examples of felonies. Misdemeanors call for a lighter penalty, such as a fine or jail sentence in a place other than a state prison. Disturbing the peace, simple assault, and petty larceny are examples of misdemeanors.

ACCOMPLICES

The crime of **conspiracy** is when two or more people agree to commit an unlawful act. A conspiracy exists even when the crime or unlawful act that was agreed upon is never carried out. In some states, proof of an agreement between the parties to commit a criminal or unlawful act is all that is necessary to convict the parties of conspiracy. In many states, however, to obtain a conviction it is necessary to prove, in addition, that the parties took some action toward the commission of the crime or unlawful act. Anyone who takes part with another in the commission of a crime is called an **accomplice**.

Principal in the First Degree

A **principal in the first degree** is a person who actually commits a felony either by his or her own hand or through an innocent agent. A principal in the first degree is the one, for instance, who pulls the trigger or strikes the blow. One who intentionally places poison in a glass, for example, would be considered a principal in the first degree even if the glass containing the poison was delivered to the victim by an innocent third person.

Principal in the Second Degree

A **principal in the second degree** is one who did not commit the act, but who was actually or constructively present, aiding and abetting another in the commission of a felony. **Aiding and abetting** means participating in the crime by giving assistance or encouragement. One who is positioned outside as a lookout, for example, while his or her companions are inside committing burglary would be considered **constructively** present—that is, made present by legal interpretation. In a Nevada case (*State v. Nevada, 13 Nev. 386 (1878)*) well over a hundred years ago, a lookout stationed miles away sent a smoke signal to fellow robbers, signaling that a stagecoach was coming. The court found the lookout guilty as a principal in the second degree, holding that the lookout was constructively present even though he was miles away from the scene of the crime.

At common law, and in many states today, a principal in the second degree is subject to the same punishment as that given to a principal in the first degree.

Accessory before the Fact

An **accessory before the fact** is one who procures, counsels, or commands another to commit a felony, but who is not present when the felony is committed. Mere knowledge that a crime is going to be committed by another person is not enough to become an accessory before the fact to the crime that is subsequently committed by the other person, however. It must be shown that the accessory before the fact was active in inducing or bringing about the felony.

An accessory before the fact will be responsible for the natural and probable consequences that ensue from the crime that he or she induced, but not for a crime of a substantially different nature. This is known as the Pinkerton doctrine, coming from a Supreme Court case in 1946. Thus, if one person procures another to beat someone up and the beating results in death, the one who arranged for the beating would be an accessory before the fact to the killing because death is a natural and probable consequence of beating someone up. Conversely, in the situation in which one person hires a man to beat up a woman and he rapes her instead, the procurer would not be an accessory before the fact to the rape, because it is a crime of a substantially different nature than that which was ordered by the procurer. The **Model Penal Code**, which was created by the American Law Institute and which serves as the template for many states' criminal codes, breaks from the common law doctrine. It makes an accessory liable only for those acts that were contemplated by the perpetrator, as opposed to those acts which were foreseeable from the plan.

Some states view a person who hires another to commit a crime as a principal in the first degree rather than an accessory before the fact, because hiring a "hit man" makes one equally as guilty of the crime as if the hiring party had committed it. Some states still follow the common law rule that an accessory before the fact cannot be tried in court until a principal is first convicted. Many states' criminal codes, however, now state that an accessory before the fact may be tried without regard to the principal and may be found guilty even though the principal is acquitted.

Word Wise
"Mal-" … "Mala"

"Mal(e)" is a prefix or word part used in many legal terms to mean "bad," "wrong," or "fraudulent."

| malconduct | malefaction | Malefactor |
| malice | malicious | Malfeasance |

"Mala" is the plural form of the Latin word "malum," which also means "bad," "evil," or "wrongful."

"Mala" appears in many legal phrases, including

mala fides	bad faith
mala in se	wrongs in themselves
mala praxis	malpractice
mala prohibita	prohibited wrongs or offenses

Accessory After the Fact

An **accessory after the fact** is one who receives, relieves, comforts, or assists another, with knowledge that the other person has committed a felony. To be convicted of being an accessory after the fact, a felony must have been committed by another person, and the accessory after the fact must intend that that person avoid or escape detention, arrest, trial, or punishment.

Historically under the common law, a wife could not be guilty as an accessory after the fact under the theory that she was under her husband's control and the assumption that he was the principal. Modern statutes have extended that exception, although for a different reason, to include close relatives as well. The reason is that it would be natural for spouses and close relatives to protect their loved ones who were in trouble with the law. Vermont and Massachusetts, for example, do not allow a criminal's spouse, parent, grandparent, child, grandchild, brother, or sister to be convicted of being an accessory after the fact to the criminal. Indiana, however, limits the family protection for "assisting a criminal" to the perpetrator's parent, child, or spouse. For example, if a mother harbors her son from the police, after knowing he has committed a felony, she would not be charged as an accessory after the fact. However, under a different fact pattern, she could be guilty as a conspirator with him.

CRIMINAL DEFENSES

Evidence offered by a defendant to defeat a criminal charge or civil lawsuit is known as a **defense**. Some common criminal defenses are alibi, entrapment, insanity, and self-defense. **Alibi** is a defense that places the defendant in a different place than the crime scene, so that it would have been impossible to commit the crime. **Entrapment** may be used as a defense when a police officer induces a person to commit a crime that the person would not have committed otherwise, and would not be predisposed to commit as demonstrated by the person's lack of criminal history. **Insanity** is a wide-ranging defense and one which is tied to the specific criminal insanity standard of the defendant's jurisdiction. Essentially, insanity is available to mentally ill defendants who can prove, that at the time of their crimes, they did not know the difference between right and wrong or did not appreciate the criminality of their conduct. **Self-defense** is a justification for the use of force in resisting an unlawful, imminent attack. Those claiming self-defense may use no more force than is reasonably necessary to stop the attack. Some states require someone claiming self-defense to have first attempted retreat from the imminent attack—if reasonably possible—except when that person is in his or her own home. One defense that rarely ever works, assuming it is allowed in a jurisdiction, is the defense of **intoxication**. This defense is based on the idea that someone might be unable to form the mens rea to commit a crime if he or she is so intoxicated (which would include being under the influence of drugs, as well). Involuntary intoxication can be a defense, but in most jurisdictions there is no defense allowed to those who voluntarily take drugs or drink alcohol before committing crimes.

TERMS IN ACTION

Woody Will Smith was charged in 2009 with the **felony** of all felonies: murdering his wife Amanda Hornsby-Smith by strangling her with an extension cord. The physical evidence against him was overwhelming and conclusive that he killed his wife. But Smith claimed in his defense that he was **insane** at the time he killed his wife, due to caffeine **intoxication**. According to his defense lawyer, Smith suspected that his wife was going to leave him weeks earlier and that, as a result of his anxiety and sleeplessness, he began drinking energy drinks and ingesting diet pills, one after another. This condition, the lawyer claimed, rendered Smith unable to form the intent (**mens rea**) to kill. The jury was unmoved by that defense. He found Smith guilty of murder in 2010 and sentenced him to life in prison. His conviction and sentence were upheld on appeal in 2012.

Source: cbsnews.com; nydailynews.com; law.justia.com

CONSTITUTIONAL PROTECTIONS FOR DEFENDANTS

The U.S. Constitution provides broad protection for criminal defendants. For example, under the Fourth Amendment, a **search warrant** (a written order of the court authorizing law enforcement officers to search and seize certain property) must, generally, be obtained before officers may enter private property without permission. A search warrant is not needed to seize items that are in plain view of a lawfully positioned police officer, under the **plain view doctrine**. Likewise, a search warrant is not needed in exigent circumstances, such as the **hot pursuit doctrine**, which is at issue when police pursue a fleeing suspect into a private area and such flight puts others' safety at risk. Similarly, under the **stop and frisk rule** a police officer who reasonably believes a person is acting suspiciously and could be armed may stop and frisk the suspect for weapons, without a search warrant. Stop and frisk policies have come under scrutiny as at least one U.S. District Court concluded New York's City's stop and frisk actions to be unconstitutional. The case is still ongoing, as of this writing. Police officers have limited rights to frisk someone who has been arrested. Police officers are also allowed to stop and search a motor vehicle and to order all passengers out of the vehicle, but only when they have **probable cause** to do so. Probable cause is a reasonable belief, based on the then-available facts, that a crime has been committed or that evidence of criminality exists.

Illegal profiling may also be used as a defense. **Illegal profiling** is a law enforcement action, such as a detention or arrest, based solely on race, religion, national origin, ethnicity, gender, or sexual orientation of the person being charged, rather than on that person's behavior or on information identifying the person as having engaged in criminal activity.

Under the **exclusionary rule** (a doctrine created by the U.S. Supreme Court), evidence obtained by an unconstitutional search or seizure cannot be used at the trial of a defendant. Similarly, under the **fruit of the poisonous tree doctrine** evidence derived from an illegal search is inadmissible. Thus, law enforcement officers could not use as evidence illegal weapons found in a building that they had unlawfully searched while looking for illicit drugs. The **good faith exception to the exclusionary rule** makes admissible any evidence discovered by unlawful searches by officers acting in good faith (sincere), but in the mistaken belief that the search was valid.

CYBERCRIMES

Cyberlaw, the area of law that concerns the use of the Internet and related networks, is a term that has recently come into common usage. **Cybercrimes**—criminal activity associated with a computer network—include such crimes as spamming, hacking, computer fraud, identity theft, stalking, blackmail, and cyber-terrorism. For instance, drug trafficking is a criminal activity that now includes operating an illegal, online pharmacy. The first federal legislation to respond to the increase of computer crime was the 1986 **Computer Fraud and Abuse Act**, which predated the Internet (at least what we think of as the World Wide Web). So many criminal acts are committed through the use of computers and the Internet that the Computer Fraud and Abuse Act has been amended at least seven times, including through the USA Patriot Act, passed after 9/11.

Web Wise

- The United States Department of Justice has a website dedicated to inform the public about computer crimes, including legal resources and news releases on the latest arrests of those accused of cybercrimes. The website can be found at ***http://www.cybercrime.gov***.
- For a critical review of the Computer Fraud and Abuse Act, including example and cases of its alleged over-reach, go to ***www.digitaltrends.com***, and type "Computer Fraud and Abuse Act" in the search bar

TERMS IN ACTION

Cybercrimes, such as hacking and online identity theft, are often committed for financial gain. Every now and then though, a cybercrime is committed for no other reason than spite. Allan Eric Carlson was a long-suffering Philadelphia Phillies fan who had had enough of the team he hated to love—the baseball team with the most losses in Major League Baseball history. Rather than writing a letter to the editor of a Philadelphia newspaper, around 2001, he sent thousands of Spam e-mails expressing his disgust. But he didn't send them from his own e-mail account. According to the Department of Justice, Carlson hacked into computers around the country, hijacking the return e-mail addresses of Philadelphia sports writers, ESPN, Fox Sports, as well as Phillies employees, and had those e-mail accounts launch his e-mail tirades. Those e-mails were then bounced back to the original victims of the hacking. Carlson was arrested in 2003 and was eventually convicted of 79 counts of identity theft and computer fraud. In 2005, Carlson was sentenced to four years in prison. In 2008, the Phillies won the World Series, and the next year they played in it again. Carlson maintains his own web log, and calls himself a "political prisoner of the United States government."

The story of Allan Schwartz shows the tragic effect the **Computer Fraud and Abuse Act** can have. Passed in 1986 and amended many times, the wide-ranging collection of laws related to computer and Internet activities has been called by a law professor "the worst law in technology," in part because it makes it a federal crime to violate a website's terms of service. In 2013, Aaron Swartz, who at the age of 14 helped write the RSS feed computer program that alerts web users to new blog posts, who was the co-founder of the website Reddit, and was a Harvard scholar, committed suicide at the age of 26, after years of fighting the U.S. Department of Justice, which charged him with multiple Computer Fraud and Abuse crimes.

In 2011, Schwartz used his academic access to download millions of pages of documents from the Massachusetts Institute of Technology library. For that violation of MIT's online terms of service, Swartz faced up to three decades in prison and a $1 million fine, even though his **intent** was not to profit from the downloads. Many in the academic and tech communities petitioned the Justice Department and President Obama to drop the felony charges, but after negotiations between his defense lawyers and the prosecutors failed in reducing the **felonies** to **misdemeanors**, Swartz hung himself in his apartment two years to the day after his arrest.

Sources: usdoj.gov; justice.gov; allancarlson.blogspot.com; huffingtonpost.com; nydailynews.com; newyorker.com

Reviewing What You Learned

After studying the chapter, write the answers to each of the following questions:

1. Who brings the action in a criminal case?

____

____

____

2. What is an ex post facto law?

____

____

____

3. How does a crime that is mala in se differ from a crime that is mala prohibita?

____

____

____

4. List the three classifications of crimes.

____

____

____

5. What is a generally accepted difference between a felony and a misdemeanor?

____

____

____

6. What is the difference between a principal in the first degree and a principal in the second degree?

____

____

7. How does the punishment of a principal in the first degree compare with that of a principal in the second degree?

____

____

____

8. What is the difference between an accessory before the fact and an accessory after the fact?

____

____

____

9. How has the law placed some limits on the extent of criminal liability for an accessory before the fact compared to a principal to a crime?

____

____

____

10. How do Vermont and Massachusetts differ from Indiana as it concerns who cannot be held liable as an accessory after the fact?

____

____

____

Understanding Legal Concepts

Indicate whether each statement is true or false. Then, change the italicized word or phrase of each false statement to make it true.

ANSWERS

_____ 1. A crime is an offense against *the individual victim alone*. It *is not* a wrong against all of society.

_____ 2. A felony is a *less* serious crime than a misdemeanor.

_____ 3. A crime that is wrong in and of itself is called a crime *mala in se*.

_____ 4. *Petit treason* is a crime that is defined in the U.S. Constitution.

_____ 5. No act is criminal unless it is both *prohibited and penalized* by the law of the jurisdiction in which it is committed.

_____ 6. One who intentionally places poison in a glass is a *principal in the first degree* even though the glass containing the poison is delivered to the victim by an innocent third person.

_____ 7. A *principal in the second degree* is one who procures, counsels, or commands another to commit a felony, but who is not present when the felony is committed.

_____ 8. Mere knowledge that a specific crime is going to be committed by another person *is enough* for someone to become an accessory before the fact.

_____ 9. At common law, a wife *could not* be held as an accessory after the fact to a crime committed by her husband, under the theory that she was under the husband's coercion.

_____ 10. In general, an *accessory before the fact* is subject to the same punishment as that given to a principal.

Checking Terminology

From the list of legal terms that follows, select the one that matches each definition.

ANSWERS

a. accessory after the fact
b. accessory before the fact
c. accomplice
d. actus reus
e. aiding and abetting
f. alibi
g. common law
h. conspiracy
i. constructively
j. cybercrime
k. cyberlaw
l. defense
m. double jeopardy
n. entrapment
o. exclusionary rule
p. ex post facto
q. felony
r. fruit of the poisonous tree doctrine
s. good faith exception to the exclusionary rule
t. high treason
u. hot pursuit doctrine
v. illegal profiling
w. incarceration
x. insanity
y. intoxication
z. mala in se
aa. mala prohibita
bb. mens rea
cc. misdemeanor
dd. penal laws

_____ 1. Evidence discovered unlawfully by officers under the reasonable but mistaken belief that a search was valid can be used in court.

_____ 2. Under the influence of alcohol or drugs—a defense that rarely works.

_____ 3. A minor crime; not a felony.

_____ 4. Wrong in and of itself.

_____ 5. Evidence offered by a defendant to defeat a criminal charge or civil lawsuit.

_____ 6. One who actually commits a felony.

_____ 7. A major crime, punishable by imprisonment in a state prison.

_____ 8. One who procures, counsels, or commands another to commit a felony, but who is not present when the felony is committed.

_____ 9. Tried twice for the same offense.

_____ 10. After the fact.

_____ 11. One who did not commit the act, but who was present, aiding and abetting another in the commission of a felony.

_____ 12. A defense available to mentally ill defendants who can prove that they did not know the difference between right and wrong or did not appreciate the criminality of their conduct.

_____ 13. Prohibited wrong.

_____ 14. The statutory and case law used in England and in the American Colonies before the American Revolution.

_____ 15. A written order of the court authorizing law enforcement officers to search and seize certain property.

_____ 16. One who receives, relieves, comforts, or assists another, with knowledge that the other has committed a felony.

_____ 17. An excuse for the use of force in resisting attack.

_____ 18. Acts against the king (under the English common law).

_____ 19. A defense that may be used when a police officer induces a person to commit a crime that the person would not have otherwise committed.

_____ 20. Participating in a crime by giving assistance or encouragement.

_____ 21. A search warrant is not needed to seize items out in the open, able to be seen by a lawfully positioned police officer.

_____ 22. A defense that places the defendant in a different place than the crime scene so that it would have been impossible for the defendant to have committed the crime.

ee. petit treason
ff. plain view doctrine
gg. principal in the first degree
hh. principal in the second degree
ii. prosecutor
jj. search warrant
kk. self-defense
ll. stop and frisk rule
mm. treason

_____ **23.** Acts against one's master or lord (under the English common law).
_____ **24.** The getting together of two or more people to plan and accomplish some criminal or unlawful act.
_____ **25.** Anyone who takes part with another in the commission of a crime.
_____ **26.** Laws that impose a penalty or punishment for a wrong against society.
_____ **27.** The person who brings charges against those whom the police have arrested for crimes.
_____ **28.** A search warrant that is not needed when police pursue a fleeing suspect into a private area.
_____ **29.** A rule that allows police officers who believe a person is acting suspiciously and could be armed to stop and check the suspect without a search warrant.
_____ **30.** Made so by legal interpretation.
_____ **31.** Evidence generated or derived from an illegal search or seizure that cannot be used at the trial of a defendant.
_____ **32.** Evidence obtained by an unconstitutional search or seizure that cannot be used at the trial of a defendant.
_____ **33.** Levying war against the United States or giving aid and comfort to its enemies.
_____ **34.** A law enforcement action, such as a detention or arrest, based solely on the race, religion, national origin, ethnicity, gender, or sexual orientation of the person charged.
_____ **35.** Criminal intent.
_____ **36.** A voluntary act.

Using Legal Language

Read the following story and fill in the blank lines with legal terms taken from the list of terms at the beginning of this chapter:

Abigail hired two ________________________, Bonnie and Clyde, to rob a bank. She waited at home while the others carried out the act, which was a(n) ________________________, because it was an offense against the public at large. Bonnie, with a state of mind known as ________________________, went into the bank and committed the robbery, while Clyde, who was ________________ and ________________, waited outside in the get-away car. Abigail would be classified as a(n) ________________, Bonnie a(n) ________________, and Clyde a(n) ________________ to robbery, which is a(n) ________________ rather than a(n) ________________. It is also a crime that is mala ________________ because it is wrong in and of itself. After the commission of the crime, Bonnie and Clyde drove to the home of their sister, Dinah, who took them in, knowing that they had robbed the bank. Dinah was found not guilty of being a(n) ________________, because she is a close relative. She could not be tried—that is, ________________—

a second time for the same offense because it would put her in ________________, which is against the U.S. Constitution. When Abigail, Bonnie, and Clyde agreed to commit the robbery and took action to carry it out, they committed the crime of ________________. Once they were convicted, they were called ________________. They had no ________________—that is, evidence to defeat the criminal charges against them—and they had no ________________ that placed them in a different place than the crime scene. Had Bonnie and Clyde been born generations later, they wouldn't have needed to physically go to a bank to access its assets. Instead, they could have ________________ into the bank's computer mainframe and transferred the bank's electronically listed deposits into their own accounts. Or, they could have sent thousands of ________________ to unsuspecting Internet users, attempting to commit ________________, which would allow Bonnie and Clyde to use other people's identities.

11

Crimes Against Property

ANTE INTERROGATORY

*The wrongful taking and carrying away of personal property
of another with the intent to steal is (A) trespassing, (B) larceny,
(C) asportation, (D) extortion.*

LEARNING OBJECTIVES

LO 1: Identify the elements of larceny, including distinguishing grand larceny from petty larceny

LO 2: Explain how embezzlement is different from traditional larceny

LO 3: Contrast larceny by false pretenses from traditional larceny

LO 4: Distinguish bribery from extortion

LO 5: Summarize the federal RICO law and explain what money laundering (a type of RICO conduct) is

LO 6: Explain the crime of receiving stolen property and how circumstantial evidence can be used to prove the crime

LO 7: Identify what forgery is and what crime just beyond forgery can be committed

KEY TERMS

animus furandi

asportation

attempted larceny

bailee

bribery

chattels

chose in action

circumstantial evidence

coercion

computer fraud

constructive possession

criminal fraud

custody

efficacy

embezzlement

extortion

forgery

fraud in esse contractus

grand larceny

larceny

larceny by false pretenses

mail fraud

money laundering

negotiable instrument

personal property

petit larceny

petty larceny

possession

prosecution

racketeering

real property

receiving stolen goods

RICO

uttering

white-collar crime

wire fraud

WEBSITES FOR PRONUNCIATION HELP

http://dictionary.cambridge.org/us/pronunciation/english/audio

https://www.howtopronounce.com

To be criminal acts, those acts must have exact definitions in addition to having to be committed voluntarily with wrongful intent. This is so that there can be no question about what is against the law. At common law, exact definitions came about by assigning specific elements to each crime. No person could be convicted of a crime unless each element of the crime was proved beyond a reasonable doubt. Most states still define crimes in this manner, but do so in legislatively created criminal codes, rather than in appellate case law. This chapter discusses the elements of some of the most commonly committed crimes against property.

LARCENY

The common law definition of **larceny** is "the wrongful taking and carrying away of personal property of another with the intent to steal." "Larceny" comes from the Anglo-French word "larcine," which is translated as "theft," and often larceny is called theft. Broken down into its elements, this crime consists of the following:

1. a wrongful taking
2. and carrying away
3. of the personal property
4. of another
5. with intent to steal

Wrongful Taking

A wrongful taking means a trespass to someone else's possession of personal property. More precisely, it is the exercise of dominion and control over the personal property in the possession of another, without the right to do so.

Carrying Away

In addition to the wrongful taking, a carrying away must occur, which is called an **asportation** in legal terminology. This act involves a removal of the property from the place it formerly occupied.

To illustrate, in a case in which a thief attempted to steal a fur coat from a store mannequin, but was unable to do so because the coat was attached to the mannequin by a chain, the court ruled there was no larceny, because the coat was not carried away. Instead, this would have been the crime of **attempted larceny** (a substantial step to commit larceny, falling short of its completion), but this offense was not placed in the original charge. Consequently, the defendant was protected by the right to freedom from double jeopardy. However, in another old case, a thief opened a cash register and picked up some bills, but dropped them back into the register drawer when he was discovered by the owner. In holding that a carrying away occurred, the Supreme Court of Ohio said, "If he had actually taken the money into his hand, and lifted it from the place where the owner had placed it, so as to entirely sever it from the spot where it was so placed, with the intention of stealing it, he would be guilty of larceny, though he may have dropped it into the place it was lying, upon being discovered, and had never had it out of the drawer." *Eckels v. State* (OH, 1870). That case is still cited as the law in Ohio on theft, as recent as 2013, in *Ohio v. Csillag.*

Personal Property

The subject matter of larceny must be **personal property** (also called goods or **chattels**), which was historically defined as "everything that is the subject of ownership not coming under the category of real estate." A **negotiable instrument** (a written, unconditional order or promise to pay money, which can be transferred by the original receiver to others), such as a check, draft, or promissory note, was not the subject of larceny at common law, as it was not personal property. Such an instrument is called a **chose in action**, which is evidence of a right to property, but not the property itself. For example, a check is evidence of the right to the amount of money for which the check is written, but it is not the money itself. Most states have enacted statutes making it a crime to commit larceny of choses in action.

To be the subject of larceny, the item stolen must be have been owned at the time of the crime. Older cases held that it was not larceny to steal a dead body, as a dead body could have no owner; however, it was larceny to steal the casket containing the body as well as the clothing on the body, as these things were owned by the personal representatives of the decedent's estate. Wild animals having no owner could not be the subject of larceny for the same reason, even if they were taken from another's land.

Real property (land or anything permanently affixed thereto) is not the subject of larceny unless made so by statute. Thus, such things as growing trees, fences, doors or other fixtures, seaweed, and minerals or stone not yet mined or quarried were not the subject of common law larceny. The cutting down and carrying away of a standing tree would not be larceny; however, the carrying away of wood already cut would be larceny. Statutes have been passed by many states making it larceny to steal many things not included in common law larceny.

Property of Another

The general rule is that a person cannot commit larceny of his or her own property, with the exception of stealing his or her own property from a **bailee** (one to whom it has been rightfully entrusted, but not given as a gift or sold). For instance, if one's car is at the mechanic and the owner takes the car from the mechanics' lot as a way of avoiding paying the bill (where upon the owner would normally get back the car keys), that could constitute theft…of one's own property. The property must be taken from the possession of another. The law, however, distinguishes between possession and custody. **Custody** is the care and keeping of anything; **possession** is the detention and control of anything. A person is said to have constructive possession of property when it is held in custody for that person by another. **Constructive possession** is not actual possession, but an assumed possession. For example, a supermarket cashier has custody of the money in the cash register. The store itself (or the store owner) has actual possession of it. Anyone stealing it from the cashier commits larceny from the possession of the owner, which is true even if the cashier is the thief.

Intent to Steal

An essential element of larceny is called **animus furandi**. This Latin term means the intent to permanently deprive the owner of the property. Thus, at common law, the borrowing of a neighbor's horse without consent, but with the intent to return it later in the day, was not considered to be larceny. (It was, if anything, a trespass to personal property.) Some more recent cases, although still requiring intent to steal, define larceny as appropriating the goods to a use inconsistent with the owner's rights, thus avoiding the problem mentioned earlier. For example, Indiana's basic theft statute focuses on the defendant's criminal intent to exert "unauthorized control over the property of another person, with intent to deprive the other person of any part of its value or use."

The intent to steal must exist at the time of the taking. A person who takes another's goods with permission or with the intent to return them, and later changes his or her mind and decides to steal them, is guilty of embezzlement rather than common law larceny. Embezzlement is discussed later.

Degrees of Larceny

By statute, larceny is divided into two degrees, **petit larceny** (usually spelled **petty larceny**) and **grand larceny**. The former is usually a misdemeanor; the latter is a felony. The common characteristic between petty and grand larceny is the value of the property that was stolen, although the states differ in their distinctions between when petty larceny becomes grand larceny. For example, in New York, when the property or services stolen is over $1,000 it becomes grand larceny. In California, the dollar limit for petty larceny is $950 but exceptions are made in the statute, such that theft of over $250 worth avocados (or other farm crops) is grand larceny.

Word Wise

"Animus" [Latin for mind; intention]

Examples	Meaning
animus cancellandi	intent to cancel or destroy (as applied to wills)
animus capiendi	intent to capture or take
animus defamandi	intent to defame
animus derelinquendi	intent to abandon or relinquish
animus lucrandi	intent to make a gain or profit (become lucrative)
animus recuperandi	intent to recover or recuperate
animus signandi	intent to sign an instrument (such as a will)
animus testandi	intent to make a will (testament)

EMBEZZLEMENT

Embezzlement, which is essentially a breach of trust, consists of the same elements as larceny except that instead of "wrongful taking," a "rightful taking" occurs. The crime did not exist at common law, but was created by statute to fill the gap in the law of larceny when someone, such as an employee or bailee, was entrusted with property of another and appropriated it to his or her own use, or when property was stolen before it came into the possession of the owner. While larceny and embezzlement share the same ending (wrongfully depriving someone of his or her property), they have different beginnings.

To illustrate, if a bank employee were to write cashier's checks to a fictitious employee and cash them himself, that would likely be embezzlement, but if that same employee were to pull cash from someone's safe deposit box, that would likely be larceny or theft. The difference in the two is that in the former, the bank employee would have a limited authority to issue cashier's checks, but not with respect to what is in safe deposit boxes.

LARCENY BY FALSE PRETENSES

Larceny by false pretenses also called **criminal fraud** is another crime created by statute to fill a gap in common law larceny. In general, it is the act of knowingly and deliberately obtaining the property of another by false pretenses with intent to defraud. The elements of this crime are quite similar to the elements of the tort of deceit, which is discussed in a later chapter.

Some states have consolidated larceny, embezzlement, and larceny by false pretenses into one statute so that the need no longer exists for the **prosecution** (the state bringing the action) to distinguish among them. The defendant is merely charged with violating that particular chapter and section of the statute, which includes all three common law crimes.

> ### TERMS IN ACTION
>
> Garth Flaherty lived near Washington State University, and living near a large university is a good place to live if, like Flaherty, you're interested in stealing women's undergarments. Throughout the apartment complexes in Pullman, Washington, many women reported their underwear and bras having been stolen from their laundry rooms. In 2007, the 24-year-old Flaherty was spotted leaving a laundry room with women's underwear, and the police tracked him down at his apartment. Inside, they found 1,613 pairs of women's underwear, bras, and other garments, which the police said weighed over 93 pounds and filled five garbage bags. Charged with 12 counts of second-degree **burglary** and one count of first-degree **larceny**, Flaherty pleaded guilty in 2008 and was sentenced to 45 days in jail.
>
> Source: msnbc.msn.com; seattletimes.com

BRIBERY, EXTORTION, AND COERCION

It is illegal to give money or other items to public officials to sway their official activity. The giving or receiving of a reward to influence any official act is called **bribery** and is against the law. The inverse of bribery is **extortion**, which is the gaining of property or money through some kind of unlawful threat to the owner of the property or money. And so, it is also illegal for public officials to demand payment from others for doing official acts. This type of extortion was historically defined as "the corrupt demanding or receiving by a person in office of a fee for services that should be performed gratuitously." Public figure extortion, which was historically the exclusive form of extortion, is now a type of extortion. For example, Washington state's general extortion statute states that extortion "means knowingly to obtain or attempt to obtain by threat property or services of the owner, and specifically includes sexual favors." **Coercion**, also a crime, means "compelling someone to do something by threat or force."

RICO

A federal statute referred to as **RICO** (an acronym for the Racketeer Influenced and Corrupt Organizations Act of 1970) is designed to stop organized criminal activity from invading legitimate businesses. Under RICO, it is illegal to conduct a legitimate business with funds obtained from a pattern of racketeering activity. **Racketeering** (activities of organized criminals who extort money from legitimate businesses) includes many kinds of criminal activity such as arson, robbery, bribery, extortion, and **money laundering**. Essentially, under federal laws, one is guilty of racketeering if that person engages in a "period of racketeering activity," which is at least two racketeering acts within a ten-year period. There are over 30 crimes listed as racketeering activities including some of the acts listed above. States also have their own RICO statutes.

"Money laundering" is a type of racketeering activity and is a metaphor to describe how money acquired through criminal activities is "washed" so that it can look like it was earned legitimately. That is usually done by putting the "dirty" money through a seemingly legitimate business, which treats it like regular income so the cash appears clean. Also included in the definition of racketeering are the crimes of **mail fraud**, **wire fraud** (a federal and state crime involving using wire communications facilities in carrying out a scheme to defraud) and **computer fraud** (the offense of using mail, wire, or computers to obtain money, property, or services, by false pretenses). Those types of crimes are part of the category of crimes commonly called **white-collar crimes**. "White-collar crime" is a term first coined by sociologist Edwin Sutherland in 1939 to refer to crimes committed by those with high status and respect, but whose crimes are committed in the course of their employment.

> ## TERMS IN ACTION
>
> The **Racketeer Influenced Corrupt Organizations Act (RICO)** laws were originally designed to combat organized crime, particularly by the mafia, even though the extent of RICO law goes beyond the traditional subjects thought of as organized crime. For instance, in 2016, a Delaware corporate lawyer was hit with a RICO indictment for his alleged role in assisting his client, a payday-lending businessman, in committing lending abuses. One of the more famous RICO cases brought against the mafia was also one of longest criminal trials in American history, known as the "Pizza Connection Trial." Following an FBI investigation into the link between Sicilian and New York mobsters and the use of pizza restaurants as outlets for **money laundering** from heroin smuggling and distribution, the U.S. Department of Justice prosecuted 24 alleged crime family members. The Pizza Connection trial began in Manhattan in October 1985 and ended in March 1987. Eighteen defendants were convicted. One of the key federal prosecutors was future New York City Mayor (and 2008 presidential candidate) Rudy Giuliani, and one of the key witnesses was Joseph Pistone, the first FBI agent to go undercover in the New York mafia, and who was played by Johnny Depp in the 1997 movie, titled after Pistone's undercover identity, *Donnie Brasco*.
>
> Source: philly.com; abajournal.com; history.com; americanmafia.com; nytimes.com

RECEIPT OF STOLEN GOODS

The crime of **receiving stolen goods** involves buying, receiving, or aiding in the concealment of stolen or embezzled property, knowing it to have been stolen. Receipt of stolen goods requires that the receiver have knowledge the goods of which he or she is taking possession were stolen, and the receiver must receive them with criminal intent.

One of the major issues in determining the guilt or innocence of people accused of this crime is whether or not they actually knew that the goods were stolen. If they either knew or believed that the property was stolen at the time it came into their possession or if at any time while it was in their possession they ascertained that it was stolen property and undertook to deprive the owner of the rightful use of it, they may be convicted of the crime. If they did not know that the goods were stolen, they cannot be found guilty. **Circumstantial evidence** is relevant here. As opposed to eyewitness testimony or other forms of direct evidence, circumstantial evidence is of an indirect nature and requires someone to draw an inference about a fact. For example, the evidence that the defendant paid an unreasonably low purchase price for stolen goods is often used—as circumstantial evidence—to prove he or she had knowledge that the goods were stolen.

> ### Web Wise
> *Need to find out what an acronym like RICO stands for?*
>
> | Web Address | Definition |
> | --- | --- |
> | **http://www.ucc.ie/ cgi-bin/acronym** | The **Acronym Servers** allows you to find out what an acronym means; you may also search for a word to see what acronyms it is used in. |
> | **www.wikipedia.org** | Type in "RICO" to learn more about it. Make sure to look for the endnotes, which have the citations to the primary authority from which the Wikipedia entry comes. |

FORGERY

Forgery is defined as "the fraudulent making or altering of a writing whereby the rights of another might be prejudiced." The subject matter of forgery must be a writing or a document that has some legal **efficacy** (effectiveness), such as a deed, mortgage, will, promissory note, check, receipt, or other writing. The forgery of a person's signature to a will that is invalid because of an improper number of witnesses would not be a forgery, because the will had no legal efficacy because of insufficient witnesses.

People can commit forgery by signing their own name if they fraudulently hold themselves out to be someone else of that same name, sign another's name with intent to defraud, or write something in a document above another's existing signature. It has also been held to be forgery to obtain someone's genuine signature by **fraud in esse contractus**—commonly called fraud in the essence, that is, fraud as to the essential nature of the contract—as when a person signs a promissory note, which evidences that the signer is agreeing to pay back a sum of borrowed money, thinking he or she is signing a receipt or other instrument.

Fraudulent intent is necessary to commit forgery. Thus, if someone is authorized to sign another's name, or reasonably believes that he or she has that authority, it would not be the crime of forgery to sign the other's name.

Uttering a forged instrument, which would include a check or promissory note, is not only a crime, it is often a separate crime from forgery, which is the making of the false or deceptive instrument. **Uttering** means offering a forged instrument to another person, knowing it to be forged and with intent to defraud.

Reviewing What You Learned

After studying the chapter, write the answers to each of the following questions:

1. List the five elements of common law larceny.

____

____

____

2. Describe a wrongful taking.

____

____

____

3. What is a carrying away?

____

____

____

4. Of what must the subject matter of larceny consist?

____

____

____

5. Describe and give an example of a chose in action.

____

____

____

6. As mentioned in the chapter, why did the court hold that it was not larceny to steal a dead body?

____

____

____

7. When is real property the subject of larceny?

____

____

____

8. Under what circumstances is it considered larceny to steal one's own property?

____

____

____

9. Describe the difference between possession and custody.

____

____

____

10. Define "intent to steal."

____

____

____

11. At common law, is borrowing with intent to return considered to be larceny? Why or why not?

____

____

____

12. Under what circumstances must the intent to steal exist for the action to constitute larceny?

____

____

____

13. Name the two degrees of larceny.

____

____

____

14. What is the amount that divides the two degrees of larceny, by statute in some states?

____

____

____

15. In comparing the crimes of larceny and embezzlement, what is the one element that differs?

____

____

____

16. What have some states done, by statute, to larceny, embezzlement, and larceny by false pretenses so that no need exists to distinguish among them?

____

____

____

17. In what way does bribery differ from extortion?

____

____

____

Understanding Legal Concepts

Indicate whether each statement is true or false. Then, change the italicized word or phrase of each false statement to make it true.

ANSWERS

______ **1.** In addition to a wrongful taking, a carrying away must occur to constitute *larceny*.

______ **2.** The subject matter of larceny must be *personal property*.

______ **3.** Older cases held that it *was* larceny to steal a dead body.

______ **4.** The cutting down and carrying away of a standing tree *was* larceny, at common law.

______ **5.** One cannot commit larceny of *one's own* property except from a bailee.

______ **6.** To constitute larceny, the property must be taken from another's *custody*.

______ **7.** An essential element of *larceny* is an intent to steal.

______ **8.** Petty larceny is usually a *misdemeanor* and grand larceny is a *felony*.

______ **9.** Embezzlement includes a *wrongful* taking.

______ **10.** The crime of bribery is *the same as* the crime of extortion.

Checking Terminology

From the list of legal terms that follows, select the one that matches each definition:

ANSWERS

a. animus furandi
b. asportation
c. attempted larceny
d. bailee
e. bribery
f. chattels
g. chose in action
h. circumstantial evidence
i. coercion
j. computer fraud
k. constructive possession
l. criminal fraud
m. custody
n. efficacy
o. embezzlement
p. extortion
q. forgery
r. fraud in esse contractus
s. grand larceny
t. larceny
u. larceny by false pretenses
v. mail fraud
w. money laundering
x. negotiable instrument
y. personal property
z. petit larceny
aa. possession
bb. prosecution
cc. racketeering
dd. real property
ee. receiving stolen goods
ff. RICO
gg. uttering
hh. white-collar crime
ii. wire Fraud

_____ 1. Using email or websites to obtain money, property, or services by false pretenses.

_____ 2. Using mail to obtain money, property, or services by false pretenses.

_____ 3. The care and keeping of anything.

_____ 4. A federal statute designed to stop organized criminal activity from invading legitimate businesses.

_____ 5. One to whom personal property is given under a bailment contract.

_____ 6. Activities of organized criminals who extort money from legitimate businesses.

_____ 7. Everything that is the subject of ownership not coming under the category of real estate. (Select two answers.)

_____ 8. The corrupt demanding or receiving by a person in office of a fee for services that should be performed gratuitously.

_____ 9. Possession not actual, but assumed to exist.

_____ 10. The party by whom criminal proceedings are started or conducted; the state.

_____ 11. A written, unconditional promise to pay money which can be transferred by the original receiver to others.

_____ 12. Effectiveness.

_____ 13. Compelling someone to do something by threat or force.

_____ 14. Using wires, such as telephone wires, to transmit false pretenses in order to improperly obtain money, property, or services.

_____ 15. At common law, the wrongful taking and carrying away of personal property of another with the intent to steal.

_____ 16. The giving or receiving of a reward to influence any official act.

_____ 17. The detention and control of anything.

_____ 18. Crimes of racketeering, mail fraud, wire fraud, and computer fraud.

_____ 19. Knowingly and deliberately obtaining the property of another by false pretenses, with intent to defraud. (Select two answers.)

_____ 20. Making money look like it was earned legitimately.

_____ 21. The fraudulent misappropriation of property by a person to whom it has been entrusted.

_____ 22. The ground and anything permanently attached to it, including land, buildings, and growing trees, and the airspace above the ground.

_____ 23. Evidence of a right to property, but not the property itself.

_____ 24. Larceny that is a misdemeanor rather than a felony.

_____ 25. An attempt to commit larceny, but falling short of its commission.

_____ 26. Evidence of an indirect nature.

_____ 27. Offering a forged negotiable instrument to another person, knowing it to be forged and intending to defraud.

_____ 28. The fraudulent making or altering of a writing whereby the rights of another might be prejudiced.

_____ 29. The carrying away of goods.

_____ 30. Larceny that is a felony.

_____ 31. An intent to steal.

Using Legal Language

Read the following story and fill in the blank lines with legal terms taken from the list of terms at the beginning of this chapter:

A blind woman named Rachel bought some items of stolen furniture from a corrupt salesperson. Because she did not know that the goods were stolen, Rachel could not be convicted of ________________________ The salesperson committed ________________________ when he told Rachel that she was signing a receipt, because she was actually signing a check made out to the crook. Even though Rachel signed her own name, the crime of ________________________ was committed, although not by her. The salesperson committed the crime of ________________________ when he tried to cash the check at a local bank. At the time the devious salesperson was at the bank, an automobile was stolen from the bank's parking lot, Depending on the value of the car, one of two crimes was committed: ________________________ or ________________________. The defense lawyer argued her client wasn't guilty, because there was a missing element to the crime, in that there was no ________________________ because her client only wanted to borrow the car. Furthermore, the defense lawyer argued that because the car broke down in the lot while the defendant tried to drive it away, the element of ________________________ was also missing. Unfortunately, the crime of ________________________ occurred, however, because later on the thief paid the prosecuting attorney $1,000 to drop the case. It would have been ________________________ if the thief had coerced the prosecuting attorney by threat or force to drop the case.

12

Crimes Against the Person and Human Habitation

ANTE INTERROGATORY

Statutory Rape requires (A) force, (B) the victim to be under a certain age, (C) lack of consent, (D) specific intent

LEARNING OBJECTIVES

LO 1: Identify and summarize the common law elements of robbery

LO 2: Contrast mayhem from robbery

LO 3: Distinguish assault from battery and characterize various degrees or types of each crime

LO 4: Explain the common law elements of rape, and contrast common law rape with some of the modern aspects of the crime

LO 5: Define stalking and the various cyber versions of it

LO 6: Identify the two common crimes against habitation

LO 7: Contrast the modern view of burglary with the common law requirements for burglary

LO 8: Explain how the statutory version of arson is more liberal than common law arson

KEY TERMS

aggravated assault

arson

assault

attempted arson

battery

breaking

burglary

carnal knowledge

convicted

curtilage

cyberbullying

cyberharrassment

cyberstalking

dangerous weapon

deadly weapon

domestic violence

dwelling house

lesser included offense

maim

mayhem

nighttime

rape

rape shield laws

restraining order

robbery

sexual assault

stalking

statutory arson

statutory burglary

statutory rape

summarily

threat of force

WEBSITES FOR PRONUNCIATION HELP

http://dictionary.cambridge.org/us/pronunciation/english/audio

https://www.howtopronounce.com

Crimes against the person were considered to be more serious than crimes against property at common law and were subject to a harsher punishment. In modern criminal codes, crimes against persons are classified more seriously than those against property. This is because crimes against the person involve face-to-face confrontation, increasing the chance for violence against the victim.

ROBBERY

Robbery is defined as the wrongful taking and carrying away of the personal property of another from the other's person or personal custody, and against the other's will by force and violence, or by threat of force. The essence of the crime is the exertion of force (or threat) against another to steal personal property from that person. The common elements of robbery consist of the following:

1. wrongful taking and
2. carrying away
3. of the personal property of another
4. from the person or their personal custody
5. against the other's will by the use of force or threat of force

> ### Web Wise
>
> - Go to **www.justia.com** for links to the text of the U.S. Constitution, state constitutions, criminal codes, as well as general research on many legal topics, including criminal law.
> - Look up robbery (and other crime) statistics throughout the world at **www.nationmaster .com**, and use the website's search bar. America is not the leading country in crimes of robbery, by the way.

Because all of the elements of larceny are included in the crime of robbery, larceny is a lesser included offense of robbery. A **lesser included offense** is a crime that contains some, but not all, elements of a greater offense, making it impossible to commit the greater offense without also committing the lesser offense. One can be convicted of either the greater or the lesser offense, but not both. The first three elements of robbery are discussed in the prior chapter under the heading "Larceny." Understand, though, that while larceny and robbery share some elements, robbery is more serious than larceny because it involves a personal confrontation with the victim. The last two elements of robbery are discussed here.

Taking from the Person or Personal Custody

One of the principal differences between larceny and robbery is that in robbery a taking "from the person" occurs, whereas in larceny it does not. To constitute robbery, the taking must be from the person or in the presence of the one in possession of the goods at the time of the robbery.

A Massachusetts case from 1902, which has been cited even in the 21st century by other state courts, spoke to the issue of robbery involving the act of taking something from a person's possession: "A thing is in the presence of a person, in respect to robbery, which is so within his reach, inspection, observation, or control, that he could, if not overcome by violence or prevented by fear, retain his possession of it" (*Commonwealth v. Homer*). And as recently as 2014, the 2nd Circuit Court of Appeals approved of that same standard in a carjacking case, where the defendants argued to no avail that robbing a woman of her car keys while she was inside her home wasn't a carjacking (*U.S. v. Soler*). Furthermore, when the owner is kept in one room of the house and is forced to tell where his or her property may be found in another room, and the assailant goes there and takes the property, it has been held that such a taking is a robbery.

Taking Against the Other's Will

The taking must be against the will of the person in possession of the goods. If the person from whom the goods are stolen is unaware of the crime's occurrence, as when a pocket is picked, the crime is larceny rather than robbery. In a case from New Mexico, a drunken man knocked over a woman whose purse was separated from her possession when she fell to the ground, whereupon he then picked up her purse and ran away. The man was convicted of robbery, but got a new trial on appeal, arguing that he didn't form the intent to take her purse until after he accidentally knocked her down. The appellate court reversed the conviction, finding that if the man could convince a new jury that he didn't intend to knock her over so that he could take her purse, then his crime would be larceny instead (*State v. Curley* 939 P.2d 1103 (1997).

Force and Violence

Some force or violence must be used against the possessor of the goods to constitute robbery. The degree of force is immaterial so long as it is sufficient to obtain the victim's property against his or her will. A court, for example, held that the dispensing of a drug to a person so as to make him unconscious in order to steal his property was enough force to constitute robbery.

An intimidation, or a putting in fear, commonly called a **threat of force**, is equivalent to force and will replace the force requirement. Thus, even though no actual force is used, if victims are put in fear, as when threatened by one with superior strength or by one who displays a weapon to the victim, the element of force and violence will be satisfied.

Penalty for Robbery

In general, the penalty for robbery is greater than that for larceny. For example, in Massachusetts, the punishment for robbery (whether armed or unarmed) is "imprisonment in the state prison for life or for any term of years." In contrast, one form of larceny, shoplifting, is punished by "a fine of not more than one thousand dollars or by imprisonment in the house of correction for not more than two and one-half years, or by both such fine and imprisonment."

MAYHEM

At common law, **mayhem** was violently depriving others of the use of such members as may render them less able in fighting, either to defend themselves or to annoy their adversary. Examples of mayhem were cutting off a person's hand, foot, or finger and putting out an eye. Therefore, it was not mayhem to cut off another's nose or ear or to disfigure a person in a way that did not interfere with the ability to fight. Interestingly, it was mayhem to knock out a person's front tooth, but it was not mayhem to knock out a back tooth, because such a tooth was not needed to bite someone while fighting. Mayhem was a misdemeanor at common law, except for castration, which was a felony.

In modern times, mayhem has become a felony in most states and includes many types of disfiguration beyond that which would render the victim generally unable to physically defend himself or herself. It is commonly called **maim**, which means to cripple or mutilate in any way. To illustrate, California's mayhem statutes read in part (Cal. Penal Code §§ 203-204), in part, as follows:

> Every person who unlawfully and maliciously deprives a human being of a member of his body, or disables, disfigures, or renders it useless, or cuts or disables the tongue, or puts out an eye, or slits the nose, ear, or lip, is guilty of mayhem. Mayhem is punishable by imprisonment in the state prison for two, four, or eight years.

ASSAULT AND BATTERY DISTINGUISHED

An **assault** is an attempt to commit a battery, or putting someone in fear of being battered; a **battery** is the actual contact or touching of another without permission or privilege. Thus, raising one's arm with a knife in hand is the assault; the knife stabbing the victim is the battery. An assault can and often does occur without a battery. Likewise, a battery can occur without an assault, such as if the victim is stabbed from behind and without warning. In the tort law, battery is an unlawful touching, and assault is putting someone in fear of an unlawful touching. For example, kissing a stranger on the lips who is sleeping while riding a train is battery, while lunging at a waitress standing behind the counter of a diner is an assault—regardless of whether or not the waitress is actually touched. Not all states treat assault and battery as separate crimes. For example, the Texas criminal code has merged the separate crime of battery into the state's definition of assault and included threatening to assault someone as part of that crime.

Battery

A battery is the physical contact with another person, without that person's permission, in an angry, revengeful, rude, insolent, or reckless manner. It may also be thought of as the unlawful application of force on another person. The intentional pushing or hitting of someone or grabbing someone's purse or wallet would be a battery. An accidental bumping of another in a crowded room, however, would not be a battery because the crime requires a general criminal intent or reckless behavior on the part of the perpetrator. Battery is classified in various ways in many jurisdictions, including aggravated battery, domestic battery, sexual battery, and even battery by bodily waste.

Assault

An assault is an attempt, real or apparent, to commit a battery. Some overt act, such as the movement of an arm or pointing of a gun toward the victim, is required to accomplish the crime. Mere threats or words alone are not enough to commit the offense. A criminal assault may occur even though a battery is impossible, as when an unloaded gun is aimed at another, or even if the victim is unaware of the offense and is not put in fear.

Simple assault and battery is generally a misdemeanor. **Aggravated assault**, which is an assault committed with the intention of committing some additional crime, is a felony by statute in most states. Examples of aggravated assault are assault with intent to murder, assault with a **dangerous** or **deadly weapon** (an item that is, from the way it is used, capable of causing death or serious bodily injury), assault with intent to commit unarmed robbery, and assault with intent to commit a felony.

To illustrate, in October 2000, Boston Bruins hockey player Marty McSorley was found guilty by a Canadian court of *assault with a weapon* when he hit Vancouver Canucks player Donald Brashear in the head with a hockey stick, with three seconds left in the game. Brashear was knocked unconscious and suffered a concussion and memory lapse. McSorley was sentenced to 18-months probation.

RAPE

At common law, **rape** was defined as the unlawful, forcible carnal knowledge by a man of a woman, against her will, or without her consent. The essential elements of the crime follow:

1. carnal knowledge and
2. the use of force by the man and
3. nonconsent by the woman

Carnal knowledge meant the slightest penetration of the sexual organ of the woman by the sexual organ of the man. The force by the man had to be such that it would overcome physical resistance by the woman, and historically under the common law the woman had to resist "to the uttermost" to prove that force occurred and that she did not consent to the act. The punishment for rape was death, as was the case for many common law felonies centuries ago.

It was impossible, under the common law, for a woman to commit the crime of rape, because the definition required carnal knowledge "by a man of a woman." A woman could be **convicted** (found guilty) of rape, however, as a principal in the second degree or as an accessory to the crime if she aided another in its commission. Similarly, a husband could not be convicted of raping his wife; however, he could be found guilty as a principal in the second degree by assisting another to do the act. Spousal rape is now considered rape in all states and the District of Columbia.

Sexual assault is a crime (or collection of crimes) much broader than rape, and is sometimes defined as any unwanted sexual contact. Some states have replaced the crime of "rape" with various types of "sexual assault." Many states today have changed the definition of rape to include unwanted sexual acts on men as well as women and to include the threat of bodily harm as well as actual force on the victim. In 2012, the U.S. Justice Department modernized its definition of rape (for the purposes of national crime collection data) and it now states, "The penetration, no matter how slight, of the vagina or anus with any body part or object, or oral penetration by a sex organ of another person, without the consent of the victim." Notice this definition focuses on the lack of the victim's consent, rather than the defendant's use of force or threat of force against the victim. Likewise, many states have shifted the standard in their own statutes on rape or sexual assault from force to lack of consent.

Word Wise
Prefix "Carn-" (Latin for "flesh")

Term	Meaning
carnal	Fleshly; of or pertaining to the flesh or body (adjective)
carnage	Destruction of life; slaughter of many people as in battle (noun)
carnaged	Covered with carnage or slaughtered bodies (adjective)
carnalism	The practice of what is carnal; sensualism (noun)
carnalist	A person who pursues sensual, especially sexual, pleasure (noun)
carnality	State of being flesh; fleshiness (noun)
carnalize	To make carnal or rob of spirituality; to sensualize (verb)
carnally	Corporeally; bodily (adverb)
carnalness	Carnal quality or state; sensuality (noun)
carnivorous	Flesh-eating (adjective)

Rape shield laws have been passed to help prevent rape victims from being re-victimized, by prohibiting a defendant from using the victim's sexual history as evidence against her own credibility, with limited exceptions. An example of an exception is the victim's prior consensual sexual history with the defendant. In addition, some states require people charged with rape to be tested for HIV, or allow the victim to demand the defendant be tested for HIV.

Statutory Rape

Statutory rape is sexual intercourse with a child under the age set by the particular state statute, regardless of whether the child consented or not. At one time under the common law, a child under the age of 10 was considered incapable of consenting, and sexual intercourse with a child under that age was deemed rape even if an argument could be made that the child could be considered to have consented. Present-day statutory rape statutes vary from state to state and have increased the age to 16 and even 18 years. Thus, sexual intercourse with a person under that particular age is rape even if the victim consented to or encouraged the act. Because of the sexual risks inherent in teen dating, some states have created what are known as "Romeo and Juliet" defenses. This Shakespeare-inspired defense permits statutory rape charges to be dropped where the victim is above an age threshold (15, for instance) and the defendant is not more than four years older than the victim and was in a dating relationship with the victim at the time of the sexual encounter. For example, Indiana's Romeo and Juliet defense is found in Ind. Code § 35-42-4-9(e).

TERMS IN ACTION

Rape is a crime that traditionally involved the use of force or threat of force against the victim. But some states, including Tennessee, Alabama, and California, have added **sex by deception** (or by fraud) as conduct that also constitutes **sexual assault**. In a strange case from Tennessee, a man dubbed "The Fantasy Man" by the press was convicted of rape by fraud. Robert Mitchell, III, of Nashville, called hundreds of women late at night, talking in a hushed voice, pretending to be their boyfriends or fiancés. Although most women hung up on him, eight of them believed that he was their boyfriend, and they followed his requests to unlock their doors and put on blindfolds, or meet him in black-as-night hotel rooms. Reportedly one victim had blindfolded sex with him twice a week for two months, mistakenly thinking he was her significant other. Mitchell was eventually caught when the blindfold of one of his victims slipped off her eyes during one of their encounters. He was **convicted** of rape by fraud and of attempted rape by fraud, and sentenced to 15 years in prison. At least one other country ciminalizes what would otherwise be consensual sex if it were not deceptively induced. In 2010, a married Palestinian man was convicted in Israel of sex by deception for having told an Israeli woman in Jerusalem with whom he had sex that he was single and Jewish.

Source: nbcnews.com; Nashvillescene.com; *State v. Mitchell*, 1999 WL 559930; cnn.com

---

DOMESTIC VIOLENCE AND STALKING

In recent years, states have enacted laws attempting to decrease the amount of **domestic violence** (the abuse of a closely related person such as a present or former spouse or cohabitant). Among other things, states have made it easier for victims to obtain restraining orders against their attackers. A **restraining order** is an order forbidding a person from doing a particular act. A temporary restraining order is often given **summarily** (quickly), followed by a hearing, which may or may not result in a permanent restraining order. In California, police officers must give domestic violence victims a "Victims of Domestic Violence" card, notifying them of their rights and of the availability of counseling centers and 24-hour counseling service telephone numbers. Many states in recent years have made it a crime, called **stalking** to follow someone around, threatening him or her with violence. **Stalking** is the willful, malicious, and repeated following, harassing, and threatening of another person, intending to place the person in fear of death or serious bodily injury.

Because the Internet has made stalking or harassing someone even easier, jurisdictions have passed laws against **cyberstalking** and **cyberbullying**. Some states interchangeably use the terms **cyberharassment** and cyberbullying. Cyberharassment is using the Internet to repeatedly interfere with someone's life; cyberbullying is using the Internet to malign or threaten someone; and cyberstalking is using the Internet to put another person in fear for their—or their loved ones'—safety or life.

CRIMES AGAINST HABITATION

The crimes of burglary and arson were considered to be crimes against habitation under the common law. For this reason, their definitions include, among other elements, "a dwelling house."

Burglary

Burglary under common law, is defined as the breaking and entering of a house (dwelling house) of another, in the nighttime, with intent to commit a felony. All of the following elements of the crime must be proved by the state to convict someone of the crime of common law burglary:

1. a breaking
2. and entering of
3. a dwelling house of another
4. in the nighttime
5. with the intent to commit a felony

BREAKING.   A **breaking** is the forced entry of a secured dwelling house, that which is the security against intrusion. It can consist of such an activity as opening a door or window (whether locked or unlocked), opening a screen, opening a shutter or blind, digging under a sill, or even climbing down a chimney. At common law, it was held not to be a breaking when a window was left partly open and a burglar raised it further to enter. Modern court interpretations of the breaking requirement, however, have held such an act to be a breaking.

ENTERING.   To constitute a burglary, an entry must occur by some part of the defendant's body or of some instrument by which the felony is sought to be accomplished. The entry may consist of an arm, leg, head, or the slightest part of the body such as a finger or foot. An interesting case arose when a person bored a hole with an auger up through the floor of a grain storage area that was part of a dwelling house, causing the grain to spill out of the hole into a sack placed below it. The court held that an entry occurred when the auger entered the storage area.

DWELLING HOUSE OF ANOTHER.   A **dwelling house** is a house in which the occupier and his or her family usually reside and includes all outbuildings within the curtilage, such as a garage or other outbuilding. **Curtilage** means the enclosed space of ground and buildings immediately surrounding a dwelling house, sometimes enclosed by a fence or wall. The requirement that the dwelling house be of another refers to occupancy rather than ownership. A landlord, for example, may be guilty of burglary for entering a house owned by him or her, but rightfully occupied by tenants, if the other elements of burglary are present.

NIGHTTIME.   In ancient times, **nighttime** was defined as that period between sunset and sunrise during which the face of a person could not be discerned by the light of day (not including moonlight). In modern times, the word "nighttime" has been defined more precisely. For example, one state statute (Mass. Gen. Laws ch. 278 § 10) defines it as follows:

If a crime is alleged to have been committed in the nighttime, nighttime shall be deemed the time between one hour after sunset on one day and one hour before sunrise on the next day; and the time of sunset and sunrise shall be ascertained according to mean time in the place where the crime was committed.

INTENT TO COMMIT A FELONY.   Under the common law definition of burglary, the breaking and entering must be done with the intent to commit a felony within the house. If the person breaking in intended merely to commit a misdemeanor, the crime would not be common law burglary. In an odd case from the early 19th century, a group of men broke into and entered a man's home at night with the intent to cut off his ear. That sounds like burglary. Yet, the burglary indictment was dismissed because cutting off someone's ear was not a felony at that time. It was simply a misdemeanor, under both the common law and that state's recently enacted statute … on cutting off a person's ear (*Commonwealth v. Newell*).

STATUTORY BURGLARY.   Many states have enacted statutes making it a criminal offense to do certain acts similar to, but not included in, the common law crime of burglary. Such crimes are sometimes referred to as **statutory burglary**. They include breaking and entering a building other than a dwelling house, and breaking and entering with the intent to commit a misdemeanor. And the nighttime requirement is often eliminated. Furthermore, many states' burglary statutes focus on the burglar's intent to commit a "crime" once inside the structure, rather than a "felony," thus broadening the scope of acts after the breaking and entering that could constitute burglary. As it concerns the breaking and entering, many statutes have liberalized those elements and, instead, consider "surreptitiously remaining" in a building sufficient for the common law breaking and entering requirements. For example, trying to hide in a store bathroom until the store closed for the day so that you could steal merchandise could qualify as surreptitiously remaining for burglary.

TERMS IN ACTION

Jean Thomas, of Boynton Beach, Florida, decided to take matters into her own hands after her house had been **burglarized** once in 2008. So, she set up a surveillance camera in her home and put it on a live-feed over the Internet, allowing her to monitor the sanctity of her home from nearly anywhere. Thanks to her technological skills, in April 2009, she was able to watch on her Fort Lauderdale office computer (live and in color, with sound) two men committing burglary at her home. The two burglars entered her house by way of the doggie door, and as she and her two dogs—who were in the house, lounging on her couch at the time—watched the **breaking and entering**, she called 911. The police arrived in time to catch the burglars. A total of four defendants were charged with **statutory burglary**. Not only was Ms. Thomas's five-minute video of the crime in action the best evidence the police could have hoped for, it also was posted on YouTube, naturally.

Source: Thesmokinggun.com

Arson

The common law definition of **arson**, which is still followed in many states, is "the willful and malicious burning of the dwelling house of another." Broken down into its elements, common law arson consists of the following elements:

1. the malicious
2. burning
3. of a dwelling house
4. of another

The mere scorching or blackening of the wood of a dwelling house was not enough to constitute arson under the common law. Some portion of the house must actually have been on fire, so that the wood or other building material is charred, to constitute the crime of arson. If someone attempts to commit the crime of arson, but falls short of its commission, the crime of **attempted arson** is committed. Because the common law crime of arson was directed toward the protection of people rather than property, the burning of a building other than a dwelling house was not considered to be arson. The dwelling house must have been occupied by someone other than the perpetrator of the crime, and the fire must have been set intentionally and not through negligence or by accident.

Statutory arson. Although many states have retained the common law definition of arson and still follow it, they have added, by statute, other forms of arson such as the burning of a building other than a dwelling house and the burning of one's own house to collect insurance. This act is referred to as **statutory arson** in contrast to common law arson. For instance, in some states' arson statutes, such as Indiana, damaging by fire is sufficient to constitute the burning requirement for arson.

Reviewing What You Learned

After studying the chapter, write the answers to each of the following questions:

1. List the elements of robbery.

   ____

   ____

   ____

2. The first three elements of robbery are the same as those for what other crime?

   ____

   ____

   ____

3. What is one of the principal differences between larceny and robbery?

   ____

   ____

   ____

4. In addition to the use of force, what else could constitute robbery, instead of larceny?

   ____

   ____

   ____

5. What is the difference between assault and battery?

   ____

   ____

   ____

6. What is the difference between simple assault and battery and aggravated assault?

   ____

   ____

   ____

7. List the three essential elements of rape at common law.

   ____

   ____

   ____

8. Explain how a husband in earlier times could be guilty of rape, even where there was a marital rape exception.

   ____

   ____

   ____

9. In what ways have many states changed the common law definition of rape?

____

____

____

____

10. How does statutory rape differ from ordinary rape?

____

____

____

____

11. List the elements of common law burglary.

____

____

____

____

12. Describe the present law with respect to a breaking when a burglar enters a partially open window.

____

____

____

13. Would it be burglary if you entered an open garage during the afternoon to avoid a hailstorm and then stole an expensive tool that you noticed while standing in the garage?

____

____

____

14. What is statutory burglary, and why does a need for the term exist?

____

____

____

15. List the elements of common law arson.

____

____

____

____

16. Describe the amount of burning that must occur to constitute common law arson.

____

____

____

17. Describe statutory arson.

____

____

____

Understanding Legal Concepts

Indicate whether each statement is true or false. Then, change the italicized word or phrase of each false statement to make it true.

ANSWERS

_______ **1.** At common law, crimes against the person were *not as serious as* crimes against property.

_______ **2.** One of the principal differences between larceny and robbery is that in *robbery* a taking "from the person" occurs, whereas in *larceny* it does not.

_______ **3.** A *battery* is an attempt to commit an *assault.*

_______ **4.** The accidental bumping of another in a crowded room *is* a battery.

_______ **5.** If the person from whom goods are stolen is unaware of the crime's occurrence, the crime is *larceny* rather than *robbery.*

_______ **6.** Many states today have changed the definition of rape to include *unnatural sexual acts* on men as well as women.

_______ **7.** Sexual intercourse with a child under the age set by state statute *is* rape even though the child consented to or encouraged the act.

_______ **8.** Opening an *unlocked* door or window is considered a breaking.

_______ **9.** A landlord *may be* guilty of burglary for entering a house owned by him or her, but rightfully occupied by a tenant, if the other elements of burglary are present.

_______ **10.** Cyberbullying *is not* considered a crime, although it is a tort.

Checking Terminology

From the list of legal terms that follows, select the one that matches each definition.

ANSWERS

a. aggravated assault
b. arson
c. assault
d. attempted arson
e. battery
f. breaking
g. burglary
h. carnal knowledge
i. convicted
j. curtilage
k. cyberbullying
l. cyberharassment
m. cyberstalking
n. dangerous weapon
o. deadly weapon
p. domestic violence
q. dwelling house
r. lesser included offense
s. maim
t. mayhem
u. nighttime
v. rape
w. rape shield laws
x. restraining order
y. robbery
z. stalking
aa. statutory arson
bb. statutory burglary
cc. statutory rape
dd. summarily
ee. threat of force
ff. unlawful sexual intercourse

_____ 1. Using the Internet to put someone in fear for their own or their loved ones' safety or lives.

_____ 2. The willful, malicious, and repeated following, harassing, and threatening of another person, intending to place the person in fear of death or serious bodily injury.

_____ 3. An item that is, from the way it is used, capable of causing death or serious bodily injury. (Select two answers.)

_____ 4. Laws passed to help prevent rape victims from being victimized.

_____ 5. At common law, violently depriving others of the use of such members as may render them less able in fighting.

_____ 6. An intimidation or putting in fear; equivalent to force.

_____ 7. Using the Internet to malign or threaten someone.

_____ 8. The unprivileged touching, not permitted, of another person; the unlawful application of force on another person.

_____ 9. An assault committed with the intention of committing some additional crime.

_____ 10. An order forbidding a person to perform a particular act.

_____ 11. The abuse of a closely related person such as a present or former spouse or cohabitant.

_____ 12. The wrongful taking and carrying away of the personal property of another from the other's person or personal custody, against his or her will, by force and violence.

_____ 13. At common law, the unlawful, forcible carnal knowledge by a man of a woman against her will or without her consent.

_____ 14. Sexual intercourse; the slightest penetration of the sexual organ of the woman by the sexual organ of the man.

_____ 15. A crime that contains some, but not all, the elements of a greater offense.

_____ 16. Sexual intercourse with a child under the age set by state statute regardless of whether the child consented or not. (Select two answers.)

_____ 17. Use of force against someone to steal personal property from that person.

_____ 18. The willful and malicious burning of the dwelling house of another.

_____ 19. Trying, unsuccessfully, to maliciously burn the dwelling house of another.

_____ 20. The burning of a building other than a dwelling house, or the burning of one's own house to collect insurance.

_____ 21. At common law, the breaking and entering of a dwelling house of another, in the nighttime, with intent to commit a felony.

_____ 22. The forced entry of a secured dwelling.

_____ 23. A house in which the occupier and family usually reside, including all outbuildings within the curtilage.

_____ 24. The enclosed space of ground and buildings immediately surrounding a dwelling house.

_____ 25. Burglary that does not contain all of the elements of common law burglary.

_____ 26. Found guilty of a crime.

_____ 27. A real or apparent attempt to commit a battery.

_____ 28. Quickly.

_____ 29. Using the Internet to repeatedly interfere with someone's life.

_____ 30. To cripple or mutilate in any way.

Using Legal Language

Read the following story and fill in the blank lines with legal terms taken from the list of terms at the beginning of this chapter:

The suspect was charged with ________________________ when he sexually attacked a young woman late at night as she entered her house. Since the young woman was an adult, it was not the crime of ________________________, which is called ________________________. The suspect was not ________________________ of the crime, because the state could not prove the element of ________________________. The state was able to prove, however, a(n) ________________________ and a(n) ________________________ because the suspect had lunged at the young woman with a knife, which struck her hand. The suspect was found guilty of ________________________ and also ________________________, which was called ________________________ at common law, because the knife had cut off the tip of the young woman's finger. The entire incident was not considered to be ________________________ because the force was not used against the woman in order to steal from that person. Also, it was not ________________________ because the suspect had not repeatedly followed and harassed the young woman. In addition, after ________________________ into the woman's garage, which was part of the ________________________ because it was within the ________________________, the suspect deliberately set fire to a pile of rubbish. The fire scorched some molding before it went out. Because the wood did not char, the suspect could be convicted of ________________________ but not ________________________ along with the crime of ________________________.

Homicide

ANTE INTERROGATORY

The killing of a human being by another human being is the definition of (A) euthanasia, (B) homicide, (C) manslaughter, (D) murder.

LEARNING OBJECTIVES

LO 1: Distinguish homicide from justifiable homicide, including listing examples of justifiable homicide

LO 2: Explain the elements needed to establish self-defense

LO 3: Define the year-and-a-day rule and its evolution as a common law exclusion to homicide

LO 4: Identify the characteristic that makes felonious killing a murder

LO 5: Explain how the law has evolved with respect to suicide as a felonious murder

LO 6: Summarize what distinguishes first-degree murder from second-degree murder

LO 7: Explain manslaughter and distinguish voluntary manslaughter from involuntary manslaughter

KEY TERMS

adequate provocation

capital crime

castle doctrine

corpus delicti

euthanasia

excusable homicide

felon

felonious homicide

felony murder

feticide

first-degree murder

fratricide

genocide

homicide

imminent danger

infanticide

involuntary manslaughter

justifiable homicide

malice aforethought

manslaughter

matricide

murder

patricide

premeditated malice aforethought

proximate cause

right-to-die laws

self-defense

sororicide

suicide

uxoricide   voluntary manslaughter
viable   year-and-a-day rule

WEBSITES FOR PRONUNCIATION HELP

http://dictionary.cambridge.org/us/pronunciation/english/audio
https://www.howtopronounce.com

Homicide is the killing of a human being by another human being. The term comes from the Latin *homo* (man) and *cidere* (to kill). Other terms with the same suffix include the following:

feticide: killing a fetus in the womb—abortion

fratricide: killing one's brother

genocide: killing a racial or political group

infanticide: killing an infant soon after birth

matricide: killing one's mother

patricide: killing one's father

sororicide: killing one's sister

suicide: killing oneself

uxoricide: killing one's wife

mariticide: killing one's husband

JUSTIFIABLE HOMICIDE

Justifiable homicide (which is also known as **excusable homicide** in some jurisdictions) is the taking of human life when a legal justification exists. A justification defense involves a defendant arguing that he or she is responsible for the act committed, but is not wrong. It includes the legal execution of murderers, the killing of other solders during battle, the killing of a dangerous felony suspect by a police officer to prevent bystanders from being harmed or killed, and the killing of another in self-defense.

Self-Defense

Self-defense is a justification for the use of force in resisting attack, including when the force used kills the assailant. Before it can be used as a justification for homicide, the one claiming self-defense must establish that he or she was in **imminent danger** (that the unlawful attack was just about to happen) so that the only possible way to escape death or bodily injury was to kill the assailant. In addition, in some states defendants must seek to retreat from deadly confrontations, where reasonable, before engaging in self-defense. When in one's own house, however, one need not retreat before using self-defense, including deadly force, when being attacked. Frequently referred to as the **castle doctrine**, the rule is based on the common law principle that one's home is one's castle.

TERMS IN ACTION

Can someone kill in **self-defense**, and yet be wrong in believing that an unlawful deadly attack is imminent? Yes. Self-defense requires a **reasonable belief**, but not necessarily a correct belief. In the middle of the night on October 2, 2009, in Winter Springs, Florida, John Tabutt awoke to the sound of someone in his house. So, he got out of his bed, grabbed his handgun and then shot at the intruder standing in his hallway, whose form he could barely make out in the darkness. His aim was correct but his belief was wrong, because Tabutt shot and killed his fiancée, Nancy Dinsmore. They were supposed to be married the next day.

A grand jury was convened, and in July 2010 it announced that it would not indict Tabutt for murder. Tabutt had claimed from the beginning he thought that his fiancé was in bed with him at the time he got out of bed, and that—at the time he fired—he believed an intruder was in his home. Although he was not in **imminent danger** when he fired his gun, Tabutt was the beneficiary of Florida's **castle doctrine**, which grants greater freedom to engage in deadly force self-defense in one's home. And the grand jury believed that Tabutt was sincere about his mistaken belief and, therefore, did not indict him.

Sources: foxnews.com; truecrimereport.com

Homicide Exclusions Under the Common Law

At common law, the killing of an unborn child in its mother's womb was not homicide because to be homicide, the child must have had a circulation independent of its mother—that is, it must have breathed and thus have supplied oxygen to its own lungs. Such an act, however, could amount to criminal abortion. Modern decisions in many states have changed this rule, making it homicide to kill an unborn child in its mother's womb when the child is **viable**—that is, having a reasonable ability to live outside the womb.

At common law, the death of the victim must have occurred within a year and a day after the blow occurred for the defendant to be convicted of a homicide. This rule, known as the **year-and-a-day rule** is still followed in some states. Many other states, including Indiana, Massachusetts, New Jersey, New York, Ohio, Oregon, and Pennsylvania, have abolished the year-and-a-day rule because modern medical techniques allow injured people to be kept alive for long periods. California has increased the time under the rule to three years and one day, but it still allows a prosecutor to charge someone with murder even if the victim lived longer than three years and a day, by overcoming the presumption that the victim died of natural causes.

PROXIMATE CAUSE

To win a conviction of homicide, the prosecution must show that the defendant's act was the **proximate cause**—that is, the dominant cause of death. It need not, however, be the sole cause of death. For example, a defendant who inflicted a gunshot wound on another was found guilty of the homicide even though the victim was negligently treated by a physician and died from lockjaw. In addition, the **corpus delicti** (the body on which a crime has been committed) must be accounted for to convict someone of homicide. Proof of death must exist. The term "corpus delicti" also refers to all of the elements that must be proved in a particular crime. As discussed in **Chapter 12**, for example, the corpus delicti of robbery consists of five elements: (1) wrongful taking, (2) and carrying away, (3) of personal property of another, (4) from the person or personal custody, and (5) against the other's will with force and violence.

TERMS IN ACTION

The **year-and-a-day rule** is a centuries-old rule that controls the doctrine of causation in murder cases. But many states have abandoned it in favor of allowing the jury to decide whether the defendant's conduct was the **proximate cause** of the victim's death, regardless of the time between the attack and death. In 2009, Walter Hutchinson, Jr. was convicted in New Hampshire of **first-degree murder** for beating and strangling his girlfriend, Kimberly Ernest, whom he suspected of cheating on him. Had New Hampshire followed the year-and-a-day rule, Hutchinson could not have been convicted, because he strangled her in 1991, leaving her in a vegetative state, until her death in 2005. At the time of his murder conviction, Hutchinson was due to have been released from prison, having been convicted of attempted murder 18 years earlier. He lost the legal argument—before his murder trial—that he was the victim of double jeopardy, and then he lost the trial. This time, he was sentenced to life behind bars. In 2011, the New Hampshire Supreme Court unanimously upheld Hutchinson's conviction, concluding there was ample evidence to connect his murderous intent and actions to Ms. Ernst's death 14 years later.

Sources: unionleader.com; wmur.com; nashuatelegraph.com; *State v. Hutchinson* (10 A.3d 972 (2011))

FELONIOUS HOMICIDE

Felonious homicide is homicide done with the intent to commit a felony. A person who commits a felony is called a **felon**. Felonious homicide is a **capital crime** in some states—that is, one that is punishable by death. It is divided into two kinds: murder and manslaughter.

Murder

Murder is defined as "the unlawful killing of a human being by another with **malice aforethought**." Malice aforethought is evil intent, which was historically referred to as "depraved state of mind." It is the state of mind that involves predetermination of an act with knowledge of its harmfulness or reckless indifference to the legal rights of others. It is a state of mind that prompts one to take the life of another without just cause or provocation. When malice is present, the person is motivated by cruelty, hostility, or revenge.

Suicide

Suicide was held to be murder at common law, and the punishment was the forfeiture of the deceased's goods to the state and burial under the highway leading into town so that, henceforth, every person, wagon, and animal going in and out of town would run over the body. Suicide is not punished in the United States and generally is not considered a crime because of the fact that the perpetrator cannot be punished. In some states, anyone who counsels another to commit suicide and who is present when the act is committed would be considered a principal in the second degree to the crime of murder. In 1997, the U.S. Supreme Court decided in *Washington v. Glucksberg* that states may ban doctor-assisted suicides, and most states have done so. Florida law, for example, states the following:

> Every person deliberately assisting another in the commission of self-murder shall be guilty of manslaughter, a felony of the second degree.... (Florida Statutes §782.08)

As of this writing, physician-assisted suicide is legal in five states: California, Oregon, Vermont, and Washington. Referred to as Death with Dignity statutes, these types of laws (or court decisions) allow doctors to prescribe lethal doses of medication to terminally ill people who have six months (or less) left to live. In 2006, the U.S. Supreme Court impliedly upheld Oregon's Death with Dignity Act, in *Gonzales v. Oregon*, by striking a regulation by the U.S. Attorney General that prohibited doctors from prescribing such dosages.

Euthanasia, which is not the same as physician-assisted suicide because a doctor is not involved, is the act of painlessly putting to death someone suffering from an incurable disease, as an act of mercy, and it is illegal in the United States. However, **right-to-die laws**, which allow dying people to refuse extraordinary treatment to prolong life, are very popular. Right-to-die laws are discussed in Chapter 25.

Degrees of Murder

No degrees of murder existed at common law; however, by statute in many states, the crime has been divided into two and, sometimes, three degrees. Under early statutes, the punishment for murder in the first degree was death, and the punishment for murder in the second degree was life imprisonment. Today, punishment for the crime varies from state to state.

FIRST-DEGREE MURDER.   With some variations from state to state, **first-degree murder** is defined as murder committed in any of the following ways:

1. with deliberately premeditated malice aforethought,
2. with extreme atrocity or cruelty, or
3. while in the commission or attempted commission of a felony, which is sometimes referred to as a **felony murder**

Premeditated malice aforethought means thinking over, deliberating on, or weighing in the mind beforehand. Examples of murder committed with extreme atrocity or cruelty are those committed with repeated violent blows, sexual attacks, or repeated stabbing. Examples of felony murders are those committed in connection with rape, robbery, kidnapping, and, sometimes, arson and burglary.

SECOND-DEGREE MURDER.   In some states, murder that is not found to be in the first degree is charged as **murder in the second degree**. Other states differentiate between the two degrees depending on whether the malice was express or implied, the latter being second-degree murder. Still others base the difference on whether or not deliberation or premeditation occurred. For example, Kansas states that second-degree murder is "the killing of a human being committed: (1) Intentionally; or (2) unintentionally but recklessly under circumstances manifesting extreme indifference to the value of human life" (Kan. Stat. Ann. § 21-5403).

Manslaughter

Manslaughter is the unlawful killing of one human being by another without malice aforethought. The major difference between murder and manslaughter is that malice is essential in all degrees of murder, whereas it is not present in manslaughter. Manslaughter is either voluntary or involuntary.

VOLUNTARY MANSLAUGHTER.   **Voluntary manslaughter** occurs when an intention to kill exists, but through the violence of sudden passion (which concerns uncontrolled emotional outbursts, not necessarily sexual emotions), occasioned by what the law recognizes as **adequate provocation**. To be considered adequate, the provocation must be such that a reasonable person might naturally be induced to commit the act after losing self-control. For example, suppose that a wife comes home unexpectedly and finds her husband in the act of adultery with the wife's best friend. She becomes enraged and, in a fit of irresistible passion, kills the husband or the best friend. That is an unfortunate and classic example of the provocation considered adequate in most if not all jurisdictions. When voluntary manslaughter occurs, an intent to kill exists, but the killing is done in the heat of passion, without malice. Indiana's voluntary manslaughter definition (Ind. Code § 35-42-1-3), for example, is nearly identical to the state's definition of murder, except the manslaughter statute includes the "sudden heat" aspect. Later, the statute explains the difference between the two crimes by saying, "The existence of sudden heat is a mitigating factor that reduces what otherwise would be murder under section 1(1) of this chapter to voluntary manslaughter."

INVOLUNTARY MANSLAUGHTER.   **Involuntary manslaughter** is the unintentional killing of another while in the commission of an unlawful act that is not a felony, or in the commission of a wanton or reckless act. For example, the accidental killing of a pedestrian while driving at a high speed along a densely populated, residential street could be involuntary manslaughter. Not all accidents resulting in someone's death are involuntary manslaughter. The key to this crime is that the unintentional act be inherently dangerous to others or committed in a way that shows a reckless disregard for human life. And remember, like all crimes, involuntary manslaughter is defined in a criminal code.

Word Wise
"Manslaughter"—A Sexist Term

Should we continue to use the term "manslaughter" even though it is sexist? *The Dictionary of Bias-Free Usage: A Guide to Nondiscriminatory Language* (1991) recommends continuing to use the word until a nonsexist term is created to replace it. The language associated with English and American law, courts, and government is largely male oriented because men, in the past, dominated the field. American women, for example, were not granted a constitutional right to vote until the 19th Amendment in 1920. Myra Bradwell, of Illinois, is thought to be the first American woman to pass a state's bar exam, in 1869. But both the Illinois Supreme Court and the U.S. Supreme Court denied her submission to the bar. At the U.S. Supreme Court in 1872, Mrs. Bradwell's lawyer argued that she shouldn't be denied the right to practice law even though she was (at that time) lawfully being denied the right to vote (*Bradwell v. Illinois*, 83 U.S. 130). When the Founding Fathers wrote that "all men are created equal" in the Declaration of Independence, they meant men specifically, not generically—and even more precisely, white, male, property owners. In government, terms such as "city fathers," "favorite-son candidate," and "gentlemen's agreement" remain in common usage. Can you suggest a gender-neutral term that might realistically replace the word "manslaughter"? Would it be "humanslaughter" or "personslaughter?"

Reviewing What You Learned

After studying the chapter, write the answers to each of the following questions:

1. What is the difference between justifiable homicide and felonious homicide?

2. What must appear before self-defense can be used as a justification for homicide?

3. What must be shown to win a conviction of homicide?

4. At common law, what was the punishment for suicide?

5. In some states, what happens to one who counsels another to commit suicide and is present when the act is committed?

6. At common law, what were the degrees of murder?

7. Under early statutes, what was the punishment for murder in the first degree and murder in the second degree?

8. Generally, what are the three ways in which first-degree murder can be committed?

9. What is second-degree murder?

____

____

____

10. What is the difference between murder and manslaughter?

____

____

____

____

11. Under what circumstances does voluntary manslaughter occur?

____

____

____

12. Under what circumstances does involuntary manslaughter occur?

____

____

____

____

Understanding Legal Concepts

Indicate whether each statement is true or false. Then, change the italicized word or phrase of each false statement to make it true.

ANSWERS

_____ **1.** Legal execution is an example of *felonious* homicide.

_____ **2.** Except when a person is in his or her own home, he or she *must* retreat, if possible, before killing an assailant in self-defense.

_____ **3.** At common law, the killing of an unborn child in its mother's womb *was not* homicide.

_____ **4.** The corpus delicti *must be* accounted for to convict someone of homicide.

_____ **5.** *Malice* is defined as the unlawful killing of a human being by another.

_____ **6.** *Three* degrees of murder existed at common law.

_____ **7.** Deliberately *premeditated malice aforethought* means thinking over, deliberating on, or weighing in the mind beforehand.

_____ **8.** The major difference between murder and manslaughter is that malice is essential in all degrees of *murder,* whereas it is not present in *manslaughter.*

_____ **9.** *Involuntary manslaughter* includes an intent to kill, but it is done in the heat of passion, without malice.

_____ **10.** The accidental killing of a pedestrian while violating the speed limit is an example of *voluntary manslaughter.*

Checking Terminology

From the list of legal terms that follows, select the one that matches each definition.

ANSWERS

a. capital crime
b. castle doctrine
c. corpus delicti
d. euthanasia
e. excusable homicide
f. felon
g. felonious homicide
h. felony murder
i. feticide
j. first-degree murder
k. fratricide
l. genocide
m. homicide

_____ **1.** The killing of a human being by a human being.

_____ **2.** The taking of a human life when a valid excuse exists. (Select two answers.)

_____ **3.** Homicide done with the intent to commit a felony.

_____ **4.** A body on which a crime has been committed.

_____ **5.** The unlawful killing of a human being by another with malice aforethought.

_____ **6.** Evil intent; that state of mind that is reckless of law and of the legal rights of others.

_____ **7.** A person who commits a felony.

_____ **8.** Murder committed with deliberately premeditated malice aforethought, with extreme atrocity or cruelty, or while in the commission of a crime punishable by life in prison.

_____ **9.** The situation in which an unlawful attack is just about to happen.

_____ **10.** The unlawful killing of one human being by another without malice aforethought.

_____ **11.** The unlawful killing of another without malice when an intention to kill exists, but provoked by the violence of sudden passion.

n. imminent danger
o. infanticide
p. involuntary manslaughter
q. justifiable homicide
r. malice aforethought
s. matricide
t. manslaughter
u. murder
v. patricide
w. proximate cause
x. right-to-die laws
y. second-degree murder
z. self-defense
aa. sororicide
bb. suicide
cc. uxoricide
dd. viable
ee. voluntary manslaughter
ff. year-and-a-day rule

_____ **12.** The unintentional killing of another while in the commission of an unlawful act or while in the commission of a reckless act.

_____ **13.** A valid excuse for the use of force in resisting attack, especially for killing an assailant.

_____ **14.** The dominant cause that produces an injury or death.

_____ **15.** The act of painlessly putting to death someone suffering from an incurable disease, as an act of mercy.

_____ **16.** Killing oneself.

_____ **17.** Laws that allow dying people to refuse extraordinary treatment that would prolong life.

_____ **18.** Killing a fetus in a womb—abortion.

_____ **19.** Killing one's brother.

_____ **20.** Killing a racial or political group.

_____ **21.** Killing an infant soon after birth.

_____ **22.** Killing one's mother.

_____ **23.** Killing one's father.

_____ **24.** Killing one's sister.

_____ **25.** Killing one's wife.

_____ **26.** death must have occurred within a year and a day after the blow occurred for a defendant to be convicted of homicide.

_____ **27.** Murder committed while in the commission or attempted commission of a felony.

_____ **28.** Having the appearance of being able to live.

_____ **29.** A crime that is punishable by death.

_____ **30.** when being attacked in one's house, a person need not retreat before using deadly force against the assailant.

_____ **31.** Murder that is not found to be in the first degree.

Using Legal Language

Read the following story and fill in the blank lines with legal terms taken from the list of terms at the beginning of this chapter:

A gruesome killing was discovered when the maid found the _____________________, on the floor, riddled with bullet holes. The victim was not an infant or a father or a mother; therefore, the crime could not have been _____________________, _____________________, or _____________________. It turned out that the butler shot his wife, making the crime _____________________. Even though the maid may have harmed the victim by failing to properly stop the flow of blood from the wound, the shooting was held to be the _____________________, or dominant cause that produced the death. This case was not one in which the killer had a valid excuse for the use of force in resisting attack; therefore, he could not claim _____________________. The killer was eventually executed by the state, which itself was a type of _____________________ known as _____________________ or _____________________. The _____________________ had been convicted of _____________________, which is the kind committed with deliberately premeditated _____________________ aforethought. Although it found malice, the jury decided against _____________________, because premeditation had occurred.

At trial, the killer unsuccessfully argued that he committed _____________________ instead of murder because he killed his wife due to her unkind comments about his lot in life as a butler. That, however was legally insufficient to serve as _____________________ for killing his wife.

14

2

Crimes Against Morality and Drug Abuse

ANTE INTERROGATORY

With some variations, most states prohibit marriage between people who are related by (A) fornication, (B) affinity, (C) consanguinity, (D) miscegenation.

LEARNING OBJECTIVES

LO 1: Explain the evolution of adultery and fornication laws

LO 2: Distinguish bigamy from polygamy and identify any defense to a prosecution for bigamy

LO 3: Identify how consanguinity and affinity affect marriages that are illegal because of incest laws

LO 4: Contrast the historical, legal definition of sodomy from its more modern understanding

LO 5: Summarize key Supreme Court cases dealing with the legalization or criminialization of abortion

LO 6: Identify the characteristics that distinguish pornography from obscenity

LO 7: Explain the key provisions of the Controlled Substances Act and the Anti-Drug Abuse Act

LO 8: Explain how states deal with drug laws, compared to the federal government

KEY TERMS

abortion

adultery

affinity

bestiality

bigamy

consanguinity

controlled substance

copulation

drugs

drug trafficking

fornication

impediment

incest

miscegenation

obscenity

ordinance

polygamy

pornography

preponderance of evidence

pro-choice

pro-life

prurient interest

reasonable doubt

sodomy

WEBSITES FOR PRONUNCIATION HELP

http://dictionary.cambridge.org/us/pronunciation/english/audio
https://www.howtopronounce.com

ADULTERY AND FORNICATION

Adultery is consensual sexual intercourse by a married person with someone other than his or her spouse or by an unmarried person with a married person. While it is not surprising to think of adultery as a reason for divorce, it may be surprising to realize adultery is a crime in at least 10 states. Minnesota is one of those states and its adultery statute reads as follows:

> When a married woman has sexual intercourse with a man other than her husband, whether married or not, both are guilty of adultery and may be sentenced to imprisonment for not more than one year or to payment of a fine of not more than $3,000, or both…. No prosecution shall be commenced under this section except on complaint of the husband or the wife, except when such husband or wife lacks the mental capacity, nor after one year from the commission of the offense. (MSA § 609.36)

Notice that Minnesota's statute seems on its face to be discriminatory against married women. Maryland still has an adultery statute (MD Criminal Code § 10-501), which simply prohibits it and makes the punishment ten dollars. To convict someone of the crime of adultery, the prosecution must prove beyond a **reasonable doubt** that the illegal act occurred. In contrast, to obtain a divorce on the ground of adultery, it is merely necessary to prove by a **preponderance of evidence** that the illegal act occurred. **Preponderance** of evidence is evidence of the greatest weight, indicating that it is more likely than not that the act occurred. The subject of adultery is discussed further in Chapter 38.

TERMS IN ACTION

Suzanne Corona, of Batavia, New York, was charged with **adultery** in June 2010. Surprisingly, New York is a state that still has in its penal code (Section 255.17) such a crime. Unsurprisingly, adultery is a charge that is rarely brought in New York. According to the news accounts, a distraught woman first spotted Mrs. Corona and Justin Amend on top of a picnic table in the park, and when the police arrived they viewed what they believed was a public act of sexual intercourse. So, Corona and Amend were charged with public lewdness. But because one of the officers knew that Corona was married, he charged her with adultery, making her the 13th New Yorker to be so charged since 1972. There must no longer be a **fornication** law in New York, because Amend, who was single, was not charged with that, but he did get 30 days in jail for the lewdness charge. The adultery charge was dropped as part of a plea bargain on the public lewdness count, for which Mrs. Corona was given probation. But she went to jail in 2011 for violating her probation, after she was arrested for shoplifting. Some years earlier in a state next door to New York, the New Hampshire Supreme Court ruled that a married woman whose husband sought a divorce on the grounds of adultery didn't commit adultery because her affair was with another woman and therefore, technically, she did not have sexual intercourse.

Sources: nydailynews.com; abcnews.go.com; thedailynewsonline.com; *Blanchflower v. Blanchflower*, 150 N.H. 226 (2003)

Fornication, which is sexual intercourse between two unmarried persons, is also a crime in some states. The Massachusetts statute declares: "Whoever commits fornication shall be punished by imprisonment for not more than three months or by a fine of not more than thirty dollars" (M.G.L.A. 272 § 18). Multiple attempts have been made to repeal Massachusetts's fornication law. Very few states, including Michigan (M.C.L.A. § 750-335), still have laws prohibiting an unmarried man and woman from living together as if they were married. Florida's law, originating in 1868, was repealed in 2016. Many states have done away with laws that made adultery and fornication crimes. Many other states have kept the laws on their books, but seldom enforce them. Because of the outcome of a Supreme Court case, *Lawrence v. Texas*, discussed later in the chapter, it is doubtful whether laws prohibiting adultery or fornication are constitutional.

BIGAMY AND POLYGAMY

Bigamy is the state of a man who has two wives, or of a woman who has two husbands, living at the same time. **Polygamy** is the state of having several wives or husbands at the same time. All states in the United States consider bigamy and polygamy to be criminal offenses. In addition, a marriage contracted while either party thereto has a wife or husband is void and of no legal effect unless the previous marriage has been terminated by annulment, divorce, or death of that spouse. In some states, if one of the parties entered the marriage in good faith without knowledge of the **impediment**—that is, the hindrance to the making of a contract (the fact that the other spouse is married)—the second marriage will become valid upon the death or divorce of the former spouse if the parties continue to live together in good faith on the part of one of them.

Word Wise
Numbers

Word Element	Meaning	Examples
uni-	one	unilateral, universe
bi-, di-, du-	two	bilateral, dichotomy, duet
tri-	three	trifurcate, tricycle
quadr-, quart-	four	quadrangle, quartet
quint-, penta-	five	quintuplets, pentagon
ses-, sext-, hexa-	six	sestet, sextet, hexagon
sept-	seven	septet
oct-	eight	octagon, octet
non-, nov-	nine	nonagon, novena
deca-	ten	decathlon, decade

INCEST AND SODOMY

Incest is sexual intercourse between people who are related by **consanguinity** (blood) or affinity in such a way that they cannot legally marry. **Affinity** is the relationship that one spouse has to the blood relatives of the other.

At common law, people could not marry the following relatives:

Consanguinity	**Affinity**
mother or father	stepmother or stepfather
grandmother or grandfather	step-grandmother or step-grandfather
daughter or son	stepdaughter or stepson
granddaughter or grandson	step-granddaughter or step-grandson

Consanguinity	**Affinity**
aunt or uncle	mother-in-law or father-in-law
sister or brother	grandmother-in-law or grandfather-in-law
niece or nephew	daughter-in-law or son-in-law granddaughter-in-law or grandson-in-law

Today, many states no longer prohibit all marriages between people who are related by affinity. With some variations, most states still prohibit marriages between people who are related by consanguinity. For example, Delaware's incest statute (11 Del C. § 766) prohibits marriage between 22 categories of related persons, whether by blood or adoption.

Sodomy was formerly referred to in many state statutes as the "abominable and detestable crime against nature." Although that is a nonspecific description, the crime of sodomy has been interpreted by the courts as referring to oral intercourse, anal penetration, and **bestiality**, the later being carnal **copulation** (sexual intercourse) by a man or woman with an animal. In 2003, the U.S. Supreme Court case of *Lawrence v. Texas* (539 U.S. 558) held anti-sodomy laws to be unconstitutional. The Court said that the parties' right to liberty under the due process clause gives them the full right to engage in private conduct without government intervention. But the court's majority opinion limited itself to non-commercial, heterosexual and homosexual sodomy, and so it does not affect the constitutionality of laws against bestiality or those against prostitution.

MISCEGENATION AND ABORTION LAWS

At one time, many states prohibited marriage between people of different races, which was called **miscegenation**. Such marriages were often held to be illegal and void, and the parties thereto were punished, until the U.S. Supreme Court unanimously ruled in 1967, in *Loving v. Virginia*, that anti-miscegenation statutes were unconstitutional. As the court stated, such laws violate the equal protection clause and the due process clause of the Fourteenth Amendment of the U.S. Constitution.

The subject of **abortion** (the act of preventing a live birth by terminating a pregnancy) is extremely emotional. Many people are **pro-life**—they believe that abortions should not be allowed except in the case of rape or incest and when necessary to save the life of the mother. They believe that an abortion takes the life of a human being and is no different from killing someone who is alive. Many others are **pro-choice**—they believe that a pregnant woman should have the choice of having an abortion or not, without interference from the government.

In 1973, in *Roe v. Wade* (413 U.S. 113), the U.S. Supreme Court held that laws prohibiting abortion were unconstitutional. The Court said that during the first three months of pregnancy, a woman can have an abortion; the decision is up to her, without interference by the state. States are allowed to pass laws to protect the mother's health during the second three months of pregnancy by making rules as to who can perform abortions and where they can be performed. State laws may prohibit abortions during the last three months of pregnancy, the Court said, with exceptions to protect the life or health of the mother.

In 1989, the U.S. Supreme Court held, in *Webster v. Reproductive Health Services* (492 U.S. 490) that states may ban public employees from performing abortions in public hospitals other than to save the life of the mother and that states may pass laws requiring doctors to determine through various tests whether a fetus at least 20 weeks old is viable. In the 1991 case *Rust v. Sullivan* (500 U.S. 173), the U.S. Supreme Court upheld laws which prohibit agencies that receive federal or state funding from giving information on or performing abortions. In 1992, in the case *Planned Parenthood v. Casey* (505 U.S. 833), the U.S. Supreme Court reaffirmed its essential holdings in the *Roe v. Wade* case. In addition, the Court upheld laws that require minors seeking an abortion to obtain a parent's or guardian's consent, but struck down laws that require wives to notify husbands of an intended abortion.

In 2003, in *Scheidler v. National Organization for Women* (537 U.S. 393), the U.S. Supreme Court held that federal racketeering laws, such as RICO laws, could not be used as the foundation for criminal charges against pro-life protesters who rally outside abortion clinics. Four years later, in 2007, the same court held in *Gonzales v. Carhart* (550 U.S. 124) that the Partial Birth Abortion Ban Act passed by Congress in 2003 was constitutional. The court's majority ruled the ban did not violate a woman's right to have an abortion even though it contains no exception to allow an abortion if needed to preserve a woman's life.

PORNOGRAPHY AND OBSCENITY

Pornography in general, refers to material or conduct showing or describing some kind of sexual activity and which is designed to cause sexual arousal. The term that is more commonly used by courts and legislatures to describe pornography is **obscenity**, although one could make the technical, legal distinction that pornography is that which is intended to sexually arouse and is subject to regulation, whereas obscenity is a subset of pornography and is that which is patently offensive and subject to criminalization.

The First and Fourteenth Amendments to the U.S. Constitution, which give to all Americans the right of free speech and free expression, do not protect obscenity. Each individual state may, under a U.S. Supreme Court decision, enact laws regulating obscenity. In 1970, the Court issued a decision, in *Miller v. California* (413 U.S. 15), that established a three-part test to determine whether material is obscene, and all three parts of the test must be present for material to be deemed obscene. The three-part test follows:

1. An average person, applying modern community standards, would find that the work, taken as a whole, appeals to prurient interests. **Prurient interest** means "a shameful or morbid interest in sex." Local, rather than national, standards may be used as a guide.
2. The matter must show or describe sexual conduct in a way that is openly offensive. The sexual conduct that is not allowed to be shown or described must also be clearly defined by state law. This guideline exists so that people will know exactly what the state considers to be obscene.
3. The work, taken as a whole, has no serious literary, artistic, political, or scientific value.

In 1975, the U.S. Supreme Court issued a decision in an obscenity case that is worthy of a summary: A drive-in theater showed a movie in which people were nude. The theater was located in such a way that the screen could be seen from two public streets and a nearby church parking lot. A local **ordinance** (law passed by a city council) made it unlawful for a drive-in theater to show films containing nudity when the screen was visible from a public street or public place. The theater was charged by the city with violating the ordinance. The U.S. Supreme Court held that the city ordinance was unconstitutional because it was too broad. As written, the ordinance prevented drive-in theaters from showing movies containing any nudity at all, however innocent or educational. The court said, "clearly, all nudity cannot be deemed obscene even as to minors" (*Erznoznik v. City of Jacksonville*, 422 U.S. 205).

ILLEGAL DRUG USE

The abuse of **drugs** (chemical substances that have an effect on the body or mind) has been a major national concern since the 1930s. Both federal and state laws deal with drug abuse.

Federal Drug Use and the Controlled Substances Act

The Federal Controlled Substances Act, passed in 1970 (21 U.S.C. § 812), places strict controls on drugs. Under the act, five schedules have been established. Drugs are placed on one of five schedules, depending on their medical use, potential for abuse, and potential for dependence. A drug that is included on any of the five schedules is called a **controlled substance**. Drugs that are placed on Schedule I, such as heroin and marijuana, are strictly controlled. They have little or no medical use, are usually addictive, and have a high potential for abuse. Drugs that are placed on Schedule V, such as low-dose codeine cough medicine, are not as strictly controlled.

Penalties for violating federal drug abuse laws are found in the United States Sentencing Guidelines. They range from imprisonment for one year and a $1,000 fine, to imprisonment for life. Penalties also include the forfeiture of personal property (such as motor vehicles, boats, and aircraft) and real property used to facilitate the possession of a controlled substance or obtained from the proceeds of a controlled substance.

The Anti-Drug Abuse Act of 1988 has a provision for allowing minor punishment without giving the offender a criminal record if an offender is in possession of only a small amount of drugs. In such cases, the government has the option of imposing a civil fine of up to $10,000 rather than a criminal penalty. In determining the amount of the fine, the offender's income and assets are considered. For a first offense for which the offender has paid all fines, can pass a drug test, and has not been convicted of a crime after three years since the conviction, the proceedings can be dismissed. When this occurs, the drug offender can lawfully say that he or she had never been prosecuted, either criminally or civilly, for a drug offense. This law may not be used if (1) the drug offender has been previously convicted of a federal or state drug offense; or (2) the offender has been fined twice under this special program.

The federal act imposes penalties on persons for illegal **drug trafficking**. This activity is the unauthorized manufacture or distribution of any controlled substance, or the possession of such a substance with the intention of manufacturing or distributing it illegally. The penalty for being convicted of a first offense of drug trafficking of a Schedule I or II drug is not less than 5 years or more than 40 years in prison. The penalty increases to not less than 10 years or more than life in prison for a second offense. The penalty increases even more for the trafficking of very great quantities of illegal drugs. The Drug Enforcement Administration (DEA) enforces the federal drug laws. It also strives to cut off the sources of supply of illegal drugs before they reach people who might use them.

Web Wise
• For a detailed look at the five schedules of drugs under the Controlled Substance Act, go to the website of the U.S. Drug Enforcement Agency's Diversion Control Division: **https://www.deadiversion.usdoj.gov/index.html** and look for the "Controlled Substance Schedule" inside the "Resources Tab" • For more information on the federal Asset Forfeiture Program, including an overview of the various federal agencies having a role or authority over asset seizures, **go to https://www.justice.gov/afp**

State Drug Use Laws

Many states have adopted the Uniform Controlled Substances Act and have made it part of their state law. The uniform law is similar to the Federal Controlled Substances Act. It contains the same five Schedules that are found in the federal act and provides a procedure for adding, removing, and transferring drugs from one Schedule to another. It also contains controls that are similar to those found in the federal act. It does not, however, establish penalties for violation of the law. Instead, the act leaves it up to each state to set its own penalties, and those punishments vary considerably. According to the website drugabuse.com, the average incarceration length in Georgia for drug trafficking is 122 months, while in New Mexico the average incarceration 34 months. Furthermore, some states have begun to decriminalize the possession and sale of marijuana. See the "Terms in Action" below for more on states contradicting federal law on marijuana.

TERMS IN ACTION

Marijuana is the most famous and most popular of the **controlled substances**. Under the Controlled Substances Act marijuana is classified as a Schedule I drug, which is the most serious of the five categories, or Schedules. Marijuana comes from female Cannabis plants and has been used for centuries. In America, marijuana was a legal substance until the early twentieth century, when states began criminalizing it. In 1913, California became the first state to criminalize marijuana, and many states followed suit. The federal government first began regulating marijuana with the passage of the Marijuana Tax Act of 1937. To many in America, marijuana usage or **trafficking** is no big deal, but in New York City in 2010, over 50,000 people were arrested for marijuana, making it the cause of 15 percent of all NYC arrests that year. In 2014, though, a new mayor and police commissioner changed the arrest policy for marijuana possession, cutting the arrests by about one-half. Believing that marijuana is not nearly as dangerous as the federal government believes, some states have de-criminalized it or even legalized it in recent years. As of this writing Colorado, Washington, Oregon, Alaska, and the District of Columbia have legalized marijuana, while many other states have decriminalized it. But federal law still controls; that is the essence of the 6th Amendment's Supremacy Clause. The reason those states can get away with legalization is that the Obama administration issued guidelines allowing states to—in essence and under certain restrictions—do their own thing with marijuana. That doesn't mean federal law has no place in those states. In 2015, the Colorado State Supreme Court ruled that a man who was fired for using medical marijuana (which was legal under Colorado law) had no wrongful termination claim against his employer because federal law made such drug use unlawful.

Sources: justice.gov; drugpolicy.org; drugabuse.gov; gothamist.com; governing.com; *Coats v. Dish Network, LLC* 350 P.3d 849 (Col0. 2015).

Reviewing What You Learned

After studying the chapter, write the answers to each of the following questions:

1. What is the difference between fornication and adultery?

   ____

   ____

   ____

2. What is the status of a marriage contracted while either party has a spouse still living?

   ____

   ____

   ____

3. Under what circumstance will a bigamous marriage become valid in some states?

   ____

   ____

   ____

4. Name five relationships by consanguinity in which one cannot legally marry.

   ____

   ____

   ____

5. Name three relationships by affinity in which one could not legally marry at common law.

____

____

____

6. What is the difference between being related by consanguinity and being related by affinity?

____

____

____

7. Explain the present legal status of miscegenation statutes.

____

____

____

8. Under what circumstances is abortion legal?

____

____

____

9. Describe the three-part test that must be used to determine whether or not material is obscene.

____

____

____

10. The Federal Controlled Substances Act places drugs on different Schedules depending on what three considerations?

____

____

____

11. Give an example of a drug that is placed on Schedule I of the Federal Controlled Substances Act.

____

____

____

12. In what ways does the Uniform Controlled Substances Act deal with penalties for drug abuse?

____

____

____

Understanding Legal Concepts

Indicate whether each statement is true or false. Then, change the italicized word or phrase of each false statement to make it true.

Answers

_____ **1.** In addition to being a ground for divorce, adultery is a *crime* in many states.

_____ **2.** Fornication *is not* a crime in *any* state.

_____ **3.** All states in the United States consider bigamy, *but not polygamy*, to be criminal.

_____ **4.** Incest and sodomy are *synonymous.*

_____ **5.** With some variations, most states *still prohibit* marriage between people who are related by consanguinity.

_____ **6.** The U.S. Supreme Court has held miscegenation statutes to be *valid and legal.*

_____ **7.** During the first *six* months of pregnancy, a woman can have an abortion without interference by the state, under the 1973 Supreme Court decision.

_____ **8.** The First and Fourteenth Amendments to the U.S. Constitution *do not* protect obscenity.

_____ **9.** The penalties are *greater* for the illegal trafficking of drugs on Schedule I than they are for drugs on Schedule V, under the Federal Controlled Substances Act.

_____ **10.** The Uniform Controlled Substances Act *establishes* penalties for violation of the law.

Checking Terminology

From the list of legal terms that follows, select the one that matches each definition.

ANSWERS

a. abortion
b. adultery
c. affinity
d. bestiality
e. beyond a reasonable doubt
f. bigamy
g. consanguinity
h. controlled substance
i. copulation
j. drugs
k. drug trafficking
l. fornication
m. impediment
n. incest
o. miscegenation
p. obscenity
q. ordinance
r. polygamy
s. pornography
t. preponderance of evidence
u. pro-choice
v. pro-life
w. prurient interest
x. reasonable doubt
y. sodomy

_____ 1. Voluntary sexual intercourse by a married person with someone other than his or her spouse or by an unmarried person with a married person.

_____ 2. The state of a man who has two wives, or of a woman who has two husbands, living at the same time.

_____ 3. Sexual intercourse by a man or woman with an animal.

_____ 4. Disability or hindrance to the making of a contract.

_____ 5. The act that state statutes often describe as an "abominable and detestable crime against nature."

_____ 6. Material or conduct that shows or describes some kind of sexual activity and is designed to make people become sexually aroused. (Select two answers.)

_____ 7. A law passed by a city council.

_____ 8. The act of ending a pregnancy.

_____ 9. The unauthorized manufacture or distribution of any controlled substance or the possession of such a substance with the intention of manufacturing or distributing it illegally.

_____ 10. Sexual intercourse between two unmarried persons.

_____ 11. The state of having several wives or husbands at the same time.

_____ 12. Sexual intercourse between people within the prohibited degrees of consanguinity or affinity.

_____ 13. The relationship that one spouse has to blood relatives of the other.

_____ 14. Marriage between people of different races.

_____ 15. Chemical substances that have an effect on the body or mind.

_____ 16. Sexual intercourse between people within the prohibited degrees of consanguinity or affinity.

_____ 17. A shameful or morbid interest in sex.

_____ 18. Favoring legislation that disallows abortion.

_____ 19. A drug that is included in any of the five Schedules established by the Federal Controlled Substances Act.

_____ 20. Sexual intercourse.

_____ 21. Favoring legislation that allows abortion.

_____ 22. Related by blood.

Sharpening Your Latin Skills

In the space provided, write the definition of each of the following legal terms, referring to the glossary when necessary:

actio criminalis _______________________________

actus reus _______________________________

animus furandi _______________________________

corpus delicti _______________________________

doli capaz _______________________________

ex post facto _______________________________

mala in se _______________________________

mala prohibita _______________________________

mens rea _______________________________

nolle prosequi _______________________________

Using Legal Language

Read the following story and fill in the blank lines with legal terms taken from the list of terms at the beginning of this chapter:

Janice's husband, Rodney, who was white, became acquainted with some people who were taking _______________________, which is the name for illegal drugs. Because he did not manufacture or distribute the _______________________, he could not be convicted of _______________________ Rodney's friends often watched X-rated movies, which were allowed by a local _______________________—that is, a law passed by the city—but which were close to being _______________________, because, among other points, they appealed to _______________________, which means a shameful or morbid interest in sex. Without divorcing Janice, Rodney married another woman, thereby committing the crime of _______________________. Both of these marriages were later dissolved. Rodney then met Doris, an Asian woman, with whom he had sexual intercourse. This crime was one of _______________________ because they were not married to each other. Because neither of them was married to anyone else, it was not the crime of _______________________, and because they were not related by _______________________ or _______________________, it was not the crime of _______________________. When she became pregnant, Doris decided to carry the baby to term—that is, not have a(n) _______________________. The fact that the two were of different races did not prohibit them from getting married, because all _______________________ statutes are now illegal.

PART THREE

Terms Used in Tort Law

Stockbyte/Getty Images

CHAPTER 15
Torts and Tortfeasors

CHAPTER 16
Intentional Torts

CHAPTER 17
Negligence and Product Liability

3

Some wrongful acts are not criminal but still cause injuries to others. To provide monetary relief to people who suffer losses from the wrongs of others, the law of torts has developed over the years. Chapter 15 defines the elements of a tort action and then discusses imputed liability, liability of minors, immunity from tort liability, and joint tortfeasors. Chapter 16 explains the intentional torts of assault and battery, infliction of emotional distress, deceit, defamation, malicious prosecution, trespass, and conversion. The most common tort—negligence—is saved for last, and its elements, degrees, and defenses are examined in Chapter 17.

Torts and Tortfeasors

ANTE INTERROGATORY

*A tort is defined as (A) a breach of contract, (B) a wrong against
the public at large, (C) a wrong against a town government,
(D) a wrong against an individual.*

LEARNING OBJECTIVES

LO 1: Identify the element of a tort action

LO 2: Explain imputed liability its application in the doctrine of respondeat superior

LO 3: Explain if and when minors can be liable for their torts

LO 4: Explain the doctrine of sovereign immunity

LO 5: Explain how liability is apportioned among joint tortfeasors

KEY TERMS

agent

cybertort

damages

doctrine of charitable immunity

doctrine of respondeat superior

doctrine of sovereign immunity

Good Samaritan statutes

immune

imputed liability

joint liability

joint tortfeasors

master

principal

right of contribution

servant

several liability

tort

tortfeasor

vicarious liability

WEBSITES FOR PRONUNCIATION HELP

http://dictionary.cambridge.org/us/pronunciation/english/audio

https://www.howtopronounce.com

A **tort**, which comes from the Latin word *tortus*, meaning "twisted" or "crooked," is a wrong against an individual (a private wrong), as opposed to a crime, which is a wrong against the public at large. A tort action is a civil suit brought by the injured party to recover **damages**, which is money intended to compensate the injured party for losses caused by the tortious act of the **tortfeasor** (the one who commits the tort). It differs from a criminal action, which is brought by the state to prosecute and then punish the defendant for the wrongdoing. In some situations, such as with assault and battery, the act is both a tort and a crime. In such a case, the state can bring a criminal action against the defendant, and the injured party can bring a separate tort action against the defendant for the same occurrence. The constitutional concept of double jeopardy would not prevent a plaintiff for suing one for a tort even though the defendant was acquitted in a criminal court related to the same underlying action. The term **cybertort** means a tort associated with a computer or the Internet.

To contrast a tort with a breach of contract, a tort is a breach of duty imposed by law (whether it is common law doctrines or statutes), whereas a breach of contract is a breach of duty imposed by a legally agreement between the parties.

ELEMENTS OF A TORT ACTION

Although each tort has its own particular elements that must be alleged and proved by the plaintiff in order for the plaintiff to win a case, four basic elements are common to all torts. In general, the plaintiff must allege and prove all of the following:

1. the existence of a duty owed to the plaintiff by the defendant;
2. a violation of that duty;
3. a showing that the violation was the cause of the plaintiff's injuries; and
4. damages.

It is important to realize the significance of the first element: duty. If one doesn't owe a duty of care to an individual, it matters not that injury or death could have been avoided had the defendant acted differently. In a case from Mississippi, a teenager visiting his uncle at the uncle's apartment complex drowned in the apartment complex's swimming pool, and the teen's mother sued the apartment complex's owner for negligence (a tort to be discussed later). The Mississippi Supreme Court ruled in favor of the owner, finding that the apartment complex owed no duty of care to the teen because, even though he was his uncle's "guest" at the apartment, he was a "trespasser" at the pool because he went to the pool unaccompanied by his uncle. Generally, the only duty landowners owe trespassers is the duty to not intentionally or recklessly harm them (*Handy v. Nejam*, 111 S.O.3d 610, 2013).

The rule that people owe no legal duty to trespassers does have some limitations. For example, the owner of an apartment building was held to be negligent when its janitor failed to turn off the electricity to an elevator after the janitor was told that a child had climbed through the opening in the elevator car's roof and was stuck in the elevator shaft. The child was killed when an unsuspecting person set the elevator in motion soon thereafter. In that case, the court held that the janitor owed a duty to aid the trespassing child by shutting off the electricity once the janitor realized the child was in danger (*Pridgen v. Boston Housing Authority*, 364 Mass. 696 (Mass. 1974)).

Word Wise
Homonyms

Homonyms are words that have the same pronunciation, but that differ in meaning. Here are some examples:

Word	Meaning	Examples
principle	Rule; precept	It would be contrary to my *principles* to vote for that person.
		There were no guiding *principles* to follow when we landed on the moon.
principal	Chief; main	The *principal* of the school was the *principal* objector to the plan to invest the *principal* at 3 percent.
counsel	Advice; deliberation; one who gives advice	I asked for *counsel* from my aunt's *counsel* before making my investments.

Word	Meaning	Examples
		The defendant consulted his *counsel* before answering the question.
council	An assembly	The city *council* discussed the matter at its last meeting.
		Council Bluffs, Iowa, commemorates the *council* that Lewis and Clark held with the Indians on the high bluffs.

Although in most cases people are not legally bound to help others, if they do so and are negligent, they will be liable for any injuries that they may cause. For this reason, people in the medical field would, in the past, sometimes refuse to assist injured people at accident scenes or in other emergencies. States have passed laws, known as Good Samaritan statutes, to alleviate this problem. **Good Samaritan statutes** generally provide that physicians, nurses, and certain other medical personnel will not be liable for negligent acts that occur when they voluntarily and without a fee render emergency care or treatment outside of the ordinary course of their practice. For instance, Colorado's Good Samaritan Statute (C.R.S. §13-21-108) also covers non-medical personnel as well, and states as follows:

> Any person licensed as a physician and surgeon under the laws of the state of Colorado, or any other person, who in good faith renders emergency care or emergency assistance to a person not presently his patient without compensation at the place of an emergency or accident, including a health care institution as defined in section 13-64-202 (3), shall not be liable for any civil damages for acts or omissions made in good faith as a result of the rendering of such emergency care or emergency assistance during the emergency, unless the acts or omissions were grossly negligent or willful and wanton.

IMPUTED LIABILITY

Although all people are responsible for their own torts, in some situations one person may be held responsible for the torts that are committed by another person; this is known as **imputed liability**. Often, the term **vicarious liability** is used interchangeably with the term "imputed liability." Vicarious liability applies most frequently when an employee commits a tort while working for an employer. Under the **doctrine of respondeat superior**, **masters** (employers) can be held responsible for the torts of their **servants** (employees) that are committed within the scope of employment. A tort committed within the scope of employment is a wrongful act committed by an employee that is nonetheless committed inside the zone of that person's employment authority. Similarly, **principals** (people who authorize others to act for them) can be held responsible for the torts committed by their **agents** (people authorized to act) while acting within the scope of the principals' authority. Similarly, a business partner may be held liable for torts committed by another partner while acting in the ordinary course of the partnership.

TERMS IN ACTION

Predicting when **imputed liability** or **vicarious liability** applies in employment situations can be difficult. Try a couple of examples. In the first scenario, a woman who was being transported to a hospital in Washington, D.C., was sexually assaulted in the ambulance by one of the ambulance employees. Six months later, another Washington, D.C., woman was sexually assaulted under the same circumstances, allegedly by the same man. And in Virginia, an employee—who five minutes earlier had left an employer-sponsored Christmas party where he had been drinking alcohol served by the employer—injured someone while driving drunk. In the first two cases, the District of Columbia, as the employer of the ambulance company, was sued under the doctrine of **Respondeat Superior**, as was the employer in the Virginia case. In the first ambulance case, the jury returned a verdict for the District of Columbia, because it was not aware of the possibility of such an act (which was not within **the scope of employment**), but the same jury awarded a $180,000 verdict for the second woman, because the District was on notice from the first allegation. In the Virginia case, the jury awarded the plaintiff $11 million in damages, but the trial judge reversed the verdict (which was upheld on appeal), concluding that the employee was not within the scope of employment at the time of the accident. That decision was affirmed by the Virginia Supreme Court.

Sources: washingtonpost.com; *Sayles v. Piccadilly Cafeterias, Inc.*, 410 S.E.2d 632 (Va. 1991).

LIABILITY OF MINORS

Minor children (those under the age of 18) are just as liable for their torts as adults. At one time under the common law, children under a certain age (7, for example) could not be liable for their actions. When children were between the minimum age and adulthood, there was a rebuttable presumption of nonliability that plaintiffs had to overcome by showing the child's actions met the requirements of tort liability. But the modern view tends to be that children of any age can be liable in tort. In fact, in 2010, a Manhattan judge ruled that a 4-year-old girl could be sued in tort law for allegedly negligently riding her training wheels-connected bike too fast and hitting an 87-year-old woman, who broke her hip in the fall and died three months later. The estate of the woman sued the girl and her biking buddy (who was 5), with whom the girl was racing down the street on her bike with training wheels at the time she hit the woman. The mothers of both children were also sued for negligence in supervising their children's bike riding.

It is usually impossible to collect court judgments from minors, because in most cases they have no money. Under the common law, parents were not responsible for the torts of their minor child unless the act was committed in the parents' presence or while the minor was acting as the agent or servant of the parents. Some states have modified this rule by enacting statutes that make parents liable up to a limited amount of money for the willful torts committed by their minor children. Additionally, parents can be liable for the negligent supervision of their children when those children commit torts that reasonably would not have occurred under careful supervision.

IMMUNITY FROM TORT LIABILITY

In the past, charitable and governmental institutions could not be sued, with some exceptions, for their wrongdoings.

Charitable Immunity

Until recently, charitable institutions such as hospitals and churches were **immune**—that is, exempt—from tort liability. They could not be sued in tort for the wrongdoings of their agents or employees that occurred in the course of the charitable activity. This regulation was known as the **doctrine of charitable immunity**. By 1969, most U.S. states had abolished the doctrine of charitable immunity. To illustrate, in 1969, the Massachusetts Supreme Judicial Court (the highest court in that state) declared that it would abolish the doctrine in the next case involving that issue unless the legislature acted on the matter. This decision caused the Massachusetts legislature to pass a statute in 1971 abolishing the doctrine of charitable immunity in cases arising from a charity's commercial activity.

> ### TERMS IN ACTION
>
> The doctrine of **sovereign immunity** applies to a variety of government employees, including judges. The most infamous case of **judicial immunity** is *Stump v. Sparkman*, a 1978 U.S. Supreme Court case. In that case, an Indiana trial judge granted the request of a mother that her "somewhat retarded" 15-year-old daughter be sterilized. When the daughter went in for surgery, she was told that she was having her appendix taken out. Later, when she married and couldn't get pregnant, she then learned what had been done to her. She sued the judge for violating her civil rights and due process rights by granting a sterilization order, something over which he had no jurisdiction. Judge Sparkman got the case dismissed on the basis of sovereign immunity, but the 7th Circuit of Appeals reversed the decision. Then, the Supreme Court reversed, holding that the judge was absolutely immune from liability because he had been performing a function normally performed by a judge and acting in his official capacity when granting the wrongful sterilization order. *Stump v. Sparkman* was cited by the same court years later when it ruled another judge was immune from liability for wrongfully ordering the police to arrest a lawyer who failed to appear in the judge's courtroom as scheduled. Obviously peeved that the lawyer was absent, the judge ordered the police to "forcibly and with excessive force," an order they clearly obeyed. Despite the wrongfulness of such a **tortious** order, the Supreme Court, once again, concluded that the judge could not be sued because his arrest order was the kind of official act judges make.
>
> Source: *Stump v. Sparkman*, 435 U.S. 349 (1978).

Sovereign Immunity

The **doctrine of sovereign immunity**, which makes a governmental body immune from tort liability unless the government agrees to be held liable, stems from the old common law rule that "the king can do no wrong." For hundreds of years, under this doctrine, individuals could not sue the federal, state, or local government for its torts unless a statute allowed a suit for that particular wrong. This doctrine has also been modified by the U.S. Congress, and by statute in many states.

For example, the U.S. government has waived its sovereign immunity in order to allow civil suits for actions arising out of negligent acts of its agents. To bring such an action, strict rules under the Federal Tort Claims Act must be followed precisely.

Under the Massachusetts Tort Claims Act, public employers (Mass. Gen. Law, Chapter 258) state and local governmental agencies) are liable up to $100,000 for personal injury, property damage, or death, caused by the negligent or wrongful act or omission of any public employee while acting within the scope of employment. In addition, the public employee whose negligent or wrongful act or omission caused the claim cannot be sued if the act occurred while he or she was acting within the scope of employment and if it was not an intentional tort. Before suit may be brought under the act, a claim must be presented in writing, within two years after the cause of action arose, to the executive officer of the public employer involved. The public employer has six months in which to pay the claim, deny it, refer it to arbitration, or reach a settlement. Only then may the suit be brought against the public employer, and it must be brought within three years after the cause of action arose.

JOINT TORTFEASORS

If more than one person participate in the commission of a tort, they are called **joint tortfeasors**. They may be held either jointly or severally liable for their wrongdoings. **Joint liability** means that all joint tortfeasors must be named as defendants in the lawsuit and, if found liable, together they owe the damages awarded to the plaintiff. **Several liability** means that the joint tortfeasors may be sued separately for the wrongdoing. Suppose that two drag-racing teens wreck into a home situated next to the highway, causing extensive property damage, and one of the teens joins the armed services the next day, leaving the jurisdiction. The plaintiffs sue the other teen, who is now the only one around. If that teen-driver is found liable, he or she owes the entire damages. By statute in some states, if one joint tortfeasor is required to pay more than his or her share to the injured party, he or she may sue the other joint tortfeasor for the excess. This regulation is known as the **right of contribution** between joint tortfeasors.

Reviewing What You Learned

After studying the chapter, write the answers to each of the following questions:

1. What is the difference between a tort and a crime?

2. Give an example of a wrong that is both a tort and a crime.

3. How does a tort differ from a breach of contract?

4. What four basic requirements must the plaintiff allege and prove in order to recover damages for a tort?

5. Describe and name the term for the situation in which one person may be held responsible for the torts that are committed by another person.

6. What liability do minor children have for their torts?

7. In what way are parents liable for torts committed by their children?

8. Describe the statute enacted in 1971 by the Massachusetts legislature, dealing with the tort liability of a charitable organization.

9. Describe the main features of the Massachusetts Tort Claims Act. _______________________________________

____

____

____

10. What is the difference between joint liability and several liability? _______________________________________

____

____

____

Understanding Legal Concepts

Indicate whether each statement is true or false. Then, change the italicized word or phrase of each false statement to make it true.

ANSWERS

_____ **1.** A tort is a wrong against *society*.

_____ **2.** Under the doctrine of *respondeat superior*, a governmental body is immune from tort liability.

_____ **3.** In the past, charitable institutions and government bodies were immune from *tort* liability.

_____ **4.** "Master" is the legal name that means *employer*.

_____ **5.** *Several* liability means that all joint tortfeasors must be named as defendants in a lawsuit.

_____ **6.** Minor children are liable for their *torts* just the same as adults.

_____ **7.** In comparing a tort with a breach of contract, a tort is a breach of duty imposed by *the parties*, whereas a breach of contract is a breach of duty imposed by *law*.

_____ **8.** A *tort* is a criminal action brought by the state to punish the defendant for the wrongdoing.

_____ **9.** If one joint tortfeasor is required to pay more than his or her share to the injured party, he or she *may* sue the other joint tortfeasor for the excess.

_____ **10.** An *agent* is a person who is authorized to act on behalf of another and subject to the other's control.

Checking Terminology

From the list of legal terms that follows, select the one that matches each definition.

ANSWERS

a. agent
b. doctrine of charitable immunity
c. doctrine of respondeat superior
d. doctrine of sovereign immunity
e. Good Samaritan statutes
f. immune
g. imputed liability
h. joint liability
i. joint tortfeasors
j. master
k. principal
l. right of contribution
m. servant
n. several liability
o. tort
p. tortfeasor
q. vicarious liability

_____ **1.** A wrong against an individual.

_____ **2.** One who commits a tort.

_____ **3.** Vicarious responsibility for the torts committed by another person. (Select two answers.)

_____ **4.** A legal doctrine under which a master is responsible for the torts of his or her servants, that are committed within the scope of employment.

_____ **5.** An employer.

_____ **6.** An employee.

_____ **7.** A person who authorizes an agent to act on his or her behalf and subject to his or her control.

_____ **8.** A person authorized to act on behalf of another and subject to the other's control.

_____ **9.** Exempt.

_____ **10.** A legal doctrine under which charitable institutions and immune from tort liability.

_____ **11.** A legal doctrine under which governmental bodies and immune from tort liability.

_____ **12.** Two or more people who participate in the commission of a tort.

_____ **13.** Liability under which all joint tortfeasors must be named as defendants in a lawsuit.

_____ **14.** Liability under which joint tortfeasors may be sued separately in a lawsuit.

_____ **15.** The right to share a loss among joint tortfeasors or other codefendants.

_____ **16.** Laws providing that physicians, nurses, and certain other medical personnel will not be liable for negligent acts that occur when they voluntarily, without a fee, render emergency care or treatment outside of the ordinary course of their practice.

Using Legal Language

Read the following story and fill in the blank lines with legal terms taken from the list of terms at the beginning of this chapter:

Amy and Barry, while working for the Red Cross, committed a _____________________ when they violated a duty imposed on them by law. Because they committed the wrongful act together, they were joint _____________________, but because they could be sued separately, their liability was _____________________ rather than _____________________. Because the doctrine of _____________________ no longer applies, the Red Cross, which is the _____________________ of Amy and Barry, has _____________________ liability for the torts of its _____________________ under the doctrine of _____________________. If it turns out that Amy is required to pay more than Barry for the damages they caused, Amy has the right of _____________________ to recover the excess from Barry. This case is not one involving the doctrine of _____________________, because it does not involve a governmental body being _____________________ from tort liability, nor does it involve a(n) _____________________ or _____________________ that is, a person who authorizes another to act or one who is authorized to act.

Intentional Torts

ANTE INTERROGATORY

A defamatory statement that is made by an online message or Internet communication is called (A) slander, (B) libel, (C) defamation, (D) invasion of privacy.

LEARNING OBJECTIVES

LO 1: Contrast the torts of assault and battery

LO 2: Define false imprisonment and explain the exception related to store owners

LO 3: Summarize intentional infliction of emotional distress, including discussing the physical contact requirement

LO 4: Explain the five elements of fraud

LO 5: Compare and contrast the two classes of defamation, being sure to include any defenses or privileges against defamation

LO 6: Identify the categories of invasion of privacy

LO 7: Identify the elements of malicious prosecution

LO 8: Define trespass and identify both types of trespass

LO 9: Explain how conversion is different from trespass

LO 10: Define nuisance, including both categories

KEY TERMS

acquitted

actionable

assault

battery

conversion

damages

deceit

defamation

false arrest

false imprisonment

fraud

intentional infliction of emotional distress

intentional torts

invasion of privacy

libel

malicious prosecution

misrepresentation

nuisance

per se

private nuisance

public nuisance

right of privacy

scienter

slander

special damages

tortious

trespass

trespass de bonis asportatis

unintentional torts

waste

willful torts

WEBSITES FOR PRONUNCIATION HELP

http://dictionary.cambridge.org/us/pronunciation/english/audio
https://www.howtopronounce.com

Tortious (wrongful) acts may be committed either intentionally or unintentionally. Those that are committed intentionally—that is, deliberately rather than by accident or mistake—are known as **intentional** or **willful torts**. Conversely, those that are committed accidentally, such as negligence, are referred to as **unintentional torts**. Some of the key intentional torts are discussed below.

ASSAULT AND BATTERY

Assault and battery are examples of intentional torts that are also crimes, as was mentioned in an earlier chapter. In such cases, the state can bring a criminal action; additionally, victims can file a tort suit against the wrongdoer. **Battery** is defined as the intentional contact with another person without that person's permission and without justification. **Assault** is an act that intentionally creates in the victim a reasonable apprehension of an imminent battery. Pointing a gun at someone is an assault; the bullet striking the person is a battery.

Generalized verbal threats alone are not enough to constitute an assault in most states. To convert a threat into an assault requires some act to indicate that the battery will ensue immediately. Although every battery includes an assault, an assault does not necessarily require a battery.

FALSE IMPRISONMENT

False imprisonment (also called **false arrest**) is the intentional confinement of a person without legal justification. It is a restraint on a person's liberty. The person who is confined need not be held within an enclosure of any kind or even touched by the other person. It is considered to be a confinement if a person apprehends that physical force will be used if he or she attempts to leave.

Many cases of false imprisonment arise out of situations in which suspected shoplifters are detained by store proprietors without reasonable grounds for doing so. The person who is detained may sue the store for **damages** arising from the false imprisonment.

Store owners, in some states, have the protection of statutes that allow the detention, for a reasonable length of time and in a reasonable manner, of a person suspected of shoplifting if reasonable grounds for such suspicion exist. For example, Pennsylvania's retail theft statute includes a subsection that provides authority to merchants and their employees who have probable cause that someone committed or is committing shoplifting to detain that person in a reasonable manner and for a reasonable time to investigate whether shoplifting occurred and, if so, to recover the merchandise and contact the police (18 Pa.C.S. § 3929). Generally, it is reasonable to detain a person if goods that were not purchased are concealed in the clothing or among the belongings of a shopper.

INFLICTION OF EMOTIONAL DISTRESS

Historically, except in the case of false imprisonment, one could not recover damages from another for the infliction of emotional distress unless the emotional suffering was accompanied by some outer physical injury such as a break in the skin or a broken bone.

This original legal doctrine was changed by court decisions and state statutes, as they began to no longer require physical contact of the victim as a prerequisite for liability when the defendant engages in extreme and outrageous conduct. For example, in a 1976 case, the manager of a restaurant called a meeting of the waitresses and told them that some stealing was occurring and that the identity of the person responsible was unknown. He said that until the person responsible was discovered, he would begin firing all the present waitresses in alphabetic order.

He then fired a waitress whose name began with the letter "A," even though the manager had no evidence that she had been stealing from the restaurant. She became greatly upset and began to cry, sustaining emotional distress and mental anguish, as well as lost wages from being randomly fired. The court allowed her to sue for her emotional suffering even though she sustained no physical injury from the manager's actions (*Agis v. Howard Johnson, Co.*, 355 N.E.2d 315 (Mass. 1976)).

The tort of **intentional infliction of emotional distress** (IIED) is defined as "emotional suffering caused by the infliction of extreme and outrageous intentional conduct by another." By contrast, there is an unintentional tort called "negligent infliction of emotional distress (NIED)." NIED occurs where a defendant commits an accidental act that is foreseeable to lead to the plaintiff's emotional distress, and where such distress occurs—even in the absence of physical injury. Because NIED allows for the recovery of damages even where there is no physical harm from the negligence, NIED has been criticized and limited in many states.

Word Wise
Suffixes

Many words in this chapter are a combination of the basic part of a word, called a root, and a suffix, which is a word element that follows the root. Some of the words use suffixes to form nouns; others form adjectives. Some suffixes form both nouns and adjectives.

Suffixes That Form Nouns

Suffix	Meaning	Examples
-ment	state, quality, act of	imprisonment, statement
-sion, -tion	act or state of	defamation, recognition

Suffixes That Form Adjectives

Suffix	Meaning	Examples
-able, -ible	capable of	actionable, visible
-al	like, relating to	emotional, intentional

Suffixes That Form Nouns or Adjectives

Suffix	Meaning	Examples
-ery, -ary, -ory, -ry	relating to, connected with	robbery (noun) customary (adjective)
-ful	full of	spoonful (noun) plentiful (adjective)

FRAUD

The tort of **fraud** or *fraudulent misrepresentation*, which is also known as **deceit**, occurs when one person, by false representation of material facts, induces another to act and thereby suffer a financial loss. To recover for this tort, the plaintiff must allege and prove all of the following five elements:

1. a misrepresentation of a material, existing fact;
2. made with knowledge of its falsity;
3. made with the intent that it be relied on;
4. that it was reasonably relied on; and
5. damages.

To be actionable, the **misrepresentation** (false or deceptive statement or act) must be of a material, existing fact. It is not actionable if it is an opinion or a promise of something to happen in the future.

The misrepresentation must be made with knowledge of its falsity. This act is known as the **scienter** requirement, which is from the Latin word meaning "knowingly." This element of deceit may be satisfied if the person who made the misrepresentation had actual knowledge of its falsity or made it recklessly without regard to its truth or falsity. In some states, it may also be satisfied if the person who made the misrepresentation actually had no knowledge of its falsity, but was susceptible of knowledge—that is, was in a position in which he or she was expected to know.

To illustrate the latter, in some states if a buyer asks a homeowner who is selling a house, "Does the house have termites?" and the homeowner does not know whether it does or not, but replies, "No, it does not have termites," the court will hold that the homeowner was susceptible of such knowledge and therefore satisfied the knowledge requirement.

The person who makes the misrepresentation must intend that the other person rely on it. Suppose, for example, that A made false representations in order to induce a sale of the goods to B. Then B sold the goods to C. C would have no right of action against A for the misrepresentations because A did not intend that C rely on them.

In addition, the person to whom the misrepresentation was made must reasonably rely on it. Suppose, for example, that a prospective buyer of a house says to the owner, "Does the house have termites?" and the owner replies, "No, it does not have termites." If the buyer, before buying, has the house inspected by a termite inspector who negligently fails to discover termites that are actually in the house, the buyer could not sue the seller for deceit because the buyer, having done an independent inspection, did not rely on the seller's misrepresentation.

To recover for deceit, the injured party must prove that he or she suffered some **damage** (financial loss) as a result of the misrepresentation.

DEFAMATION

Defamation is the wrongful act of damaging someone's character or reputation by making or repeating a false statement about that person. It is divided into two classes: libel and slander. **Libel** is defamation that is communicated by a writing, drawing, photograph, television program, Internet posting, or other broadcast-based defamation, including defamation made on the radio. **Slander** is oral defamation, notwithstanding that defaming someone by spoken word on radio or television is libel.

To be **actionable**—that is, to furnish legal ground for a lawsuit—both libel and slander must be communicated to a third person. Unless a third person hears or sees the defamatory material, no one can sue.

Libel

Because of its more longer lasting form of defamation (books, for example) and its ability to reach more people (TV and the Internet, for example), libel is considered to be more serious than slander. It is actionable **per se**—that is, in and of itself, and, therefore, a suit can be brought in all instances of libel.

Slander

Slander, conversely, is not actionable per se. It is actionable only in the following situations:

1. when the injured person can prove that he or she suffered **special damages** (damages that are capable of exact dollar-amount calculations) from the slanderous statements;
2. when someone is falsely accused of committing a crime of moral turpitude (immorality);
3. when someone is falsely accused of having a contagious disease, such as leprosy, AIDS, or venereal disease; or
4. when someone makes a false statement that injures a person in his or her business, profession, or trade.

Slander that does not fall within one of the preceding four categories is not actionable.

TERMS IN ACTION

Sunda Croonquist is a stand-up comedian and television personality who was sued by her mother-in-law in 2009 for **defamation**. Ms. Croonquist, who is half-black and half-Swedish and who was raised Catholic, didn't tell ordinary mother-in-law jokes; she told jokes focusing on her in-laws as Jews. And not just that, but the jokes made it seem that her in-laws were racists. One of her jokes about the first time she went to her mother-in-law's house, went this way: "I walk in, I say, 'Thank you so much for having me here, Ruthie.' She says, 'The pleasure's all mine, have a seat. Then, she said to her husband in a loud voice, 'Harry, put my pocketbook away!'" Croonquist's stand-up act took aim at other members of her husband's family; she compared her sister-in-law's voice to a cat in heat. It was actually the sister-in-law who first sued her for **slander** and **libel** (because of Croonquist's website), but the mother-in-law joined the lawsuit in 2009, and it was moved to federal court in Los Angeles. In May 2010, the case was dismissed. The judge ruled that Croonquist's statements weren't assertions of fact, but simply opinions, which aren't subject to defamation claims. Making the matter even more awkward for thanksgiving dinners and other family gatherings, Croonquist was represented by the law firm where her husband works.

Sources: nydailynews.com; abajournal.com

Web Wise

- To read current information about defamation, go to **www.findlaw.com**. At that site, type "defamation, libel and slander" in the search bar.
- For a detailed look at various types of common fraud schemes, go to the following webpage of the FBI: **https://www.fbi.gov/scams-and-safety/common-fraud-schemes**

Privileges and Defenses to Defamation

The law gives privileges to certain people, making them immune from suit for slander and libel. Judges, lawyers, and witnesses while they are participating in trials, and members of the legislature during its sessions, have an absolute privilege against defamation suits. They cannot be sued for libel or slander.

Newspapers have a qualified privilege when they report about public events and matters of public concern. Actual malice on the part of the newspaper must be proved for someone to recover damages from the newspaper in such cases. Public figures such as actors, actresses, and politicians must prove that the defamatory material was spoken or written with actual malice before they can recover damages against others for defamation.

Truth is an absolute defense against libel or slander. Regardless of how it may harm someone's reputation, a truthful statement is not defamatory. It might, however, qualify as an invasion of privacy, the tort discussed in the next section.

INVASION OF PRIVACY

The **right of privacy** encompasses the right to be left alone, the right to be free from uncalled-for publicity, and the right to live without unreasonable interference by the public in private matters. A violation of the right of privacy is known as **invasion of privacy**. Using someone's photograph without permission for advertising purposes, wiretapping someone's house, and publishing someone's medical or financial condition are examples of invasion of privacy.

Invasion of privacy has four distinct types of claims: (1) Intrusion of Solitude (peeping on someone in a private location); (2) Appropriation of Identity (using the likeness or name of another, often a celebrity, without permission); (3) Public Disclosure of Private Facts (revealing sensitive and private information of an individual that is not of public concern and which is offensive to make public); and (4) False Light (the media's public disclosure of information about someone that, while not technically false, creates a misleading impression about the individual). As Internet use, text-messaging, and social media have become more prevalent, examples of online invasion of privacy have increased. But whether the Internet is used as the conduit for libel or invasion of privacy, online service providers (e.g., Google, Yahoo, Facebook) are immune from being sued, due to Section 230 of the Communications Decency Act. For example, if someone used their Facebook account to libel a former friend, the victim can sue the Facebook user who posted the false statements, but not Facebook, itself.

TERMS IN ACTION

One of the more disturbing trends in the issue of **invasion of privacy** is the use of secretly-placed video equipment to spy on others. In Miami, Florida, Kenneth Ryals, a 60-year-old IRS agent, placed an ad on Roommates.com, under the screen name "Buttercup," seeking to rent out one of the furnished bedrooms of his home. A 27-year-old woman responded and rented the room, which came with a TV and DVD player. While living in Ryals's home, the woman confronted Ryals about what she thought was his inappropriate behavior in the house, some of which occurred near her room. Ryals then asked her to move out within a month. While cleaning her room in preparation for leaving, the woman noticed a small hole in the DVD/VCR player, which was pointed at her bed. She called the police, who found a mini-wireless camera implanted in the DVD player. Ryals admitted what he had done, but, somehow, the misdemeanor criminal charges against him were dropped. The former tenant did win her invasion of privacy civil suit, and in 2011 a jury awarded her $476,000 in damages.

Sources: miamiherald.com; abajournal.com; articles.sun-sentinel.com

---

MALICIOUS PROSECUTION

The right of action for the tort of **malicious prosecution** arises when one person has unsuccessfully brought criminal or civil charges against another, with malice and without probable cause. The one against whom the original charges were brought may bring a tort suit for malicious prosecution against the person who brought the original charges. To bring such a suit, all of the following must be proved:

1. Criminal or civil charges were brought by the defendant against the plaintiff.
2. The plaintiff was **acquitted**—that is, discharged from accusation.
3. The defendant brought the charges maliciously and without probable cause.

TRESPASS

The intentional and unauthorized entry on the land of another is called **trespass**. Suit may be brought against a trespasser by the one who is in possession of the land whether or not he or she has suffered any damages from the trespass. It has been held to be a trespass to do any of the following: step on another's land without permission, hit a golf ball into another's airspace, and string a wire into another's airspace.

Trespass to personal property is a tort called **trespass de bonis asportatis** (trespass for goods carried away). To recover for this tort, it is necessary to prove that actual damages occurred as a result of the trespass. Trespass is an example of a wrongful action that is both a tort and a crime.

CONVERSION

Conversion is the wrongful exercise of dominion and control over the personal property in the possession of another. It is different from trespass in that it is using another's property as though it belonged to the wrongdoer, rather than interfering with the owner's possession as in trespass. Some examples of conversion are misdelivery of goods by a carrier, theft of goods, failure to return borrowed goods, and sale of goods belonging to another without authority.

NUISANCE AND WASTE

The tort of **nuisance** involves the use of one's property in a way that causes annoyance, inconvenience, or discomfort to another. The emission of smoke, offensive odors, and loud noises often generate nuisance lawsuits. Airlines are sometimes sued, for example, by people who live near airports, because of the loud noise, smoke, and odors of the planes taking off. The tort is called a **public nuisance** when the disturbance affects the community at large and a **private nuisance** when it disturbs one neighbor only.

Another tort, called **waste**, is the abuse or destructive use of property that is in one's rightful possession. A tenant who damages the landlord's property, for example, commits the tort of waste.

Reviewing What You Learned

After studying the chapter, write the answers to each of the following questions:

1. What must occur to convert a verbal threat into an assault?___

2. Out of what situations do many false imprisonment cases arise? _______________________

3. What five elements must the plaintiff allege and prove to recover for fraud or deceit? _______________________

4. Give an example of a person not relying on a misrepresentation and thus not being able to recover for fraud or deceit. ___

5. What is the difference between libel and slander? _______

6. To whom must libel and slander be communicated to be actionable? _______________________

7. Under what circumstances is libel actionable? _______

8. Under what circumstances is slander actionable?_______

9. In what positions do people enjoy an absolute privilege against defamation suits? _______________________

____

____

10. What must be proved for someone to recover for libel from a newspaper when it reports about public events and matters of public concern? _______________________

____

____

11. What three elements must be proved for one to recover for malicious prosecution? _______________________

____

____

12. What are the types of invasion of privacy torts? _______________________

____

____

13. Give three examples of conversion. _______________________

____

____

____

Understanding Legal Concepts

Indicate whether each statement is true or false. Then, change the italicized word or phrase of each false statement to make it true.

ANSWERS

_____ **1.** In the case of false imprisonment, the person confined *must be* held within an enclosure of some kind.

_____ **2.** Although every battery includes an assault, an *assault* does not necessarily require a battery.

_____ **3.** Verbal threats alone *are* enough to be an assault.

_____ **4.** To be actionable fraud, the misrepresentation *must be* an opinion or a promise of something to happen in the future.

_____ **5.** To recover for emotional suffering, the plaintiff must prove that the emotional suffering was caused by the *extreme and outrageous* intentional conduct of the defendant.

_____ **6.** To be actionable, *both* libel and slander must be communicated to a third person.

_____ **7.** *Libel* is defamation that is directed toward the sense of hearing.

_____ **8.** *Slander* is actionable per se.

_____ **9.** Hitting a golf ball into another's airspace is *not* a trespass.

_____ **10.** Failing to return borrowed goods is an example of *conversion*.

Checking Terminology

From the list of legal terms that follows, select the one that matches each definition.

ANSWERS

a. acquitted
b. actionable
c. assault
d. battery
e. conversion
f. damages
g. deceit
h. defamation
i. emotional distress
j. false arrest
k. false imprisonment
l. fraud
m. intentional infliction
 of emotional distress

_____ **1.** The wrongful act of damaging another's character or reputation by the use of false statements.

_____ **2.** Defamation that is communicated by a writing or by other means that is directed toward the sense of sight.

_____ **3.** Defamation that is communicated by the spoken word.

_____ **4.** In and of itself; taken alone.

_____ **5.** Prosecution begun in malice without probable cause.

_____ **6.** The intentional and unauthorized entry on the land of another.

_____ **7.** The wrongful exercise of dominion and control over the personal property in another's possession.

_____ **8.** Wrongful; implying or involving tort.

_____ **9.** Torts that are committed intentionally. (Select two answers.)

_____ **10.** The intentional contact with another person without that person's permission and without justification.

n. intentional torts
o. invasion of privacy
p. libel
q. malicious prosecution
r. misrepresentation
s. nuisance
t. per se
u. private nuisance
v. public nuisance
w. right of privacy
x. scienter
y. slander
z. tortious
aa. trespass
bb. trespass de bonis asportatis
cc. unintentional torts
dd. waste
ee. willful torts

_____ **11.** The intentional creation of a reasonable apprehension of an imminent battery.

_____ **12.** The intentional confinement of a person without legal justification. (Select two answers.)

_____ **13.** A misrepresentation of a material, existing fact, knowingly made, that causes someone reasonably relying on it to suffer damages. (Select two answers.)

_____ **14.** A false or deceptive statement or act.

_____ **15.** The monetary loss suffered by a party as a result of a wrong.

_____ **16.** Discharged from accusation.

_____ **17.** That which creates or affords a basis to sue.

_____ **18.** Trespass for goods carried away.

_____ **19.** Emotional suffering caused by the infliction of extreme and outrageous intentional conduct by another.

_____ **20.** Knowingly.

_____ **21.** Negligent or accidental torts.

_____ **22.** A violation of the right of privacy.

_____ **23.** The use of one's property in a way that causes annoyance, inconvenience, or discomfort to another.

_____ **24.** A nuisance that affects the community at large.

_____ **25.** The right to be left alone, the right to be free from uncalled-for publicity, and the right to live without unreasonable interference by the public in private matters.

_____ **26.** The abuse or destructive use of property that is in one's rightful possession.

_____ **27.** A nuisance that disturbs one neighbor only.

_____ **28.** Emotional suffering caused by the infliction of extreme and outrageous intentional conduct by another.

Using Legal Language

Read the following story and fill in the blank lines with legal terms taken from the list of terms at the beginning of this chapter:

While looking at cars in a used car lot, Henry recognized a car that had once belonged to his friend Sam. He knew that the car had been abused by Sam and was in poor condition. A salesperson, noticing Henry looking at the car, went up to Henry and said, "This car's a beauty! It belonged to a little old lady who took it out only on Sunday morning to drive to church." Angered by this _____________________ and knowing that the salesperson was committing _____________________, which is also known as _____________________, Henry picked up a hubcap that was on the ground and threw it at the salesperson, but missed. Legally, this action was _____________________ but not _____________________. In any case, it was a(n) _____________________ act. The salesperson, now enraged, grabbed an innocent passerby, thinking she was with Henry. He detained the passerby in his office for 10 minutes, thereby committing the tort of _____________________, which is also called _____________________. Later that day, Henry accidentally sold his next-door neighbor's lawn mower to a stranger at his yard sale. When his next-door neighbor, Martha, learned of the _____________________, she called up her friend Mildred and told her that Henry was a no-good dirty rat. Although this statement was a form of _____________________, it was not actionable _____________________, because it was not one of the four situations for which suit may be brought. Later, Martha wrote a letter to the editor of the local newspaper, saying that Henry was a no-good dirty rat. The newspaper refused to print the letter because it did not want to be sued for _____________________, which is actionable _____________________. When Henry heard that Martha had written the letter to the newspaper, he went outside, picked up a huge pile of trash from his yard, and dumped it all over Martha's front lawn, thereby committing the tort of _____________________. He then swore out a criminal complaint against Martha for disturbing the peace. Martha was tried for the crime and found not guilty. She then sued Henry in tort for _____________________.

Negligence and Product Liability

ANTE INTERROGATORY

The tort doctrine that makes land owners liable when children trespass on the land owners' property and are injured because of the children's inability to appreciate the risk posed by their trespass is called the (A) attractive nuisance doctrine, (B) contributory negligence doctrine, (C) comparative negligence doctrine, (D) assumption of the risk doctrine.

3

LEARNING OBJECTIVES

LO 1: Identify the elements of a negligence action

LO 2: Explain how a landowner's duty of care been applied to those who might be on the landowner's property

LO 3: Explain the doctrine of res ipsa loquitur

LO 4: Categorize the types of compensatory damages

LO 5: Summarize the concept of proximate cause

LO 6: Identify five key defenses to a negligence claim

LO 7: Compare and contrast contributory negligence and comparative negligence

LO 8: Explain the defense of assumption of risk

LO 9: Compare and contrast a statute of limitations with a statute of repose

LO 10: Summarize what product liability is

KEY TERMS

absolute liability

affirmative defense

assumption of risk

attractive nuisance doctrine

bare licensee

business invitee

causation

comparative fault

comparative negligence

compensatory damages

contributory negligence

culpable negligence

damages

dangerous instrumentalities

design defect

duty of care

fact finder

failure to warn

foreseeable

general damages

gratuitous guest

gross negligence

humanitarian doctrine

last clear chance doctrine

liability

malpractice

manufacturing defect

negligence

ordinary negligence

pain and suffering

privity of contract

product liability

proximate cause

prudent

reasonable care

res ipsa loquitur

special damages

statute of limitations

statute of repose

strict liability

supervening cause

willful, wanton, and reckless
conduct

wrongful death action

wrongful death statutes

WEBSITES FOR PRONUNCIATION HELP

http://dictionary.cambridge.org/us/pronunciation/english/audio
https://www.howtopronounce.com

Negligence occurs when one person causes a loss or injury because of his or her own carelessness. It is an unintentional tort and is the subject matter of more lawsuits than any other tort. **Negligence** is generally defined as the failure to use the amount of care and skill that a reasonably prudent person would have used under the same circumstances and conditions.

ELEMENTS OF NEGLIGENCE

To win a negligence case, the injured party must prove all of the following:

1. Duty of care owed by the defendant to the plaintiff;
2. Breach of duty (negligent act);
3. Damages; and
4. Causation.

Duty of Care

In order to be liable to another for a harmful action (or inaction), the person who commits the harm must first owe a **duty of care** to the injured party. Although difficult to define, a duty of care is a legal obligation of carefulness or prudence owed to those who are likely (or foreseeably likely) to be injured by one's conduct. For instance, a parent owes a duty of care to his or her child, but not to someone else's child generally. But duties change according to the circumstances. So, if that parent's child has a friend over for a visit, then the parent has now voluntarily undertaken a duty of care to the other child. A duty of care is generally created through relationships (parent to child), through statute (drivers of cars to others on the road or in their paths), or through contract (lifeguards employed to keep watch over swimmers).

Until recently, the law recognized different *degrees of care* owed to different people. The duty of care owed to a **business invitee** (one invited on the premises for a business or commercial purpose) was to refrain from **ordinary negligence** (the want of ordinary care). The duty of care owed to a **gratuitous guest** (one invited on the premises for nonbusiness purposes) was to refrain from gross negligence. **Gross negligence** is extreme negligence. Under this older legal doctrine, a gratuitous guest could not recover for damages caused by a host's ordinary negligence. The duty of care owed to a trespasser and a **bare licensee** (a person allowed on another's premises by operation of law, such as a firefighter or police officer) was to refrain from **willful, wanton, and reckless conduct**. This conduct, also called **culpable negligence** is the intentional commission of an act that a reasonable person knows would cause injury to another. It is more serious than gross negligence.

Some states have eliminated the different degrees of care discussed above. Instead, they hold that property owners owe a duty to use **reasonable care** toward everyone who is rightfully on their premises. This degree of care is one that a reasonable person would have used under the circumstances then known. Because a trespasser is not rightfully on the premises, the duty of care owed to such a person is to refrain from willful, wanton, and reckless conduct.

One exception to the principle regarding the degree of care owed to trespassers is the **attractive nuisance doctrine**, which protects children who are enticed to trespass on another's property because of an attraction that exists there, such as a swimming pool in a backyard. In states that follow the doctrine, property owners owe a duty to refrain from ordinary negligence, rather than simply from willful, wanton, and reckless conduct, toward children who are attracted to the premises by a condition that normally attracts children, even though the children are trespassers. For instance, Florida has an attractive nuisance statute that declares discarded or abandoned refrigerators, iceboxes, clothe washers or dryers, and other airtight units with the doors still attached to be attractive nuisances to children, and another statute makes it a misdemeanor to leave on one's property such discarded units with the doors still attached (§ 823.07-.09 Fla. Stat.).

Breach of Duty (Negligent Act)

Whether or not an act is negligent and, therefore, breaches the duty of care owed to the plaintiff, is normally a question of fact to be decided by the fact finder, rather than a question of law to be decided by the judge. The **fact finder** (or trier of fact) is the jury in a jury trial or the judge in a nonjury trial. The fact finder must ask the question, "Did the defendant do (or fail to do) that which a reasonably **prudent** (cautious) person would have done under the same circumstances and conditions?" If the defendant is a child, the fact finder must ask, "Did the defendant exercise the degree of care that a reasonably prudent child of the same age, intelligence, and experience would have exercised under the same circumstances and conditions?" If the defendant is a physician, the fact finder must ask, "Did the defendant exercise the degree of care and skill of the average qualified physician, considering the advances in the medical profession?" Negligence of a physician, attorney, or other professional is commonly referred to as **malpractice**. In many states, medical expert testimony is required for the plaintiff to establish medical malpractice, and in some states a plaintiff must first present her or his claim to a state-run medical review panel before filing a lawsuit.

DOCTRINE OF RES IPSA LOQUITUR.   To recover for negligence, evidence must be introduced by the plaintiff to prove the negligent act of the defendant. Sometimes, the plaintiff has no evidence to prove that a negligent act was committed by the defendant; however, the plaintiff can prove that he or she was injured by an act that normally does not occur unless someone is negligent, such as in a rear-end automobile collision. The doctrine of **res ipsa loquitur**, which means "the thing speaks for itself," can sometimes be used by the plaintiff when he or she cannot prove an actual negligent act of the defendant, but can argue that the type of injury suffered normally would not occur unless the defendant was negligent. Under this doctrine, the mere fact that an act occurred can be used by the jury (or by the judge in a nonjury trial) to infer that the defendant was negligent. When the doctrine is used, the case can go to the jury if it is probable (not just possible) that a negligent act of the defendant caused the plaintiff's injury. The first and, therefore, most famous case to apply this doctrine was *Byrne v. Boadle*, a British case from 1863. A man was walking down the street and— out of nowhere!—a barrel of flour fell on the his head. He had no way of proving that the warehouse next to the sidewalk and from whose second-floor window the barrel came was negligent in storing its barrels. But the court ruled the plaintiff could allege that such a thing wouldn't have happened had it not been for the warehouse's negligence.

ABSOLUTE LIABILITY.   People who handle **dangerous instrumentalities** such as explosives or wild animals are liable, regardless of fault, for injuries to others caused by the dangerous item. Such liability regardless of fault is known as **absolute or strict liability**.

> ### Word Wise
> *Res Ipsa Loquitur ("the thing speaks for itself")*
>
> The "ipsa" in *res ipsa loquitur* is a form of the Latin term *ipse* meaning "myself, himself, herself, or itself." Here are some other uses of the term:
>
> > *ipse dixit* = he himself said it (something asserted, but not proved).
> >
> > *ipso facto* = by the fact (or act) itself (by the mere effect or nature of an act or fact).
> >
> > *ipso jure* = by the law itself (by the mere operation of the law).

Damages

To recover for negligence, the plaintiff must prove **damages**—that is, some actual loss. Even though the defendant may have committed a negligent act, the plaintiff cannot recover unless he or she suffers damages. Various kinds of damages are discussed in Chapter 18.

The amount of **compensatory damages**, sometimes called actual damages, that the plaintiff can recover is the amount of money that will place the plaintiff in the same position that he or she was in before the negligent act occurred. **Special damages** are measurable, quantifiable amounts of losses and include the cost of hospital and medical treatment, and any lost wages. **General damages** are money meant to compensate the plaintiff for **pain and suffering** (physical discomfort and emotional trauma) that she or he endured.

When someone dies as a result of another's negligence, the suit that is brought is called a **wrongful death action**. This suit is brought by the decedent's personal representative against the negligent party for the benefit of the decedent's heirs. Such suits are governed by **wrongful death statutes** found in each state.

Causation

To recover for negligence, the plaintiff must prove **causation**—that is, that the negligent act of the defendant was the direct and **proximate cause** (the dominant, or primary, cause) of the plaintiff's injuries. In determining proximate cause, the important issue is whether the harm that resulted from the conduct was **foreseeable** (known in advance; anticipated) when it took place. Proximate cause is about that which is probable, rather than that which is possible (because anything is possible). So, the more likely or probable an outcome, the more foreseeable it is. Suppose a bar serves liquor to a clearly intoxicated person who after leaving the bar negligently drives into another car, killing that driver. Even before statutes were passed making the server liable (those laws are often called dram shop laws), one can see that the bartender's act of serving a drink to the intoxicated person was a proximate cause of death. A jury could conclude the bartender could have foreseen that the intoxicated person would be driving home and might cause death or injury to another.

Conversely, the plaintiff cannot recover damages if a break in the chain of causation exists. For example, when a car owner leaves the key in a car (which is a statutory violation in some states) and a thief steals the car and injures someone while driving negligently, the car owner's act of leaving the key in the car is not the direct and proximate cause of the injury. Rather, the negligent act of the thief was a **supervening cause**—that is, a new occurrence that becomes the proximate cause of the injury. The injured party cannot recover from the car owner. These types of superseding intervening causes are determined based on the uniqueness of each fact pattern, but the doctrine is consistent: where an unforeseen, unanticipated event follows the defendant's negligent conduct and injures the plaintiff, that subsequent event can mitigate or even eliminate the defendant's liability.

DEFENSES TO NEGLIGENCE

The principal defenses to negligence actions are (1) contributory negligence, (2) comparative negligence, (3) assumption of the risk, (4) discharge in bankruptcy, and (5) running of the statute of limitations.

Contributory Negligence

Contributory negligence is negligence on the part of the plaintiff that contributed toward the injuries and was a proximate cause of them. Under the traditional doctrine of contributory negligence, if the defendant can prove that the plaintiff was also negligent, no matter how slightly, and that the plaintiff's negligence contributed to the injury or loss, the plaintiff will lose at trial. An exception exists under a rule known as the **last clear chance doctrine** in some states and as the **humanitarian doctrine** in others. Accordingly, a defendant who had the last clear chance to have avoided injuring the plaintiff is liable even though the plaintiff had also been responsible for contributory negligence.

Many states no longer follow the doctrine of contributory negligence, because of its unfairness to plaintiffs who were only slightly negligent. These states have adopted the doctrine of comparative negligence in its place.

Comparative Negligence

In **comparative negligence** jurisdictions (called **comparative fault** in some jurisdictions), the negligence of all parties is compared, and the plaintiff's damages are reduced in proportion to his or her negligence. In determining by what amount the plaintiff's damages are to be diminished, the negligence of the plaintiff is compared with the total negligence of all persons against whom recovery is sought. The combined total of the plaintiff's negligence and all of the negligence of all defendants must equal 100 percent. For example, in a case in which the total damages are $100,000, if the jury finds that the plaintiff was 40 percent negligent and the defendant was 60 percent negligent, the plaintiff will recover $60,000. Likewise, if the jury finds that each party was 50 percent negligent, the plaintiff will recover $50,000. In many comparative negligence jurisdictions, if the jury finds that the plaintiff was 51 percent negligent and the defendant was 49 percent negligent, the plaintiff will recover nothing.

TERMS IN ACTION

In 2003, a man riding the train home from his job in Chicago exited his passenger car at his stop and immediately fell to the ground because the train had overshot the platform. The man, who was riding in the first car, fell to the ground, severely injuring his knee, including tearing his anterior cruciate ligament (ACL) and his lateral meniscus cartilage. He sued the railroad company for **negligence**, not only because the train conductor failed to stop the train at the platform correctly, but also because the train car doors opened, which isn't supposed to happen when the train overshoots the platform. At the trial a few years later, the judge gave a directed verdict to the man, but ordered the jury to determine how much of the man's own conduct contributed to his injuries. Although the railroad company failed to use **reasonable care** and was the **proximate cause** of the accident, the jury determined that the man was **comparatively negligent** for immediately exiting his train car when he knew the car wasn't at the platform and yet didn't ask for help. The jury calculated his comparative fault at 50 percent and reduced his **damages** from $250,000 to $125,000. Curiously, the man who was stung by the doctrine of comparative negligence was an attorney.

Sources: passenlaw.com; *Richard C. Moenning v. Union Pacific Railroad, et al.* No. 1-08-0543 (unpublished, 2009).

Assumption of Risk

In a suit for negligence, if the defendant can show that the plaintiff knew of the risk involved and took the chance of being injured, he or she may claim **assumption of risk** as a defense. Assumption of risk is an **affirmative defense**, and when a defendant raises an affirmative defense, the defendant bears the burden of proving it. Namely, assumption of risk involves proving the plaintiff's injuries were a result of the plaintiff's voluntary and intentional exposure to a known dangerous condition. For example, assumption of risk has been raised against persons hit by foul balls (or flying baseball bats) while sitting in the stands at baseball games. In fact, this defense has been so often used by baseball teams, the defense was occasionally called the baseball rule.

Discharge in Bankruptcy

A lawsuit alleging negligence cannot be brought against a defendant if the defendant has been discharged in a bankruptcy proceeding and the plaintiff's claim is included among the defendant's debts.

Statutes of Limitations and Repose

Every cause of action has a time limit for bringing suit. A **statute of limitations** is a time limit, set by statute, within which a suit must be commenced after the cause of action accrues. A cause of action accrues when a suit may be brought for damages. In negligence cases, the statute of limitations begins to run either on the date of the injury or on the date that the injury was, or should have been, discovered. For example, if the statute of limitations for a personal injury suit is two years and a person had no way of knowing of the injury until three years after the incident, the plaintiff would theoretically have five total years from the date of the incident to file a suit. A **statute of repose** on the other hand, places an absolute time limit for bringing a cause of action regardless of when the cause of action accrues. The following is Arizona's Statute of Repose for certain kinds of suits over real estate:

> Notwithstanding any other statute, no action or arbitration based in contract may be instituted or maintained against a person who develops or develops and sells real property, or performs or furnishes the design, specifications, surveying, planning, supervision, testing, construction or observation of construction of an improvement to real property more than eight years after substantial completion of the improvement to real property. (A.R.S. § 12-552)

Notice that the statute places an eight-year maximum time limit on the types of claims listed, regardless of when a plaintiff might discover that it has a cause of action.

PRODUCT LIABILITY

Liability (legal responsibility) of manufacturers, sellers, and lessors (those who lease products) to compensate people for injuries suffered because of defects in their products is a tort known as **product liability**. Under modern legal theory, people who are injured by defective products can bring suit against the manufacturers or sellers of the products whether or not the injured persons purchased the products. There is no requirement of **privity of contract** (the legal relationship between contracting parties) to recover for injuries from defective goods. In addition, it is not always necessary to prove a negligent act on the part of the manufacturer or seller. Product liability is based on alternative theories of liability. **Design defect** is the theory that the product was negligently designed or could have been designed more safely. **Manufacturing defect** is the theory that the product was negligently built or built with substandard materials. **Failure to warn** (also called inadequate warnings) is the theory that the product's dangers were inadequately labeled or communicated to the consumer or user.

Under a theory of strict liability, which was first applied in America in 1963 by the California Supreme Court in *Greenman v. Yuba Power Products* (59 Cal. 2d 57), manufacturers and sellers can be liable without regard to fault. This type of liability is applied if it is shown that the product was sold in a defective condition, that it was unreasonably dangerous to the user or consumer, and that the defective condition was the proximate cause of the injury or damage. The rationale of strict liability is that if neither the plaintiff nor the defendant is at fault, the defendant should pay the damages because it is a corporation and therefore is more able to absorb the costs of injury.

TERMS IN ACTION

George Allen Ward brought a **product liability** lawsuit against the maker of ARM & HAMMER Baking Soda in 2003, seeking a total of $425 million dollars. This was not a class action suit, where Ward was suing on behalf of thousands of other plaintiffs. In fact, Ward was representing himself *pro se*, and typed the complaint…from federal prison. What could baking soda have done that caused so much harm? According to Ward's complaint, Arm & Hammer was the **proximate cause** of his 200-month prison sentence for having been made and sold crack cocaine. Crack is relatively simple to make (once one has cocaine) and baking soda is one of its ingredients. Ward alleged that ARM & HAMMER, which had put five warnings on its baking soda boxes (including, "do not administer to children under 5 years of age."), failed to provide adequate notice to him that using its product for illegal drug manufacturing is illegal would be harmful to his freedom. Furthering his **failure to warn** theory, Ward stated in his complaint, "I feel as if I was forewarned by this company that I'd never used this product as I was charged with…." Ward's case was dismissed in 2004, wherein the U.S. District Judge said that a manufacturer of a product has no duty to warn of the potential consequences of its criminal misuse.

Sources: legalreader.com; overlawyered.com; abovethelaw.com

Reviewing What You Learned

After studying the chapter, write the answers to each of the following questions:

1. Name the tort that is the subject matter of more lawsuits than any other tort. _______________________________

   ____

   ____

   ____

2. List three elements that an injured party must prove to recover for negligence. _______________________________

   ____

   ____

   ____

3. Who is the fact finder in a jury trial? In a nonjury trial? _____

   ____

   ____

   ____

4. What degree of care must be exercised by a child to avoid negligence? _______________________________

   ____

   ____

   ____

5. What degree of care must be exercised by a physician to avoid negligence? _______________________________

   ____

   ____

   ____

6. Until recently, what degree of care was owed to a business invitee? To a gratuitous guest? To a bare licensee? _______

   ____

   ____

7. What degree of care is owed to the parties named in question 6, under modern law in many states? _______________________

____

____

____

8. What degree of care is owed to a trespasser? ___________

____

____

____

9. When may the doctrine of res ipsa loquitur be used to prove negligence? _______________________________________

____

____

____

10. What is the difference between special damages and general damages?_______________________________________

____

____

____

11. What must the plaintiff prove relative to causation in order to recover for negligence?_______________________________

____

____

____

12. List four defenses to negligence. _______________________

____

____

____

13. What is the difference between contributory negligence and comparative negligence?_______________________________

____

____

____

14. What defense is sometimes used by a baseball club when it is sued by a spectator for being injured by a ball that is hit into the stands?_______________________________________

____

____

____

15. What is the difference between a statute of limitations and a statute of repose?_______________________________________

____

____

____

16. List and explain three product liability theories. ___________

____

____

____

Understanding Legal Concepts

Indicate whether each statement is true or false. Then, change the italicized word or phrase of each false statement to make it true.

ANSWERS

_______ 1. Whether or not an act is negligent is normally a question of *law*.

_______ 2. For a *negligent* act to occur, a duty of care must be owed by the defendant to the plaintiff, and a breach of that duty must occur.

_______ 3. In states that follow the attractive nuisance doctrine, property owners owe a duty to refrain from *gross negligence* toward children who are attracted to the premises by a condition that normally attracts children.

_______ 4. When the doctrine of res ipsa loquitur is used, the case can go to the jury if it is *probable* that a negligent act of the defendant caused the plaintiff's injury.

_______ 5. Even though a negligent act may be committed by the defendant, no recovery by the plaintiff can occur unless he or she *suffers damages*.

_______ 6. When a thief steals a car with keys left in it and injures a pedestrian, the pedestrian *can* recover from the car owner for damages.

_____ **7.** Many states *no longer* follow the doctrine of contributory negligence, because of its unfairness to plaintiffs who were only slightly negligent.

_____ **8.** Contributory negligence is negligence on the part of the *defendant,* which contributed toward the injuries and was a proximate cause of them.

_____ **9.** In a case involving comparative negligence, if the jury finds that the plaintiff was 51 percent negligent and the defendant was 49 percent negligent, the plaintiff will recover *nothing.*

_____ **10.** *No* time limit exists for bringing suit for the tort of negligence.

_____ **11.** Money for the plaintiff to compensate for pain and suffering is called *special damages.*

_____ **12.** *Manufacturing defect* is the theory that a product was negligently designed.

Checking Terminology

From the list of legal terms that follows, select the one that matches each definition.

ANSWERS

a. absolute liability
b. assumption of the risk
c. attractive nuisance doctrine
d. bare licensee
e. business invitee
f. causation
g. comparative fault
h. comparative negligence
i. compensatory damages
j. contributory negligence
k. culpable negligence
l. damages
m. dangerous instrumentalities
n. design defect
o. duty of care
p. fact finder
q. failure to warn
r. foreseeable
s. general damages
t. gratuitous guest
u. gross negligence
v. humanitarian doctrine
w. last clear chance doctrine
x. liability
y. malpractice
z. manufacturing defect
aa. negligence
bb. ordinary negligence
cc. pain and suffering
dd. privity of contract
ee. product liability
ff. proximate cause
gg. prudent
hh. reasonable care
ii. res ipsa loquitur
jj. special damages
kk. statute of limitations
ll. statute of repose
mm. strict liability
nn. supervening cause
oo. willful, wanton, and reckless conduct
pp. wrongful death action
qq. wrongful death statutes

_____ **1.** Extreme negligence.

_____ **2.** One invited on the premises for a business or commercial purpose.

_____ **3.** The thing speaks for itself.

_____ **4.** A time limit, set by statute, within which a suit must be commenced after the cause of action accrues.

_____ **5.** The intentional commission of an act that a reasonable person knows would cause injury to another. (Select two answers.)

_____ **6.** A relationship between contracting parties.

_____ **7.** The failure to use that amount of care and skill that a reasonably prudent person would have used under the same circumstances and conditions.

_____ **8.** A person allowed on another's premises by operation of law, such as a firefighter or police officer.

_____ **9.** A doctrine under which a defendant who had the last clear chance to have avoided injuring the plaintiff is liable even though the plaintiff had also been responsible for some contributory negligence. (Select two answers.)

_____ **10.** A monetary loss suffered by a party as a result of a wrong.

_____ **11.** The situation wherein the plaintiff assumes consequences of injury; the employee agrees that dangers of injury shall be at his or her own risk.

_____ **12.** Professional misconduct; negligence of a professional.

_____ **13.** The degree of care that a reasonable person would have used under the circumstances then known.

_____ **14.** Liability of manufacturers and sellers to compensate people for injuries suffered because of defects in their products.

_____ **15.** The proportionate sharing between the plaintiff and the defendant of the legal responsibility for injuries, according to the relative negligence of the two. (Select two answers.)

_____ **16.** A new occurrence that became the proximate cause of the injury.

_____ **17.** One invited on the premises for nonbusiness purposes.

_____ **18.** The jury in a jury trial or the judge in a nonjury trial.

_____ **19.** Physical discomfort and emotional trauma.

_____ **20.** Liability for an act that causes harm without regard to fault or negligence.

_____ **21.** A suit brought by a decedent's personal representative for the benefit of the decedent's heirs, claiming that death was caused by the defendant's negligent act.

_____ **22.** Cautious.

_____ **23.** Hazardous items such as explosives and wild animals.

_____ **24.** Legislative enactments that govern wrongful death actions.

_____ **25.** Measurable amounts of losses including the cost of medical treatment and loss of wages.

_____ **26.** A doctrine establishing property owners' duty to use ordinary care toward trespassing children who might reasonably be attracted to their property.

_____ **27.** Negligence on the part of the plaintiff, which contributed toward the injuries and was a proximate cause of them.

_____ **28.** An absolute time limit for bringing a cause of action regardless of when the cause of action accrues.

_____ **29.** Money meant to compensate the plaintiff for pain and suffering he endured.
_____ **30.** The theory that a product was negligently built.
_____ **31.** The direct and proximate cause of someone's injuries.
_____ **32.** Legal responsibility.
_____ **33.** The amount of money that will place the plaintiff in the same position that he was in immediately before the negligent act occurred.
_____ **34.** A legal obligation of carefulness owed to those who are likely to be injured by one's conduct.
_____ **35.** A theory that the product was negligently designed or could have been designed more safely.
_____ **36.** A theory that the product's dangers were inadequately labeled.
_____ **37.** The dominant or primary cause.
_____ **38.** Known in advance; anticipated.
_____ **39.** The failure to exercise ordinary care.

Sharpening Your Latin Skills

In the space provided, write the definition of each of the following legal terms, referring to the glossary when necessary.

per se _________________________________   respondeat superior _________________________________

res _________________________________   scienter _________________________________

res ipsa loquitur _________________________________

Using Legal Language

Read the following story and fill in the blank lines with legal terms taken from the list of terms at the beginning of this chapter:

While shopping in a grocery store, Alison slipped on some liquids that had accumulated in the floor where samples of a new iced tea were being given away. Alison was a(n) _________________________ (customer), and the _________________________ (carelessness) of the store employees, who were not _________________________ (cautious), caused the accident. Because the wrongful act was not extreme, the degree of wrong would probably be considered _________________________ rather than _________________________. The physician who treated Alison for her injuries was capable and not responsible for _________________________, although the amount of the physician's bill became part of Alison's _________________________. When Alison arrived home, she noticed a police car in front of her house and saw a police officer inside. The officer, who was a(n) _________________________, told her that a neighborhood child had wandered without permission into Alison's pool area and had almost drowned. A friend of Alison, who was visiting at the time, had rescued the child from drowning. The legal status of the friend was that of a(n) _________________________. Because the child was a trespasser, Alison's obligation to her would normally have been to refrain from _________________________ unless the _________________________ doctrine required her to use ordinary care. Should the case go to court, the jury, which is the _________________________, will have to determine whether the child was negligent if the state follows the doctrine of _________________________ or the percentage of negligence of each party if the state follows the doctrine of _________________________. Because it is not probable, but merely possible, that Alison was negligent, the plaintiff would not be able to use the doctrine of _________________________ to prove the case. Similarly, it is doubtful that Alison can use the defense of _________________________ _________________________ or _________________________ if suit is brought promptly.

PART FOUR

Terms Used in Law of Contracts

Thinkstock/Stockbyte/Getty Images

CHAPTER 18
Formation of Contracts

CHAPTER 19
Contract Requirements

CHAPTER 20
Third Parties and Discharge of Contract

CHAPTER 21
The Uniform Commercial Code and Sales of Goods Contracts

4

The law of contracts lies at the core of most personal and business transactions that we become involved with during our lifetime. A contract occurs whenever we buy or sell something, provide or receive services for a fee, employ someone or become employed, rent an apartment, attend college, and in many other contexts during our lives. **Chapter 18** breaks down the subject of contracts into various classifications. Contract requirements, including consideration, writing essentials, defective agreements, and illegality, are examined in Chapter 19. After discussing the subjects of assignment and delegation of contracts, Chapter 20 surveys the various methods of ending contractual obligations and Chapter 21 provides an overview of a particular, but often-made type of contract: sales of goods contracts—which are governed by the Uniform Commercial Code.

18

Formation of Contracts

ANTE INTERROGATORY

In most cases, contracts made by minors are (A) misdemeanors,
(B) void, (C) voidable, (D) unenforceable.

LEARNING OBJECTIVES

LO 1: Explain how a contract is formed

LO 2: Identify the four classifications of contracts

LO 3: Contrast an express contract from an implied contract

LO 4: Contrast a bilateral contract from a unilateral contract

LO 5: Explain the difference between a void, voidable, and unenforceable contract

LO 6: Contrast an executed contract from an executor contract

LO 7: Distinguish the ways in which e-contracts can entered

KEY TERMS

acceptance
avoid
bargain
bilateral contract
browsewrap contract
capacity
clickwrap agreement
condition precedent
contract
contract implied in fact
contract implied in law
counteroffer
digital signature
disaffirm
e-contract
executed
executory
express contract

implied contract
infant
invitation to deal
invitation to negotiate
majority
minor
necessaries
nullity
offer
offeree
offeror
quasi
quasi contract
ratify
rejection
restitution
revocation
shrinkwrap contract
suretyship

4

unenforceable contract	valid
unilateral contract	void
unjust enrichment	voidable

WEBSITES FOR PRONUNCIATION HELP

http://dictionary.cambridge.org/us/pronunciation/english/audio
https://www.howtopronounce.com

CONTRACT FORMATION

In its simplest terms, a **contract** is any agreement that is enforceable in a court of law.

To reach an agreement, one party (called the **offeror**) makes an **offer** (a proposal) to another party (called the **offeree**) to enter into a legally enforceable (binding) agreement. If the offeree assents to the terms of the offer, an **acceptance** occurs and an agreement, sometimes called a **bargain** comes into existence. To illustrate, if one person says to another, "I'll sell you my car for $2,500" (the offer), and the other person replies, "I'll buy it" (the acceptance), a contract is formed the moment the words of acceptance are spoken. If instead, the other person replies, "No way!" that is a **rejection**—the offeree's refusal of an offer. A rejection terminates the offer. When the other person responds with a different offer instead of accepting the one that was made, that is called a **counteroffer**. For instance, if instead of saying, "No way!" the offeree says, "I like your old car, but not that much. I'll give you $2,000 for it," that would be a counteroffer. Like a rejection, a counteroffer extinguishes an offer. A **revocation** occurs when the offeror has a change of mind and takes back the offer before the offeree accepts it. Suppose that, before the offeree can say yes or no to the offer of the car for $2,500, the seller says, "Never mind. I don't feel like selling it today." That would be a revocation, which terminates the offer.

When an offer (or contract) contains a condition precedent, the other party is not obligated to perform until the prerequisite is carried out. For example, if I agree to buy your car only if you have the brakes fixed, I would have no obligation to buy it unless you have the repairs made. A **condition precedent** is an event that must first occur before an agreement (or deed or will) becomes effective.

TERMS IN ACTION

Is getting engaged a **contract**, and if it is, then does breaking off an engagement constitute a breach of contract? Few, if any, contracts questions are more personal than those relating to agreements to marry. Most jurisdictions stay out of romantic disputes because those types of agreements are thought to not include the kind of **consideration** that courts want to measure. Likewise, no-fault divorces can be obtained without the party seeking the divorce having to prove a breach of any promise by the other spouse. But in 2008, a six-man six-woman jury in Georgia awarded a woman $150,000 because her fiancé called off their wedding. Evidently, RoseMary Shell (the **offeree**) agreed to marry Wayne Gibbs (the **offeror**) and then moved from Pensacola, Florida, to Gainesville, Georgia, where Gibbs lived. She left behind an $81,000-per-year job and found a job paying $34,000 annually. Three months later, Gibbs broke off the engagement. He had contemplated it even earlier, but shortly before the wedding, Gibbs let Shell know of his change of heart through a conspicuously-placed note in their bathroom, and a $5,000 check. In his defense at the trial, Gibbs testified that he had made some of Shell's mortgage payments and paid off $30,000 of Shell's debts, but when he realized she had even more debt than he originally realized, he broke off the wedding. The trial judge instructed the jury that "breach of a promise to marry is a common law contract action. By the very nature of this action, there must be an actual promise to marry and **acceptance** of that promise before one can be held liable for a breach." The $150,000 damages amount was based on Shell's old salary, bonuses, and benefits.

Sources: gainesvilletimes.com; today.msnbc.msn.com; abajournal.com

Advertisements, including price tags, prices on merchandise, signs, and prices in catalogs are not usually treated as offers. Instead, such an advertisement is called an **invitation to negotiate** or an **invitation to deal**. Although it seems counterintuitive to think this way, the common law of contracts treats an advertisement—such as listing your car for $2,500 in a classified ad—as being your invitation to the reader to find you and then "offer" you $2,500 for your car. For this reason, a contract does not usually arise when a customer offers to buy a mismarked product unless the store accepts the customer's offer and agrees to sell the product at the mismarked price. Stores might honor the mismarked price for the sake of customer relations, but that does not affect the underlying doctrine that, generally, advertisements are not offers.

CONTRACT CLASSIFICATIONS

Contracts may be classified in the following ways:

1. express and implied
2. bilateral and unilateral
3. valid, void, voidable, and unenforceable
4. executed and executory

Express and Implied Contracts

An **express contract** is one in which the terms of the contract are stated by the parties, either orally or in writing. An **implied contract** is one in which the terms of the contract are not stated by the parties, but their behavior shows them to be in a contract. For instance, if a business has for many months delivered parts that the receiving company uses to make a product and then resell, and the two parties have long since stopped exchanging terms (because the price hasn't gone up, let's say), the parties are in an implied contract.

Two types of implied contracts are a contract implied in fact and a contract implied in law. A **contract implied in fact** is a contract that arises from the conduct of the parties rather than from their express statements. For example, when you board a bus and pay the fare without saying anything to the driver, and the driver says nothing to you, no express contract exists because the terms were not stated; however, a contract implied in fact exists that the bus driver will take you to a destination along that bus's particular route.

Unjust enrichment occurs when one person retains money, property, or other benefit that in equity and justice belongs to another. Situations involving unjust enrichment can occur when a party receives contract-like benefits without having paid for them, which seems somewhat like the tort of conversion. Sometimes, to prevent unjust enrichment, the court will impose a contract on the parties when one actually does not exist or when an express contract cannot be enforced. This court-imposed obligation is called a **contract implied in law** or **quasi contract**. The term **quasi** means "as if" or "almost as it were." For example, if a cable TV customer gets premium channels for a year that the customer didn't order (or protest), but has paid only the standard rate for a year, the customer has been unjustly enriched and could be required to pay 12 months of premium-channel prices. A person who has been unjustly enriched at the expense of another is required to make **restitution**—that is, restore the other person to his or her original position prior to the loss.

Bilateral and Unilateral Contracts

The primary distinction between an unenforceable agreement and an agreement qualifying as a contract is that a contract involves an exchange between the parties, and at least one of the things being exchanged has to be a promise. Contracts are classified according to the number of promises made by the parties. A **bilateral contract** is a contract containing two promises, one made by each party to the contract. One party makes a promise in exchange for the other party's promise. For example, if someone says, "I'll sell you my laptop computer for $400," and the other party replies, "I'll buy it," a bilateral contract has been made because both parties made and

Carol M. Highsmith's America, Library of Congress, Prints and Photographs Division [LC-DIG-highsm-04756]

FIGURE 18-1   A reward offer is an example of a unilateral contract, which comes into existence when the offer is accepted by the performance of an act.

exchanged promises. Notice that a bilateral contract doesn't need the word "promise" to be used for there to be an exchange of promises. It is the form of the agreement, not the exact words, that make a particular contract bilateral.

A **unilateral contract** is a contract containing only one promise in exchange for an act, often referred to as a performance. Suppose, for example, that a person offers a $100 reward for the return of a lost dog. The only way that the offer can be accepted is by the actual return of the lost dog to the offeror. When that happens, the offer is accepted.

In a bilateral contract, consideration (which is discussed in Chapter 19) is found in the promises of each party. In a unilateral contract, consideration is found in the promise of the offeror and the act of the offeree. Winning a prize for being first in a contest or race (think of the Indianapolis 500) is the result of a unilateral contract, because promising to win the contest or promising to try to win the contest has no bearing on the prize being given.

TERMS IN ACTION

Karen Kershaw, of Akron, Ohio, couldn't afford to pay the remaining $600 for a truck she wanted to buy from Rick Remmy, a used car dealer. So, according to her lawsuit, Remmy presented to her—on Valentine's Day, 2000—a **contract** allowing her to pay for the truck by performing certain "favors" for him. The value of each performance-payment was based on its type of favor. Although Kershaw denied agreeing to such a contract, she made two of these types of personal-services payments, and Remmy kept track of her remaining balance on the front of an envelope. She also helped to pay for the truck by giving him cigarettes, and she got a receipt for that payment. Eventually, Ms. Kershaw went to the police, who told her that she was committing prostitution. Since that is illegal, their alleged **bilateral contract** would be **void**. Yet, Ms. Kershaw filed a small claims court suit seeking $212. Both parties then agreed to resolve their dispute on the television show "The People's Court," whose judge at that time was Jerry Sheindlin, the husband of TV's "Judge Judy." Judge Jerry awarded Ms. Kershaw $125 (paid by the show's producers). When Remmy returned home from the TV show's taping in New York, he was arrested—not for compelling prostitution, but for violating his probation (stemming from a 1998 car theft conviction) by leaving the state. He was sentenced to nine months in jail.

Sources: thesmokinggun.com; nydailynews.com

Valid, Void, Voidable, and Unenforceable Contracts

A **valid** contract is one that meets all of the requirements of an enforceable agreement. In a sense, the term "valid contract" is redundant because an agreement that is unenforceable isn't a contract, so it couldn't be valid. A **void** contract, conversely, is a **nullity** and has no legal effect. For the same reason that an agreement having the required elements of enforceability doesn't need to be called a "valid" contract, but simply a contract, an alleged agreement that fails to qualify as a contract is considered void, but is commonly referred to as a void contract. For instance, an illegal contract, such as one for the sale of an item that is prohibited to be bought and sold (marijuana, for instance), is void.

A **voidable** contract is one that may be **disaffirmed** or **avoided** (repudiated; gotten out of) by one of the parties, if he or she wishes, because of some rule of law that excuses that party's performance. It is sometimes said that a voidable contract is one that is valid unless voided. For example, a contract entered into between an **infant** (the legal name for a **minor**) and an adult is voidable by the minor, but not by the adult. For example, if a 16-year-old buys a car from an adult, the minor may disaffirm the contract and return the car in exchange for the money paid (even if the seller spent the money). An exception to the doctrine that minors may disaffirm their contracts while they are still minors concerns contracts that minors make for necessaries. **Necessaries** (sometimes called necessities, as mentioned in the "Word Wise" below) include food, clothing, shelter, and medical care that are needed by the minor, but not being supplied by the parent or guardian.

Although minors are responsible for paying for the fair value of their necessaries, at their option they may disaffirm most other contracts on the ground that they lack **capacity** (legal competency) to contract. When minors reach **majority** (adulthood, which is 18 years old in most jurisdictions), they may **ratify**—that is, approve or confirm—earlier contracts made during their minority and thus be bound by them. Ratification can be made by continuing to make payments for an item purchased during infancy, or even by failing to disaffirm a contract within a reasonable time after reaching majority status. Some states make exceptions to the general rule on minors' contracts, including allowing the other party to offset the money to be returned to the minor by an amount equivalent to any depreciation in the item the minor is returning. And some states grant minors the authority to make certain types of contracts. For example, despite having 18 as the cutoff age for being a minor, North Carolina has a statute that allows certain 16-year-olds to make the following type of contract:

> A minor who is 16 years of age or older and who is in the legal custody of the county department of social services shall be qualified and competent to contract for the purchase of an automobile insurance policy with the consent of the court with continuing jurisdiction over the minor's placement…. (N.C.G.S.A. § 48A-4)

An **unenforceable contract** is one that is valid, but cannot be enforced for some legal reason. An oral contract for the sale of real property is an example of an unenforceable contract, because a real estate contract is required to be in writing to be enforceable. Statutes often declare what contracts need to be in writing (and signed) in order to be enforceable, known as statutes of frauds. Typically, the contracts included in a statute of frauds are:

1. Contracts for the sale of real estate
2. Contracts in consideration of marriage (prenuptial agreements)
3. Contracts that, by their terms, cannot be completed within one year from the date of making the contract
4. Promises to a creditor to pay someone else's debts (called **suretyship)**
5. Promises by the executor of the estate of a dead person to personally pay for the estate's debts
6. Contracts for sales of goods where the purchase price is at least $500 (discussed in more detail in Chapter 21)

Where parties have already acted as if they were in an enforceable contract, courts will not undo their past contractual transactions, because unenforceability is about being able to avoid future contract performance. To illustrate, if a buyer is unhappy about the price paid for a house after moving into the house, she or he cannot seek a refund from the seller based on the Statute of Frauds because the contract has been performed. There is no enforceability to avoid. The Statute of Frauds is discussed in more detail in Chapter 19.

Word Wise
Necessaries v. Necessities

The definition of "necessities" in standard dictionaries lists food, clothing, and shelter as specific items necessary to sustain life. In legal dictionaries, however, the term is often given a broader meaning as well as a different spelling. For example, a "see necessaries" reference is listed under the term "necessities" in *Black's Law Dictionary*. This is because in the legal use of the term, "necessaries" include not only what maintains life, but also what is required to preserve the standard of living to which an individual is accustomed. Thus, "necessaries" often relate to the standard established by the rank, position, and earning power of a buyer or those of his or her parent or spouse.

Web Wise

- For an overview of contract law, with links to recent, contracts court decisions, go to www.law.cornell.edu/wex/contract, which is part of the Legal Information Institute web site, of the Cornell University School of Law

Executed and Executory Contracts

Contracts that are completely carried out (both sides' performance duties have been fully completed) are said to be **executed**. Those that have come into existence (i.e., there has been offer and acceptance), but are not yet fully carried out are **executory**. For example, if one student agrees to sell her textbook to another student for $50, and the seller gives the book to the buyer, but the buyer has to wait until getting paid on Friday to pay for the text, the contract is valid, but is executory. When the buyer pays the seller $50, the contract is executed.

E-CONTRACTS

Because so many items are bought and sold on the Internet, including the licenses to use software, contracts entered into over such a medium have been termed **e-contracts**. There is no separate body of contract law that governs e-contracts, but the traditional contract doctrines have been applied to e-contracts. Statutes and case law have been developed to respond to specific issues related to making contracts by way of the Internet. One key issue needing to be addressed is how someone signs an e-contract when it is the kind of contract that, for statute of fraud purposes, has to be signed. In 2000 Congress created the E-Sign Act (15 U.S.C § 7001), which establishes that electronic signatures, contracts and other records used in interstate commerce are valid, per standard agreement between the parties. In response, 47 states and the District of Columbia have adopted some version of the Uniform Electronic Transaction Act (UETA), which creates a framework for determining the legality of e-signatures in commercial and government transactions. The three states that haven't adopted the UETA (Illinois, New York, and Washington) created their own laws to deal with the same issue.

An online acceptance or signature can be established in a variety of ways. Regardless of what it means to "sign" something online, the intent of the signer and the establishment of authenticity of the signing are more important than the actual signature. But when one has agreed to the terms on an online contract, it can still require court analysis. For instance, how do users know whether hitting the "Enter" bar on their laptop while viewing an item on eBay is a binding acceptance to a valid offer? Furthermore, what makes an offer on the Internet sufficient to be binding? In a 2007 federal case dealing with such an issue, a lawyer who paid to advertise on Google.com and was billed $100,000 over three years, sued Google. Google's contract with advertisers required the advertisers to pay Google every time someone using Google clicked on selected keywords leading to the advertiser's website. The advertising contract was, naturally, online and is known as a **"clickwrap" agreement**, because the offeree enters into the contract by clicking on a dialog box, which is on the screen. In the case, the lawyer claimed Google's clickwrap contract was fraudulent because the terms weren't clearly identified. The court disagreed, in part, because Google provided the entire contract by way of a web page link, which then placed the entire agreement in a text box. Furthermore, the contract's clickwrap was preceded by a button with text that said, "Yes, I agree to the above terms and conditions," and that had to be clicked before the user could enter into the contract. The court ruled in favor of Google (*Feldman v. Google, Inc.*, 513 F.Supp.2d 229).

Another type of e-contract is the **browsewrap**. Unlike the clickwrap, where the Internet user agrees to the other party's terms by way of an e-signature or even a **digital signature** (some algorithmically created message that is unique for the recipient, allowing the recipient to respond electronically in some cryptographic way so as to confirm that the actual recipient was the one "signing" online), a browsewrap is less stringent. In a browsewrap contract, the terms of the online agreement (downloading software, for instance) are available to review, or browse, but explicitly accepting the terms isn't necessary. Browsewrap agreements are looked upon less favorably than clickwraps because of the lack of clarity that the user, or buyer, was adequately presented the terms of the contract. For example, in 2014, the 9th Circuit Court of Appeals ruled against an arbitration agreement placed in Barnes and Noble's browsewrap online terms of service, concluding that the hyperlink for the website's "Terms of Use" (which included the arbitration clause) was insufficient (*Nguyen v. Barnes and Noble, Inc.*, 763 F.3d 1171 (9th Cir. 2014)).

Not all legal documents have their own online-equivalent versions. For instance, as of now, no jurisdiction recognizes the validity of an online will, codicil or other online testamentary trust, much less an online eviction or foreclosure notice.

Word Wise
-wrap

Ever wonder where "clickwrap" and "browsewrap" came from? Glad you asked. It's one thing to click on or click through something, or to browse information online, but why is "wrap" added? You can thank the software companies, because before there was an Internet, computer software makers often put the terms of their software licenses inside the boxes with the software disks. And how were the boxes prepared for sale? They were "shrinkwrapped" which meant that one couldn't find the fine print of the contract between the seller and consumer until after tearing and discarding the plastic wrap. Essentially, the terms inside the shrinkwrapped box stated that use of the software was evidence of agreement with the terms. The law was split on **shrinkwrap contracts**, with some courts concluding they were unenforceable because buyers hadn't agreed to the terms prior to making the purchase.

Reviewing What You Learned

After studying the chapter, write the answers to each of the following questions:

1. Explain how a contractual agreement is reached. __________

2. Why does a contract not usually arise when a customer offers to buy a mismarked product? __________

3. Give an example of a contract implied in fact. __________

4. For what reason does the court impose a contract on the parties when a quasi contract arises? __________

5. What is the difference between a bilateral contract and a unilateral contract? __________

6. Give an example of a void contract, a voidable contract, and an unenforceable contract. __________

7. How does an executory contract differ from an executed contract?

8. Explain how a clickwrap and browsewrap agreements work.

Understanding Legal Concepts

Indicate whether each statement is true or false. Then, change the italicized word or phrase of each false statement to make it true.

ANSWERS

_____ 1. A *rejection* occurs when an offeror has a change of mind and calls back an offer before it is accepted.

_____ 2. Prices on merchandise and in catalogs are usually treated as *offers*.

_____ 3. Boarding a bus and putting money in the coin slot without saying anything to the driver is a *quasi contract*.

_____ 4. A *bilateral contract* results when someone says, "I'll sell you my stereo for $100," and the other party replies, "I'll buy it."

_____ 5. A *voidable* contract is one that is valid unless voided.

_____ 6. An oral contract for the sale of real property is an example of a contract that is *void*.

_____ 7. Infants *may* ratify contracts at any time during their minority.

_____ 8. When someone says, "I'll sell you my stereo for $100," and the other party replies, "I'll buy it," a contract comes into existence, and it is in its *executory* stage.

_____ 9. It is known as a *rejection* when the offeree declines an offer.

_____ 10. A *void* contract is said to be a nullity.

Checking Terminology

From the list of legal terms that follows, select the one that matches each definition.

ANSWERS

a.	acceptance
b.	avoid
c.	bargain
d.	bilateral contract
e.	capacity
f.	clickwrap agreement
g.	condition precedent
h.	contract
i.	implied in fact contract
j.	implied in law contract
k.	counteroffer
l.	disaffirm
m.	e-contract
n.	executed
o.	executory
p.	express contract
q.	implied contract
r.	infant
s.	invitation to deal
t.	invitation to negotiate
u.	majority
v.	minor
w.	necessaries
x.	nullity
y.	offer
z.	offeree
aa.	offeror
bb.	quasi
cc.	quasi contract
dd.	ratify
ee.	rejection
ff.	restitution
gg.	revocation
hh.	unenforceable contract
ii.	unilateral contract
jj.	unjust enrichment
kk.	valid
ll.	void
mm.	voidable

_____ 1. Any agreement that is enforceable in a court of law.

_____ 2. A contract in which the terms are stated or expressed by the parties.

_____ 3. The refusal by an offeree of an offer.

_____ 4. A proposal inviting someone to enter into a contract.

_____ 5. A contract containing two promises, one made by each party.

_____ 6. A contract entered into over the Internet.

_____ 7. The assent to the terms of an offer.

_____ 8. Approve; confirm.

_____ 9. A contract in which an offeree enters into a contract by clicking on a dialog box on an Internet web site.

_____ 10. Occurs when one person retains money, property, or other benefit that in equity and justice belongs to another.

_____ 11. Full age; adulthood.

_____ 12. Carried out or performed.

_____ 13. The legal name for a minor.

_____ 14. A contract that cannot be enforced for some legal reason.

_____ 15. To get out of a voidable contract; to repudiate. (Select two answers.)

_____ 16. Not good; having no legal effect.

_____ 17. The taking back of an offer by an offeror before it has been accepted by an offeree.

_____ 18. One who makes an offer.

_____ 19. Good; having legal effect.

_____ 20. Capable of being disaffirmed or voided.

_____ 21. A contract in which the terms are not stated or expressed by the parties.

_____ 22. A response to an offer in which the terms of the original offer are changed.

_____ 23. A contract that is imposed by the court to prevent unjust enrichment. (Select two answers.)

_____ 24. As if; almost as it were.

_____ 25. Under the age of majority; usually under 18.

_____ 26. Legal competency.

_____ 27. A contract containing one promise in exchange for an act.

_____ 28. That which is yet to be executed or performed.

_____ 29. One to whom an offer is made.

_____ 30. Agreement.

_____ 31. Restore an injured person to his or her original position prior to a loss.

_____ 32. A request to an individual or the public to make an offer. (Select two answers.)

_____ 33. A contract that arises from the conduct of the parties rather than from their express statements.

_____ 34. Food, clothing, shelter, and medical care that are needed by an infant, but not supplied by a parent or guardian.

_____ 35. Nothing; as though it had not occurred.

Using Legal Language

Read the following story and fill in the blank lines with legal terms taken from the list of terms at the beginning of this chapter.

Monica placed a sign on her car that read, "FOR SALE: $1,000." Seeing the sign, Alex approached Monica and said, "I'll give you $800 for it." Monica replied, "I'll take $900 for it." The sign was a(n) _____________, or _____________. Alex's statement was a(n) _____________, and Monica's response was a(n) _____________, which required a(n) _____________ on the part of Alex to create a(n) _____________. Alex did not answer immediately, causing Monica to change her mind about the $900 offer and to take it back. However, before she voiced her ___________________, Alex answered with a(n) ___________________ by saying, "I don't want it at that price." Alex left Monica and took a bus to visit his nephew. This action resulted in a(n) ___________________ between Alex and the bus company, because the terms of the contract were not stated. Because the contract arose from the conduct of the parties, it was a contract ___________________. When Alex got off the bus, he noticed that he was being followed by a small poodle that looked just like one that was advertised as being lost, in the newspaper he had just read. The advertisement offered a reward of $150 to anyone who returned the lost poodle to its owner. Alex went to the address given in the newspaper and returned the dog to its owner, thus creating a(n) ___________________. While there, he noticed a car for sale in front of the house and said to the dog owner, "I'll take that car instead of the $150 reward." Alex was the ___________________; the dog owner was the ___________________. The dog owner replied, "It's a deal." At this point, the contract was in its ___________________ stage, because it had not been carried out completely. When the dog owner turns the car over to Alex, the contract will be ___________________. In addition, because the terms of the contract were stated, this agreement was a(n) ___________________. It was not a contract ___________________ (which is also known as a(n) ___________________), because no unjust enrichment occurred. Because both parties made promises, it was a(n) ___________________. The contract met the requirements of law; therefore, it was ___________________. Alex said to his 14-year-old nephew, Otto, "I'll sell you my baseball glove for $15." Otto replied, "I'll buy it." This contract was ___________________ because of Otto's age. He was still a(n) ___________________ and could disaffirm all contracts except for ___________________ unless he ___________________ them after reaching ___________________. Otto then said to Alex, "I'll bet you $2,000 that the Chicago Cubs will win the World Series this year." Alex asked, "Where will you get the money if you lose?" "From a loan shark at 50% per year interest," Otto answered. This loan would involve charging a greater amount of interest than is allowed by law. Such a contract is a(n) ___________________ because it is illegal. This type of agreement is *not* an example of a(n) ___________________ contract, which is a contract that is valid, but that cannot be enforced for some legal reason.

Contract Requirements

ANTE INTERROGATORY

A binding promise by an offeror to hold an offer open, requiring consideration from the offeree to make it binding, is called a (an) (A) firm offer, (B) option contract, (C) promissory estoppel, (D) nundum pactum.

LEARNING OBJECTIVES

LO 1: Identify what capacity to make a contract means

LO 2: Explain what consideration for a contract is, as well as explaining key exceptions to the requirement of consideration

LO 3: Explain what contracts are generally included in a statute of frauds and what is required to be considered a written contract

LO 4: Distinguish what makes certain agreements defective, such as fraud, duress and undue influence, and contracts that are unconscionable

LO 5: Identify what types of agreements are unenforceable because they are illegal

KEY TERMS

adhesion contract

affirm

avoid

bilateral mistake

boilerplate

charitable subscription

consideration

contractual capacity

duress

e-signature

exculpatory clause

failure of consideration

firm offer

forbearance

fraud

fraud in the execution

fraud in the inducement

in pari delicto

lack of consideration

locus

locus sigilli

memorandum

mutual mistake

nudum pactum

option contract

parol evidence rule

promisee

promisor

promissory estoppel

public policy

quid pro quo

rescind

rescission

seal

4

statute of frauds

unconscionable

undue influence

unilateral mistake

usury

WEBSITES FOR PRONUNCIATION HELP

http://dictionary.cambridge.org/us/pronunciation/english/audio

https://www.howtopronounce.com

CONTRACTUAL CAPACITY

As discussed in Chapter 18, minors make voidable contracts, because their age makes them legally incapable of making an initially binding contract. While an adult is generally presumed competent to make a contract, age is not the only impediment to **contractual capacity,** which is the legal standard for being able to make a contract. One can lack the mental capacity to make a contract due to being too drunk (or otherwise under the influence of drugs) to realize she or he is making a contract. A judicial declaration of insanity also makes one incapable of legally entering into a contract.

CONSIDERATION

The key ingredient that, when added to an unenforceable agreement, turns that agreement into a binding contract is **consideration**. Consideration is the exchange of benefits and promises by the parties to the agreement. It is the glue that binds the parties to the contract. The Latin phrase describing this concept is **quid pro quo**, meaning "this for that" or "one thing in return for another."

Contracts are, in a metaphoric sense, two-way streets, imposing both an obligation to perform (the duty) and a right to receive (the benefit). Consideration is both sides of that street. By contrast, a promise to make a gift to someone is unenforceable (a one-way street), because the other side hasn't promised something in return. There are exceptions to the gift-promise rule, such as the **charitable subscription**. A charitable subscription is a promise to make a donation or gift to a charitable organization (religious, civic, educational, etc.), and those gratuitous promises are binding. So, if someone isn't bound to keep a promise (such as when the other side hasn't promised anything in return) the agreement lacks consideration. The difference between "Please, take my coat" and "Please take my coat for $100" is more than a comma. The money in the second sentence represents the other half of the exchange, and consideration is all about an exchange.

Promising not to do something that one has a right to do is known as **forbearance**, and it can be consideration, just as promising to do something that one has a right to do can be consideration. For example, in exchange for a huge plate of chocolate chip cookies promised by a next-door neighbor, the other neighbor could promise not to use his charcoal grill to cook hamburgers for a particular week when the cookie-making neighbor has vegan family members visiting.

When one who made the promise (the **promisor**) is under no legal obligation to give the object to the one to whom the promise was made (the **promisee**), the agreement is a **nudum pactum**—that is, a barren promise with no consideration, or literally translated: a naked agreement.

In a bilateral contract, the consideration is the promises exchanged by each party. In a unilateral contract, the consideration is the promise of one and the act or performance of the other. Therefore, the contract isn't made, technically, until the act is performed.

In the past, and today in some states, a **seal** on a contract establishes consideration when none existed. This mark, impression, the word "seal," or the letters "L.S." is placed on a written contract next to the party's signature. "L.S." stands for **locus sigilli**, which means the place of the seal.

An **option contract** is a binding promise by an offeror to hold an offer open, and it requires consideration from the offeree to make it binding. For instance, someone who wants to buy a home, but does not immediately know whether financing can be arranged, might offer the seller a sum of money to take the home off the market to other prospective buyers for, let's say, 30 days,

> **Word Wise**
> *One "Locus"; Several "Loci"*
>
> Most nouns in the English language form plurals by adding "s" to the singular. However, some nouns adapted from Latin, Greek, French, or Italian rely on the original language for the plural. Here are some examples:
>
> | *Singular* | *Plural* |
> | --- | --- |
> | locus | Loci |
> | medium | media |
> | datum | data |
> | beau | beaux |
> | memorandum | memoranda |
> | criterion | criteria |
> | phenomenon | phenomena |
> | stimulus | stimuli |
> | radius | radii |
> | larva | larvae |
> | crisis | crises |
> | matrix | matrices |

so that bank financing may be sought. If the seller accepts the money, an option contract has been created (for 30 days). An exception occurs when a merchant promises in writing to hold an offer open for the sale of goods. This promise by a merchant (someone, according to the Uniform Commercial Code, who is in the business of buying and selling goods) is known as a **firm offer** and requires no consideration to be binding. This will be discussed again in Chapter 21, which concerns the Uniform Commercial Code and contracts for sales of goods.

In a lawsuit, the defense of **lack of consideration** refers to a barren promise containing no consideration in the agreement. In contrast, the defense of **failure of consideration** refers to a contract that originally had consideration but that, after the contract was made, the consideration was not provided to the party being sued. Failure of consideration could be used when a buyer of goods is sued for failing to pay them, and then claims the goods weren't paid for because when they arrived to the buyer they had become worthless through the fault of the seller.

Under an equitable doctrine known as **promissory estoppel** no consideration is necessary when someone makes a promise that induces the other person's detrimental and reasonable reliance on the promise, and injustice can be avoided only by enforcing the promise. Suppose that a man works in a catering business and offers to buy the business when the owner retires. The owner says, "I tell you what, I'll sell it to you," but she then suggests that the employee get a degree in culinary arts first. So, the employee borrows money to go to culinary school, which takes a few years. Then, the owner mentions that caterers should understand business and says, "You'll need to have a business degree, too." So, the employee borrows more money to earn a business degree and spends more years studying. Then, the owner says that to be the owner of her catering business, the employee would have to move to the city where the business is located rather than live in the cheaper town 15 miles away. So, the employee moves to the city, increasing his housing costs by 30 percent. When the owner finally retires, she refuses to sell her business to her long-suffering employee. This could likely be a case for promissory estoppel. However, if that employee were to win a promissory estoppel case, the damages would be the money the employee lost by relying on the promise that the catering business would be his to buy; the damages wouldn't be the forced sale of the business to the employee or money equaling what the business is worth.

TERMS IN ACTION

Allen Iverson was one of the most gifted scorers in NBA history, averaging 26.7 points per season over a 13-year career, most of it spent with the Philadelphia 76ers. Iverson won a Rookie of the Year award in 1997, a Most Valuable Player award in 2001, and was inducted into the Basketball Hall of Fame in 2016. Iverson's nickname was "The Answer," and this name was the source of a breach of contract claim made by one of Iverson's close friends. Jamil Blackmon was a family friend who had a mentor-like relationship with Iverson when Iverson was still in high school. Before Iverson went to the University of Georgetown in 1994, Blackmon suggested that Iverson take for his nickname "The Answer"—as in, Iverson would be the answer to all of the NBA's woes. Iverson loved the idea and promised Blackmon 25 percent of all of the money Iverson might make from future merchandising of that nickname. Iverson repeated that promise as he began profiting from using "The Answer" as his marketing nickname. The promises were repeated through 2001, but never honored, so Blackmon sued Iverson. But the trial judge dismissed the case in 2003, concluding that there was no **consideration** for the promise. As the court examined the allegations made in Blackmon's complaint, Iverson's promises to pay Blackmon came *after* Blackmon, in effect, gave him the nickname. There was no exchange, because promises made after one has already performed are insufficient to create a contract. It was **nudum pactum**. Blackmon then refiled his complaint, alleging **promissory estoppel**, but lost again. No evidence showed that Blackmon detrimentally and reasonably relied on Iverson's 1994 promise.

Source: *Blackmon v. Iverson*, 324 F.Supp.2d 602 (E.D. Pa. 2003), affirmed in an unpublished opinion, 317 Fed. Appx. 123 (3rd Cir. 2008)

CONTRACTS REQUIRED TO BE IN WRITING

Although it makes sense for a variety of reasons to put a contract in writing, the law requires only certain contracts to be in writing; others are fully enforceable even though they are oral.

Statute of Frauds

Under a rule of law coming from 17th-century England known as the **statute of frauds**, certain contracts must be in writing to be enforceable. With some variations from state to state, the following contracts must be in writing to be enforceable:

1. contracts whose performance cannot be completed within a year after the contract was formed
2. promises to answer for the debt or default of another (sometimes known as a collateral promise)
3. contracts for the sale of an interest in real property
4. contracts in consideration of marriage (such as prenuptial agreements)
5. promises by personal representatives of estates to pay debts of the estate personally (a type of collateral promise)
6. with certain exceptions, contracts for the sale of goods of $500 or more (discussed in Chapter 20)

Requirements of a Writing

The writing that is necessary to satisfy the statute of frauds is called a **memorandum**. It may consist of any writing (such as words on a piece of scrap paper, receipt, or check) so long as it meets the following requirements:

1. identifies the parties to the contract
2. states the terms of the contract

3. for real estate contracts, identifies the **locus** of land—that is, the exact parcel of land under contract
4. states the price
5. is signed by the person against whom enforcement is sought

As stated in Chapter 18, federal law and many state laws allow contracts to be signed with an **e-signature** (electronic signature)—a method of signing an electronic message that identifies the sender and signifies his or her approval of the message's content.

TERMS IN ACTION

In the world of American contract law, very few cases are more famous than *Lucy v. Zehmer*. This 1954 case involves the **statute of frauds**, the unwitting sale of the family farm, and lots of whiskey. It seems that Mr. and Mrs. Zehmer owned a 471-acre farm in Virginia, a farm that Mr. Lucy wanted for quite some time. One time, Zehmer reneged on a promise to sell the farm to Lucy for $20,000, which he got away with because his promise was oral and real estate contracts need to be in writing to be enforceable. On another occasion, Lucy came armed with a bottle of whiskey to the restaurant–gasoline station that Zehmer owned, called the "YE OLD VIRGINNIE RESTAURANT," and began to drink with Zehmer. While talking about Zehmer's farm, Lucy said to Zehmer, "I bet you wouldn't take $50,000 for that place." Zehmer responded, "Yes, I would, too; you wouldn't give fifty." Lucy said that he would, and Zehmer wrote a one-sentence contract on the back of a restaurant check. However, Lucy noticed that Zehmer wrote "I agree to sell," rather than "We," and the farm was owned by Zehmer and his wife. So Zehmer ripped up the paper, wrote it again and had his wife—who was actually working in the restaurant—sign the document with him and Lucy. You probably know where this is going. By the time Zehmer realized Lucy was serious about paying for and taking possession of the farm, Zehmenr cried foul—that he never actually intended to sell it. But Virginia's statute of frauds had been met, and the Virginia Supreme Court failed to find any substance to Zehmer's claims of lacking **contractual capacity** to make a contract due to drunkenness, or his claim that he was just joking when making the contract.

Source: *Lucy v. Zehmer*, 84 S.E.2d 516 (Va. 1954)

Parol Evidence Rule

The law assumes that when a contract is reduced to writing, and signed, all of its terms are contained in the writing. Consequently, under a special rule of evidence known as the **parol evidence rule** oral evidence of prior or contemporaneous negotiations between the parties is not admissible in court to alter, vary, or contradict the terms of a written agreement. Because of this rule, it is important to include all terms that are orally agreed upon whenever a contract is reduced to writing. If one believes that he or she was lied to during negotiations because the contract doesn't reflect what was stated by the other party, the party making the accusation of lying will not be able to testify about what was supposed to be in the contract. There are exceptions to the parol evidence rule, including allowing testimony to help clear up an acknowledged ambiguity in the terms in the contract, lending it to reasonable but alternate meanings.

DEFECTIVE AGREEMENTS

Certain agreements that initially seem to be legitimate are, in fact, defective and therefore not recognized as valid, binding contracts. The most common of these are agreements involving mutual mistake, fraud, duress, and undue influence. Contracts that are unconscionable may also be declared unenforceable by courts.

Mistake

When both parties are mistaken about an essential aspect of an agreement they entered into, which is also known as being mistaken as to a material fact of the contract, a **bilateral** or **mutual mistake** has been made and the contract is voidable at the option of either party. Occasionally, courts might refer to a contract as requiring a "meeting of the minds," which would not be the case in a mutual mistake. In contrast to a mutual or bilateral mistake, when only one of the parties makes a mistake as to a material element of the contract, it is known as a **unilateral (one-sided) mistake** and, generally, the mistaken party cannot have the contract **avoided** (made void) or **rescinded** (cancelled). One factor courts look to in considering if a contract can be rescinded because of mistake is if the party claiming mistake bore the risk of mistake. To illustrate, suppose a buyer of a $2,000 acoustic guitar made of mahogany wood seeks to rescind the contract on the grounds that the buyer thought he actually was buying a rosewood-made guitar. If the terms of the sales contract state the buyer's purchase indicates satisfactory inspection of the guitar, then the buyer explicitly bore the risk of mistake.

Fraud

Fraud (which also exists in tort law) occurs when one party to the contract makes a misrepresentation of a material, existing fact, which the other party to the contract relies on and thereby suffers damages. If the defrauded party was induced by fraud to enter into the contract, it is called **fraud in the inducement** and the contract is voidable at the option of the injured party. If, conversely, fraud as to the essential nature of the transaction occurred, such as telling a blind man that he is signing a receipt when the document is really a check from the blind man's checkbook, that is **fraud in the execution** (originally, "fraud in esse contractus") and the contract is void. A defrauded party always has the right to rescind the contract and to return any consideration received. Thus, **rescission** restores the parties to their original positions. A defrauded party may choose, instead, to keep the consideration and **affirm** (approve) the contract and bring suit for damages.

The elements that must be proved by the party claiming fraud are discussed in more detail in Chapter 16 in the section on fraud.

Duress vs. Undue Influence

Contracts entered into because of duress or undue influence may also be avoided by the injured party. **Duress** is the overcoming of a person's free will by the use of an unlawful threat or physical harm. "Sign this contract or I'll ruin your credit history" is duress. **Undue influence** is the overcoming of a person's free will by misusing a position of trust and taking advantage of the other person who is relying on the trust relationship. Undue influence starts by way of a relationship that is unequal, where the "stronger" one in the relationship takes advantage of the "weaker" one by abusing the trust. Undue influence would be at issue when a nephew, caring for his elderly and forgetful aunt, persuades her to sell her million-dollar house to him for $100,000.

Unconscionable Contracts

Some contracts (or parts of them) are so harshly one-sided and unfair that they—as is the operative legal phrase—shock the conscience of the court. Such contracts are considered **unconscionable** by the courts and will not be enforced. This is because unconscionable contracts (in some cases called **adhesion contracts**) are drawn by one party to that party's lopsided benefit and must be accepted as is, on a take-it-or-leave-it basis if a contract is to result. Sometimes, adhesion contracts fall into this category. Adhesion contracts often contain **boilerplate**, which is standardized language commonly used in similar legal documents. Although no longer descriptive of its history, boilerplate is still alive and well, and is usually found at the end of contracts, with such heading titles as "Attorney's Fees," "Waiver," "Arbitration," or "Limitations on Damages." Boilerplate can be found in legal form books or stored on law-office computers for use in the drafting of legal documents. **Exculpatory clauses** (clauses that limit or eliminate legal responsibility for the party drafting the contract) are generally used in boilerplate. Courts generally look disfavorably at exculpatory clauses. However, such clauses will usually be enforced if they do not offend public policy (defined below) and if the bargaining power between the parties is equal.

> **Web Wise**
>
> • Learn more about standardized terms in contracts, including common boilerplate, by going to *www.nolo.com* and typing "boilerplate" into the search bar.

AGREEMENTS UNENFORCEABLE DUE TO ILLEGALITY

To be valid and enforceable, contracts must be about that which is legal to do or perform. Illegal contracts are void; they have no legal effect. For example, **Usury**, which is the charging of a higher amount of interest than is allowed by consumer protection laws, is illegal in every state. Gambling is illegal in many states, with exceptions such as state lotteries, horse and dog racing, and bingo. Sunday contracts (contracts to purchase on Sundays certain items like alcohol or automobiles) are illegal in some states, with certain specific exceptions. Contracts in restraint of trade, such as agreements not to compete, are also illegal, along with other types of contracts that are opposed to public policy. **Public policy** is a doctrine that is often difficult to identify, but it is generally thought to be underlying, foundational principles that bind various peoples into a close-knit society. It represents those ideas that reflect the moral or cultural fabric of a jurisdiction. For instance, a contract prohibiting someone from marrying is thought to be against public policy and would be void.

Except when the parties are not **in pari delicto** (which means, in equal fault), the court will not aid either party to an illegal contract. It will leave the parties where they placed themselves.

4

Reviewing What You Learned

After studying the chapter, write the answers to each of the following questions:

1. Give an example of consideration in a contract._____________

   ____

   ____

   ____

2. Give an example of an agreement that does not contain consideration. _________________________

   ____

   ____

   ____

3. Where is consideration found in a bilateral contract? In a unilateral contract?_____________________

   ____

   ____

   ____

4. List six kinds of contracts that must be in writing in order to be enforceable. _______________________

   ____

   ____

   ____

5. What are the requirements of a memorandum that will satisfy the statute of frauds?_____________________

   ____

   ____

   ____

6. Explain the meaning and significance of the parol evidence rule.

   ____

   ____

   ____

7. Describe the kind of contract that is voidable because of a mistake, and compare it with the kind of contract that is not voidable because of a mistake. _______________

____

____

____

8. List the elements of fraud. _______________

____

____

____

9. Provide an example of an unconscionable contract._______

____

____

____

10. Describe three kinds of contracts that are illegal and void in many states._______________________

____

____

____

Understanding Legal Concepts

Indicate whether each statement is true or false. Then, change the italicized word or phrase of each false statement to make it true.

ANSWERS

____ **1.** A binding contract *comes* into existence when one person says to another, "I'm going to give you my stereo as a gift," and the other replies, "Fine, I'll accept it."

____ **2.** In the past, and still today in some states, a seal on a contract *furnishes* consideration when none exists.

____ **3.** Under a rule of law known as the *statute of limitations*, certain contracts must be in writing to be enforceable.

____ **4.** Contracts for the sale of an interest in *real property* must be in writing to be enforceable.

____ **5.** With four exceptions, contracts for the sale of goods of *$600* or more must be in writing to be enforceable.

____ **6.** A memorandum *may* consist of words on a piece of scrap paper, receipt, or check.

____ **7.** The law assumes that when a contract is reduced to writing, *all* of its terms are contained in the writing.

____ **8.** When a mutual mistake occurs, a contract *cannot* be avoided by the parties.

____ **9.** When a person is induced by fraud to enter into a contract, it is called *fraud in the execution*, and the contract is void.

____ **10.** Illegal contracts are *void*; they have no legal effect.

Checking Terminology

From the list of legal terms that follows, select the one that matches each definition.

ANSWERS

a. adhesion contract
b. affirm
c. avoid
d. bilateral mistake
e. boilerplate
f. consideration
g. contractual capacity
h. deceit
i. duress
j. e-signature
k. exculpatory clause
l. failure of consideration
m. firm offer
n. forbearance
o. fraud
p. fraud in the execution
q. fraud in the inducement

____ **1.** The giving up of a legal right.

____ **2.** Place; locality.

____ **3.** Cancellation.

____ **4.** In equal fault.

____ **5.** Standard language commonly used in documents of the same type.

____ **6.** The overcoming of a person's free will by misusing a position of trust and taking advantage of the other person who is relying on the trust relationship.

____ **7.** Underlying foundational principles which bind various peoples into a close-knit society.

____ **8.** Oral evidence of prior or contemporaneous negotiations between the parties is not admissible in court to alter, vary, or contradict the terms of a written agreement.

____ **9.** Refraining from taking action.

____ **10.** The overcoming of a person's free will by the use of threat or physical harm.

____ **11.** A clause that is used in a contract to escape legal responsibility.

____ **12.** A contract that is drawn by one party to that party's benefit and must be accepted, as is, on a take-it-or-leave-it basis if a contract is to result.

____ **13.** A misrepresentation of a material, existing fact, knowingly made, that causes someone reasonably relying on it to suffer damages. (Select two answers.)

r. in pari delicto
s. lack of consideration
t. locus
u. locus sigilli
v. memorandum
w. mutual mistake
x. nudum pactum
y. option contract
z. parol evidence rule
aa. promisee
bb. promisor
cc. promissory estoppel
dd. public policy
ee. quid pro quo
ff. rescind
gg. rescission
hh. seal
ii. statute of frauds
jj. unconscionable
kk. undue influence
ll. unilateral mistake
mm. usury

_____ **14.** The writing that is necessary to satisfy the statute of frauds.
_____ **15.** A mark, impression, the word "seal," or the letters "L.S." placed on a written contract next to the party's signature.
_____ **16.** Approve.
_____ **17.** So harshly one-sided and unfair that the court's conscience is shocked.
_____ **18.** Fraud as to the essential nature of the transaction.
_____ **19.** A defense available when the consideration provided for in an agreement is not in fact given to the party being sued.
_____ **20.** A mistake made by only one party to a contract.
_____ **21.** To annul, cancel, or make void.
_____ **22.** One to whom a promise is made.
_____ **23.** A defense available to a party being sued when no consideration is contained in the agreement that is sued on.
_____ **24.** Cancel.
_____ **25.** A binding promise to hold an offer open.
_____ **26.** A doctrine under which no consideration is necessary when someone makes a promise that induces another's action or forbearance and injustice can be avoided only by enforcing the promise.
_____ **27.** A merchant's written promise to hold an offer open for the sale of goods.
_____ **28.** Capability of making a fully binding contract.
_____ **29.** When both parties are mistaken about an important aspect of an agreement. (Select two answers.)
_____ **30.** Certain contracts must be in writing to be enforceable.
_____ **31.** Barren promise with no consideration.
_____ **32.** An exchange of benefits and detriments by the parties to an agreement.
_____ **33.** Fraud that induces another to enter into a contract.
_____ **34.** The charging of a greater amount of interest than is allowed by law.
_____ **35.** A method of signing an electronic message.
_____ **36.** One thing in return for another
_____ **37.** One who makes a promise.
_____ **38.** Place of the seal.

Using Legal Language

Read the following story and fill in the blank lines with legal terms taken from the list of terms at the beginning of this chapter:

The smooth-talking salesperson promised a free cataract operation to an elderly woman who was almost blind. Contractually speaking, the salesperson was the _____________________ and the elderly woman was the _____________________; however, because the elderly woman promised nothing in exchange for the cataract operation, she suffered no _____________________. Had the promise been in writing and put under _____________________ by the use of the letters "L.S." (which stand for _____________________), it would have been binding in some states. The salesperson also committed _____________________ or _____________________ when he lied to the elderly woman. He talked her into buying some worthless land with a shack on it by telling her that the _____________________ was beautiful, high ground; actually, it was swampland. The type of fraud was _____________________, because the salesperson's lie induced the woman to enter into the contract. Because the salesperson was not in a position of trust, the wrongful act was not _____________________ and it was not _____________________, because the woman's free will was not overcome by threats or physical harm. It was _____________________, however, when the salesperson told the woman that she was signing a second copy of the contract when she was actually signing a check for $10,000. The writing that the woman signed met the requirements of a(n) _____________________ and, for that reason, was sufficient to satisfy the ___________________. Because it was drawn up by the seller to the seller's advantage and offered to the woman on a take-it-or-leave-it basis, the court might consider the contract to be a(n) ___________________ ___________________. In addition, the court might consider the contract to be ___________________, because the woman agreed to buy a shack on an acre of worthless swampland for $250,000. Under the terms of the contract, she was to pay $100,000 in cash and sign a note for the balance at 50 percent per annum interest, which is ___________________.

Although the ___________________ does not allow prior oral statements by the parties into evidence in court to alter the terms of a written agreement, an exception exists when fraud is committed. In addition, because both parties were mistaken as to the existence of the subject matter when they signed the contract (the shack on the property had burned down two days before the contract was signed), the contract was voidable. The mistake was a(n) ___________________, which is also known as a(n) ___________________, not a(n) ___________________.

20

Third Parties and Discharge of Contracts

ANTE INTERROGATORY

*Damages that are agreed upon by the parties at the time of the execution
of the contract in the event of a subsequent breach are called
(A) consequential damages, (B) exemplary damages, (C) incidental damages,
(D) liquidated damages.*

LEARNING OBJECTIVES

LO 1: Explain how a third-party beneficiary would acquire rights to a contract

LO 2: Summarize the distinction between an assignment and delegation

LO 3: Identify the five primary ways that contractual obligations end

LO 4: Contrast the legal significance between full performance and substantial performance

LO 5: Explain accord and satisfaction

LO 6: Explain what is needed for the defense of impossibility of performance

LO 7: Identify two key ways that contractual obligations can be extinguished by operation of law

LO 8: Identify and explain the categories of contract damages

KEY TERMS

accord and satisfaction
anticipatory breach
assignee
assignment
assignor
bankruptcy
breach of contract
compensatory damages
consequential damages
damages
delegation
exemplary damages

impossibility
incidental beneficiary
incidental damages
intended beneficiary
legal tender
liquidated damages
material breach
mitigate
nominal damages
novation
performance
privity of contract
punitive damages

reasonable time

specific performance

statute of limitations

substantial performance

tender of payment

tender of performance

third-party beneficiary

time is of the essence

toll

WEBSITES FOR PRONUNCIATION HELP

http://dictionary.cambridge.org/us/pronunciation/english/audio

https://www.howtopronounce.com

THIRD-PARTY BENEFICIARIES

A **third-party beneficiary** is someone who is not a party to a contract (offeror or offeree), but is benefited by a performance of the contract. Being benefited by a contract performance does not necessarily give that beneficiary legal rights under the contract, because **privity of contract**— the term for the legal relationship that exists between contracting parties—is generally required in order to acquire rights under the contract. In order to have rights to sue under a contract, the third-party beneficiary must be an **intended beneficiary**, which means that the contract was made with the purpose of benefiting the third party. The child whose birthday cake (with his name on it) is made by a bakery is a third-party beneficiary, but a child who eats a piece of cake at the birthday party is only an **incidental beneficiary** (one who is indirectly benefited by a contract; for example, a homeowner is the incidental beneficiary of the contract between the city and the construction company that improves the sidewalks alongside the homeowner's property).

ASSIGNMENT AND DELEGATION

Parties who enter into contracts receive rights and incur duties. (Remember, from Chapter 19, that consideration is like a two-way street.) For example, if a woman offers to sell her car for $5,000 and another person agrees to buy it for that price, the seller receives the right to the money and incurs the duty to supply the car. The buyer's rights and duties are the opposite. With some exceptions and unless otherwise agreed by the parties, contract rights and duties can be transferred to other people.

The transfer of a contract right is an **assignment**. The person who transfers the right is the **assignor** and the person to whom the right is transferred is the **assignee**. In the preceding example, if before receiving the $5,000 from the buyer, the seller assigns her right to the money under the contract to a third person, the buyer would have to pay the money to the third person upon learning of the assignment.

The transfer of a contract duty is known as a **delegation**. When the performance under the contract is standardized, delegation can be done, generally. For example, a commercial painter hired to paint the walls inside an office building would be able to delegate that performance to a different painter. Remember, though, a contract's terms can prohibit delegation of duties. Duties to perform personal services or duties that require the use of personal judgment cannot be delegated without the consent of the person for whom the duty is to be performed. For instance, an artist hired to paint someone's portrait cannot delegate the job to another painter without the client's permission.

One who delegates duties under a contract is still liable under the contract for the performance. So, the commercial painter, from the above paragraph, would be in breach of contract if the second commercial painter failed to paint the office walls as required by the contract. But when two contracting parties agree that one of them will transfer both rights and duties to a third person, and the remaining party and the third person agree to deal solely with each other, privity of contract changes, and a novation occurs. A **novation** is an agreement whereby an original party to a contract is replaced by a new party, creating a completely new agreement and ending the original one.

<table>
<tr><td>

Web Wise

</td></tr>
<tr><td>

• To learn some of the fun and sometimes curious things that musicians and celebrities insist upon having when they travel, or perform at concerts or speaking engagements, go to *www.thesmokinggun.com* and then click on the "Backstage" tab. There you will find many contracts to examine, organized by style of music and other categories.

</td></tr>
</table>

ENDING CONTRACTUAL OBLIGATIONS

The principal ways that contractual obligations end are as follows:

1. performance
2. agreement
3. impossibility
4. operation of law
5. breach of contract

Performance

Most contracts come to an end by **performance**—that is, the parties do as they agreed to do under the terms of the contract. At common law, the parties were required to do absolutely everything they agreed to do, without exception, to be able to file suit against the other party for breach of contract. That was known as full performance. However, the modern legal doctrine of **substantial performance** focuses on if the party failing to fully perform has committed a **material breach**, which occurs when a major or essential part of the contract has not been performed. If the breaching party's failure is not material (which is fact-dependent unless detailed in the contract), then that party has substantially performed and the other party would still be obligated to perform. But the other party's performance could be offset by the decreased value that arose because of the nonmaterial breach. To illustrate, if the performing party's performance could be quantified as 10% less than called for in the contract, the paying party would be obligated to pay but could deduct 10% from the original price.

The time for performance of a contract is sometimes important to the parties. If a time for performance is stated in a written contract, the court may allow additional time for its performance without recognizing a breach. If a time for performance is stated in the writing and the words **time is of the essence** (meaning that time is critical) are added, however, a breach of contract will occur at the end of the stated time if the contract has not been performed. If no time for performance is put in the contract, it must be performed within a **reasonable time**. What is reasonable is ultimately left to the discretion of the judge or jury, and varies depending on the circumstances.

To be in a position to bring a suit against another for breach of contract, it is necessary for that party to make tender. **Tender of performance** means to offer to do that which one has agreed to do under the terms of the contract. **Tender of payment** means to offer to the other party the money owed under the contract. For the sale of goods under the Uniform Commercial Code, tender of payment may be made by any means or in any manner that is commonly used in the ordinary course of business. The seller may demand legal tender, but must give the buyer a reasonable time to obtain it. **Legal tender** is coin, paper, or other currency that is sufficient under law for the payment of debts.

Agreement

Sometimes when there is a dispute about a contract, instead of completing the terms, the parties will agree to end the contract altogether. Other times, they will agree to perform in a different manner from that agreed upon originally. This latter arrangement is called an accord. When the agreed-upon performance is completed, a satisfaction occurs. Together, this arrangement is known as an **accord and satisfaction**. For accord and satisfaction to be legitimate, there must be a legitimate dispute about the contract's terms. One who borrows $10,000 can't claim accord and satisfaction by writing on a check for $1,000 "paid in full," even if the lender cashes the smaller check. But suppose there is a real dispute about the value of someone's services; say the replacing of a furnace in a home. Imagine the bill is $5,000 and the homeowner thinks he was overcharged by $1,000, in light of the work done. If the homeowner issues a $4,000 check and writes "paid in full" on the check, that would be the "accord" (the offer). If the plumbing and heating company endorses and cashes the check, that is the "satisfaction" (the acceptance), and the $5,000 contract has been extinguished for $4,000.

Impossibility

Contracts that are impossible to perform, not merely difficult or costly to do so, may be discharged by a defense called **impossibility**. Legal reasons for this kind of discharge of performance include the following:

1. death or incapacity of a person who was to perform personal services;
2. destruction of the exact subject matter of the contract (the boat to be transferred to the buyer is destroyed in a hurricane);
3. subsequent illegality of the performance, which would make the future performance a crime;
4. defense against a breach of contract claim, based on the inability of the defendant to perform the contract, whose inability wasn't the defendant's fault.

Some courts use the word "impracticability" interchangeably with "impossibility," in order to deal with situations where in absolute terms something isn't impossible to do, but it has become useless to try and perform because of an unforeseeable and extreme change in circumstances.

Operation of Law

Sometimes, contracts will be discharged by operation of law. The filing of bankruptcy, for example, discharges the contractual obligations of the debtor. **Bankruptcy** (discussed in Chapter 41) is a legal process under the Federal Bankruptcy Act that aims to give debtors who are overwhelmed with debt a fresh start and to provide a fair way of distributing a debtor's assets among all creditors.

Contract rights are also discharged by the operation of **statutes of limitations**, the laws establishing time limits for bringing legal actions. For example, the Uniform Commercial Code states a suit for breach of contract for the sale of goods must be brought within four years from the date of the breach, but can be reduced by the parties to not less than one year (UCC § 2-725). Other time limits vary from state to state for different causes of actions. Washington State, for instance, establishes a three-year limit for bringing a suit for breach of an oral contract (RCW 4.16.080), and a six-year limit for suing for breach of a written contract (RCW 4.16.040).

Statutes of limitations are usually tolled—that is, they do not run—while a plaintiff is under a disability such as infancy or mental illness. Similarly, they do not run while a defendant is out of the state and not under the jurisdiction of the court. In the case of a lawsuit for money owed, partial payment of the debt has the effect of starting the full statutory period running all over again from the beginning. The word **toll** means to bar, defeat, or take away. Thus, to toll the **statute of limitations** means to show facts that would prevent a lawsuit from being dismissed due to its being filed too late.

TERMS IN ACTION

When does being too sick to work become impossibility of performance? A case from Indiana sheds some light on the matter. Rose Acre Farms was an egg company that produced 250,000 dozen eggs per day and attempted to motivate its 300 employees through unique bonus programs. Employees had been paid car-payment bonuses for three years for buying new, white cars that advertised Rose Acre Farms and were always kept clean, or had been paid bonuses for wearing a silver feather at work. In all the bonus programs at Rose Acre Farms, employees forfeited the money if they ever missed work for any reason—illness included—or even

(Continued)

if they were tardy for work by one minute. All employees who competed in these bonus programs were made aware of the exact requirements. Mark Dove worked at Rose Acre Farms and participated in a bonus program to help construct a building in 12 weeks, for an extra $6,000. Because he was going to law school before the 12th week, he was allowed to compete for a $5,000 bonus for 10 weeks of work. But on Thursday of his 10th week, Dove got strep throat with a 104-degree temperature, and missed the remaining days of work. After being paid no bonus, Dove sued for breach of contract, claiming that he had **substantially performed**, as well as claiming that his illness qualified as impossibility of performance. Dove lost on both counts. The Indiana Court of Appeals concluded that substantial performance didn't apply, because the bonus program was specifically and strictly based on full performance. Moreover, the court held that impossibility of performance didn't apply for the same reason that substantial performance didn't, and for a more important reason, as well: Impossibility is a defense raised by defendants, not a claim made by plaintiffs.

Source: *Dove v. Rose Acre Farms, Inc.*, 434 N.E.2d 931 (Ind. App. 1982)

Word Wise
Prefixes That Mean "Not"

Prefix	Examples
dis-	disbelief, disaffirm, dishonor
in-	indirect, intestate
im- (before *p, b, m*)	immature, impeach, impossibility
il- (before *l*)	illegal, illegitimate child
ir- (before *r*)	irregular, irreconcilable differences, irrevocable trust
non-	nonliving, nonsuit
un-	unscrupulous, unconscionable, undisclosed principal, unenforceable

Web Wise

- To research your jurisdiction's common statute of limitations, go to www.nolo.com and type "statutes of limitations" in the search bar. One of the results should be a statewide listing of statutes of limitations.

Breach of Contract

As stated earlier in the chapter, a **breach of contract** occurs when one of the parties fails to carry out the terms of the contract. When the breaching party announces before the time for performance that he or she is not going to perform, it is known as an **anticipatory breach**. Some states allow suit to be brought at that moment; other states require the injured party to wait until the time for performance before bringing suit, to test the breaching party's ability to perform.

When a breach of contract occurs, the injured party may bring suit for **damages**, which is the money lost as a result of the breach. **Nominal damages**—that is, damages in name only—are token or trivial amounts of money awarded to the party who wins a lawsuit by proving that the defendant breached the contract, but suffers no actual monetary loss. **Compensatory damages** compensate the plaintiff for actual losses resulting from the breach. **Punitive** or **exemplary damages** such as those that are double or triple the amount of actual damages, are occasionally awarded to the plaintiff as a measure of punishment for the defendant's egregious acts related to breaching the contract. **Liquidated damages** are damages that are agreed upon (pre-determined) by the parties at the time of the creation of the contract, in the event of a subsequent breach. **Incidental damages** may be awarded to the injured party to cover reasonable expenses that indirectly result from a breach of contract. Examples of incidental damages includes legal fees or costs to store or transport defective goods that were sent to the buyer. **Consequential damages** are losses (such as lost profits) that flow from the consequences of the breach, rather than the direct damages that are for the breach itself. In order for a plaintiff to win consequential damages, the losses must be a foreseeable (likely) result of the breach (such as the inability to resell a damaged vehicle delivered to the dealer two days late), and the parties must have taken the possibilities into account when making the contract.

Whenever a contract is breached, the injured party owes a duty to the breaching party to **mitigate** the damages—that is, to try and minimize the negative effects of the breach and get them as low as possible. For example, if a tenant breaches a lease agreement by leaving the property six months early, the landlord has a duty to try and find a new tenant, in order to mitigate the damages. If the landlord did nothing for six months, the tenant would not owe six months of unpaid rent because of the doctrine of mitigation.

Sometimes, the court will order the breaching party to do that which he or she agreed to do according the terms of the contract. This is known as **specific performance** and is used only when the subject matter of the contract is either unique or rare so that money damages are not an adequate remedy for the injured party. Because real estate has uniformly been viewed to be unique, for the purposes of specific performance, courts will often order a breached contract for the purchase or sale of real property to be specifically performed.

TERMS IN ACTION

The legal world was rocked in 1985 with the news that a jury had awarded a plaintiff over $10 billion in total **damages**. That lawsuit pitted two oil companies, Pennzoil against Texaco. In 1984, Pennzoil sought to purchase the Getty Oil Company, which had been founded by J. Paul Getty, a reclusive billionaire who was so cheap he kept a payphone in his mansion. Gordon Getty, one of Getty's sons and the CEO of the Getty Oil Company, verbally agreed to the sale, and the picture of his handshake with Pennzoil executives ran in many newspapers. But Getty Oil had not officially agreed to the sale, and Texaco offered more money to Getty Oil than Pennzoil had. So, Getty Oil broke its deal with Pennzoil. Pennzoil sued Texaco for tortuous interference of a contract, rather than suing Getty Oil for **breach of contract**, because Texaco's offer to Getty included covering any breach of contract legal costs. Texaco argued at trial that Gordon Getty's informal intent to enter into a contract with Pennzoil wasn't sufficient to form a contract. But Pennzoil was represented by Houston's Joe Jamail, one of the best trial lawyers on the planet. The jury ruled in favor of Pennzoil and awarded it $3.53 billion in **compensatory damages** and $7 billion in **punitive damages,** making it then the biggest damages award ever. Eventually, the parties reached a deal in 1987, with Texaco agreeing to pay Pennzoil $3 billion. Joe Jamail's legal fee has never been confirmed, but is believed to be in the hundreds of millions of dollars. Jamail was so successful in court that he repeatedly made the Forbes Magazine list of American billionaires, and was such a significant donor to the University of Texas at Austin, his alma mater, that the football field, a swim center, a law school pavilion and a law library bear his name. He died in December 2015, at the age of 90.

Source: forbes.com; lawnix.com; *Economic Foundations of Law and Organization*; nytimes.com

Reviewing What You Learned

After studying the chapter, write the answers to each of the following questions:

1. Explain the difference between an assignment and a delegation.______________________________________

____

____

2. List the five ways that contractual obligations may come to an end. _____________________________________

____

____

3. If the time for performance is not mentioned in a contract, when must the contract be performed?______________

____

____

____

4. What is necessary for a person to be in a position to bring suit against another for breach of contract?______________

____

____

5. Explain the difference between accord and satisfaction.

____

6. List three legal reasons for discharging a contract because of impossibility.______________________________

____

____

____

7. Describe two situations that toll the statute of limitations. ___

____

____

____

8. Explain the difference between nominal damages, punitive damages, liquidated damages, incidental damages, and consequential damages. ________________________

____

____

____

9. Under what circumstances may a court order specific performance of a contract? ____________________________

____

____

____

Understanding Legal Concepts

Indicate whether each statement is true or false. Then, change the italicized word or phrase of each false statement to make it true.

ANSWERS

_____ **1.** The transfer of a *duty* is known as an assignment.

_____ **2.** With some exceptions and unless otherwise agreed, rights and duties *cannot* be transferred to other people.

_____ **3.** Most contracts come to an end by *agreement*.

_____ **4.** If a time for performance is stated in a written contract, the court *may* allow additional time for its performance.

_____ **5.** If no time for performance is put in a contract, it must be performed within a *reasonable* time.

_____ **6.** When parties agree to perform in a different manner than originally agreed upon and the new performance is completed, it is called an accord and *completion*.

_____ **7.** The law of *bankruptcy* aims to give a fresh start to debtors who are overwhelmed with debt.

_____ **8.** In the case of a breach of contract for the sale of goods, suit must be brought within *six* years from the date of the breach, to be actionable.

    9. Whenever a contract is breached, the *breaching* party owes a duty to keep the damages as low as possible.

    10. *Specific performance* is used only when the subject matter of a contract is either unique or rare so that money damages are not an adequate remedy for the injured party.

Checking Terminology

From the list of legal terms that follows, select the one that matches each definition.

ANSWERS

a. accord and satisfaction
b. anticipatory breach
c. assignee
d. assignment
e. assignor
f. bankruptcy
g. breach of contract
h. compensatory damages
i. consequential damages
j. damages
k. delegation
l. exemplary damages
m. impossibility
n. incidental beneficiary
o. incidental damages
p. intended beneficiary
q. legal tender
r. liquidated damages
s. mitigate
t. nominal damages
u. novation
v. performance
w. privity of contract
x. punitive damages
y. reasonable time
z. specific performance
aa. statute of limitations
bb. substantial performance
cc. tender of payment
dd. tender of performance
ee. third-party beneficiary
ff. time is of the essence
gg. toll

    1. The transfer of a right from one person to another.

    2. One who transfers a right by assignment.

    3. One to whom a right is transferred by assignment.

    4. The transfer of a duty by one person to another.

    5. Coin, paper, or other currency that is sufficient under law for the payment of debts.

    6. An agreement to perform in a different manner than originally called for and the completion of that agreed-upon performance.

    7. A defense against a breach of contract claim, based on the inability of the defendant to perform the contract, whose inability wasn't the defendant's fault.

    8. A legal process that aims to give a fresh start to debtors who are overwhelmed with debt and to provide a fair way of distributing a debtor's assets among all creditors.

    9. The failure of a party to a contract to carry out the terms of the agreement.

    10. The announcement, before the time for performance, by a party to a contract that he or she is not going to perform.

    11. Compensation in money for loss or injury.

    12. Damages as a measure of punishment for the defendant's wrongful acts (also called punitive damages).

    13. Damages that are agreed upon by the parties at the time of the execution of a contract, in the event of a subsequent breach.

    14. Reasonable expenses that indirectly result from a breach of contract.

    15. Losses that flow not directly from a breach of contract, but from the consequences of it.

    16. The relationship that exists between two or more contracting parties.

    17. An agreement whereby an original party to a contract is replaced by a new party.

    18. Discharging a contract by doing that which one agreed to do under the terms of the contract.

    19. A doctrine allowing a contracting party to sue the other party for breach even though slight omissions or deviations were made in his or her own performance of the contract.

    20. Time is critical.

    21. A period, left to the discretion of the judge or jury, that may be fairly allowed depending on the circumstances.

    22. To offer to do that which one has agreed to do under the terms of a contract.

    23. To offer to the other party the money owed under a contract.

    24. Law that sets forth time limits for bringing legal actions.

    25. To bar, defeat, or take away.

    26. One who is indirectly benefited by a contract.

    27. Damages as a measure of punishment for the defendant's wrongful acts (also called *exemplary* damages).

    28. The condition that exists when a contract is made with the purpose of benefiting the third party.

    29. An order by the court ordering a breaching party to do that which he or she agreed to do under the terms of the contract.

    30. Damages that compensate the plaintiff for actual losses resulting from the breach.

    31. Someone for whose benefit a promise is made, but who is not a party to the contract.

    32. Lessen; keep as low as possible.

    33. Damages in name only.

Sharpening Your Latin Skills

In the space provided, write the definition of each of the following legal terms, referring to the glossary when necessary:

assumpsit _______________________________

ex contractu _______________________________

gratis _______________________________

in pari delicto _______________________________

locus sigilli _______________________________

non assumpsit _______________________________

nudum pactum _______________________________

quasi _______________________________

Using Legal Language

Read the following story and fill in the blank lines with legal terms taken from the list of terms at the beginning of this chapter:

Needing a car for a trip she was planning, Holly entered into a contract to buy a late-model Toyota from Enrique for $7,000. Time was of the _______________________________ with regard to this contract, because Holly planned to leave on the trip the next day. Before she could carry out the contract, however, Holly's trip was canceled. She decided to transfer her right to the car to her friend Maxine. The transfer of a right is called a(n) _______________________________ rather than a(n) _______________________________, which is a transfer of a duty. Holly was the _______________________________, and Maxine was the _______________________________. Enrique agreed to deal solely with Maxine and to release Holly from all obligations under the contract, thus creating a(n) _______________________________. Enrique and Maxine were in _______________________________, which is the legal name for the relationship that existed between them. When the time for _______________________________— that is, the carrying out of the contract—arrived, Enrique made _______________________________ by offering to turn the car over to Maxine. She offered to pay him with Mexican pesos, which is not _______________________________ in the United States. Enrique refused the _______________________________ but then reached an agreement with Maxine to change the price for the car to $6,000 and to postpone the time for performance for a week. This agreement to change the performance is called a(n) _______________________________. The next day Maxine told Enrique that she had changed her mind and was not going to buy the car. Because this occurred before the time for performance had arrived, it is known as a(n) _______________________________. Enrique would not be able to ask the court to order _______________________________, because the subject matter of the contract was not unique. Similarly, because the parties had not agreed on damages at the time of the execution of the contract, no _______________________________ existed. If Enrique suffered no actual monetary loss because of the _______________________________ by Maxine, he would be able to recover only _______________________________ from her in court, plus _______________________________ to take care of any reasonable expenses resulting from the breach. Enrique owed a duty to Maxine to _______________________________ the damages—that is, keep them as low as possible. This case was not one involving _______________________________ or _______________________________ such as double or triple the amount of actual damages. Thankfully for Maxine and her lawyer, the _______________________________ _______________________________—that is, the time limit for bringing suit—had not run out.

The Uniform Commercial Code and Sales of Goods Contracts

ANTE INTERROGATORY

A seller's right to fix the problem when the goods delivered to the buyer are damaged is called (A) cover, (B) perfect tender, (C) merchantability, (D) cure.

LEARNING OBJECTIVES

LO 1: Summarize the purpose of the Uniform Commercial Code and its organizational structure

LO 2: List what kinds of contracts would and would not be governed by Article 2 of the UCC

LO 3: Define goods and explain what set of law governs a mixed contract of goods and services

LO 4: Define a sale and distinguish between a sale on approval and a sale or return

LO 5: Explain what a merchant is and why it matters to know whether one is a merchant

LO 6: Compare and contrast an express warranty from an implied warranty

LO 7: List Article 2's Statute of Fraud requirement and its exceptions

LO 8: Describe the kinds of remedies available to nonbreaching sellers and buyers in sales of goods contracts

KEY TERMS

article

bill of sale

breach of contract

conforming goods

consequential damages

contract to sell

cover

cure

damages

destination contract

donee donor

express warranty

f.o.b. the place of destination

f.o.b. the place of shipment

full warranty

fungible goods

future goods

goods

identified goods

implied warranty

incidental damages

4

limited warranty

merchant

nonconforming goods

output contract

puffing

requirements contract

remedies

risk of loss

sale

sale on approval

sale or return

shipment contract

specific performance

Statute of Frauds

title

Uniform Commercial Code (UCC)

warranty of fitness for a particular purpose

warranty of merchantability

warranty of title

WEBSITES FOR PRONUNCIATION HELP

http://dictionary.cambridge.org/us/pronunciation/english/audio
https://www.howtopronounce.com

The **Uniform Commercial Code (UCC)** was first created in 1952 through a joint effort of the National Conference of the Commissioners on Uniform State Laws and the American Law Institute. It is a collection of model statutes designed to bring uniformity across the country to common commercial transactions. The UCC is transformed from being a model code (like the Model Penal Code or the Uniform Partnership Act) that, by itself, has no authority to becoming "law" when states adopt it, which has been done in whole or in part in every state. When adopted by a jurisdiction, the UCC's legal rules replace that jurisdiction's common law doctrines. However, since state courts have to interpret the meaning of statutes, state case law must be considered when one researches any section of a state's UCC. As drafted, the UCC consists of 11 parts, called **Articles**, in a statutory framework (an article is a discrete collection of laws on the same general topic), on subjects like leases of personal property (Article 2A), negotiable instruments (which concerns written unconditional promises or orders to pay money, located Article), and the subject of this chapter, sales of goods (Article 2).

SALES OF GOODS

A commonplace commercial activity that happens everywhere is a contract for the sale of goods. The UCC expressly covers sales of goods through the UCC's Article 2. In fact, Article 2 of the UCC has been legislatively adopted everywhere in America, except Louisiana. Consequently, Article 2 governs all sales of goods, whether the contracts are made by businesses for commercial purposes or made by persons for non-business reasons. It is important to remember that Article 2 doesn't apply to all contracts, including all contracts where something is sold. For example, an employment contract (a services contract) is not covered under Article 2, and a contract for the sale of real estate would be outside the scope of Article 2. Contracts outside Article 2's coverage are governed by the common law or applicable legal doctrines of the controlling jurisdiction. Also, bear in mind that the rules in Article 2 don't have to automatically apply to sales contracts. While that may seem counterintuitive, the UCC provides throughout its rules that parties to a contract can make an agreement that differs from the UCC's de facto rules. For example, the statute of limitations (the legally established time for bringing a lawsuit) for a lawsuit for **breach of contract** (the failure of a party to a contract to carry out the terms of the agreement) in a sales of goods case is four years, but parties are allowed to include in their sales contracts an agreement to reduce the time period to as short as one year (UCC 2-725).

Goods

The starting point for understanding what Article 2 covers is the word, "goods." **Goods** are defined in UCC 2-105. Essentially, goods are movable, tangible personal property. This book, clothing, motor vehicles, computers, furniture, food, animals, and growing crops are all examples of goods. If the goods are not yet in existence (such as goods not yet manufactured) or owned by the seller (such as fish not yet caught), they are known as **future goods**. If they are the type of goods that are usually sold by weight or measure and are stored in bulk quantities, such as grain or oil, they are called **fungible goods**. These are defined as goods of which any unit is the same as any like unit. **Identified goods** is the name given to specific goods that have been selected as the subject matter of a contract. Goods must be identified as those goods to which a contract refers before title to them can pass from a seller to a buyer.

Some contracts involve the sale of goods and also services associated with the goods (in-home installation of a new appliance, for instance). This creates the question of whether such a mixed contract is or is not governed by Article 2. Although the UCC is silent on this question, courts have crafted an answer, and if the "predominate factor" in the contract is the sales of goods, the entire contract is governed by the UCC. If not, the entire contract is governed by the traditional contract doctrines of the given jurisdiction. Appellate courts are tasked with determining what the predominate factor is for those types of contracts. For example, thinking back to the appliance example, a customer doesn't buy a stove to get it installed; the customer gets installation services and a warranty because he or she bought a stove. And a stove—which is moveable personal property—is "goods." By contrast, one doesn't buy a pacemaker in a hospital, so much as one is getting medical services that include the correct placement by doctors and other trained medical service providers of a pacemaker in one's body. Therefore, the predominate factor in the first example would be the sale of the stove, and in the second example, the predominate factor is the medical services.

Sales

A **sale** is defined by in UCC 2-106 as "the passing of **title** from the seller to the buyer for a price." Title means ownership. Sometimes, a **bill of sale**, which is a signed writing evidencing the transfer of personal property from one person to another, is given by the seller to the buyer. If title to goods is to pass at a future time, the transaction is called a **contract to sell** rather than a sale. A gift is not a sale, because the person receiving the gift (the **donee**) pays no price to the person making the gift (the **donor**).

There are times when a sale is made conditionally and either title doesn't transfer to the buyer or the buyer has the right to return the goods to the seller even after buying and taking title to the goods. For example, a **sale on approval** (UCC 2-326) occurs when the goods are for the buyer's use (consumer goods) rather than for resale (commercial goods), and they may be returned even though they conform to the contract. Such goods remain the property of the seller until the buyer's approval is expressed or a reasonable time elapses. In contrast, a **sale or return** (2-326) occurs when the goods are primarily for resale and may be returned even though they conform to the contract. In this latter instance, title passes to the buyer at the time of sale, but reverts to the seller if and when the goods are returned. The key distinction between a sale on approval and a sale or return is that the buyer bears the **risk of loss** (responsibility in case of damage or destruction) in a sale or return until the goods have been returned to the seller (2-327).

▎ TERMS IN ACTION

After noticing an advertisement for a mail order coin club, a New York man joined the club and ordered some coins valued at almost $600 (which was a lot of money in 1976). The coin company sent the coins by registered mail, which required someone to sign for the package. The postal service delivered the coins to the man's address and someone signed for the package, but the man claimed he never received them and refused to pay for the coins. The coin company sued him for breach of contract, and the legal issue came down to whether the coins, which are **goods** and therefore covered by New York's **Uniform Commercial Code**, were sold as a **sale on approval** or a **sale or return**. The appellate court concluded that,

(Continued)

> because the buyer was a coin collector but wasn't in the business of selling coins, he didn't qualify as a **merchant**. Therefore, the sale was a sale on approval, which makes a seller liable for the goods until they have been received and approved (accepted). Even though the coin company could prove the package was signed for at the buyer's address, the buyer wasn't the one who signed for them. In fact, at the time of the delivery of the coins, the buyer was having some remodeling done at his home, but the general contractor testified that neither he nor his employees were at the buyer's property when the coins were delivered. Because there was no proof that the buyer ever had the coins, then he never accepted them or took **title** to them. Therefore, he didn't have to pay for them.
>
> Source: *First Coinvesters, Inc. v. Coppola*, 388 N.Y.S.2d 833 (N.Y. Dist. Ct. 1976)

Unique terms are used to describe certain contracts for goods. A contract to sell all the goods a company manufactures is called an **output contract** (2-306). In contrast, a contract to buy an unspecified amount of goods from the seller (such as all the goods the buyer might need) is called a **requirements contract** (also 2-306). A contract under which the seller turns the goods over to a carrier for delivery to a buyer is termed a **shipment contract** and is often designated **f.o.b. the place of shipment** (such as Chicago), meaning free on board (no delivery charges) to the stated place of shipment (2-319). In a shipment contract, title to the goods and **risk of loss** pass to the buyer when the goods are turned over to a carrier. On the other hand, a contract that requires the seller to deliver goods to a destination is called a **destination contract** and is designated **f.o.b. the place of destination** (such as Philadelphia). In a destination contract, title and risk of loss pass to the buyer when the goods are tendered at their destination, and the shipper (e.g., in Boston) assumes ownership responsibility until then.

Merchants

While Article 2 covers all that would be considered sales of goods, not all of Article 2's rules apply to everyone. The UCC has certain rules that only apply to **merchants**. A merchant is defined in UCC 2-104 as "a person who deals in goods of the kind or otherwise by his occupation holds himself out as having knowledge or skill peculiar to the practices or goods involved in the transaction or to whom such knowledge or skill may be attributed by his employment of an agent or broker…." A reading of that rule shows there are three ways to be considered a merchant and the significance is that the UCC holds merchants to a higher standard in their transactions in certain situations. For instance and as will be discussed later, more implied warranties are imposed on merchant sellers than non-merchant sellers.

Warranties

Sellers of goods often guarantee their products by making promises or statements of fact about them. Sometimes, sellers say positive things about the goods they're trying to sell in an attempt to entice prospective buyers. Putting goods in the best light possible and making statements of opinions are not considered warranties, but instead are known as **puffing**. For example, the phrase "Absolutely the best chocolate cookies you will ever eat!" is puffing and not a warranty.

Article 2 distinguishes between express and implied warranties. According to 2-313, an **express warranty** is one that is a promise or assurance about the goods and which is part of the bargain (the sale), or is a description about the goods that is part of the bargain, or is a sample or model of the goods that is made part of the bargain. Notice, the words "warranty" or "guarantee" aren't required to make an express warranty. Under the federal Magnuson-Moss Warranty Act, when a **full warranty** is given for consumer goods, the seller must repair or replace, without cost to the buyer, defective goods or else refund the purchase price. Any express warranty that does less must be labeled a **limited warranty**.

An **implied warranty** is one that is imposed by law rather than given expressly by the seller. The UCC establishes certain implied warranties that all sellers make, such as the **warranty of title** (2-312; that the seller owns the goods being sold and that the transfer is rightful and that no unknown liens on the goods exists). Another implied warranty all sellers are capable of making is the **warranty of fitness for a particular purpose** (2-315), which is made when a buyer relies on a seller's skill and judgment in selecting the goods in choosing goods that are capable of meeting the buyer's unique needs, and the seller is aware of this reliance. When this happens, the seller impliedly warrants that the goods are fit for the purpose for which they are to be used.

Merchants make certain implied warranties not made by non-merchant sellers, including the **warranty of merchantability** (2-314). Merchantability is sometimes called fitness for ordinary use, and it means that goods are warranted as fit for the ordinary purpose for which they are to be used. Merchantability does not mean the goods will be perfect. In a famous case from Massachusetts, a woman sued a Boston restaurant for breach of the implied warranty of merchantability after eating a bowl of the restaurant's fish chowder that had a bone in it. The bone lodged in the woman's throat, requiring two surgeries. Despite her misfortune, the Massachusetts Supreme Court ruled in favor of the restaurant, concluding there was no implied warranty of merchantability, such that every New Englander knew that a well-known chowder made in the New England tradition for centuries likely could have bones in it (*Webster v. Blue Ship Tea Room*, 198 N.E.2d 309, Mass. 1964).

Express warranties are only made when sellers choose to provide them. And even though the UCC imposes certain implied warranties, sellers may exclude or disclaim implied warranties, provided the exclusions are done clearly. According to 2-316, the expression "as is" or "with all faults" is sufficient, but in order to disclaim a warranty of fitness, the exclusion must be in writing and conspicuous.

TERMS IN ACTION

It can be difficult to know when a seller's positive statements about the quality of its goods become a **warranty**. In a case from Indiana, a farming corporation that made a substantial portion of its revenues from selling watermelons, ordered 40 pounds of watermelon seeds from a seed company, costing $85.40 per pound. The watermelon seeds were "Prince Charles," a type of seed known for its resistance to disease. On the top of the cans in which the seeds were shipped was a label that described the seeds as "top quality seeds with high vitality, vigor and germination." But when the watermelons grew and became diseased, the buyer sued the seller for breach of express and implied warranties. In interpreting Indiana's version of the UCC's warranty requirements, the Indiana Supreme Court held that the phrase "top quality seeds" didn't qualify as a warranty, because it lacked a definite assertion of fact about the quality of the seeds. That statement was considered **puffing**. But the court concluded that the seller's claim that the seeds had "high vitality, vigor and germination" could qualify as an express warranty, as well as the **implied warranty of merchantability**, which is an implied warranty applying only to **merchants**.

Source: *Martin Rispens & Son v. Hall Farms, Inc.*, 621 N.E.2d 1078 (Ind. 1993), abrogated by a later case on grounds distinct from the issues presented here

Statute of Frauds

As discussed in Chapter 19, according to the **Statute of Frauds** certain contracts need to be in writing to be enforceable. Those contracts include real estate contracts, prenuptial agreements, and contracts that can't be completed within a year from the date of making the contract. Article 2 of the Uniform Commercial Code has its own requirement on written contracts, and here the focus is on the price of the goods. According to UCC 2-201, "a contract for the sales of goods for the price of $500 or more is not enforceable…" unless it is in writing. But as is the same with the traditional Statute of Frauds, it isn't a written contract alone that is sufficient; the contract must be "signed by the party against whom enforcement is sought or by his authorized agent or broker." So, if someone sells her or his old car for $499, that sale is fully enforceable as an oral contract. But if the price is $500 or higher, then if the buyer has buyer's remorse before taking possession of the car and paying the money, the buyer can back out of the deal if the contract wasn't in writing and signed by the buyer. Likewise, if that contract is oral and the seller gets a better offer after the buyer agreed to buy the car but before anything was actually exchanged, the seller is not in breach of contract when making a more lucrative deal with a second buyer.

As is the case with almost everything in the law, there are exceptions to Article 2's Statute of Frauds. A later part of 2-201 provides three exceptions: (1) when the goods are made specifically for the buyer's needs and are not suitable for sale in the ordinary course of the seller's business, and the seller has made substantial effort toward making or procuring the goods; (2) if in the course of litigation, the party against whom enforcement is sought admits under oath (such as in testimony) that a sales contract was made between the parties; and (3) when the seller accepts payment for the goods or, conversely, the buyer accepts the goods.

A part of Article 2's Statute of Frauds has an application exclusive to merchants, and it is significant. If two merchants are dealing with each other and one of them sends the other what 2-201 refers to as a "written confirmation of the contract" and the other party receives the written confirmation, the parties are in a binding contract even if the party receiving the written confirmation didn't sign the confirmation … *unless* the receiving party sends a written objection to the confirmation within 10 days of receiving it.

> ### Web Wise
>
> - The entire UCC can be accessed at the following webpage of the Legal Information Institute (created by Cornell University Law School): **https://www.law.cornell.edu/ucc**
> - More information on the UCC can be found at: **https://uniformcommercialcode.uslegal.com**
> - The Wikipedia page for the Uniform Commercial Code is a good starting point for further research, and is located at: **https://en.wikipedia.org/wiki/Uniform_Commercial_Code**
> - More information on federal warranty law can be found at the following Federal Trade Commission's web page: **https://www.ftc.gov/tips-advice/business-center/guidance/businesspersons-guide-federal-warranty-law**

Remedies

Article 2 provides various **remedies** for both sellers and buyers in the event either party breaches the sales contract. Remedies are the types of relief or justice a court can award to a litigant who has established a violation of a legal right committed by the defendant. Remedies can be legal in nature, such as monetary **damages**, or equitable in nature, like a restraining order. While Article 2 has specific rules on remedies, the buyer and seller to a sales contract are free to create in their agreement any suitable remedy.

Where the buyer is in breach of contract by failing to pay for goods or by wrongfully rejecting them, 2-703 provides the seller with a number of options, including withholding delivery of the goods, selling the goods to an alternate buyer and the suing the breaching buyer for the difference between the contract price of the goods and what the seller received from the alternate sale, or even canceling the contract. Sellers are also allowed to recover **incidental damages** from a breaching buyer, which 2-710 states include reasonable costs of transporting or storing the goods after the buyer's breach.

If the goods are delivered to the buyer in accordance with the contract terms, the goods are known as **conforming goods**. In contrast, if the goods are not the same as those called for under the contract or are defective or damaged, they are called **nonconforming goods**. Consequently, sellers are in breach of contract for delivering nonconforming goods, or for failing to deliver the goods. Before a buyer would have a remedy because of the seller's delivery of nonconforming goods, 2-508 states that when buyers reject nonconforming goods, sellers are allowed to **cure** (correct) the defect if they do so within the contract time. If the defect is not cured, 2-712 states that buyers have the right to obtain **cover**—that is, the purchasing of similar goods from someone else followed by a suit for the difference between the contract price and the cost to purchase the substitute goods (if the second purchase was more expensive). And according to 2-711, buyers have the right to cancel the contract when the seller is in breach. UCC 2-716 states that where the goods are unique or so rare that money damages would be an insufficient remedy, buyers have the option to seek **specific performance** from the seller, which is to sue for the goods themselves.

UCC 2-715 allows buyers to seek **incidental damages** and **consequential damages** from the breaching seller. Incidental damages are reasonable expenses incurred because of the seller's breach (which can include legal fees), and consequential damages are damages that flow from the seller's breach and which the seller had reason to know about and which can't be prevented by the buyer obtaining cover. In an illustrative case from California, a commercial fruit grower bought from a tree nursery 1100 peach trees that turned out to have been diseased at the time of the sale. In the litigation, the seller of the peach trees argued its damages were limited to the difference between the value of the land with the diseased trees on it and what it would be worth if the trees were healthy. But the appellate court agreed with the buyer that the damages can include the lost profits (consequential damages) resulting from the buyer being unable to sell the peaches that would have grown on the trees had they not been diseased (*Serian Brothers, Inc. v. Agri-Sun Nursery*, 30 Cal.Rptr.2d 382 (Ct. App. 1994)).

Reviewing What You Learned

After studying the chapter, write the answers to each of the following questions:

1. Explain the purpose of the Uniform Commercial Code._____

____

____

____

2. What is included in the definition of "goods?"___________

____

____

____

3. What is the difference between identified goods and future goods?____

____

____

____

4. Give an example of a sale on approval contract and a sale or return contract? _______________________________

____

____

5. According to Article 2, what makes someone a merchant and why does it matter?

____

____

____

6. What makes something an express warranty?_____________

____

____

____

7. What are two implied warranties generally required to be made by Article 2 sellers?___________________________

____

____

____

8. What are three exceptions for Article 2's Statute of Frauds? _

____

____

____

9. What remedies are available to a seller when the buyer is in breach of contract? _______________________________

____

____

____

10. Given an example of where consequential damages would be an appropriate remedy for a buyer when the seller is in breach of contract? _______________________________

____

____

____

Understanding Legal Concepts

Indicate whether each statement is true or false. Then, change the italicized word or phrase of each false statement to make it true.

ANSWERS

_____ **1.** The Uniform Commercial Code is organized by *Articles*.

_____ **2.** *Future goods* are specific goods that have been selected as the subject matter of a contract.

_____ **3.** If the predominate factor in a mixed contract is *services*, the entire contract is governed by the UCC.

_____ **4.** A conditional sale where the buyer is purchasing goods for resale is by default a *sale or return*.

_____ **5.** An *express warranty* is made by operation of law.

_____ **6.** Merchants make the warranty of *fitness for ordinary use*.

_____ **7.** Article 2 requires a sales of goods contract to be in writing when the purchase price is *at least* $500.

_____ **8.** The type of relief a court can grant a winning plaintiff is called *damages*.

_____ **9.** Legal fees incurred in suing a breaching party to a sales of goods contract is an example of *consequential damages*.

_____ **10.** When a seller is in breach, the buyer has the option of obtaining *cover*.

Checking Terminology

From the list of legal terms that follows, select the one that matches each definition.

ANSWERS

a. article
b. bill of sale
c. breach of contract
d. consequential damages
e. cover
f. cure
g. damages
h. express warranty
i. fungible goods
j. future goods
k. goods
l. implied warranty
m. incidental damages
n. merchant
o. nonconforming goods
p. puffing
q. remedies
r. sale
s. sale on approval
t. sale or return
u. specific performance
v. title
w. warranty of fitness for a particular purpose
x. warranty of merchantability

_____ **1.** A warranty that is specifically made a part of the bargain.

_____ **2.** Tangible, moveable personal property.

_____ **3.** One whose business is to sell goods.

_____ **4.** Putting goods in the best light possible, but without making a warranty.

_____ **5.** The kinds of relief or justice a court can award.

_____ **6.** When the goods are for the buyer's use rather than for resale, and they may be returned even though they conform to the contract. Here, the seller bears the risk of loss.

_____ **7.** A warranty imposed by the operation of law.

_____ **8.** When the goods are primarily for resale and may be returned even though they conform to the contract. Here, the buyer bears the risk of loss.

_____ **9.** The failure of a party to a contract to carry out the terms of the agreement.

_____ **10.** A signed writing evidencing the transfer of personal property from one person to another.

_____ **11.** A type of remedy that is compensation in money for loss or injury.

_____ **12.** The right the seller has to fix or make right the nonconforming goods.

_____ **13.** Reasonable expenses that indirectly result from a breach of contract.

_____ **14.** Losses that flow from a breach of contract, but which are from special circumstances that result from the breach and which the seller had reason to know about, like lost profits.

_____ **15.** The transfer of title by way of a contract.

_____ **16.** A type of remedy where the buyer can seek from the seller the goods that weren't delivered, rather than money damages.

_____ **17.** A type of goods that are usually sold by weight or measure and are stored in bulk quantities.

_____ **18.** A warranty made when a buyer relies on a seller's skill and judgment in selecting the goods that meet the buyer's unique needs, and the seller is aware of this reliance.

_____ **19.** Goods that are defective or damaged in any way.

_____ **20.** Purchasing similar goods from someone else after the seller fails to provide conforming goods and bringing suit for the difference between the contract price and the cost to purchase the substitute goods.

_____ **21.** Ownership of goods.

_____ **22.** In a statutory framework, a discrete collection of laws on the same general topic

_____ **23.** A warranty that the goods are fit for the ordinary purpose for which they are to be used.

_____ **24.** Goods are not yet in existence or owned by the seller.

Using Legal Language

Read the following story and fill in the blank lines with legal terms taken from the list of terms at the beginning of this chapter:

Rachel owned a bakery specializing in cupcakes. She had started out making cupcakes for friends' birthdays but with their encouragement she began selling her cupcakes and then rented a storefront in town. Cupcakes qualify as _____________________, according to _____________________, and so her cupcake _____________________ are transactions governed by the UCC. She buys a lot of flour and sugar for her business, and those types of bulk goods, sold by weight or measurement, are known as _____________________. Once Rachel began her business, she qualified as a _____________________, and so certain rules of Article 2 only apply to her but not necessarily her customers. When she makes a contract for a large order of cupcakes, she formalizes the agreement by drafting a _____________________. Customers should be careful to read that document, because in it Rachel makes all sales final, meaning that her sales are not conditional, meaning they are neither a _____________________ nor a _____________________.

Rachel got a huge order for 250 cupcakes from a company hosting an employee gathering, and that contract needed to be in writing (and signed) in order to satisfy the _____________________, because the purchase price was at least _____________________. Rachel provided the company a few samples of her cupcakes, which meant she was making an _____________________ that the cupcakes would be like her samples. At the tasting, Rachel said that her cupcakes were the most delicious "from here to the Food Network!" which is known as _____________________, or just putting her cupcakes in the best light possible.

Unfortunately, the stove she had bought the prior week broke and she was unable to fulfill the order! As a buyer of goods (the stove), she realized that the seller, who was a kitchen supply company, had breached the _____________________, sometimes called the _____________________, because the stove obviously didn't work the way it was ordinarily supposed to. And because she lost the large order, she considered suing the stove seller for her _____________________, which would include the lost profits of that order. The company that was supposed to receive the cupcakes had to think fast and so it bought substitute cupcakes from a bakery in another town. That type of purchase is known as cover, and because the substitute cupcakes cost more than what Rachel was charging, the company considered suing Rachel for the difference. If that company were to use an attorney to sue Rachel for breach of contract, those legal fees would be _____________________, which is a type of _____________________, which means the types relief or justice a court can order to a plaintiff. Fortunately, Rachel got a new stove from the seller, and she got an even bigger order from the company who never got its 250 cupcakes from her. As it turns out, her samples were really as good as she claimed.

PART FIVE

Terms Used in the Law of Personal Property and Agency

Konstantin Chagin/Shutterstock

CHAPTER 22
Personal Property
and Bailments

CHAPTER 23
Intellectual Property

CHAPTER 24
Law of Agency

5

We are surrounded by personal property from the moment we are born to the moment we die. In fact, whether for good or bad, much of our lives is spent in the pursuit of more personal property of one kind or another. In addition, we are touched by the law of agency in many aspects of our lives, either by dealing with people who are principals, agents, employers, and employees, or by being involved in those roles ourselves. Chapter 22 discusses personal property and how it is acquired, and then gives an explanation of bailments. Chapter 23 covers the subject of intellectual property, including patents, copyrights, trademarks, and trade secrets. Chapter 24 begins by distinguishing among the different kinds of agency relationships and continues with an examination of the various kinds of agents, the authority of agents, and the subject of vicarious liability.

Personal Property and Bailments

ANTE INTERROGATORY

*When you borrow a cup of sugar from a neighbor, with the intention
of returning the same amount of sugar, it is known as a
(A) bailment for the sole benefit of the bailor, (B) mutuum, (C) mutual benefit
bailment, (D) bailment for the sole benefit of the bailee.*

LEARNING OBJECTIVES

LO 1: Categorize personal property and real property

LO 2: List the various methods by which one can acquire personal property

LO 3: Contrast an auction with reserve with an auction without reserve

LO 4: Explain the elements of a valid gift

LO 5: Contrast an inter vivos gift with a gift causa mortis

LO 6: Summarize the differences between lost, mislaid, and abandoned property

LO 7: List the three types of bailments and explain the liability distinction between each type

KEY TERMS

abandoned property

auction sale

auction with reserve

auction without reserve

bailee

bailment

bailment for the sole benefit of the bailee

bailment for the sole benefit of the bailor

bailor

bidder

chattels

chose in action (singular)

donee

donor

fixture

gift causa mortis

gratuitous bailment

intangible personal property

intellectual property

inter vivos gift

lost property

mislaid property

mutual benefit bailment

mutuum

personal property

personalty

shop right

tangible personal property

title

tortious bailee

trade fixture

WEBSITES FOR PRONUNCIATION HELP

http://dictionary.cambridge.org/us/pronunciation/english/audio
https://www.howtopronounce.com

PERSONAL PROPERTY VS. REAL PROPERTY

Broadly speaking, anything that can be owned is property. **Personal property**, also called **personalty** or **chattels**, is anything subject of ownership other than real property, which is the second class of property. Real property, also known as real estate, includes land and the building or other permanent things put on the land, including fixtures, which are discussed below. **Tangible personal property** is property that has substance and that can be touched, such as a flat screen television, an item of clothing, or an automobile. **Intangible personal property**, conversely, is property that is not perceptible to the senses and cannot be touched, such as ownership interests in partnerships or corporations, patents, copyrights, and trademarks; and checks or promissory notes. One can have a personal property right by way of an enforceable claim against another, both in tort and in contract. Such an intangible interest or claim is called a **chose in action** (singular; the plural is choses in action), which is a comprehensive term suggesting a property right or a right to possess something only obtainable by a legal action.

When personal property is physically attached to real property, it is known as a **fixture** and becomes part of the real property. A built-in dishwasher or a permanently installed lighting unit is an example of fixtures. In contrast, when a business tenant physically attaches personal property, such as machinery, that is necessary to carry on the trade or business to real property, it is called a **trade fixture**. It does not become part of the real property and may be removed by the business tenant upon termination of the tenancy. Whether something has been affixed or annexed to real estate sufficiently to be considered a fixture is determined on a case-by-case basis, but a key factor is the intent of the owner of the personal property that was affixed. Intent is often determined by inference. For example, one can safely conclude that a homeowner who puts a new toilet in his or her bathroom intends for it to stay even if the homeowner were to sell the home and leave.

Methods of Acquiring Personal Property

One can possess and yet not own personal property. Ownership is a legal concept and presumes the owner has **title** to the property, even if the owner does not have possession. Title is evidence of ownership and for many items of personal property, possession would be sufficient to prove ownership. For instance, do you have all the receipts for the socks and shoes you own? If not, does that mean you're not the owner? Of course you are, unless you stole them. But for other types of personal property, such as a car or boat, tangible evidence of ownership—like the "title"—is required to prove lawful ownership.

Personal property can be acquired through the following methods:

1. Purchase, including by auction
2. Gift
3. Creation
4. Inheritance
5. Abandonment

Purchase of Personal Property

To acquire property by purchase requires a buyer and seller, obviously. And as earlier chapters have discussed, including the prior chapter on the UCC, a sale of personal property involves the acceptance of an offer for sale of the item. Title to property (whether a document or certificate of title or simply, legal ownership) transfers to the buyer at the time of purchase.

An **auction sale** is a sale of property to the highest **bidder**. In an **auction with reserve** the auctioneer may withdraw the goods without accepting the highest bid, if the bids fail to reach the stated reserve price. By contrast, in an **auction without reserve** (sometimes referred to as an **absolute auction**), the auctioneer may not withdraw the goods after one bid has been placed. According to Section 2-238 of the UCC, auctions are presumed to be *with reserve* unless otherwise explicitly stated at the auction or when the goods are put up. Beyond that, some states have auction rules clearly establishing what is required for an auction to be considered with reserve. In an auction with reserve, the offeror is the bidder. But in an auction without reserve, the offeror is the person placing the item up for bidding. This distinction is important because it is the offeree who has the power to reject an offer, which is why in a with-reserve auction the seller/auctioneer can reject the bidders' offers. But in a without-reserve auction, the first bid would qualify as an acceptance, which explains why the item can't be withdrawn after one bid. All that is left in this type of auction is determining who is the highest bidder/acceptor. Those who sell goods through online bidding sites, such as eBay, need to be clear in communicating the type of auctions in which they are engaged.

Gift

Property acquired by an **inter vivos gift** requires a living **donor** (the giver of the gift) and a **donee** (the recipient of the gift). But unlike a purchase of property, which is a transfer that is the consequence of contractual consideration, gifting involves donative intent. The elements of a gift are generally considered the following: 1) the donor's intent to make a gift (as opposed to a loan); 2) delivery of the gift; and 3) the donee's acceptance of the gift. Disputes about whether something was a loan or a gift (as in between friends) turn on evidence that there was intent expressed that the item being given was not to be returned. Delivery of a gift can be made symbolically or constructively. For example, one might give away a car stored in a garage by giving all the car's keys to the friend who will be the car's next owner.

Creation

Property through creation is the result of one's intellectual activities. Common types of **intellectual property** are trademarks, patents, and copyrights. (See Chapter 23 on intellectual property.) An issue for those whose work involves the creation of intellectual property is who owns the property. If one's job involves creating intellectual property (a software engineer) or if one is specifically hired as an independent contractor to create intellectual property (a website designer), that which is created is generally owned by the employing or hiring party. This is known as the **shop right** doctrine and often has applicability in patent law for those whose employment involves inventing products and who use company resources in the creation of their patentable property. Of course, employment contracts can grant to the hiring party any intellectual property rights related to the work the hired party creates.

Inheritance

Part Six of this textbook is focused on the law related to inheritance, but at this point it is worth pointing out that one's right to inherited property is only a contingent right until the party from whom the property is given has passed away. Unlike a will or other estate-planning device, which is a written mechanism for giving property away upon death, a **gift causa mortis** involves a person, in anticipation of impending death, attempting to give property to someone. "Causa mortis" is Latin for "because of death," and for a gift causa mortis to be valid, the requirements of an inter vivos gift must exist and the donor must die from the event that precipitated the causa mortis gift. Some states limit the extent of property that may be given by causa mortis, For example, Indiana does not allow real property to be the subject of a gift causa mortis.

TERMS IN ACTION

Gustav Klimt is a renowned 19th-century Austrian symbolist painter whose works include a painting that sold for a then-record $135 million in 2006. That work is the subject of the film, *The Woman in Gold*, which tells how an heir of the original owner of the painting had to sue the Austrian government to get it back, decades after the Nazis stole it during World War II. Another famous legal case involving Klimt's work comes from New York. There, a wealthy

New York City architect wrote a letter to his son at college, on the son's 21st birthday, telling him that he was getting as his birthday present a Klimt oil painting the father owned, titled *Schloss Kammer am Attersee II*. But there was a catch: the father was keeping the painting in his possession until his death. The father died 17 years later, and at the time of his passing he was living in Austria. When the son requested the painting from his stepmother, she refused. In the ensuing lawsuit, the stepmother argued that, because her husband, the father, kept the painting until his death, there was insufficient intent to make an **inter vivos gift** and inadequate delivery of the painting. The court ruled otherwise, finding that the letter and subsequent letters the father wrote about the painting showed his **donor's** intent to make a gift of the painting, as well as its symbolic delivery—even though he wanted to keep it for the remainder of his life. Furthermore, the son's possession of the letters during the interim years was sufficient to show the son's acceptance of the painting. According to the appellate case, the father bought the painting in 1959 for $8,000. When the court awarded it to the son in the mid-1980s, it was valued at $2,500,000. In 1997, the painting was sold at **auction** for $23,590,000.

Source: *Gruen v. Gruen*, 68 N.Y.2d 48 (N.Y. 1986); christies.com

Abandonment

Property can be involuntarily transferred when someone finds property, but whether the finder is the keeper or the weeper depends on how the property was separated from its owner—if it was lost, mislaid, or abandoned. **Lost property** is that which the owner doesn't realize has accidentally left her or his possession. For example, if a wallet falls out of a man's back pocket, the wallet has been lost. **Mislaid property** is that which the owner has set aside somewhere, but later forgets. For example, if one puts a wedding ring in a drawer for safekeeping but later forgets where he or she put it, the ring is mislaid. **Abandoned property** is that which the owner had intentionally discarded, having no desire to keep it. One's trash in a garbage can sitting outside a house or apartment is abandoned property. Where property has been abandoned, the finder is the new owner, but one who finds lost or mislaid property generally has a possession right that can be trumped by the true owner. In fact, some jurisdictions refer to such possessors as **bailees** (bailments is discussed later in the chapter). But knowing whether property has been intentionally abandoned or is lost or mislaid isn't always easy.

TERMS IN ACTION

Justin Gawronski should have been frightened enough to be reading George Orwell's *1984*. Perhaps the greatest political novel of the 20th century (unless it's Orwell's *Animal Farm*), *1984* focuses on a horrifying world where the government is constantly watching the citizenry through technology, so much so that what most people think of when they think of *1984* is the phrase "Big Brother is watching you." But for Gawronski, a teenager from Michigan reading the novel on his Kindle for a school project in July 2009, fiction came to life when—all of a sudden—Amazon.com deleted from his electronic **possession** the book he **purchased**. Furthermore, Gawronski had made his own personal notes on his e-book copy and they were gone as well. Earlier that year, the same thing happened to another teenage student, Antoine Brugier of California, who at least got an email from Amazon announcing his refund at the time of the deletion. For its part, Amazon believed that it had unwittingly allowed an e-vendor to sell an unauthorized version of *1984*, a type of property that is both **intellectual property** and **intangible personal property**. Yet, if the boys had bought paper copies of the novel, one can hardly imagine an Amazon employee coming to their homes to repossess their **personal property**, or to the homes of the other 2,000 Kindle owners whose e-books by Orwell, including *Animal Farm*, were deleted. The boys brought a class-action suit against Amazon for breach of contract and violation of the federal Computer Fraud and Abuse Act. Consequently, Jeff Bezos,

(Continued)

> Amazon.com's founder and CEO, personally apologized, acknowledging, "we deserve the criticism we've received." In October 2009, the case was settled, with Amazon agreeing to pay plaintiffs' $150,000 legal fees and promising not to unilaterally delete e-books from Kindles anymore.
>
> Sources: pcmag.com; phys.org

BAILMENTS

A **bailment** occurs whenever one person temporarily places personal property in the possession of another person without intending to transfer title to that person. For example, a bailment exists when someone leaves a car with an auto repair shop to be fixed, loans a lawnmower to a neighbor, or takes care of a friend's golden retriever for a week. The one who owns the goods and places them in the possession of another person is the **bailor**. The one who takes possession of the goods is the **bailee**. It is not a bailment when someone borrows something (such as a cup of sugar) and intends to return a similar amount of the same goods. This is because the exact thing borrowed will not be returned. Instead of a bailment, this is a loan for the purposes of consumption and is known as a **mutuum**, which is a word one can trace back to Roman law.

Someone is benefited by a bailment and the benefit determines the type of bailment. Bailments are either for the sole benefit of the bailor, for the sole benefit of the bailee, or are mutual benefit. A **mutual benefit bailment**, which is the typical commercial bailment, is when both the bailor and the bailee receive something valuable from the transaction. For example, when someone leaves a watch with a jeweler to be repaired, the watch owner receives the benefit of having the watch repaired, and the jeweler receives the benefit of being paid for the service rendered. In a mutual benefit bailment, the bailee owes a duty to use ordinary care toward the bailed goods and would be responsible for ordinary negligence if the goods were lost or damaged while in the bailee's care or custody. But a bailee can only be liable when it is aware, or should be aware, that it possesses the bailor's property. In a case from Alabama, a car was stolen right out from under the control of the employees of a drive-through car wash, just before the car was given back to the owner. The driver's employer, a jewelry company, sued the car wash business for the value of the $850,000 in jewelry that was in the trunk of the car, alleging mutual benefit bailment liability. But the problem for the plaintiff was that its employee—who was a traveling jewelry salesperson—never told the car wash employees what was in the car's trunk, and so the court ruled that, without such knowledge, the car wash wasn't a bailee of the contents of the trunk even though it was a bailee of the car (*Ziva Jewelry, Inc. v. Car Wash Headquarters, Inc.*, 897 So.2d 1011(Ala. 2004)).

When, for instance, someone stores his or her car in a friend's garage for safekeeping while away on a trip, and the friend expects nothing back in return, that would be a **bailment for the sole benefit of the bailor**. This is sometimes known as a **gratuitous bailment**, because the bailee is not being tangibly compensated for taking possession of the personal property. In this type of bailment, the bailee owes a duty to exercise only slight care over the property and would be responsible just for gross negligence or recklessness. Conversely, when someone loans (without compensation) a camera or other item to a friend, that is a **bailment for the sole benefit of the bailee**. Here, the bailee owes a duty to use great care with the property and would be responsible for even slight negligence in the event of loss or damage to the bailed property.

A **tortious bailee** is one who has intentional, wrongful possession of another's goods. For example, a person who takes another's goods without authority, keeps another's goods after they should be returned, or uses another's goods for a purpose other than agreed upon is a tortious bailee. Such a bailee is liable for the conversion and for any damage to the property.

Word Wise
More Words Ending in "or" and "ee"

assignor (ass·en·OR)	a person who transfers contract rights or property to another
assignee (ass·en·EE)	one to whom contract rights or property is transferred
bailor (bay·LOR)	one who transfers goods to another temporarily
bailee (bay·LEE)	one to whom goods are transferred temporarily
consignor (kon·sine·OR)	a party shipping goods under a bill of lading
consignee (kon·sine·EE)	a party to whom goods are shipped under a bill of lading
donor (doh·NOR)	one who makes a gift
donee (doh·NEE)	one to whom a gift is made

Reviewing What You Learned

After studying the chapter, write the answers to each of the following questions:

1. Name and give an example of each of the two classes of personal property.

2. Name three kinds of intangible property.

3. What is the difference between a fixture and a trade fixture?

4. What is the difference between an auction that is with reserve and one that is without reserve?

5. Who is the offeror in an auction that is with reserve?

6. What are the elements of a valid inter vivos gift?

7. Explain the shop right doctrine.

8. What makes a gift causa mortis valid?

9. What is the difference between lost, mislaid, and abandoned property?

____

____

____

10. Who owns mislaid property?

____

____

____

11. What is a bailment?

____

____

____

12. Give an example of a bailment for the sole benefit of the bailee?

____

13. Why is it not a bailment when someone borrows a cup of sugar from a neighbor?

____

____

____

14. What is the standard of care in a mutual benefit bailee?

____

____

____

15. Give an example of a bailment for the sole benefit of the bailor.

____

____

____

Understanding Legal Concepts

Indicate whether each statement is true or false. Then, change the italicized word or phrase of each false statement to make it true.

ANSWERS

_____ **1.** *Tangible* personal property is property that is not perceptible to the senses and cannot be touched.

_____ **2.** *Ownership* of goods is represented by title.

_____ **3.** When someone physical attaches personal property to his or home, the personal property becomes a *trade fixture*.

_____ **4.** An auction that is *with reserve* allows the seller to withdraw the item even if there have been bids.

_____ **5.** An *inter vivos* gift can be made through constructive delivery.

_____ **6.** A gift *causa mortis* is only valid if the donor dies from the impending peril or sickness.

_____ **7.** It is a *bailment* when someone borrows a cup of sugar from a neighbor.

_____ **8.** In a mutual benefit bailment, the bailee owes a duty to use *slight* care toward the property.

_____ **9.** In a bailment for the sole benefit of the bailee, the bailee owes a duty to use *great* care with the property.

_____ **10.** A person who uses another's goods for a purpose other than agreed upon is a *tortious bailee*.

Checking Terminology

From the list of legal terms that follows, select the one that matches each definition.

ANSWERS

a. abandoned property
b. auction sale
c. auction with reserve
d. auction without reserve
e. bailee
f. bailment

_____ **1.** Offeror in a without reserve auction.

_____ **2.** Another word for personal property.

_____ **3.** A loan of goods, on the agreement that the borrower may consume them and will return to the lender an equivalent in kind and quantity.

_____ **4.** Personal property that is physically attached to real property and becomes part of the real property.

g. bailment for the sole benefit of the bailee
h. bailment for the sole benefit of the bailor
i. bailor
j. bidder
k. chattels
l. chose in action
m. donee
n. donor
o. fixture
p. gift causa mortis
q. gratuitous bailment
r. lost property
s. mislaid goods
t. mutual benefit
u. bailment
v. mutuum
w. tortious bailee
x. trade fixture

_____ **5.** An auction in which the auctioneer may withdraw the goods without accepting the highest bid.

_____ **6.** Property that has unbeknownst to the owner become separated from the owner's possession.

_____ **7.** A gratuitous bailment benefiting only the owner of the goods.

_____ **8.** An auction in which the auctioneer must sell the goods to the highest bidder.

_____ **9.** Property that the owner has intentionally discarded without intent to reclaim.

_____ **10.** An auction in which the auctioneer must sell the goods to the highest bidder.

_____ **11.** The relationship that exists when possession (but not ownership) of personal property is transferred to another for a specific purpose.

_____ **12.** A sale of property to the highest bidder.

_____ **13.** A gift of personal property made in contemplation of impending death.

_____ **14.** A person who receives a gift.

_____ **15.** The owner of personal property that has been temporarily transferred to a bailee under a contract of bailment.

_____ **16.** A bailment in which both the bailor and the bailee receive some benefit.

_____ **17.** Evidence of the right to property, but not the property itself.

_____ **18.** Personal property, necessary to carry on a trade or business, that is physically attached to real property, but does not become part of the real property.

_____ **19.** The person to whom personal property is delivered under a contract of bailment.

_____ **20.** A person who gives a gift.

_____ **21.** A bailment that does not benefit the bailee for taking possession of the property.

_____ **22.** A person who is wrongfully in possession of another's personal property.

_____ **23.** A gratuitous bailment benefiting only the person receiving the bailed goods.

_____ **24.** Property that the owner has set aside and can't remember where it is.

Using Legal Language

Read the following story and fill in the blank lines with legal terms taken from the list of terms at the beginning of this chapter.

One of the Christmas presents Kent and Karen bought for their 11-year-old son Reagan was a go-kart, which is a type of _____________________. Another name would be _____________________ or _____________________. Had he wanted a Dallas Cowboys ceiling light for his room (which is a great idea, by the way), the light would needed to have been installed in such a fashion that it would cease being personal property, and would have become a _____________________. As it concerned its acquisition, the go-kart first was _____________________ and then it was _____________________ to Reagan. Had Reagan been given a Porsche Panamera instead of a go-kart (which is ridiculously awesome and wrong all at the same time), one way to accomplish that gift—inside a house—would be to give Reagan the keys to the car, which is an example of _____________________ or _____________________.

Reagan decided to put his go-kart up for sale, so he could use the money to buy a golden retriever. The method he attempted was an _____________________, more specifically the kind where he would be allowed to withdraw the go-kart from the bidding if the bids weren't satisfactory to him. This is known as an _____________________, and the auction ended without a sale. A few weeks later, Reagan couldn't remember where he had put his go-kart, which meant it was _____________________. Had he decided it wasn't worth having any longer and left it on the sidewalk for someone else to have, the go-kart would have been _____________________. Because Reagan drove the go-kart like it was a Porsche Panamera, it needed to be repaired, so Kent took it to a mechanic. Obviously, Kent wasn't giving the go-kart away, so the mechanic was a _____________________ of the go-kart, instead of being a _____________________. This arrangement is known as a _____________________, because both parties are receiving something of value from the temporary transfer of possession.

When Kent went to the mechanic to pay the bill for the go-kart's repair, the shop owner told him that the go-kart had been stolen by a very small and lightweight man named Nolan, who had since been arrested. Nolan claimed he didn't actually steal it, but instead was just borrowing it to see how fast it went. Evidently, the go-kart was fast enough for Nolan to wreck. Regardless if Nolan was a thief, he qualified as a _____________________ and was liable for the destroyed go-kart. Reagan took the money Nolan had to pay him and used it to buy the golden retriever he had wanted all along.

Intellectual Property

ANTE INTERROGATORY

The exclusive right given to an author, composer, artist, or photographer to exclusively publish and sell a work for the life of the author plus 70 years is called (A) a copyright, (B) a trademark, (C) a patent, (D) a trade secret.

LEARNING OBJECTIVES

LO 1: Identify the four kinds of intellectual property

LO 2: Explain the three types of patents and their terms of length

LO 3: Distinguish a trademark from a service mark and identify in what ways a mark might qualify as distinctive

LO 4: Contrast trademark infringement from trademark dilution

LO 5: Explain what a copyright is for, when copyright protection begins, and for how long it lasts

LO 6: Summarize how a trade secret differs from the traditional intellectual property

KEY TERMS

confidentiality agreement

copyright

copyright infringement

design patent

enjoin

fair use doctrine

generic term

injunction

intellectual property (IP)

nondisclosure agreement

patent

patent infringement

plant patent

public domain

secondary meaning

service mark

trademark

trademark dilution

trade secret

treble damages

utility patent

WEBSITES FOR PRONUNCIATION HELP

http://dictionary.cambridge.org/us/pronunciation/english/audio
https://www.howtopronounce.com

Intellectual property (IP) is a category of intangible property that is the result of intellectual creativity. The term, intellectual property, is broad, encompassing property in the fields of patents, copyrights, trademarks, and trade secrets. Examples of intellectual property are literary and artistic works, inventions, audio and video recordings, computer programs, and trade secrets (for example, the 11 secret herbs and spices used in Kentucky Fried Chicken). Owners of such property are given protection by the government to prevent their creative works from being taken and used without permission by others. In fact, in Article I, Section 8 of the U.S. Constitution, Congress is given authority to "promote the Progress of Science and useful Arts" by protecting the creation of intellectual property, which is done by granting authors and inventors some form of a limited monopoly over their work. Intellectual property law is often abbreviated "IP law." Trade secrets, however, aren't protected by traditional intellectual property law, and are discussed at the end of the chapter.

PATENTS

According to the United States Patent and Trademark Office, a **patent** is the grant of a property right to the inventor. For protection of their inventions, inventors must receive a patent issued by the U.S. Patent and Trademark Office. What is patentable is determined by federal statute, wherein it states any person "who invents or discovers any new and useful process, machine, manufacture, or composition of matter, or any new and useful improvement thereof, may obtain a patent" (35 § U.S.C. 101).

There are three types of patents: (1) Utility patents; (2) **Design patents**; and (3) **Plant patents**. A *utility patent* is granted for the invention of a new process or item of manufacture, and lasts for 20 years from the date the application is filed. In contrast, a *design patent* issued prior to May 13, 2015 lasts 14 years from the date of the patent being issued and is granted for the way an item is fashioned; that is, an ornamental design (i.e., its shape) for an article of manufacture. For example, the curvy shape of the Coca-Cola bottle was granted a design patent in 1915. Utility and design patents can be obtained for the same invention. For patents issued for applications filed on or after May 13, 2015, design patents have a 15-year term. A *plant patent* may be granted for the discovery or invention of an asexually reproducing plant, meaning, by other than the use of seeds—for example, by grafting. Plant patents last 20 years from the date the application is filed.

When the patent protection period expires, the patent owner loses exclusive protection and the invention becomes part of the **public domain**—which means no one may claim ownership over it. When an invention falls into the public domain, the invention may be made, used, or sold by anyone, including the original inventor. Confusion can arise as to who has the patent when two inventors claim the same prize. In 2013, U.S. patent law was dramatically changed, when a key federal statute went into effect, granting protection to the first inventor to file for patent protection, not the first inventor to invent.

A **patent infringement** is the unauthorized making, using, or selling of a patented invention during the term of the patent. Federal courts have the power to enjoin anyone from infringing on another's patent. **Enjoin** means to require a person to perform or to abstain from some act, and it is usually done by the court's issuance of an **injunction**, which is an order to do or refrain from doing a particular act. One who succeeds in winning a patent infringement case can recover damages, which could include a reasonable royalty paid for the unauthorized use, as well as lost profits, **treble damages** (triple the damages amount, which is granted by the Patent Act).

TERMS IN ACTION

The U.S. Patent and Trademark Office employs over 10,000 people and some of those employees determine when an inventor's application is worthy of a patent. In order to qualify for **patent** protection, an invention must be deemed "useful." Evidently, that was the case for the invention of Albert Cohen, who received U.S. Patent No. 5,356,330 on October 18, 1994, for his device: a spring-loaded mechanical high-five device. Intended to satisfy the desires of people who watch sports at home alone, the "Hi-5" can be attached onto the wall, allowing the solo sports enthusiast to turn and slap an enthusiastic high-five after a home run or touchdown, or whatever suits the fan's fancy. The device has a hand and forearm facing up, with the rest of the arm above the elbow at a 90-degree angle. Unfortunately, it does not pat you on the shoulder if your team loses. Other curious **utility patents** have been granted for a fireplace waterfall (US 6901925), tubes for dogs' ears, called animal ear protectors (US 4233942) that protect them from getting dirty when bending down into a dog-food dish, and for a sun mask towel (US 7051371), which looks like a cloth with holes for eyes and a mouth, that one can put on their face to protect it from the sun while … laying in the sun.

Sources: findarticles.com; uspto.gov; inc.com

TRADEMARKS

A **trademark** is any word, name, symbol, or device used by a business to identify goods and distinguish them from those manufactured or sold by others. The Nike swoosh on the side of its shoes is a trademark example. A **service mark** is the term used to describe trademark protection for those words, names, symbols, or combinations of them, which are used to identify service providers. Summarily, a trademark in any form is a brand name. Sounds can qualify as a mark, and the sound of a roaring lion is the service mark for MGM (Metro-Goldwyn-Mayer), the movie studio whose lion loudly and sternly announces the beginning of their films.

In addition to being established by usage under the common law, trademarks may be obtained from state governments by following state trademark laws. The most common type of trademark, however, is one obtained by registering with the U.S. Patent and Trademark Office. A federal trademark provides protection for 10 years and may be renewed for additional 10-year periods. Under federal law, an application to register a trademark may be filed six months before the mark is used in commerce. The mark then becomes reserved and cannot be used by anyone else for six months. An additional six-month reservation period is allowed, and other extensions may be obtained by showing good cause. The trademark registration becomes effective when the mark is actually used in the ordinary course of commerce.

Although not required by law, notice that a trademark is registered with the federal government may be given by using the symbol ® or by using the phrase "Registered in U.S. Patent & Trademark Office" or "Reg. U.S. Pat. & Tm. Off." Failure to give notice of a trademark registration can result in a limitation of monetary damages under the Lanham Act. If the mark is not federally registered, the symbol ® may not be used. The symbol ™ or SM may be used, however, to give notice of the trademark or service mark established by usage under the common law. No symbol has been established to designate state-registered trademarks.

Trademark protection qualifies for those marks that are used in commerce and which are distinctive. What actually is distinctive can be difficult to ascertain. According to federal case law, distinctiveness includes that which is:

1. fanciful (made up for the purpose of being used as a trademark, like "Kodak")
2. arbitrary (using a common word in a particularly uncommon way, like "Apple" for a computer company)
3. suggestive (using a word or term that indirectly describes a characteristic of the underlying product or service, like "Coppertone" for sun tan lotion
4. descriptive (using a word or term that directly describes a characteristic the product or service, like "Holiday Inn" for the hotel chain; descriptive marks are generally not distinctive unless, over time, the mark has acquired a very strong identification, which is known as a **secondary meaning**

In 2017, the U.S. Supreme Court issued a significant decision on trademark qualifications when it ruled unanimously in *Matal v. Tam* (582 U.S. ____) that the U.S. Trademark Office couldn't deny a trademark to an American-Asian rock bank that called itself "The Slants." The Trademark Office had denied the trademark registration on the grounds that the band's name was disparaging to "persons of Asian descent," in violation of the disparagement clause of the Lanham Act of 1946 (also known as the Trademark Act). But the Supreme Court ruled that such a prohibition created by the Lanham Act's disparagement clause (Section 2(a)) was a clear violation of the Free Speech clause of the First Amendment. The Slants victory also benefited the National Football League's Washington Redskins team, whose trademark was cancelled in 2014 on the grounds that it was "disparaging to Native Americans."

Otherwise protected trademarks can be lost by nonuse or because the mark has become a generic term used by a large segment of the public for a long period. A **generic term** is a term that relates to, or is characteristic of, a whole group. "Corn flakes," "nylon," "escalator," "bikini," "aspirin," and "yo-yo" are examples of former trademarks that were lost by becoming generic terms. To prevent products from losing their trademarks, some businesses use the their trademarks as an adjective and then use the word "brand" after their product name. Businesses also place advertisements in journals reminding people that their products are trademarked. For example, the Xerox Corporation advertised the following in a 1991 issue of the *ABA Journal*: "You can't Xerox a Xerox on a Xerox, but we don't mind if you copy a copy on a Xerox copier." And in March, 2010, Xerox Corporation placed an ad in the *Hollywood Reporter*, asking that the word, "Xerox" be used only as an adjective (a Xerox copy), not a noun ("a Xerox") or a verb ("Xerox this for me").

Once trademark infringement is proven, a trademark holder can seek an injunction to prevent the infringer from further damaging the original trademark. As well, damages for trademark infringement can be recovered and could include the profits the infringer made from unauthorized trademark use, as well as the economic loss the trademark holder suffered (lost profits), or even treble damages and attorneys' fees. Connected to trademark infringement is **trademark dilution**, which is the unauthorized use of a trademark in a commercially similar way that reduces or is likely to reduce the public's perception of the trademark. According to the Trademark Dilution Revision Act of 2006, a mark must be nationally well-known to qualify for dilution protection. For example, if a manufacturer of bicycles were to name them "BMW," that would likely qualify as trademark dilution of the trademark the automobile manufacturer, BMW, has.

COPYRIGHTS

A **copyright** is the exclusive right given to an author, composer, artist, or photographer to publish and sell a creative work. The works that qualify for copyright protection include the following: literary works; pantomime and choreographic works; pictorial, graphic, and sculptural works; motion pictures and other audiovisual works; and sound recordings (17 U.S.C. § 102). Computer programs fall under the category of literary works and may also be copyrighted. For all works created after January 1, 1978, copyright protection lasts for the life of the author plus 70 years. If there is more than one author ("author" includes all creators of copyrightable works), the copyright lasts for 70 years after the death of the last author. For works for hire and copyrights owned by corporations, the term is 95 years from the year of its first publication or 120 years from the year of its creation, whichever expires first.

Copyright law does not protect ideas and commonly known facts; rather, it protects original works of authorship and does so automatically the moment the work is created in a tangible medium of expression. For example, a great idea for a novel isn't protected; so don't tell a friend your great plot points. But the writing of the novel is automatically copyrighted as it is being written. One does not need to publish the work or register the work with the U.S. Copyright Office to be protected as the copyright owner. However, registration is advisable as a means of helping to establish ownership, if a dispute were to arise. And registration is necessary for a copyright holder to qualify for statutory damages and the recovery of attorney's fees. To register a copyright, one must complete the correct government form and send it with the proper fee and a copy of the work to the U.S. Copyright Office in Washington, D.C. That can be done online now. Although formerly required, it is now optional to put the symbol © or the word "copyright," followed by the date and the name of the owner, on the work.

Copyrighted works may not be reproduced without permission (such as a license) of the copyright owner. The unauthorized use of copyrighted material is known as **copyright infringement**. There are exceptions to copyright infringement, including what is known as the **fair use doctrine**. The fair use doctrine (statutorily created in 17 U.S. § 107, but heavily influenced by case law) allows for the limited, noninfringing use of another's copyrighted work for purposes such as criticism, comment, news reporting, teaching (including making multiple copies for classroom use), scholarship, or research. Whether using someone's copyrighted work qualifies as "fair use" is up to the judicial interpretation of the factors listed in the four-part fair use test, found in 17 U.S.C. § 107.

TERMS IN ACTION

Fred Lawrence, of Racine Wisconsin, was like most grandfathers: completely unaware of what his grandchildren do on his computer. So when his 12-year-old grandson downloaded four movies onto Lawrence's computer, the Motion Picture Association of America (MPAA) came calling. In 2005, it sued Mr. Lawrence for **copyright infringement**, seeking over $600,000 in damages, an amount allowed by federal law. Electronic copyright infringement is blamed on the IP address, not necessarily the one who is illegally downloading the files. In the case at hand, Mr. Lawrence's grandson acknowledged downloading "The Grudge," "I Robot," "The Incredibles," and "The Forgotten," even though his family already owned three of those movies. The MPAA initially sought $4,000 from Lawrence, but when he refused to pay, it sued him for the much higher amount. After a publicity ruckus, a settlement was reached, requiring the boy to publicly apologize and to speak at a school assembly about the risks of illegally downloading copyrighted materials.

Sources: msnbc.msn.com; p2pnet.net; foxnews.com

Web Wise

- For more information on all things related to patents and trademarks, go to the U.S. Patent and Trademark Office, at www.uspto.gov
- Google offers its own international patent search webpage and it can be found at https://patents.google.com
- For more information on all things related to copyrights, go to the U.S. Copyright Office, at www.copyright.gov

TRADE SECRETS

A **trade secret** is a plan, process, formula, pattern, or device that is used in business and provides an economic benefit over the trade secret owner's competitors who do not know or use it. Examples of trade secrets include customer lists, chemical formulas, food recipes, manufacturing processes, marketing techniques, and pricing methods. Unlike the aforementioned forms of intellectual property, trade secrets take their value from *not* being disclosed and from the trade secret holder's reasonable attempts to protect the secrecy of the information. Trade secrets aren't "protected" by federal statute in the way patents, trademarks, and copyrights are. States, however, have their own trade secrets statutes, and every state but New York and Massachusetts have adopted some version of the Uniform Trade Secrets Act. In 2016, the U.S. Congress passed the "Defend Trade Secrets Act," which, among other features, criminalizes certain trade secret misappropriations and allows trade secret owners to file civil suits in federal court.

Businesses often protect trade secrets by having employees sign **nondisclosure** or **confidentiality agreements** consenting to refrain from disclosing trade secrets to others. Even without such an agreement, however, courts prohibit employees from disclosing their employer's trade secrets both while they are employed and after they leave the employment. When this employee duty is violated, courts will often enjoin the use of the trade secret by others to whom the secret has been given. Verdicts in trade secret cases can be quite high. For example, in 2012, a jury ordered electronics retailer Best Buy to pay $27 million dollars to California software company TechForward, after the jury concluded Best Buy had stolen TechForward's trade secret for what became Best Buy's Guaranteed Buyback program.

Word Wise
The "Gen" in "Generic"

The root "gen-" may mean "birth, origin, or race" as in

> gene
>
> generation
>
> genesis
>
> Or it may mean "type" as in
>
> gender
>
> generic
>
> genus

How the word is used in the context of a sentence will generally show whether "gen-" indicates "birth" or "type" in a particular word. Consider the use of "gen-" in the following terms found in the text:

> miscegenation
>
> general agent
>
> primogeniture
>
> genocide
>
> generic term

Reviewing What you Learned

After studying the chapter, write the answers to each of the following questions:

1. Name the fields that "intellectual property" describes.

____

____

____

2. What are the requirements for an invention to be patented?

____

____

____

3. What happens to an invention when the protection period covered by a patent expires.

____

____

____

4. What may a court do when a patent infringement occurs?

____

____

____

5. Explain the procedure to copyright an original work.

____

____

6. When is the copying of a copyrighted work not an infringement?

____

____

____

7. In what three ways may a trademark be obtained?

____

____

____

8. What qualifies something for trademark protection?

____

____

____

9. When does a trademark registration become effective?

____

____

____

10. For how long may the federal trademark protection period be renewed?

____

____

____

11. How may trademark protection be lost?

____

____

____

12. Give three examples of trade secrets.

____

____

____

13. How do businesses often protect their trade secrets?

____

____

____

14. In what other way are trade secrets protected?

____

____

____

Understanding Legal Concepts

Indicate whether each statement is true or false. Then, change the italicized word or phrase of each false statement to make it true.

ANSWERS

______ **1.** A patent owner has the exclusive right to make, use, and sell an invention for *50 years.*

______ **2.** *State* courts have the power to enjoin anyone from infringing on another's patent.

______ **3.** Copyright protection lasts for *the life of the author.*

______ **4.** It is now *optional* to put the symbol © or the word "copyright," followed by the date and the name of the owner, on a copyrighted work.

______ **5.** The fair use of copyrighted work for purposes of teaching, *including making multiple copies for classroom use,* is allowed.

______ **6.** *Trademark* is the term used to describe protection for services.

______ **7.** Trademark protection may be obtained from *state governments.*

______ **8.** The most common type of trademark is obtained by *usage under the common law.*

______ **9.** A registered trademark provides protection for *15 years.*

______ **10.** Trademark protection *can* be lost by the mark's becoming a generic term.

Checking Terminology

From the list of legal terms that follows, select the one that matches each definition.

ANSWERS

a. confidentiality agreement
b. copyright
c. copyright infringement
d. enjoin
e. fair use doctrine
f. generic term
g. injunction
h. intellectual property
i. nondisclosure agreement
j. patent
k. patent infringement
l. public domain
m. service mark
n. trademark
o. trade secret

_____ 1. To require a person to perform or to abstain from some act.

_____ 2. An order to do or refrain from doing a particular act.

_____ 3. A term used to describe trademark protection for services.

_____ 4. The unauthorized use of copyrighted material.

_____ 5. A grant by the U.S. government of the exclusive right to make, use, and sell an invention for 20 years.

_____ 6. A rule stating that the use of a copyrighted work for purposes such as criticism, comment, news reporting, teaching, scholarship, or research is not a copyright infringement.

_____ 7. Any word, name, symbol, or device used by a business to identify goods and distinguish them from those manufactured or sold by others.

_____ 8. An agreement to refrain from disclosing trade secrets to others. (Select two answers.)

_____ 9. An original work fixed in a tangible medium of expression.

_____ 10. Owned by the public.

_____ 11. A term that means relating to or characteristic of a whole group.

_____ 12. A secret plan, process, or device that is used in business and is known only to employees who need to know the secret to accomplish their work.

_____ 13. The unauthorized making, using, or selling of a patented invention during the term of the patent.

_____ 14. The exclusive right given to an author, composer, artist, or photographer to publish and sell a work for the life of the author plus 70 years.

Using Legal Language

Read the following story and fill in the blank lines with legal terms taken from the list of terms at the beginning of this chapter:

Franklin, an inventor, obtained _________________ on two products that she had invented, giving her the exclusive right to make, use, and sell them for 20 years. Since she had obtained one of them more than 20 years ago, it was now in the _________________. The other type of intellectual property (original work fixed in a tangible medium of expression) was much newer and was copied by a competitor, causing Franklin to bring a(n) _________________ suit for the unauthorized making of the product. Franklin won the case, and the court _________________ the competitor by issuing a(n) _________________ ordering it to refrain from making Franklin's product. When Franklin began to sell the product, she obtained a(n) _________________ for it to identify it and to distinguish it from products made by others. She did not obtain a(n) _________________, because the product was a good rather than a service. To prevent the product from becoming a(n) _________________, Franklin used the word "brand" in all product advertisements. For further protection, Franklin required all of her employees to sign _________________, also called _________________, agreeing to refrain from disclosing _________________ to others. The product turned out to be so successful that she wrote a book about her success. A(n) _________________ gave her the exclusive right to publish the book except for a limited amount of copying that could be done by others under a rule known as the _________________.

Law of Agency

ANTE INTERROGATORY

One who performs services for another but whose work methods are not directly controlled by the hiring party is known as a(n) (A) factor, (B) independent contractor, (C) employee, (D) consignee.

LEARNING OBJECTIVES

LO 1: Distinguish the relationships of principal–agent, employer–employee, and employer–independent contractor

LO 2: Explain the ramifications of an agent representing an undisclosed principal, as opposed to a partially disclosed principal

LO 3: Explain the difference between a general agent and a special agent

LO 4: Identify the distinctions between an agent's express authority, implied authority, and apparent authority

LO 5: Explain under what circumstances principals and employers can be vicariously liable for the torts of their agents or employees

KEY TERMS

agency
agency by estoppel
agency by ratification
agent
apparent authority
attorney-in-fact
consignee
consignment
consignor
del credere agent
dummy corporation
employee
employer
express authority
factor
fiduciary
general agent

implied authority
impute
independent contractor
malfeasance
master
misfeasance
nonfeasance
partially disclosed principal
power of attorney
principal
respondeat superior
scope of employment
servant
special agent
third party
undisclosed principal
vicarious liability

5

WEBSITES FOR PRONUNCIATION HELP

http://dictionary.cambridge.org/us/pronunciation/english/audio
https://www.howtopronounce.com

I t is common to have one person act on behalf of another in dealing with third parties, whether it be for business or non-business purposes. Very few businesspeople transact all business on their own behalf. For example, when salespeople sell goods and collect various forms of payment, they are acting on behalf of the owner of the establishment; when corporate executives sign contracts, they are acting on behalf of the stockholders who own the business.

RELATIONSHIPS DISTINGUISHED

When discussing agency law, three types of relationships will be distinguished: (1) principal–agent, (2) employer–employee, and (3) employer–independent contractor.

An **agency** relationship exists when one person, called an **agent**, agrees to act on behalf of and under the control of, another person called a **principal**. The person with whom the agent deals is known as the **third party**. Traditional agency relationships are **fiduciary** in nature, meaning that at least one party in the relationship (the fiduciary, a word which can be an adjective or noun) owes a duty to act for the benefit of another. For example, parent are fiduciaries to their minor children. When a principal authorizes an agent to enter into a contract on the principal's behalf, the resulting contract is between the principal and the third party. The authorized agent is not a party to the contract and cannot be sued for its breach. Generally, an agent can be liable on a contract to the third party only when an agent acts without authority or fails to disclose the existence of the agency relationship.

When a third party deals with an agent and is not aware of the agency relationship, the principal is known as an **undisclosed principal**. In such a case, privity of contract exists between the third party and the agent, rather than the principal and the third party, and the agent can be held liable on the resulting contract. In the event the principal is discovered after the transaction, the third party may elect to hold liable either the agent or also the principal, since the principal is the real party in interest. Occasionally, a principal will conceal its identity even beyond being an undisclosed principal, and have the agent act on behalf of a **dummy corporation**, which is a lawful corporation created to take title to assets while safeguarding the owner corporation's identity and liability. At times, a principal might send an agent to do business on the principal's behalf, but doesn't want its identity known. If the third party is aware the agent is acting as an agent, then the principal is said to be a **partially disclosed principal**. In some states, an agent can still be liable for a contract made on behalf of a partially disclosed principal.

TERMS IN ACTION

Suppose that you're Walt Disney. You want to create a much larger theme park than Disneyland, and you want it in central Florida, but you want to pay as little for the land as possible. You realize that if your plans were known, the price of land would skyrocket. How would you buy the land? If you were as shrewd as Walt Disney, you would use secret **agents** and **dummy corporations** to buy small tracts of land in the Orlando area, which is exactly what Mr. Disney did in 1964 and 1965. Dubbed "Project X," the plan involved sending buyers to the farmlands around Orlando, who purchased small plots from sellers who did not know that there was an **undisclosed principal** behind the buyers. One of the dummy corporations was named "M. T. Lott Real Estate Investments." (Think about that name for a second.) Eventually, title to the land was turned over to the Disney Corporation.

By October 1965, word began to spread throughout Orlando that something was going on—27,000 acres had changed hands in a matter of months—and after the *Orlando Sentinel* made its guess, land prices increased around 1000 percent. By the time the buying spree ended, Disney owned 43 square miles, about twice the size of Manhattan. One of the agents who worked on behalf of Disney (the **principal**), was an Orlando real estate broker named Nelson Boice, who passed away in 2009.

Sources: *Economics: Private and Public Choice*; ehow.com; lifthill.com

An employment relationship exists when one person, called an **employee** (formerly known as a **servant**), performs services under the direction and control of another, called an **employer** (formerly known as a **master**). Employees may also be agents if they have been authorized to enter into contracts with third parties on behalf of their employers.

Independent contractors differ from employees in that they perform services for others, but are not under the methodology control of the hiring party. People who have independent contractors perform work for them do not withhold taxes from their pay and are not responsible for their work-related wrongdoings. For example, a lawyer is an independent contractor to her or his client (who hires a lawyer for a desired outcome), whereas the lawyer's paralegal or legal assistant is the lawyer's employee (because the lawyer has management authority over the paralegal's or legal assistant's "process" and work outcomes). But a lawyer who works for a corporation's in-house legal department is no longer an independent contractor, but is an employee, just like any paralegals or legal assistants who also work at the company.

KINDS OF AGENTS

A **general agent** is one who is authorized to conduct all of a principal's activity in connection with a particular business. A person hired to manage a business would be an example of a general agent. A **special agent**, conversely, is one who is authorized to carry out a single transaction or to perform a specified act. For example, a person authorized to sell a house for someone who is away on a trip would be a special agent.

Sometimes, goods are sold on **consignment**—that is, they are left by a bailor (**consignor**) with a bailee (**consignee**) who tries to sell them. Title to the goods does not pass between these parties, and the goods may be returned if not sold. The bailee to whom the goods are consigned for sale is a type of agent called a **factor**, which is Latin for "doer, maker." If the factor sells consigned goods on credit and guarantees to the consignor that the buyer will pay for them, the factor is known as a **del credere agent**. Ultimately, a del credere agent may become liable for uncollected money that was to be paid and transmitted to the bailor/consignor.

AUTHORITY OF AGENTS

Agents are often given their authority expressly, which may be done either orally or in writing. **Express authority** is authority that is given explicitly. A job description attached to an employment contract is a type of express authority, as would be the order, "Stand here and take the tickets for people entering Gate 3 of the arena." Sometimes, agents are appointed formally by a written instrument known as a **power of attorney**, which authorizes an agent to act for a principal and perform certain acts or functions. When a power of attorney is used, the agent is referred to as an **attorney-in-fact**.

In addition to the express authority given them, agents have a certain amount of **implied authority**. This is the type of authority that the agent customarily and reasonably needs in order to perform incidental functions that enable the agent to accomplish the overall purpose of the agency. Namely, an agent often needs implied authority to perform the duties that are the result of the grant of express authority. For instance, a bus driver who is hired to drive tourists to the Grand Canyon has the implied authority to fuel up the bus when the tank gets low or to have a mechanic fix the air conditioner if it breaks.

Apparent authority comes about when a principal, through some act or statement, makes it appear that an agent has authority beyond the agency's limit or when the agent has no authority. This type of authority is also known as **agency by estoppel** because the principal will be stopped from denying that an agency relationship existed if he or she attempts to do so.

Word Wise

Negative Prefixes—A Further Clarification

Prefix	Meaning	Examples
mis-	incorrect; improper	misspell
		misfeasance
		misdemeanor
		mistrial
		misrepresentation
mal-	bad; evil	malice
		malfeasance
		malpractice
non-	not	nonentity
		nonfeasance
		nonmarital child
		nonconforming use

When an agent acts on behalf of a principal without authority to do so, but the principal later approves of the act, it is known as an **agency by ratification**. For ratification to be effective, the principal must be aware of the key facts of the agent's unauthorized action, and must ratify in total and within a reasonable time.

Sometimes, agents fail to act when they are supposed to, or they act improperly. Three terms are used to describe such situations. **Misfeasance** is the improper doing of an act, **malfeasance** is the doing of an act that ought not to be done at all, and **nonfeasance** is the failure to do an act that ought to have been done.

VICARIOUS LIABILITY

The doctrine of **respondeat superior** (which means, "let the superior respond") holds that principals and employers are responsible for the torts of their agents and employees committed within the scope of authority (in the case of agents) and within the **scope of employment** (in the case of employees). Principals and employers are said to have **vicarious liability**, which means that the wrongdoings of their agents and employees are **imputed** (charged) to them, even if those principals or employers had no knowledge of the wrongful actions or even had rules prohibiting them. Employer–employee liability was once referred to as the master–servant rule. And as discussed in the "Terms in Action" below, the scope of employment doctrine can be applied to organizations whose unpaid volunteers commit torts while in the course of their volunteer activities.

It is not always easy to see when an employee's wrongful actions are still inside the scope of employment, which is why courts are employed to declare and modify the doctrine of *respondeat superior*. Essentially, the scope of employment is acknowledged to be broader than the employee's stated job description or given work tasks. When one's actions can be thought to be in furtherance of the employer's objectives or which are foreseeable in light of what the employee is hired to do, then the employee would be in the scope of employment. For example, if a taxi driver (employed by the taxi company) injures patrons when driving recklessly in a rainstorm, the driver is in the scope of employment because driving the taxi is exactly what the company hired the driver to do. Likewise, if the taxi driver injures a pedestrian while negligently driving the taxi on the way to lunch at a restaurant within the driver's geographic range of work, that act of driving is still in the scope of employment. Injured parties may recover damages from the employee who committed the tort (the agent) and from the employer (the principal), because of vicarious liability. Usually, plaintiffs will recover from the employer, because that person or business is in a better financial position to pay the damages. Some refer to this as the employer having the "deep pockets."

TERMS IN ACTION

While it is true that, under the doctrine of **respondeat superior**, employers are vicariously liable for the torts of their employees, it is not always easy to determine under what circumstances an employee's misconduct is still within **the scope of employment**. In what one would hope is a rare occurrence, an employee at a Bronx bar called the Pot Belly Pub, poked a patron in the eye with a knife, blinding the man in that eye. The injured patron sued the bar for vicarious liability and the employee for negligence. Even stranger than the story so far is how the injury occurred. The employee in question was talking with the patron about the increase of muggings in the area, and during their discussion the employee got out his pocketknife to show what he carried for personal protection. After opening the knife, the employee began to flip it in the air and catch it by its handle. The last of his flips was too strong and somehow the knife hit the patron in the eye. At trial, the employer argued that there was no **vicarious liability** on the employer's part because nothing the employee did in stabbing the plaintiff was even close to being in the scope of employment. However, the jury awarded the patron $200,000. On appeal, the New York Court of Appeals concluded that the employee was acting in the scope of employment when he struck the plaintiff in the eye. The court's rationale was that the employee—who only worked part-time in the small bar—was someone who would occasionally work in the kitchen (where knives were), and part of his job involved mingling with customers so that they would stay longer (and order more drinks). Therefore, the jury could have thought the employee was in the scope of employment at the time, and the employer could have anticipated such a type of **malfeasance**.

Even though the term is the scope of "employment," volunteers can make their organizations vicariously liable. In a case from Indiana demonstrating this, a church was held liable for the negligent driving of one of its volunteers, delivering Christmas cookies to hospital patients and nursing home residents. In the case, a man and his wife were delivering cookies baked by the church's Ladies Guild, whose Guild members included the wife, and on the December day in question, the man turned his car into the path of a motorcyclist. As a result of the accident, the motorcyclist's left leg was amputated above the knee. The motorcyclist sued the driver and the church, winning a judgment against both and on appeal the church argued that respondeat superior didn't apply. But the Indiana Court of Appeals affirmed the jury verdict, concluding the facts showed respondeat superior. Namely, what the court called the master-servant rule was in effect because the Ladies Guild of the church baked the cookies, sought the volunteer drivers, picked the delivery date and provided the driver (and the other drivers) with the lists and addresses of those to whom the driver was to deliver the cookies. So, for the sake of respondeat superior, the driver was in the scope of the Ladies Guild's purposes when he struck the motorcyclist. The appellate court also affirmed the trial judge's refusal to give instructions to the jury on whether the driver could be considered an **independent contractor**.

Source: *Riviello v. Waldron*, 391 N.E.2d 1278 (N.Y. 1979); *Trinity Lutheran Church, Inc. of Evansville v. Miller*, 451 N.E.2d 1099 (Ind. Ct. App. 1983).

Reviewing What You Learned

After studying the chapter, write the answers to each of the following questions:

1. Name the three relationships that need to be distinguished when discussing agency law.

2. When a principal authorizes an agent to enter into a contract, who are the parties to the contract?

3. When can a third party hold an agent liable on a contract?

4. When an undisclosed principal is involved, whom may a third party hold liable in the event of a suit for breach of contract?

5. Under what circumstances may employees also be agents?

6. Describe two advantages of hiring independent contractors.

7. Give an example of a general agent and a special agent.

8. What is the term for those who sell goods on consignment?

9. Why is apparent authority also called *agency by estoppel?*

10. From whom may injured parties recover damages when employees commit torts within the scope of their employment?

11. What is a dummy corporation and when might it be used?

Understanding Legal Concepts

Indicate whether each statement is true or false. Then, change the italicized word or phrase of each false statement to make it true.

ANSWERS

_____ 1. When a principal authorizes an agent to enter into a contract on the principal's behalf, the resulting contract is between the *agent* and the third party.

_____ 2. An agent who contracts on behalf of an undisclosed principal *can* be held liable on the contract.

_____ **3.** Employees *may also be* agents if they have been authorized to enter into contracts with third parties on behalf of their employers.

_____ **4.** People who have independent contractors perform work for them *must* withhold taxes from their pay.

_____ **5.** A person hired to manage a business is an example of a *special* agent.

_____ **6.** When goods are sold on consignment, title to the goods *does not pass* between the consignor and the consignee.

_____ **7.** Agents may be appointed expressly, *either orally or in writing.*

_____ **8.** When agents are given express authority to perform certain acts, they have *no* implied authority.

_____ **9.** Apparent authority comes about when *an agent* makes it appear that the agent has authority when none exists.

_____ **10.** Someone injured by the wrongful conduct of an employee *may sue* the employee and also his or her employer.

Checking Terminology

From the list of legal terms that follows, select the one that matches each definition.

ANSWERS

a. agency
b. agency by estoppel
c. agency by ratification
d. agent
e. apparent authority
f. attorney in fact
g. consignee
h. consignment
i. consignor
j. del credere agent
k. dummy corporation
l. employee
m. employer
n. express authority
o. factor
p. general agent
q. implied authority
r. impute
s. independent contractor
t. malfeasance
u. master
v. misfeasance
w. nonfeasance
x. power of attorney
y. principal
z. respondeat superior
aa. scope of employment
bb. servant
cc. special agent
dd. third party
ee. undisclosed principal
ff. vicarious liability

_____ **1.** A rule of law that makes principals and employers responsible for the torts of their agents and servants committed within the scope of their authority or employment.

_____ **2.** To charge; to lay the responsibility or blame.

_____ **3.** Liability that is imputed to principals and employers because of the wrongdoings of their agents and employees.

_____ **4.** A relationship that exists when one person is authorized to act under the control of another person.

_____ **5.** A factor who sells consigned goods on credit and who guarantees to the consignor that the buyer will pay for the goods.

_____ **6.** A bailee to whom goods are consigned for sale.

_____ **7.** One who is authorized to act for another.

_____ **8.** One who authorizes another to act on his or her behalf.

_____ **9.** One who performs services under the direction and control of another. (Select two answers.)

_____ **10.** One who performs services for another, but who is not under the other's control.

_____ **11.** An agent who is authorized to conduct all of a principal's activity in connection with a particular business.

_____ **12.** An agent who is authorized to carry out a single transaction or to perform a specified act.

_____ **13.** Authority that is given explicitly.

_____ **14.** A formal writing that authorizes an agent to act for a principal.

_____ **15.** Authority of an agent to perform incidental functions that are reasonably and customarily necessary to enable the agent to accomplish the overall purpose of the agency.

_____ **16.** Authority that comes about when a principal, through some act, makes it appear that an agent has authority when none actually exists. (Select two answers.)

_____ **17.** The failure to do an act that ought to be done.

_____ **18.** A relationship that occurs when someone performs an act on behalf of another without authority to do so, but the other person later approves of the act.

_____ **19.** The process of delivering goods to a bailee, called a factor, who attempts to sell them and who may return those that are unsold.

_____ **20.** One who is not known by a third party to be a principal for an agent.

_____ **21.** The doing of an act that ought not to be done at all.

_____ **22.** In agency law, one who deals with an agent in making a contract with the agent's principal.

_____ **23.** An agent who is authorized to act under a power of attorney.

_____ **24.** One who makes a consignment.

_____ **25.** That zone in which employees operate.

_____ **26.** One who employs the services of others in exchange for wages or salaries. (Select two answers.)

_____ **27.** A lawful corporation created to take title to assets while safeguarding the corporation owner's identity and liability.

_____ **28.** The improper doing of an act.

_____ **29.** An agent to whom a consignment is made.

Sharpening Your Latin Skills

In the space provided, write the definition of the following legal terms, referring to the Glossary when necessary.

caveat _______________________   nulla bona _______________________

caveat emptor _______________________   respondeat superior _______________________

caveat venditor _______________________

Using Legal Language

Read the following story and fill in the blank lines with legal terms taken from the list of terms at the beginning of this chapter:

Darlene, who was the general manager and thus a(n) _______________________ for Johnson Service Co., hired Amos to work as a(n) _______________________ or _______________________ under the company's direction and control. The company was the _______________________ or _______________________ of Amos. One year later, Amos took a three-week vacation trip to Europe. Because his house was for sale at the time, he appointed Betsy to be his _______________________ solely for the purpose of selling the house in the event that a buyer might come along while he was away. Because he used a formal written instrument called a(n) _______________________ to make the appointment, Betsy became known as a(n) _______________________. Claude learned that the house was for sale and went to look at it. Betsy, meanwhile, was at the house and had just removed the well cover to see how much water was in it when Claude arrived. She introduced herself to him and showed him around, not telling him that she was not the owner. Claude decided to buy the house and signed a contract agreeing to do so. Betsy signed as the seller, not telling Claude that this was a(n) _______________________ relationship and that she was a(n) _______________________ acting on behalf of Amos, the _______________________, and that Claude was a(n) _______________________. Amos would be described as a(n) _______________________, because Claude was not aware of the particular relationship. As he walked from the house, Claude fell into the uncovered well and was injured. Under a doctrine known as _______________________, Amos would be _______________________ liable—that is, Betsy's negligent act of leaving the well uncovered would be _______________________ to him. After recuperating from his injuries, Claude converted part of his new house into a small gift shop where he sold other people's goods on _______________________, which is an arrangement under which title to the goods did not pass to Claude and he could return those that did not sell. People who left goods in his store for sale were called _______________________. Claude, who was known as a(n) _______________________, was also a type of agent called a(n) _______________________. Whenever he sold goods on credit and guaranteed payment, he was a(n) _______________________. Claude hired Eva to paint the shop for him. She was a(n) _______________________, because she was not under Claude's control in doing the work. One day, Claude left the gift shop to go fishing and told Eva to look after business while she painted. Eva had _______________________ to take care of incidental functions that were reasonably and customarily necessary to accomplish her purpose. Before Claude returned, Eva sold an expensive antique for one-tenth of its value to a knowledgeable customer. Claude attempted to rescind the sale on the ground that Eva had no authority, but he failed in his attempt because Eva had _______________________; this was a(n) example of _______________________, because Claude made it appear that Eva had authority by leaving the store in her care.

PART SIX

Terms Used in the Law of Wills and Estates

Stockbyte/Getty Images

The drafting of wills is a customary part of the practice of most law offices because many people realize that a will is an important document and should be drafted professionally. Even law offices that specialize in other areas of law often draft wills as part of their practice. Litigation relating to the settling of estates is also common in the United States. Chapter 25 explains who may make a will, describes the requirements of drafting and executing a proper will, and examines advance directives. Chapter 26 discusses the methods of revoking a will and explains the failure of legacies and devises, including lapse and ademption. The principal clauses in a will are outlined in Chapter 27. Spousal protection, dower and curtesy, pretermitted children, distinctive relationships, and the law of intestacy comprise Chapter 28. The types of personal representatives are discussed in Chapter 29 and the procedure for settling an estate is outlined in Chapter 30. The parties to a trust and the various kinds of trusts are explored in Chapter 31.

6

Wills, Testaments, and Advance Directives

ANTE INTERROGATORY

A gift of personal property by way of a will is a (A) devise, (B) springing power, (C) proponent, (D) legacy.

LEARNING OBJECTIVES

LO 1: Identify the parties to a will

LO 2: Identify the common requirements for executing a will

LO 3: Summarize the two ways in which one's age qualification to make a will is calculated

LO 4: Explain the characteristics that go into determining if a testator is of sound mind

LO 5: Contrast a holographic will from a nuncupative will

LO 6: Explain how and where a testator might sign a will

LO 7: Explain what is expected of a competent witness to a will

LO 8: Summarize what it means to attest and subscribe a will

LO 9: Explain what it means for a witness to sign a will in the testator's presence

LO 10: Identify the common types of advance directives

KEY TERMS

advance directive

agent

attest

attesting witness

beneficiary

bequeath

bequest

decedent

devise

devisee

devisor

directive to physicians

disinterested witness

do not resuscitate order

durable power of attorney

estate planning

euthanasia

exordium clause

health care declaration

health care proxy

holographic will

instrument

intestate share

legacy

legatee

legator

living will

medical directive	subscribe
medical power of attorney	surrogate
nuncupative will	testament
personal property	testamentary capacity
physician orders for scope of treatment	testamentary disposition
proponent	testate
real property	testator
right-to-die laws	testatrix
self-proving will	Uniform Probate Code (UPC)
soundness of mind	will
springing power	will and testament

WEBSITES FOR PRONUNCIATION HELP

http://dictionary.cambridge.org/us/pronunciation/english/audio
https://www.howtopronounce.com

The branch of the law known as **estate planning** involves arranging a person's assets in a way which fulfills that person's desires about protecting her or his assets during life and passing them on at death. The fields of taxation, insurance, property ownership, trusts, and wills are important facets of estate planning.

The word, **will**, is an Anglo-Saxon word that originally referred to an **instrument** (a formal or written legal document, such as a deed or contract or will) that disposed of **real property** (land and anything that is permanently attached to it). Even today, a gift of real property in a will has a special name. It is called a **devise**. The person who makes the gift of real property is called the **devisor**, and the person to whom the gift is made is called the **devisee**.

The term **testament**, which is Latin, referred to an instrument that disposed of **personal property** (things other than real property) under early English common law. A gift of personal property in a will today is known as a **bequest** or a **legacy**. The person who makes a gift of personal property in a will is called a **legator**, and the person to whom the gift is made is called a **legatee**.

Over time, the distinction between a will and a testament disappeared, and now a **will and testament** (or simply, a will) disposes of both real and personal property. In practice today, the distinction between the two terms is not made. It is common, however, to see the phrase "I give, devise, and bequeath…." in a will referring to both real and personal property, as the verb **bequeath** means "to give personal property in a will."

PARTIES TO A WILL

Historically, a person who makes a will is called a **testator** if a man and a **testatrix** if a woman. That distinction has begun to fall out of favor and "testator" is often used interchangeably. A **beneficiary** is someone who receives a gift under a will. The word **testate** refers to the state of a person who has made a will, and the phrase **testamentary disposition** means a gift of property that is not to take effect until the one who makes the gift dies.

STATUTORY REQUIREMENTS FOR A WILL

Today in the United States, each state has enacted its own statutes governing the formalities of executing wills. Seventeen states (see Figure 25-1) have adopted the entirety of the **Uniform Probate Code (UPC)**, which is a uniform law, originally published in 1969 and revised several

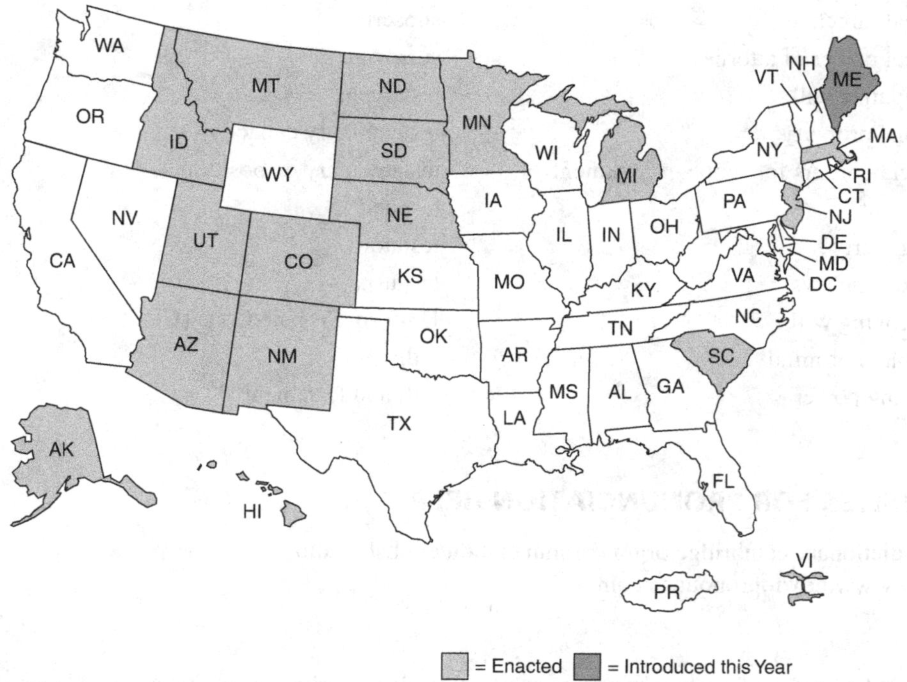

FIGURE 25.1 States that have adopted the Uniform Probate Code, as of 2016

times, that attempts to standardize and modernize laws relating to the affairs of **decedents** (deceased persons), minors, and certain other people who need protection. In fact, most states have adopted at least some part of the UPC. The UPC has changed the definitions of some commonly used legal terms. For example, in states that have adopted the UPC, the term **devise** refers to a gift under a will of either real or personal property, and the term **devisee** refers to a person who receives a gift of either real or personal property under a will.

For an example of a non-UPC statute on the various requirements for a will, consider the following from Mississippi:

> Every person eighteen (18) years of age or older, being of sound and disposing mind, shall have power, by last will and testament, or codicil in writing, to devise all the estate, right, title and interest in possession, reversion, or remainder, which he or she hath, or at the time of his or her death shall have, of, in, or to lands, tenements, hereditaments, or annuities, or rents charged upon or issuing out of them, or goods and chattels, and personal estate of any description whatever, provided such last will and testament, or codicil, be signed by the testator or testatrix, or by some other person in his or her presence and by his or her express direction. Moreover, if not wholly written and subscribed by himself or herself, it shall be attested by two (2) or more credible witnesses in the presence of the testator or testatrix. (Miss. Code Ann. § 91-5-1)

An analysis of the preceding statute, as well as recognition of Uniform Probate Code directives, reveal the following common requirements for executing a will in in many states:

1. eighteen years of age
2. sound mind
3. writing
4. signed
5. two or more competent witnesses
6. attested
7. subscribed in the testator's presence

Eighteen Years of Age

Although most state laws set the minimum age for making a will at 18, a few states allow wills to be made at an earlier age for military personnel, emancipated minors or married persons. In fact, Georgia allows someone as young as 14 to make a will (Ga. Code Ann., § 53-4-10).

> ### Word Wise
> *To Write*
>
> Both the root "graph" used in "holographic" and the root "scrib" used in "subscribe" mean "to write." Other words with these roots are the following:
>
> | Word | Meaning |
> | --- | --- |
> | circumscribe [*circum* (around) + *scribe*] | To draw a line around |
> | manuscript [*manu* (by hand) + *script*] | A document written by hand |
> | telegraph [*tele* (far) + *graph*] | Message sent over a distance |
> | autograph [*auto* (self) + *graph*] | Written with one's own hand |

You probably have never asked yourself this question: when exactly does someone turn 18, or any age? If your birthday is September 9, then are you a year older on September 8? In some states, the answer is yes. Under the common law, people become 18 years of age on the day before their 18th birthday because the law considers persons as having lived an entire day if they live any part of that day. And because one's day of birth is counted, a child will have lived 365 days on the day before the child's first birthday. Some states (New Jersey and Texas, for example) follow the common law rule on calculating age. At the federal level, the Social Security Agency considers one to have reached "a particular age on the day before your birthday." (20 CFR § 404.102). Yet, other states (California and Kansas, for example) have rejected the common law rule and subscribe to what can best be called the "birthday rule" for calculating when one reaches a certain age.

Sound Mind

Soundness of mind, which is also referred to as **testamentary capacity**, exists when, at the time of the execution of the will, the testator was able to:

1. Understand the nature of his or her act in the making of a will
2. Know the "natural objects of his or her bounty," which means to realize who the testator's family and close relatives (i.e., one's proposed heirs, which doesn't mean all the heirs must inherit something)
3. Know the general nature and value of his or her property
4. Have the ability to connect these elements in order to form a testamentary plan

Generally, if the question of soundness of mind is raised in a contested will case, only the following people are allowed to testify as to the testator's mental condition: the witnesses to the will, the testator's family physician, and experts in the area of mental diseases or cognitive impairments. The **proponent** of the will—that is, the one who presents the will to the court for allowance—has the burden of proving the soundness of mind of the testator.

TERMS IN ACTION

Is it possible that the kinds of **bequests** a person leaves in his or her **will** demonstrates he or she lacks **testamentary capacity**? Generally, no. William Shakespeare's will was written in 1616, and after his death later that year it passed on many assets to Shakespeare's family, including his daughters, his sister, and his friends. But to his wife Anne, Shakespeare gave only his "second best bed." Julia H. Egan, a woman from New York City who had once been put in what then was called an "asylum," died with a will that left her husband $5, as retaliation because he had called her crazy. Canadian lawyer and investor Charles Vance Millar died in 1926, leaving a will that has become famous for its **testator's** bequests that demonstrated—after death—his love of irony. His will opens by stating that it is "proof of my folly in gathering and retaining more than I required in my lifetime." He gave shares of

(Continued)

his stock in a Catholic-run beer company to some Methodist ministers, provided that they participate in management of the company (which included beer tasting). And he gave his Jamaican vacation home to three men known to hate each other. But the bequest that eventually became the subject of the movie "The Stork Derby" was the one that gave the bulk of his estate to the Canadian woman who would bear the most children during the decade after his death. More than a few of his distant relatives attempted to have his will set aside, but after a decade of litigation, Millar's will, which had been **attested** to and **subscribed** to by **attesting witnesses,** was proven to be airtight. Four women eventually shared the estate prize, valued at over $250,000, each having had nine children during that prosperous decade.

Sources: timemagazine.com; archives.gov.on.ca; william-shakespeare.info; nytimes.com

Writing

The writing that is sufficient for a will may be printed, typewritten, or written entirely in the hand of the testator. A will that is written entirely by the testator and signed by the testator, but has no witnesses, is called a **holographic will.** Because of the lack of witnesses, holographic wills are not recognized as valid in some jurisdictions, but the UPC authorizes the use of holographic wills. It is believed that the shortest valid will on record is one written by a German, Herr Karl Tausch, whose 1967 holographic will was two words, but in English, three: "All to wife." On the opposite end of the spectrum is the will of Frederica Evelyn Stilwell Cook, a British woman who died in 1925. Her will was 95,940 words and put in four bound volumes, and is thought to be the unofficial record-holder as the longest.

In many states, a **nuncupative will,** which is an oral will, is an invalid method to dispose of one's property at death. (Bear in mind, one can give property away during life by way of an oral expression.) Even where disallowed, exceptions are often made for soldiers in military service or mariners at sea. Where nuncupative wills are allowed by statute or state common law, strict requirements attach to their validity, including that the statements of donation be made during the testator's impending fatality, that the dying declarations be witnessed by a required number of people who are not beneficiaries, and that the property given away be limited to personal property. For example, notice Indiana's limitations on its allowance of nuncupative wills:

(a) A nuncupative will may be made only by a person in imminent peril of death, whether from illness or otherwise, and shall be valid only if the testator died as a result of the impending peril, and must be

   (1) Declared to be his will by the testator before two (2) disinterested witnesses;

   (2) Reduced to writing by or under the direction of one (1) of the witnesses within thirty (30) days after such declaration; and

   (3) Submitted for probate within six (6) months after the death of the testator.

(b) The nuncupative will may dispose of personal property only and to an aggregate value not exceeding one thousand ($1,000) dollars, except that in the case of persons in active military, air or naval service in time of war the aggregate amount may be ten thousand ($10,000) dollars.

(c) A nuncupative will does not revoke an existing written will. Such written will is changed only to the extent necessary to give effect to the nuncupative will. (Ind. Code § 29-1-5-4)

Signature

A testator must sign a will, but where? Some states require that the testator sign at the end of the will, but if there are no statutory stipulations, one can imagine there are cases where courts have allowed the probate of a will where the testator signed his or her name in the **exordium clause** (the first paragraph of a will, which includes identifying the testator, identifying his or her state of residence, and revoking any prior wills) but failed to sign it at the end.

The testator's signature need not be in any particular form. It may be made by an "X" or any other similar mark, so long as it is intended to be the testator's signature. In fact, in some states an attesting witness to a will may sign the testator's name at the testator's request in the testator's presence.

Two or More Competent Witnesses

All but two states require two witnesses to a will. Pennsylvania has no witness requirement unless the testator is unable to sign the will at all or if the testator signs by mark (meaning that the testator is unable to sign his or her name); then in either case two witnesses are needed. And Louisiana requires two witnesses plus a notary public. Vermont used to require three witnesses, but reduced the requirement to two in 2005. Witnesses to a will need to be competent, which often means being at least 18 and being of sound mind. Notwithstanding the requirement for witnesses, remember that in some states in some states, holographic wills are valid.

Generally a witness to a will needs to be a **disinterested witness**, meaning he or she will not inherit any property from the will or gain financially by signing it. Some states require the witnesses to be disinterested, while others allow witnesses who are named as beneficiaries to inherit under the will. Still others, including California, Indiana, and Texas, allow witnesses who are named as beneficiaries in a will to inherit only an amount that does not exceed their **intestate share** (the amount they would have inherited had the decedent died without a will). And Florida takes the view that a will is not invalid because an interested witness signed it.

Attestation and Subscription

To **attest** means to bear witness to the testator's signature. To **subscribe** means to write below or underneath. An early English case held that "to attest" and "to subscribe" are different actions. Attestation is the act of the senses; subscription is the act of the hand. The one is mental; the other mechanical. To attest to a will is to know that it was published as a will; to subscribe is only to write on the same paper the names of the witnesses for the sole purpose of identification.

What qualifies as effective attestation and subscription varies based on the court. In one case, a will was held to be properly executed when the testator acknowledged his signature, which he had previously placed thereon, by showing the paper to the witness, stating that it was his will, and requesting the person to sign it as a witness. In another case, a court disallowed a will because the testator intentionally covered up his signature so that the witnesses could not see it. In that case, the court said that a person does not acknowledge a signature to be his when the witness can see no signature. In a contrasting case, however, a will was allowed by the court when the signature of the testator was unintentionally covered up by a fold in the paper.

Attesting witnesses (people who witness the signing of a document and then sign the document as the witnesses) should sign below the testator's signature and after the testator signs the instrument. They may subscribe either by making a mark or by writing their names in full, as long as they do so with the intent of subscribing to the will. In a case from the early 20th century in which a witness wrote his correct first name, but accidentally wrote the middle initial and last name of the person who signed above his name, the court allowed the will, stating that any form of writing adopted by the witness showing it was his signature was sufficient to satisfy the statute. (*Smith v. Buffum*, 115 N.E 669 (Mass. 1917))

Witnesses who sign a will might ultimately have to testify if the will is contested regarding the authenticity of the will and the soundness of mind of the testator at the time the will was executed. That can be difficult and time consuming, and even impossible if the witnesses predecease the testator. The solution for this is the **self-proving will**. A self-proving will is one that includes not only the witnesses' signatures but also has a self-proving clause or an affidavit attached to it wherein the witnesses certify that the will and its signatures are authentic. Often, states that allow self-proving wills have statutorily-created self-proving clauses that should be used in order to make the self-proved wills effective. Not every state allows a self-proved will. As of this writing, those states are Vermont, Ohio, Maryland, as well as the District of Columbia.

Testator's Presence

The witnesses must subscribe in the presence of the testator. It has been said that witnesses are not in the presence of the testator unless they are within the testator's sight; however, a person may be aware of the presence of another by the other senses, such as hearing or touch. (If two blind people, for example, are in the same room talking together, no question exists that they are in each other's presence.) But be careful to know your jurisdiction's peculiarities about what it means to be in the testator's presence. In one case from New York (*In re Banta's Will*, 128 N.Y.S.2d 334, 1953), probate was denied because one of the witnesses signed the will of a seriously ill man outside the room where the man was laying in his bed. Despite the testimony in the case that the witnessing woman heard the man acknowledge the document she was signing was his will, the court strictly held that the witness did not subscribe in the presence of the testator.

ADVANCE DIRECTIVES

Right-to-die laws have become prevalent in recent years. These are laws that allow dying people to refuse extraordinary life-prolonging treatment. In *Cruzan* v. *Director, Missouri Department of Health* (497 U.S. 261 (1990)), the U.S. Supreme Court held that the right to refuse medical treatment is protected by the Fourteenth Amendment of the U.S. Constitution. In the *Cruzan* case, the court encouraged people to make **advance directives**—that is, written statements specifying whether one wants life-sustaining medical treatment if one become desperately ill—and if so, what types of treatments. Moreover, many states have *surrogate decision-making laws* that permit a close relative or friend to make healthcare decisions for patients who have no advance directives and are unable to make their own decisions.

Individual state laws regulate advance directives. Those advance directives include the use of the **living will**, which is a written expression of a person's wishes to be allowed to die a natural death and not be kept alive by heroic or artificial methods in certain critical care situations. In some states a health care proxy can be used for the same purpose. A **health care proxy**, also called a **medical power of attorney**, is a written statement authorizing an **agent** or **surrogate** (person authorized to act for another) to make medical treatment decisions for an individual in the event of that individual's inability to do so. Still other states use a durable power of attorney for this purpose. A **durable power of attorney** is a document authorizing another person to act on one's behalf, with language indicating that the authorization either is to survive one's incapacity or is to become effective when one becomes incapacitated. In the latter instance, the power is called a **springing power**, because it does not become effective until the person making it actually becomes incapacitated. A durable power of attorney is not limited to health care issues in most states. A living will is sometimes called a **directive to physicians**, a **medical directive**, or a **health care declaration**.

Recently, some states have adopted laws to provide for the use of a "**Physician Orders for Scope of Treatment**" form, or POST, as it is commonly known. A POST is a direct physician order expressing one's treatment preferences at the time one is nearing the end of his or her life due to terminal illness. While similar in underlying purposes, a POST is different from a living will, which is broader than a POST and can be made by any adult and those in good health. As well, a POST is different from a **Do Not Resuscitate order** (DNR), which is narrower than a POST and expresses (usually in the hospital medical chart of a terminally ill patient, written by a doctor) that one does not want to receive CPR.

TERMS IN ACTION

A **living will** is likely the most well known of the **advance directives**, but unlike a **will**, whose genesis can be traced as far back as Ancient Greece, living wills are more recent estate planning devices. Luis Kitner, an attorney and human rights activist from Chicago, is credited with having been the inventor of the living will. It is thought that Kitner was prompted to begin drafting living wills in 1967 after watching the agonizingly slow death of a good friend

(Continued)

who had been violently beaten while being robbed. California was the first state, in 1976, to authorize living wills by way of legislation and by 1993 all 50 states and the District of Columbia recognized the validity of living wills. Kitner was a brilliant attorney who entered law school at 15, worked while in law school for Clarence Darrow (considered by many to be the greatest criminal defense lawyer in American history), and co-founded the human rights organization Amnesty International.

Sources: nytimes.com; medicinenet.com

One controversial and confusing issue regarding end-of-life law is whether someone has the legal authority to enlist another person to assist in a suicide attempt. Today, in many jurisdictions, attempted suicide is a crime. Physician-assisted suicide is commonly called **euthanasia** (an active procedure to hasten the death of one who is terminally ill or in immense suffering) and has been illegal in America. In 1997 the Supreme Court unanimously declared in *Washington v. Glucksberg* (521 U.S. 702) that there is no constitutional right to an assisted suicide. But in the 2006 case, *Gonzales v. Oregon* (546 U.S. 243), the Supreme Court decided that the federal government could not intervene by prohibiting doctors in Oregon from over-prescribing drugs to terminally ill patients who would then overdose the drugs to take their own lives. The *Gonzales* case was the result of a suit filed after a law known as the "Death with Dignity Act" passed in Oregon in 1997. As opposed to traditional euthanasia, which involves actively taking another's life for altruistic reasons and at the request of the victim, statutes similar to Oregon's authorize what some have called "physician assisted dying," Other states, including Washington, Vermont and California, have passed legislation legalizing this passive form of physician-assisted suicide through the over-prescription of drugs to those terminally ill patients who qualify under the statutes as eligible to receive the fatal prescriptions.

Web Wise

- Find out about the U.S. Living Will Registry, where one can register a living will online at **www.uslivingwillregistry.com**
- To learn more about advance directives, including downloading your state's advance directives, go to the website of the National Hospice and Palliative Care Organization: **www .caringinfo.org**

Reviewing What You Learned

After studying the chapter, write the answers to each of the following questions:

1. What was the difference between a will and a testament under early law?

2. List the seven requirements for executing a will under a typical state statute.

3. What are the possibilities of determining when one becomes 18 years old?

4. What establishes the soundness of mind of a testator?

5. Generally, who is considered competent to give an opinion of the testator's mental condition?

____

____

____

6. Generally, who may make an oral will? To what is it limited?

____

____

____

7. What is the difference between "attest" and "subscribe"?

____

8. What can be confusing about the requirement that a witness sign a will in the testator's presence?

____

____

____

9. Name three advance directives that are in common use.

____

____

____

Understanding Legal Concepts

Indicate whether each statement is true or false. Then, change the italicized word or phrase of each false statement to make it true.

ANSWERS

______ **1.** Originally, the term *will* referred to an instrument that disposed of personal property, and the term *testament* referred to an instrument that disposed of real property.

______ **2.** A devise is a gift of *personal* property in a will.

______ **3.** The word "testate" refers to the state of a person who dies *without* a will.

______ **4.** According to the Social Security Administration, a person becomes 18 years of age on the *day before* his or her 18th birthday.

______ **5.** If the question of soundness of mind is raised in a contested will case, the witnesses to the will *may not* testify.

______ **6.** A nuncupative will is limited to the disposition of *real* property.

______ **7.** A will *may never be* signed by an "X."

______ **8.** Attestation is the act of the *senses;* subscription is the act of the hand.

______ **9.** In *all* states, a witness to a will must be disinterested.

______ **10.** Witnesses *must* subscribe in the presence of the testator.

Checking Terminology

From the list of legal terms that follows, select the one that matches each definition.

ANSWERS

a. advance directive
b. agent
c. attest
d. attesting witnesses
e. beneficiary
f. bequeath
g. bequest
h. decedents
i. devise
j. devisee
k. devisor
l. directive to physicians
m. durable power of attorney
n. estate planning

______ **1.** Originally, a legal instrument stating a person's wishes as to the disposition of real property at death, but now referring to both real and personal property.

______ **2.** A legal instrument stating a person's wishes as to the disposition of personal property at death.

______ **3.** Someone who actually receives a gift under a will; also, one for whose benefit a trust is created.

______ **4.** A gift of real property in a will.

______ **5.** A woman who makes or has made a testament or will.

______ **6.** An oral will.

______ **7.** A gift of property that is not to take effect until the one who makes the gift dies.

______ **8.** A male who makes or has made a testament or will.

______ **9.** A person to whom real property is given by a will.

______ **10.** Land and anything that is permanently attached to it.

______ **11.** Things other than real property.

o. euthanasia

p. exordium clause

q. health care declaration

r. health care proxy

s. holographic will

t. intestate share

u. legacy

v. legatee

w. legator

x. living will

y. medical directive

z. medical power of attorney

aa. nuncupative will

bb. personal property

cc. proponent

dd. real property

ee. right-to-die laws

ff. soundness of mind

gg. springing power

hh. subscribe

ii. surrogate

jj. testament

kk. testamentary capacity

ll. testamentary disposition

mm. testate

nn. testator

oo. testatrix

pp. Uniform Probate Code (UPC)

qq. will

rr. will and testament

_____ **12.** A gift of personal property in a will. (Select two answers.)

_____ **13.** A person who gives real property by will.

_____ **14.** The state of a person who has made a will.

_____ **15.** Under early English law, a legal instrument that disposed of both real and personal property at death.

_____ **16.** A person who receives a gift of personal property under a will.

_____ **17.** Deceased persons.

_____ **18.** An amount that is inherited when a decedent dies without a will.

_____ **19.** A law attempting to standardize and modernize laws relating to the affairs of decedents, minors, and certain other people who need protection.

_____ **20.** Sufficient mental ability to make a will. (Select two answers.)

_____ **21.** A will written entirely in the hand of the testator.

_____ **22.** To bear witness to.

_____ **23.** A person who makes a gift of personal property by will.

_____ **24.** To sign below or at the end; to write underneath.

_____ **25.** The introductory paragraph of a will.

_____ **26.** To give personal property in a will.

_____ **27.** Laws allowing dying people to refuse extraordinary treatment intended to prolong life.

_____ **28.** A written expression of a person's wishes to be allowed to die a natural death and not be kept alive by heroic or artificial methods. (Select four answers.)

_____ **29.** A written statement specifying whether a person wants life-sustaining medical treatment if he or she becomes desperately ill.

_____ **30.** A power in a durable power of attorney that does not become effective until the person making it actually becomes incapacitated.

_____ **31.** A document authorizing another person to act on one's behalf, with language indicating that it either is to survive one's incapacity or is to become effective when one becomes incapacitated.

_____ **32.** A written statement authorizing an agent or surrogate to make medical treatment decisions for another in the event of the other's inability to do so. (Select two answers.)

_____ **33.** A person authorized to act for another. (Select two answers.)

_____ **34.** People who witness the signing of a document.

_____ **35.** Arranging a person's assets in a way that maintains and protects the family most effectively both during and after a person's life.

_____ **36.** One who proposes or argues in support of something.

_____ **37.** An active procedure to hasten the death of one who is terminally ill or undergoing immense suffering.

Using Legal Language

Read the following story and fill in the blank lines with legal terms taken from the list of terms at the beginning of this chapter:

When Jason signed his last ________________________ and ____________________, he was not aware that the term "will" originally referred to an instrument that disposed of ____________________ and that the term "testament" originally referred to an instrument that disposed of ____________________. He was glad to be ____________________, however, which refers to the state of a person who has made a will. Jason is called a(n) ____________________, because he is a man. When his wife Julia signed her will, she was referred to as a(n) ____________________ in her state. These wills were not oral; therefore, they were not ____________________. They were not entirely in their own handwriting; therefore, they were not ____________________. The wills were witnessed by two ____________________. Jason and Julia both ____________________ (willed) their real estate to their children, which made them ____________________ and their children ____________________. They made a special ________________________ of their automobile to Julia's brother James. This made them ________________________, and James was a(n) ________________________ as to this ________________________. Because they were both of sound mind, they had ________________________, and the ________________________ was valid. Because Jason and Julia were concerned about end-of-life decisions, they both created what is generally called an ________________________. Specifically, each created a ________________________, which is a set of written instructions regarding medical treatments they wanted to refuse in the event they were unable to personally make those decisions.

Revocation, Lapse, and Ademption

ANTE INTERROGATORY

A legacy of money is called a (A) demonstrative legacy, (B) pecuniary legacy, (C) specific legacy, (D) lapsed legacy.

LEARNING OBJECTIVES

LO 1: Categorize the ways in which a will can be revoked

LO 2: Explain the ways in which a will can be revoked by destruction

LO 3: Identify the formalities associated with a codicil

LO 4: Explain how a subsequent marriage and divorce or annulment affect the testator's will

LO 5: Summarize the consequences to a will in the event of a lapsed legacy or devisee

LO 6: Contrast an ademption by satisfaction with an ademption by extinction

LO 7: Explain how the Uniform Simultaneous Death Act deals with the problem of being unable to clearly determine if the beneficiary predeceased the testator

LO 8: Explain what a slayer statute does and why

KEY TERMS

adeemed

ademption

antilapse statute

codicil

collateral descendent

demonstrative legacy

execute

extinction

general legacy

general pecuniary legacy

intestate

intestate succession

issue

lapsed devise

lapsed legacy

lineal ascendant

lineal descendent

pecuniary gift

predeceased

republishing a will

residuary clause

revocable

revocation

revoke

satisfaction

simultaneous deaths

slayer statute

specific legacy

6

WEBSITES FOR PRONUNCIATION HELP

http://dictionary.cambridge.org/us/pronunciation/english/audio

https://www.howtopronounce.com

REVOCATION

The term **revoke** means to cancel or rescind. **Revocable** means capable of being revoked, and **revocation** means the act of revoking. With variations from state to state, a will may be revoked in the following ways:

1. destruction of the will (burning, tearing, cancelling, or obliterating)
2. execution of a new will (To **execute** means to complete, to make, to perform, or to do, such as signing a will.)
3. subsequent marriage
4. divorce or annulment of marriage (but only as to gifts made in a will to a former spouse)

Revocation of a will by a subsequent marriage or by divorce of annulment is generally considered revocation by operation of law (which means something occurring automatically). The Uniform Probate Code covers those changes of circumstances resulting in revocation, but does provide that a will can state it is to remain in effect "notwithstanding any subsequent marriage" (UPC 2-301(a)(2)).

Destruction of Will

When a will is revoked by burning, tearing, canceling, or obliterating it, the act must be done with the intent to revoke the will. Thus, a will destroyed in a house fire would not be revoked simply because it burned along with the other contents in the house. In such a case, a copy of the signed will, if available, could be used in court as evidence of the unrevoked will.

To destroy a will often means more than striking a line through it or portions of it, even if the requisite intent to destroy exists. In a case from Ohio, a court disallowed the claimed revocation of the testator's will, even though the testator marked an "X" across portions of the first page of the will, blackened language involving giving property to her daughter, and wrote new language in the margins to replace hand-stricken text. The problem was, though, the statute on revoking a will requires physical destruction of a will to be accomplished by "tearing, canceling, obliterating or destroying it...." (*Horst v. Horst*, 920 N.E.2d 441). In another case, a testatrix left a sizable **pecuniary gift** (gift of money) in her will to a friend. Later, she decided to leave her friend a larger sum of money in the will. Without consulting a lawyer, she drew a line through the first amount and wrote above it the larger amount. When the testatrix died, her friend received nothing. The line drawn through the smaller amount effectively canceled that gift and the larger amount written above had no effect because the court ruled the will had not been reexecuted by the testator or reattested and resubscribed by the proper number of witnesses after the change was made. Other cases in various jurisdictions, however, have held that lines drawn through a line of text, paragraph, or portion of a will were effective to revoke those particular parts of the will that were marked out.

TERMS IN ACTION

Bill Groza of Arkansas died in 2006, leaving no will behind, at least so he thought. But relatives of his wife, who had died a few years before Bill, had a copy of Groza's will, claiming that it made them beneficiaries of his estate. However, Groza had **revoked** his will prior to his death. Among the things he did to show his intent to revoke was he used liquid paper over the names of certain beneficiaries listed in his will, he wrote "void" on every paragraph, and he even wrote "bastard" and "get nothing" throughout the will. As if that wasn't enough, he put the will through a paper shredder in front of his insurance agents. But his dead wife's relatives, who were the obvious object of his revocation desires, claimed that Groza suffered from insane delusions at the time he attempted to disinherit them, such that he lacked the **testamentary capacity** to revoke his will. The jury disagreed with those relatives, and so did the appellate court. Part of its opinion included the following, wonderful sentence: "The evidence clearly showed that Bill was an irascible, angry, suspicious, controlling, profane, and difficult man for most of his adult life; however, we cannot say that the trial court erred in refusing to find that he labored under insane delusions."

Source: *Goza v. Potts*, 374 S.W.3d 132 (Ark. App. 2010)

Execution of a New Will

It is a good idea to review one's will after significant life changes (marriage, divorce, children or grandchildren, taking title to significantly valued property), or to review one's estate plan every five years or so. One way to revoke or change a will is to make and execute a new will. Another way is to make a **codicil**, which is an alteration or addition to an existing will. A codicil must be executed with the same formalities as a will (signed and attested by the testator, and subscribed in the testator's presence by two or more competent witnesses) and must refer specifically to the existing will so as to identify it.

A will and codicil are read together as one instrument. A properly executed codicil has the effect of **republishing a will**, which means that it will reestablish a will that has been formerly revoked or improperly executed.

Subsequent Marriage

In many states, the marriage of a person after that person has executed a will has no effect on the will. That does not necessarily mean that the surviving spouse automatically inherits any of the testator's estate. Of course, if the surviving spouse was named in the will as a beneficiary before marrying the testator (and the will isn't automatically revoked, as is the case in many states), the surviving spouse would receive whatever the will provides. In states where a later marriage revokes a will, if it appears within the body of the will that it was made in contemplation of marriage, then the will is not revoked. Under the Uniform Probate Code, a surviving spouse who was not married to the testator at the time of the will's execution can receive whatever portion would go to the surviving spouse as his or her intestate share, which would be what a surviving spouse would receive if the testator died without a valid will, and which is determined by intestacy statutes.

Divorce or Annulment

In most states, a divorce or annulment revokes a gift in an unchanged will made to the former spouse. It does not revoke the entire will; it instead treats the surviving ex-spouse as if he or she predeceased the testator, and the contingent beneficiaries receive what would have gone to the ex-spouse. Similarly, a divorce or annulment revokes any nomination of the former spouse as executor, trustee, conservator, or guardian, unless the will expressly provides otherwise.

FAILURE OF LEGACIES AND DEVISES

A gift made in a will may fail in two ways. The first occurs when the person who is to receive the gift (the devisee or legatee) dies before the testator. The second occurs when, at the time of death, the testator no longer owns the gift. These two situations are discussed subsequently.

Lapsed Legacies and Devises

When a legatee or devisee dies before the testator, the bequest or devise in the will to that person is called a **lapsed legacy** or **lapsed devise** and takes no effect. Instead, it falls into the residuary fund of the estate, which is established by the will's residuary clause. The **residuary clause** is the clause in a will that disposes of property not successfully or expressly disposed of by other parts of the will. A sample residuary clause might state that it leaves "all the rest, residue and remainder" of the estate to named beneficiaries after specific gifts, if any, are provided for. If no residuary clause is in a will and the legatees and devisees have **predeceased** (died before) the testator, the lapsed gift passes to the heirs according to the laws of **intestate succession**. These state statutes govern the distribution of property of one who dies without a will—that is, dies **intestate**. As will be discussed in more detail in Chapter 28, intestacy statutes generally give first priority of the intestate decedent's estate to a surviving spouse and surviving children, and then (if those persons don't exist) to the decedent's **lineal ascendants** (parents, grandparents) or **lineal descendants** (children, grandchildren, etc.) and if they don't exist, to the decedent's **collateral descendants** (siblings, cousins, aunts, uncles, etc.). These descendants can collectively be thought of as **heirs**.

ANTILAPSE STATUTES.   Some states have enacted **antilapse statutes** designed to minimize the effect of lapse. Here is an example, in part, from Indiana:

> Whenever any estate, real or personal, shall be devised to any descendant of the testator, and such devisee shall die during the lifetime of the testator, whether before or after the execution of the will, leaving a descendant who shall survive such testator, such devise shall not lapse, but the property so devised shall vest in the surviving descendant of the devisee as if such devisee had survived the testator and died intestate. The word "descendant," as used in this section, includes children adopted during minority by the testator and by the testator's descendants and includes descendants of such adopted children. (Ind. Code § 29-1-6-1(g))

Under this statute, a gift that is made in a will to a descendant who predeceases the testator does not lapse. Instead, it passes to the issue of the child or other relative of the testator. **Issue** are all people who have descended from a common ancestor such as the decedent's children, grandchildren, great-grandchildren, and so forth.

If the testator does not want the issue of a deceased legatee or devisee to receive a gift under the antilapse statute, a statement to that effect must be made in the will. For example, a clause in a will leaving a gift "To my daughter, Shirley, if she shall survive me," would prevent the antilapse statute from taking effect. As well, listing a contingent beneficiary if the named beneficiary (descendant or otherwise) predeceases the testator accomplishes the effect of avoiding an antilapse statute.

Ademption

If the thing that is bequeathed or devised is not in existence or has been disposed of by the time of the testator's death, the legacy or devise is **adeemed** (taken away), and the legatee's or devisee's rights are gone. This is known as **ademption** and occurs in either of two ways: satisfaction or extinction.

SATISFACTION.   **Ademption by satisfaction** occurs if a testator were to give away during his or her life a gift that is listed in the will as going to that person by way of a bequest. In some jurisdictions, if the person who receives the gift (and is named in the will also as to receive that gift) is a child or grandchild of the testator, there is a presumption of ademption by extinction. Thus, a satisfaction takes place when all or part of the amount of a **general pecuniary legacy** (a gift of money out of the general assets of the estate) is paid to the legatee during the testator's life with the intent that such payment is in lieu of the legacy. In such a case, the legatee will not receive the legacy when the testator dies because the gift is said to have been adeemed. It was given to the legatee while the testator was alive. For example, if a grandmother gives her granddaughter $20,000 soon before her death and the grandmother's will gives $30,000 to that granddaughter, there is a presumption of an ademption by satisfaction of $20,000 and the granddaughter would receive $10,000 under the will.

Word Wise
Prefixes That Mean "Against"

Prefix	Examples	Meaning
ant-	antonym	A word of opposite meaning
anti-	antilapse	To minimize lapse
contra-	contradict	To say the opposite
contro-	controversy	A dispute
ob-	obstruct	To block
oc- (before *c*)	occupy	To seize
of- (before *f*)	offend	To insult
op- (before *p*)	oppose	To set against
o- (before *m*)	omit	To neglect

Legacies and devises are classified into three types—specific, general, and demonstrative. A **specific legacy** is a gift by will of a particular piece of personal property. For example, if a clause in a will reads, "I leave my 2014 Audi A7 to my son, Timothy," the gift is a specific legacy. A **general legacy** is a gift (usually, of money) that comes out of the estate generally. For example, if a clause in a will reads, "I leave $10,000 to my daughter, Jennifer," the gift is a general legacy. A **demonstrative legacy** is a combination of the two. When it is used, the testator intends to make a general gift, but wishes to have it satisfied out of specific property. An example of a demonstrative legacy is a clause in a will that reads, "I bequeath $10,000 to my son, Matthew, and I direct that my shares of Apple stock be sold and the proceeds applied to the payment of this gift."

EXTINCTION. Ademption by **extinction** occurs when the testator during his or her life disposes of, loses or destroys a specific legacy. Thus, in the first example given earlier, if the testator does not own the 2014 Audi at death, the legacy will adeem by extinction. Timothy will not receive the car because it is not part of the decedent's estate. Nor would he receive an amount equivalent to the sales price of the car had the testator sold it and kept the money in a specific account.

A general legacy does not adeem by extinction unless the general assets of the estate are not enough to pay it. Similarly, a demonstrative legacy does not adeem. In the third example given earlier, if the testator does not own any shares of Apple stock at the time of death, Matthew could still receive the $10,000 gift because it will then come out of the general assets of the estate – assuming the asset size is sufficient.

Simultaneous Deaths and Slayer Statutes

Simultaneous deaths are the deaths of two or more people in such a way that it is impossible to determine who died before whom. All states have adopted some version of the Uniform Simultaneous Death Act (USDA). This law comes into effect when the disposition of the decedents' property depends on who died first and that fact cannot be determined. Often, such an unfortunate situation exists when two or more people who are each other's heirs die in a common disaster. To deal with this, the USDA creates a default rule requiring a person to survive another by 120 hours or else both are considered to have predeceased the other, unless the parties' wills say otherwise. This allows the property of each decedent to be distributed as if he or she had survived, unless a will or trust provides otherwise.

As one would hope, murderers are not allowed to inherit from those who they kill. Instead, state laws called **slayer statutes** regard a murderer as having died before the victim, thus preventing any inheritance from going to the wrongdoer. Slayer statutes are not generally limited to those who are convicted of murder, which is a specific intent homicide committed with malice aforethought. Rather, it could include those convicted of voluntary manslaughter and it could include those who, as Florida's Slayer Statute puts it, "intentionally kills or participates in procuring the death of the decedent…" (F.S.A. § 732.802).

TERMS IN ACTION

Slayer statutes prevent killers from inheriting the estates of their victims. But even before statutes were enacted to prevent such unjust inheritances, the common law prohibited it. In 1886, the U.S. Supreme Court first ruled that an insurance company did not have to pay life insurance proceeds to the estate of a man who had been hanged for killing a person six weeks after the killer bought a life insurance policy on the victim. Three years later, the New York Court of Appeals ruled, in a case not involving life insurance, that a grandson who murdered his grandfather could not qualify as a beneficiary of the grandfather's estate. The **Uniform Probate Code** created a slayer statute in the 1960s, and many states then followed suit. In 2004, the Maryland Supreme Court was faced with the question of whether the children of a man who murdered his own father could inherit their dead grandfather's estate through **intestate succession**, since the grandfather died without a will. The court ruled against the grandchildren, finding that because their father (the murderer) had no current right to inherit and was still alive, then his children could not have any intestacy rights through him. But in 2009, the Georgia Supreme Court ruled that two lawyers who represented a woman accused of murdering her husband could keep the $75,000 she paid them from her husband's estate to prepare her defense, which was paid before she pled guilty to murder. At the time she paid them, she wasn't—legally speaking—a murderer. Not all states have comprehensive prohibitions on the inheritance rights of killers. Texas's Constitution and a statute expressly forbid the application of what was once under English common law called "corruption of blood" for those convicted of murder. But the statute denies insurance benefits to those who are convicted of "willfully bringing about the death of the insured."

Sources: *Mutual Life Insurance Co. v. Armstrong*, 117 U.S. 591 (1886); *Riggs v. Palmer*, 22 N.E. 188 (N.Y. 1889); *Cook v. Grierson*, 845 A.2d 1231 (Md. 2004); *Levenson v. Ward*, 686 S.E.2d 236 (Ga. 2009); TX Constitution Art. 1, § 21; Tex. Estates Code § 201.0582.

Reviewing What You Learned

After studying the chapter, write the answers to each of the following questions:

1. What four ways may a will be revoked, depending on state statute?

   ____

   ____

   ____

2. To revoke a will by burning, tearing, canceling, or obliterating, what must accompany the act?

   ____

   ____

3. How must a codicil be executed?

   ____

   ____

   ____

4. A properly executed codicil republishes a will that is defective in what two ways?

   ____

   ____

5. Generally, what effect does a subsequent marriage have on a will made before the marriage?

____

____

____

6. What effect does a divorce or annulment have on a will made before the divorce or annulment?

____

____

____

7. What effect does a divorce have on the appointment of the former spouse as executor, trustee, conservator, or guardian, unless the will expressly provides otherwise?

____

____

____

8. In what two ways may a gift in a will fail?

____

____

____

9. Who will receive a gift that is made in a will to a legatee who dies before the testator if a residuary clause is in the will? What if there is no residuary clause is in the will?

____

____

____

10. Under the antilapse statute, what will happen to a gift made in a will to a child or other relative who predeceases the testator? What language can be used in a will to keep this from happening?

____

____

____

11. In what two ways may an ademption occur?

____

____

____

12. When might a gift adeem by satisfaction?

____

____

____

13. Give an example of a specific legacy, a general legacy, and a demonstrative legacy.

____

____

____

14. How may a gift adeem by extinction?

____

____

____

Understanding Legal Concepts

Indicate whether each statement is true or false. Then, change the italicized word or phrase of each false statement to make it true.

ANSWERS

_______ **1.** A *codicil* must be signed by the testator and attested and subscribed in the testator's presence by two or more competent witnesses.

_______ **2.** A properly executed codicil *will reestablish* a will that has been formerly revoked or improperly executed.

_______ **3.** In *every state,* it is important for a person to make a new will after becoming married if he or she had a will before the marriage.

_______ **4.** In most states, a divorce revokes a *will* that was made before the divorce.

_______ **5.** When a legatee or devisee dies before the testator, the bequest or devise in the will to that person *falls into the residuary fund* of the estate.

_____ **6.** Under an antilapse statute, a gift that is made in a will to a *friend* who predeceases the testator does not lapse.

_____ **7.** A clause in a will leaving a gift "to my daughter, Linda, if she shall survive me," would *cause* the antilapse statute *to take* effect.

_____ **8.** A *satisfaction* occurs when all or part of the amount of a general pecuniary legacy is paid to a legatee during the testator's life with the intent that such payment is in lieu of the legacy.

_____ **9.** If a clause in a will reads, "I leave $10,000 to my daughter, Deborah," the gift is a *specific* legacy.

_____ **10.** An *extinction* occurs by a destruction or disposal of a specific legacy by the testator during his lifetime.

Checking Terminology

From the list of legal terms that follows, select the one that matches each definition:

ANSWERS

a. adeemed
b. ademption
c. advancement
d. antilapse statute
e. codicil
f. demonstrative legacy
g. execute
h. extinction
i. general legacy
j. general pecuniary legacy
k. intestate
l. intestate succession
m. issue
n. lapsed devise
o. lapsed legacy
p. pecuniary gift
q. predeceased
r. republishing a will
s. residuary clause
t. revocable
u. revocation
v. revoke
w. satisfaction
x. simultaneous deaths
y. slayer statutes
z. specific legacy

_____ **1.** The act of revoking.

_____ **2.** Cancel or rescind.

_____ **3.** Capable of being revoked.

_____ **4.** To complete, to make, to perform, or to do, such as sign a will.

_____ **5.** Gift of money.

_____ **6.** An amendment to a will that must be executed with the same formalities as the will itself.

_____ **7.** Reestablishing a will that has been formerly revoked or improperly executed.

_____ **8.** The clause in a will that disposes of all of the testator's property not otherwise distributed.

_____ **9.** A gift of personal property in a will that fails because the legatee predeceased the testator.

_____ **10.** The act or process of an heir's becoming beneficially entitled to the property of one who dies without a will.

_____ **11.** Died before.

_____ **12.** Having made no valid will.

_____ **13.** All people who have descended from a common ancestor.

_____ **14.** A bequest of a certain sum of money with a direction that it be paid out of a particular fund.

_____ **15.** Taken away.

_____ **16.** The testator's disposing of or giving to a beneficiary, while alive, that which was provided in a will, so as to make it impossible to carry out the will. (Select two answers.)

_____ **17.** Laws designed to minimize the effect of lapse.

_____ **18.** The discharge of a legal obligation by paying a party what is due.

_____ **19.** A gift of money out of the general assets of the estate. (Select two answers.)

_____ **20.** A gift by will of a particular article of personal property.

_____ **21.** The act of extinguishing or putting to an end.

_____ **22.** A gift of real property in a will that fails because the devisee predeceased the testator.

_____ **23.** Laws enacted by legislatures stating that murderers cannot inherit from their victims.

_____ **24.** The deaths of two or more people in a way that it is impossible to determine who died before whom.

Using Legal Language

Read the following story and fill in the blank lines with legal terms taken from the list of terms at the beginning of this chapter:

Because Jason sold the automobile that he had bequeathed to James before he (Jason) died, a(n) _____________________ occurred. The automobile, which was a(n) _____________________ (kind of gift), _____________________ by extinction. The gift of money—that is, the _____________________, which is also known as a(n) _____________________ or _____________________—went to his children, who were his _____________________. Because they did not _____________________ (die before) him, it was not a(n) _____________________, and the house they inherited was not a(n) _____________________. The gift of $1,000 to Jack, the brother of Julie, Jason's wife, to be taken from the sale of

Jason's Netflix stock, was a(n) _________________. Because Jason died with a will, he did not die _________________, and the laws of _________________ did not apply to him. He had not made a(n) _________________— that is, an addition to his will. Because he did not

_________________ (cancel or rescind) the instrument after he had _________________ (signed) it, no _________________ of the instrument had occurred. The _________________ of the will gave all the rest, residue, and remainder of Jason's estate to his wife, Julie.

Principal Clauses in a Will

ANTE INTERROGATORY

The clause or clauses in a will that provides the testator's bequests is called the (A) residuary clause/s, (B) dispositive clause/s, (C) attestation clause/s, (D) exordium clause/s.

LEARNING OBJECTIVES

LO 1: Identify the purposes of an exordium clause

LO 2: Identify the common source for paying the debts and funeral expenses

LO 3: Summarize objectives to be accomplished in the dispositive clauses, including distinguishing a monetary bequest that is per stirpes from one that is per capita

LO 4: Explain what happens to the residue of an estate if there is no residuary clause

LO 5: Distinguish an executor from a guardian from a conservator

LO 6: Explain the effects of a no surety on bond clause

LO 7: Identify the purpose of a clause giving fiduciaries' powers

LO 8: Explain the purpose of a tax apportionment clause

LO 9: Summarize the pros and cons of a no contest clause

LO 10: Identify the basics of a testimonium clause

LO 11: Identify the best location for an attestation clause

LO 12: Explain the purpose and substance of a self-proving affidavit

KEY TERMS

administrator
administratrix
attestation clause
bond
conservator
dispositive clauses
domicile
executor
executrix
exordium clause
fiduciary
guardian
guardian ad litem

incorporation by reference
in terrorem clause
no-contest clause
per capita
per stirpes
publication clause
residuary clause
residuary estate
self-proving affidavit
signature clause
surety
testimonium clause
trustee

6

WEBSITES FOR PRONUNCIATION HELP

http://dictionary.cambridge.org/us/pronunciation/english/audio

https://www.howtopronounce.com

A will need not follow a singular format, beyond having the necessary elements required in the testator's jurisdiction. In fact, a properly drawn will is a highly individualized instrument tailored to the particular needs of the testator and the testator's family. Although one can draft his or her own will or use various will templates available for purchase online, a will drafted by a lawyer will contain many of the following clauses:

EXORDIUM CLAUSE

The **exordium clause**, also called the **publication clause**, is the introductory paragraph setting out the full name and **domicile** (principal residence) of the testator and stating that he or she revokes all previous wills and codicils made at an earlier time and declares the document to be his or her will.

DEBTS AND FUNERAL EXPENSES

A will commonly contains a clause directing that the just debts and funeral expenses be paid out of the residuary estate. The **residuary estate** is the estate—if any—remaining after all individual items have been given by the will.

DISPOSITIVE CLAUSES

The **dispositive clauses** make up the main part of the will. In these clauses, the testator names his or her beneficiaries and states exactly what each is to receive. Often, when the testator leaves the entire estate to one person or in equal shares to several people, the only dispositive clause is the residuary clause discussed later.

A gift made in a will to one's issue then living **per stirpes** (by right of representation, or as members of a group) means that the children of any deceased heirs inherit their deceased parent's share. For example, if, at death, the testator has two children and each child has two children, the two children would each get equal portions of the estate and the grandchildren would get nothing. But if one of the children (let's call her A) had predeceased the testator, then the surviving child would get that same certain portion of the estate as earlier stated and the two grandchildren from A would share their mother's share (so to speak) by getting half of their mother's allotted portion each. In contrast, a gift made to one's issue then living **per capita** (per head) means that heads are counted and all living issue share the amount of the gift equally. Going back to the example, if the testator has two children and four grandchildren alive at the time that the will is probated, each of them would get 1/6 of the estate in a per capita gift. If, however, A is also dead, then B and the four grandchildren would each get 1/5 of the estate.

A will's reference to another document, such as a list of items to be given to someone, makes the other document a part of the will; this inclusion is known as **incorporation by reference**. The Uniform Probate Code acknowledges incorporation by reference and doesn't require the extraneous document to be in existence at the time the will is executed. Under the common law, however, for incorporation by reference to be valid, the document referred to in the will must be in existence at the time that the will is executed. Regardless of whether the document must exist at the time of the will, many states require that the document be in the testator's handwriting or signed by the testator.

RESIDUARY CLAUSE

The **residuary clause** disposes of all of the testator's property not otherwise given out. If the residuary clause is omitted from the will, or if all of the residuary legatees and devisees predecease the testator, the residue usually passes to the heirs according to the law of intestate succession.

PERSONAL REPRESENTATIVE, GUARDIAN, AND TRUSTEE

Separate clauses are used to appoint the personal representative, guardian, and trustee in a will.

The **executor** is the personal representative of the estate and is responsible for settling the estate. (Remember, in some jurisdictions "executor" is used if a man and "**executrix**" is used if a woman.) He or she gathers the assets of the estate, pays the debts (including taxes and cost of administration), and distributes the remainder according to the testamentary provisions of the will. This distribution is done under the supervision of the probate court. If a testator fails to appoint an executor or if the executor predeceases the testator or otherwise fails to carry out the responsibility (or declines serving as executor or executrix), a court will appoint someone else to perform the task. The person whom the court appoints to be the personal representative of the estate is called an **administrator** (or **administratrix**).

It is common for people to name someone in their will to serve as guardian of their minor children, in the event both parents are deceased while the children are still minors. Additionally, adults sometimes need the services of a guardian. A **guardian** is one who legally has the responsibility over the care and management of the person, or person and property, of a minor or someone who is incompetent. A **guardian ad litem** (meaning "for the suit") is a guardian appointed by a court to protect a minor who brings or defends a lawsuit. In some jurisdictions, the word, **conservator**, is used to mean one who legally has the care and management of the property, but not the person, of someone who is incapacitated or has been declared incompetent.

A **trustee** is someone who is appointed in a will to hold property for the benefit of another when one or more of the gifts are left in trust. (Trusts will be discussed in more detail in a later chapter.)

NO SURETY ON BOND

A will usually contains a clause stating that the executor (often, the guardian and trustee) is to serve without giving surety on his or her bond (or use some other language that doesn't require the executor to post a bond). In some states, without this clause in the will, the executor will have to have pay a bond to the court, which is like an insurance policy for the benefit of the estate, which protects the estate against loss due to the executor's fraud or embezzlement. More officially, a **bond** is a promise by the personal representative and the sureties (if any) to pay the amount of the bond to the probate judge if the representative's duties are not faithfully performed. A **surety** is a person or organization that agrees to pay the debts of another in the event of default.

POWERS GIVEN TO FIDUCIARIES

A clause is often included in the will to give the **fiduciaries** (people in positions of trust who have a duty to act in the best interest of others, such as the executor, guardian, and trustee) specific power and authority to conserve and manage the property under all foreseeable conditions. Without such a clause, the executor—who is a fiduciary—would be required to obtain permission (sometimes, a license) from the court each time he or she wished to carry out an extraordinary administrative function such as selling real property belonging to the estate.

TAX APPORTIONMENT CLAUSE

As it is that applicable federal and state estate or inheritance taxes are mandatory, a will does not need a tax clause in order for the executor to have the authority to pay any owed taxes. One purpose of the tax clause is to establish the source for the payment of estate taxes, which are sometimes called death taxes. That source could be the residuary clause or it could be, as is required by some states, apportioned to the beneficiaries. Of course, this presumes the estate is sizeable enough to owe estate taxes. If so, the testator can use the tax apportionment clause to direct how the beneficiaries are to pay any estate taxes.

NO-CONTEST CLAUSE

A **no-contest clause**, also known as an **in terrorem (in terror or warning) clause**, attempts to disinherit any legatee, devisee, or beneficiary who contests the provisions of the will. In states that have adopted the Uniform Probate Code, such a clause is unenforceable if there is probable cause to contest the will. Some states, like California and Massachusetts enforce no-contest clauses (Cal. Probate Code § 21310-21315; Mass. Gen Law 190B § 2-517), whereas Florida and Indiana specifically do not (Fla. Stat. §732.517; Ind. Code § 29-1-6-2).

TERMS IN ACTION

Texas oilman Alfred C. Glassell, Jr., died in 2008 at the age of 95, leaving behind an estate valued at around $500 million. Over his life, he had executed and revoked 12 wills, but his 13th will, from 2003, was the source of a lawsuit by his 52-year-old daughter Curry Glassell, who attempted to set it aside in favor of her father's 1998 will. In the 1998 will, Curry Glassell was slated to receive millions more than the $3 million that she would have received under her father's 2003 will. That will split most of his fortune between the Glassell family foundation and Houston's Museum of Fine Arts. Curry's brother, Alfred, III, opposed his sister's claim that their ailing and weak father had been coerced by his lawyers into changing his will in 2003. If she won the 2009 trial, it would have meant a $100 million difference in her inheritance. If she lost, she would have received nothing, thanks to her father's **in terrorem clause**. She lost. The jury took 40 minutes to decide against her, including the time it took for lunch.

Sources: chron.com; bloomberg.com

TESTIMONIUM CLAUSE

The clause immediately preceding the testator's signature is called the **testimonium clause** or the **signature clause**. It is a declaration that the testator's signature is attached in testimony of the preceding part of the instrument and begins with the words "IN WITNESS WHEREOF" or "IN TESTIMONY WHEREOF." Often, it contains a statement that the testator has initialed each of the previous pages.

Word Wise
Per

The Latin word *per* means "by," "through," "by way of," or "by means of."

per annum = by the year; annually (*annum* means "year")

per autre vie (also spelled pur autre vie) = for or during another's life; for the period that another person is alive (*autre* means "other"; *vie* means "life")

per capita = by heads; for each person; as individuals (*capita* means "heads")

per centum = (usually shortened to percent) by the hundred (*centum* means "hundred")

per curiam = by the court; an opinion of the whole court rather than an opinion of any one judge (*curiam* means "court")

per diem = by the day; an allowance or amount of so much per day (*diem* means "day")

per formam doni = by the form of a gift; by designation of the giver rather than by the operation of the law (*formam* means "form"; *doni* means "gift")

per fraudem = by fraud (*fraudem* means "fraud")

per infortunium = by misadventure or misfortune (*infortunium* means "misfortune")

6

> per se = by itself, by herself, by himself, in isolation; unconnected to other matters (*se* means "itself," "herself," or "himself")
>
> per stirpes = by (family) roots; by representation (*stirpes* means "stems" or "roots")

ATTESTATION CLAUSE

The **attestation clause** precedes the witnesses' signatures and recites that the will was witnessed at the request of the testator and that it was signed by the witnesses in the presence of the testator and in the presence of each other.

The most desirable arrangement of the signature page of a will is to have at least three lines of space of the will on the same page with the testimonium clause, the testator's signature, the attestation clause, and the witnesses' signatures. This accomplishes having the signatures on the same page.

SELF-PROVING AFFIDAVIT

As stated in Chapter 25, in some states, courts will allow a will to go through probate without the testimony of witnesses if it contains a **self-proving affidavit** and no one objects to its allowance. This clause contains an affidavit (a written statement made under oath) by the testator that the testator declared the instrument to be his last will and that he signed it willingly as his free and voluntary act. It also contains affidavits by the witnesses that they signed the will as witnesses and that to the best of their knowledge the testator was 18 years of age or older, of sound mind, and under no constraint or undue influence.

Here is a sample self-proof affidavit from Arizona:

STATE OF ARIZONA   )

County of ______________________________) ss.

)

We, the Testator/Testatrix and the witnesses, whose names are signed to the foregoing instrument, being first duly sworn, do hereby declare to the undersigned authority that the Testator/Testatrix signed and executed the instrument as his/her Last Will and Testament and that he/she had signed willingly, and that he/she executed it as his/her free and voluntary act for the purposes therein expressed, and that each of the witnesses, in the presence of the Testator/Testatrix was at the time eighteen (18) or more years of age, of sound mind and under no constraint or undue influence.

_______________________________   _______________________________
Signature of Testator/Testatrix   Signature of Witness

____
Signature of Witness

SUBSCRIBED, SWORN TO AND ACKNOWLEDGED before me on the _______________

day of _______________, _______________ by the Testator/Testatrix and the witnesses, whose names are subscribed above.

_______________________________   _______________________________
Notary Seal and Expiration Date   Signature of Notary Public

TERMS IN ACTION

Elizabeth Edwards was the wife of John Edwards, who was a former trial lawyer, U.S. Senator from North Carolina, vice presidential nominee, and Democratic presidential candidate in 2008. At the time of Mrs. Edwards's death from cancer on December 7, 2010, she was estranged from John Edwards due to his infidelity with a former campaign employee with whom he fathered a child—a child whom John Edwards originally denied was his. Mrs. Edwards, who was also a lawyer, executed a **will** six days before her death, and the absence of any mention of her husband on the five-page document was something to be noticed. Mrs. Edwards's will, which was first made publicly available by the television show "Inside Edition," opens with the required **exordium clause** and makes provisions to pay for her debts and funeral expenses. She appointed her daughter Catherine Elizabeth Edwards to be her **executor**. Mrs. Edwards directed in her first **dispositive clause** that all her personal tangible property be distributed to her three children, **per stirpes**, in a manner over which her executor had sole discretion. The **residuary estate** was then directed to be distributed to a trust Mrs. Edwards had established in 1992. The **attestation clause** included the signature of two witnesses, and the will concluded with a **self-proving affidavit**.

Sources: forbes.com; huffingtonpost.com

Reviewing What You Learned

After studying the chapter, write the answers to each of the following questions:

1. What particular form must a will follow?

2. What is the name given to the first clause of a will in which the testator sets forth his or her name and domicile and states that he revokes all previous wills and codicils made by him or her?

3. Why is the clause directing that the just debts and funeral expenses be paid out of the residuary estate often included from the will?

4. On what occasion is the residuary clause the only dispositive clause in a will?

5. What will happen to the residue of an estate if the residuary clause is omitted from a will?

6. What are the principal duties of the executor or executrix?

7. On what occasions, when a person dies testate, will the court appoint an administrator or administratrix?

6

8. In some states, what will be required if a will does not state that the executor is to serve without giving surety on his or her bond?

____

____

9. If there is no "powers" clause in a will, what will the executor be required to do each time he or she wishes to carry out an extraordinary administrative function?

____

____

10. What is the purpose of the tax apportionment clause in a will?

____

____

11. Where, on a will, is the testimonium clause located? What are the first few words of the testimonium clause?

12. Where, on a will, is the attestation clause located?

____

____

____

13. What is the most desirable arrangement of the signature page of a will?

____

____

____

14. Explain the reason for using a self-proving affidavit in a will.

____

____

____

Understanding Legal Concepts

Indicate whether each statement is true or false. Then, change the italicized word or phrase of each false statement to make it true.

ANSWERS

_______ **1.** Will *must* follow a particular form.

_______ **2.** The exordium clause is the *last* clause in a will.

_______ **3.** The *residuary* estate is the estate remaining after individual items have been given out by the will.

_______ **4.** Often, when the testator leaves the entire estate to one person or in equal shares to several people, the only dispositive clause is the *residuary* clause.

_______ **5.** If the residuary clause is omitted from a will, the residue will usually pass to the heirs according to the law of *intestate succession.*

_______ **6.** In some states, the court will allow a will *without* the testimony of witnesses if it contains a self-proving affidavit and no one objects to its allowance.

_______ **7.** The clause that precedes the witnesses' signatures is called the *testimonium* clause.

_______ **8.** If a testator fails to appoint an executor in a will, the court will appoint a *trustee* to perform the task.

_______ **9.** Unless a will contains a clause stating that the executor is to serve without giving surety on his or her bond, the *executor* will have to have a surety on the bond.

_______ **10.** The clause preceding the testator's signature is called the *attestation* clause.

Checking Terminology

From the list of legal terms that follows, select the one that matches each definition.

ANSWERS

a. administrator

b. administratrix

c. attestation clause

d. bond

_______ **1.** The estate remaining after individual items have been given out by a will.

_______ **2.** A person's principal place of abode; the place to which, whenever a person is absent, he or she has the present intent of returning.

_______ **3.** The introductory paragraph of a will. (Select two answers.)

e. conservator
f. dispositive clauses
g. domicile
h. executor
i. executrix
j. exordium clause
k. fiduciary
l. guardian
m. guardian ad litem
n. incorporation by reference
o. in terrorem clause
p. no-contest clause
q. per capita
r. per stirpes
s. publication clause
t. residuary clause
u. residuary estate
v. self-proving affidavit
w. signature clause
x. surety
y. testimonium clause
z. trustee

_____ **4.** A man nominated in a will of a decedent to carry out the terms of the will; a personal representative of an estate.

_____ **5.** A person in a position of trust, such as an executor, administrator, guardian, or trustee.

_____ **6.** A woman nominated in a will of a decedent to carry out the terms of the will; a personal representative of an estate.

_____ **7.** The clause in a will that disposes of all of the testator's property not otherwise given out.

_____ **8.** The clause in a will that states exactly what each beneficiary is to receive.

_____ **9.** A clause in a will containing an affidavit that allows the will to be recognized by the court without the testimony of witnesses.

_____ **10.** A man appointed by the court to administer the estate of an intestate decedent.

_____ **11.** A woman appointed by the court to administer the estate of an intestate decedent.

_____ **12.** One who legally has the care and management of the person, property, or both, of a minor or incompetent.

_____ **13.** A person who holds property in trust for another.

_____ **14.** A clause in a will that attempts to disinherit any legatee, devisee, or beneficiary who contests the provisions of the will. (Select two answers.)

_____ **15.** One who undertakes to stand behind another—that is, pay money or do any other act—in the event that his or her principal fails to meet an obligation.

_____ **16.** The clause in a will that precedes the witnesses' signatures.

_____ **17.** A written instrument promising the payment of a sum of money if certain duties are not performed.

_____ **18.** The clause in a will that precedes the testator's signature. (Select two answers.)

_____ **19.** By right of representation.

_____ **20.** One who legally has the care and management of the property, but not the person, of someone who is incompetent.

_____ **21.** Per head.

_____ **22.** A guardian appointed by a court to protect a minor who brings or defends a lawsuit.

_____ **23.** Making a document part of another document by referring to it in the second document and stating the intention of including it.

Using Legal Language

Read the following story and fill in the blank lines with legal terms taken from the list of terms at the beginning of this chapter:

In his will, Jason named his wife, Julie, to be the _____________________—that is, the personal representative of his estate—and said that she was to serve without giving _____________________ (naming someone to stand behind) on her official _____________________. Had he died without a will, Julie probably would have been appointed _____________________. The _____________________ in Jason's will set forth his name and _____________________—that is, his principal residence—and stated that he revoked all previous wills and codicils made by him. The _____________________ in his will listed the items that each beneficiary was to receive. The _____________________ gave all the rest, residue, and remainder of Jason's estate, called the _____________________, to his

wife, Julie, who was named _____________________ to care for their minor daughter, Jennie, and _____________________ to hold property for Jennie's benefit. These latter positions made her a(n) _____________________, because she was in a position of trust. A(n) _____________________, also called a(n) _____________________, was not needed because Jason expected no beneficiary to contest the will (and it would have been invalid in Jason's state). The will contained a(n) _____________________ preceding the testator's signature and a(n) _____________________ preceding the witnesses' signatures. The will ended with a(n) _____________________ that contained an affidavit by Jason that he declared the instrument to be his last will and that he signed it willingly as a free and voluntary act.

6

Disinheritance and Intestacy

ANTE INTERROGATORY

When property reverts to the state, it is said to (A) escheat, (B) lapse, (C) adeem, (D) vest.

LEARNING OBJECTIVES

LO 1: Explain how spouses are typically protected against disinheritance

LO 2: Contrast dower from curtesy

LO 3: Summarize how the law generally deals with pretermitted children

LO 4: Explain the purpose and the workings of a homestead exemption

LO 5: Identify the common distinctive relationship that might be affected by the testator's death

LO 6: Summarize the general scheme states employ in the event of intestacy

KEY TERMS

adoption
adoptive parents
affiliation proceeding
collateral relatives
coparceners
coverture
curtesy
decedent
degree of kindred
descendants
descent
disinheritance
distribution
dower
elective share
escheat
forced heir
forced share

half blood
homestead exemption
illegitimate children
intestacy
intestate
intestate succession
kindred
legal fiction
life estate
lineal ascendants
lineal descendants
next of kin
nonmarital children
paternity proceeding
pretermitted child
primogeniture
vested
waive a spouse's will

6

WEBSITES FOR PRONUNCIATION HELP

http://dictionary.cambridge.org/us/pronunciation/english/audio

https://www.howtopronounce.com

SPOUSAL PROTECTION

Surviving spouses are protected against being disinherited by their husbands or wives. State laws allow surviving spouses to disclaim the provisions made for them in their deceased spouse's will and instead take a statutorily designated amount, called an **elective share** (also known as a **statutory share** or a **forced share**).

Some states allow a disinherited spouse to take the amount that he or she would have inherited had the spouse died without a will. Other states use a different formula to determine the amount of a spouse's inheritance. For example, in Massachusetts, the surviving husband or wife who wishes to **waive a spouse's will**—that is, renounce or disclaim it—will be entitled to receive the following from the estate of the deceased spouse:

1. the entire intestate estate if: (i) no descendant or parent of the decedent survives the decedent; or (ii) all of the decedent's surviving descendants are also descendants of the surviving spouse and there is no other descendant of the surviving spouse who survives the decedent;
2. the first $200,000 plus 3/4 of any balance of the intestate estate if no descendant of the decedent survives the decedent, but a parent of the decedent survives the decedent;
3. the first $100,000 plus 1/2 of any balance of the intestate estate, if all of the decedent's surviving descendants are also descendants of the surviving spouse and the surviving spouse has 1 or more surviving descendants who are not descendants of the decedent;
4. the first $100,000 plus 1/2 of any balance of the intestate estate, if 1 or more of the decedent's surviving descendants are not descendants of the surviving spouse. (M.G.L.A. 190B § 2-102)

DOWER AND CURTESY

Centuries ago in England, the rights of dower and curtesy developed as a way to protect the interest of a surviving spouse of one who owned real property. These rights were especially important in those days, when land was the chief form of income from either rents or profits from the land. **Dower** was a right that a widow had to a **life estate** (ownership of property for the duration of a named person's life) in 1/3 of all real property owned by her husband during **coverture** (marriage). **Curtesy** was a right that a widower (a man) had, only if issue of the marriage were born alive, to a life estate in all real property owned by his wife at any time during coverture. Both dower and curtesy were exempt from the claims of the decedent's creditors—an important consideration today.

Many states today have either abolished common law dower and curtesy or amended it to treat men and women equally. They also apply it only to real property that was owned by a spouse upon death rather than during coverture. This change eliminates the need to obtain a release of dower or curtesy of a spouse on a married person's deed.

Usually, a person cannot accept dower and, at the same time, waive the will of a deceased spouse. In states that follow this rule of law, a surviving spouse of a person who dies testate has a choice of (1) accepting the provisions of the will, (2) waiving the will and taking the amount provided for by statute, or (3) taking the right of dower or curtesy. Usually, the last would not be elected unless the decedent's estate was insolvent, because the second choice would normally provide a greater inheritance.

> ## TERMS IN ACTION
>
> When does a surviving spouse lose her or his right to an **elective** or **statutory share**? When that person is, technically, not married, according to her or his state's requirements. Here is a telling case from Florida. Rose Zyontz married Isaac Litzky on May 13, 1971. The wedding ceremony was performed by an orthodox Rabbi in conformity to the couple's Orthodox Jewish faith, and the Rabbi issued them a Hebrew marriage certificate, called a Ksuba. On October 1, 1971, Isaac died, leaving behind no will. Because Isaac died **intestate**, Rose sought her **statutory share** (or **dower** rights), but was denied because the court concluded that she wasn't Mr. Litzky's legal spouse. Even though Rose took Litzky's last name, and even though their apartment mailbox was labeled "Mr. and Mrs. Isaac Litzky," the couple never obtained a marriage license from the State of Florida. Florida invalidated common law marriage in 1968, and so a valid marriage license on file with the state is what determines legal marriage between two people. Another fact hurting Rose's claim to her dead "husband's" intestate estate was that, while living with Mr. Litzky, Rose was still receiving the Social Security checks sent to her as the widow of a Mr. Nathan Zyontz. Rose even accepted the Social Security checks after Mr. Litzky died. If you're wondering how Social Security checks meant for a Mrs. Zyontz could be mailed to the address of Mrs. Litzky, the apartment's mailbox actually said "Mr. and Mrs. Isaac Litzky and Rose Zyontz."
>
> Source: *In re Litzky's Estate*, 296 So.2d 638 (Fl. App. 1974)

PRETERMITTED CHILDREN

The statutory share for surviving spouses to protect them against being disinherited does not apply to children, except in Louisiana. In that state (whose legal heritage is more French-based than English), children under 24 at the time of the testator's death or children at any age who are permanently incapacitated have limited protection against disinheritance, qualifying them as **forced heirs**.

While it is possible to expressly and purposely **disinherit** one's children by language in a will, sometimes, a testator or testatrix inadvertently leaves a child out of a will. This situation can also occur when a child of the testator is born or adopted after the testator's will was created. When this occurs, the omitted child, called a **pretermitted child**, is usually protected by pretermitted heir statutes, which often provide such children an intestate share or some other formulaic distribution, unless the omission from the will is intentional. To avoid a will contest when a child is disinherited, it is best to mention in the will that the child was omitted intentionally and that it was not done by accident or mistake.

> ## TERMS IN ACTION
>
> Joan Crawford was one of the biggest movie stars of all time. Beginning in 1928, she made over 70 movies throughout a six-decade career, was one of the highest-paid women in America, and won an Academy Award for Best Actress in 1945. She was ambitious and driven, so much so that after being declared "box office poison" in 1933, she made an Oscar-winning comeback in the following decade. Joan Crawford adopted four children and was married four times. Her last husband was the CEO of Pepsi, and she sat on its board of directors after his death. But Crawford is probably most famous for being "Mommie Dearest," which was the title of the book and movie about her, written by her oldest child, Christina. The book and movie were particularly unflattering portraits of a bitter, mean-spirited, cleanliness-obsessed woman who was a physically and emotionally abusive mother to Christina and her brother

Christopher. What might have prompted a daughter to write such a tell-all about her own mother? **Disinheritance**, maybe. Joan Crawford's will was executed on October 28, 1976, and was opened after her death on May 10, 1977. It was a will not written in a way that could subject it to a claim by a **pretermitted child**. Although Ms. Crawford gave $77,000 bequests to her two younger children, her will's dispositive clauses end with this line: "It is my intention to make no provision herein for my son Christopher or my daughter Christina for reasons which are well known to them." *Mommie Dearest* was published in 1978.

Sources: imdb.com; answers.com

HOMESTEAD PROTECTION

To allow families to remain in their homes when tragedy strikes and to keep those home out of the complete reach of creditors, states have **homestead exemptions**, which allow a homeowner (or homeowners) to designate a house and land as a homestead, provided it is used by the owner as a home. In many states, a homestead allowance up to a certain amount of money continues after the death of the head of household to provide a residence for the surviving spouse and minor children. For example, Minnesota's homestead exemption applies to up to 160 acres of property, and the value is up to $390,000; however, if the property is used for farming, the exemption is $975,000 (M.S.A. § 510.02). Theoretically, if a home is worth less than the stated homestead exemption, creditors couldn't force a sale of the house against a surviving spouse. If, however, a home is valued beyond the exemption, creditors could force a sale but the surviving spouse would be entitled to the dollar amount from the sale equal to the exemption.

DISTINCTIVE RELATIONSHIPS

Half-blood relatives have one parent in common. For example, a half-sister might have the same mother, but not the same father, as her half-brother. Under the laws of many states, half-blood relatives inherit the same as whole-blood relatives. In a few states, half-blood relatives inherit only when there are no whole-blood relatives. In Florida, half-blood **kindred** receive only half as much as whole-blood kindred unless there is no one of the whole blood.

Adoption is the legal process by which a child's legal rights and duties toward his or her natural parents are replaced by similar rights and duties toward his or her adopting parents. Under most state laws today, adopted children inherit from and through their **adoptive (adopting) parents** and not from their natural parents. The term **descendants** means those who are of the bloodstream (including adopted children) of a common ancestor. This paradox is known as a **legal fiction**—an assumption, for purposes of justice, of a fact that does not exist.

Children born out of wedlock (formerly called bastards but now referred to as **illegitimate children** or **nonmarital children**) inherit from their mother and any maternal ancestors. In addition, they inherit from and through their fathers who have acknowledged paternity, have been adjudicated to be their fathers in paternity proceedings, or have married the children's mothers. A **paternity proceeding**, also called an **affiliation proceeding**, is a court action to determine whether a person is the father of a child born out of wedlock.

INTESTACY

Historically, when people die without a will—that is, **intestate**—their personal property passed to others according to the law of the state where they were domiciled when they died and their real property passed according to the law of the state in which the property is located. Under early English law, these laws were called the **laws of descent and distribution** and distinguished real property from personal property. Real property descended to the eldest son of the **decedent** (deceased person) under a doctrine known as **primogeniture**. If parents had no sons, all daughters took the property together as a single heir (as **coparceners**, or joint heirs). Personal property of the decedent, in those early days, was distributed by church officials "for the good of the soul of the deceased." Thus, the word **descent** technically refers only to real property, and the word **distribution** refers to personal property.

Today, the law of **intestacy** (the circumstance of dying without having made a valid will) is called the law of **intestate succession**. The early distinction between real and personal property is still followed in some jurisdictions. There, ownership of real property becomes **vested** (fixed or absolute) in the decedent's heirs at the moment of death; ownership of personal property, however, passes to the administrator or administratrix to be distributed by him or her.

Many American statutes of intestate succession are based on the English Statute of Distribution of 1670 and apply to both real and personal property. According to most state laws, after an amount is allotted to a surviving spouse, any balance passes to the decedent's lineal descendants. **Lineal descendants** are people who are in a direct line of descent (downward) from the decedent—children, grandchildren, and great-grandchildren. When there are no living lineal descendants, the balance passes to the decedent's lineal ascendants. **Lineal ascendants** are people who are in a direct line of ascent (upward) from the decedent—parents, grandparents, and great-grandparents. When there are no living descendants or ascendants, the balance passes to the decedent's **collateral relatives**—those not in a direct line, such as brothers, sisters, nieces, nephews, uncles, aunts, and cousins. Remember: A will is for your loved ones, which could include your family; intestate succession is for your relatives. Although the statutes differ from state to state, a fairly typical one is discussed here.

Rights of Surviving Spouse

While intestate succession statutes are varied throughout the country, Delaware's can serve as an example of how surviving spouses are treated. Delaware's statute for surviving spouses grants the following to the surviving spouse:

1. If there is no surviving issue or parents of the decedent, the entire intestate estate;
2. If there is no surviving issue but the decedent is survived by a parent or parents, the first $50,000 of the intestate personal estate, plus one half of the balance of the intestate personal estate, plus a life estate in the intestate real estate;
3. If there are surviving issue all of whom are issue of the surviving spouse also, the first $50,000 of the intestate personal estate, plus one half of the balance of the intestate personal estate, plus a life estate in the intestate real estate;
4. If there are surviving issue, one or more of whom are not issue of the surviving spouse, one half of the intestate personal estate, plus a life estate in the intestate real estate. (12 Del. C. § 502)

Rights of Other Heirs

Continuing with Delaware, its intestate succession statute for other heirs states that the intestate estate not going to the surviving spouse, or the entire estate if there is no surviving spouse, passes as follows:

1. To the issue of the decedent, per stirpes;
2. If there is no surviving issue, to the decedent's parent or parents equally;
3. If there is no surviving issue or parent, to the brothers and sisters and the issue of each deceased brother or sister, per stirpes;
4. If there is no surviving issue, parent, or issue of a parent, then to the next of kin of the decedent, and to the issue of a deceased next of kin, per stirpes;
5. Any property passing under this section to 2 or more persons passes to such persons as tenants in common. (12 Del. C. § 503)

A review of the above requires a little explanation. One's **next of kin** would be those most nearly related by blood. To determine the closest relatives, each relationship is assigned a number called a **degree of kindred**. The relationship with the lowest number usually inherits to the exclusion of all others. For example, first cousins (fourth-degree kindred) would inherit before second cousins (sixth-degree kindred). Finally, if there are no heirs or any kindred who can inherit the intestate estate, the estate's property will **escheat** to the state, which means the state will take title to and possession of it (12 Del. C. § 1101).

Word Wise
The Prefix "Co-"

This Latin prefix meaning "together" appears in hundreds of English words. Its four spelling variations (col-, com-, con-, and cor-) make pronunciation easier before various roots. Some examples are as follows:

Word	*Meaning*
collaborate [*col* + *laborare* (to work)]	To work together
companion [*com* + *panis* (bread)]	Someone who accompanies another; originally, someone who shared bread
contact [*con* + *tact* (to touch)]	Touch by meeting
coparceners	Joint heirs
corroborate [*cor* + *roborare* (strength)]	To make certain; confirm

---

Reviewing What You Learned

After studying the chapter write the answers to each of the following questions:

1. If a testator fails to provide for a spouse in a will and the surviving spouse waives the will, how much will the surviving spouse be entitled to receive, in a state that follows the statute excerpted in this chapter?

    a. If the deceased was survived by issue?

    ____

    ____

    ____

    b. If the deceased was survived by no issue?

    ____

    ____

    ____

2. For what reason did the rights of dower and curtesy develop in early England?

    ____

    ____

3. What was the difference between dower and curtesy years ago in England?

    ____

    ____

    ____

4. What choices are available to a surviving spouse who does not like the provisions of the will of his or her spouse?

    ____

    ____

    ____

5. What must a pretermitted child prove to inherit from a parent's estate?

    ____

    ____

6. What should testators do to avoid a will contest when a child is purposely omitted from a will?

____

____

____

7. Differentiate between the words "descent" and "distribution" as they are used historically.

____

____

____

8. Explain the difference between the vesting of real property and the passing of personal property under today's law.

____

____

____

9. What is the purpose of homestead exemptions?

____

____

____

10. How do half-blood relatives inherit under the laws of many states?

____

____

____

11. From whom do adopted children inherit?

____

____

____

12. Under what circumstances do nonmarital children inherit from and through their fathers?

____

____

____

13. Who will inherit, and in what amount, under Delaware's intestate succession statutes, from the estate of a person who dies intestate survived by the following:

   a. A spouse and two children ($120,000 estate)?

____

____

____

   b. A spouse and a father and mother ($260,000 estate)?

____

____

____

   c. A spouse and no issue or kindred ($120,000 estate)?

____

____

____

   d. No spouse and three children ($120,000 estate)?

____

____

____

   e. A spouse and a 96-year-old uncle ($400,000 estate)?

____

____

____

Understanding Legal Concepts

Indicate whether each statement is true or false. Then, change the italicized word or phrase of each false statement to make it true.

ANSWERS

_____ **1.** Under today's laws, if a surviving spouse is unhappy with the provisions of his or her spouse's will, he or she can *do nothing about* it.

_____ **2.** Under the state statute referred to earlier, a will *cannot be* waived by the surviving spouse if the deceased testator or testatrix had obtained a legal separation from his or her spouse before death.

_____ **3.** Years ago in England, *dower* was a right that a widower had if issue of the marriage were born alive, but not otherwise, to a life estate in all real property owned by his wife at any time during coverture.

_____ **4.** Both dower and curtesy were exempt from the claims of the decedent's *creditors*.

_____ **5.** A child who is omitted from a parent's will can receive nothing from the parent's estate unless the child can prove that the omission was *unintentional.*

_____ **6.** A person can bring a lawsuit by himself or herself at *any age.*

_____ **7.** If a person dies without a will and is survived by heirs, the property will pass *to the state.*

_____ **8.** Today, real property vests in the decedent's heirs at the moment of death of the owner, whereas *personal property* passes to the administrator or administratrix to be distributed by him or her.

_____ **9.** Under some state statutes, illegitimate children inherit from their *father* and any *paternal* ancestor.

Checking Terminology

From the list of legal terms that follows, select the one that matches each definition:

ANSWERS

a. adoption
b. adoptive parents
c. affiliation proceeding
d. bastards
e. collateral relatives
f. coparceners
g. coverture
h. curtesy
i. decedent
j. degree of kindred
k. descent
l. disinherited
m. distribution
n. dower
o. elective share
p. escheat
q. forced heir
r. forced share
s. full age
t. half-blood
u. homestead
v. homestead exemption
w. illegitimate children
x. intestacy
y. intestate
aa. intestate succession
bb. kindred
cc. legal fiction
dd. life estate
ee. lineal ascendants
ff. lineal descendants
gg. majority
hh. next friend
ii. next of kin

_____ **1.** Relatives who have one parent in common, but not both.

_____ **2.** To die without a will.

_____ **3.** A statutory sum given to a surviving spouse who disclaims the provisions made for him or her in a deceased spouse's will. (Select two answers.)

_____ **4.** At common law, the right of a widow to a life estate in 1/3 of all real property owned by her husband during coverture.

_____ **5.** At common law, the right of a widower, if issue of the marriage were born alive, to a life estate in all real property owned by his wife during coverture.

_____ **6.** Renounce or disclaim a spouse's will.

_____ **7.** Blood relatives.

_____ **8.** An ownership interest whose duration is limited to the life of some person.

_____ **9.** A court action to determine whether a person is the father of a child born out of wedlock. (Select two answers.)

_____ **10.** Children born out of wedlock. (Select three answers.)

_____ **11.** The legal process in which a child's legal rights and duties toward his or her natural parents are replaced by similar rights and duties toward his or her adopting parents.

_____ **12.** One acting for the benefit of an infant in bringing a legal action.

_____ **13.** A child who is omitted by a testator from a will.

_____ **14.** Time married.

_____ **15.** Adulthood. (Select two answers.)

_____ **16.** The act or process of an heir's becoming beneficially entitled to the property of one who dies without a will.

_____ **17.** Succession to the ownership of real property by inheritance (early English law).

_____ **18.** The apportionment and division of the personal property of an intestate among his or her heirs (early English law).

_____ **19.** The state of being the firstborn son among several children of the same parents (early English law).

_____ **20.** Persons to whom an estate of inheritance descends jointly; joint heirs (early English law).

_____ **21.** The state of dying without having made a valid will.

_____ **22.** A surviving spouse who elects to disclaim the provisions of a deceased spouse's will.

_____ **23.** Parents who adopt a child.

_____ **24.** Those most nearly related by blood.

_____ **25.** The reversion of property to the state if the property owner dies without heirs.

_____ **26.** Fixed or absolute; not contingent.

_____ **27.** A deceased person.

_____ **28.** Proved and allowed by the court.

_____ **29.** Property that is beyond the reach of creditors' and others' claims as long as the family uses the property as a home.

_____ **30.** The relationship between a decedent and his or her relatives to determine who are most nearly related by blood.

jj.	nonmarital children	
kk.	paternity proceeding	
ll.	pretermitted child	
mm.	primogeniture	
nn.	probated	
oo.	vested	
pp.	waive a spouse's will	

_____ **31.** Relatives not in a direct line, such as brothers, sisters, nieces, nephews, uncles, aunts, and cousins.

_____ **32.** Those who are of the bloodstream (including adopted children) of a common ancestor.

_____ **33.** An assumption, for purposes of justice, of a fact that does not exist.

_____ **34.** People who are in a direct line of ascent (upward) from the decedent—parents, grandparents, and great-grandparents.

_____ **35.** People who are in a direct line of descent (downward) from the decedent—children, grandchildren, and great-grandchildren.

_____ **36.** Purposely omitted from a will.

_____ **37.** **The provision that** allows a homeowner to designate a house and land as a homestead.

Using Legal Language

Read the following story and fill in the blank lines with legal terms taken from the list of terms at the beginning of this chapter:

When Jason, the ____________________, died testate, his wife, Julie, who was of ____________________—that is, an adult—could choose to accept the provisions of the will, ____________________ (renounce or disclaim) the will, or take her right of ____________________, which at common law was the right to a(n) ____________________ in 1/3 of all real property owned by Jason during ____________________. Had she been a man, this right would be called ____________________. Jason's real property passed under the will by ____________________ to his devisee, and ____________________ at the moment of death. His personal property passed by ____________________ through his personal representative to his legatees. The will had to be ____________________—that is, proved and allowed by the court. Jason did not fail to provide for any of his children; therefore, no ____________________ would, if he or she had not reached ____________________, have to bring suit by a ____________________. He had no ____________________—that is, children born out of wedlock—and none of his children were of the ____________________—that is, had one parent in common, but not both. Had Jason died without a will, on death, his personal property would have passed to his heirs according to the law of ____________________ in the state where he died domiciled. His ____________________—that is, those most nearly related by blood and sometimes referred to as ____________________—would have inherited from his estate along with his surviving spouse.

Personal Representative of the Estate

ANTE INTERROGATORY

An official who administers the estate of a person who dies intestate and no relative, heir, or other person appears who is entitled to act as administrator is called a(n) (A) public administrator, (B) special administrator, (C) ancillary administrator, (D) voluntary administrator.

LEARNING OBJECTIVES

LO 1: Identify the type of court that oversees the task of settling an estate

LO 2: Identify the titles given to the personal representative for an estate

LO 3: Identify the various names for successor personal representatives

LO 4: Identify the various names for particular-purpose administrators

KEY TERMS

administrator
administrator ad litem
administrator c.t.a.
administrator cum testamento annexo
administrator d.b.n.
administrator d.b.n.c.t.a.
administrator de bonis non
administrator de bonis non cum testamento
  annexo
administrator pendente lite
administrator with the will annexed
administrator w.w.a.
administratrix
ancillary administrator
Court of Ordinary
executor
executor de son tort
executrix
fiduciary capacity
Orphan's Court
personal representative
Probate and Family Court
public administrator
special administrator
successor personal representatives
summary administration
Surrogate's Court
voluntary administrator
will contest

6

WEBSITES FOR PRONUNCIATION HELP

http://dictionary.cambridge.org/us/pronunciation/english/audio

https://www.howtopronounce.com

ESTATE SETTLEMENT

When a person dies owning any property by himself or herself (as opposed to co-owning property, such as with a surviving spouse), that decedent's estate must be settled. A court oversees that task, but it acts through an executor or administrator (called the **personal representative**), who is appointed for that purpose and who acts in a **fiduciary capacity**—that is, a position of trust. The court that exercises this function is called by different names in different states. For example, in New York it is called the **Surrogate's Court**, in Pennsylvania the **Orphan's Court**, in New Jersey also the Surrogates' Court (for most cases and with an apostrophe placed after the "s" instead of before it as in New York), in Massachusetts the **Probate and Family Court**, and in Georgia the Probate Court, (formerly it was called the **Court of Ordinary**). In California, the Superior Court has jurisdiction over probate proceedings.

TITLES OF PERSONAL REPRESENTATIVES

In states that have adopted the Uniform Probate Code (see Chapter 25), a personal representative is referred to as the same, a **personal representative**. In other states, personal representatives are given different titles, depending on the method by which they gained their position or the particular task that they are to perform. An **executor** (if a man) or **executrix** (in a state that still uses that word for a female) is a person nominated in the will of a decedent to carry out the terms of the will. An **administrator** (if a man) or **administratrix** (if a woman, where used in such jurisdictions) is a person appointed by the court to administer the estate of an intestate decedent.

TERMS IN ACTION

When Doris Duke's father died in 1925, she inherited a $100 million fortune at the age of 13. Her tobacco tycoon father, James Buchanan Duke, was so rich that a certain university in North Carolina to which he had given so much of his fortune took his last name in 1924. Doris's life of hyper-wealth was fraught with sadness, oddness, and tragedy. She gave birth to a daughter in 1940 who only lived for a day, and in 1966 Doris accidentally ran over and killed a friend while he was opening the gates to a mansion so that she could enter the driveway. By the time of her death in 1993, she was a secluded, gravely ill, and highly medicated 80-year-old woman whose constant companion was her Irish butler, Bernard Lafferty. Because her will made that butler the **executor** of her billion-dollar estate, many disgruntled beneficiaries filed lawsuits against Lafferty, alleging that the barely literate man had applied undue influence on the mentally incompetent Duke to get her to put her estate under his control. After three years of litigation, Lafferty agreed in April 1996 to a settlement, giving up control of Doris Duke's estate in exchange for $4.5 million and an annual payment of $500,000 for as long as he lived. He lived seven months longer.

Source: nytimes.com

Successor Personal Representatives

An **administrator de bonis non** (Latin for administrator of goods not administered), also known as **administrator d.b.n.**, is appointed by the court to complete the settlement of an estate in which a previously appointed administrator has died, has resigned, or has been removed.

An **administrator cum testamento annexo** (**administrator with the will annexed**), also known as **administrator c.t.a.** or **administrator w.w.a.**, is appointed by the court to administer a testate estate in which no executor is nominated, or in which the person named to be executor, before being appointed, either has died, has been adjudged incompetent, or refuses or neglects to perform the task. An **administrator de bonis non cum testamento annexo** (administrator of goods not administered with the will annexed), also known as **administrator d.b.n.c.t.a.**, is appointed by the court to take the place of a previously appointed executor or administrator cum testamento annexo who has died, has resigned, or has been removed. The Uniform Probate Code states, all of these people are referred to as **successor personal representatives**. They are appointed to succeed previously appointed personal representatives.

Particular-Purpose Administrators

A **special administrator** is one who is appointed by the court to handle the affairs of an estate for a limited time only, such as when a delay occurs in the allowance of a will or dispute over the appointment of an executor. The special administrator takes care of affairs that are in need of immediate attention.

A **public administrator** is an official who administers the estate of a person who dies intestate and no relative, heir, or other person appears who is entitled to act as administrator.

A **voluntary administrator** is a person who undertakes the informal administration of a small estate. Some states allow this provision as an easy method of settling small estates. For example, in Massachusetts, if a decedent's estate consists entirely of personal property the total value of which does not exceed an $25,000, not counting an automobile, then a surviving spouse (or a child, parent, sibling, or even a niece or nephew of the decedent) may, after the expiration of 30 days from the date of death, file certain information and become a voluntary administrator. The powers of a voluntary administrator cease if a regular administrator or executor is appointed to settle the estate. In California, a similar procedure, known as **summary administration**, is used to settle estates that do not exceed $150,000.

Word Wise
The Prefix "Ad-"

The Latin prefix "ad" means "to" or "toward." Its spelling variations facilitate different pronunciations before different roots.

Prefix	*Example*
ad-	administrator
a- (before *sc, sp, st*)	ascend, aspect, astride
ac- (before *c* or *q*)	accept, acquit
af- (before *f*)	affect
ag- (before *g*)	aggravated
an- (before *n*)	annulment
ap- (before *p*)	approve
ar- (before *r*)	arraignment
as- (before *s*)	assault
at- (before *t*)	attempt

An **ancillary administrator** is one who is appointed by the court to handle the affairs of a decedent in a foreign state. For example, if a decedent domiciled in New York dies owning real property in Connecticut, ancillary administration will have to be taken out in Connecticut, to settle the Connecticut real property in addition to there being a New York executor or administrator. It is also necessary to take out ancillary administration if one is to bring suit or collect debts of a nonresident decedent. In Florida, for example, there is an abbreviated procedure for ancillary administration if the Florida real estate owned at death by a non-resident decedent is less than $75,000.

An **administrator pendente lite** (pending suit) is a temporary administrator appointed by the court to protect estate assets when there is a **will contest** (a suit over the allowance or disallowance of a will). In contrast, an **administrator ad litem** (for the suit) is appointed by the court to supply a necessary party to a suit in which the estate has an interest, as when the estate is a party to a lawsuit.

An **executor de son tort** is the name given to a person who performs the duties of an executor without authority to do so. Notice that the word "tort" is in the name. Such a person is said to be an intermeddler and is held responsible for his or her acts.

TERMS IN ACTION

When Herman Rockefeller, of Melbourne Australia, failed to return home three days after a business trip that ended on January 21, 2010, his wife Victoria made a public plea for help. Unfortunately, Mrs. Rockefeller subsequently had to endure both the news that her husband had been killed and also the circumstances surrounding his death and dismemberment. The 52-year-old businessman was thought to be worth $400 million, but he wasn't killed for his money. Unbeknownst to his wife and two children, Rockefeller frequented swingers' parties and attended one on the night he returned from his last business trip. At that party, Rockefeller angered a couple whom he had already known from a prior party. They expected Rockefeller to bring a woman with him, as he had earlier promised them while at a prior party. Their argument escalated until the couple beat him to death. Once the couple realized whom they had just killed, they moved his body to a secluded location and then dismembered and burned it. Despite his immense wealth, Rockefeller died **intestate**; so, after his death his wife went to court in July 2010 to seek the appointment as the **administrator** of her husband's estate. She was made the administrator in February 2011. Then Mrs. Rockefeller learned that her husband allegedly also had a long-time mistress, who not only claimed ignorance of his secret lifestyle, but also rights to his estate as well. The two women reached a confidential settlement in 2012.

Sources: heraldsun.com.au; dailytelegraph.com.au; nzherald.co.nz

Reviewing What You Learned

After studying the chapter, write the answers to each of the following questions:

1. Name the title of the personal representative who is nominated in a will.

____

____

____

2. Name the title of the personal representative of an intestate estate.

____

____

____

3. If the original personal representative of an intestate estate dies before completing the task, what is the title given to the person who is appointed to take his or her place?

____

____

4. If the personal representative who is nominated in the will dies before the testator, and then the testator dies, what is the title given to the person who is appointed to settle the estate?

____

____

____

5. If the personal representative who is nominated in the will begins, but does not complete, the task, what is the title given to the person who is appointed to settle the estate?

____

____

____

6. What kind of affairs does the special administrator usually handle?

____

____

____

7. Under what circumstances does a public administrator administer an estate?

____

____

8. Under what circumstances would an ancillary administrator be appointed in one state for a person who dies while domiciled in another state?

____

____

____

9. What is the difference between an administrator pendente lite and an administrator ad litem?

____

____

____

10. Why would you think that an executor de son tort is said to be an intermeddler?

____

____

____

Understanding Legal Concepts

Indicate whether each statement is true or false. Then, change the italicized word or phrase of each false statement to make it true.

ANSWERS

_____ 1. Another name for an executor or administrator is *personal representative.*

_____ 2. The court that undertakes the settlement of estates is called the *Surrogate's Court.*

_____ 3. An *executor* is a male appointed by the court to administer the estate of an intestate decedent.

_____ 4. An *administratrix* is a woman nominated in a will to carry out the terms of the will.

_____ 5. An *administrator de bonis non* is appointed by the court to complete the settlement of an estate in which a previously appointed administrator has died, has resigned, or has been removed.

_____ 6. An administrator cum testamento annexo is also called an *administrator with the will annexed.*

_____ 7. An administrator de bonis non cum testamento annexo is appointed by the court to take the place of a previously appointed *executor* who has died, has resigned, or has been removed.

_____ 8. A *public* administrator is a person who undertakes the informal administration of a small estate.

_____ 9. The powers of a voluntary administrator *cease* if a regular administrator or executor is appointed to settle the estate.

_____ 10. A *voluntary* administrator is one who is appointed by the court to handle the affairs of a decedent in a foreign state.

Checking Terminology

From the list of legal terms that follows, select the one that matches each definition.

ANSWERS

a. administrator
b. administrator ad litem
c. administrator cum testamento annexo (c.t.a.)
d. administrator d.b.n.
e. administrator d.b.n.c.t.a.
f. administrator de bonis non
g. administrator de bonis non cum testamento annexo
h. administrator pendente lite
i. administrator with the will annexed (w.w.a.)
j. administratrix
k. ancillary administrator
l. Court of Ordinary
m. executor
n. executor de son tort
o. executrix
p. fiduciary capacity
q. Orphan's Court
r. personal representative
s. Probate and Family Court
t. public administrator
u. special administrator
v. successor personal representatives
w. summary administration
x. Surrogate's Court
y. voluntary administrator
z. will contest

_____ 1. A man nominated in a will of a decedent to carry out the terms of the will; a personal representative of an estate.

_____ 2. A woman appointed by the court to administer the estate of an intestate decedent.

_____ 3. A person appointed by the court to complete the settlement of an estate in which a previously appointed administrator has died, has resigned, or has been removed. (Select two answers.)

_____ 4. A person who undertakes the informal administration of a small estate.

_____ 5. A woman nominated in a will of a decedent to carry out the terms of the will; a personal representative of an estate.

_____ 6. A person appointed by the court to administer a testate estate in which no executor is nominated or in which the executor has died or for some other reason does not settle the estate. (Select two answers.)

_____ 7. A person who performs the duties of an executor without authority to do so.

_____ 8. A temporary administrator appointed by the court to protect estate assets when there is a will contest.

_____ 9. A position of trust.

_____ 10. People appointed to succeed previously appointed personal representatives.

_____ 11. An administrator appointed by the court to supply a necessary party to a suit in which the estate has an interest.

_____ 12. A suit over the allowance or disallowance of a will.

_____ 13. A male appointed by the court to administer the estate of an intestate decedent.

_____ 14. A person appointed by the court to replace a previously appointed executor who has died, has resigned, or has been removed. (Select two answers.)

_____ 15. A person appointed by the court to handle the affairs of an estate, for a limited time only, to take care of urgent affairs.

_____ 16. An official who administers the estate of a person who dies intestate when no relative, heir, or other person appears who is entitled to act as administrator.

_____ 17. A person appointed by the court to handle the affairs of a decedent in a foreign state.

_____ 18. The executor or administrator of a deceased person.

_____ 19. The name given to the court that exercises the function of settling a decedent's estates. (Select five answers.)

_____ 20. An informal procedure used to settle estates that do not exceed $30,000.

Using Legal Language

Read the following story and fill in the blank lines with legal terms taken from the list of terms at the beginning of this chapter:

In his will, Kevin named Katherine to be the person who would settle his estate when he died. She was called a(n) _____________________, which is the name given to a female _____________________ of an estate. In her will, Katherine named Kevin to be the _____________________. Kevin was killed in an automobile accident. His huge vegetable garden, from which he made a living, was just about to be harvested when Kevin died and needed immediate attention; thus, the court appointed a(n) _____________________ to take care of the garden at once. Because Kevin was domiciled in Georgia when he died, Katherine was given her fiduciary appointment by the Court of _____________________. Six months later, Katherine died. Because she had not completed the settlement of Kevin's estate, Katherine's brother-in-law, Keith, was appointed _____________________ to finish the job. Keith was also appointed the fiduciary to settle Katherine's estate. In that position, he was known as a(n) _______________________________ because the person Katherine had named to complete the task had predeceased her. Katherine's newborn child, Kelley, who had inherited a sizable estate from her mother, lived only for six days and then died. Because Kelley died without a will, Katherine's sister, Karen, was appointed _______________________________ by the court to settle Kelley's estate. Before completing her task, Karen became mentally ill and could not complete the job. Her friend, Kaleb, was appointed a(n) _______________________________ by the court to finish the task. No need existed to appoint a(n) _______________________________, because relatives could settle all of the estates involved here. A(n) _______________________________ was not needed, because no out-of-state property was involved. None of these estates was small; therefore, none met the requirements for the appointment of a(n) _______________________________.

Settling an Estate

ANTE INTERROGATORY

A promise by the personal representative to pay an amount of money to the probate judge if the representative's duties are not faithfully performed is called a (A) covenant, (B) surety, (C) decree, (D) bond.

LEARNING OBJECTIVES

LO 1: Identify the key steps in settling an estate

LO 2: Contrast the titles of the person who petitions the court to settle an estate, depending whether the decedent died testate or intestate

LO 3: Explain the purpose of a fiduciary's bond

LO 4: Explain the federal estate tax and the relationship the estate tax exemption has to the estate tax

LO 5: Explain how the federal gift tax credit relates to the federal estate tax exemption

LO 6: Summarize what a sponge tax is

LO 7: Explain under what circumstances one might contest a will

KEY TERMS

bond

burden of proof

decree

estate tax

fiduciary

first and final account

gifts causa mortis

gifts made in contemplation of death

gift tax

gross estate

heir

heirs at law

inheritance tax

inter vivos

inventory

judgment

letters of administration

letters testamentary

marital deduction

proponent

sponge tax

sureties

tax credit

WEBSITES FOR PRONUNCIATION HELP

http://dictionary.cambridge.org/us/pronunciation/english/audio

https://www.howtopronounce.com

STEPS IN ESTATE SETTLEMENT

Several steps are involved in settling an estate. These include petitioning the court for appointment, filing a bond, filing an inventory, making out tax returns, paying debts and expenses of administration, making distribution of the assets of the estate, and filing an account with the court.

Petitioning the Court

If the decedent died testate, the executor named in the will or some other interested person petitions the court for the allowance of the will and for appointment as executor or administrator cum testamento annexo of the will. If the decedent died intestate, one or more of the heirs, next of kin, or creditors petition the court for appointment as administrator of the estate. An **heir**, in the broadest usage of the term, is a person who inherits property from a decedent's estate, whether through intestacy or by someone's will.

Notice of a hearing on the petition is given to all interested parties, including heirs at law, by service of process, mail, or newspaper publication, depending on the particular state statute. **Heirs at law** are people who would have inherited had the decedent died intestate. After a waiting period (usually, three weeks), a hearing is held to decide on the petition, and the court issues a **decree** (a word that has its roots in courts of equity and means a final decision) or **judgment** (decision of a court of law) that either allows or disallows the will, if one exists, and appoints the executor of the will or the administrator of the estate.

> ### Word Wise
> *Variations of "Heir": Related Terms and Spellings*
>
> heir [the *h* is silent; pronounced "air"]
>
> > heirdom *(AIR·dum)*
> >
> > heirloom *(AIR·loom)*
>
> The *i* disappears and the *h* is pronounced in these words:
>
> > heredity *(her·ED·i·tee)*
> >
> > hereditament *(herr·e·DIT·a·ment)*
> >
> > hereditary *(her·ED·i·terr·ee)*
>
> A prefix is added in these words:
>
> > inherit *(in·HER·it)*
> >
> > inheritance *(in·HER·i·tense)*
> >
> > inheritor *(in·HER·i·tor)*

Fiduciary's Bond

Before being appointed, the executor or administrator (called a **fiduciary**, meaning a person who holds a position of trust) must file a bond with the court. A **bond** is a promise by the personal representative and the sureties (if any) to pay the amount of the bond to the probate judge if the representative's duties are not faithfully performed. **Sureties** are people who stand behind the personal representative in the event that he or she fails to do the job. The amount of a probate bond is usually twice the value of the personal property of the estate. Sureties on the bond are often required unless the will otherwise provides or unless all interested parties consent to a bond without sureties.

Letters

When a satisfactory bond with sufficient sureties has been filed, the court issues a certificate of appointment to the personal representative. The certificate is known as **letters testamentary** in a testate estate and **letters of administration** in an intestate estate. For example, in California, the judge signs an "order for probate" and the personal representative is given a form explaining the duties and liabilities of the position.

Inventory

After his or her appointment, one of the first duties of the personal representative is to file an inventory with the court. The **inventory** is a document that lists the assets of the estate together with their appraised value.

A multi-month waiting period elapses to give time for creditors to present their claims. After this period runs out, creditors are barred from bringing claims, and the debts of the estate may be paid. For instance, the waiting period to file most types of claims against a probate estate in Ohio is six months (Ohio Rev. Code § 2117.06).

Federal Estate Tax

An **estate tax** is a tax imposed on the estate of a deceased person. The key question for estate taxes is how big must an estate be to qualify for being taxed, and then at what rate. A federal estate tax return (Form 706) must be filed within nine months after the date of death in cases in which the gross estate exceeds an amount that is exempt from the tax. The exempt amount was $3.5 million in 2009, but the federal estate tax disappeared altogether in 2010, which, as the "Terms in Action" describes more fully, would have been a great year to die, financially speaking. Congress then passed a late-term bill in December 2010 for the 2011 tax year, which exempted the first $5 million of an estate from taxation, and anything over that amount is subject to a 35 percent tax. For the 2016 tax year, the exclusionary amount was $5.45 million (and then any amount over that was subject to a maximum tax rate of 40 percent) and for 2017 was increased to $5.49 million. The **gross estate** for tax purposes includes all property that the decedent owned at death, including individually owned real or personal property, jointly owned real or personal property, life insurance, **inter vivos** (between the living) trusts, and **gifts made in contemplation of death**. Gifts made within three years of the date of death are presumed to be made in contemplation of death unless shown to the contrary. They are sometimes referred to as **gifts causa mortis**.

The following are deductible from the gross estate: debts of the decedent, funeral expenses, administration expenses, amounts given by will to charity, amounts inherited by a surviving spouse (called the **marital deduction**), and other miscellaneous items.

TERMS IN ACTION

Whereas there is never a good time to die, there is a better time to die: it is better to die when there are no **estate taxes**. As far back as 700 B.C., estate taxes existed. The ancient Egyptians levied a 10 percent tax on property transferred at the owner's death. The first inheritance tax in America was the 1797 Stamp Act, although it was repealed in 1802. Estate taxes seemed to be permanent by the 1920s—that is, until Congress passed a law in 2001 that effectively lowered the estate tax every year until it disappeared in 2010, but only in 2010. In 2011, the federal estate tax reappeared. So when Dan Duncan, of Houston, Texas, died on March 28, 2010, he became the first billionaire to completely escape the estate tax. Born in 1933 and raised by his grandmother, the once-poor Duncan started his oil services business in 1968 with $10,000 and a truck. At his death, he was the 74th richest person in the world, with an estimated **gross estate** of $9.8 billion. Had he died in 2009, or even worse, in 2011, his family members would have lost up to $4 billion of their inheritance.

Sources: heritage.org; forbes.com; thetrustadvisor.com

Federal Gift Tax

With exceptions, a federal **gift tax** is imposed on gifts made during one's lifetime that total more than $5.45 million (for those dying in 2016). That means that the donor would owe no gift taxes unless the total amount of gifts made during the donor's life exceeds a $5.45 million **tax credit** (which is a sum of money that is used to offset what is owed in taxes). The federal gift tax exclusion is unified with the federal estate tax, meaning that the dollar-amount exclusion singularly applies to both estate and gift tax situations. However, anyone can make gifts of up to $14,000 per donee per year without incurring gift tax calculations. Married persons may give $28,000 per donee per year. Any gift tax due is collected from the donor's estate, if the estate is large enough to be taxable, when the donor dies.

State Death Taxes

In addition to the federal estate tax, many states impose their own death taxes. They are called either **estate or inheritance taxes**, depending on whether the tax is imposed on the estate or on the people receiving the inheritance. An inheritance tax is a tax imposed on a person who inherits from a decedent's estate. Some states impose an estate tax equal to the credit allowed for state death taxes on the federal estate tax return if it is required to be filed. It is called a **sponge tax** because it soaks up money for the state that the estate is being given credit for in any event.

Distribution and Accounting

After the taxes and debts have been paid and the time has expired for creditors to submit claims, the remaining assets for the estate are distributed according to the terms of the will or the laws of intestate succession. Finally, an accounting, called the **first and final account** if it is the only one, is prepared. This report details the amounts received and distributed by the personal representative of the estate. When the court allows the final account, the estate is settled.

CONTESTING A WILL

A will may be contested on one of the following grounds: (a) the will was improperly executed; (b) the testator was of unsound mind; or (c) the will's execution was obtained through the use of undue influence or fraud. If a will is contested on either of the first two grounds, the **proponent** of the will—that is, the person offering it for probate—has the **burden of proof** (the duty of proving a fact) either that the will was properly executed or that the testator was of sound mind. In contrast, if a will is contested on the ground of undue influence or fraud, the person claiming those acts must prove that they took place. A will may be contested only by someone who has an interest in opposing it, such as an heir at law or a devisee or legatee of an earlier-made will.

TERMS IN ACTION

At his death in 1877, Cornelius Vanderbilt was the richest man on the planet. His fortune was built on shipping and railroads, and he was so rich that his estate of around $100 million would, in today's dollars, be worth well over $180 billion. Known as "The Commodore," Vanderbilt's foray into the rough and tumble New York business world began when he borrowed $100 from his mother for the purpose of ferrying passengers between New York and New Jersey on the Hudson River. Although he fathered 13 children (to one wife, who died before he did), at his death he had 10 living children. He gave 95 percent of his estate to his oldest son, William, and the rest to his eight daughters and his other son, named Cornelius

(Continued)

Jeremiah Vanderbilt, a disfavored son who suffered from epilepsy. A few of the disgruntled daughters and Cornelius contested their father's will on the grounds that he lacked the testamentary capacity when his will was drafted and executed in 1875, and was at that time under the undue influence of a spiritualist. The tawdry and scandalous lawsuit, known as "The Great Will Contest," lasted well over a year. At its conclusion in 1879, the judge ruled in favor of William Vanderbilt, the will's **proponent**. William then paid the legal fees of his losing siblings and also enlarged their bequests. Three years later, Cornelius shot himself in a hotel room and died a few hours later, with his older brother at his bedside.

Sources: americanheritage.com; forbes.com; nytimes.com

Reviewing What You Learned

After studying the chapter, write the answers to each of the following questions:

1. What is the first step in administering an estate if the decedent dies testate?

____

____

____

2. How is notice of a hearing given to all interested parties?

____

____

____

3. What is the significance of the decree or judgment that is issued after the court hearing?

____

____

____

4. Under what circumstances are sureties required on a personal representative's bond?

____

____

____

5. What is the usual amount of a probate bond?

____

____

6. On what grounds may a will be contested?

____

____

____

7. If a will is contested on the ground that the testator was not of sound mind, who has the burden of proof?

____

____

____

8. After being appointed, what is one of the first duties of the personal representative of an estate?

____

____

____

9. What is the length of time that creditors have to make claims against a decedent's estate?

____

____

____

10. In general, when must a federal estate tax return be filed?

____

____

11. What does the gross estate include?

12. What is the final report that is prepared to close an estate?

Understanding Legal Concepts

Indicate whether each statement is true or false. Then, change the italicized word or phrase of each false statement to make it true.

ANSWERS

_____ **1.** If the decedent died *intestate,* the executor named in the will or some other interested person petitions the court for the allowance of the will and appointment as executor.

_____ **2.** Notice of a hearing on the petition is given to *all interested parties* by service of process, mail, or newspaper publication.

_____ **3.** Before being appointed, the executor or administrator will always be required to file a *bond* with the court.

_____ **4.** The amount of the bond is usually *three times* the value of the personal property of the estate.

_____ **5.** Sureties on the fiduciary's bond are *never* required.

_____ **6.** A certificate of appointment of the personal representative in a *testate* estate is known as letters of administration.

_____ **7.** After being appointed, one of the first duties of the personal representative is to file an *inventory* with the court.

_____ **8.** A waiting period from nine months to *a year* elapses to give creditors time to present their claims.

_____ **9.** The gross estate, for tax purposes, *does not* include jointly owned property.

_____ **10.** When the *final account* is allowed by the court, the estate is settled.

Checking Terminology

From the list of legal terms that follows, select the one that matches each definition.

ANSWERS

a. bond
b. burden of proof
c. decree
d. estate tax
e. fiduciary
f. first and final account
g. gifts causa mortis
h. gifts made in contemplation of death
i. gift tax
j. gross estate
k. heir
l. heirs at law
m. inheritance tax
n. inter vivos
o. inventory
p. judgment
q. letters of administration
r. letters testamentary
s. marital deduction
t. proponent
u. sponge tax
v. sureties
w. tax credit

_____ **1.** A person who inherits property.

_____ **2.** The decision of a court of law.

_____ **3.** People who undertake to pay money or to do any other act in the event that their principal fails to meet an obligation.

_____ **4.** A certificate of appointment as executor of a will.

_____ **5.** A detailed list of articles of property in an estate, made by the executor or administrator thereof.

_____ **6.** A promise made by the personal representative to pay an amount of money to the probate judge if the representative's duties are not faithfully performed.

_____ **7.** A person in a position of trust, such as an executor, administrator, guardian, or trustee.

_____ **8.** People who would have inherited had a decedent died intestate.

_____ **9.** A person offering a will for probate.

_____ **10.** The decision of a court of equity.

_____ **11.** A certificate of appointment as administrator of an estate.

_____ **12.** Gifts made within three years of the date of death and subject to the federal estate tax. (Select two answers.)

_____ **13.** Amounts inherited from the estate of one's spouse, not subject to the federal estate tax.

_____ **14.** All property that the decedent owned at death, including individually and jointly owned property, life insurance, living trusts, and gifts made in contemplation of death.

_____ **15.** Between the living.

_____ **16.** A tax imposed on the estate of a deceased person, to be paid prior to distribution.

_____ **17.** An accounting, if it is the only one, presented to the court in final settlement of a decedent's estate.

_____ **18.** A tax imposed on a person who inherits from a decedent's estate.

_____ **19.** A tax that soaks up money for the state that the estate is being given credit for in any event.

_____ **20.** The duty of proving a fact.

_____ **21.** A federal tax that is imposed (with exceptions) on gifts totaling more than $5 million made during one's lifetime.

_____ **22.** A sum of money used to offset an amount owed in taxes.

Using Legal Language

Read the following story and fill in the blank lines with legal terms taken from the list of terms at the beginning of this chapter:

Soon after Kevin died, Karen filed a petition for the probate of the will and for the allowance of her ________________, which is her promise to pay an amount of money to the probate judge if her duties are not faithfully performed. She was not required to have ________________—that is, people who would stand behind her in the event that she failed to do her job. She then notified Kevin's next of kin and all of his ________________—that is, the people who inherited from his estate. After a waiting period, a hearing was held, and the court issued its decision, called a(n) ________________ or ________________, allowing the will. The court then issued Karen a certificate of her appointment, called ________________, because this was a testate case, rather than ________________, which would have been issued had Kevin died intestate. She

could now be called a(n) ________________—that is, a person who holds a position of trust. Karen's first job was to file a(n) ________________ listing the assets of the estate. Her next task was to file a federal estate tax return listing the ________________, which includes the value of all property Kevin owned at his death, both in his own name and jointly with others, as well as life insurance, ________________ (between the living) trusts, and gifts made within three years of death, called ________________ or ________________. Anything left to Kevin's surviving spouse, which is known as the ________________, was not taxable. Some states have a(n) ________________, which is a tax equal to the credit allowed for state death taxes on the federal estate tax return.

31

Trusts

ANTE INTERROGATORY

A trust that allows the trustee to use discretion to decide how much will be given to each beneficiary is a/(an) (A) cestui que trust, (B) inter vivos trust, (C) sprinkling trust, (D) trust res

LEARNING OBJECTIVES

LO 1: Identify the parties to a trust

LO 2: Contrast a testamentary trust from a living trust

LO 3: Summarize the key aspects of a spendthrift trust

LO 4: Explain what is required for a trust to qualify as a charitable or public trust

LO 5: Identify what qualifies a trust as a sprinkling or spray trust

LO 6: Compare and contrast two types of implied trusts: a resulting trust and a constructive trust

LO 7: Explain a precatory trust and how it comes into existence

LO 8: Explain why the term "pour-over-trust" is a misnomer

LO 9: Summarize how a marital deduction trust works

KEY TERMS

A–B trust

beneficial title

beneficiary

bypass trust

cestui que trust

charitable remainder annuity trust

charitable remainder trust

charitable remainder unitrust

charitable trust

constructive trust

conveyance in trust

corpus

credit-shelter trust

Crummey powers

cy pres doctrine

declaration of trust

discretionary trust

domestic asset protection trust (DAPT)

donor

equitable title

exemption equivalent trust

grantor

implied trust

inter vivos trust

irrevocable living trust

legal title

living trust

marital deduction

marital deduction trust

payable on death (POD) account

pour-over trust

precatory trust

public trust

qualified terminable interest property (QTIP)
 trust

resulting trust

revocable living trust

rule against perpetuities

settlor

spendthrift

spendthrift trust

spray trust

sprinkling trust

testamentary trust

Totten trust

trust

trust deed

trustee

trust fund

trust indenture

trustor

trust principal

trust property

trust res

vest

WEBSITES FOR PRONUNCIATION HELP

http://dictionary.cambridge.org/us/pronunciation/english/audio
https://www.howtopronounce.com

PARTIES TO A TRUST

A **trust** is a form of property ownership in which someone controls and manages the property, but does so for the benefit of another. When a trust is established, the **legal title** (full, absolute ownership) in a particular item of property is separated from the **equitable** or **beneficial title** (the right to beneficial enjoyment) in the same property. The person who establishes the trust is called the **settlor** (or the **trustor**, the **grantor**, or the **donor**). The person who holds the legal title to the property for the other's benefit is called the **trustee**. The person who holds the equitable or beneficial title is known as the **beneficiary**. The beneficiary, also known as the **cestui que trust**, is the one for whom the trust is created and who receives the benefits from it. The property that is held in trust is called the **corpus** (or the **trust res**, the **trust fund**, the **trust property**, or the **trust principal**).

Generally, there are no limitations on who can be a trustee, assuming that the person has the legal capacity to own and transfer property. Trustees do not have to be human persons; corporations can serve as trustees. In fact, banks offer trust services through their trust departments.

An example that is typical of how a married couple could use a trust is as follows: A husband married for a second time but with children by his first marriage gives property to a trustee—either during his lifetime or by will when he dies—to be held in trust with instructions to pay the income from the property to his wife for as long as she lives and, on her death, to divide what remains among his children.

KINDS OF TRUSTS

Trusts go back as far as the Roman era. For common law purposes, trusts as we think of them take their heritage from the Middle Ages and the Crusades, and many different kinds of trusts exist. The most common ones are described briefly in this chapter.

Testamentary Trust

A **testamentary trust** is a trust that is created by a will. It comes into existence only on the death of the testator. The terms of the trust, together with the names of the trustee and the beneficiaries, are set out in the body of the will itself. Here is the beginning of a typical trust clause in a will:

> I direct that each share of my residuary estate payable to an individual under the age of 25 shall be held in trust for that individual under Article III. (Article III of the will contains the provisions of the trust.)

Living Trust

A **living trust**, also called an **inter vivos trust**, is created by the settlor while he or she is alive and is established by either a conveyance in trust or a declaration of trust. The instrument creating the trust is called a **trust deed** or a **trust indenture**. In a **conveyance in trust**, the settlor conveys away the legal title to a trustee to hold for the benefit of either the settlor or another as beneficiary. In a **declaration of trust**, the settlor declares in writing that he or she is holding the legal title to the property as trustee for the benefit of some other person (the beneficiary) to whom he or she now conveys the equitable (beneficial) title.

Word Wise

Cestui Que Trust (Ses·twee kay trust) ("trust beneficiary")

Cestui is a French term meaning "to him" or "to her." Here are some other "cestui" phrases:

cestui que use = someone for whose use and benefit land, tenements, etc., are held by another. The *cestui que use* may receive profits and benefits of the estate, but the legal title and possession rest with the other.

cestui que vie = the person whose life determines the duration of the trust, gift, estate, or insurance contract. The *cestui que vie* is the person on whose life the insurance is written.

A living trust may be either irrevocable or revocable. If it is an **irrevocable living trust**, the settlor loses complete control over the trust corpus during his or her lifetime and cannot change the trust. The advantage of an irrevocable trust is that the income from the trust is not taxable to the settlor. The trust itself or the beneficiaries pay the taxes on the trust's income. Such a trust has a disadvantage, however, in that it is irrevocable. In most situations, it is impossible to change or terminate an irrevocable trust. Where it is possible, court involvement is often required as is the consent of all the trust's beneficiaries.

TERMS IN ACTION

One of the more interesting forms of **trusts** that have been gaining popularity is what is known as a gun trust. Certain kinds of weapons are classified as Title II weapons under federal law, and the purchase of those weapons (a machine gun, for instance) is more difficult than for the purchase of traditional weapons. So, rather than buying such a weapon, a person becomes a **settlor** and forms an **irrevocable trust**, which takes title to the gun. Such a form of ownership avoids some of the red tape associated with buying Title II firearms, including fingerprinting. It also allows the trust-owned weapons to be possessed by heirs of the settlor without any parties having to actually take title (or risk losing title). A gun trust, formally known as a National Firearms Act Trust, was the creation in 2007 of David M. Goldman, an attorney from Jacksonville, Florida. He has since copyrighted his gun trust and licensed its use to other attorneys in at least 20 states.

Sources: abajournal.com; guntrustlawyer.com

A **revocable living trust** may be rescinded or changed by the settlor at any time during his or her lifetime. It has neither estate tax nor income tax benefits. Such a trust, however, can serve the purpose of relieving the cares of management of money or property, as well as other purposes, including protecting the assets in the trust from loss due to the beneficiary's negligence.

This type of trust can provide privacy at the time of death, unlike a will, which must be probated and therefore becomes part of the public record.

Spendthrift Trust

A **spendthrift** is one who spends money wastefully and without any self-control. Accordingly, a **spendthrift trust** is designed to provide resources for the maintenance of a beneficiary and, simultaneously, to secure those resources against the beneficiary's improvidence or incapacity. In some states, including New York, there is a presumption that a trust is a spendthrift trust unless it declares otherwise. In other states, such as Massachusetts, to create a spendthrift trust requires that a clause be placed in the trust instrument to the effect that the beneficiary cannot assign either the income or the principal of the trust, and that neither the income nor the principal of the trust can be reached by the beneficiary's creditors. (Of course, once money is paid to a beneficiary, her or his creditors can generally access the money.) Oklahoma's spendthrift trust statute authorizes creation of trusts with language that prohibits the interest (meaning, any right to the trust) of a beneficiary from being subject to "voluntary or involuntary alienation by such beneficiary" (Oklahoma §60-175.25). But the statute allows for certain exceptions, including accessing the trust's income for spousal support or child support.

Generally, spendthrift trusts may not be created to exclusively benefit the trust's grantor or settlor. However, at least 16 states have followed Alaska and Delaware, which became the first and second states—in 1997—to allow self-settled trusts, called **domestic asset protection trusts (DAPT)**, which are self-settled trusts that have independent trustees. A DAPT allows higher net worth individuals to protect their assets from creditors without having to use offshore trusts and their use is controversial.

Charitable Trust

A **charitable** or **public trust** is one established for express charitable purposes, such as the advancement of education; relief to the aged, ill, and poor; and promotion of religion. For a charitable trust to be valid, it must benefit a class of beneficiaries (such as the children of American veterans killed in Iraq or Afghanistan), but it cannot benefit a specific person within that class. A **charitable remainder trust** is a trust in which the donor, or a beneficiary, retains the income from the trust for life or other period, after which the trust corpus is given to a charity. Under a **charitable remainder annuity trust**, a fixed *amount* of income is given annually to a beneficiary, and the remainder is given to a charity. Under a **charitable remainder unitrust**, a fixed *percentage* of income (at least 5 percent of the trust corpus) is given annually to a beneficiary, with the remainder going to a charity.

A charitable trust can be written to last indefinitely; it is not affected by the rule against perpetuities. The **rule against perpetuities** is one of the most difficult common law rules to understand. Essentially, it provides that every interest in property is void unless it must **vest**, if at all, not later than 21 years after some life in being, plus the period of gestation, at the time of the creation of the interest. To "vest" means that a future right or benefit becomes presently owned. By way of example, the right to vote is contingent when you're not yet 18. But at 18, the right to vote is vested, even if the next election is months away. Going back to the rule against perpetuities, a trust established for "my grandchildren who shall reach the age of 21" would be void because other children yet may be born to the settlor and they would not be "lives in being" when the trust was created. Some states have rewritten the rule to provide that property interests must vest either no later than 21 years after some life in being at the time of the creation of the interest or within 90 years of such creation.

When the original purpose of a charitable trust can no longer be fulfilled, instead of causing the trust to end the court may apply the **cy pres doctrine**, a doctrine meaning "as near as possible." Under this doctrine, the court allows the trust fund to be held for another purpose that meets as nearly as possible the intent of the settlor.

Sprinkling Trust

A **sprinkling** or **spray trust** allows the trustee to use discretion to decide how much will be given to each beneficiary. Such a trust is also called a **discretionary trust**. The advantage of this type of trust is that the trustee can determine the tax brackets of the beneficiaries and pay a lesser tax amount by giving more money to those beneficiaries in the lowest tax brackets. It also has built-in spendthrift provisions. A sprinkling trust's chief advantage (trustee discretion) can be its primary disadvantage, in that it can lead to disputes among the beneficiaries about the trustee's control over the distribution of the trust property.

TERMS IN ACTION

Leona Helmsley was one of the more notable characters of New York City's high society in the 1970s and 1980s. After becoming a real estate broker in Manhattan, she met and eventually married real estate developer Harry Helmsley. Leona Helmsley acquired in the press the memorable nickname: the "Queen of Mean," in part because she was exceptionally unkind to her employees. In 1992 Mrs. Helmsley was sentenced to 19 months in prison for tax evasion, and her conviction was based in part on the testimony of her maid, who reported that Helmsley said about the rich, "We don't pay taxes, only the little people pay taxes." She died in 2007, leaving behind an estate valued at around $8 billion. While giving next to nothing in her will to her relatives, Mrs. Helmsley left $12 million in a **testamentary trust** for her dog, a Maltese poodle named Trouble. Helmsley left the remainder of her estate to a **charitable trust** named after her and her husband, established for the care and welfare of stray dogs. That would make the Helmsley trust larger than the combined assets of all of the 7,000-plus animal-related non-profit groups in America. At the request of the **trustees**, a judge in 2008 reduced the $12 million trust for Helmsley's dog to $2 million. And in 2009, a judge ruled that Helmsley's charitable trust wasn't limited to caring for stray dogs, but that the trustees could distribute the money in any charitable manner that they saw fit. This was due to the phrasing in the trust documents and mission statement that were vague enough to allow for the care of people, as well as animals, making a **sprinkling trust** for dogs into a fully **discretionary trust**. Although Trouble the dog died in 2010, in 2013 it got a Manhattan cocktail bar named in its honor: Trouble's Trust, where patrons can order a $19 whiskey drink named the "Queen of Mean."

Sources: wsj.com; nytimes.com; abajournal.com; nypost.com

Implied Trust

A trust that arises by implication of law from the conduct of the parties is known as an **implied trust**. Two examples of implied trusts are resulting trusts and constructive trusts.

A **resulting trust** arises when one unsuccessfully attempts to create a trust or whose created trust is deficient in some significant respect and a court attempts to carry out the wishes of the grantor by establishing a resulting trust. For example, suppose a person creates a trust to pay income from the trust principal to that person's child but has no instructions on what to do in the event of the child's death. If that child dies before the trust has been fully drained, the trustee can do nothing with the assets but would need court intervention to determine what should be done with the trust. Another type of resulting trust occurs when a buyer purchases property but transfers the property's title to another person for the purposes of a third person. The intent is to create a trust but without a trust document, and so a resulting trust would have to be created to make official the grantor's wishes.

A **constructive trust** is imposed by a court to avoid the unjust enrichment of one party at the expense of the other when the legal title to the property was obtained by fraud. For example, if someone embezzles money from his employer and then uses the money to buy a luxury beach house, the employer could ask a court to declare a constructive trust, which would transfer the property from the embezzler to his employer. Notice that in a constructive trust, the trust is a fiction created to prevent the fraudulent one from continuing to wrongfully own property. In fact, the only duty of a trustee of a constructive trust is to transfer the trust property to the newly named beneficiary.

> ### Totten Trusts and Crummey Powers
>
> Two legal terms used in the law of trusts are derived from the names of cases. A **Totten trust** is a bank account in the name of the depositor as trustee for another person. While alive, the depositor can deposit and withdraw from the account. Upon the depositor's death, the account belongs to the named beneficiary. The name of the trust comes from a 1904 New York case, *In re Totten*, 71 N.E. 748. Also known as a **payable on death (POD) account**, this kind of trust is sometimes referred to as a "poor man's trust" because a Totten trust costs next to nothing to create and administer. Those who call it a poor man's trust might need a history lesson, because the Totten trust was created by a woman—who wasn't poor or named Totten.
>
> **Crummey powers** give trust beneficiaries the right to withdraw each year the money that is contributed to the trust during that year. This term comes from the case of *Crummey v. Commissioner*, 397 F.2d 82 (1968).

Precatory Trust

A **precatory trust** is an express trust that sometimes arises from the use of polite language by a testator in a will that is not worded strongly enough to be a trust, on its face. For example, a testatrix wrote the following in her will in 1859: "I give and bequeath unto my husband, George Bates, … the use, income, and improvement of all the estate … for and during the term of his natural life, in the full confidence that upon my decease he will, as he has heretofore done, continue to give and afford my children [naming them] such protection, comfort and support as they or either of them may stand in need of." When the wife died, the husband disregarded his wife's wishes for her children and gave the estate to himself and his brother, among others. But one of the woman's children (the husband's step-child) sued and the court held that the woman's will was, in effect, a trust for the benefit of the children (*Warner v. Bates*, 1867). This type of trust, like a constructive trust, is a trust by decree, rather than by design.

Pour-Over Trust

A **pour-over trust** is a misnomer. It is actually a provision in a will leaving a bequest or devise to the trustee of an existing living trust, and so it might best be thought of as a pour-over will. When the testator dies, the will pours the particular gift into the trust—thus the name "pour-over trust."

Marital Deduction Trust

A **marital deduction trust** is a trust arranged to make maximum use of the marital deduction that is found in the federal estate tax law. The **marital deduction** is the amount that passes from a decedent to a surviving spouse and is not taxable under the federal estate tax law, provided the surviving spouse is a U.S. citizen.

One type of marital deduction trust, called a **credit-shelter trust**, an **A–B trust**, a **bypass trust**, or an **exemption equivalent trust**, reduces the taxation of the second spouse to die by limiting the amount in that person's estate to a sum that is not taxable. With this type of trust, the property of the first spouse to die passes to a two-part trust rather than to the surviving spouse. Trust A is an irrevocable trust that provides only income to the surviving spouse for life, with the principal passing to someone else (such as children) upon the surviving spouse's death, tax free. Trust B, for an amount that is tax exempt (see Chapter 30), is for the benefit of the surviving spouse. When the surviving spouse dies, that estate is not large enough to be taxable.

Another marital deduction trust, called a **qualified terminable interest property (QTIP) trust**, gives all trust income to a surviving spouse for life, payable at least annually, with the principal passing to someone else upon the spouse's death. This type of trust was the example used near the start of the chapter, and it provides for the surviving spouse for life, yet leaves the principal untouched for someone else when the surviving spouse dies.

Reviewing What You Learned

After studying the chapter, write the answers to each of the following questions:

1. When a trust is created, how is title to the property separated?

2. List four names that are used to describe a person who establishes a trust.

3. List five names that are used to describe the property that is held in trust.

4. How is a testamentary trust created? Under what circumstances does it come into existence?

5. What is another name for a living trust?

6. Describe what occurs when a conveyance of trust is created.

7. Describe what occurs when a declaration of trust arises.

8. What are the advantages and disadvantages of an irrevocable living trust?

9. What is necessary for a charitable (or public trust) to be valid?

10. What is the advantage of a sprinkling (or spray) trust?

11. What is the difference between a resulting trust and a constructive trust?

____

____

____

12. Why is the term pour-over trust a misnomer?

____

____

____

Understanding Legal Concepts

Indicate whether each statement is true or false. Then, change the italicized word or phrase of each false statement to make it true.

ANSWERS

_____ 1. When a trust is established, the *legal title* in a particular item of property is separated from the equitable or beneficial title in the same property.

_____ 2. A *testamentary* trust comes into existence only on the death of the testator.

_____ 3. An *inter vivos* trust is a trust that is created by a will.

_____ 4. In a *declaration of* trust, the settlor conveys away the legal title to a trustee to hold for the benefit of either the settlor or the beneficiary.

_____ 5. The advantage of a *revocable* living trust is that the income from the trust is not taxable to the settlor.

_____ 6. A *spendthrift* trust is designed to provide a fund for the maintenance of a beneficiary and, simultaneously, to secure it against his or her improvidence or incapacity.

_____ 7. For a *charitable* trust to be valid, the person to be benefited must be uncertain.

_____ 8. The chief objection to a sprinkling or spray trust is that it gives the *trustee* too much control over the distribution of the trust property.

_____ 9. A *resulting* trust is imposed by law to avoid the unjust enrichment of one party at the expense of the other when the legal title to the property was obtained by fraud.

_____ 10. A precatory trust is an *implied* trust that sometimes arises from the use of polite language by a testator in a will.

Checking Terminology (Part A)

From the list of legal terms that follows, select the one that matches each definition.

ANSWERS

a. A–B trust
b. beneficial title
c. beneficiary
d. bypass trust
e. cestui que trust
f. charitable remainder annuity trust
g. charitable remainder trust
h. charitable remainder unitrust
i. charitable trust
j. constructive trust
k. conveyance in trust
l. credit-shelter trust
m. Crummey powers
n. cy pres doctrine
o. declaration of trust
p. equitable title
q. exemption equivalent trust
r. implied trust
s. inter vivos trust
t. irrevocable living trust

_____ 1. A trust that is created by the settlor when he or she is alive. (Select two answers.)

_____ 2. A trust established for charitable purposes. (Select two answers.)

_____ 3. A bank account in the name of the depositor for the benefit of another person. Upon death, the account belongs to the named beneficiary and avoids estate taxes.

_____ 4. An express trust that arises from the use of polite, non-commanding language by a testator in a will.

_____ 5. The amount that passes from a decedent to a surviving spouse and is not taxable under the federal estate tax law.

_____ 6. A trust in which a fixed amount of income is given annually to a beneficiary and the remainder is given to a charity.

_____ 7. A written declaration by a settlor that he or she is holding legal title to property as trustee for the benefit of another person.

_____ 8. The right to beneficial enjoyment. (Select two answers.)

_____ 9. Authority that gives trust beneficiaries the right to withdraw each year the money that is contributed to the trust during that year.

_____ 10. An implied trust that arises in favor of one who is defrauded when title to property is obtained by fraud.

_____ 11. A future right or benefit becomes presently owned.

_____ 12. A type of marital deduction trust that reduces the taxation of the second spouse to die by limiting the amount in that person's estate to a sum that is not taxable. (Select four answers.)

u. legal title
v. living trust
w. marital deduction
x. marital deduction trust
y. payable on death account
z. pour-over trust
aa. precatory trust
bb. vest

_____ **13.** A trust which is arranged to make maximum use of the marital deduction that is found in the federal estate tax law.

_____ **14.** A trust in which a fixed percentage of income (at least 5 percent of the trust corpus) is given annually to a beneficiary and the remainder is given to a charity.

_____ **15.** A provision in a will leaving a bequest or devise to the trustee of an existing living trust.

_____ **16.** A trust that may not be rescinded or changed by the settlor at any time during his or her lifetime.

_____ **17.** A trust that arises by implication of law from the conduct of the parties.

_____ **18.** A trust in which the donor, or a beneficiary, retains the income from the trust for life or other period, after which the trust corpus is given to a charity.

_____ **19.** A transfer of legal title to property by the settlor to a trustee to hold for the benefit of a beneficiary.

_____ **20.** One for whose benefit a trust is created. (Select two answers.)

_____ **21.** Full, absolute ownership.

_____ **22.** As nearly as possible.

Checking Terminology (Part B)

From the list of legal terms that follows, select the one that matches each definition.

ANSWERS

a. corpus
b. discretionary trust
c. donor
d. grantor
e. qualified terminable interest property (QTIP) trust
f. resulting trust
g. revocable living trust
h. rule against perpetuities
i. settlor
j. spendthrift
k. spendthrift trust
l. spray trust
m. sprinkling trust
n. testamentary trust
o. Totten trust
p. trust
q. trust deed
r. trustee
s. trust fund
t. trust indenture
u. trustor
v. trust principal
w. trust property
x. trust res

_____ **1.** A trust that may be rescinded or changed by the settlor at any time during his or her lifetime.

_____ **2.** A person who establishes a trust. (Select four answers.)

_____ **3.** A person who holds legal title to property in trust for another.

_____ **4.** A trust designed to provide a fund for the maintenance of a beneficiary and, at the same time, to secure it against the beneficiary's improvidence or incapacity.

_____ **5.** The principle that no interest in property is good unless it must vest, if at all, not later than 21 years after some life in being, plus the period of gestation, at the creation of the interest.

_____ **6.** A bank account in the name of the depositor as trustee for another person.

_____ **7.** A marital deduction trust that gives all trust income to a surviving spouse for life, payable at least annually, with the principal passing to someone else upon the spouse's death.

_____ **8.** The body, principal sum, or capital of a trust. (Select five answers.)

_____ **9.** A trust that is created by will and that comes into existence only on the death of the testator.

_____ **10.** An instrument that creates a living trust. (Select two answers.)

_____ **11.** An implied trust that arises in favor of the payor when property is transferred to one person after being paid for by another person.

_____ **12.** A right of ownership to property held by one person for the benefit of another.

_____ **13.** A trust that allows the trustee to decide how much will be given to each beneficiary at the trustee's discretion. (Select three answers.)

_____ **14.** One who spends money profusely and improvidently.

Using Legal Language

Read the following story and fill in the blank lines with legal terms taken from the list of terms at the beginning of this chapter:

Leon decided to put $10,000 in ________________________ for the benefit of his daughter, Lois. He created a(n) ________________________, which is also known as a(n) ________________________, while he was alive, by the use of an instrument called either a(n) ________________________ or a(n) ________________________. It was not called a(n) ________________________, because it was not created by a will. Because Leon transferred legal title to the money to another, the transaction was known as a(n) _______________________ rather than a(n) _______________________, which it would have been called had he retained legal title to the money. Leon could rescind this trust whenever he wished; therefore, it was known as a(n) _______________________ rather than a(n) _______________________. Because he established it, Leon could be referred to as the _______________________, the _______________________, the _______________________, or the _______________________. Lois was known as the _______________________. Leon's wife, Laura, was given legal title to the money; therefore, she was called the _______________________. The money itself could be termed the _______________________, the _______________________, the _______________________, the _______________________, or the _______________________. Called a(n) _______________________, the instrument was designed to provide a fund for Lois and, at the same time, to protect against her improvidence because she was a(n) _______________________—that is, one who spends money profusely. It was not a(n) _______________________ or _______________________, because it was not for charitable purposes; thus, the rule known as the _______________________ was applicable. Leon did not give Laura discretion in the trust to decide how much would be given to different beneficiaries. For that reason, this was not a(n) _______________________ or a(n) _______________________. Because the trust did not arise by implication of law from the conduct of the parties, it was not either one of the _______________________—that is, a(n) _______________________ or a(n) _______________________. In addition, because it did not arise from the use of polite but insufficient language in a will, it was not a(n) _______________________.

Terms Used in Law of Real Property

RzymuR/Shutterstock

Some law firms specialize in the field of real property law, other firms work in the field as part of a general practice, and still others work in the field only occasionally or not at all. Knowledge of real property law, in any event, is important for everyone because we all must reside somewhere, whether we own the property, rent it, or live there with someone else who does. Chapter 32 explains the various estates in real property that are available to property owners. Co-ownership of real property is discussed in Chapter 33, and the methods of acquiring title to real property are outlined in Chapter 34. The requirements of a valid deed and the different types of deeds are examined in Chapter 35, followed by a discussion of mortgages in Chapter 36. Finally, Chapter 37 provides an overview of landlord and tenant law.

7

Estates in Real Property

ANTE INTERROGATORY

The estate in real property that is capable of coming to an end automatically because of the happening of some event is (A) fee simple estate, (B) estate pur autre vie, (C) life estate, (D) fee simple determinable.

LEARNING OBJECTIVES

LO 1: Identify the types of freehold estates

LO 2: Identify what language makes an estate a fee simple estate

LO 3: Characterize the purpose behind a fee tail estate

LO 4: Explain the relationship the feudal system has to real property law

LO 5: Summarize the ways in which a determinable fee estate is created

LO 6: Summarize what a life estate is, how it is created and what limitations are on a life tenant's ownership

LO 7: Compare and contrast the four types of leasehold estates

KEY TERMS

apt words
condition subsequent
defeasible estate
determinable fee
determine
esquire
estate
estate pur autre vie
estate tail male
estate tail special
fee
fee simple absolute
fee simple determinable

fee simple estate
fee tail estate
fixture
freehold estate
leasehold estate
life estate
life tenant
possibility of reverter
real property
remainder interest
reversionary interest
revert
waste

WEBSITES FOR PRONUNCIATION HELP

http://dictionary.cambridge.org/us/pronunciation/english/audio
https://www.howtopronounce.com

Ownership of interests in **real property**—that is, the ground and anything permanently attached to it—in the United States follows the estate concept that developed under the English feudal system. **Estates** (ownership interests) in real property are divided into two groups: freehold estates and leasehold estates. Personal property that is permanently attached to real property becomes part of the real property and is known as a **fixture**. Something as slight as a bathroom towel rack, or as heavy as a marble countertop, has its status changed by its placement in a home (or on the property, like a shed). Fixtures, generally, stay with or on noncommercial property when real estate is sold or otherwise transferred.

FREEHOLD ESTATES

A **freehold estate** is an estate in which the holder owns the land for life or some other indefinite time period without interference from others. At common law, only freehold estates were considered to be real property. There are four types of freehold estates:

1. fee simple
2. fee tail
3. determinable fee
4. life

Fee Simple Estate

The **fee simple estate** (sometimes called **fee** or **fee simple absolute**) is the largest estate that one can own in land, giving the holder absolute ownership that descends to the owner's heirs on his or her death. In addition, it can be sold or granted out by the owner at will during the owner's lifetime. In early conveyances, a fee simple estate was created by a deed containing the words "To (a person) and his heirs." If the words "and his heirs," called the **apt words** (the suitable words), were omitted from the deed, the grantee received only a life estate. Today, real estate statutes declare that the words "and his heirs" are no longer required to be in a deed to create a fee simple estate. This type of ownership is old enough to be mentioned in Shakespeare's *Romeo and Juliet*, wherein a character states, "An I were so apt to quarrel as thou art, any man should buy the fee simple of my life for an hour and a quarter."

Fee Tail Estate

A **fee tail estate** restricts ownership of real property to a particular family bloodline. It was created by statute in England in 1285 (when land was the basis for the family fortune) as a way to keep real property in the family forever. Under the statute, the property could not be alienated. If the bloodline became extinct, the property reverted to the original owner's line.

Gradually, statutes were passed in England allowing tenants to transfer their property rights to others without permission of the lord and also to pass their interest in the land to their heirs. The feudal system was finally abolished in England in 1660 during the reign of King Charles II, with the passage of the Tenures Abolition Act.

At common law, an estate tail was created by the apt words in a deed "to (the grantee) and the heirs of his body" and was often given by a parent to a child as part of a marriage settlement. The word "tail" comes from the French word *tailler,* meaning "to carve." The idea was that the grantor was carving an estate to his liking. Variations included the **estate tail special**, in which land was given to both the husband and wife and the heirs of their two bodies, and the **estate tail male**, which restricted ownership to men in the family line.

Origin of Real Property Law

THE FEUDAL SYSTEM

Under the feudal system in England, which began in the year 1066 when William the Conqueror of Normandy took over England after the Battle of Hastings, the king was the personal owner of all land in the kingdom. In exchange for services, the king granted land in large tracts to his tenants-in-chief (barons) who, in turn, granted land to lesser lords. These lesser lords granted land to still lesser noblemen. In exchange for use of the land, continuous services were required. Thus was created a pyramid with the king at the top and the people who worked the land at the bottom. Rights in the land moved down the pyramid (each step down being a lesser right), while a constant flow of services moved up.

In its early stage, feudalism was a military system designed to protect the king. Since the king was often short of money, he used land to purchase military services. Thus, the highest type of ownership of land was a military tenure called knight's service. The vassal swore allegiance to the king and also agreed to give him the services of a number of knights and squires (depending on the amount of land received) for 40 days in the year, known as the feudal levy. The services were perpetual. The land reverted to the king if the knights were not productive.

Today in the United States, the term **esquire** is used as a title (abbreviated Esq.) following the name of an attorney, in place of the prefixes Mr., Mrs., Miss, or Ms. In English nobility, esquire (abbreviated squire) was a social rank higher than a gentleman, but lower than a knight.

Oath of Fealty

In return for land, each tenant down the line swore *fealty* (allegiance) and agreed to do *homage* (a particular service) to his landlord in a ceremony called *feoffment*. The landlord was called the *feoffor* and the tenant was called the *feoffee*. The feoffee made the following oath of fealty:

> I become your man from this day forward of life and limb and of earthly worship, and unto you shall be true and faithful, and bear to you faith for the tenements that I claim to hold of you, saving the faith that I owe unto our sovereign lord the king.

Tenant's Service

The tenant's service to his lord varied greatly. *Cornage* required the tenant to blow a horn to warn the country on the approach of the king's enemies. *Villeinage* required the tenant to plow the lord's land and make his hedges. A *tenant in sergeanty* was a servant such as a chamberlain, an armorer, a cook, or an esquire. Churches held land in *frank-almoign* (free alms) in exchange for services such as the saying of masses for the donor. *Socage* tenure required the oath of faithfulness, but only nominal services for the land such as the giving of one red rose at midsummer, or the delivery of one peppercorn annually. This was often done when a father parceled out land to his children. The word *nominal* means "in name only; not real or substantial."

Life Estate

In the early feudal period, the greatest estate that one could own was a life estate, and that could not be transferred by a tenant without his lord's assent. When the tenant died, the lord was under no obligation to accept the tenant's heir as successor; however, he customarily did so in exchange for a payment called *relief*. This payment was the forerunner of our present estate tax. When a tenant died leaving an infant heir, the child became the ward of the lord, who kept the child's income and profit from the land, during minority, in exchange for support, education, and protection. The lord also had the power to choose the minor's spouse. Wardships and marriages were bought and sold by the lord, and upon his death, they passed by will or intestate succession to the lord's heirs.

Fee Simple Estate

As time went on, a lord could accept, if he wished, the tenant's heir in advance by granting land "to him and his heir." The heir at that time would usually be the tenant's eldest son. If the grant was "to him and his heirs," it was a grant to the tenant, then the tenant's heir, then the heir's heir, and on down the line. These words eventually became the term that created a *fee simple estate* (absolute ownership of property). When a tenant died without heirs, his property *escheated,* that is, reverted to the lord. Unfortunately, none of this applied to women who, in those days, had almost no legal rights.

TERMS IN ACTION

The **fee tail estate** was eradicated in most jurisdictions because it can create a perpetual restriction on real estate. The statutes that abolish the fee tail estate tend to use language that is similar in construction. Pennsylvania's statute abolishing the fee tail states, "Whenever by any conveyance an estate in fee tail would be created according to the common law of the Commonwealth, it shall pass an estate in **fee simple**, and as such shall be inheritable and freely alienable." Michigan's abolishment of the fee tail includes the effective date and says, "All estates tail are abolished, and every estate which would be adjudged a fee tail, according to the law of the territory of Michigan, as it existed before the second day of March, 1821, shall for all purposes be adjudged a fee simple; and if no valid remainder be limited thereon, shall be a fee simple absolute."

Source: 20 Pa. Cons. Stat. § 6116, Mich. Comp. Laws 554.3

As time went on in England, methods were devised that allowed property in an estate tail to be alienated from the family line. Today, the estate tail has been either abolished or made ineffective by state statutes.

Determinable Fee Estate

A **determinable fee**, also called a **fee simple determinable**, is an estate in real property that is capable of coming to an end automatically because of the happening of some event. If the event occurs, the estate will **determine**—that is, will come to an end. If the event never occurs, the estate will be absolute. To illustrate, if a person conveys real property to a particular church "so long as the premises shall be used for church purposes," the church has a fee simple determinable. The property will **revert** (go back) to the grantor or his or her heirs if it is not used for church purposes. The grantor has a **possibility of reverter** interest in the property because it is always possible that the event will occur.

A similar type of **defeasible estate**—that is, one that can be lost or defeated—is called a *fee simple subject to a* **condition subsequent** (a qualification that comes later). This exists when a condition is placed in a deed, making it possible to have the ownership terminated at a future time. For example, if a deed contains the language "subject to the condition that the premises never be used for the sale of alcohol" and the property is later used for the sale of alcohol, the former owner (or his or her heirs) could bring legal action to take back the property. The estate does not automatically come to an end, as in the case of a determinable fee; rather, legal action must be taken to end it.

Word Wise
The "Vert" in Revert

The Latin root "vert" and its variation "vers" mean "turn." For example, the term "revert" [*re* (back) + *vert* (turn)] means "to go back" or "to return."

"Vert" may mean "turn" in the physical or literal sense, as in the word "invert" [*in* + *vert* = to turn in], which could include turning inside out or upside down or reversing the order.

"Vert" may also be used in a non-physical sense, as in the word "advertise," meaning that consumer attention is hopefully "turned" toward a product or service.

Consider how the root functions in these words: adversary, vertigo, perverse, diversion.

Life Estate

A **life estate** is an estate limited in duration to either the life of the owner or the life of another person. It may be created by deed, will, or operation of law.

If A either deeds or wills real property "to B for life and on B's death to C," B will own an estate for life, and C will own a **remainder interest** (an interest that takes effect after another estate is ended) in fee simple. Life tenants may convey their interest to others; however, they can convey only that which they own, nothing greater. Thus, if B conveys his or her interest (a life estate) to D, D will own a life estate for the duration of B's life, after which the property will belong to C, the holder of the fee. It is known as an **estate pur autre vie** when one holds property for the duration of the life of another person.

When a person grants a life estate, either by will or by deed, to another and retains the fee, he or she is said to have a **reversionary interest** (a right to the future enjoyment of property that one originally owned). On the death of the life tenant, the estate reverts to the owner or the owner's heirs.

Legal life estates are created by the operation of some law. For example, the rights of dower (legal grants of property rights for widows) and curtesy (legal grants of property rights for widowers) and the right of a surviving spouse to waive the will of a deceased spouse sometimes create life estates, depending on the existence and language of those state statutes.

Owners of life estates, known as **life tenants**, own legal title to the property during their lifetime. They must pay the taxes, but are entitled to possession of the property and to any income that comes from it. Life tenants are responsible to the owners of the fee for the commission of **waste**, which is the destruction, alteration, or deterioration of the premises, other than from natural causes or from normal usage. In an illustrative case from Florida, a woman conveyed her property to a married couple but reserved a life estate for herself. While still living on her own property, the woman was sued by the couple for cutting down timber on the property and selling the timber. The couple argued such deforestation constituted waste. In ruling for the couple, the Florida Court of Appeals held that unless the life tenant was holding the proceeds of the timber sales for the benefit of couple, she had no right to cut the timber. Interestingly, the court noted that, while the life tenant's cutting of timber for commercial gain was waste, she could have cut the timber…to use as fuel (*Sauls v. Crosby*, 258 So.2d 326, 1972).

TERMS IN ACTION

Dr. Kirk Deibert and his wife Lillian owned a 170-acre farm in **fee simple absolute** in Florence, Alabama. They bought the property in 1952 and turned it into a beautiful horse farm called Rolling Acres. Having no children and desiring that more parks be created in their town, decades later the Deibert granted to themselves **life estates** in the property and gave the city a **remainder interest**, with the condition that the city turn their property into a public park. Another **condition subsequent** on the transfer of their property to the city was that the property never be used for commercial development. Dr. Deibert passed away in 1993, and eventually Mrs. Deibert decided to give up her life estate so that before she passed away the city could begin its work on what was now the city's property in **fee simple determinable**, Mrs. Deibert continued to live at her home on the property, watching her gift to the public become reality, until February 9, 2011, when she died at the age of 94. She was buried in the park, which has a playground, ponds, pavilions, paved walking trails, and a children's museum.

Sources: timesdaily.com; flpl.org

LEASEHOLD ESTATES

A **leasehold estate** is an estate that is less than a freehold estate, in that it provides a temporary right to property. At common law and in most states today, leasehold estates are treated as personal property rather than real property. There are four types of leasehold estates:

1. *Tenancy for years*—an estate for a definite or fixed period of time, such as "for two years," or "for nine months," or even, "until the crops have been harvested."

2. *Periodic tenancy*—an estate that continues for successive periods until one of the parties terminates it by giving notice to the other party. The phrase "month-to-month tenancy" or "week-to-week tenancy" is an alternative term to "periodic tenancy" and, unlike the tenancy for years, there is no stated ending date, even though there is a specified term.

3. *Tenancy at will*—an estate for an indefinite period. A tenant at will might rent for years, but what distinguishes the tenancy at will from the aforementioned tenancies is that there is no fixed or set period established at the start of the tenancy. A difference between a tenancy at will and a periodic tenancy, discussed above, is that in a periodic tenancy there is an agreed upon term of the occupancy, while in both there is no stated ending date of the occupancy.

4. *Tenancy at sufferance*—a "hold-over" tenancy wherein the tenant continues to occupy the premises after the lease has expired. A tenant at sufferance is not breaking the law until the landlord has asked the tenant to vacate the premises, and such a tenant will be liable for the past rent, and is bound by the terms of the prior lease. A difference between a tenancy at sufferance and a tenancy at will, discussed above, is that the tenancy at will is the result of an agreement between landlord and tenant.

Landlord and tenant law are discussed in detail in Chapter 37.

Reviewing What You Learned

After studying the chapter, write the answers to each of the following questions:

1. Estates in real property are divided into what two groups?

   ____

   ____

   ____

2. List four types of freehold estates. ___________________

   ____

   ____

   ____

3. What will happen to an estate owned solely by an individual in fee simple when the owner dies? Under what circumstances may the owner sell or grant out the property? ___________

   ____

   ____

   ____

4. What was the original purpose of the estate in fee tail?

   ____

   ____

   ____

5. Give an example of a conveyance that is a determinable fee.

   ____

   ____

   ____

6. In what three ways may a life estate be created?

   ____

   ____

   ____

7. What is the difference between a remainder interest and a reversionary interest? ___________________________

   ____

   ____

   ____

8. If A conveys her interest in real property to B for B's life, and upon B's death to C, and B thereafter conveys her interest to D, who will own the property when B dies? ___________

   ____

   ____

9. What is the difference between a freehold estate and a leasehold estate? _________________________________

____

____

____

10. List four types of leasehold estates. _________________________________

____

____

____

Understanding Legal Concepts

Indicate whether each statement is true or false. Then, change the italicized word or phrase of each false statement to make it true.

ANSWERS

_____ 1. Ownership of interests in land in the United States follows the estate concept that developed under the *English feudal system*.

_____ 2. A freehold estate is an estate in which the holder owns the land *only for life*.

_____ 3. A fee simple estate *cannot* be sold during the owner's lifetime.

_____ 4. Today, by statute, the words "and his heirs" are *no longer required* to be in a deed to create a fee simple estate.

_____ 5. Today, the *estate tail* has been either abolished or made ineffective by state statutes.

_____ 6. A determinable fee is an estate in real property that *never comes to an end*.

_____ 7. Legal action *must be* taken to end an estate in fee simple subject to a condition subsequent if the condition occurs.

_____ 8. A life estate may *not be* created by will.

_____ 9. When a person grants a life estate to another and retains the fee, he or she is said to have a *remainder* interest.

_____ 10. Life tenants are responsible to the owners of the fee for the commission of *waste*.

Checking Terminology

From the list of legal terms that follows, elect the one that matches each definition.

ANSWERS

a. apt words
b. condition subsequent
c. defeasible estate
d. determinable fee
e. determine
f. esquire
g. estate
h. estate pur autre vie
i. estate tail male
j. estate tail special
k. fee
l. fee simple absolute
m. fee simple estate
n. fee tail estate
o. fixture
p. freehold estate
q. leasehold estate
r. life estate
s. life tenant
t. possibility of reverter
u. real property
v. remainder interest
w. reversionary interest
x. revert
y. waste

_____ 1. Ownership interest.

_____ 2. The largest estate that one can own in land, giving the holder the absolute ownership and power of disposition during life and descending to the owner's heirs at death. (Select three answers.)

_____ 3. A freehold estate that restricts ownership of real property to a particular family blood line.

_____ 4. A freehold estate restricting ownership to men in the family line.

_____ 5. Come to an end.

_____ 6. An estate that can be lost or defeated.

_____ 7. An estate limited in duration to either the life of the owner or the life of another person.

_____ 8. A right to the future enjoyment of property that one originally owned.

_____ 9. Destruction, alteration, or deterioration of a premises other than from natural causes or normal use.

_____ 10. An estate in which the holder owns the land for life or forever.

_____ 11. Suitable words.

_____ 12. A freehold estate restricting ownership to a husband and wife and the heirs of their two bodies.

_____ 13. An estate in real property that is capable of coming to an end automatically because of the happening of some event. (Select two answers.)

_____ 14. Go back.

_____ 15. A qualification that comes later.

_____ 16. An interest that takes effect after another estate is ended.

_____ 17. Personal property that is permanently attached to real property.

_____ 18. An estate that is less than a freehold estate.

_____ 19. An interest in property that could be returned to the grantor as the result of the occurrence of an event.

_____ **20.** The ground and anything permanently attached to it.

_____ **21.** An estate that a person holds for the duration of the life of another person.

_____ **22.** A title following the name of an attorney in place of the prefixes Mr., Mrs., Miss, or Ms.

_____ **23.** The owner of a life estate.

Using Legal Language

Read the following story and fill in the blank lines with legal terms taken from the list of terms at the beginning of this chapter:

Harvey owned a(n) _________________ in real property, which was limited to the duration of his life. It is not a(n) _________________—that is, an estate that a person holds for the duration of the life of another. He was known as a(n) _________________ and was responsible to others for the commission of _________________, which is the destruction or deterioration of the premises. On Harvey's death, the _________________—that is, the ownership interest—went to Harriet, a new owner who had a(n) _________________, which took effect after Harvey's estate ended. It was not a(n) _________________, because title did not _________________—that is, go back—to an earlier owner. Similarly, it was not a(n) _________________ designed to restrict ownership of real property to a particular family blood line, with its variations of _________________ and _________________. The deed conveying title to Harriet contained the _________________—that is, the suitable words—to give her the largest estate that one can own in land. This estate has various names, including _________________, _________________ and just plain _________________. The estate was not a(n) _________________—that is, an estate in real property that is capable of coming to an end—nor was it _________________, meaning one that can be lost or defeated. It was not a fee simple, subject to a(n) _________________, because no conditions were in the deed. In addition, it was not a(n) _________________, because it was not less than a(n) _________________, which is an estate in which the holder owns the land for life or forever.

7

Multiple Ownership of Real Property

ANTE INTERROGATORY

When two or more persons own real property as jointly but as a single estate, holding the same interest, it is known as (A) joint tenancy, (B) community property, (C) tenants in common, (D) unity of interest.

LEARNING OBJECTIVES

LO 1: Summarize the various ways in which real property can by co-owned

LO 2: Explain the key characteristics of owning property as tenants in common

LO 3: Contrast joint tenancy with tenancy in common

LO 4: Identify what it means for a state to be a community property state

LO 5: Explain the key aspects of tenancy by the entirety

LO 6: Compare and contrast tenancy by the entirety with tenancy in partnership

LO 7: Compare and contrast condominiums with cooperative apartments

LO 8: Identify how timesharing is different from traditional real estate ownership

KEY TERMS

common areas

community property

concurrent ownership

condominium

condominium association

cooperative apartment

co-ownership

co-tenants

covenants, conditions, and restrictions (CC&Rs)

creditors

estate in severalty

homeowners association

interval ownership

joint tenancy

joint tenancy with the right of survivorship

joint tenants

levy on execution

master deed

moiety

partition

proprietary lease

several

tenancy by the entirety

tenancy in partnership

tenants in common

timesharing

unit deed   unity of possession
units   unity of time
unity of interest   unity of title

WEBSITES FOR PRONUNCIATION HELP

http://dictionary.cambridge.org/us/pronunciation/english/audio
https://www.howtopronounce.com

CO-OWNERSHIP OF REAL PROPERTY

When real property is owned separately by one person, it is referred to as **estate in severalty** (or **severally**, as an alternative). In contrast, when real property is owned by more than one person, this is known as **concurrent ownership** or **co-ownership**, and the owners are known as **co-tenants**. Notice that "tenant" can have more than one meaning; it does not just apply to renters. It used to be said that co-owners of property own by moieties. **Moiety** means a part, portion, or fraction. The most common co-tenant relationships are tenants in common, joint tenants, tenants by the entirety, and tenants in partnership.

Tenants in Common

When two or more persons own real property as **tenants in common**, each person owns an undivided share, and on one owner's death that person's share passes to his or her heirs. Tenants in common have **unity of possession**, which means that each owner is entitled to possession of the entire premises. This tenancy may be created by deed or by will, but more commonly it comes about by operation of law, such as when a person dies intestate, leaving real property to two or more heirs. Such heirs will take the property as tenants in common.

Any of the tenants in common may sell or grant out their interests to others without permission of the other co-tenants, and any new owners become tenants in common with the remaining owners. To say that each tenant in common has an undivided share does not automatically mean that each co-tenant has an equal share. For example, a will might make a child and two cousins tenants in common, and the child owns a ½ interest in the property and the two cousins each own a ¼ interest. As tenants in common, they own a unified right to be on the property, but they individually own a financial stake (based on their given share), which they can sell (or give) to someone else, not comprehended by the grantor of the tenancy in common. From the preceding example, one of the cousins could sell his or her ¼ share to a neighbor, without the other co-tenants being able to prevent the sale.

Tenants in common may separate their interests in the property by petitioning the court for a partition of the premises. When a **partition** occurs, the court either divides the property into separate parcels so that each co-tenant will own a particular part outright, or orders the property sold and divides the proceeds of the sale among the co-tenants. **Creditors** (people or businesses who are owed money) may reach the interest of a tenant in common and have the interest sold or hold it with the remaining tenants in common.

Joint Tenants

When two or more persons own real property as joint tenants, the estate created is a single estate with multiple ownership. This is known as **joint tenancy** or **joint tenancy with the right of survivorship**. **Joint tenants** are two or more persons holding one and the same interest, accruing by one and the same conveyance, commencing at one and the same time, and held by one and the same undivided possession. Each tenant owns the entire estate, subject to the equal rights of the other joint tenants. Joint tenancy requires four different "unities" of ownership. All joint tenants' interests are equal (**unity of interest**), and all have the right to possession of the entire estate (**unity of possession**). All owners must take title at the same time (**unity of time**), and each must receive title from the same instrument or conveyance, such as a will or a deed (**unity of title**).

A joint tenant may not transfer his or her own ownership to someone else, including by using a will, and at the death of any joint tenant, the surviving tenant(s) owns the property in its entirety.

A joint tenant may petition the court for a partition of the estate, which would end the joint tenancy. Creditors may levy on the interests of a joint tenant on execution and take over the joint tenant's interest as a tenant in common with the remaining joint tenants. To **levy on execution** means "to collect a sum of money by putting into effect the judgment of a court."

TERMS IN ACTION

Joint tenancy with the right of survivorship isn't dependent on which of the joint tenants paid how much for the property. In a 1997 case from Pennsylvania, two people bought real estate and titled it as joint tenants with rights of survivorship. Later, one of the joint tenants went to court to have the property partitioned, as an alternative to first seeking credit for the amount of his extra contribution toward buying the property. The joint tenant seeking **partition** argued that it was warranted because he had paid more than five times the amount of money that his joint tenant had paid. But the court ruled that unless there is evidence of fraud, disproportionate contributions toward buying the property aren't court-reimbursable acts and don't warrant partition of such a joint tenancy.

Source: *D'Arcy v. Buckley*, 71 Bucks Co. L. Rep. 167 (1997)

Word Wise
The "Cur" in Concurrent

The Latin root "cur," or "cour," means "to run." Other words with this root are as follows:

Word	Meaning
concur (verb) [*con* (together) + *currere* (to run)]	to run or happen together
concurrent (adjective) [*concur* + *ent* (that has, shows, or does)]	occurring at the same time
cursory (adjective) [*currere* (to run) + *ory* (relating to)]	hastily, superficially
incur (verb) [*in* (toward) + *currere* (to run)]	to run into
precursor (noun) [*pre* (before) + *currere* (to run) + that *or* (person or thing that)]	person or thing that goes before
recur (verb) [*re* (again) + *currere* (to run)]	to occur again
recurrent (adjective) [*recur* + *ent* (that has, shows, or does)]	occurring again

Community Property

Influenced by the Roman Civil Law system (in contrast to the English Common Law system) in the 5th century Spain, through its Visigothic Code, there originated a form of marital property ownership we now call community property. It has been adopted as the default from of marital property ownership in the nine states indicated on the map in **Figure 33-1**. Alaska and Tennessee are thought of as opt-in community property states, which means spouses can create a community property agreement and designate what property they want considered as community property. **Community property** is property acquired by a husband or wife during marriage that belongs to both spouses equally. Under this system, property acquired by the efforts of either spouse during marriage belongs to both spouses equally—that is, each spouse owns an undivided one-half interest in the whole premises. Common exceptions to community property

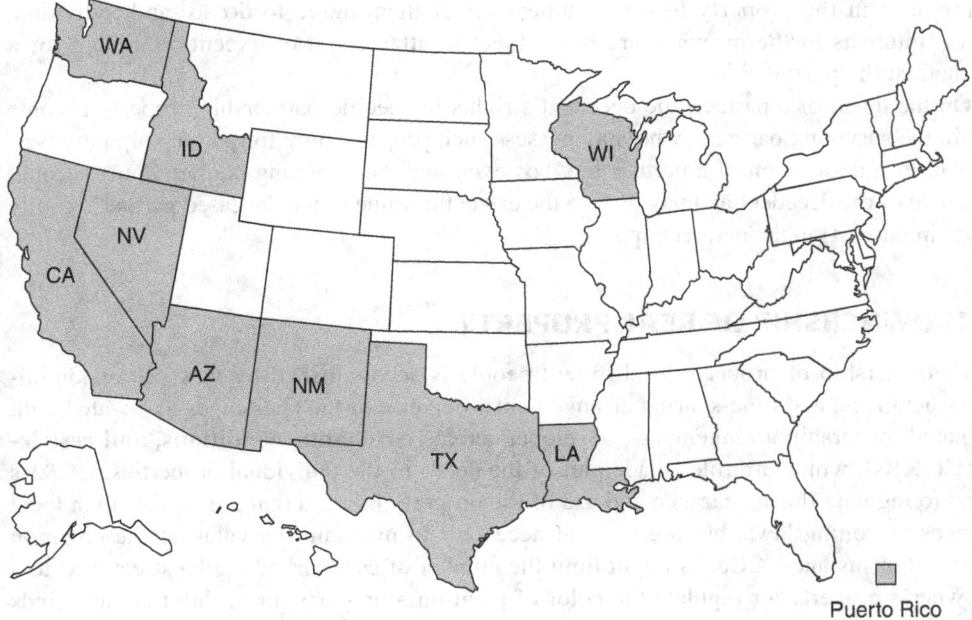

Figure 33-1 Community property jurisdictions

include property a spouse acquires before marriage, property given as an individual gift to a spouse, and property a spouse has inherited.

Tenants by the Entirety

A **tenancy by the entirety** may be held only by a husband and wife (and same sex spouses, as of recent changes in the law) and is based on the common law doctrine that a husband and wife are regarded, in law, as one person. Under common law doctrine, each spouse owns the entire estate, which neither spouse can destroy by any separate act. (While no longer the case, originally under the common law application of tenancy by the entirety, a husband, had the entire control over the marital estate, including the exclusive right to possession and the right to all rents and profits.) On the death of either spouse, the survivor owns the entire estate outright.

In recent years, some states have modified the common law version of tenancy of the entirety—because of the unfair rights given to the husband—in order to give equal rights to the spouses, while at the same time retaining the feature of protection against attachment by creditors. Here is an example of a part of a modern state statute, in this case Massachusetts:

> A husband and wife shall be equally entitled to the rents, products, income or profits and to the control, management and possession of property held by them as tenants by the entirety. The interest of a debtor spouse in property held as tenants by the entirety shall not be subject to seizure or execution by a creditor of such debtor spouse so long as such property is the principal residence of the non-debtor spouse; provided, however, both spouses shall be liable jointly or severally for debts incurred on account of necessaries furnished by either spouse or to a member of their family. (M.G.L.A. ch. 209 §1)

A divorce, by operation of law, automatically nullifies a tenancy by the entirety for the former spouses. The terms of the divorce will determine what happens to the property.i

Tenants in Partnership

Tenancy in partnership is a form of ownership of real property that is available to business partners if they choose to use it. The Uniform Partnership Act (UPA) or the Revised Uniform Partnership Act (RUPA) governs a tenancy in partnership in those states have adopted either the UPA or RUPA. According to the act, individual partners cannot transfer their interests in the property to others unless all of them agree to do so, and individual partners' interests in the property are not subject to attachment or execution except for a claim against the partnership.

On the death of a partner, the decedent's rights in specific partnership property become vested in the surviving partners, who may possess such property only for partnership purposes. Death causes a dissolution of a partnership, however, and the surviving partners must account to the estate of the decedent and pay over to the estate the value of the deceased partner's equity (ownership interest) in the partnership.

MULTI-OWNERSHIP OF REAL PROPERTY

Separate ownership of property by different people is accomplished by way of condominiums, cooperatives, and time-sharing arrangements. Because of the challenges associated with coordinated ownership arrangements, developers create **covenants, conditions, and restrictions (CC&Rs)**, which are rules made part of the deeds to the individual properties. CC&Rs are used to regulate the appearance and use of the property in ways that are stricter than local ordinances or zoning laws, but are thought necessary to maintain the value of the common properties. For instance, CC&Rs might limit the number of cars parked on the street next to a homeowner's property, or regulate the color of paint on a property, or prohibit certain kinds of trees or shrubs from being grown. Developers often incorporate **homeowners associations** as nonprofit corporations, for the purposes of marketing and managing the housing developments. When a buyer purchases a property that is part of a multi-ownership development, the buyer becomes a member of the homeowners association and then is subject to its covenants, conditions, and restrictions.

Condominiums

A **condominium** is a parcel of real property, portions of which, called **units**, are owned separately in fee simple by individual owners, and the remainder of which, called the **common areas**, is owned as tenants in common by all of the unit owners. Common areas include entrances, hallways, sidewalks, swimming pools, yards, roofs, and outside walls, and are maintained and managed by a **condominium association** consisting of unit members. Unit owners pay monthly maintenance fees in addition to real property taxes. An ownership interest in a condominium is considered to be real property. A **master deed**, describing the entire property that is owned by the condominium association, is recorded at the registry of deeds, together with restrictions that are placed on the use of the property. The transfer of ownership of each unit is accomplished by the use of a **unit deed**, which is a deed to the individual unit being transferred.

Cooperatives

A **cooperative apartment** (commonly called a co-op)is a dwelling unit in which the occupants lease individual units and, at the same time, own shares of stock in the corporation that owns the building housing the individual units. The corporation owns the complex, which is occupied by the tenants who are the stockholders of this nonprofit corporation. The lease is known as a **proprietary lease** because it is a lease to an owner of the property. Tenants pay rent to the corporation, and the corporation maintains the property and pays the real property taxes. An ownership interest in a cooperative is personal property rather than real property, and a transfer of ownership is accomplished by sale of stock in the controlling corporation. Co-ops are still prevalent in places like New York City. In fact, the largest co-op in America is Co-Op City, located in the Bronx and which has about 50,000 residents. Because a co-op board controls the process of getting into (and leaving) a co-op, the rules can be burdensome. Some exclusive co-ops in Manhattan have famously rejected more than a few celebrities, including Madonna, Barbra Streisand, and Rush Limbaugh.

TERMS IN ACTION

Smoking is quite expensive, especially in New York, where the price of a pack of cigarettes is around $15. But for Harry Lysons, the cost of smoking in his apartment in an Upper East Side Manhattan **cooperative apartment** building became nearly priceless. He enjoyed smoking cigars in his apartment, but some of his neighbors—Amanda and Russell Poses, who have two small children—did not enjoy inhaling his secondhand smoke. The tensions persisted for over a year, with Lysons installing multiple air cleaners in his apartment. Then the Poses sued Lysons in 2011 for $2 million, claiming they were being harmed in their apartment, which shared a common wall with his, by the invasion of his "foul and noxious odors." Lysons settled with the Poses quickly, agreeing to pay them $2,000 dollars every time he lit up a cigar in his apartment. According to the court-approved agreement, if the Poses suspect that Lysons has been smoking in his apartment, they may request to come over and conduct a smell test. If Lysons doesn't pay his $2,000 fine within 15 days, he will be on the hook for an additional $1,500. Lysons's lawyer claimed that no payments will need to be made, because Lysons will find somewhere else to smoke.

Sources: nypost.com; cbsnews.com

Timesharing

Timesharing, also called **interval ownership**, is a fee simple ownership of a unit of real property in which the owner can exercise the right of possession for only an interval of time, such as a week or two, each year. Other people possess the property at other intervals of the year. Like condominium owners, interval owners have the right to use the common areas of the property. An ownership interest in a time-share is considered to be real property, unless it is established by a lease, and the transfer of ownership is accomplished with the use of a deed to the individual unit being transferred. Timesharing is popular in vacation and resort areas of the country. As an alternative to deeded timeshare ownership, some timeshares are offered as a "right to use" vacation option. In such arrangements, the developers retain all ownership rights but grant purchasers a contractual right to property access for a specific interval and for a specific number of years, often denominated in decades.

Reviewing What You Learned

After studying the chapter, write the answers to each of the following questions:

1. List the four most common co-tenant relationships.

____

____

____

2. Each tenant in common is entitled to possession of what part of the premises?

____

____

3. What happens to the interest in real property of a tenant in common at death?

____

____

____

4. May tenants in common grant out their interests in real property without permission to do so from the other co-tenants? May joint tenants do so?

____

____

____

5. Name the four unities in a joint tenancy.

____

____

____

6. What happens to a joint tenant's interest in real property at death?

____

____

____

7. Who may own real property as tenants by the entirety?

____

____

____

8. Describe ownership rights of a husband and a wife under the community property system.

____

____

____

9. What jurisdictions follow the community property system?

____

____

____

10. Why is a tenancy by the entirety a popular method of ownership by a husband and wife?

____

____

____

11. In what way have some states modified the common law version of the tenancy by the entirety?

____

____

____

12. When a partner dies, who owns the property under tenancy in partnership?

____

____

____

13. Explain the difference between covenants, conditions, & restrictions and a homeowners association.

____

____

____

14. Explain the differences between a condominium and a cooperative apartment.

____

____

____

Understanding Legal Concepts

Indicate whether each statement is true or false. Then, change the italicized word or phrase of each false statement to make it true.

ANSWERS

_____ **1.** Real property may be owned severally—that is, by *two or more persons.*

_____ **2.** When two or more people own real property as tenants in common, each owner is entitled to the possession of *his or her part of the premises only.*

_____ **3.** Any of the tenants in common *may* grant out their interests to others without permission of the other co-tenants.

_____ **4.** All joint tenants' interests *are* equal.

_____ **5.** If a joint tenant grants out his or her interest to a new owner, the new owner becomes a *joint tenant* with the remaining joint tenants.

_____ **6.** Under the common law historically, the husband, in a tenancy by the entirety, had the *exclusive* right to possession of the premises.

_____ **7.** Under the common law, a wife *can* transfer her interest in a tenancy by the entirety to someone else without her husband's consent.

_____ **8.** The court *has no power* to partition a tenancy by the entirety.

_____ **9.** A divorce, by operation of law, automatically converts a tenancy by the entirety into a *joint tenancy.*

_____ **10.** In a *tenancy in partnership,* individual partners cannot transfer their interests in the property to others unless all of them do so.

Checking Terminology

From the list of legal terms that follows, select the one that matches each definition:

ANSWERS

a. common areas
b. community property
c. concurrent ownership
d. condominium
e. condominium association
f. cooperative apartment
g. co-ownership
h. co-tenants
i. covenants, conditions, & restrictions (CC&Rs)
j. creditors
k. joint tenancy
l. joint tenancy with the right of survivorship
m. joint tenants
n. levy on execution
o. master deed
p. moiety
q. partition
r. proprietary lease
s. several
t. tenancy by the entirety
u. tenancy in partnership
v. tenants in common
w. timesharing
x. unit deed
y. units
z. unity of interest
aa. unity of possession
bb. unity of time
cc. unity of title
dd. homeowners association

_____ 1. Property (other than a gift or inheritance) acquired by a husband or wife during marriage that belongs to both spouses equally.

_____ 2. Two or more owners of real property.

_____ 3. The individual portions of a condominium that are owned separately in fee simple by individual owners.

_____ 4. Equal interest in property by all owners.

_____ 5. A dwelling unit in which the occupants lease individual units and, at the same time, own shares of stock in the corporation that owns the building.

_____ 6. Separate, individual, and independent.

_____ 7. The division of land held by joint tenants or tenants in common into distinct portions so that they may hold them separately.

_____ 8. The part of a condominium or cooperative apartment building that is owned as tenants in common by all of the unit owners.

_____ 9. Two or more persons holding one and the same interest, accruing by one and the same conveyance, commencing at one and the same time, and held by one and the same undivided possession.

_____ 10. Ownership in which each person has an interest in partnership property and is a co-owner of such property.

_____ 11. A lease to an owner of the property.

_____ 12. Ownership by more than one person. (Select two answers.)

_____ 13. All owners of property taking title at the same time.

_____ 14. The estate owned by joint tenants. (Select two answers.)

_____ 15. People who are owed money.

_____ 16. A type of joint tenancy held by a husband and wife that offers protection against attachment and that cannot be terminated by one spouse alone.

_____ 17. A group of condominium unit owners that manages and maintains a condominium.

_____ 18. Equal rights to possession of the entire property by all owners.

_____ 19. Two or more persons holding an undivided interest in property, with each owner's interests going to his or her heirs on death rather than to the surviving co-owners.

_____ 20. A fee simple ownership of a unit of real property in which the owner can exercise the right of possession for only an interval, such as a week or two, each year. (Select two answers.)

_____ 21. A deed to the individual unit being transferred.

_____ 22. A parcel of real property, portions of which are owned separately in fee simple by individual owners, and the remainder of which is owned as tenants in common by all of the unit owners.

_____ 23. All owners of property receiving title from the same instrument.

_____ 24. To collect a sum of money by putting into effect the judgment of a court.

_____ 25. Regulates the appearance and use of property in ways that are stricter than local ordinance and zoning laws.

_____ 26. A deed to a condominium that describes the entire property that is owned by the condominium association.

_____ 27. A part, portion or fraction.

_____ 28. Markets and manages housing developments.

Using Legal Language

Read the following story and fill in the blank lines with legal terms taken from the list of terms at the beginning of this chapter:

James and Kathleen, who were business partners, took title to a parcel of real property as ________________________ to protect their interests from being attached except on a claim against the partnership. When the partnership was dissolved, Kathleen bought out James's interest and owned the property ________________________—that is, separately. She sold the property to Larry, Mary, and Nancy, who took title as ________________________, which means that on the death of one of them, the entire ownership would remain in the surviving owners. They were called ________________________, because of the ________________________ ownership, and they had the following unities: ________________________, ________________________, ________________________, and ________________________. Mary decided to sell her interest in the property, but couldn't find a buyer. To avoid having the court ________________________ the property—that is, divide it into separate parcels—Larry and Nancy bought Mary's share. They decided to take title as ________________________ so that if one of them died, his or her share would go to his or her heirs. Later, however, when Larry and Nancy got married, they had their attorney change the way in which they owned the property to ________________________ so that they would have protection against attaching ________________________ (people who are owed money), who could ________________________ to collect money owed them by putting into effect a court judgment. They did not live in a(n) ________________________ jurisdiction in which all property (other than a gift or inheritance) acquired by either of them during marriage would belong to both equally. Eventually, Larry and Nancy sold the property and bought a ________________________, which is a parcel of real property, portions of which, called ________________________, are owned separately in fee simple by individual owners, and the remainder of which, called the ________________________, is owned as tenants in common by all the owners.

34

Acquiring Title to Real Property

ANTE INTERROGATORY

A formal written instrument used to transfer title from one person to another is a (A) convey, (B) deed, (C) reliction, (D) seisin

LEARNING OBJECTIVES

LO 1: Identify the various ways in which title to real property may be acquired

LO 2: Summarize the history of original grants of real property, including the 1862 Homestead Act

LO 3: Explain what a deed is and who are the parties to a deed

LO 4: Summarize how one acquires real property by inheritance

LO 5: Define a sale on execution

LO 6: Summarize the process of a foreclosure sale

LO 7: Summarize the process for a taxing authority to take title to real property

LO 8: Explain the purpose of and method of taking title by adverse possession

LO 9: Define the key terms associated with acquiring title by the slow action of water

KEY TERMS

accretion

adverse possession

alluvion

attachment

convey

conveyance

deed

disseised

divested

erosion

foreclose

Homestead Act

infancy

mortgagee

mortgagee's foreclosure sale

mortgagor

record owner

reliction

right of redemption

seal

seisin

sheriff's sale

tacking

vendee

vendor

WEBSITES FOR PRONUNCIATION HELP

http://dictionary.cambridge.org/us/pronunciation/english/audio

https://www.howtopronounce.com

Title to real property may be acquired in the following ways:

1. original grant
2. deed
3. inheritance
4. sale on execution
5. mortgagee's foreclosure sale
6. tax title
7. adverse possession
8. slow action of water

ORIGINAL GRANT

Originally, land in America was owned by the various foreign governments that had settled there, such as England, France, Spain, and Mexico. Individuals obtained title to the land by grants from the crowns of those countries. After the American Revolution, any land that was not owned by individuals became the property of either the state or the federal government, which **conveyed** (transferred) much of it out by public grant to homesteaders or settlers under laws enacted by Congress. Perhaps the most famous of these land grants was the 1862 **Homestead Act**, signed into law by President Lincoln. It allowed anyone who was at least 21 years old and who had never taken up arms against the United States to get up to 160 acres of public, undeveloped land. An application first had to be filed, and then the applicant had to demonstrate improvements on the land for a five-year period, as well as build a 12-by-14-foot dwelling. Finally, the applicant then could seek a deed. Success wasn't guaranteed, however; over half of the homesteaders failed, due in part to the harsh weather and lack of natural vegetation sufficient to feed livestock. A shorter alternative to getting the property allowed homesteaders to buy their property from the government for $1.25 per acre after six months of living on the land. Following the Civil War, Union soldiers could apply the time they served in uniform toward the residency requirement. By the turn of the 19th century, over 80 million acres moved from public to private ownership.

DEED

The most common method of acquiring title to real property is by the use of a deed signed by the grantor and delivered to the grantee. A **deed** is a formal written instrument used to transfer a title from one person to another. It is also known as a **conveyance**. The transfer can be as a result of a sale, a gift, or an inheritance. A person who transfers property or goods by sale is a **vendor**. A purchaser or buyer of property or goods is a **vendee**. Traditionally, a deed was required to be under seal to be effective; however, many states statutorily have done away with that requirement. A **seal** is a mark or impression (originally made with wax) placed next to the party's signature. Some states require that a deed be witnessed; others have no such requirement. The deed is discussed in detail in Chapter 35.

INHERITANCE

In some states, when people die owning real property either separately or with others as tenants in common, title (legal ownership) to the property vests in their heirs or devisees, according to any estate plan or intestacy, at the moment of death. No deed is necessary for them to receive title, because ownership passes to them by operation of law. Such vesting of title, however, is subject to being **divested** (taken away) by the executor or administrator of the estate if it is necessary to obtain money from the sale of the property to pay estate taxes, administrative expenses, and other claims against the estate. In states where there is not automatic transfer of ownership, and for the sake of expediency everywhere, it is advisable to have the certificate of title of the decedent's property changed at the behest of the executor. This change will make it easier for the inheriting party to obtain insurance or to sell the property.

When someone dies owning real property with others as joint tenants (see the prior chapter on joint tenancy), the surviving joint tenants own the entire property outright at the moment of death of the decedent. In this case, it is not necessary to probate the estate to obtain title because title passes automatically to the surviving joint tenants. It is usually necessary to obtain estate tax releases for the surviving joint tenants to have clear title to the property, however.

SALE ON EXECUTION

At the beginning of a lawsuit, the plaintiff will often attach the defendant's real property. An **attachment** has the effect of bringing the property under the jurisdiction of the court as security for the debt. If the defendant loses the case and does not pay the amount of the judgment to the plaintiff, the sheriff may levy and sell on execution the real property that was attached. This is often referred to as a **sheriff's sale** and is done by public auction after notice and a prescribed amount of time, set by state statute, is given to the property owner.

MORTGAGEE'S FORECLOSURE SALE

A **mortgagee's foreclosure sale** occurs when the holder of a mortgage on real property (known as the **mortgagee** and usually a bank or lender to the homeowner) is not paid and decides to sell the property to obtain the amount owed by the homeowner (the **mortgagor**). The mortgagee's foreclosure sale is the last stage of **foreclosure**, which is the legally established judicial process for obtaining title to property that is the collateral for an unpaid loan or is available to satisfy an outstanding judgment against the property owner. The sale is by auction and occurs under the jurisdiction of the court. The proceeds of the sale are applied to the payment of the mortgage debt, with any surplus going to the mortgagor. Many states have a statutory power of sale provision for mortgages that regulates the foreclosure sale and must be strictly followed when a foreclosure sale occurs. Foreclosure sales under a deed of trust (see Chapter 36) typically are not subject to court supervision.

TERMS IN ACTION

In 2015, there were 1.1 million foreclosure filings, which is over 70% less than the record 3.92 million foreclosure filings made in 2011. About half of those record **foreclosures** from 2011 took place in five states: California, Florida, Michigan, Arizona, and Illinois. Most foreclosures involve one person or family losing one home, but this is not necessarily so with celebrities. Between 2009 and 2010, Nicholas Cage was foreclosed upon four times. The Academy Award-winning actor of "Leaving Las Vegas" and star of such films as "The Rock" and "National Treasure" was hard hit by the international financial meltdown of 2008 and became beset by unpaid taxes and mortgage payments. In 2009, he sued his manager for swindling him out of millions of assets. That case settled. In November 2009, Cage lost to a **mortgagee's foreclosure sale** the two homes he owned in New Orleans, one of which was located in the famous French Quarter. Both homes brought a total of $5.7 million, although their appraisals totaled $6.8 million. In January 2010, Cage's Las Vegas home sold for $4.95 million, nearly half the price of the $8.5 million that Cage had paid in 2006 for the 14,000-square-foot home, which has an elevator and an underground 16-car garage.

> And then in November 2010, Cage's Bel Air, California, mansion was sold in foreclosure for $10.5 million. This 12,000-square-foot, home built in 1940 for $110,000, was originally listed for auction at $34 million. It had once been owned by legendary singer and film star Dean Martin, and then later by the Welsh singer Tom Jones, who between 1968 and 2010 was one of the biggest acts in—you guessed it—Las Vegas.
>
> Sources: statisticsbrain.com; zillow.com; realtytrac.com; tampabay.com; money.cnn.com; latimesblogs.latimes.com; huffingtonpost.com

TAX AUTHORITY TITLE

Municipalities have the power to take real property for unpaid taxes, after acquiring a tax lien against the property for delinquent property taxes. Once the lien has been in existence for the statutorily required time (assuming the delinquency still exists), the municipality will institute proceedings against the property. In some jurisdictions, a city or town will make a demand for payment on the record owner of the property for the tax delinquency. The **record owner** is the person who appears to be the owner of the property according to the records at the registry of deeds. If the tax is not paid within a certain number of days after demand, the tax collector may take the property for the city or town, or sell it at a public auction. In some states, this is done by a foreclosure suit brought by the taxing authority. And in some jurisdictions, the taxing authority has the right to execute its lien by taking the property in order to sell it.

A purchaser of real property at a tax sale, however, takes the property subject to the former owner's **right of redemption** (right to take the property back). The latter can get the property back upon payment to the city or town of the back taxes, interest, and expenses incurred in the tax title sale. The purchaser of tax title property, to obtain clear title, must petition the court to **foreclose** (terminate) the right of redemption. Only when the court does this does a title become absolute in the owner who purchased it at the tax sale.

ADVERSE POSSESSION

Title to real property may be obtained by taking actual possession of the property, under the following generally required conditions: (1) open and notorious possession (visible and apparent use that is not granted by the landowner); (2) exclusively (not concurrent with the land owner's use); (3) under a claim of right (not attempting to steal that which is obviously under someone else's control); and (4) continuously for the statutory period (which is 20 years in many states). This method of obtaining title to real property, called **adverse possession**, developed at common law under the theory that two persons (unless they are co-owners) could not have **seisin** (possession of a freehold) of the same land at the same time. If one person took possession of land under a claim of right, the real owner was said to be **disseised** (dispossessed) and would have to bring an action to regain possession within 20 years (or whatever the statutory length is) or be forever barred from doing so. For instance, a homeowner might incorrectly but sincerely believe he or she owns property on which he or she has built a fence, which is actually one foot in width of the neighbor's property. If the conditions for adverse possession are met, that length of property on which the fence was built can belong to the fence's builder.

In calculating the 20-year or other statutory period, any uninterrupted continuous use by previous non-owner occupiers may be added to the time. Such an accumulation of possession by different occupiers who are not record owners is called **tacking**.

Certain disabilities on the part of the true owner (including **infancy**—that is, under the age of majority—insanity, imprisonment, and absence from the United States), if they occur at the beginning of the adverse possession, will give the true owner a longer time to regain possession of the premises.

In some states, obtaining clear title by adverse possession may be had by simply filing an affidavit with the proper office. Other states require a court proceeding to obtain clear title. Some states impose additional requirements for adverse possession in addition to those listed earlier, including that the adverse possessor have paid the property taxes for the subject property during the designated time.

TERMS IN ACTION

Adverse possession can be traced as far back as the Babylonian Code of Hammurabi, circa 1780 B.C., and it has a long history in America. Adverse possession was based on the idea that allowing a trespasser to take title to someone else's property, after enough time, was beneficial because the trespasser has made the property more useful. But an adverse possession case from Boulder, Colorado, shows that times have changed. In 2006, Richard McLean, retired judge and former Boulder mayor, and his wife Edith Stevens, an attorney, sought title by adverse possession to 1/3 of the 4,750-square-foot lot of Don and Susie Kirlin, who had purchased the undeveloped property in 1980, planning eventually to build their dream home. McLean and Stevens sued in 2006, claiming that that their use of the property entitled them to ownership. Their evidence of "use" was the claim that they had trespassed on the property sufficiently to create a path on the undeveloped lot, had hosted political events around the area of the path, and had been using the property as if it were their own for the statutorily required uninterrupted 18-year time frame. The Kirlins countered that the politically connected neighbors were trying to steal what was valued to be an $800,000 lot. After a few years and $400,000 in legal fees, the Kirlins finally settled the case, agreeing to transfer ownership of 12 percent of what was once their land. The outcry over what happened to the Kirlins resulted in the Colorado legislature's passing a stricter adverse possession law in 2008, which, among other things, requires those claiming adverse possession to have a "good faith belief" that the land is theirs. It also increases the burden of proof in an adverse possession case to "clear and convincing evidence."

Sources: denverpost.com; fwlaw.com; dailycamera.com

Word Wise
Seise or Seize?

The legal term "seisin" means "possession"; the term "disseised" means "dispossessed." "Seise" is the legal variation of the word "seize," which has the broader meaning of "grasping something suddenly and forcibly." Both words have the same pronunciation.

SLOW ACTION OF WATER

Any addition to the soil made by nature, such as the gradual accumulation of soil on land next to a stream caused by the action of water, is called **accretion**. Another term used to describe this addition to the soil is **alluvion**. Such addition to the soil belongs to the owner of the soil to which it is added. In contrast, when one side of a stream gains soil by the slow action of water, the opposite side of the stream often loses soil. This process is known as **erosion**, which is the gradual eating away of the soil by the operation of currents or tides.

Real property owners sometimes gain additional land when adjoining water permanently recedes. This gradual recession of water, leaving land permanently uncovered, is referred to as **reliction**.

Reviewing What You Learned

After studying the chapter, write the answers to each of the following questions:

1. List the ways that title may be acquired to real property.

   ____

   ____

   ____

2. From whom did individuals originally obtain title to land in America?

   ____

   ____

   ____

3. What happened, after the American Revolution, to land that was not owned by individuals?

   ____

   ____

   ____

4. What were the particular conditions of the Homestead Act of 1862?

   ____

   ____

   ____

5. What is the most common method of acquiring title to real property, and what are the requirements of this method?

   ____

   ____

   ____

6. When an individual owner of real property dies, who becomes the immediate owner of the property? To what is this ownership subject?

   ____

   ____

   ____

7. Briefly describe a sale on execution.

   ____

   ____

   ____

8. When does a mortgagee's foreclosure sale occur?

   ____

   ____

   ____

9. Why does the purchaser of real property at a tax sale take a risk?

   ____

   ____

   ____

10. How long in many states must one possess real property to own it by adverse possession?

    ____

    ____

    ____

11. Who becomes the owner of soil that is gradually added to land adjoining a stream as a result of the slow action of water?

    ____

    ____

    ____

Understanding Legal Concepts

Indicate whether each statement is true or false. Then, change the italicized word or phrase of each false statement to make it true.

ANSWERS

_____ 1. Originally, land in America was owned by the various *foreign governments* that had settled here.

_____ 2. Traditionally, a deed was required to be under seal to be effective; however, many states *have* done away with that requirement.

_____ 3. *Some* states have no requirement that a deed be witnessed.

_____ 4. When people die owning real estate separately, *a deed* is necessary to pass legal ownership to their heirs.

_____ 5. For title to pass to a surviving joint tenant, it *is necessary* to probate the estate of a deceased joint tenant.

_____ 6. An attachment has the effect of bringing property under the jurisdiction of *the court* as security for a debt.

_____ 7. A mortgagee's foreclosure sale is a *private sale* that occurs under the jurisdiction of the court.

_____ 8. A purchaser of real property at a tax sale takes the property subject to the former owner's right to *take the property back.*

_____ 9. In calculating the period required to obtain title by adverse possession, any uninterrupted use by previous non-owner occupiers *may not be* added to the time period.

_____ 10. Any addition to the soil made by nature, such as the *very rapid* accumulation of soil on land next to a stream, is called accretion.

Checking Terminology

From the list of legal terms that follows, select the one that matches each definition.

ANSWERS

a. accretion
b. adverse possession
c. alluvion
d. attachment
e. convey
f. conveyance
g. deed
h. disseised
i. divested
j. erosion
k. foreclose
l. Homestead Act
m. infancy
n. mortgagee
o. mortgagee's foreclosure sale
p. mortgagor
q. record owner
r. reliction
s. right of redemption
t. seal
u. seisin
v. sheriff's sale
w. tacking
x. vendee
y. vendor

_____ 1. A formal, written instrument used to transfer title to real property from one person to another. (Select two answers.)

_____ 2. A mark or impression, originally made with wax, placed next to a party's signature.

_____ 3. The act of taking or seizing property by the use of a writ, summons, or other judicial order and bringing it into the custody of the court.

_____ 4. One who borrows money and gives a mortgage—that is, pledges property—to the lender as security for the loan.

_____ 5. A sale of property at public auction conducted by a sheriff.

_____ 6. Right to take property back.

_____ 7. Title to real property obtained by taking actual possession of it openly, notoriously, exclusively, under a claim of right, and continuously for a period set by statute.

_____ 8. Dispossessed.

_____ 9. Any gradual addition to the soil made by nature, such as the gradual accumulation of soil on land next to a stream caused by the action of water. (Select two answers.)

_____ 10. To transfer.

_____ 11. Taken away.

_____ 12. One who lends money and takes back a mortgage as security for the loan.

_____ 13. One who appears to be the owner of real property according to the records at the registry of deeds.

_____ 14. A sale of real property that terminates all rights of the mortgagor in the property covered by the mortgage.

_____ 15. A federal land grant that encouraged people to improve the land over five years in order to gain a deed to the property.

_____ 16. Possession of a freehold.

_____ 17. The addition of previous occupants' possession to one's own possession to meet the statutory period for adverse possession.

_____ 18. The gradual eating away of the soil by the operation of currents or tides.

_____ 19. The gradual recession of water, leaving land permanently uncovered.

_____ 20. Under the age of majority.

_____ 21. A purchaser or buyer of property or goods.

_____ 22. Terminate.

Using Legal Language

Read the following story and fill in the blank lines with legal terms taken from the list of terms at the beginning of this chapter:

Arlene inherited some real property that adjoined a river. Title to the property vested in Arlene at the moment of death of the decedent, but was subject to being _________________________ to pay claims against the estate. Arlene was the _________________________, because she was the person who appeared to be the owner according to the records at the Registry of Deeds. She received a notice in the mail from her bank saying that a(n) _________________________ was about to occur, because she was behind in her mortgage payments. She was the _________________________; the bank was the _________________________. Arlene took the money that she had saved to pay property taxes and other creditors and used it to pay the money owed on the mortgage. One of her creditors brought suit against her and placed a(n) _________________________ on her property, which had the effect of bringing it under the jurisdiction of the court as security for the debt. To prevent a(n) _________________________—that is, a sale on execution of the property—Arlene paid the amount that was owed to the creditor. She then had the property lines surveyed and discovered that the garage belonging to her next-door neighbor, Ben, extended four feet onto her land. Although Ben had owned the property for 10 years, the garage had been placed there by Carl, the previous owner, 22 years earlier. Ben can add his 10 years of ownership to that of Carl's under a method called _________________________. Ben obtained title to the land under the garage by _________________________, a method which had developed at common law under the theory that two persons could not have _________________________ of the same land at the same time. If one person took possession of land under a claim of right, the real owner was said to be _________________________—that is, dispossessed—of the property. Because Arlene had failed to pay the property tax, the local tax collector took the property and sold it at a public auction to Darlene. The _________________________— that is, the transfer to Darlene—was made by the use of a(n) _________________________, which is a formal written instrument used to transfer title from one person to another. The instrument was under _________________________, which is a mark or impression next to the party's signature. Darlene bought the property subject to Arlene's _________________________ that is, the right to take the property back—unless Darlene is successful in petitioning the court to _________________________ (terminate) that right. By then, a considerable amount of land had been added to the property by _________________________, which is also called _________________________, caused by the slow action of the adjoining river.

Deeds

ANTE INTERROGATORY

The most desirable form of a deed, which gives assurances that title is good, is a (A) bargain and sale deed, (B) quitclaim deed, (C) special warranty deed, (D) general warranty deed.

LEARNING OBJECTIVES

LO 1: Summarize the evolution of the transfer of title to real property, from the use of the sealed instrument to the deed

LO 2: Identify the requirements of a modern deed

LO 3: Explain the three principal systems used to describe real property

LO 4: Identify the four common types of deeds

LO 5: Explain the key covenants of a general warranty deed

LO 6: Distinguish a special warranty deed from a general warranty deed

LO 7: Identify the chief characteristic of a quitclaim deed, as well as who would grant one

LO 8: Distinguish a bargain and sale deed from a quitclaim deed

KEY TERMS

acknowledgment
bargain and sale deed
base lines
bounds
conveyancing
covenant
deed
deed without covenants
encumbrance
fiduciary deed
full covenant and warranty deed
general warranty deed
government survey system
grantee
grantor
habendum clause
heirlooms
hereditaments
limited warranty deed
locus
locus sigilli
meridians
metes
metes and bounds
monuments

notary public

plat

plat book

plat map

plot

quitclaim deed

range

rectangular survey system

section

special warranty deed

tenements

title insurance

township

tract of land

warrant

WEBSITES FOR PRONUNCIATION HELP

http://dictionary.cambridge.org/us/pronunciation/english/audio

https://www.howtopronounce.com

Centuries ago in feudal England, before the use of the deed, real property was transferred from one person to another in a public ceremony known as *livery of seisin*. The one transferring the property would hand the other a clod of dirt or a twig from a tree, symbolizing the transfer. The ceremony was called *livery in deed* when it took place on the property itself, and *livery in law* when it was done in sight of the property, but not actually on it.

SEALED INSTRUMENT

As time went on and more people learned to read and write, the written deed replaced the formal ceremony of transferring real property. In those days, a person's seal was of foremost importance. One reason is that the seal was more difficult to forge than a handwritten signature. Any contract that was under seal and contained **covenants** (promises) was called a **deed**.

Later, but still under the common law, a deed became defined as "a writing under seal by which lands, tenements, or hereditaments are conveyed for an estate not less than freehold." (This definition can originally be found in the famous *Commentaries on the Laws of England*, published in the mid-18th century by Sir William Blackstone, an English judge and its first legal scholar. Blackstone's *Commentaries*, of which there four volumes, were highly influential to the development of the common law in England and America.) **Tenements** were defined as "everything of a permanent nature which may be holden, and in a more restrictive sense, houses or dwellings." **Hereditaments** were "things capable of being inherited, including not only lands and everything thereon, but also **heirlooms**" (valued possessions with sentimental value passed down through generations within a family).

Originally, a seal was an impression on wax, paper, wafer, or some other firm substance upon which an impression could be made. Eventually, the impression was replaced by a round, red, paper seal pasted on the instrument, or the word "seal," or a phrase such as "Witness my hand and seal," or the letters "L.S." (the abbreviation for **locus sigilli**—the place of the seal) written beside a party's signature. Whatever method is used to put a deed under seal is not the same as a **notary public's** seal used by a notary (a person authorized by his or her state to serve as an official, impartial witness to those acts requiring a witness's signature; also known as a public notary) to acknowledge an instrument. These two types of seals are separate and distinct, one having nothing to do with the other.

Today, a **deed** may be defined as a formal, written instrument by which title to real property is transferred from one person to another. The deed is the most common method of **conveyancing** (transferring title to real property from one person to another). By statute, in many states, a deed is no longer required to be under seal.

The person who transfers title is known as the **grantor**, and the person to whom title is transferred is known as the **grantee**.

REQUIREMENTS OF A MODERN DEED

A deed must convey a present ownership interest to the grantee, even though the grantee's right to possess the premises may be delayed until a later time. For a conveyance to be valid, a deed must meet the following requirements:

1. be in writing
2. identify the grantor
3. be signed by the grantor
4. identify the grantee
5. contain words of conveyance, such as "grant," "convey," or "transfer"
6. describe the **locus** (exact parcel) being conveyed
7. be delivered to the grantee
8. be accepted by the grantee

To be effective as to third parties, a deed must also be recorded. To be recorded, a deed must be acknowledged. An **acknowledgment** is a formal declaration before an authorized official, by a person who executes an instrument, that it is his or her free act and deed. A certificate of acknowledgment, signed and sealed by the official (usually, a notary public), is placed at the bottom of the deed following the signature of the grantor.

DESCRIBING REAL PROPERTY

There are three principal systems in use today by which to describe real property in a deed: (1) the metes and bounds system, (2) the rectangular survey system, and (3) by reference to a plat or survey.

Metes and bounds is a system of describing real property by its outer boundaries, with reference to courses, distances, and **monuments** (visible marks indicating boundaries). **Metes** are the distances between points, and **bounds** are the directions of the boundaries that enclose a parcel of land. This system came from England and is used in the eastern part of the United States, where the original 13 colonies were located. Here is an example:

> Beginning at the Southwesterly corner of the wall, by Haverhill Road, (Main Street) and land now owned by Raymond Pearl (formerly owned by B. Ford Parsons) and thence running
>
> | | |
> |---|---|
> | Easterly | by said wall and fence and by land of said Pearl about four hundred thirty-four (434) feet to a corner of the fence by land now of Charles M. Moulton; thence running |
> | Northerly | by the wall, and by land of said Moulton, one hundred sixty-seven feet (167) to land now or formerly of Charles F. Austin; thence running |
> | Westerly | by said land about four hundred and forty-four feet (444) to said Haverhill Road (Main Street); thence running |
> | Southerly | by said Haverhill Road (Main Street) one hundred eighty-eight feet (188) to the point begun at. |

Following the Revolutionary War, the United States Congress ordered a survey of the vast area of land west of the original 13 colonies. The **rectangular survey system**, also known as the **government survey system**, was established at that time. It is a method of describing real property according to the property's relationship to intersecting lines called **base lines** (running east and west) and *principal* or *prime* **meridians** (lines running north and south). The intersections of the lines create 24-mile squares, which are further divided into 6-mile squares called **townships**. Each township is divided into 26 equal squares called sections. A **section** is a square mile of land, containing 640 acres. A row of townships running north and south is called a **range**.

A third method of describing real property is by reference to a recorded survey that is made when a **tract of land** (a large piece of land) is subdivided. A map of the subdivision, called a **plat, plat map,** or **plot**, is drawn. The size and shape of each lot is designated, and the plat is given a name or number so that it can be identified. When it is recorded, the plat is entered into a **plat book** at the registry of deeds. This method is also known as the lot and block survey system

TYPES OF DEEDS

There are four types of deeds in general use today:

1. general warranty deed
2. special warranty deed
3. quitclaim deed
4. bargain and sale deed

As shown by their names, the first two deeds contain warranties. The latter two do not.

General Warranty Deed

A **general warranty deed**, sometimes known as a **full covenant and warranty deed**, is the most desirable form of deed, from the viewpoint of the grantee, because it **warrants** (gives assurances) that the title is good. The typical general warranty deed contains the following four covenants made by the grantor to the grantee:

1. The grantor has good title.
2. No **encumbrances** (liens against the property or claims by others against the grantor that affect the title) exist.
3. The grantor has good right to sell and convey the property.
4. The grantor will warrant and defend the title against the claims of all persons.

Because of its lengthy covenants, the warranty deed is extremely long and wordy. To illustrate, the clause called the **habendum clause**, which defines the extent of ownership, reads as follows in a long-form warranty deed:

> TO HAVE AND TO HOLD THE GRANTED PREMISES, with all the privileges and appurtenances thereto belonging, to the said (grantee), and his [or her] heirs and assigns, to their own use and behoof forever.

Similarly, the clause containing the covenants in a long-form general warranty deed reads as follows:

> And I hereby, for myself and my heirs, executors, and administrators, COVENANT with the grantee and his [or her] heirs and assigns that I am lawfully seized in fee simple of the granted premises; that they are free from all encumbrances; that I have good right to sell and convey the same as aforesaid; and that I will, and my heirs, executors, and administrators shall, WARRANT AND DEFEND the same to the grantee and his [or her] heirs and assigns forever against the lawful claims and demands of all persons.

To avoid the use of such lengthy and complicated language, many states have created short forms of deeds, which give the same warranties as the long forms, but use fewer words. For example, the words "convey and warrant" create a general warranty deed in states including Alaska, Illinois, Kansas, Michigan, Minnesota, and Wisconsin. The words "warrant generally" mean the same in Pennsylvania, Vermont, Virginia, and West Virginia deeds. The words "grant, bargain, and sell" create a general warranty deed in Arkansas, Florida, Idaho, Missouri, and Nevada. Finally, the words "with warranty covenants" mean the same in Massachusetts deeds.

TERMS IN ACTION

Seven thousand properties in Taos County, New Mexico, were put in real estate limbo in 2011 after someone filed two **warranty deeds** to all of the properties in the county. The claimants filing the deeds asserted that they were the heirs of the 42,000 acres in question, citing title documents going as far back as the 1848 Treaty of Guadalupe Hidalgo, which ended the Mexican–American war and made New Mexico an American territory. But the treaty also honored land grants that had been made to individuals by the Spanish King and Mexican government. To file a warranty deed in New Mexico, one only has to preset the proper form stamped by a **notary**

public identifying the property being deeded and the names of the **grantee** and **grantor**. Proof of ownership isn't required. Because of the warranty deed filings, title companies were stymied; real estate brokers didn't know what to do; sellers and buyers couldn't close on their transactions; homeowners couldn't even refinance their mortgages. Then it came to light that the parties asserting the title claim were two trustees of one of the land grants (Arroyo Hondo Land Grant) and heirs of the original **grantees** from that 1848 treaty. Some of the stated reasons for filing the deeds was annoyance that no one ever attended the trustees' meetings, as well as a claim that the properties in the hands of the current owners were wrongfully transferred centuries earlier. In 2013, a local judge quashed the warranty deeds, seemingly bringing an end to the conflict, and one of the land grant trustees pled guilty to fraud in connection to the warranty deeds.

Sources: abajournal.com; taosnews.com; hcn.org; latino.foxnews.com

---

Word Wise
More Words Ending in "or" and "ee"

grantor (*gran·TOR*)	One who transfers real property to another.
grantee (*gran·TEE*)	One to whom real property is transferred.
mortgagor (*more·gej·OR*)	One who borrows money and gives a mortgage as security.
mortgagee (*more·gej·EE*)	One who lends money and takes a mortgage as security.
obligor (*ob·li·GOR*)	One bound by contract to perform an obligation.
obligee (*ob·li·GEE*)	One to whom an obligation is owed under a contract.
pledgor (*plej·OR*)	One who gives property to another as security for a loan.
pledgee (*plej·EE*)	One to whom property is given as security for a loan.
promisor (*prom·i·SOHR*)	One who makes a promise.
promisee (*prom·i·SEE*)	One to whom a promise is made.

Special Warranty Deed

A **special warranty deed**, sometimes called a **limited warranty deed**, warrants that no defects arose in the title during the time that the grantor owned the property, but no warranty is made as to defects that may have arisen before the grantor owned the property. In a special warranty deed, the grantor warrants the following:

1. The premises are free from all encumbrances made by the grantor.
2. The grantor will warrant and defend the title only against claims through him or her.

As in the case of the general warranty deed, many states have created short forms of special warranty deeds. For example, the words "warrant specially" create a special warranty deed in Mississippi, Pennsylvania, Vermont, Virginia, and West Virginia. The word "grant" means the same in California, Idaho, and North Dakota deeds. The words "with quitclaim covenants" are used to create a special warranty deed in Massachusetts.

Quitclaim Deed

A **quitclaim deed** (called a **deed without covenants** or a **fiduciary deed** in some states) conveys only the grantor's interest, if any, in the real property and contains no warranties. It is commonly used when a deed is necessary to cure a defect in the chain of title or when the grantor is not sure whether his or her title is good or bad. Executors, administrators, and other fiduciaries often use this form of deed when conveying real property.

> ### ▎TERMS IN ACTION
>
> The **quitclaim deed** lacks the guarantees of the traditional **warranty deed**, but one would think that the quitclaim deed would, at least, guarantee that the signatures were authentic. That isn't always the case. In 2005, a Minnesotan named Marc Stuart Smyth sought to refinance the home he and his wife owned in an exclusive beach-front community on Alabama's Ono Island. But Smyth and his wife were divorcing at the time, and she didn't know that he had applied for a $496,000 refinance loan on that property. She also didn't know that her ex-husband-to-be found a female friend in Alabama who used Mrs. Smyth's driver's license and then forged Mrs. Smyth's signature on a quitclaim deed that purported to give Mr. Smyth sole ownership of the property, providing him the qualification to apply for the refinance loan by himself. He then used the loan from the mortgage company to pay off the mortgage on the home and to buy a $225,000 boat. Mr. Smyth was caught and indicted for fraud and identity theft in 2010. Smyth's by-then ex-wife and the mortgage company sued him for fraud, for which they won an $800,000 default judgment in 2008, and in 2011, he pled guilty to the criminal charges and was sentenced to five years of probation. Believe it or not, the defrauded mortgage company didn't lose any money; in fact, it foreclosed on the Smyth property and then sold it at a profit.
>
> Source: www.blog.al.com

Bargain and Sale Deed

A **bargain and sale deed** conveys the land itself rather than merely the interest that the grantor has in the property, as is done in a quitclaim deed. The form is the same as a warranty deed except that the covenants (warranties) are omitted. Even though the recipient of a bargain and sale deed acquires property with knowledge that someone might have an encumbrance against it, if the buyer can obtain **title insurance** for the property (an insurance policy sold by a title company that protects the purchaser against past problems or defects with the title, as opposed to traditional insurance, which protects policyholders against future problems), such a policy would warrant good title and protect the buyer. Consideration is required in a bargain and sale deed, which means that a bargain and sale deed may not be used to transfer land by way of a gift. States that are known to use bargain and sale deeds include New York, Vermont, Colorado, and Washington.

Reviewing What You Learned

After studying the chapter, write the answers to each of the following questions:

1. What was considered to be a deed under the early days of common law?

2. List the requirements of a valid deed.

3. What are the four types of deeds that are in general use today?

4. Why is a general warranty deed the most desirable form of deed, from the viewpoint of the grantee? How many covenants are made in a general warranty deed?

5. What have many states done to avoid the use of long and complicated language in a deed?

____

____

____

6. Describe the two warranties made in a special warranty deed.

____

____

____

7. Under what circumstances is a quitclaim deed commonly used?

____

____

____

8. Describe the form of a bargain and sale deed.

____

____

____

Understanding Legal Concepts

Indicate whether each statement is true or false. Then, change the italicized word or phrase of each false statement to make it true.

ANSWERS

_______ **1.** In the early days of common law, a deed and a sealed instrument were *practically synonymous*.

_______ **2.** For a conveyance to be valid, a deed must be *delivered* to the grantee.

_______ **3.** A general warranty deed *is not* the most desirable form of deed, from the viewpoint of the grantee.

_______ **4.** A general warranty deed *does not* contain a warranty that the grantor has good title.

_______ **5.** To avoid use of lengthy and complicated language, many states have created *short forms* of deeds.

_______ **6.** The *habendum clause* begins with the words "TO HAVE AND TO HOLD."

_______ **7.** A special warranty deed protects against defects that arose *before* the grantor owned the property.

_______ **8.** A quitclaim deed contains *a warranty that title is good*.

_______ **9.** A *quitclaim* deed is commonly used when a deed is necessary to cure a defect in the chain of title.

_______ **10.** Consideration *is not* required in a bargain and sale deed.

Checking Terminology

From the list of legal terms that follows, select the one that matches each definition.

ANSWERS

a. acknowledgment
b. bargain and sale deed
c. base lines
d. bounds
e. conveyancing
f. covenant
g. deed
h. deed without covenants
i. encumbrance
j. fiduciary deed
k. full covenant and warranty deed
l. general warranty deed
m. government survey system
n. grantee
o. grantor
p. habendum clause
q. heirlooms
r. hereditaments
s. limited warranty deed
t. locus

_______ **1.** Valued possessions with sentimental value passed down through generations within a family.

_______ **2.** A place.

_______ **3.** A map designating the size and shape of a specific land area. (Select three answers.)

_______ **4.** To give assurance.

_______ **5.** A claim, lien, charge, or liability attached to and binding real property.

_______ **6.** A square mile of land, containing 640 acres, in the United States government survey.

_______ **7.** A system of describing real property by its outer boundaries, with reference to courses, distances, and monuments.

_______ **8.** A deed that conveys land itself, rather than people's interests therein, and requires consideration.

_______ **9.** The portion of a deed beginning with the words "To have and to hold," which defines the extent of the ownership of the property granted.

_______ **10.** A person to whom real property is transferred.

_______ **11.** Visible marks indicating boundaries.

_______ **12.** A row of townships running north and south in the United States government survey.

_______ **13.** A promise or assurance.

_______ **14.** A six-square-mile portion of land in the United States government survey.

_______ **15.** Horizontal lines running east and west in the United States government survey.

_______ **16.** Vertical lines running north and south in the United States government survey.

u. locus sigilli
v. meridians
w. metes
x. metes and bounds
y. monuments
z. notary public
aa. plat
bb. plat book
cc. plat map
dd. plot
ee. quitclaim deed
ff. range
gg. rectangular survey system
hh. section
ii. special warranty deed
jj. tenements
kk. township
ll. tract of land
mm. warrant

_____ **17.** A deed containing warranties under which the grantor guarantees the property to be free from all encumbrances made during the time that he or she owned the property and to defend the title only against claims through him or her. (Select two answers.)

_____ **18.** A method of describing real property according to the property's relationship to intersecting lines running east and west and lines running north and south. (Select two answers.)

_____ **19.** Transferring title to real property.

_____ **20.** A formal written instrument by which title to real property is transferred from one person to another.

_____ **21.** A person who transfers real property to another.

_____ **22.** A large piece of land.

_____ **23.** A deed containing warranties under which the grantor guarantees the property to be free from all encumbrances and to defend the title against the claims of all persons. (Select two answers.)

_____ **24.** Everything of a permanent nature that may be possessed and, in a more restrictive sense, houses or dwellings.

_____ **25.** Directions of the boundaries that enclose a parcel of land.

_____ **26.** A book that is recorded at the registry of deeds, containing plat maps.

_____ **27.** Things capable of being inherited, including not only lands and everything thereon, but also heirlooms.

_____ **28.** A deed to real property in which the grantor transfers only his or her interest, if any, in the property and gives no warranties of title. (Select three answers.)

_____ **29.** Distances between points.

_____ **30.** A formal declaration before an authorized official, by a person who executes an instrument, that it is his or her free act and deed.

_____ **31.** A person authorized as an official witness to acts requiring a witness's signature.

Using Legal Language

Read the following story and fill in the blank lines with legal terms taken from the list of terms at the beginning of this chapter:

Clifford purchased a parcel of real property from Diane, who was the executrix of an estate. In the ______________________, which was the formal written instrument by which title was transferred, Diane was the ______________________ and Clifford was the ______________________. The instrument, which conveyed only the grantor's interest and contained no warranties, is called a(n) ______________________ in some states, a(n) ______________________ in others, and a(n) ______________________ in still others. The ______________________ system is used to describe the property by its outer boundaries, with reference to courses, distances, and ______________________ (visible marks indicating boundaries). ______________________ are the distances between points, and ______________________ are the directions of the boundaries that enclose a parcel of land. Later, Clifford sold the property to Emily, who was schooled in the subject of ______________________that is, transferring title to real property—and wanted the kind of deed that ______________________ (gives assurances) that title is good. Emily insisted that Clifford give her a deed containing four promises, or guarantees, called ______________________.This type of deed is known as a(n) ______________________ in some states and a(n) ______________________ in others. The ______________________ in this deed begins with the words "To have and to hold." The day after receiving title, Emily transferred the exact parcel—that is, the ______________________ to Frank by giving him a(n) ______________________, which is called a(n) ______________________ in some states and warrants that the premises are free from all ______________________ made by the grantor. In her state, the ______________________, which conveys the land itself and requires consideration, is not used.

Mortgages

ANTE INTERROGATORY

A mortgage whose interest rate is subject to being adjusted, based upon an interest index to which it is tied is a(n) (A) variable rate mortgage, (B) graduated payment mortgage, (C) fixed rate mortgage, (D) alternating mortgage.

LEARNING OBJECTIVES

LO 1: Identify the historical background of the word "mortgage"

LO 2: Distinguish the two prevailing mortgage theories

LO 3: Identify the types of mortgages in use

LO 4: Contrast a mortgage from a deed of trust

LO 5: Summarize the process of mortgage foreclosure

LO 6: Explain the relationship between mortgage redemption and mortgage foreclosure

LO 7: Summarize the process of transferring mortgaged premises

LO 8: Define a junior, or second, mortgage

LO 9: Identify how a mortgage is discharged

KEY TERMS

acceleration clause

adjustable rate mortgage

amortization

balloon mortgage

collateral

common law theory

court of equity

deed of release

deed of trust

default

defeasance clause

deficiency judgment

equitable theory

equity of redemption

fixed-rate mortgage

flexible-rate mortgage

foreclose

graduated-payment mortgage

junior mortgage

lien

lien theory

mortgage

mortgage assignment

mortgage assumption

mortgage deed

mortgage discharge

mortgagee

mortgage take-over

mortgagor

partial release of mortgage

power of sale clause

<table>
<tr><td>promissory note</td><td>second mortgage</td></tr>
<tr><td>redeem</td><td>security</td></tr>
<tr><td>refinance</td><td>short sale</td></tr>
<tr><td>reverse mortgage</td><td>title theory</td></tr>
<tr><td>right of redemption</td><td>variable-rate mortgage</td></tr>
</table>

WEBSITES FOR PRONUNCIATION HELP

http://dictionary.cambridge.org/us/pronunciation/english/audio

https://www.howtopronounce.com

Most people who buy real estate do not have enough money to pay for the property outright. They must borrow it. Lenders, however, wish to have some **security** for their loan—that is, something they can sell to get their money back in case borrowers default. A security interest is also known as **collateral**, and collateral is either possessory (meaning that the lender takes physical possession of the collateral or security interest until the loan is repaid) or non-possessory. A **mortgage**, sometimes called a **mortgage deed**, meets the lender's need for a security interest, because a mortgage is a conveyance of real property for the purpose of securing a debt. The one who borrows money and gives a mortgage to the lender as security for the loan is the **mortgagor**. The one who lends money and takes back a mortgage as security for the loan is the **mortgagee**. In addition to signing a mortgage deed when the loan is made, the mortgagor signs a **promissory note**, which is a written promise by the borrower to pay a sum of money to the lender.

HISTORICAL BACKGROUND

Mort means "dead" and *gage* means "pledge." In early times, a mortgage was a "dead pledge." The mortgagor pledged the property to the mortgagee and gave up possession of the property, as well as all income from it, until the debt was paid. In addition, the mortgagor lost all title to the property if the debt was not paid precisely when it was due. As time went on, the **court of equity**, which is a court originally created as alternative to English common law courts and designed to do that which is just and fair, allowed the mortgagor additional time after a default to **redeem** (buy back) the property. Current legal theories governing mortgages follow.

PREVAILING MORTGAGE THEORIES

Two principal legal theories relating to mortgages are followed in the United States. They are the common law theory and the lien theory.

Under the **common law theory** (called the **title theory** in some states), a mortgage is a conveyance of title by the mortgagor to the mortgagee. A clause in the mortgage, known as the **defeasance clause** provides that the mortgage deed shall be void on payment of the obligation. The mortgagor has the right to possession of the premises and the right to all rents and profits from the property. The mortgagee has no right to enter the premises unless a **default** (the failure to perform a legal duty) by the mortgagor occurs, but he or she does have the right to prevent waste through court action. Prior to foreclosure statutes granting some protections to borrowers who were in default, under the common law theory a mortgagee's title could become a fee simple absolute if the mortgagor missed the payment by one day.

Under the **lien theory** (called the **equitable theory** in some states), a mortgage is not regarded as a conveyance of title to the mortgagee, but merely a lien against the property. A **lien** is a claim or charge on the property for the payment of a debt. Under this mortgage theory, the mortgagor retains legal title to the premises. A lien theory state makes foreclosure more difficult to complete, because the title remains with the borrower rather than being transferred to the lender, as is the case in title theory states. A majority of states are lien theory states.

TERMS IN ACTION

Dorothy Rhue Allen purchased a home in Deptford, New Jersey, in 1976, signing a **promissory note** and obtaining a 30-year **mortgage** for the $40,000 she borrowed from LaSalle Bank. She never missed any of the 359 payments, but on her 360th—the final payment—the 85-year-old widow was in the hospital and the $432 she owed wasn't sent to the bank on time. So, LaSalle Bank began **foreclosure** proceedings against her in 2006. When she tried to cure the **default**, the bank's law firm told her attorney that she needed to pay almost $5,800. Dorothy's attorney then filed a class-action lawsuit against LaSalle Bank and its law firm, alleging that they violated the Fair Debt Collections Practices Act by demanding she pay exorbitant and unlawful fees, including title recording fees and the bank's attorney fees, which were close to $2,400. In response, the law firm argued it didn't violate the Fair Debt Collection Practices Act because it communicated with Mrs. Allen's lawyer and not her, which wasn't a violation of the federal consumer protection law. But in 2011, the 3rd Circuit Court of Appeals ruled the law firm could be sued, because such suits comport with the deterrent purpose of the Fair Debt Collection Practices Act. The law firm then sought an appeal with the U.S. Supreme Court, which in 2012 refused to grant certiorari.

Sources: courthousenews.com; abajournal.com; 4closurefraud.org; 629 F.3d 364 (3d Cir. 2012)

Word Wise
The Prefix "Equi-" in Equity

The Latin prefix *equi* means "equal" and is used in many English words. Here are some examples:

Words	Meaning
equiangular	equal angles
equidistant	equally distant
equilateral	equal sides
equinox	equal nights
equity	equal treatment

TYPES OF MORTGAGES

There are a variety of mortgages in use today. A **fixed-rate mortgage** is a mortgage with an interest rate that does not change during the life of the mortgage. A **variable-rate mortgage**, also called a **flexible-rate mortgage** or **adjustable rate mortgage (ARM)**, is a mortgage with an interest rate that fluctuates according to changes in an index (tied to market forces and published by a neutral party) to which it is connected. The loan documents of an ARM will state what index to which the ARM is connected and what the interest rate cap is. A **graduated-payment mortgage** is a mortgage under which payments increase gradually over the life of the loan. A **balloon mortgage** is a mortgage with low, fixed payments during the life of the loan, ending with one large final payment. A **reverse mortgage** is one in which a bank pays a homeowner the equity in his or her home in exchange for taking title to the home. Instead of borrowing to buy a home, the borrower—who must be at least 62 years old, according to federal law—is, in effect, borrowing to stay in a home. But, rather than being required to pay back the "loan" in monthly installments or otherwise, the homeowner has no obligation to repay until the homeowner moves from the home or dies. In the latter instance, the bank (or other lender) takes title to the property, per the reverse mortgage agreement, which could include the alternative requiring the executor to sell the home to pay back the reverse mortgage (assuming there is sufficient equity in the home).

Deed of Trust

In some states, a **deed of trust** is used instead of a mortgage. This instrument conveys title to a third party (often, a title insurance company), called a **trustee** who holds it as security for the debt. When the debt is paid, title is returned to the borrower. If the borrower defaults, however, the trustee can sell the property, without going to court, in order to pay the amount of the debt to the lender. Because deed of trust states use non-judicial foreclosures, which are faster than judicial foreclosures (see later in the chapter), more states are converting to deed of trust jurisdictions. Deed of trust states include California, Colorado, Georgia, Idaho, Mississippi, Nevada, North Carolina, Oregon, Texas, and West Virginia.

MORTGAGE FORECLOSURE

Foreclose means to "shut out," "bar," or "terminate." Thus, a foreclosure proceeding terminates the mortgagor's equity of redemption in the property. The mortgagee has a right to foreclose when the mortgagor defaults in the payment of the debt or fails to follow a condition (requirement) of the mortgage. An **acceleration clause** in the mortgage or note causes the entire balance of the loan to become due when a default occurs.

The most common method of foreclosure is by judicial sale, which is a sale at public auction under the jurisdiction of the court. Another method of foreclosure is by "power of sale" under the terms of a **power of sale clause** found in the mortgage instrument. This clause allows the mortgagee to hold the foreclosure sale alone, without involving the court. Still another method of foreclosure found in a few states allows the mortgagee to enter and possess the premises for a specific period. This method may be used only when the entry and possession can be made peaceably.

Sometimes, a foreclosure sale does not bring enough money to pay off the amount owed to the mortgagee. When this occurs, the court may issue a deficiency judgment against the mortgagor. A **deficiency judgment** is a judgment for the amount remaining due on the mortgage after a foreclosure sale. Not all states permit deficiency judgments, particularly states that allow non-judicial foreclosures. If a deficiency judgment is ordered, such debt would be unsecured, unlike the mortgage or deed of trust, in that there is no collateral securing the payment of the deficiency judgment amount.

Because of the severity of the downturn in the real estate market, which began in 2007 and lasted for a number of years, many homeowners who could not afford their mortgages but wanted to avoid foreclosure sought to sell their homes, even though the sales prices would be less than the loan balances. This type of sale is known as a **short sale** and can be done only if the lender allows it. A lender might allow a short sale because it avoids the costs associated with foreclosure. Lenders who allow homeowners to short sell their homes can still require the sellers to be liable for the difference between the sale price and the remaining loan balance. Borrowers who are the beneficiaries of loan forgiveness need to pay income taxes on the amount forgiven, but Congress passed a law, the Mortgage Foreclosure Relief Act of 2007, which provided relief to those taxpayers whose loan forgiveness related to their primary residences. The original version of the Mortgage Foreclosure Relief Act had an expiration year, but Congress has renewed it as recently as for the 2017 tax year.

MORTGAGE REDEMPTION

Under modern laws, the mortgagor has the **equity of redemption**, which is the right to redeem the property any time before the completion of a foreclosure proceeding by paying the amount of the debt, interest, and costs. In addition, in some states, the mortgagor has the **right of redemption**, which is a statutory right to redeem the property even after a foreclosure sale. In states that recognize this latter right, a buyer at a mortgage foreclosure sale does not receive good title to the premises until the time for the mortgagor's right of redemption elapses, which ranges from six months to two years after the foreclosure sale, depending on the state.

> **Web Wise**
>
> To see a list of the lengths of time states provide for redemption of foreclosed homes, see http://www.alllaw.com/articles/nolo/foreclosure/right-of-redemption.html, or go to alllaw.com and search under "Foreclosure Law" under the listing of "Legal Topics & Resources."

TERMS IN ACTION

Of the many tragedies associated with America's 2008–09 subprime mortgage crisis and its related economic fallout, one of them seems almost impossible: homeowners with **reverse mortgages** being **foreclosed** upon. A reverse mortgage allows persons who are at least 62 years old to be paid the equity in their homes without having to move from the home, unlike the way a buyer would take possession in a traditional sale. With a reverse mortgage, the homeowner borrows the equity from a bank, which takes title to the property in exchange for providing cash to the borrower. In 2011, approximately 30,000 homeowners in America were in **default** on their reverse mortgages, with Florida having just under 20 percent of the total number of those in default. According to the researchers who discovered this sad fact, many elderly homeowners take their equity payments in one lump sum and spend the money, not realizing that they will need some of that cash to continue to pay the insurance and real estate taxes on their homes. The Federal Housing Administration responded by proposing new rules that would minimize the chance of reverse mortgage default, including as recently as 2016. And Congress passed the Reverse Mortgage Stabilization Act of 2013, which in part grants the Department of Housing and Urban Development more power to enact more rules to reduce reverse mortgage foreclosures.

Sources: orlandosentinel.com; usnews.com; reversemortgagedaily.com; huffingtonpost.com

TRANSFER OF MORTGAGED PREMISES

Usually, when mortgagors sell real property, they convey it free and clear of the mortgage by paying it off out of the proceeds of the sale. Sometimes, however, a buyer will agree to buy property with the mortgage still on it—that is, "subject to the mortgage." This agreement means that the new buyer takes the property subject to the mortgagee's rights. Only the equity of redemption is sold. The original mortgagor must still pay the mortgagee, and the mortgagee can foreclose against the new buyer if a default of the mortgage payments by the new mortgagor occurs.

> **Web Wise**
>
> Mortgage information abounds on the Web. Here are a few reliable choices:
>
> Bank Rate (a website with information related to all things involving in borrowing money)
> **www.bankrate.com**
>
> Homefair.com (a comprehensive website on everything from looking for homes to investigating the school systems in locations where one might be buying a home)
> **www.homefair.com**
>
> Homepath (a property foreclosure listing service from Fannie Mae, which is formally known as the Federal National Mortgage Association, a government-sponsored company)
> **www.homepath.com**
>
> Interest.com (a thorough website providing interest rate information, interest rate calculators, and articles on buying and selling homes)
> **www.interest.com**

Sometimes, a mortgagor will sell the premises "subject to the mortgage that the grantee assumes and agrees to pay." This is commonly referred to as a **mortgage take-over** or a **mortgage assumption**. In this situation, the new buyer not only takes the property subject to the mortgagee's rights, but also agrees to pay the balance of the mortgage payments to the mortgagee as they fall due. Generally, such a mortgage transfer is subject to the approval of the lender. The original mortgagor is still liable on the debt, however, and becomes a surety on the loan. Unless released from liability by the lender, he or she must pay the mortgage if the new buyer, who took it over, fails to do so.

It is common for banks who are mortgagees to put "due on sale" clauses in their mortgages, stating if title to the property vests in someone other than the mortgagor, the mortgage is immediately due and payable. This language prevents the assumption of a mortgage by another person without the bank's permission.

Mortgagees often transfer their interests in mortgages to other parties. This transfer is done by the use of an instrument known as a **mortgage assignment**. When this occurs, the original mortgagor makes the mortgage payments to the new mortgagee to whom the mortgage has been assigned.

JUNIOR MORTGAGES

A **junior mortgage**, also called a **second (or third) mortgage**, is a mortgage on the equity of redemption, or a mortgage subject to a prior mortgage. A junior mortgagee may foreclose only on the mortgagors' equity of redemption, and because a junior mortgage is subordinate to a first mortgage, such a foreclosure is subject to the rights of the first mortgagee. If a first mortgagee forecloses, the second mortgagee's recourse is to pay the mortgagor's debt and then foreclose also. As a practical matter, however, both mortgages are foreclosed in the same proceeding; the proceeds of the sale are paid to the first mortgagee, and any balance remaining is paid to junior mortgagees. As interest rates drop, especially as they did between 2007 and 2012, homeowners often **refinance** their mortgages. Refinancing involves extinguishing a debt obligation and replacing it with a new debt that has different terms, such as a different interest rate or **amortization** schedule. "Amortization" is a Middle English word that originally meant to kill, but today means to reduce or decrease over time. In lending, amortization shows how the loan balance is reduced until it is paid off.

MORTGAGE DISCHARGE

When a mortgage debt is paid, the mortgagor signs a **mortgage discharge**, a document stating that the mortgage debt is satisfied. The mortgage discharge is recorded at the registry of deeds (or whatever similar name is used in a given jurisdiction). A **deed of release** (a deed releasing property from an encumbrance) is sometimes used for this purpose, especially by a trustee of a deed of trust, to divest the trustee of legal title and revest title in the original owner. A **partial release of mortgage** is used to show that specified parcels are released from the encumbrance, as opposed to the entire real estate.

Reviewing What You Learned

After studying the chapter, write the answers to each of the following questions:

1. What need does the mortgage meet? _________________

2. In addition to signing a mortgage deed when a loan is made, what else does a mortgagor sign? _________________

3. What was a mortgage in early times? ____________________

____

____

____

4. Who is the mortgagor and who is the mortgagee? ________

____

____

____

5. Who holds the legal title to the property under the common law mortgage theory? Under the lien theory? __________

____

____

____

6. Who has the right to possession under the common law mortgage theory? ____________________

____

____

____

7. Name five types of mortgages and give a short definition of each. ____________________

____

____

____

8. What is the difference between the equity of redemption and the right of redemption? ____________________

____

9. Name three methods of foreclosure. ____________________

____

____

____

10. If a new buyer takes the property subject to a mortgage, what can the mortgagee do if a default of the mortgage payments by the new mortgagor occurs? ____________________

____

____

11. If a first mortgagee forecloses on the mortgage, what is the second mortgagee's recourse? ____________________

____

____

____

12. Describe the way that a deed of trust is used to provide security for a debt. ____________________

____

____

____

13. What does "refinancing" mean? ____________________

____

____

Understanding Legal Concepts

Indicate whether each statement is true or false. Then, change the italicized word or phrase of each false statement to make it true.

ANSWERS

______ **1.** The mortgagor is the *lender*.

______ **2.** In early times, a mortgage was a *dead pledge* because the property owner gave up possession of the property until the debt was paid.

______ **3.** As time went on, the court of equity allowed the *mortgagor* additional time after a default to redeem the property.

______ **4.** Under the *lien* theory of mortgages, a mortgage is a conveyance of title by the mortgagor to the mortgagee.

______ **5.** Under the common law theory of mortgages, the *mortgagee* has the right to possession of the premises.

______ **6.** The right of redemption is the right to redeem the property *any time before* the completion of a foreclosure proceeding.

______ **7.** The most common method of foreclosure is by *entry and possession* of the premises.

______ **8.** When property is sold "subject to the mortgage," the *original mortgagor* must still pay the mortgagee.

______ **9.** When a *mortgagee* transfers an interest in a mortgage to another, it is known as a mortgage assignment.

______ **10.** A junior mortgagee's foreclosure is subject to the rights of the *first mortgagee*.

Checking Terminology

From the list of legal terms that follows, select the one that matches each definition.

ANSWERS

a. acceleration clause
b. adjustable rate mortgage
c. amortization
d. balloon mortgage
e. collateral
f. common law theory of mortgages
g. court of equity
h. deed of release
i. deed of trust
j. default
k. defeasance clause
l. deficiency judgment
m. equitable theory of mortgages
n. equity of redemption
o. fixed-rate mortgage
p. flexible-rate mortgage
q. foreclose
r. graduated-payment mortgage
s. junior mortgage
t. lien
u. lien theory of mortgages
v. mortgage
w. mortgage assignment
x. mortgage assumption
y. mortgage deed
z. mortgage discharge
aa. mortgagee
bb. mortgage take-over
cc. mortgagor
dd. partial release
ee. power of sale clause
ff. promissory note
gg. redeem
hh. refinance
ii. reverse mortgage
jj. right of redemption
kk. second mortgage
ll. security
mm. short sale
nn. title theory of mortgages
oo. variable-rate mortgage

______ **1.** Assurance (usually in the form of a pledge or deposit) given by a debtor to a creditor to make sure that a debt is paid.

______ **2.** One who lends money and takes back a mortgage as security for the loan.

______ **3.** Buy back.

______ **4.** The right of a mortgagor to redeem the property any time before the completion of a foreclosure proceeding by paying the amount of the debt, interest, and costs.

______ **5.** A clause in a mortgage providing that the mortgage deed shall be void on payment of the obligation.

______ **6.** A claim or charge on the property for the payment of a debt.

______ **7.** A statutory right to redeem the property even after a foreclosure sale.

______ **8.** An agreement by a new owner of real property to pay the former owner's mortgage. (Select two answers.)

______ **9.** A mortgage with an interest rate that fluctuates according to changes in an index to which it is connected. (Select three answers.)

______ **10.** A clause in a mortgage or note that causes the entire balance of the loan to become due when a default occurs.

______ **11.** A mortgage with an interest rate that does not change during the life of the mortgage.

______ **12.** A mortgage subject to a prior mortgage. (Select two answers.)

______ **13.** A conveyance of real property for the purpose of securing a debt. (Select two answers.)

______ **14.** One who borrows money and gives a mortgage to the lender as security for the loan.

______ **15.** A court designed to do that which is just and fair.

______ **16.** A failure to perform a legal duty.

______ **17.** To shut out, bar, or terminate.

______ **18.** The transfer of a mortgagee's interest in a mortgage to another person.

______ **19.** A mortgage with low, fixed payments during the life of the loan, ending with one large, final payment.

______ **20.** A written promise by a borrower to pay a sum of money to a lender.

______ **21.** A mortgage under which payments increase gradually over the life of the loan.

______ **22.** An instrument used in some states that replaces a mortgage, by which the legal title to real property is placed in a trustee to secure the repayment of a debt.

______ **23.** A judgment for the amount remaining due on the mortgage after a foreclosure sale.

______ **24.** A deed releasing property from an encumbrance.

______ **25.** A document stating that a mortgage debt is satisfied.

______ **26.** The legal theory that a mortgage is a conveyance of title, which becomes void on payment of the obligation. (Select two answers.)

______ **27.** The legal theory that a mortgage is not a conveyance of title, but merely a lien against the property. (Select two answers.)

______ **28.** A clause in a mortgage allowing the mortgagee to hold a foreclosure sale without involving the court when a default in payment of the mortgage occurs.

______ **29.** A document stating that specified parcels of property are released from an encumbrance.

______ **30.** To reduce or decrease over time.

______ **31.** A bank pays a homeowner the equity in his or her home in exchange for taking title to the home.

______ **32.** Security interest for a loan, such as a mortgage deed.

______ **33.** Extinguishing one debt obligation and replacing it with a new debt with different terms.

______ **34.** With permission of the lender, selling a home for a sale price lower than the loan balance.

Using Legal Language

Read the following story and fill in the blank lines with legal terms taken from the list of terms at the beginning of this chapter:

When Steve and Linda bought their house, they gave a(n) ________________—that is, a conveyance of real property for the purpose of securing a debt—to the bank as ________________ for the loan. They were called the ________________; the bank was the ________________. The instrument contained a(n) ________________ providing that the mortgage deed would be void on payment of the obligation. It also contained a(n) ________________, which allows the mortgagee to hold a foreclosure sale without involving the court when a default in payment of the mortgage occurs. Steve and Linda hold the ________________, which is the right to ________________ (buy back) the property any time before the completion of a foreclosure proceeding. The state where they live does not recognize the ________________, which is the right to redeem the property even after a foreclosure sale. Similarly, their state does not use the ________________ in place of a mortgage, which involves conveying title to a third party to hold as security for the debt. Steve and Linda gave a(n) ________________, also known as a(n) ________________, which is a mortgage subject to a prior mortgage, to Elliott, who sold them their house. Soon thereafter, Elliott made a(n) ________________—that is, a transfer of his mortgage interest—to an out-of-town lending institution. The instrument represented a(n) ________________, which is a claim or charge on the property for the payment of a debt. Possibly, when Steve and Linda sell their house, a(n) ________________ or a(n) ________________ will occur, wherein the new owner agrees to pay their existing mortgage. They were very careful not to ________________—that is, fail to perform their legal duty—on either of their obligations, because they did not want anyone to ________________ (shut out, bar, or terminate) their equity of redemption.

Landlord and Tenant

ANTE INTERROGATORY

A tenancy that continues for successive periods until one of the parties terminates is a tenancy (A) at will, (B) at sufferance, (C) for years, (D) from year to year.

LEARNING OBJECTIVES

LO 1: Identify the types of leasehold estates

LO 2: Explain why a tenancy for years doesn't have to be for a "year"

LO 3: Explain what distinguishes a periodic tenancy from a tenancy for years

LO 4: Compare and contrast a tenancy at will and a periodic tenancy

LO 5: Compare and contrast a tenancy at sufferance from a tenancy at will

LO 6: Explain how a license to occupy property is different from a lease

LO 7: Explain how a sublease is accomplished

LO 8: Identify what rights a tenant acquires in a lease, and summarize the warranty of habitability

KEY TERMS

constructive eviction
deed-poll
demise
dispossessory warrant proceedings
ejectment
eviction
forcible entry and detainer
holdover tenant
indenture
landlord
lease
leasehold estate
lessee
lessor
license
licensee
periodic tenancy
quiet enjoyment
retaliatory eviction
sublet
sublease
summary ejectment
summary process
tenancy at will
tenancy for years
tenancy from year to year
tenant
tenant at sufferance
underlease
unlawful detainer
warranty of habitability

WEBSITES FOR PRONUNCIATION HELP

http://dictionary.cambridge.org/us/pronunciation/english/audio
https://www.howtopronounce.com

A real estate **lease** is a contract granting the use of certain real property by its owner (called the **lessor** or **landlord**) to another (called the **lessee** or **tenant**) for a specified period in return for the payment of rent. In their strictest meaning, the terms *lessor* and *lessee* refer only to the parties to a lease, which would include leasing more than real property. In contrast, the terms *landlord* and *tenant* are broad terms that refer to the parties under a tenancy at will as well as the parties under a lease.

LEASEHOLD ESTATES

The interest that is conveyed by a lease is called a **leasehold estate** and was treated as personal property at common law. The common types of leasehold estates are as follows:

1. tenancy for years
2. periodic tenancy
3. tenancy at will
4. tenancy at sufferance

Tenancy for Years

A **tenancy for years** is an estate for a definite or fixed period, no matter how long or how short. Such a tenancy can be for 1 month, 6 months, 1 year, 5 years, 99 years, or any period, so long as it is ascertained. While the custom of a 99-year lease limit exists in some jurisdictions, a few states prohibit by statute leases longer than 99 years, including Alabama (Ala. Code § 35-4-6).

Word Wise
Compound Words

Compound words are made by joining two or more words already in usage to create a new word with a new meaning. Some compound words found in this chapter are the following:

Word	Meaning
holdover	To hold over from a previous period
landlord	A lord (person with authority or power) over land
leasehold	To hold by lease
sublease	A lease that is "sub" (less than) the full period
underlease	A lease that is under (less than) the full period

Some states require that a tenancy for years be in writing to be enforceable; others require a writing only if the period exceeds one year. For example, Indiana requires leases longer than three years to be in writing, to satisfy the statute of frauds (Ind. Code § 32-21-1-1). In some states, leases for long periods must be recorded to be effective as to third parties. For example, a lease for seven years or more (or a notice thereof) must be recorded at the registry of deeds, under Massachusetts law, to be valid as to persons other than the lessor. Under this statute, if the owner of a building rents the building to a lessee for 10 years and the lease is not recorded, the owner can sell the building to someone else and the new owner will not be bound by the lease. Alabama's statute, referred to above, which prohibits leases longer than 99 years also requires leases longer than 20 years to be recorded at the property county office where the property is located, so as to protect an innocent purchaser of the property who didn't know the property was actually owned by someone else.

Periodic Tenancy

A **periodic tenancy**, which is also called a **tenancy from year to year** (or from month to month, or from week to week), is a tenancy that continues for successive periods until one of the parties terminates it by giving notice to the other party. It is created when a lease agreement has no specified ending date. The notice requirement differs from state to state, but is typically the period between rent payment due dates. This tenancy may be created by implication if the landlord accepts rent payment from a tenant whose lease has run out or who is wrongfully in possession of the premises. Some states that do not recognize periodic tenancies treat the latter situation as a tenancy at sufferance (to be explained shortly).

Tenancy at Will

A **tenancy at will** is an estate in real property for an indefinite period. No writing is required to create this tenancy, and it may be terminated at the will of either party by issuance of the proper statutory notice. A landlord may seek to increase the rent in a tenancy at will by providing notice one payment period in advance. That does not mean, however, that the rent may be raised unilaterally, because the tenant may refuse the increase. But the refusal will result in the landlord's either seeking to terminate the tenancy or keeping the rent the same. A difference between a tenancy at will and a periodic tenancy, discussed above, is that in a periodic tenancy there is an agreed upon term of the occupancy, while in both there is no stated ending date of the occupancy.

Tenancy at Sufferance

A tenant who wrongfully remains in possession of the premises after the tenancy has expired is called a **holdover tenant** or a **tenant at sufferance**. Such a tenant has no estate or title, but holds possession wrongfully. A tenant at sufferance is not breaking the law until the landlord has asked the tenant to vacate the premises, and such a tenant will be liable for the past rent, and is bound by the terms of the prior lease. A difference between a tenancy at sufferance and a tenancy at will, discussed above, is that the tenancy at will is the result of an agreement between landlord and tenant.

LICENSE

A lease conveys an interest in land and transfers possession, whereas a **license** to real estate conveys no property right or interest to the land, but merely allows the licensee to do certain acts that would otherwise be a trespass. Lodgers who occupy rooms and advertisers who place signs on buildings are examples of **licensees** (people who have permission to do certain acts).

THE LEASE

A lease is an express contract between the parties in which real property is **demised** (leased) by the lessor to the lessee. The lease is usually executed in duplicate and signed by both parties (called an **indenture**, which simply means an official document executed in two or more identical copies), although a lease signed by the lessor only (a **deed-poll**) will be binding if accepted by the lessee. No particular form is necessary so long as the instrument identifies the parties, describes the demised premises, sets out the terms of the lease, provides for possession by the lessee, and contains consideration.

An *assignment* of a lease occurs when the lessee conveys the interest in the demised premises to another person for the balance of the term of the lease. It is called a **sublease** (or **underlease**) if the transfer is for a part of the term, but not for the remainder of it. The word **sublet** is sometimes used instead of "sublease." A tenant's ability to sublet the property is subject to the landlord's approval of it (as provided in the lease), including approving the subtenant.

TENANTS' RIGHTS

Tenants have the right to **quiet enjoyment** of the leased premises, which means that they have the right to possess the property and to be undisturbed in that possession. Thus, if the landlord locks out the tenant or interferes with the tenant's possession in any way, it is a breach of the tenant's right to quiet enjoyment.

When real property is rented for residential purposes, an implied warranty exists by the landlord that the premises are fit for human habitation, which is known as the implied **warranty of habitability**. In general, to be habitable, the property must meet the sanitary code of the local community. Legislation in some states allows the tenant to pay the rent to the court, instead of to the landlord, when the property is not fit for human habitation and violates the sanitary code. This action places the court in a position to prevent tenants from being evicted for complaining that the property which they rent is uninhabitable. In other states, the tenant, after giving notice to the landlord, can correct a sanitary code defect at the tenant's own expense and withhold rent up to the cost of having the defect corrected.

TERMS IN ACTION

Does a landlord's implied **warranty of habitability** extend to a tenant's automobile? In Montpelier, Vermont, heavy snow isn't a surprise, but surprise is just one of the emotions Karen Weiler experienced in February 2008 when a heavy pile of snow and ice slid off the roof of the apartment she rented, landing on her van and destroying it as it sat in the parking space that was designated for her in her apartment **lease**. So, the single mother of six sued her landlord, Richard Hooshiari, alleging that the warranty of habitability, expressly granted by statute in 9 V.S.A. § 4457, extended to a landlord-provided parking space. She won at trial, which would have made Vermont the first state to apply the warranty of habitability to a renter's parking space, but lost in the Vermont Supreme Court. In concluding that the warranty of habitability applies only to human habitation in the livable space, the Supreme Court wrote as follows: "[Weiler] maintains that a conventional lifestyle involving children and employment requires ready transportation, meaning that a secure parking place is a critical component of human habitation. While it may be exceptionally inconvenient not to have access to a parking space and therefore access to a car, the absence of a parking space is not an equivalent threat to health and safety as that posed by clogged toilets, raw sewage, and poisoned water."

Sources: benningtonbanner.com; *Weiler v. Hooshiari*, 19 A.3rd. 124 (Vt. 2011)

EVICTION

An **eviction** is the act of depriving a person of the possession of real property, either by reentry or by legal process. A landlord may not use force to evict a tenant. Instead, the landlord must give the tenant whatever notice is required by state law and use legal process (described later) to evict a tenant. For example, Pennsylvania requires a 10-day notice for eviction because of nonpayment of rent and a 15-day notice for eviction because of a breach of the lease agreement (other than nonpayment). In Oregon requires a 30-day eviction notice for fixed-term renters, whereas in the city of Portland, Oregon, similarly situated renters are owed 90 days of notice.

Retaliatory eviction is the eviction of a tenant for reporting to the authorities sanitary-code or building-code violations in the rented property. This type of eviction is illegal in most states today.

A **constructive eviction** occurs when the landlord does some act that deprives the tenant of the beneficial enjoyment of the premises. Examples are depriving the tenant of heat, light, power, or some other service that was called for under the lease. When a constructive or other illegal eviction occurs, the tenant has the right to leave the premises without being in breach of the lease. The tenant may also withhold rent for the length of the eviction.

The legal action used by landlords to evict tenants was called **ejectment** at common law. Today, the name given to the action varies from state to state and includes **summary process**, **summary ejectment**, **forcible entry and detainer**, **dispossessory warrant proceedings**, and **unlawful detainer**.

The landlord is required to give the proper statutory notice to the tenant before commencing such action, and the court, in its discretion, may allow time for the tenant to find another place to live.

TERMS IN ACTION

President Donald Trump was sued by the Trump Plaza in 2009, when its co-op board sought to **evict** him from one of its apartments. Trump built the 175-unit co-operative apartment building on the Upper East Side of New York in 1984, but one of his companies, Trump Corporation, also rented apartment units from it. According to the eviction lawsuit, Trump Corporation missed rent payments on its units, totaling $87,000, in April and May of 2009. According to the complaint, the **lease** terminated on May 6, five days after Trump Corporation missed its May rent deadline. Notice of default had been sent on April 10th, after April's rent had gone unpaid. Whereas those may seem like harsh termination terms, the lease contract was created by Trump's attorneys, and, according to Andrew Perel, President of the Trump Plaza Owners, Inc. co-op at the time, "If you don't pay the rent when Donald Trump is your landlord, he comes down on you like a hammer. Well, lo and behold, he signed a lease that was his own lease and he's the tenant. And he missed April and May." Perel is a lawyer, so it likely came as no shock to him that a few days after the co-op sued Trump, Trump sued the co-op—for $18.1 million in damages for what seemed very much like a **constructive eviction** allegation. Part of the allegations Trump leveled against his own building's co-op was shoddy repairs and water damage to the units that his company occupies, going back as far as 2007.

TORT LIABILITY

When a person is injured on rented or leased property, the one who is in control of that part of the premises where the injury occurs is generally responsible if the injury was caused by negligence. For example, the landlord may be responsible for injury to others caused by a defect in the common areas over which he or she has control, such as hallways, stairways, and so forth. Likewise, the tenant may be responsible for injury to persons caused by defects in the portion of the premises over which he or she has control.

Legislation in some states has changed this common law rule of liability by allowing the tenant to give notice to the landlord of any unsafe conditions in that part of the premises under the tenant's control and making the landlord responsible thereafter for injury caused by the unsafe condition if the landlord fails to correct the condition. For example, California makes a tenant responsible to notify the landlord of inoperable dead bolt locks or window security or other premises locking devices, whereupon the landlord has a legal duty to repair the defects within a reasonable time (Cal. Civil Code § 1941.3).

Reviewing What you Learned

After studying the chapter, write the answers to each of the following questions:

1. What are the differences between the terms *landlord* and *tenant* and the terms *lessor* and *lessee*?

2. A leasehold estate was what kind of property at common law?

3. List the four types of leasehold estate.

4. For what length of time may a tenancy for years last?

5. What does a tenancy for 100 years create in some states?

6. How may a periodic tenancy be created by implication?

7. Describe a tenancy at will, including the method for its termination.

8. What is another name for a tenant at sufferance? How much notice must be given to evict such a tenant?

9. Compare a lease with a license.

10. Who usually signs a lease?

11. Differentiate between an assignment of a lease and a sublease.

12. Recent legislation in some states provides for what remedy to a tenant if the premises are not fit for human habitation?

13. What is the difference between a retaliatory eviction and a constructive eviction?

14. List five names, given by different states, for the eviction action.

____

____

____

b. In an area of the building that is controlled by a tenant?

____

15. Who is responsible for a negligently caused injury that takes place

____

a. In the common areas of an apartment building?

____

____

Understanding Legal Concepts

Indicate whether each statement is true or false. Then, change the italicized word or phrase of each false statement to make it true.

ANSWERS

_____ **1.** The terms *lessor* and *lessee* are broad terms that refer to the parties under a tenancy at will as well as the parties under a lease.

_____ **2.** A *tenancy for years* can be for any period so long as it is ascertained.

_____ **3.** A periodic tenancy continues for *successive periods* until one of the parties terminates it by giving notice to the other party.

_____ **4.** A writing *is necessary* to create a tenancy at will.

_____ **5.** A tenant at sufferance *is not* entitled to notice to vacate.

_____ **6.** A lease differs from a license in that a *license* conveys an interest in land and transfers possession.

_____ **7.** An *assignment* occurs when the lessee conveys part of the term of a lease, but not the remainder of it, to another person.

_____ **8.** *Quiet enjoyment* means that a tenant has the right to possess the property and to be undisturbed in that possession.

_____ **9.** A *retaliatory* eviction occurs when the landlord deprives the tenant of heat, light, power, or some other service called for under the lease.

_____ **10.** When a person is injured on leased property, the one in control of that part of the premises where the injury occurs *is generally responsible* if the injury was caused by negligence.

Checking Terminology

From the list of legal terms that follows, select the one that matches each definition.

ANSWERS

a. constructive eviction
b. deed-poll
c. demise
d. dispossessory warrant proceedings
e. ejectment
f. eviction
g. forcible entry and detainer
h. holdover tenant
i. indenture
j. landlord
k. lease
l. leasehold estate
m. lessee

_____ **1.** A contract granting the use of certain real property by its owner to another for a specified period in return for the payment of rent.

_____ **2.** A person who owns real property and who rents it to another under a lease. (Select two answers.)

_____ **3.** A person who has temporary possession of, and an interest in, real property of another under a lease. (Select two answers.)

_____ **4.** The interest that is conveyed by a lease.

_____ **5.** An estate in real property for a definite or fixed period of time no matter how long or how short.

_____ **6.** An estate in real property that continues for successive periods until one of the parties terminates it by giving notice to the other party. (Select two answers.)

_____ **7.** A lease given by a lessee to a third person conveying the same interest for a shorter term than the period for which the lessee holds it. (Select two answers.)

_____ **8.** The right of a tenant to possess the rented property and to be undisturbed in that possession.

n. lessor
o. license
p. licensee
q. periodic tenancy
r. quiet enjoyment
s. retaliatory eviction
t. sublease/sublet
u. summary ejectment
v. summary process
w. tenancy at will
x. tenancy for years
y. tenancy from year to year
z. tenant
aa. tenant at sufferance
bb. underlease
cc. unlawful detainer
dd. warranty of habitability

______ **9.** A legal action used by landlords to evict tenants. (Select six answers.)

______ **10.** An estate in real property for an indefinite period.

______ **11.** A tenant who wrongfully remains in possession of the premises after a tenancy has expired. (Select two answers.)

______ **12.** A person who has permission to do certain acts.

______ **13.** A grant or permission to do a particular thing.

______ **14.** To lease.

______ **15.** A deed or lease to which two or more persons are parties.

______ **16.** A deed or lease in which only the party making the instrument executes it.

______ **17.** Dispossession caused by an act of the landlord that deprives the tenant of the beneficial enjoyment of the demised premises.

______ **18.** The act of depriving a person of the possession of real property either by reentry or by legal process.

______ **19.** The eviction of a tenant for reporting to the authorities sanitary code or building code violations of the leased property.

______ **20.** An implied warranty by a landlord that the premises are fit for human habitation.

Sharpening Your Latin Skills

In the space provided, write the definition of each of the following legal terms, referring to the glossary when necessary.

et al. _______________________________

et seq _______________________________

et u _______________________________

fructus industriales _______________________________

fructus naturalis _______________________________

habendum _______________________________

lis pendens _______________________________

locus _______________________________

locus sigilli _______________________________

pendente lite _______________________________

Using Legal Language

Read the following story and fill in the blank lines with legal terms taken from the list of terms at the beginning of this chapter:

Priscilla rented an apartment to Peter under a one-year _______________________ (contract). Priscilla was the _______________________ or _______________________, and Peter was the _______________________ or _______________________ of the _______________________ that is, the interest that was conveyed by the lease. Both parties signed the contract; therefore, it was a(n) _______________________ rather than a(n) _______________________, which is signed only by one party. Because the arrangement was for a definite period, it was called a(n) _______________________ rather than a(n) _______________________ (or _______________________), which continues for successive periods until one party terminates it by giving notice to the other party. A month later, Peter transferred his interest in the tenancy to Paul for a three-month period by the use of a(n) _______________________, which is also called a(n) _______________________. It was not a(n) _______________________, because Peter was to return to finish the remainder of the lease. Priscilla did not deprive Paul of heat, light, power, or other services called for under the lease; therefore, no _______________________ occurred. Paul did not pay the rent, however, which caused Priscilla to seek a(n) _______________________, which is the act of depriving him of the possession of the property. Paul continued to stay on even after being evicted, thus becoming a(n) _______________________, which is also called a(n) _______________________. After Paul left, Priscilla _______________________ (leased) the premises to Prudence for an indefinite period, creating a(n) _______________________. Prudence allowed Pauline to live with her as a lodger, the latter being a(n) _______________________, because she had no property right or interest in the premises.

PART EIGHT

Terms Used in Family Law

Comstock/Stockbyte/Getty Images

CHAPTER 38
Marriage, Divorce, and Dissolution of Marriage

CHAPTER 39
Divorce Procedure

8

lthough many unmarried couples today live together, the institution of marriage remains firmly embedded in our culture and legal system. While divorce rates seem to have dropped, compared to the almost 50% rate for those who married in the 1970s and 1980s, divorce courts are still booked and lawyers specializing in family law are heavily occupied. After a discussion of prenuptial agreements and marriage formalities, Chapter 38 compares annulment with marriage dissolution. It then examines the principal grounds for divorce. Chapter 39 discusses domicile and residence, foreign divorce, defenses to divorce actions, alimony, and support and custody of children.

38

Marriage, Divorce, and Dissolution of Marriage

8

ANTE INTERROGATORY

A judicial declaration that a marriage never existed is a/n (A) anullment, (B) no-fault divorce, (C) fault divorce, (D) prenuptial agreement.

LEARNING OBJECTIVES

LO 1: Explain what is generally required of a valid prenuptial agreement

LO 2: Describe key aspects of marriage formalities, including discussing common law marriage

LO 3: Summarize the evolution of the legal status of same sex marriages

LO 4: Contrast an annulment with a divorce and provide reasons why an annulment may be granted

LO 5: Define a legal separation of spouses

LO 6: Explain the basics of a no-fault divorce

LO 7: Summarize the key grounds on which fault divorces can be granted

KEY TERMS

adultery

age of consent

alienation of affections

alleged

annulment

antenuptial agreement

banns of matrimony

breach of promise to marry

civil union

cohabit

common law marriage

community property

conjugal

consortium

copulate

co-respondent

covenant marriage

crime of moral turpitude

criminal conversation

cruelty

desertion

discretion

dissolution of marriage

divorce

divorce from bed and board

gay marriage

heart balm statutes

impotency

incompatibility

irreconcilable differences

irretrievable breakdown

limited divorce

marriage

marriage banns

no-fault divorce

polygamy

premarital agreement

prenuptial (prenup) agreement

proxy marriage

reconciliation

same-sex marriage

separation of spouses

solemnized

WEBSITES FOR PRONUNCIATION HELP

http://dictionary.cambridge.org/us/pronunciation/english/audio

https://www.howtopronounce.com

PRENUPTIAL AGREEMENTS

A **prenuptial agreement**, also called a **premarital** or **antenuptial agreement**, is a written contract, required to comport with states' statute of frauds, made in contemplation of marriage between prospective spouses and, setting forth, among other points, the rights each spouse will have to property brought into the marriage. A prenuptial agreement (commonly called a prenup) takes effect on marriage. To be upheld by the court, the contract must be fair and reasonable and the parties must fully disclose their assets to each other. While parties are free to draft and sign a prenuptial agreement without attorney involvement, in many states, if the parties employ an attorney each party must be given the opportunity to have independent counsel. One attorney should not represent both parties, because a prenuptial agreement is a contract, and a lawyer representing both sides to the same contract has a severe conflict-of-interest problem. For instance, suppose that the wife-to-be (the wealthier side of the relationship) hires her lawyer to represent her and her fiancé in drafting a prenuptial agreement. How would that lawyer protect the interests of the husband-to-be, while also protecting the interests of the one paying the legal bill?

TERMS IN ACTION

Bill Murray, famous Chicago Cubs fan and star of such films as *Caddy Shack*, *Stripes*, *Ghost Busters* (the first one) and *Lost in Translation*, was sued for **divorce** in May 2008 by his wife of 10 years, Jennifer. In the filing, she accused him of infidelity, abusive behavior, marijuana abuse, and abandonment. But their divorce was finalized a month later, most likely as the result of the **prenuptial agreement** that they entered into in July 1997. The 23-page agreement stated that both parties waived the right to have any review of each other's separate assets or financial documents, and waived the right to alimony or any marital property distribution, in the event of divorce. As consideration for signing the agreement, Bill promised to buy a $1 million home in South Carolina for Jennifer that was to be titled only in her name. The prenuptial agreement states that in the event of a divorce, Jennifer Murray would receive a $7 million payment within 60 days after the divorce decree. Each party waived the right to the other's retirement accounts. The prenuptial agreement stated that each spouse had independent legal representation. Ironically, even though the divorce got off to a very public and ugly start, the prenuptial agreement's opening paragraph states that "this Agreement will enhance and encourage a harmonious marital relationship between them and will enable them to avoid any conflict or controversy in the future arising out of any dissolution of the marriage." According to the legal self-help website Legalzoom.com, some prenuptial agreements have had interesting, if not curious, requirements in them. Legalzoom didn't explain how the prenuptial agreements were discovered, but its examples included a husband's promise to only watch one football game with his friends per Sunday, another

(Continued)

husband's promise to pay a $10,000 fee every time he was rude to his in-laws, a wife who agreed to keep her weight no higher than 120 pounds, at the risk of giving to her husband $100,000 of separate property not covered by the prenup, and a husband who was bound to keep his weight at 180 pounds. And of course, there was a couple whose prenup included a promise to have sex 3-4 times a week—a promise that is completely unenforceable for reasons that should be obvious to anyone who read the contracts chapters.

Sources: www.slate.com; thesmokinggun.com; legalzoom.com

MARRIAGE FORMALITIES

The term **marriage** is defined by the federal government and most states as "a legal union of one man and one woman as husband and wife." (As of this writing, this definition is found in 1 U.S.C. § 7, which has been rendered unconstitutional by virtue of the 2013 U.S. Supreme Court case, *U.S. v. Windsor* discussed later in the chapter in the section on same sex marriage.) Despite the continual evolution of the law, men and women who live together without being married have few, if any, rights beyond those given to single persons. In contrast, people who are married have legal rights beyond the **conjugal** rights (the mutual rights and privileges of cohabitation, sexual relations, and companionship) that are deeply embedded in the law. These rights include protection of property, provisions for maintenance and support, and the right of inheritance.

Most states require marriages to be **solemnized**—that is, performed in a ceremonial fashion with witnesses present. Although no particular form of ceremony is required, state laws determine who is authorized to perform a marriage ceremony. In a unique ceremony in 2007, a Minnesota National Guardsman deployed in Iraq beyond his commitment term married his fiancée in Minnesota by the use of video teleconferencing and the help of a chaplain.

A **common law marriage** is a marriage without a formal ceremony or marriage license. It is currently allowed in a minority of states and the District of Columbia[1], and five other states[2] permit certain common law marriages if they were valid before statutes prohibiting common law marriage were enacted in those states. Where allowed, common law marriage has the same legal effect as a ceremonial marriage. To enter into a common law marriage, the couple must (1) agree by words to each other in the present tense that they are married, (2) **cohabit** (live together), and (3) hold themselves out to the community as husband and wife. In order to qualify as common law married, the couple has to continuously live together as common law spouses for a required period, usually 7 or 10 years.

Word Wise
Prefix Review

Key Term	Prefix	Prefix Meaning
prenuptial (*pre·NUP·shel*)	pre-	before
antenuptial (*an·tee·NUP·shel*)	ante-	before
cohabit (*koh·HAB·it*)	co-	together
incompatibility (*in·kom·pat·e·BIL·i·tee*)	in-	not
irretrievable (*ir·ree·TREE·ve·bel*)	ir-	not
impotency (*IM·pe·ten·see*)	im-	not
reconciliation (*rek·on·sil·ee·AY·shun*)	re-	again

---

[1] According to the National Conference of State Legislatures and the Legal Information Institute, those states include Alabama, Colorado, the District of Columbia, Iowa, Kansas, Montana, Oklahoma, Rhode Island, South Carolina, Texas, and Utah.

[2] According to the National Conference of State Legislatures and the Legal Information Institute, those states are Georgia, Idaho, New Hampshire, Ohio, and Pennsylvania.

The Uniform Marriage and Divorce Act, which has been adopted in some states, allows a marriage by proxy when a party to the marriage cannot be present. A **proxy marriage** is a ceremonial marriage in which one of the parties is absent, but represented by an agent who stands in his or her place for the purpose of solemnization. Such a wedding took place in 1810 in Vienna, where the 19-year old great niece of the ill-fated Marie Antoinette, named Marie Louise (the Archduchess of Austria) was married to Napoleon Bonaparte, becoming his second wife. Napoleon had yet to meet his future wife and wasn't in attendance, so the bride's uncle, Archduke Charles, stood in for him at the ceremony.

The **covenant marriage** was adopted in Arizona, Arkansas, and Louisiana (the first state to have it, in 1997) in an attempt to decrease the divorce rate and to safeguard children from traumatic experiences, although its use is rare. It is a form of marriage whose roots are religious in nature. Whereas it is not the only form of marriage in those states, couples who choose a covenant marriage agree to go through counseling before the marriage and also during the marriage to resolve conflicts. With exceptions, covenant marriage spouses can divorce only after a two-year separation, and causes for divorce are limited to domestic violence, adultery, or a felony with incarceration.

Some religions require public notice of a marriage contract, called **banns of matrimony**, or **marriage banns**, for a certain number of weeks before the wedding date. This Middle English term, which means "proclamation," provides anyone the time and opportunity to object to the marriage if there is just cause to do so. In addition, many state laws require a waiting period ranging from one to five days after the wedding license is issued before the wedding can occur. Also, many states require the couple to have blood tests to determine the presence of rubella (German measles), venereal disease, sickle cell anemia, and/or HIV.

SAME-SEX MARRIAGE AND CIVIL UNIONS

Historically, marriage has been exclusively recognized only between one man and woman. In fact, **polygamy** (marriage between more than two spouses) is illegal in America, even if considered to be allowed in one's religion. Until recently, the same could be said for **same-sex marriage**, also called **gay marriage**, which was prohibited in all jurisdictions until Massachusetts became the first state to recognize same-sex marriage, in 2004. In 1996 the U.S. Congress passed a law, signed by President Clinton, called the Defense of Marriage Act, which defined marriage as between one man and one woman and declared that if a given state recognizes gay marriage, no other state would have to recognize it as valid marriage. Approximately 15 years later, statutes in 36 states prohibited gay marriage and many states also had constitutional amendments defining marriage as heterosexual.

Going in the opposite direction of the majority of states that had prohibited same-sex marriage, the states of Vermont, Connecticut, and New Jersey passed laws making civil unions legal. A **civil union** is a relationship in which same-sex couples have the same rights and duties as married couples. California's domestic partners law is a variation of the laws regarding civil union.

However, by the latter part of the first decade of the 21st century, some state and federal courts began to recognize gay marriage, despite the laws or voter referendums in those states that called to prohibit it. Massachusetts's highest court held that its marriage law violated the Massachusetts constitution, leading to the recognized validity of same-sex marriages in that state. And, whereas California voters passed a direct referendum and change in the California constitution in 2008 (known as Proposition 8), which declared marriage to be only between a man and a woman, federal courts in California (including the 9th Circuit Court of Appeals) concluded that Proposition 8 violated the constitutional rights of gays and lesbians. But three U.S. Supreme Court cases, each of them 5-4 decisions, negated most laws that negatively affected the marriage rights of same-sex couples. In 2013, the Supreme Court effectively struck down Proposition 8 in *Hollingsworth v. Perry* (570 U.S. __), and in *U.S. v. Windsor* (570 U.S. __), also in 2013, the Supreme Struck down the federal law application of the Defense of Marriage Act. In 2015 in *Obergefell v. Hodges*, the Supreme Court held that state laws that deny same sex couples from marrying violated the due process and equal protection clauses of the Fourteenth Amendment. As such, civil unions have become unnecessary.

ANNULMENT OF MARRIAGE

Marriages may be dissolved either by divorce or by annulment. An **annulment** is a judicial declaration that no valid marriage ever existed.

The principal grounds for annulment, which vary from state to state, are underage marriage, lack of marital intent, duress, fraud, pregnancy by someone other than the husband, incurable venereal disease, mental illness at the time of marriage, and physical incapacity.

At common law, the marriage of a girl under 12 or a boy under 14 was voidable. The marriage could be annulled by the court. Today, a marriage of a person below the age allowed by state law (called the **age of consent**) can be annulled at the court's **discretion**. The power of discretion is one that judges have to make decisions based on their own judgment and conscience.

With some exceptions, courts have held that a marriage entered into as a joke without any intent that the marriage be binding may be annulled as long as the parties to the marriage do not cohabit. For example, Delaware's annulment statute expressly allows for an annulment because "[o]ne or both parties entered into the marriage as a jest or dare" (13 Del.C. § 1506). By contrast, a Connecticut case shows that marrying on a dare isn't always annullable. In the 1937 case, a woman married a man on a dare made by the man as he was driving her and another couple to the couple's wedding ceremony. At the time, the woman was actually engaged to another man, which may have been conclusive proof that she simply married for the sake of the dare. The woman sought an annulment on the grounds that the marriage was made in jest and that there never was consummation of the marriage. But the Connecticut Superior Court denied the annulment, ruling that the parties intended to get married and understood the consequences of their act. (*Trotta v. Trotta*, 5 Conn.Sup. 218) See the "Terms in Action" below for more on annulments.

▌ TERMS IN ACTION

An **annulment** is in some way a legal fiction; if a person has entered into a lawful marriage, concluding later that it never existed is a curious thing. But where divorce is against one's religion, annulment is a possible option. King Henry VIII created the Church of England because the pope wouldn't grant Henry an annulment to Catherine of Aragon so that he could marry Anne Boleyn. Catherine had been married to Henry's brother Arthur for a few months before Arthur's death. Because of that, Henry needed and got a special dispensation to marry Catherine in the first place, since, at the time, marrying one's brother's wife was considered incest. Henry's first claim for annulment, which was officially Catherine's claim, was that Catherine never consummated her five-month marriage to Arthur, allowing her to marry Henry. So, when the Catholic Church refused to grant Henry his annulment—for the reason that Catherine had lied about not consummating her prior marriage with Arthur— Henry was convinced that he could grant himself an annulment if he were the head of his own church. Henry split from Catholicism, and in 1530 Parliament declared the king head of the Church of England. When the very-Catholic Sir Thomas More (the king's Lord Chancellor) refused to support the annulment, Henry had him beheaded. After Anne Boleyn failed to give birth to a male heir, which was Catherine's marital blemish, Henry had her accused of incest and treason and she was beheaded. Centuries later, Britney Spears got a much less-violent annulment. She was actually once married to someone before she married and divorced Kevin Federline. In January 2004, Spears married a high-school classmate named Jason Alexander, at the Little White Wedding Chapel in Las Vegas, at 5:00 a.m. Fifty-five hours later she got the marriage annulled. Her stated reason for being deserving of an annulment—as opposed to a divorce—was that "she lacked the understanding of her actions to the extent that she was incapable of agreeing to the marriage." That may be legalese for "I was too drunk at the time to know what I was doing."

Sources: wsu.edu; forbes.com; thesmokinggun.com

SEPARATION OF SPOUSES

Instead of issuing a divorce decree, a court may order a **separation of spouses** also called a **limited divorce**, or, in some places, a **divorce from bed and board** (an arcane term), which is the discontinuance of cohabitation by the spouses. A legal separation formalizes the cessation of marital cohabitation, without going as far as a divorce—which is the formal disintegration of the legal union. If minor children are involved, a separation order will include temporary measures for support and custody. A separation for a statutory period, whether by agreement or judicial decree, is required in many states before a no-fault divorce action can be initiated.

DIVORCE OR DISSOLUTION OF MARRIAGE

A **divorce** (called **dissolution of marriage** in California and other states) is the action by a court of terminating a valid marriage. A divorce requires a valid marriage to begin with, whereas an annulment does not. The principal grounds for divorce follow:

- no-fault
- fraud or duress
- adultery
- cruelty
- desertion
- alcohol or drug addiction
- impotency
- nonsupport
- conviction of a felony

No-Fault Divorce

The Soviet Union first instituted no-fault divorce in 1918, but California was the first state to enact **no-fault divorce** in 1970. Now, all states have enacted statutes that provide for the dissolution of marriage whereby the spouse seeking the divorce doesn't have to prove fault against the other spouse. For example, Nevada has for many years allowed a divorce on the ground of **incompatibility**. In that state, instead of requiring a showing of fault, it is necessary to show only that the couple has a personality conflict so deep that no chance for a **reconciliation** (the renewal of amicable relations) exists. Common grounds for a no-fault divorce are **irretrievable breakdown** of the marriage and **irreconcilable differences**.

In some states, a choice exists between two procedures that may be followed to obtain a no-fault divorce. One procedure is used if both parties agree to the divorce; the other procedure is followed if the parties do not agree to it. The procedures differ from state to state.

In California, couples who, among other requirements, have no children, have been married less than five years, and own less than $41,000 worth of community property may divorce without going to court, under a *summary dissolution* procedure. **Community property** is property other than a gift or inheritance, acquired by a husband or wife during marriage and which belongs to both spouses equally without regard to who "earned" the property. However, divorcing spouses may avoid the effects of community property laws by the use of prenuptial agreements.

Fraud or Duress

Although most states allow an annulment, rather than a divorce, on the grounds of fraud and duress, a few states allow a divorce on both of these grounds.

Adultery

Adultery is voluntary sexual intercourse by a married person with someone other than a spouse or by an unmarried person with a married person. In addition to being grounds for divorce, it is a crime in some states. (Remember the Terms in Action in Chapter 14 that discussed the New York woman charged with adultery in 2010.)

Because of its private nature, adultery is most commonly proved by circumstantial evidence. In a divorce action, it is ordinarily enough to show that the **alleged** (claimed) adulterer had the opportunity together with the inclination or disposition to commit the act. To protect the character and reputation of innocent third persons, the name of the **co-respondent** (the person charged with committing adultery with the defendant) may not be used in the pleadings until a judge finds probable cause in a closed hearing.

In years past, a tort action called **criminal conversation** could be brought by a husband or wife against a third party who committed adultery with the husband's or wife's spouse. Damages for loss of **consortium** (the fellowship between a husband and wife) were often sought in such cases. But courts began to be less inclined to hear such awkwardly intimate disputes, and **heart balm statutes** (or heart balm acts), as they are known, have been passed in most states abolishing this cause of action along with actions for **breach of promise to marry** (breaking off the engagement) and **alienation of affections** (willful and malicious interference with the marriage relation by a third party without justification or excuse).

Web Wise

- Find a divorce law dictionary at **http://www.divorcenet.com**
- Look for state specific divorce forms at **http://www.divorce-forms.org/index.php**
- Much information on divorce law, including jurisdiction-specific resources, can be found at http://topics.law.cornell.edu/wex/Divorce
- A trove of divorce related information can be found at **http://thedivorcecenter.org/related-websites/**

Cruelty

Cruelty is a ground for divorce. It is called by different names, including the following, in different states:

cruel and abusive treatment

cruel and barbarous treatment

cruel and inhuman treatment

cruelty of treatment

extreme and repeated cruelty

extreme cruelty

intolerable cruelty

Regardless of the name given to it, the requirements for proving cruelty are quite similar throughout the country. In general, plaintiffs must prove actual personal violence that endangers their life, limb, or health or that creates a reasonable apprehension of such danger and renders cohabitation unsafe or unbearable.

Usually, more than a single act of violence must occur to obtain a divorce on this ground. For example, a court held that a single act by a husband of slapping his wife on the back—which was not severe, left no mark, and was the only act of violence in 25 years of marriage—was not a ground for divorce (*Souza v. Souza*, 125 N.E.2d 120, Mass. 1955). However, the same court said years earlier that one single incident of violence was enough to grant a divorce when a husband, while drunk, struck, knocked down and beat his wife in an argument, resulting in bruises on the wife's back, throat, arms, and legs (*Mooney v. Mooney*, 58 N.E.2d 748, Mass. 1944).

Arguments alone, nagging, or the denial of sexual intercourse is not enough by itself to obtain a divorce on the grounds of cruelty. Mental suffering can be held to be cruelty if it impairs the health of the spouse.

Desertion

Desertion is defined as the voluntary separation of one spouse from the other, for the statutory period, without justification and with the intent of not returning. The abandoned spouse must not consent to the spouse's absence and must not have committed acts that justified the other's leaving. The time period for desertion varies from state to state, and is not to be confused with a statutorily required time of legal separation as condition to divorce. Some states include constructive abandonment as part of desertion or abandonment, and acts that could qualify range from infidelity to refusing to financially support the other spouse or family.

Alcohol or Drug Addiction

Habitual drunkenness, by either alcohol or drugs, is a ground for divorce in most states. The habit must be confirmed (well-established), persistent, voluntary, and excessive.

Impotency

Impotency is the impossibility of either party to consummate the marriage by sexual intercourse because of some physical, psychological, or other medical condition. The test is the ability to **copulate**, which means to engage in sexual intercourse. It is not related to sterility or infertility (which is the inability to beget or bear a child), or the refusal to engage in sexual relations.

Nonsupport

In many states, nonsupport is available only to the wife and not to the husband as a ground for divorce. In those states that have made the equal rights of men and women part of their state law, however, it is available to both spouses if the state recognizes it as a ground for divorce. The spouse against whom the divorce is sought must have sufficient ability to provide support and must willfully fail to do so.

Conviction of a Felony

Most states allow a divorce if either party is convicted of a felony, an infamous crime, or a **crime of moral turpitude** (a crime that is base, vile, and depraved). Pennsylvania, for example, allows a spouse to divorce based on fault on the ground that the other spouse has been convicted of a crime and sentenced to at least two years in prison, and allows a no-fault divorce where the conviction is for committing a personal injury crime against the filing spouse (23 Pa.C.S.A. § 3301). In some jurisdictions, life imprisonment automatically dissolves the marriage without further legal process; most states, however, require a divorce proceeding. For example, New York law states that a person who is sentenced to life in prison may not marry unless while on community service (i.e., parole), and that existing marriages existing prior to a spouse being sentenced to life in prison are not automatically voided (NY Civil Rights Law § 79-a).

Reviewing What You Learned

After studying the chapter, write the answers to each of the following questions:

1. What is required for a prenuptial contract to be upheld by a court? _______________________________

2. The legal rights given to people who are married include what? _______________________________

3. What are the requirements for entering into a common law marriage, where common law marriage is recognized? _____

4. List the principal grounds for an annulment. _____________

5. What is meant by "the age of consent" to be married? _____

6. What legal rights do same-sex couples have to marriage? Explain. _______________________________

7. List the principal grounds for a divorce. _______________

8. What are two common grounds for a no-fault divorce? _____

9. In a divorce action for adultery, it is ordinarily enough to show what two elements on the part of the alleged adulterer? _____

10. What is done to protect the character and reputation of innocent third persons in divorce actions for adultery?

11. What is generally required to obtain a divorce for cruelty?

12. Name three activities that, by themselves, are not enough to establish cruelty. _______________________________

13. To establish desertion, the abandoned spouse must not consent to what? _______________________________

14. Explain the difference between impotency and sterility.

15. What is required of the spouse against whom a divorce is sought on the ground of nonsupport?

____

____

____

Understanding Legal Concepts

Indicate whether each statement is true or false. Then, change the italicized word or phrase of each false statement to make it true.

ANSWERS

_____ **1.** To be upheld by the court, a prenuptial agreement must be fair and reasonable and the parties *must* fully disclose their assets to each other.

_____ **2.** Men and women who live together without being married have *many* rights beyond those given to single persons.

_____ **3.** Common law marriages are allowed in *all* jurisdictions in the United States.

_____ **4.** At common law, the marriage of a girl under *12* or a boy under 14 was voidable.

_____ **5.** An *annulment* requires a valid marriage to begin with.

_____ **6.** To prove adultery in a divorce action, it is ordinarily enough to show that the alleged adulterer had the *opportunity* together with the inclination, to commit the act.

_____ **7.** The name of the co-respondent in a divorce action involving adultery may *not be* used in the pleadings until a judge finds probable cause in a closed hearing.

_____ **8.** Arguments or nagging is usually *enough* to obtain a divorce on the grounds of cruelty.

_____ **9.** To obtain a divorce for desertion, the abandoned spouse *must not* consent to the spouse's absence.

_____ **10.** The test to determine impotency is the ability to *beget or bear a child.*

Checking Terminology

From the list of legal terms that follows, select the one that matches each definition.

ANSWERS

a. adultery
b. age of consent
c. alienation of affections
d. alleged
e. annulment
f. antenuptial agreement
g. banns of matrimony
h. breach of promise to marry
i. civil union
j. cohabit
k. common law marriage
l. community property
m. conjugal
n. consortium
o. copulate
p. co-respondent
q. covenant marriage
r. crime of moral turpitude
s. criminal conversation
t. cruelty
u. desertion
v. discretion
w. dissolution of marriage
x. divorce
y. divorce from bed and board
z. gay marriage
aa. heart balm statutes
bb. impotency
cc. incompatibility
dd. irreconcilable differences

_____ **1.** The action by a court of terminating a valid marriage. (Select two answers.)

_____ **2.** A judicial declaration that no valid marriage ever existed.

_____ **3.** The power that a judge has to make a decision based on his or her own judgment and conscience.

_____ **4.** A marriage dissolution that is not based on establishing the other spouse's wrongful conduct.

_____ **5.** The renewal of amicable relations.

_____ **6.** Voluntary sexual intercourse by a married person with someone other than a spouse or by any unmarried person with a married person.

_____ **7.** The age at which one may be married under state law.

_____ **8.** Conflicts in personalities and dispositions that are so deep as to be irreconcilable and irremediable and that render it impossible for married parties to continue to live together in a normal marital relationship. (Select three answers.)

_____ **9.** The person charged with committing adultery with the defendant in a divorce action.

_____ **10.** In a divorce action, personal violence by one spouse that endangers the life, limb, or health of the other spouse.

_____ **11.** The voluntary separation of one spouse from the other, for the statutory period, without justification and with the intent of not returning.

_____ **12.** The incapacity of either party to consummate a marriage by sexual intercourse because of some physical infirmity or disarrangement.

_____ **13.** Live together.

_____ **14.** Claimed, asserted, or charged.

_____ **15.** Public notice of a marriage contract for a certain number of weeks before the wedding date. (Select two answers.)

_____ **16.** A ceremonial marriage in which one of the parties is absent, but represented by an agent who stands in his or her place.

_____ **17.** Engage in sexual intercourse.

_____ **18.** An agreement made in contemplation of marriage between prospective spouses setting forth, among other points, the rights each spouse will have to property brought into the marriage. (Select three answers.)

<table>
<tr><td>

ee. irretrievable breakdown
 ff. limited divorce
gg. marriage
hh. marriage banns
 ii. no-fault divorce
 jj. polygamy
kk. premarital agreement
 ll. prenuptial agreement
mm. proxy marriage
nn. reconciliation
oo. same-sex marriage
pp. separation of spouses
qq. solemnized

</td></tr>
</table>

_____ **19.** Performed in a ceremonial fashion with witnesses present.

_____ **20.** A marriage without a formal ceremony.

_____ **21.** Property (other than a gift or inheritance) acquired by a husband or wife during marriage that belongs to both spouses equally.

_____ **22.** A crime that is base, vile, and depraved.

_____ **23.** The willful and malicious interference with the marriage relation by a third party without justification or excuse.

_____ **24.** The fellowship between a husband and wife.

_____ **25.** A tort action brought by a husband or wife against a third party who committed adultery with the husband's or wife's spouse.

_____ **26.** The discontinuance of cohabitation by the spouses. (Select three answers.)

_____ **27.** Laws passed in most states abolishing actions for loss of consortium, breach of promise to marry, and alienation of affections.

_____ **28.** Breaking off an engagement to marry.

_____ **29.** A marriage in which the parties agree to go through counseling before the marriage and also during the marriage in order to resolve conflicts.

_____ **30.** Pertaining to the marriage relationship.

_____ **31.** Marriage between two men or two women. (Select two answers.)

_____ **32.** Marriage between more than two spouses.

Using Legal Language

Read the following story and fill in the blank lines with legal terms taken from the list of terms at the beginning of this chapter:

Although she looked older, Sonia was only 15 when she married Seth. This was below the ___________________, which is the age at which persons were allowed by the law of her state to marry; however, the couple did ___________________—that is, live together. Whether or not she could obtain a(n) ___________________, which is a judicial declaration that no valid marriage ever existed, was in the court's ___________________. She decided to seek a(n) ___________________, which is the act of terminating a marriage. Evidence existed that Seth had the opportunity together with the inclination to commit ___________________, which is a crime in many states in addition to being a ground for divorce. It was ___________________ (claimed) that he had gone to Sarah's apartment on several occasions. If Sarah were to be charged as being a(n) ___________________, her name could not be used in the pleadings unless probable cause were found by a judge in a closed hearing. Seth had not committed ___________________, which is personal violence endangering a spouse's life, limb, or health. He had the ability to ___________________—that is, engage in sexual intercourse—ruling out Sonia's obtaining a divorce on the ground of ___________________. A divorce could not be obtained on the ground of ___________________, either, because no voluntary separation of one spouse from the other had occurred. After thinking it over, Sonia decided to seek a(n) ___________________, which provides for the ___________________ without regard to fault. She considered getting a divorce in Nevada on the ground of ___________________, which required a showing that the couple had a personality conflict so deep that no chance for a(n) ___________________ existed. But she didn't live in Nevada. In some states, this ground for divorce is called ___________________, and in others, it is known as ___________________.

39

Divorce Procedure

ANTE INTERROGATORY

Some states issue a provisional or temporary divorce decision until a statutory period is over. This is called (A) response, (B) judgment nisi, (C) comity, (D) pendent lite.

LEARNING OBJECTIVES

LO 1: List the key terms associated with the filing of a divorce

LO 2: Explain how domicile and residency relate to the filing of a divorce

LO 3: Explain the key controversies associated with obtaining a foreign divorce

LO 4: Identify key, traditional defenses to a divorce action

LO 5: Summarize the purpose behind alimony and the issues involved in determining what is paid

LO 6: Distinguish the types of child custody

KEY TERMS

alimony

appearance

bilateral foreign divorce

child support

collusion

comity

condonation

connivance

custody of children

decree

divided custody

domicile

emancipated

equitable distribution laws

ex parte foreign divorce

foreign divorce

foreign jurisdiction

forum

full faith and credit clause

interlocutory decree

joint custody

judgment nisi

libel

libelant

libelee

maintenance

pendente lite

petition

petitioner

physical custody

proceeding

recrimination

residence

respondent

response

spousal support

temporary custody

WEBSITES FOR PRONUNCIATION HELP

http://dictionary.cambridge.org/us/pronunciation/english/audio
https://www.howtopronounce.com

A s divorce law has changed throughout the past decades, many of the terms have also changed. Formerly, the person bringing a divorce action was called the **libelant** and the person against whom the divorce was sought was called the **libelee**. The pleading beginning the action was called a **libel**. Although a few states still use those terms, in others, *plaintiff* and *defendant* or *petitioner* and *respondent* describe the parties to a divorce action. The initial pleading is called a *complaint for divorce/dissolution*. The divorce court's decision, formerly called a **decree** (traditionally, a decision of a court of equity), is now called a judgment in states that have changed their terminology.

But in other states, including California, the procedure for obtaining a dissolution of marriage is called a **proceeding** and the process is begun by the filing of a **petition** (a written application for a court order) with the court. The parties to the divorce proceeding are the **petitioner** (one who presents a petition to a court) and the **respondent** (one who is called on to answer a petition). The written answer filed by a respondent is a **response**.

Instead of issuing a final decision immediately, the courts of some states issue a provisional or temporary decision, called a **judgment nisi** in some states (in Massachusetts, as an example) and an **interlocutory decree** in others. The provisional decision becomes final at the end of a statutory period unless a valid reason is shown for not issuing it.

DOMICILE AND RESIDENCE

In a divorce action or dissolution petition, jurisdiction is based on **domicile**, which is a person's permanent place of abode, rather than the state where the couple married. Notwithstanding that people move or live in different states throughout the year, one's domicile is the place to which, whenever a person is absent, he or she has the present intent of returning. It cannot be abandoned or surrendered until another is acquired. It differs from a **residence** in that where one is currently living on a long-term basis (as opposed to a vacation) is one's residence. But one's current residence may not be that person's domicile. People may have several residences, but they can have only one domicile at a particular time. For example, students may reside in a college dormitory in one state, spend their summer working at a resort in another state, yet be domiciled at their home in a third state.

The plaintiff or petitioner in a divorce action must be domiciled within the jurisdiction of the court. Whether or not a legal domicile has been established is determined by the law of the **forum**, which is the place of litigation. The states are free to determine that a specific duration of residency is the equivalent of domicile.

All states except Alaska, South Dakota, and Washington require the plaintiff in a divorce action to reside in their state for a minimum time before filing for divorce. The period ranges from six weeks in a few states (Idaho, Nevada) to one year in others (South Carolina, Maryland, for example).

TERMS IN ACTION

The second most expensive American **divorce** is thought to be that between Rupert and Anna Marie Murdoch. Mr. and Mrs. Murdoch were divorced in 1999, after 32 years of marriage. Rupert Murdoch is the Australian-born billionaire who founded News Corp., the media company that owns the Fox Broadcast Network, Fox News Network, and other media outlets including the *New York Post* and the *Wall Street Journal*. Anna Murdoch filed the divorce **petition** in California, which was the couple's **domicile** at the time, although their **residence** was New York City. Their divorce settlement was valued at $1.7 billion. Seventeen days after the divorce, Rupert Murdoch married Wendy Deng, a woman 38 years younger than himself. They divorced in 2013 and, reportedly, this time Murdoch paid $1.8 billion as part of this divorce settlement, putting him first and second.

Sources: cnbc.com; nymag.com; divorcemag.com

FOREIGN DIVORCE

Before so many states allowed no-fault divorces, people would sometimes go to a **foreign jurisdiction** (another state or country) to obtain a **foreign divorce**. They did this because they did not have grounds for a divorce in their own state or because they wanted an immediate divorce without a waiting period. Nevada was attractive because domicile could be established in six weeks and a divorce could be obtained on the ground of incompatibility. Mexico allowed quick, easy divorces (including those by mail order) at one time, but its laws have been amended, ending such practice, and case law has acknowledged the invalidity of mail order divorces from Mexico (*Cammarota v. Sec. of Health, Education and Welfare*, 329 F.Supp. 1087, N.D. NY 1971).

Haiti and the Dominican Republic were once popular places to obtain overnight divorces. Jurisdiction was established by the fact that both parties submitted themselves to the jurisdiction of the court—the plaintiff in person and the defendant, in most cases, by filing an **appearance**. This voluntary submission to the court's jurisdiction, either in person or by an agent, was often accomplished by the filing of a power of attorney with the court, without the filer being personally present. Whether such divorces are valid depend on if state courts will recognize them, especially where any foreign residency requirement as a prerequisite to divorcing in those countries has not been met.

Word Wise
Opposite Parties

appellant *(a·PEL·ent)*	a party bringing an appeal
appellee *(a·pel·EE)*	a party against whom an appeal is brought
defendant *(de·FEN·dent)*	a person against whom a legal action is brought
libelant *(lie·bel·AHNT)*	the plaintiff in a divorce action
libelee *(lie·bel·EE)*	the defendant in a divorce action
petitioner *(pe·TI·shun·er)*	one who presents a petition to a court
plaintiff *(PLAIN·tif)*	a person who brings a legal action against another
respondent *(re·SPON·dent)*	one who is called on to answer a petition

A **bilateral foreign divorce** occurs when both parties file an appearance, as mentioned earlier, in a foreign state or country. A divorce obtained in a state other than the parties' state of domicile is recognized as valid by all of the United States under the **full faith and credit clause** of the U.S. Constitution. This clause requires that full faith and credit be given by each state to the judicial proceedings of every other state. The doctrine of **comity** applies a similar rule to judicial proceedings of foreign countries. This doctrine states that the courts of one jurisdiction will give effect to the laws and judicial decisions of another jurisdiction, not as a matter of obligation, but out of deference and respect.

An **ex parte foreign divorce** occurs when one spouse appears in the foreign jurisdiction, and the other spouse does not appear and fails to respond to the notice of divorce or service of process. This type of divorce may be attacked by the spouse who did not appear and declared void on the ground of lack of jurisdiction of the court granting the divorce. Such an attack may come when a spouse brings suit for separate support or when a spouse dies and the other spouse claims an inheritance. In a 1977 case from Louisiana, a husband travelled to the Dominican Republic to obtain a divorce. His wife was not there but had granted a special power of attorney to someone else in the Dominican Republic to make a court appearance on her behalf. Later, she succeeded in having the divorce declared invalid on the grounds that it didn't meet the state's divorce requirements (*Everett v. Everett*, 345 So.2d 586, La. Ct. App., 1977).

DEFENSES TO DIVORCE ACTIONS

When one seeks a divorce on the grounds allowed for divorce, the other spouse has the opportunity to raise various defenses (described next), in an attempt to prevent the divorce from being granted. But with the adoption of no-fault divorce laws, some states have eliminated the traditional defenses to divorce actions that had been available.

Condonation

Condonation is the forgiveness of a matrimonial offense. It is a defense to a divorce action that applies as long as the offense is not repeated and the wrongdoer remains faithful thereafter. The voluntary continuance of cohabitation or the resumption of sexual intercourse with knowledge of a marital offense usually amounts to condonation.

Connivance

The plaintiff's secret cooperation in the commission of a marital wrong committed by the defendant, called **connivance**, is a defense to a divorce action. A spouse who consents to the other's adultery, for example, or facilitates such an act is guilty of connivance.

Collusion

An agreement between a husband and wife that one of them will commit a marital offense so that the other may obtain a divorce, an agreement not to defend a divorce action, and an agreement to withhold evidence in such an action are examples of **collusion**, which is a defense to a divorce action, other than no-fault.

Recrimination

The common law doctrine of **recrimination** held that neither party could obtain a divorce when both were guilty of a marital wrong. Before no-fault divorce laws, this defense was widely used in the United States. Conduct on the part of the plaintiff that constituted a ground for divorce was a defense to a divorce action. The offense by the plaintiff did not have to be the same offense alleged in the complaint for divorce; however, it did have to be a ground for divorce in that particular state.

ALIMONY AND PROPERTY DISTRIBUTION

Alimony (called **spousal support** in California) is an allowance made to a divorced spouse by a former spouse for support and maintenance. Its concept stems from the common law right of a wife to be supported by a husband during marriage. Today, however, many states award alimony or spousal support payments to either the ex-husband or the ex-wife. The power of the court to award alimony and spousal support is strictly statutory and comes solely from the statutes of the particular state making the award. In general, the court having jurisdiction to award a divorce also has the power to award alimony. Not every state provides for alimony. For instance, Indiana is a non-alimony state, although it does allow for the granting of spousal maintenance, which can be rehabilitative and temporary (to allow a spouse to complete or acquire and education necessary to seek gainful employment, for instance) or indefinite (if the health of a spouse is materially affected, which would prevent the spouse from being independently employed).

Alimony **pendente lite**, meaning litigation pending, is temporary alimony that may be granted to a spouse during the pendency of a divorce or separate support action. Temporary alimony rests largely in the discretion of the court and need not be awarded when the parties have entered into an agreement in that regard or when one spouse is voluntarily providing for the other spouse's support.

No set formula exists for determining the amount of alimony or spousal support that may be awarded. The determination rests in the sound discretion of the court. Such items as income and earning capacity, financial resources, future prospects, current obligations, dependents, and number of former and subsequent spouses are considered. Also considered are the spouse's situation in life, earning capacity, separate property, contribution to a spouse's property, age, health, obligations, and number of dependents. Some jurisdictions will not award alimony or spousal support to a spouse who has a sufficient estate to provide for himself or herself. Similarly, a spouse who was at fault during the marriage will not be awarded alimony when the divorce was obtained for that reason.

The remarriage of a person who is receiving alimony or spousal support does not necessarily end a former spouse's obligation to pay it; however, that fact is usually a persuasive reason for a court to modify its judgment. The death of either party usually terminates the obligation to pay alimony or spousal support, although some state statutes authorize the continuance of alimony payments from the estate of the deceased spouse.

Courts, in most instances, will reserve the right to modify an alimony or spousal support award. Under some state laws, if the court does not reserve the right to do so in its judgment, the judgment cannot be changed after the expiration of the appeal period. Some states allow an alimony or spousal support award to be modified by agreement of the parties.

Many states have **equitable distribution laws** that give courts the power to distribute property equitably or fairly between the parties upon divorce. Both parties are usually required to disclose their financial situation and provide paycheck stubs and income tax returns. Although the spouses are considered to jointly own the marital estate, the court is given authority to determine how to divide the property in a way that is thought to be fair and just. State statutes often provide criteria to be followed by the court in making the distribution. Equitable distribution is not used in the minority of states that are community property states, where generally all property (and debts) acquired by the spouses during their marriage is split equally at divorce.

SUPPORT AND CUSTODY OF CHILDREN

The legal obligations of parents to contribute to the economic maintenance and education of their children is known as **child support** or **maintenance**. Parents are required to support their minor children who are not **emancipated**—that is, legally freed from parental control. In a divorce proceeding, the parties may set the amount of child support by agreement, subject to approval of the court, or the court may determine the amount. Under the Uniform Reciprocal Enforcement of Support Act (1950), which has been adopted by every state in the United States in its original or revised form (1968), a support order of one state can be enforced in every state.

The welfare or best interest of the child is the most important factor in determining the **custody of children**—that is, their care, control, and maintenance. In deciding who shall have **physical custody** of a child (which is the day-to-day care the child, including the place of his or her residence), the court considers the following: the stability of the person seeking custody; the physical safety of the child; and the emotional, social, spiritual, and economic needs of the child. The child's wishes are also considered in determining who shall have custody.

Temporary custody of children is often awarded to a parent, pending the outcome of a divorce or separation action. When the court orders **divided custody** of a child, it means that the child will live with each parent part of the year, the other parent usually having visitation rights. The parent with whom the child is living has complete control over the child during that period. In contrast, when the court orders **joint custody** of a child, both parents share the responsibility and authority of child rearing regardless of where the child resides at a given time.

TERMS IN ACTION

Frequently, a **child custody** battle will be part of a divorce. The spouse who wins physical custody of the couple's child or children will also receive the child support payments that have to be made by the other spouse. **Child support** payments are based on a formula that includes as a variable the paying spouse's income. Some celebrities' child support obligations make become newsworthy, at least the entertainment news. In the Britney Spears–Kevin Federline divorce (mentioned in Chapter 38), Federline won custody of the couple's two sons, and the court ordered Spears to pay $20,000 a month in child support. The mother of one of the children of rapper Sean "P. Diddy" Combs won an increase of her child support payments in 2004, when a magistrate ordered Combs to up his $5,000 monthly payments to $35,000. Actor Charie Sheen owes an awful lot of child support: $55,00 a month for the children he shares with his second wife, Denise Richards; and $55,000 a month for the children he shares with his third wife, Brooke Mueller. In 2016, he went to court seeking reductions of both child support orders, on the grounds that his income has drastically shrunk. Entertainment mogul Russell Simmons, who was married to model and reality TV performer Kimora Lee Simmons, agreed in his divorce settlement to pay $40,000 a month in child support for the care of the couple's two daughters, until each is 19½ years old. Additionally, Mr. Simmons agreed that every three years he would provide a new car worth at least $60,000 for his daughters' use. And in 2010, billionaire Kirk Kerkorian consented to pay what may be the highest child support payment schedule … to a daughter his ex-wife acknowledged wasn't actually his biological child. Approximately 93 years old at the time, Kerkorian agreed to pay $10 million in back support to the 12-year-old girl and then $100,000 per month until she reached 19 or was a full-time student, at which time the payments would be cut in half. In 2014, a judge ruled against Kerkorian's ex-wife, who sought to have her child support payments increased to $500,000 per month. Kerkorian died in 2015, leaving behind a $4 billion estate.

Sources: usatoday.com; cnbc.com; eonline.com; nydailynews.com; nbclosangeles.com; pagesix.com; nytimes.com

Reviewing What You Learned

After studying the chapter, write the answers to each of the following questions:

1. In former years, what terms described the plaintiff, the defendant, and the initial pleading in a divorce action?

   ____

   ____

   ____

2. What factors determine jurisdiction in a divorce action or dissolution petition? _______________________________________

   ____

   ____

   ____

3. What is the difference between a residence and a domicile?

   ____

   ____

4. How many domiciles can a person have at any given time?

   ____

   ____

5. In an ex parte foreign divorce, do one, both, or neither of the parties appear in the foreign jurisdiction? _______________________________________

   ____

   ____

   ____

6. On what ground may an ex parte foreign divorce be attacked?

   ____

   ____

   ____

7. On what theory were the traditional defenses to divorce actions based? _________________________

____

____

8. What is the difference between connivance and collusion?

____

____

____

9. From what common law right does the concept of alimony and spousal support stem? _________________________

____

____

10. What is considered in determining the amount of alimony and spousal support that may be awarded? _________________________

____

____

11. What is the most important factor in determining the custody of children? _________________________

____

____

Understanding Legal Concepts

Indicate whether each statement is true or false. Then, change the italicized word or phrase of each false statement to make it true.

ANSWERS

_____ **1.** In many states, the person bringing a divorce action used to be called the *libelee.*

_____ **2.** In a divorce action, jurisdiction is based on the *residence* of the plaintiff.

_____ **3.** All states except *Alaska, South Dakota, and Washington* require the plaintiff in a divorce action to reside in their state a minimum time before filing for a divorce.

_____ **4.** The doctrine of *comity* applies to the acceptance of judicial proceedings of foreign countries.

_____ **5.** A bilateral foreign divorce may be attacked by the spouse who did not appear and declared void on the ground of *lack of jurisdiction* of the court granting the divorce.

_____ **6.** The *traditional defenses* to divorce actions were based on the theory that a divorce is granted because one party was at fault and the other was not.

_____ **7.** The common law doctrine of *connivance* held that neither party could obtain a divorce when both were guilty of a marital wrong.

_____ **8.** Today, *many* states award alimony or spousal support payments to either the ex-husband or the ex-wife.

_____ **9.** A set formula *exists* for determining the amount of alimony that may be awarded.

_____ **10.** A child's wishes *are not* considered in determining who shall have custody of the child.

Checking Terminology

From the list of legal terms that follows, select the one that matches each definition.

ANSWERS

a. alimony
b. appearance
c. bilateral foreign divorce
d. child support
e. collusion
f. comity
g. condonation
h. connivance
i. custody of children
j. decree
k. divided custody
l. domicile
m. emancipated
n. equitable distribution laws

_____ **1.** The plaintiff in a divorce action (no longer used by some states).

_____ **2.** A person's principal place of abode; the place to which, whenever one is absent, he or she has the present intent of returning.

_____ **3.** The place of litigation.

_____ **4.** The voluntary submission to the court's jurisdiction, either in person or by an agent.

_____ **5.** The initial pleading in a divorce action (no longer used by some states).

_____ **6.** A rule of law requiring that full faith and credit be given by each state to the judicial proceedings of every other state.

_____ **7.** A divorce that occurs when both parties make an appearance in a foreign state or country.

_____ **8.** A divorce that occurs when one spouse appears in a foreign jurisdiction and the other spouse does not appear and fails to respond to the notice of divorce or service of process.

_____ **9.** The forgiveness of a matrimonial offense.

o. ex parte foreign divorce
p. foreign divorce
q. foreign jurisdiction
r. forum
s. full faith and credit clause
t. interlocutory decree
u. joint custody
v. judgment nisi
w. libel
x. libelant
y. libelee
z. maintenance
aa. pendente lite
bb. petition
cc. petitioner
dd. physical custody
ee. proceeding
ff. recrimination
gg. residence
hh. respondent
ii. response
jj. spousal support
kk. temporary custody

_____ **10.** An agreement between a husband and wife that one of them will commit a marital offense so that the other may obtain a divorce.

_____ **11.** An allowance made to a divorced spouse by a former spouse for support and maintenance. (Select two answers.)

_____ **12.** The defendant in a divorce action (no longer used by some states).

_____ **13.** A decision of a court of equity.

_____ **14.** A provisional or temporary decision of a court. (Select two answers.)

_____ **15.** Another state or country.

_____ **16.** A place where a person actually lives.

_____ **17.** A doctrine stating that the courts of one jurisdiction will give effect to the laws and judicial decisions of another jurisdiction, not as a matter of obligation, but out of deference and respect.

_____ **18.** The plaintiff's secret cooperation in the commission of a marital wrong by the defendant, which is a common law defense to an action for divorce.

_____ **19.** Conduct on the part of the plaintiff that constitutes a ground for divorce, which is a common law defense to an action for divorce.

_____ **20.** Litigation pending.

_____ **21.** The procedure for obtaining a dissolution of marriage.

_____ **22.** A written application for a court order.

_____ **23.** One who presents a petition to a court.

_____ **24.** One who is called on to answer a petition.

_____ **25.** The written answer to a petition filed by a respondent.

_____ **26.** Freed from parental control.

_____ **27.** The legal obligations of parents to contribute to the economic maintenance and education of their children. (Select two answers.)

_____ **28.** The care, control, and maintenance of children.

_____ **29.** Custody in which the child will live with each parent part of the year, the other parent usually having visitation rights, but not control of the child during that period.

_____ **30.** A divorce in a state or country other than that in which the party lives.

_____ **31.** Custody in which both parents share the responsibility and authority of childrearing.

_____ **32.** Custody of a child awarded to a parent on a temporary basis, pending the outcome of a divorce or separation action.

_____ **33.** The day-to-day custody of a child, including residence.

Using Legal Language

Read the following story and fill in the blank lines with legal terms taken from the list of terms at the beginning of this chapter:

Some years ago, before no-fault divorce was readily available, Rodney brought a divorce action against Heather on the ground of adultery. He was the _____________________, she was the _____________________, and the initial pleading was called a(n) _____________________. The _____________________—that is, the place of litigation—where Rodney brought the action was located in his principal place of abode, known as his _____________________. Because it was the place where he actually, presently lived, it was also his _____________________. Before the action, Heather had agreed with Rodney to commit adultery so that he could divorce her, which unwittingly set up the defense

of _____________________ if Heather wanted to use it. In addition, Rodney secretly arranged to have his friend Rudolph spend the weekend with Heather while he was out of town, making available to her the defense of _____________________. In addition, Rodney deserted Heather, leaving her without means for support. Because this conduct was on the part of the plaintiff, which constituted a ground for divorce, it was also a defense called _____________________. Before the case went to trial, the parties forgave each other for their indiscretions, and the two resumed cohabitation, which created the defense of _____________________. Their reunion did not work out, however, and Heather decided to go to Haiti, a _____________________________, to obtain an overnight divorce. Rodney refused to voluntarily submit to that court's jurisdiction by filing a(n) ________________________, which meant that this was a(n) ________________________ action rather than a(n) _____________________ action. As a result, the doctrine of ________________________, stating that the courts of one jurisdiction will give effect to the laws and judicial decisions of another jurisdiction, did not apply. Heather did not ask for _________________________—that is, an allowance for support and maintenance—as part of the court's ______________________ (decision).

PART NINE

Terms Used in Business Organizations and Bankruptcy

George Doyle/Stockbyte/Getty Images

CHAPTER 40
Business Organizations

CHAPTER 41
The Law of Bankruptcy

9

Before opening a business, an entrepreneur should give serious thought to the type of business organization best suited for her or his particular endeavor. Similarly and unfortunately, when a business fails or an individual suffers financial loss, consideration must be given to the need for and benefits of filing for bankruptcy. Chapter 40 discusses the principal kinds of business organizations, including the sole proprietorship, the partnership, the corporation, the limited liability company, the joint venture, and the franchise. Chapter 41 explains bankruptcy proceedings generally, including pointing out some of the sweeping changes made by the U.S. Congress in 2005 when it overhauled the federal bankruptcy code. Included in that chapter is a discussion of exemptions provided by the bankruptcy code and an examination of the different types of bankruptcy proceedings.

40

Business Organizations

ANTE INTERROGATORY

A business that combines limited liability for all owners with single taxation, but requires the creators to choose a jurisdiction in which to register is a (A) limited liability company, (B) partnership, (C) C corporation, (D) limited partnership.

LEARNING OBJECTIVES

LO 1: Define a sole proprietorship and list a primary advantage and disadvantage of a sole proprietorship

LO 2: Define a partnership and distinguish it from a limited partnership

LO 3: Contrast a limited partnership from a limited liability partnership

LO 4: Summarize the process a partnership goes through when it is in dissolution

LO 5: Explain what a corporation is, including how it is created and who owns it, how it is owned, and who manages it

LO 6: Compare and contrast a limited liability company with a partnership and corporation

LO 7: Define a joint venture

LO 8: Summarize what a franchise is and how it comes into existence

KEY TERMS

articles of incorporation
articles of organization
benefit corporation
blue sky laws
C corporation
certificate of incorporation
charter
close corporation
common stock
co-partnership
corporation
co-venture
de facto corporation
de jure corporation

derivative action
directors
dissociation
dissolution
dividends
domestic corporation
dormant partner
double taxation
eleemosynary corporation
foreign corporation
franchise
franchisee
franchiser
franchise disclosure document
general partner

general partnership	ostensible partner
incorporators	partnership
joint enterprise	preferred stock
joint venture	promoters
limited liability company (LLC)	S corporation
limited liability limited partnership (LLLP)	secret partner
limited liability partnership (LLP)	shareholders
limited partner	silent partners
limited partnership	sole proprietorship
liquidate	stock certificate
managers	stockholders
members	syndicate
nominal partner	ultra vires act
not-for-profit corporation	unlimited liability
operating agreement	winding-up period

WEBSITES FOR PRONUNCIATION HELP

http://dictionary.cambridge.org/us/pronunciation/english/audio

https://www.howtopronounce.com

There are almost limitless ways to make money in business endeavors, but only a select number of business organizations or entities to use in which to operate a business. The principal kinds of business organizations are the sole proprietorship, partnership, corporation, and limited liability company. Joint ventures and franchises are also commonly used.

SOLE PROPRIETORSHIP

A **sole proprietorship** is a form of an unincorporated business that is owned and controlled by one person. Because one shareholder can own a corporation, it is important to think of a sole proprietorship as a one-owner, unincorporated business. It is the least formal type of business organization, having few requirements for its establishment and being subject to less government regulation than more elaborate forms of business ownership. Generally, no state statutes exist regulating the creation and operation of sole proprietorships (except where the type of business created requires a certain registration or license), unlike what exists for partnerships and corporations and limited liability companies. Everything from a lemonade stand in the front yard to a lawyer practicing law without any other law partners can qualify as a sole proprietorship. According to the Center for Tax Policy, there are more than 23 million sole proprietorships in America, overwhelmingly the highest number of business organizations.

Although a sole proprietor owns and controls the business, a sole proprietor may hire employees and outside business consultants. Unlike a partnership (to be discussed later), the employees are not owners. A sole proprietor receives all profits and incurs all losses, and is taxed personally on business profits. Single taxation is one of the historical advantages of an unincorporated business, such as a sole proprietorship. In contrast, corporations are subject to double taxation: corporate taxes for the corporate income; and if the net income is then paid to the shareholders as dividends, the shareholders must pay personal income taxes on that income. Double taxation is discussed later in this chapter in the section on corporations. The biggest disadvantage of a sole proprietorship is that the proprietor has **unlimited liability** for all debts and liabilities incurred from its operation, which means that the proprietor is personally liable for every debt and judgment against the business, no matter how large. Unlimited liability is liability without boundaries. A sole proprietorship comes to an end at the owner's death, but the business assets can pass to the proprietor's heirs.

PARTNERSHIPS

A **partnership** (sometimes called a **co-partnership**) is an association of two or more persons for the purpose of carrying on as co-owners in a business for profit. It may be created by an oral or written agreement of the parties, by an informal arrangement between them, or by their conduct. Simply doing business together with another person can be enough to create a partnership whether or not the parties intend such an arrangement. Partnership law is based on either the Uniform Partnership Act (UPA), which was adopted by every state except Louisiana, or the Revised Uniform Partnership Act (RUPA), which itself has been revised numerous times and is enacted in over 35 states and the District of Columbia. The significance of the existence of these laws is that a state's version of the UPA or RUPA will control what happens in partnership matters (between the partners), unless the partners have a written partnership agreement that covers those issues.

A **general partnership** is one in which the parties carry on a business for the joint benefit and profit of all partners. In this type of partnership, every partner is an agent of the partnership for business purposes, which means that every general partner has equal management authority. Similarly, every partner is personally liable for the debts and wrongdoings caused by every other partner while transacting partnership business. This is known as unlimited liability and is the principal disadvantage of a partnership. For instance, if a partner is out of town when the other partner commits negligence while working on partnership business, both partners are personally liable.

A **limited partnership** is a partnership formed by two or more persons and having as members one or more general partners and one or more limited partners. **General partners** manage the business and are personally liable for its debts and obligations. **Limited partners** invest money or other property in the business, but are not personally liable for the limited partnership's debts or obligations. Their liability is limited to the extent of their financial investments. As a condition of their limited liability, they may not participate in the operation of the business. Also, the surname of a limited partner may not be used in the partnership name unless it is also the name of a general partner. Unlike a general partnership, a limited partnership must have a partnership agreement and can't come into existence without state approval. In order to create a limited partnership, the partners must file a certificate of limited partnership with their state and pay the required fees. Included in a certificate of limited partnerships are the name of the limited partnership and the name and address of any general partner.

Word Wise
Hyphenated Words

A hyphen is often used to join two words to form a compound word. Some words join together to describe a noun, as in "well-known actress," "winding-up period," "English-speaking people," and "blue-sky laws."

A hyphen usually separates a prefix from a capital letter, as in "un-American" or "non-European." Some prefixes, such as "self-," "all-," and "ex-," always require hyphens, as in "self-control," "all-inclusive," and "ex-parte foreign divorce."

A hyphen facilitates reading when the same vowels appear together, as in "de-emphasize" (rather than "deemphasize") and helps to clarify meaning when a prefix causes confusion, as in the homonymous "recreation" (a pleasurable activity) and "re-creation" (a new creation).

There is a type of partnership that removes the aspect of unlimited liability—the chief disadvantage of a general partnership. This is the **limited liability partnership (LLP)**, a partnership in which only the partnership as a whole, and not the individual partners, is liable for the *tort* liabilities of the partnership. In some states, only the partnership as a whole, and not the individual partners, is liable for the *contractual* liabilities of the partnership as well. First created in Texas in 1991 but now allowed in many states, a limited liability partnership is established by filing the required registration form and paying a filing fee to the appropriate state office, usually the Secretary of State. Essentially, a partner in an LLP has personal liability for her or his own negligence, but would have limited liability for another partner's negligence. LLPs are popular business forms for those providing professional services (attorneys and doctors, for example) and some states limit the use of LLPs to named professions. The combination of a limited partnership and a limited liability partnership is called a **limited liability limited partnership (LLLP)**. Not every state recognizes an LLLP and where allowed, they are common for real estate businesses.

Various and often interchangeable words are used to refer to partners, which can be confusing to distinguish. **Nominal partners**, also called **ostensible partners**, are partners in name only. Their names appear in some way in connection with the business in order to make it appear that they are partners, including allowing their credit to as if they were partners, but they have no real interest in the partnership. Those who qualify as nominal or ostensible partners open themselves up to partnership liability. **Silent partners** are ones who may be known to the public as partners, but who take no active part in the business in the way a limited partner doesn't. **Dormant partners** are not known to the public as partners and take no active part in the business, similar to limited partners. **Secret partners** take an active part in the business, but are not known to the public as partners.

Partners cannot transfer their interest in the partnership to other people without the consent of all other partners. In addition, any partner may end a partnership at any time by withdrawing from it. Partnerships do not last forever and begin to end when **dissolution** occurs. Dissolution is an act or occurrence that requires the partnership to eventually terminate. The causes of dissolution range from acts of the partners (voting to dissolve) to an act of a court (ordering dissolution) to automatic dissolution by operation of law. For example, the UPA states that when any partner dies, the partnership goes into dissolution. The RUPA takes a different approach to dissolution and doesn't require it when a partner dies. It uses the term "**dissociation**" in addition to dissolution and creates situations where events that under the UPA would have required dissolution now, under the RUPA, provide for dissociation. Dissociation means a change in the relationship caused by a partner ceasing to be associated in carrying on the business. Death of a partner is part of dissociation, and the RUPA provides that the surviving partners can buy out the dead partner's share of the business and continue the partnership. Bear in mind, though, that under either a UPA or RUPA jurisdiction, a partnership agreement can provide for continuation of the partnership despite the death of a partner (except where there is only one surviving partner).

After a partnership is in dissolution, a **winding-up period** occurs next. During this time, an accounting is made to determine what the value of each partner's share is, assets are **liquidated** (turned into cash), notification is made to alert creditors and the world at large that the partnership will cease to be in business on a certain date. Partnership assets are liquidated (reduced to cash by selling them) and any remaining assets are distributed among the partners or the heirs of deceased partners according to the terms of the partnership agreement. The UPA provides the following order for distributing the partnership's assets: (1) outside creditors (banks, etc.); (2) inside creditors (partners who have loaned money to the partnership; (3) payment of capital contributions; and (4) payment of retained profits. At the conclusion of the winding-up period, the partnership is said to be terminated.

TERMS IN ACTION

Some of the biggest publicly traded **corporations** in America began as **partnerships**. The movie studio Warner Bros. was formed by four brothers, Sam, Jack, Albert, and Harry Warner, Polish Jews who had immigrated to America in 1889. They revolutionized the film industry when they released "The Jazz Singer" in 1927, the first movie with live talking (called a "talkie"). Before Ray Krok bought the entire McDonald's business for $2.7 million in 1961, it was a fast-food **franchise** created by Richard and Maurice McDonald in 1948. Ice cream favorite Ben & Jerry's is now owned by the Dutch conglomerate Unilever, but it began when Ben Cohen and Jerry Greenfield, who met in the seventh grade, opened their first ice cream shop in Vermont in 1978 after taking a $5 correspondence course in ice cream making from Penn State University. Their initial venture cost them $12,000, and that ice cream shop was in a former gasoline station. Computer giant Hewlett-Packard is considered

(Continued)

the first Silicon Valley tech company and is the offspring of the partnership of Bill Hewlett and David Packard, who began working part-time out of a rented garage, making sound equipment. They eventually formed a partnership in 1939, flipping a coin to determine whose name would be first. But later they transformed their partnership into a corporation, which was listed on the New York Stock Exchange in 1961. Other Silicon Valley tech giants got their start as partnerships, including Google (now formally known as Alphabet), founded by Larry Page and Sergey Brin in 1998. Twitter was founded as a partnership in 2006 by Evan Williams, Biz Stone, and Jack Dorsey. Although Bill Gates—the richest person in the world, as of this writing—is whom one naturally thinks of when it comes to Microsoft, he co-founded that original partnership with Paul Allen, who first met Gates in 1968 at the private school in Seattle they both attended. And fittingly, Apple wasn't started just by Steve Jobs. His partner was Steve Wozniak, whom Jobs met in the early 1970s through Wozniak's employment—at Hewlett-Packard. In 1976, Jobs and Wozniak took on a third partner, Ronald Wayne, who was the elder statesman of the three (he was 42 and Jobs was 21). He was given 10% of the partnership. Wayne not only drafted Apple's partnership agreement, he designed the first Apple logo, which lasted a year. Wayne lasted 12 days at Apple, being frightened off by the prospect of being saddled with the suppliers' bills if Apple's initial customers didn't pay theirs. Jobs and Wozniak had no money at that time and Wayne had experienced such business debts five years earlier. So Wayne returned his 10% and was paid $800. When Apple incorporated in 1977, Wayne was paid $1500 to give up any claims he might ever have against the company. Doing the math on how much Ronald Wayne would be worth today had he not left Apple will make you as gobsmacked as it no doubt has done to him a time or two.

Source: images.businessweek.com; businessinsider.com; imakenews.com; mercurynews.com; edibleapple.com; visual.ly

CORPORATIONS

A **corporation** is a legal entity, created under state law, with the power to conduct its affairs as though it were a person. It is distinct from a sole proprietorship and a partnership in that, as a true entity, it has a life distinct of its owners. (Corporations can be created as nonprofit, but this chapter's primary focus is on business corporations.) It comes into existence when the state government issues a **certificate of incorporation** (sometimes called **articles of incorporation** or **charter**), which is applied for by one or more persons known as **incorporators**. **Promoters** are people who are used sometimes to begin a corporation by obtaining investors and taking control up to the time of the corporation's existence.

When a corporation is established in strict compliance with the law, it is called a **de jure corporation**. In contrast, if a technical defect in its establishment occurs (such as if the incorporators neglected to properly file the article of incorporation), the result is a **de facto corporation**. It exists in fact, although not by right, and it must be recognized as a valid corporation unless set aside by the state. Any corporate act done outside of the corporation's authority as set forth in its charter is called an **ultra vires act** and can be challenged by a stockholder or other affected party. For example, if a corporation's bylaws state that the chief executive officer (CEO) may not be paid more than 15 times the salary or wages of the lowest-paid employee, then the corporation would be engaged in an ultra vires act if it hired a new CEO and paid him or her a salary 20 times that of the lowest-paid employee. A corporation that is created for charitable and benevolent purposes is known as an **eleemosynary corporation**, or, more commonly, a **not-for-profit corporation**. A **domestic corporation** is organized in the state in which it is operating. In contrast, a **foreign corporation** is organized in a state other than that in which it is operating.

Stockholders (also called **shareholders**) own a corporation. They are not personally responsible for the debts and liabilities of the corporation and can lose only their investment in the company's shares, in a worst-case scenario of the corporation ending in bankruptcy. This rule of law is the essence of the advantage of limited liability that corporations have and is a primary reason for incorporating a business, but its benefit is for the shareholders. When stockholders die, their shares of stock pass to their heirs and the corporation continues in existence. Shares of stock may be sold or given away to other people by stockholders at any time unless the corporation is a **close corporation**, which has restrictions on the transfer of shares. In a close corporation (sometimes known as a closely held corporation), a stockholder who wishes to sell stock to someone else often must first offer to sell it to the corporation or to another shareholder. In this way, the ownership of the corporation can be kept within a limited group of people. Close, or closely held, corporations are often family-owned or owned by a few shareholders.

Because the income that a corporation earns is taxed directly by the federal government and because dividends paid to stockholders are also taxed, corporate income is taxed twice, a process referred to as **double taxation**. A corporation that is taxed in this manner is called a **C corporation**, a corporation governed by Subchapter C of the Internal Revenue Code. To avoid double taxation, small corporations can elect to be treated as S corporations. An **S corporation** is governed by Subchapter S of the Internal Revenue Code, which stipulates that the income of the corporation will be taxed directly to the shareholders rather than to the corporation itself. Requirements for S corporation status include the corporation having no more than 100 shareholders, all of whom must be U.S. citizens or resident aliens.

At one time, every stockholder was issued a **stock certificate**, which was physical evidence of ownership of stock in the corporation. Now, most stockholders don't receive stock certificates; instead, a shareholder's ownership is noted electronically. **Common stock** is voting stock with no preferences. Common stockholders have the right to vote, the right to receive profits (called **dividends**) if the board of directors declares them, and the right to receive their proportionate share of capital when the corporation is dissolved. **Preferred stock** is stock that has a superior right to dividends and to capital when the corporation is dissolved. Preferred stockholders usually have no voting rights.

A company's board of directors is legally obligated to manage the corporation, and to do so as a fiduciary for the shareholders. Members of the board of directors are elected by the shareholders at their annual meeting. **Directors** are given legal responsibility to manage the corporation in the best interests of the shareholders. Corporate officers, including a president and a chief financial officer, are appointed by the board of directors and are responsible for the daily operation of the corporate business.

When directors refuse to bring a lawsuit on behalf of the corporation against a third party to which it is entitled, a stockholder can bring a derivative action to enforce the right of the corporation. A **derivative action** is a suit by a stockholder to enforce a corporate cause of action. If a shareholder wins the derivative action, the damages are paid back to the corporation, not to the shareholders personally. See the Terms in Action below for a quick summary of an especially famous shareholders' derivative action

Both federal and state law (statutes, regulations and case law) regulates the sale corporate stock, when those corporations are over a certain financial size. State laws that regulate corporate stock are known as **Blue Sky Laws** and part of their purpose is to protect the public from the sale of worthless stocks. A more recent type of business corporation is the benefit corporation. In 2010, Maryland became the first state to provide a statutory scheme for the creation of benefit corporations. As of this writing and according to the website, benefitcorp.net, 33 states and the District of Columbia allow for benefit corporations. Essentially, a benefit corporations differs from a traditional for-profit corporations in three primary ways: 1) their purpose must be to provide a general benefit to society or the environment; 2) their accountability standards require that major decisions be made after considering the effects such decisions will have on stakeholders (more than shareholders, this would include

TERMS IN ACTION

Two shareholders of the Disney Corporation sued the Disney Board of Directors in 1997, seeking $260 million in a derivative action. At the heart of the lawsuit was the allegation that the board members were negligent in their duty to the shareholders when, in 1995, the board approved of a $140 million severance payment to President Michael Ovitz, who had been fired by CEO Michael Eisner, after just 14 months of working for Eisner. When he hired Ovitz, Eisner referred to him as "my best friend," but a little over a year later, Eisner concluded that Ovitz had to go. Ovitz's contract called for that gigantic payment to be made if he was fired without cause (which he was, since no formal accusation of wrongdoing precipitated his firing), and the shareholders claimed that by

(Continued)

failing to carefully inspect Ovitz's employment contract before approving it, and by failing to fire him for cause due to his wasteful spending and inactivity during his time at Disney, the board was liable for such mismanagement and should have to pay that money back to the corporation (rather than to the shareholders, personally), which is the purposes of a derivative action. The suit was filed in the Delaware Court of Chancery in 1997, and in 2005 the judge ruled in favor of the Disney Board. He concluded that the directors (which included Michael Eisner, who was the Chairman of the Disney Board, and also included Ovitz, himself, although the judge ruled Ovitz had no fiduciary duty to Disney when he negotiated his employment contract because he wasn't a Disney employee at that time) didn't violate their fiduciary duty to the shareholder and were protected by a doctrine known as the business judgment rule. But the judge didn't exactly praise the board for its actions, either, writing that the board's conduct "fell significantly short of the best practices of ideal corporate governance." In 2006, the Delaware Supreme Court affirmed the decision.

Sources: cfo.com; variety.com; latimes.com; nytimes.com; slate.com; *In re Walt Disney Co. Derivative Action*, 907 A.2d 693 (Del. Ch. 2005); *In re Walt Disney Co. Derivative Action*, 906 A.2d 27 (Del. 2006)

employees, the community, and even the environment); and 3) their transparency requirements include annually reporting on their businesses' social and environmental performance. As opposed to traditional business corporations, a benefit corporation is not legally obligated to maximize profits for shareholders exclusively. Outdoor clothing and gear company Patagonia, is a California corporation that became a benefit corporation in 2012, when California first allowed such a corporate form

LIMITED LIABILITY COMPANY

A relatively new type of business organization has developed in recent years that is neither a partnership nor a corporation, but that combines some aspects of both. A **limited liability company (LLC)** is a form of business organization that has the tax benefits of a partnership and the limited liability benefits of a corporation. Owners of a limited liability company are called **members**. Rather than having articles of incorporation, an LLC has **articles of organization**, and rather than having bylaws, a limited liability company has an **operating agreement**, which sets forth the rights and obligations of the members and establishes the rules of operation. In place of officers to run the company, the LLC is managed either by its members or by **managers**, people designated by the members to manage the LLC. Like stockholders of a corporation, members of an LLC are not liable for the contractual or tort liabilities of the business. A limited liability company is established by filing articles of organization with the Secretary of State's office and paying the required filing fee. LLCs seem similar to Subchapter S corporations in that both entities provide limited liability and single taxation, but the strict IRS rules on establishing and maintaining Subchapter S status don't apply to LLCs, such as limitations on the number of owners (members).

JOINT VENTURE

A **joint venture**, also called a **joint enterprise**, **co-venture**, or **syndicate**, is an enterprise relationship in which two or more people combine their labor or property for a single business undertaking. It differs from a partnership in that it involves only one undertaking and comes to an end at the completion of the undertaking. Like partners, joint venturers have unlimited liability. Each is responsible for the others' wrongdoings conducted within the scope of the joint venture. Hulu, the online video site, is the result of a joint venture between NBC Universal, Fox Broadcasting/News Corp., and the Walt Disney Company.

FRANCHISE

A **franchise** is an arrangement in which the owner of a trademark, trade name, or copyright licenses others, under special conditions or limitations, to use the trademark, trade name, or copyright in purveying goods and/or services. Many fast-food chains use the franchise method of conducting business. In fact, the top global franchises, as of this writing, are McDonalds, Subway, KFC, Burger King, and Pizza Hut. The **franchiser** (sometimes spelled franchisor, is the person or business who gives a franchise to another), and the **franchisee** (the person or business to whom a franchise is given) are considered to be independent contractors with respect to each other, and their respective rights and duties are governed by the contract between them as regulated by state and federal laws. The Federal Trade Commission requires franchisors to provide prospective franchisees with a **franchise disclosure document** (FDD) at least 14 days prior to the franchisee signing any franchise agreement or paying any money to the franchisor. The franchise disclosure document has 23 required sections, giving information on franchise costs and fees, estimated initial investment requirements, the franchisor's litigation history, the number of franchises in existence, and more.

Web Wise

- To do research on cases and statutes concerning partnership law, go to https://www.law. cornell.edu/wex/Partnership#
- Find the most popular stock certificates for sale (not necessarily the shares themselves) at http://www.giveashare.com
- Read more on limited liability companies, including reasons why a member could lose limited liability, at http://legaldictionary.net/limited-liability-company/
- Find more information on franchising at this webpage of the Federal Trade Commission: https:// www.ftc.gov/tips-advice/business-center/guidance/consumers-guide-buying-franchise

Reviewing What You Learned

After studying the chapter, write the answers to each of the following questions:

1. Describe what happens to a sole proprietorship when the owner dies. ____

2. In what ways may a partnership be created? ____

3. What is the principal disadvantage of a partnership? ____

4. What is the difference between a general partner and a limited partner? ____

5. In what ways do silent partners, dormant partners, and secret partners differ? ____

6. Summarize the process that occurs when a partnership is dissolved. ____

7. Under what conditions does a corporation come into existence? ____

8. What is a principal advantage of the corporate form of business organization? _______________________

____

____

____

9. Compare what happens to a corporation when a stockholder dies with what happens to a partnership when a partner dies.

____

____

____

____

10. In a close corporation, what must a stockholder do before selling stock to someone else?

____

____

____

____

____

____

11. What is the difference between common stock and preferred stock?

____

____

____

12. What is the purpose and function of a corporation's board of directors?

____

____

____

13. How does a joint venture differ from a partnership?

____

____

____

Understanding Legal Concepts

Indicate whether each statement is true or false. Then, change the italicized word or phrase of each false statement to make it true.

ANSWERS

_______ **1.** A sole proprietorship is the *most* formal type of business organization.

_______ **2.** A partnership *may only be* created by a written agreement.

_______ **3.** In a general partnership, *every partner* is an agent of the partnership for business purposes.

_______ **4.** Limited partners *are liable* for the debts or obligations of the partnership.

_______ **5.** Dormant partners take *an active* part in the business and are not known to the public as partners.

_______ **6.** When a corporation is established in strict compliance with the law, it is called a *de facto* corporation.

_______ **7.** Stockholders of a corporation *are not* personally responsible for the debts and liabilities of the corporation and can lose only the amount they paid for the stock.

_______ **8.** *Preferred* stockholders usually have no voting rights.

_______ **9.** A joint venture differs from a *partnership* in that it involves only one undertaking and comes to an end at the completion of the undertaking.

_______ **10.** Franchisers and franchisees are considered to be *independent contractors*.

Checking Terminology (Part A)

From the list of legal terms that follows, select the one that matches each definition.

ANSWERS

a. articles of organization
b. article of incorporation
c. benefit corporation
d. blue-sky laws
e. C corporation
f. certificate of incorporation
g. charter
h. close corporation
i. common stock
j. co-partnership
k. co-venture
l. de facto corporation
m. de jure corporation
n. derivative action
o. directors
p. dividends
q. domestic corporation
r. dormant partner
s. double taxation
t. eleemosynary corporation
u. foreign corporation
v. franchise
w. franchisee
x. franchiser
y. general partner
z. general partnership
aa. incorporators
bb. joint enterprise
cc. joint venture
dd. not-for-profit
ee. corporation
ff. Syndicate

_____ 1. Profits distributed to the stockholders of a corporation.

_____ 2. An arrangement in which the owner of a trademark, trade name, or copyright licenses others, under special conditions or limitations, to use the trademark, trade name, or copyright in purveying goods or services.

_____ 3. A for profit corporation whose purpose is to seek some societal or environmental goal.

_____ 4. A legal entity created under state law with the power to conduct its affairs as though it were a natural person.

_____ 5. A person who gives a franchise to another.

_____ 6. A document that gives authority to an organization to do business as a corporation. (Select four answers.)

_____ 7. Taxes on a corporation's income and on the dividends earned by the corporation's stockholders.

_____ 8. People who are elected by stockholders to manage a corporation.

_____ 9. A corporation organized in a state other than the one in which it is operating.

_____ 10. People who organize a corporation by filing articles of organization with the state government.

_____ 11. State laws designed to protect the public from the sale of worthless stocks.

_____ 12. A partner who manages the business and is personally liable for its debts and obligations.

_____ 13. A partner who is not known to the public as a partner and who takes no active part in the business.

_____ 14. A corporation that is established in strict compliance with the law.

_____ 15. An enterprise relationship in which two or more people combine their labor or property for a single business undertaking. (Select four answers.)

_____ 16. A corporation that is governed by Subchapter C of the Internal Revenue Code and that pays corporate taxes on its income.

_____ 17. A partnership in which the parties carry on a business for the joint benefit and profit of all partners.

_____ 18. A corporation that is created for charitable and benevolent purposes. (Select two answers.)

_____ 19. A corporation that has a defect in its establishment, but that must be recognized as a valid corporation unless set aside by the state.

_____ 20. A corporation that has restrictions on the transfer of shares.

_____ 21. A corporation that was organized in the state in which it is operating.

_____ 22. Stock that has no preferences, but that gives the owner the right to vote.

_____ 23. A suit by a stockholder to enforce a corporate cause of action.

Checking Terminology (Part B)

From the list of legal terms that follows, select the one that matches each definition.

ANSWERS

a. co-partnership
b. dissolution
c. limited liability company (LLC)
d. limited liability limited partnership (LLLP)
e. limited liability partnership (LLP)
f. limited partner
g. limited partnership

_____ 1. Stock that has a superior right to dividends and capital when the corporation is dissolved.

_____ 2. A partner in name only, who has no real interest in the partnership. (Select two answers.)

_____ 3. A form of business that is owned and operated by one person.

_____ 4. A general partnership in which only the partnership, and not the individual partners, is liable for the tort liabilities of the partnership.

_____ 5. People who are designated by its members to manage a limited liability company.

_____ 6. A partner who takes an active part in the business, but is not known to the public as a partner.

_____ 7. A partner who invests money or other property in the business, but who is not liable for the debts or obligations of the partnership.

h. liquidate
i. managers
j. members
k. nominal partner
l. operating agreement
m. ostensible partner
n. partnership
o. preferred stock
p. promoters
q. S corporation
r. secret partner
s. shareholders
t. silent partner
u. sole proprietorship
v. stock certificate
w. stockholders
x. ultra vires act
y. unlimited liability
z. winding-up period

_____ **8.** Liability that has no bounds.

_____ **9.** A document that evidences ownership of stock in a corporation.

_____ **10.** An association of two or more persons to carry on as co-owners a business for profit. (Select two answers.)

_____ **11.** Partners who may be known to the public as partners, but who take no active part in the business.

_____ **12.** A corporation governed by Subchapter S of the Internal Revenue Code and in which the income of the corporation is taxed directly to the shareholders rather than to the corporation itself.

_____ **13.** Turn into cash.

_____ **14.** A partnership formed by two or more persons, and having as members one or more general partners and one or more limited partners.

_____ **15.** Owners of a limited liability company.

_____ **16.** A period during which partnership assets are liquidated, debts are paid, an accounting is made, and any remaining assets are distributed among the partners.

_____ **17.** People who own shares in a corporation. (Select two answers.)

_____ **18.** A nonpartnership form of business organization that has the tax benefits of a partnership and the limited liability benefits of a corporation.

_____ **19.** A corporate act committed outside of the corporation's authority.

_____ **20.** An agreement that sets forth the rights and obligations of the members and establishes the rules for operating a limited liability company.

_____ **21.** People who begin a corporation by obtaining investors and taking charge up to the time of the corporation's existence.

_____ **22.** An act or occurrence that requires the partnership to eventually terminate.

Sharpening Your Latin Skills

In the space provided, write the definition of each of the following legal terms, referring to the glossary when necessary:

de facto _______________________________________

de jure _______________________________________

ex parte _______________________________________

pendente lite _______________________________________

ultra vires _______________________________________

Using Legal Language

Read the following story and fill in the blank lines with legal terms taken from the list of terms at the beginning of this chapter:

Julio and Juan became good friends while working for the Señor Tacos restaurant chain. The chain used a(n) _____________________________ method of operation, because its owner licensed others to use its trade name in making and selling tacos. Julio and Juan worked under the direction of Carmen, the _____________________________, who had the license to operate the business, given to her by Señor Tacos, the _____________________________. Every evening after work, Julio and Juan spent their time together inventing a greaseless taco fryer. Because this relationship involved two people combining their labor and property for a single business undertaking, it was known as a(n) _____________________________, which is also called a(n) _____________________________, a(n) _____________________________, or a(n) _____________________________. When the fryer was completed, Juan left his job with Carmen and opened a taco shop of his own. It was a(n) _____________________________, because Juan owned and operated it himself. The business thrived, and although he had no further money to invest, Juan felt it necessary to expand. His friend Julio offered to invest money in the business, but did not want to be liable for its debts or obligations. The two formed a(n) _____________________________, making Juan a(n) _____________________________ partner and Julio a(n) _____________________________ part-

ner. Because she was well-known in the trade, Carmen lent her name to the business, but because she had no real interest in it, she was a(n) _____________________________ or _____________________________ partner. Soon it became necessary to expand again, and Juan and Julio decided to establish a(n) _____________________________, which is a legal entity created under state law with the power to conduct its affairs as though it were a natural person. Juan and Julio were the _____________________________, because they applied for the _____________________________, which is also called _____________________________ or _____________________________. The organization was established in strict compliance with the law; therefore, it was a(n) _____________________________. Miguel, a friend of Juan and Julio, invested in the business, and all three became _____________________________, which are also known as _____________________________. Because restrictions were placed on the transfer of shares, the business was a(n) _____________________________. Miguel, Juan, and Julio received _____________________________ as evidence of their ownership in the business. The stock they received was _____________________________, which had no preferences and gave each owner the right to vote. All three were elected as _____________________________ to manage the business.

The Law of Bankruptcy

ANTE INTERROGATORY

*Chapter 11 bankruptcy is also called (A) involuntary bankruptcy,
(B) homestead exemption, (C) reorganization, (D) liquidation.*

LEARNING OBJECTIVES

LO 1: Summarize the history and purposes of the bankruptcy laws

LO 2: List the principal types of bankruptcy proceedings

LO 3: Summarize the purpose of a Chapter 7 bankruptcy

LO 4: Explain the means testing process that is required for Chapter 7

LO 5: Explain the homestead exemption

LO 6: Summarize the role of the bankruptcy trustee in a Chapter 7 bankruptcy

LO 7: Explain how a debtor is discharged in a Chapter 7 bankruptcy

LO 8: Summarize the purpose and process of a Chapter 11 bankruptcy

LO 9: Contrast Chapter 11 bankruptcy with Chapter 12 bankruptcy

LO 10: Contrast Chapter 13 bankruptcy with Chapter 11 and Chapter 7 bankruptcy

KEY TERMS

assets
automatic stay
automatic suspension
bankrupt
bankruptcy
bankruptcy estate
Bankruptcy Abuse Prevention and Consumer Protection Act of 2005
Chapter 7 bankruptcy
Chapter 11 bankruptcy
Chapter 12 bankruptcy
Chapter 13 bankruptcy
claim
creditors
debtor
debtor-in-possession

discharge in bankruptcy
exemptions
homestead exemption
involuntary bankruptcy
liquidate
liquidation
means testing
order for relief
preferences
proof of claim
prorated
reorganization bankruptcy
secured creditors
straight bankruptcy
trustee in bankruptcy
voluntary bankruptcy
wage earner's plan

WEBSITES FOR PRONUNCIATION HELP

http://dictionary.cambridge.org/us/pronunciation/english/audio

https://www.howtopronounce.com

One of the express powers that Article I of the U.S. Constitution grants to Congress is the power to make bankruptcy laws, which Congress first exercised with the Bankruptcy Act of 1800. It wasn't until 1841, however, that debtors were able to be in bankruptcy voluntarily. The United States Bankruptcy Code attempts to give debtors a fresh start (as opposed to a term in debtor's prison) by providing debt relief, while giving creditors an opportunity to collect some portion of the debts owed to them by bankrupt debtors. **Bankruptcy** is administered by U.S. Bankruptcy Courts, which have exclusive jurisdiction over bankruptcy cases. Bankruptcy courts are attached to district courts within the federal court system. Each state and territory in the United States has at least one federal district court within its boundaries.

In 2005, the U.S. Congress made sweeping changes to the Bankruptcy Code, with the passage of the **Bankruptcy Abuse Prevention and Consumer Protection Act (BAPCA)**. Among its many attributes, BAPCA makes it more difficult for people to declare bankruptcy and extends the time between repeat bankruptcy filings. The discussion that follows highlights some of the changes brought by the 2005 bankruptcy code amendments.

GOALS OF THE BANKRUPTCY CODE

The primary goals of the Bankruptcy Code are: (1) to give debtors a fresh start by eliminating their bankruptcy eligible debts and by leaving some of their **assets** (often referred to as nonexempt assets) untouched; and (2) to provide adequate protection to **creditors** (parties to whom money is owed) through creating a process where debtors' nonexempt assets are distributed to the creditors based on the class to which the creditors belong. The state of being **bankrupt** is not about having more debts than assets on a balance sheet; it is about having insufficient cash flow to pay off one's debts. The term **debtor** (one who owes a debt to another) is used in place of the term *bankrupt* in the Bankruptcy Code.

TYPES OF BANKRUPTCY PROCEEDINGS

There are five principal types of bankruptcy proceedings, and they are named after their respective chapter in the Federal Bankruptcy Code in which they are found: Chapter 7 (liquidation); Chapter 9 (municipalities); Chapter 11 (business reorganization); Chapter 12 (family farmers); and Chapter 13 (adjustment of debts of individuals).

Chapter 7 Bankruptcy

Chapter 7 bankruptcy, also called **liquidation** or **straight bankruptcy**, is a proceeding designed to **liquidate** (convert to cash) a debtor's property, pay off creditors, and discharge the debtor from most debts. A Chapter 7 bankruptcy may be either voluntary or involuntary. Businesses may "file Chapter 7," but the emphasis in this section will focus on non-business debtors in Chapter 7 bankruptcy.

Word Wise

"Bankrupt" Replaced by "Debtor"

A person who files for bankruptcy under today's law is called a "debtor." This is a change from earlier law, under which a person who filed for bankruptcy was referred to as "the bankrupt." In 1978, Congress passed the Bankruptcy Reform Act with the aim of giving debtors who are overwhelmed with debt a fresh start. Congress also wanted to reduce the stigma connected with the term "bankrupt" and did so by eliminating the term from the law and replacing it with the word "debtor."

VOLUNTARY BANKRUPTCY. **Voluntary bankruptcy** is a bankruptcy proceeding that is initiated by the debtor. To be eligible to file for this type of bankruptcy, debtors must

1. satisfy the *means test;* which is explained below.
2. meet with an approved nonprofit credit counselor before filing for bankruptcy;
3. furnish a federal income tax return for the most recent tax year; and
4. take a course in financial management after filing for bankruptcy.

When a debtor files a voluntary bankruptcy petition with the court, an **order for relief** (the acceptance of the case by the bankruptcy court) automatically takes place. At that time, an automatic stay goes into effect. The **automatic stay** (also called an **automatic suspension**), found in 11 U.S.C. § 362, is a self-operating postponement of debt collection proceedings against the debtor, except where the debtor has filed bankruptcy within one year of a prior bankruptcy's dismissal. Where the automatic stay applies, certain collection efforts are not prohibited, including current and back child support. Creditors, such as credit card companies and lenders of unsecured revolving loans, cannot bring suit for what is owed them.

INVOLUNTARY BANKRUPTCY. **Involuntary bankruptcy** is a bankruptcy proceeding that is initiated by one or more creditors. When there are less than 12 creditors, a single creditor who has an unsecured claim of at least $15,775 may file an involuntary bankruptcy petition. However, when there are 12 or more creditors, at least 3 of them must join in the bankruptcy petition, and the total claims of unsecured debt must be at least $15,775. The debtor has 20 days to file an objection in an involuntary case, and if this is done, a hearing is held to determine whether an order for relief will be issued.

MEANS TESTING. Perhaps the most significant change in the bankruptcy code as a result of the 2005 bankruptcy legislation is that a debtor must meet the eligibility requirements to be in Chapter 7, known as a **means test**. The purpose of means testing is to prevent people with high-enough incomes from being in Chapter 7, thus putting them in Chapter 13 bankruptcy, where at least some debts must be repaid. The means testing mechanism involves the debtor calculating a monthly average of his or her income six months prior to filing and multiplying that number times 12 (for an estimated annual income). If two spouses file a joint petition, their combined incomes are used. For means testing purposes, income is broader than taxable income. Then, the debtor compares that number (which is the result of the calculation) with the median annual income of the debtor's state (according to the U.S. Census Bureau), factoring in family size. For example, according to the latest Census Bureau information for 2017, the median income for a family of three in Indiana is $66,148. However, the median income for that family, if they lived in Pennsylvania, is $75,018.

If the debtor's average income calculation is below the state median, the debtor qualifies for a Chapter 7 filing. But if the debtor's average income calculation is above the state median, then a second means test must be performed. This one is a more detailed comparison between the debtor's aggregate current monthly expenses to an IRS-determined allowable monthly expenses number (as determined by IRS guidelines) for the debtor's county and state, taking family size into account. The purpose of this second calculation is to find the debtor's monthly disposable income (what is left over after paying one's monthly bills). If the debtor's disposable income is above a threshold amount projected over a five-year period, the debtor is presumed to be ineligible for Chapter 7. (This ineligibility is known as a presumption of abuse.) Unless the debtor can overcome that presumption by showing special circumstances that make the initial calculations unreliable, the debtor will need to file a Chapter 13 bankruptcy.

Web Wise

- The U.S. Department of Justice's U.S. Bankruptcy Trustee Program has a link that provides detailed information on means testing, including the means testing forms, which can be found at: https://www.justice.gov/ust/means-testing
- The various fees associated with filing bankruptcy can be found at: http://www.uscourts.gov/services-forms/fees/bankruptcy-court-miscellaneous-fee-schedule

TERMS IN ACTION

Those debtors who fail the Chapter 7 **means testing** must file a Chapter 13 petition. But sometimes the opposite happens: a Chapter 13 bankruptcy filer is moved to Chapter 7. In 2015, a bankruptcy judge denied the Chapter 13 filing of Minneapolis, MN, attorney Paul Hansmeier on the grounds of dishonesty. Hansmeier had filed Chapter 13 after being sanctioned over a half-million dollars and having his law license suspended indefinitely for fraudulently filing copyright lawsuits against computer owners whose IP addresses were linked to downloads of pirated movies or porn. After issuing subpoenas against Internet Service Providers to get the downloaders' names, lawyers like Hansmeier then threaten those people with public exposure for their unauthorized downloads in attempts to get quick settlements. This is called "copyright trolling" or "porn trolling" and it resulted in Hansmeier being federally indicted in 2016 for fraud and extortion. But prior to that, the bankruptcy court had to determine if he should be allowed to keep his assets, which is a key benefit of being in Chapter 13. Concluding "the debtor has a pattern and practice of dishonesty with the court," the judge converted the bankruptcy to a Chapter 7, so that Hansmeier's assets would be **liquidated** to pay his creditors. Months later, the bankruptcy trustee sued to have Hansmeier's bankruptcy case thrown out on the grounds of fraud. Among the allegations the trustee made were that Hansmeier had established a trust administered by his wife (also an attorney) and later pulled $150,000 from that trust and hid it in a closet, that he created a Delaware corporation to which he transferred $500,000 from his law firm and used to pay various expenses, and that he—without the bankruptcy court's knowledge—sold his and his wife's condominium to a federal judge.

Sources: abajournal.com; startribune.com; bloomberg.com

EXEMPTIONS.   As part of the "fresh start" policy of the Bankruptcy Code, some items of property, referred to as **exemptions**, are excepted from bankruptcy proceedings and may be retained by the debtor. Each state has its own list of exemptions and the federal bankruptcy code also has a list of exemptions. The law allows states to decide whether their debtors will use the federal exemptions or, instead, the state-granted exemptions. A majority of states require that their state exemptions be taken rather than the federal exemptions. In other states, however, debtors may choose to take either the state or the federal exemptions. The Bankruptcy Code, nevertheless, requires that a debtor be domiciled in a state for two years for that state's exemption rules to apply.

The **homestead exemption** allows for the exemption from bankruptcy of one's residence up to a certain amount depending on state or federal law. Essentially, the homestead exemption allows a debtor to keep a certain amount of equity from the sale of their home in bankruptcy (assuming the home has equity, which is a market value above the loan outstanding). The current federal homestead exemption amount is $23,675, and is double for married couples filing jointly. The bankruptcy code currently limits the state homestead exemption to $160,375 if the property was acquired within the previous 40 months from the bankruptcy filing. For example, if a debtor files bankruptcy in a state that allows its filers a homestead exemption of up to $250,000, and the debtor's home is worth $275,000, the debtor may use only $160,375 of the homestead exemption, because of the federal cap.

State bankruptcy exemptions are too varied to list here, but a sampling of the federal exemptions includes the following:

- the homestead exemption to the extent of $23,675 (unless the state exemption applies, as described previously)
- a motor vehicle: $3,775
- household furnishings and personal apparel: $600 per item and $12,625 total
- jewelry: $1,600
- tools of the trade: $2,375

- unmatured life insurance policies: $12,625
- personal injury lawsuit awards: $23,675
- Individual Retirement Account (IRA): $1,283,025.

These and other exemptions are adjusted for inflation every three years, and the exemptions outlined here were effective to bankruptcies filed on or after April, 2016.

TRUSTEE IN BANKRUPTCY.   When bankruptcy proceedings begin, the court appoints a person, called a **trustee in bankruptcy**, to hold the debtor's non-excluded assets in trust for the benefit of creditors. This collection of the debtor's property (including the debtor's spouse's community property in a community property state) is known as the **bankruptcy estate** and the extent to what is included in the bankruptcy estate is listed in Section 541 of the bankruptcy code. The trustee's duties are to collect the debtor's property and, with the exception of items that the law allows the debtor to keep, convert it to cash ("liquidate") and distribute the proceeds to the creditors according to certain priorities established by law. Among other things, the trustee has the power to invalidate **preferences**—that is, transfers made by the debtor to creditors before the bankruptcy proceeding—enabling them to receive a greater percentage of their claim than they would have otherwise received. The trustee also has the power to challenge certain creditors' claims and to even object to the debtor's bankruptcy discharge, as shown in the first Terms in Action for this chapter.

Among the papers filed by the debtor in a bankruptcy proceeding is schedule (a listing) of income and expenses, assets, as well as a schedule of creditors and the amount owed to each. The court notifies the creditors of the time and place of the first meeting of creditors, known as a 341 meeting. At this meeting, which usually takes place approximately a month after the petition is filed, the creditors are given an opportunity to question the debtor under oath. The court also notifies creditors that they must file, within 90 days after the first meeting, a **proof of claim**, which is a written, signed statement setting forth a creditor's claim together with the basis for it. A **claim** is a right to payment or other equitable right, such as the right to receive specific performance of a contract.

Once the debtor's property is collected by the trustee and liquidated, the proceeds are distributed to creditors with allowable claims. **Secured creditors** (those who hold mortgages and other liens on the debtor's property to secure repayment) receive payment to the exclusion of other creditors. After they are paid, the remaining nonexempt assets are used to pay the priority claims, which include administrative expenses, and then the unsecured creditors according to a priority list established by the Bankruptcy Code. Normally, there is not enough to pay unsecured creditors in full, so their shares are **prorated**—that is, divided proportionately. A **discharge in bankruptcy** releases the debtor from all debts that were part of the bankruptcy proceeding. Not all debts are eligible for Chapter 7 bankruptcy, otherwise being known as nondischargeable. Those "exceptions to discharge," as they are enumerated in 11 U.S.C. § 523, include taxes owed within three years of filing the bankruptcy petition, alimony or child support payments, student loans (except in very rare circumstances that qualify as "undue hardship"), debts incurred from willful or malicious injury, or debts for even negligent operation of a motor vehicle while under the influence of a drug or alcohol that results in personal injury or death.

Debtors who complete a Chapter 7 bankruptcy must wait at least eight years before discharged a second time in Chapter 7. Prior to the 2005 BAPCA, there was a six-year waiting period between Chapter 7 discharges. But a debtor who completes a Chapter 13 bankruptcy can file a Chapter 13 in order to reduce debts that weren't eligible for Chapter 7 but are for Chapter 13, which includes debts incurred to pay nondischargeable taxes. The total fees for filing a Chapter 7 bankruptcy petition are $335.

Chapter 11 Bankruptcy

Chapter 11 bankruptcy, also called **reorganization bankruptcy**, provides a method for businesses to restructure their financial affairs through debt realignment, keep their assets, and remain in business. (Chapter 11 bankruptcy isn't limited to business and although Chapter 11 bankruptcy is more costly and lengthy than a Chapter 13 bankruptcy, individuals whose debts exceed the limits allowed for Chapter 13 can choose a Chapter 11.) Because the business continues to operate, the debtor in a Chapter 11 bankruptcy case is referred to as a **debtor-in-possession**. Performing the function of a trustee, the debtor develops a reorganization plan, setting forth a method of repaying debts and separating creditors into various classes. Such a reorganization plan will involve paying less than the face value of the debt, and the debtor has the exclusive right to propose its plan. To be approved by the court, the plan must be feasible and proposed in good faith must be approved by at least one class of "impaired" claims. An impaired claim is a debt obligation that will not be paid in full if the reorganization plan is confirmed. Like Chapter 7, a Chapter 11 bankruptcy may be either voluntary or involuntary. The total fees for filing a Chapter 11 bankruptcy petition are $1,717.

TERMS IN ACTION

For millions of Americans, **bankruptcy** is the result of job loss, unforeseen medical bills, or business failure. But for many others, it is the consequence of poor money management and overspending. Even two lawyer-presidents who are on Mount Rushmore, Thomas Jefferson and Abraham Lincoln, experienced having crushing debts throughout their lives. More than a few celebrities have been in bankruptcy even after earning millions of dollars. Oscar-award-winning actress Kim Basinger filed **Chapter 11 bankruptcy** in 1993, not long after her career hit some bumpy spots, and after she and other investors bought the town of Braselton, Georgia, for $20 million. *Sports Illustrated* reported in 2009 that 78 percent of all NFL players are bankrupt within two years after retiring, and that 60 percent of all NBA players are broke within five years after retiring. Hall of Fame NBA player Scottie Pippen, who won six championships with Michael Jordan, was reported to have spent most of the $127 million that he made. Former baseball slugger Jack Clark filed **Chapter 7 bankruptcy** in 1992, while in the second year of a three-year $8.7-million contract with the Boston Red Sox. He spent much of his fortune on luxury homes and cars, and at one time had 18 cars and 17 car payments. The king of all sports bankruptcies is Mike Tyson. Despite earning over $400 million from boxing, he filed Chapter 11 bankruptcy in 2003. **Chapter 13 bankruptcy** wasn't an option for Tyson or the other celebrities listed here, because their debts exceeded what is allowed in Chapter 13. At the time of his filing, Tyson listed $27 million in debts. Among other debts, he owed the IRS over $13 million in back taxes, he owed $52,000 in back child support obligations, and he owed a limousine company over $300,000. Tyson was and is an avid lover of pigeons, and those birds cost him a lot of money to maintain, but not as much as the $140,000 that he spent on two Bengal tigers. Pigeons can make a person dirty, which might explain the $2 million bathtub Tyson bought for his first wife. In 2015, rapper and actor 50 Cent filed a Chapter 11 bankruptcy, listing close to $25 million in assets and over $32 million in debt. At the time of his bankruptcy filing, 50 Cent lived in a 21-bedroom estate in Connecticut he bought in 2003 for $4.1 million from—you guessed it—Mike Tyson.

Sources: variety.com; legalzoom.com; sportsillustrated.cnn.com; nytimes.com; thesmokinggun.com; washingtonpost.com; blogs.wsj.com; money.cnn.com

Web Wise

Federal bankruptcy law can change at any time. Look for information about the latest bankruptcy law at the following sites:

- www.bankruptcyaction.com
- http://www.bankruptcyinbrief.com
- http://www.uscourts.gov/services-forms/bankruptcy

Chapter 12 Bankruptcy

Chapter 12 bankruptcy provides a method for family farmers and family fishing businesses with regular income to adjust their financial affairs while continuing to operate. It is a bankruptcy process intended to eliminate some of the hurdles debtors face in Chapter 11 or Chapter 13. As it concerns how such a debtor would file a Chapter 12 petition, a family farm or fishing business can be either owned as a sole proprietorship or as a partnership or corporation. To qualify as an individually owned business, the farm or fishing business must receive more than 50 percent of their total income from farming or fishing. Also, such a family farmer must have at least 50 percent (and a family fishing business must have at least 80 percent) of its debt related to farming or fishing operations. Total debts may not exceed $4,031,575 for farming or $1,868,200 for fishing. The debtor must develop a reorganization plan, as is required in Chapter 11 bankruptcies, and serve as a debtor-in-possession, performing the functions of a trustee. The total fees for filing a Chapter 12 bankruptcy petition are $275.

Chapter 13 Bankruptcy

Chapter 13 bankruptcy provides a method for individuals with regular income to pay debts from future income over an extended period without losing their property. Debtors who do not qualify for Chapter 7 bankruptcy (discussed earlier) may file a Chapter 13 bankruptcy. To be eligible, debtors must first meet with an approved nonprofit credit counselor. Their unsecured debts may not exceed $394,725 and their secured debts may not exceed $1,184,200 (as of April 2016). Debtors must make a good-faith effort to repay their debts. They must submit a plan, sometimes referred to as a **wage earner's plan**, for the installment payments of outstanding debts, including the eventual payment in full of all claims within three to five years. An exception to paying off all claims (whether in full or in part) within the repayment period is a home mortgage. While Chapter 13 can be used to help prevent a foreclosure and to cure delinquent mortgage payments over time rather than immediately, a debtor will need to regularly pay the mortgage in order to keep the house. Furthermore, it is possible in Chapter 13 to strip down second mortgages or other junior liens on a debtor's home. Whether a Chapter 13 repayment plan is three or five years depends on what the debtor earns. Certain debts, known as priority debts, must be paid in full. Beyond one's home mortgage, priority debts include past property taxes and unpaid child support.

Chapter 13, as well as Chapter 12, bankruptcy is only voluntary. Unlike Chapter 7, there is a two-year waiting period before one can file a subsequent Chapter 13 petition. The total fees for filing a Chapter 13 bankruptcy petition are $310.

Reviewing What You Learned

After studying the chapter, write the answers to each of the following questions:

1. What are the goals of the Bankruptcy Code? _____________

   ____

   ____

   ____

2. Under what circumstances may a single creditor file an involuntary bankruptcy petition? _______________

   ____

   ____

3. Describe the duties of a trustee in bankruptcy. ___________

   ____

   ____

4. Name some papers (schedules) filed by a debtor in a bankruptcy proceeding. _______________________

   ____

   ____

5. How are the proceeds from the sale of a debtor's property distributed in a Chapter 7 bankruptcy? _______________

____

____

____

6. List five exemptions under the Federal Bankruptcy Code.

____

____

____

7. How does a Chapter 7 bankruptcy differ from a Chapter 13 bankruptcy? _______________________________

____

____

8. How does a Chapter 13 bankruptcy differ from a Chapter 11 bankruptcy? _______________________________

____

____

____

9. What is the purpose of a Chapter 12 bankruptcy? _________

____

____

____

10. How does means testing work? _______________________

____

____

____

Understanding Legal Concepts

Indicate whether each statement is true or false. Then, change the italicized word or phrase of each false statement to make it true.

ANSWERS

_______ **1.** Bankruptcy proceedings *end* with the filing of a petition with the federal court.

_______ **2.** An order for relief automatically takes place when an *involuntary* bankruptcy petition is filed.

_______ **3.** When there are *more* than 12 creditors, a single creditor who is owed more than $15,775 may file an involuntary bankruptcy petition.

_______ **4.** An *order for relief* brings into play an automatic suspension of debt collection actions, preventing further efforts by creditors to collect their debts.

_______ **5.** A trustee in bankruptcy has the power, among other things, to *invalidate* preferences.

_______ **6.** The court notifies creditors that they must file, within 90 days after the first meeting, a *proof of claim.*

_______ **7.** As part of the *nonstop* policy of the Bankruptcy Code, some items of property are exempt from bankruptcy proceedings.

_______ **8.** The federal homestead exemption is equity in one's residence to the extent of *$21,625.*

_______ **9.** *Chapter 7* bankruptcy provides a method for businesses to reorganize their financial affairs, keep their assets, and remain in business.

_______ **10.** *Chapter 13* bankruptcy provides a method by which an individual with regular income can pay his or her debts from future income over an extended period.

Checking Terminology

From the list of legal terms that follows, select the one that matches each definition.

ANSWERS

a. assets

b. automatic stay

c. automatic suspension

d. bankrupt

e. bankruptcy

f. BAPCA

g. Chapter 7 bankruptcy

h. Chapter 11 bankruptcy

i. Chapter 12 bankruptcy

_______ **1.** People to whom money is owed.

_______ **2.** A right to payment.

_______ **3.** The legal process by which the assets of a debtor are sold to pay off creditors so that the debtor can make a fresh start financially.

_______ **4.** Items of property that are excepted from bankruptcy proceedings and may be retained by the debtor.

_______ **5.** Creditors who hold mortgages and other liens.

_______ **6.** A self-operating postponement of collection proceedings against a debtor. (Select two answers.)

j. Chapter 13 bankruptcy
k. claim
l. creditors
m. debtor
n. debtor-in-possession
o. discharge in bankruptcy
p. exemptions
q. homestead exemption
r. involuntary bankruptcy
s. liquidate
t. liquidation
u. means testing
v. order for relief
w. preferences
x. proof of claim
y. prorated
z. reorganization
aa. secured creditors
bb. straight bankruptcy
cc. trustee in bankruptcy
dd. voluntary bankruptcy
ee. wage earner's plan

_____ **7.** A bankruptcy proceeding that is initiated by the debtor.

_____ **8.** The state of a person (or a business) of being unable to pay debts as they become due.

_____ **9.** A proceeding designed to liquidate a debtor's property, pay off creditors, and discharge the debtor from most debts. (Select three answers.)

_____ **10.** Divided proportionately.

_____ **11.** A person appointed by a bankruptcy court to hold the debtor's assets in trust for the benefit of creditors.

_____ **12.** Convert to cash.

_____ **13.** A method for businesses to reorganize their financial affairs, keep their assets, and remain in business. (Select two answers.)

_____ **14.** A method for family farmers to adjust their financial affairs while continuing to operate their farms.

_____ **15.** Property.

_____ **16.** A bankruptcy proceeding that is initiated by one or more creditors.

_____ **17.** One who owes a debt to another.

_____ **18.** Another name for a debtor in Chapters 11 and 13 cases.

_____ **19.** Transfers made by a debtor to creditors, before a bankruptcy proceeding, enabling them to receive a greater percentage of their claim than they would have otherwise received.

_____ **20.** A method by which an individual with regular income can pay his or her debts from future income over an extended period.

_____ **21.** A plan for the installment payments of outstanding debts under a Chapter 13 bankruptcy.

_____ **22.** In bankruptcy, the exemption of one's residence to the extent of $16,150.

_____ **23.** The acceptance of a case by a bankruptcy court.

_____ **24.** A signed, written statement setting forth a creditor's claim together with the basis for it.

_____ **25.** A release of a debtor from all debts that were included in the bankruptcy proceeding.

_____ **26.** A 2005 change in the Bankruptcy Code, making it more difficult for people to declare bankruptcy and extending the time between repeat bankruptcy filings.

_____ **27.** A comparison made to determine whether a debtor meets the eligibility requirements to be in Chapter 7.

Using Legal Language

Read the following story and fill in the blank lines with legal terms taken from the list of terms at the beginning of this chapter:

Valerie worked in a law office that specialized in ______________________ —that is, the legal process by which the assets of a(n) ______________________ (one who owes a debt to another) are sold to pay off ______________________ (people to whom money is owed) so that a fresh start can be made financially. Mr. Rodham, a client, had just left, and Attorney Jones had instructed Valerie to prepare the papers for a(n) ______________________ bankruptcy, which is also called ______________________ or ______________________, and is designed to ______________________ (covert to cash) Mr. Rodham's property, pay off his debts, and discharge him from most debts. Since the petition will be filed by Mr. Rodham, this will be a(n) ______________________ case, and a(n) ______________________ will automatically take place. When the petition is filed, a(n) ______________________, also called a(n) ______________________, occurs, which is a self-operating postponement of collection proceedings against the debtor. A(n) ______________________ will hold Mr. Rodham's assets in trust for the benefit of creditors, some of whom may receive a(n) ______________________ share—one that is divided proportionately. Creditors will be required to file a(n) ______________________ within 90 days after their first meeting. The holder of the mortgage on Mr. Rodham's house is known as a(n) ____________________________ and will receive payment to the exclusion of other creditors. Any ________________________ (earlier transfers resulting in greater percentages to some creditors) that may have occurred will be invalidated. Because of the so-called _______________________, Mr. Rodham may be able to retain an interest in his residence to the extent of $16,150. When the case is finalized, Mr. Rodham will receive a(n) ______________________ —that is, a release from all debts that were proved in the proceeding.

GLOSSARY OF LEGAL TERMS

abandoned property Personal property the owner has intentionally discarded; the finder becomes the new owner

abortion *(a·BOR·shun)* The act of stopping a pregnancy.

absolute liability *(ab·so·LOOT ly·a·BIL·i·tee)* Liability for an act that causes harm without regard to fault or negligence. Also called *strict liability.*

A–B trust A type of marital deduction trust that reduces the taxation of the second spouse to die by limiting the amount in that person's estate to a sum that is not taxable. Also called *bypass trust, credit-shelter trust,* and *exemption equivalent trust.*

acceleration clause *(ak·sel·er·AY·shun)* A clause in a mortgage or note that causes the entire balance of the loan to become due when a default occurs.

acceptance *(ak·SEP·tense)* If the offeree assents (agrees) to the terms of the offer, an acceptance occurs and an agreement comes into an existence.

accessory after the fact *(ak·SESS·o·ree)* One who receives, relieves, comforts, or assists another with knowledge that the other has committed a felony.

accessory before the fact *(ak·SESS·o·ree)* One who procures, counsels, or commands another to commit a felony, but who is not present when the felony is committed.

accomplice *(a·COM·pliss)* Anyone who takes part with another in the commission of a crime.

accord and satisfaction *(a·KORD and sat·is·FAK·shun)* An agreement to perform a contract obligation in a different manner than originally called for, and the completion of that agreed-upon performance.

accretion *(a·KREE·shun)* Any gradual addition to the soil made by nature, such as the gradual accumulation of soil on land next to a stream, caused by the action of water. Also called *alluvion.*

acknowledgment *(ak·NAWL·ej·ment)* A formal declaration before an authorized official, by a person who executes an instrument, that an act or deed is his or her free act or deed.

acquitted *(a·KWIT·ed)* Discharged from accusation; to be found not guilty.

action *(AK·shun)* Lawsuit or court proceeding.

actionable *(AK·shun·a·bel)* Furnishing legal ground for a lawsuit.

actus reus *(AK·tus REE·us)* A voluntary act.

ad damnum *(ad DAM·num)* The clause in the complaint stating the damages claimed by the plaintiff.

adeemed *(a·DEEMD)* Taken away.

ademption *(a·DEMP·shun)* The discharge of a legal obligation by paying a party what is due.

adequate provocation *(ADD-uh-kwet prah-vo-KAY-shun)* A provocation that a reasonable person might naturally be induced to commit the act after losing self-control.

adhesion contract *(ad·HEE·shen KON·trakt)* A contract that is drawn by one party to that party's benefit and whose terms must be accepted, as is, on a take-it-or-leave-it basis, if a contract is to result.

adjudicating *(a·JOO·di·kay·ting)* Determining finally by a court.

adjudication *(a·joo·di·KAY·shun)* A court judgment.

adjustment of debts of individuals *(a·JUST·ment ov dets ov in·de·VID·joo·els)* A method by which an individual with regular income can pay his or her debts from future income over an extended period. Also called and Chapter 13 *bankruptcy.*

administrator *(ad·MIN·is·tray·tor)* A male appointed by the court to administer the estate of an intestate decedent.

administrator ad litem *(ad LY·tem)* An administrator appointed by the court to represent the interests of an estate in an action.

administrator c.t.a A person appointed by the court to administer a testate estate in which no executor is nominated or in which the executor has died or for some reason does not settle the estate. (c.t.a. is an abbreviation for cum testamento annexo.) Also called *administrator with the will annexed* and *administrator w.w.a.*

administrator cum testamento annexo *(kum tes·ta·MENT·o an·EKS·o)* A person appointed by the court to administer a testate estate in which no executor is nominated or in which the executor has died or for some reason does not settle the estate. Also called *administrator c.t.a., administrator with the will annexed,* and *administrator w.w.a.*

administrator d.b.n A person appointed by the court to complete the settlement of an estate in which a previously appointed administrator has died, resigned, or been removed. (d.b.n. is an abbreviation for de bonis non.)

administrator d.b.n.c.t.a A person appointed by the court to take the place of a previously appointed executor who has died, resigned, or been removed. (d.b.n.c.t.a. is an abbreviation for de bonis non cum testamento annexo.)

administrator de bonis non *(de BO·niss non)* A person appointed by the court to complete the settlement of an estate in which a previously appointed administrator has died, resigned, or been removed. Also called *administrator d.b.n.*

administrator de bonis non cum testamento annexo A person appointed by the court to take the place of a previously appointed executor who has died, resigned, or been removed. Also called *administrator d.b.n.c.t.a.*

administrator pendente lite *(pen·DEN·tay LIE·tay)* A temporary administrator appointed by the court to protect estate assets when there is a will contest.

administrator with the will annexed *(AN·eksd)* A person appointed by the court to administer a testate estate in which no executor is nominated or in which the executor has died or for some reason does not settle the estate. Also called *administrator c.t.a., administrator cum testamento annexo,* and *administrator w.w.a.*

administrator w.w.a A person appointed by the court to administer a testate estate in which no executor is nominated or in which the executor has died or for some reason does not settle the estate. (w.w.a. is an abbreviation for with the will annexed.) Also called *administrator c.t.a.* and *administrator cum testamento annex.*

administratrix *(ad·MIN·is·tray·triks)* A female appointed by the court to administer the estate of an intestate decedent.

admiralty *(AD·mer·ul·tee)* Pertaining to the sea.

admissible evidence *(ad·MISS·e·bel EV·i·dens)* Evidence that is pertinent and proper to be considered in reaching a decision following specific rules.

adoption (*a·DOP·shun*) The legal process in which a child's legal rights and duties toward his or her natural parents are replaced by similar rights and duties toward his or her adopting parents.

adoptive parents (*a·DOP·tiv*) Parents who adopt a child.

adultery (*a·DUL·ter·ee*) Voluntary sexual intercourse by a married person with someone other than that person's spouse, or by an unmarried person with a married person.

advance directive (*ad·VANS de·REKT·iv*) A written statement specifying whether a person wants life-sustaining medical treatment if he or she becomes desperately ill.

advancement (*ac·VANSE·ment*) The testator's disposing of or giving to a beneficiary, while alive, that which was provided in a will, so as to make it impossible to carry out the will. Also called *satisfaction*.

adverse possession (*AD·verse po·SESH·en*) Title to real property obtained by taking actual possession of it openly, notoriously, exclusively, under a claim of right, and continuously for a period set by statute.

affiant (*a·FY·ent*) A person who signs an affidavit. Also called *deponent*.

affidavit (*a·fi·DAY·vit*) A written statement sworn to under oath before a notary public as being true to the affiant's own knowledge, information, and belief.

affiliation proceeding (*a·fil·ee·AY·shun pro·SEED·ing*) A court action to determine whether a person is the father of a child born out of wedlock. Also called *paternity proceeding*.

affinity (*a·FIN·i·ee*) The relationship that one spouse has to the blood relatives of the other.

affirm (*a·FERM*) Approve.

affirmative defense (*a·FERM·a·tiv de·FENSE*) A defense in civil and criminal litigation that admits the plaintiff's (or prosecutor's) allegations, but introduces another factor that avoids liability. Also called *confession and avoidance*. Defendants bear the burden of establishing affirmative defenses, such as contributory negligence (civil) or self-defense (criminal).

agency (*AY·jen·see*) A relationship that exists when one person is authorized to act under the control of another person.

agency by estoppel (*AY·jen·see by es·TOP·el*) Authority that comes about when a principal, through some act, makes it appear that an agent has authority when none actually exists. Also called *apparent authority*.

agency by ratification (*AY·jen·see by rat·i·fi·KAY·shun*) A relationship that occurs when someone performs an act on behalf of another without authority to do so, but the other person later approves of the act.

agent (*AY·jent*) A person authorized to act on behalf of another and subject to the other's control. Also called *surrogate*.

age of consent (*aje ov con·SENT*) The age at which one may be married under state law.

aggravated assault (*AG·ra·va·ted a·SAWLT*) An assault committed with the intention of committing some additional crime.

aiding and abetting (*a·BET·ing*) Participating in a crime by giving assistance or encouragement.

adjustable rate mortgage def (*a·JUSS·ta·bl rate MORE·gej*) A mortgage with an interest rate that fluctuates according to changes in an index to which it is connected.

alderpeople (*AL·der·pee·pel*) People elected to serve as members of the legislative body of a city.

alibi (*AL·i·by*) A defense that places the defendant in a different place than the crime scene so that it would have been impossible for him or her to commit the crime.

alienation of affections (*ale·ee·e·NA·shun ov a·FEK·shuns*) The willful and malicious interference with the marriage relation by a third party without justification or excuse.

alimony (*AL·i·mohn·ee*) An allowance made to a divorced spouse by a former spouse for support and maintenance. Also called *spousal support*.

allegation (*al·e·GAY·shun*) A statement or claim that the party making it expects to prove.

allege (*a·LEJ*) To make an allegation; to assert positively.

alleged (*a·LEJD*) Claimed, asserted, or charged.

alluvion (*a·LOO·vee·en*) Any gradual addition to the soil made by nature, such as the gradual accumulation of soil on land next to a stream caused by the action of water. Also called *accretion*.

alternate jurors (*AHL·ter·net JOOR·ors*) Additional jurors impaneled in case of sickness or removal of any of the regular jurors who are deliberating.

alternative dispute resolutions (*al·TERN·a·tiv dis·PYOOT res·o·LOO·shuns*) Procedures for settling disputes by means other than litigation, including mediation and arbitration.

amendments (*uh·MEND·mentz*) Parts of the U.S. Constitution which modify or invalidate earlier parts of the Constitution.

amortization (*a·MORE·ti·ZAY·shun*) Reducing or decreasing over time. In a loan, it shows how the loan balance is reduced until it is paid off.

American Bar Association (ABA) (*uh·MARE·ih·kan bar uh·so·she·A·shun*) The largest voluntary bar association in the United States; it sets academic standards for law schools and formulates a model of ethics codes related to the legal profession.

ancillary administrator (*AN·sil·a·ree ad·MIN·is·tray·tor*) A person appointed by the court to handle the affairs of a decedent in a foreign state.

animus furandi (*AN·i·mus fer·AN·day*) An intent to steal.

annulment (*a·NUL·ment*) A judicial declaration that no valid marriage ever existed.

answer (*AN·ser*) The main pleading filed by the defendant in a lawsuit in response to the plaintiff's complaint.

antenuptial agreement (*an·tee·NUP·shel a·GREE·ment*) A contract made in contemplation of marriage between prospective spouses setting forth, among other points, the right each spouse will have to property brought into the marriage. Also called *premarital agreement* and *prenuptial agreement*.

anticipatory breach (*an·TISS·i·pa·tore·ee*) The announcement, before the time for performance, by a party to a contract that he or she is not going to perform.

antilapse statutes (*an·tee·LAPS STAT·shoots*) Laws designed to minimize the effect of lapse.

apparent authority (*a·PAR·ent aw·THAW·ri·tee*) Authority that comes about when a principal, through some act, makes it appear that an agent has authority when none actually exists. Also called *agency by estoppel*.

appeal (*a·PEEL*) A request to a higher court to review the decision of a lower court.

appeal bond A bond often required as security to guarantee the cost of an appeal, especially in civil cases.

appearance (*a·PEER·ens*) The voluntary submission to the court's jurisdiction, either in person or by an agent.

appellant (*a·PEL·ent*) A party bringing an appeal.

appellate courts (*a·PEL·et*) Courts that review the decisions of lower courts. Also called *courts of appeal*.

appellate jurisdiction (*a·PEL·et joo·res·DIK·shen*) The power to hear a case when it is appealed.

appellee (*a·pel·EE*) A party against whom an appeal is brought. Also called *defendant in error* and *respondent*.

apt words Suitable words.

arbitration (*ar·be·TRAY·shun*) A method of settling disputes in which a neutral third party makes a decision after hearing the arguments on both sides.

arbitrator (*ar·be·TRAY·tor*) A neutral third party in an arbitration session who listens to both sides and makes a decision with regard to the dispute.

arbitrator's award (*ar·be·TRAY·torz uh·wohrd*) An arbitrator's final written decision in binding arbitration.

arraignment (*a·RAIN·ment*) The act of calling a prisoner before the court to answer an indictment or information.

array (*a·RAY*) The large group of people from which a jury is selected for a trial. Also called *jury panel, jury pool*, and *venire*.

arrest (*a·REST*) To deprive a person of his or her liberty.

arrest warrant (*a·REST WAR·ent*) A written order of the court commanding law enforcement officers to arrest a person and bring him or her before the court.

arson (*AR·sen*) The willful and malicious burning of the dwelling house or structure.

article (*AR·tih·cl*) In a statutory framework, a discrete collection of laws on the same general topic.

articles (*ARE·tih·clz*) The separate, original seven parts of the U.S. Constitution.

Articles of Confederation (*ARE·tih·clz ov kon·FED·er·a·shun*) The document which loosely governed the colonies and the states from 1777 until the Constitution was ratified in 1789.

articles of incorporation (*ARE·ti·clz ov in·core·pore·AY·shun*) The basic charter of a corporation, which states the name, basic purpose, incorporators, amount and types of stock that may be issued, and special characteristics such as being a not-for-profit corporation.

articles of organization (*AR·ti·kels ov or·ge·ni·ZAY·shun*) A document that gives authority to an organization to do business as a corporation. Also called *certificate of incorporation* and *charter*.

asportation (*as·por·TAY·shun*) The carrying away of goods.

assault (*a·SAWLT*) The intentional creation of a reasonable apprehension of an imminent battery. An attempt to commit a battery.

assets (*ASS·ets*) Property.

assignee (*ass·en·EE*) One to whom a right is transferred by assignment.

assignment (*a·SINE·ment*) The transfer of a right from one person to another.

assignor (*ass·en·OR*) One who transfers a right by assignment.

assumption of the risk (*a·SUMP·shun*) An affirmative defense wherein the defendant asserts (and must prove) that the plaintiff voluntarily assumed the consequences of injury that were caused by the defendant; or, when an employee agrees that the dangers of an at-work injury shall be at his or her own risk.

attachment (*a·TACH·ment*) The act of taking or seizing property by the use of a writ, summons, or other judicial order and bringing it into the custody of the court so that it may be applied toward the defendant's debt if the plaintiff wins the case.

attempted arson (*a·TEMT·ed AR·sen*) An attempt to commit the crime of arson, but falling short of its commission.

attempted larceny (*a·TEMPT·ed LAR·sen·ee*) An attempt to commit larceny, but falling short of its commission.

attest (*a·TEST*) To bear witness to.

attestation clause (*a·tes·TAY·shun*) The clause in a will that immediately precedes the witnesses' signatures.

attesting witnesses (*a·TEST·ing WIT·ness*) People who witness the signing of a document.

Attorney–client privilege (*a·turn·ee KLY·ent PRIV·lej*) The privilege related to the duty of confidentiality that an attorney has with a client, but coming from evidence law; protects a lawyer from having to testify against his or her client even when issued a subpoena.

attorney-in-fact (*a·TERN·ee*) An agent who is authorized to act under a power of attorney.

attractive nuisance doctrine (*a·TRAK·tiv NOO·sens DOK·trin*) A doctrine establishing property owners' duty to use ordinary care toward trespassing children who might reasonably be attracted to their property.

auction sale (*AWK·shun*) A sale of property to the highest bidder.

auction without reserve An auction in which the auctioneer must sell the goods to the highest bidder.

auction with reserve (*ree·ZERV*) An auction in which the auctioneer may withdraw the goods without accepting the highest bid.

automatic stay (*aw·toh·MAT·ic*) A self-operating postponement of collection proceedings against a debtor. Also called *automatic suspension*.

automatic suspension (*aw·toh·MAT·ic sus·PEN·shun*) A self-operating postponement of collection proceedings against a debtor. Also called *automatic stay*.

aver (*a·VER*) To make an allegation; to assert positively.

averments (*a·VER·ments*) Claims that the party making them expects to prove.

avoid (*a·VOID*) To annul, cancel, or make void. To get out of a voidable contract; repudiate. Also called *disaffirm*.

bail Money or property left with the court to assure that the person will return to stand trial; nonrefundable if the person "skips" bail.

bailee (*bay·LEE*) One to whom personal property is given under a bailment contract.

bailment (*BAYL·ment*) The relationship that exists when possession (but not ownership) of personal property is transferred to another for a specific purpose.

bailment for the sole benefit of the bailee (*bay·LEE*) A gratuitous bailment benefiting only the bailor.

bailment for the sole benefit of the bailor (*bay·LOR*) A gratuitous bailment benefiting only the bailor.

bailor *(bay·LOR)* The owner of personal property that has been temporarily transferred to a bailee under a contract of bailment.

balloon mortgage *(ba·LOON MORE·gej)* A mortgage with low fixed payments during the life of the loan, ending with one large final payment.

bankrupt *(BANK·rupt)* The state of a person (including a business) who is unable to pay debts as they become due.

bankruptcy *(BANK·rupt·see)* A legal process that aims to give debtors who are overwhelmed with debt a "fresh start" and to provide a fair way of distributing a debtor's assets among all creditors.

Bankruptcy Abuse and Prevention Consumer Protection Act (BAPCA) *(BANK·rupt·see uh·BEWS and pree·VEN·shun kon·SUE·mer pro·TECT·shun act)* A 2005 revision to the federal bankruptcy code that makes it more difficult for people to declare bankruptcy and that extends the time allowed between repeat bankruptcy filings.

bankruptcy estate The collection of the legal or equitable interests of the bankrupt debtor's property at the time of the bankruptcy filing. The extent of the bankruptcy estate is listed in Section 541 of the bankruptcy code.

banns of matrimony *(MAT·ri·mone·ee)* Public notice of a marriage contract for a certain number of weeks before the wedding date. Also called *marriage banns.*

Bar exam *(bar ex·AM)* The exam that lawyers have to pass in order to get licensed to practice law.

bare licensee *(ly·sen·SEE)* A person allowed on another's premises by operation of law, such as a fire-fighter or police officer.

bargain *(BAR·gen)* Agreement.

bargain and sale deed *(BAR·gen)* A deed that conveys land itself, rather than people's interests therein, and requires consideration.

base lines Horizontal lines running east and west in the United States government survey.

bastards *(BAS·terds)* An old word referring to children born out of wedlock. Also called *illegitimate children* and *nonmarital children.*

battery *(BAT·er·ee)* Intentional contact with another person without that person's permission and without justification; the unlawful application of force to another person.

benefit corporation A for profit corporation existing under benefit corporation statutes, whose purpose is to create some general public benefit and not simply to maximize shareholder profit.

bench trial *(tryl)* A trial without a jury. Also called *jury waived trial.*

beneficial title *(ben·e·FISH·el TY·tel)* The right to beneficial enjoyment. Also called *equitable title.*

beneficiary *(ben·e·FISH·ee·air·ee)* Someone who actually receives a gift under a will; also, one for whose benefit a trust is created. Also called *cestui que trust.*

bequeath *(be·KWEETH)* To give personal property in a will.

bequest *(be·KWEST)* A gift of personal property in a will.

bestiality *(bee·stee·AL·i·tee)* Sexual Intercourse by a man or woman with an animal.

beyond a reasonable doubt *(REE·zen·e·bel)* The condition that exists when the fact finder is fully persuaded that the accused has committed the crime.

bicameral *(bye·KAM·er·al)* Two chambers or houses of representation in Congress.

bidder *(BID·er)* Offeror.

bifurcated trial *(BY·fer·kay·ted tryl)* A trial that is divided into two parts, providing separate hearings for different issues in the same lawsuit.

bigamy *(BIG·a·mee)* The state of a man who has two wives, or of a woman who has two husbands, living at the same time.

bilateral contract *(by·LAT·er·el KON·trakt)* A contract containing two promises, one made by each party.

bilateral foreign divorce *(by·LAT·er·el FOR·en de·VORSS)* A divorce that occurs when both parties make an appearance in a foreign state or country.

bilateral mistake *(by·LAT·er·el mis·TAKE)* The situation that exists when both parties are mistaken about an important aspect of an agreement. Also called *mutual mistake.*

bill of particulars *(par·TIK·yoo·lars)* A written statement of the particulars of a complaint, showing the details of the amount owed.

Bill of Rights *(bil ov rites)* The first ten amendments of the U.S. Constitution.

bill of sale A signed writing evidencing the transfer of personal property from one person to another.

binding arbitration *(BINE·ding ar·be·TRAY·shun)* Arbitration in which the decision of the arbitrator is final and must be followed.

blue-sky laws State laws designed to protect the public from the sale of worthless stocks.

boilerplate *(BOY·ler·plate)* Standard language used commonly in documents of the same type.

bond A written instrument promising the payment of a sum of money if certain duties are not performed.

bounds Directions of the boundaries that enclose a parcel of land.

breach of contract *(KON·trakt)* The failure of a party to a contract to carry out the terms of the agreement.

breach of promise to marry *(PROM·iss)* Breaking off an engagement to marry.

breaking *(BRAKE·ing)* The first part of "breaking and entering," which traditionally has meant using some method to wrongfully gain entrance into a house or other occupiable structure by force, including breaking a window or picking a lock.

bribery *(BRY·be·ree)* The giving or receiving of a reward to influence any official act.

browsewrap contract *(BROWZ·rap KON·trakt)* A type of e-contract where the terms of online agreement (downloading software, for example) are available to review, or browse, but explicitly accepting the terms is not necessary. There can be lack of clarity that the use or buyer was adequately presented the terms of contract.

bulk transfer *(TRANS·fer)* A transfer, not in the ordinary course of business, in bulk, of a major part of the materials, supplies, merchandise, or other inventory of an enterprise.

burden of proof *(BER·den)* The duty of proving a fact.

burglary *(BUR·gler·ee)* At common law, the breaking and entering of a dwelling house of another, in the nighttime, with intent to commit a felony inside.

business invitee *(BIZ·ness in·vy·TEE)* One invited on the premises for a business or commercial purpose.

bypass trust *(BY·pass)* A type of marital deduction trust that reduces the taxation of the second spouse to die by limiting the amount in that person's estate to a sum that is not taxable. Also called *A–B trust, credit-shelter trust,* and *exemption equivalent trust.*

cabinet *(KAB·ih·net)* The executive department heads of government.

Canons of Professional Ethics *(KAN·onz ov pro·FEH·shun·al EH·thicks)* The first set of ethics rules created by the American Bar Association in 1908.

capacity *(ka·PASS·e·tee)* Legal competency.

capital crime *(KAP·i·tel krym)* A crime that is punishable by death.

capital criminal case *(KAP·i·tel KRIM·i·nel kase)* A case in which the death penalty may be inflicted.

carnal knowledge *(KAR·nel NOL·ej)* Sexual intercourse; the slightest penetration of the sexual organ of the woman by the sexual organ of the man.

case in chief *(cheef)* The introduction of evidence to prove the allegations that were made in the pleadings and in the opening statement.

castle doctrine *(KAS·el DOK·trin)* A doctrine that allows people to use all necessary force, without first retreating, to defend themselves when they are in their homes.

caucus *(KAW·kuss)* A private session with a mediator in which the mediator learns what the interests are behind each side's demands.

causation *(kaw·ZAY·zhun)* The direct and proximate cause of someone's injuries.

cause of action *(cawz ov AK·shun)* The grounds on which a suit is maintained.

C corporation *(kor·por·AY·shun)* A corporation governed by Subchapter C of the Internal Revenue Code, and which pays corporate taxes on its income.

cert. den. *(ser·sho·RARE·ee dee·NIDE)* Abbreviation meaning certiorari denied.

certificate of incorporation *(ser·TIF·i·ket ov in·kore·per·AY·shen)* A document that gives authority to an organization to do business as a corporation. Also called *articles of organization* and *charter.*

cestui que trust *(SES·twee kay)* One for whose benefit a trust is created. Also called *beneficiary.*

challenge *(CHAL·enj)* To call or put in question.

challenge for cause *(CHAL·enj for kaws)* A challenge of a juror made when it is believed that the juror does not stand indifferent.

challenge to the array *(CHAL·enj to the a·RAY)* A challenge to the entire jury because of some irregularity in the selection of the jury. Also called *motion to quash the array.*

Chapter 7 bankruptcy *(BANK·rupt·see)* A proceeding designed to liquidate a debtor's property, pay off creditors, and discharge the debtor from most debts. Also called *liquidation* and *straight bankruptcy.*

Chapter 11 bankruptcy *(BANK·rupt·see)* A method for businesses to reorganize their financial affairs, keep their assets, and remain in business. Also called *reorganization.*

Chapter 12 bankruptcy *(BANK·rupt·see)* A method for family farmers and family owned fishing businesses to adjust their financial affairs while continuing to operate their farms. Also called *family farmer debt adjustment.*

Chapter 13 bankruptcy *(BANK·rupt·see)* A method by which an individual with regular income can pay his or her debts from future income over an extended period. Also called *adjustment of debts of individuals.*

charitable remainder annuity trust *(CHAR·i·ta·bel re·MANE·der a·NYOO·i·tee)* A trust in which a fixed amount of income is given annually to a beneficiary and the remainder is given to a charity.

charitable remainder trust *(CHAR·i·ta·bel re·MANE·der)* A trust in which the donor, or a beneficiary, retains the income from the trust for life or other period, after which the trust corpus is given to a charity.

charitable remainder unitrust *(CHAR·i·ta·bel re·MANE·der YOO·nee·trust)* A trust in which a fixed percentage of income (at least 5 percent of the trust corpus) is given annually to a beneficiary and the remainder is given to a charity.

charitable subscription *(CHAR-i-ta-bel sub SKRIPT-shun)* A promise to make a donation or gift to a charitable organization (religious, civic, educational, etc.). Such a gratuitous promise is binding.

charitable trust *(CHAR·i·ta·bel)* A trust established for charitable purposes. Also called a *public trust.*

charter *(CHAR·ter)* A document that gives authority to an organization to do business as a corporation. Also called *articles of organization* and *certificate of incorporation.*

chattels *(CHAT·els)* Anything that is the subject of ownership other than real property. Also called *personal property* and *personalty.*

check A draft that is drawn on a bank and payable on demand.

checks and balances *(chex and BAL·en·says)* A system established in the U.S. Constitution which allows each branch of government to counteract the powers of the other branches.

child support *(su·PORT)* The legal obligations of parents to contribute to the economic maintenance and education of their children. Sometimes called *maintenance.*

chose in action *(shohz in AK·shun)* Evidence of a right to property, but not the property itself.

circuits *(SER·kits)* Name given to the division of the federal court system. There are 13 circuits in the federal system.

circumstantial evidence *(ser·kum·STAN·shel EV·i·dens)* Indirect evidence. Unlike direct evidence (e.g., eyewitness testimony), circumstantial evidence requires an inference to be drawn from the facts presented.

citation *(sy·TAY·shun)* A written order by a judge (or a police officer) commanding a person to appear in court for a particular purpose. Can also mean a reference to legal authority, like a case or a statute.

civil action *(SIV·el AK·shun)* A noncriminal lawsuit.

civil union *(SIV·el YOON·yun)* A relationship in which same-sex couples have the same rights and duties as married couples.

claim A right to payment.

class action *(klas AK·shun)* A lawsuit brought, with the court's permission, by one or more persons on behalf of a very large group of people who have the same interest in the matter.

clause *(klawz)* A distinct part of a contract or a constitutional section.

click-wrap agreement *(clik-rap a·GREE·ment)* A contract entered into online and commonly used with software licenses or web-based transactions in which the offeree enters into the contract by clicking on a dialog box that might say "I accept" or "OK"

close corporation *(klose kor·por·AY·shun)* A corporation that has restrictions on the transfer of shares. Sometimes, the term, "closely held corporation" is used, a term which also implies a limited number of shareholders.

closing argument *(AR·gyoo·ment)* Final statement by an attorney summarizing the evidence that has been introduced. Also called *summation.*

code *(KOHD)* A systematic collection of statutes, administrative regulations, and other laws.

codicil *(KOD·i·sil)* An amendment to a will that must be executed with the same formalities as the will itself.

coercion *(ko·ER·zhen)* Compelling someone to do something by threat or force.

cohabit *(koh·HAB·it)* To live together.

collateral *(co·LA·ter·al)* Something lenders can sell to get their money back in case of default; security interest for a loan.

collateral descendants (or relatives) *(ko·LAT·er·el REL·e·tivs)* Relatives not in a direct line, such as brothers, sisters, nieces, nephews, uncles, aunts, and cousins.

collusion *(ke·LOO·zhen)* An agreement between a husband and wife that one of them will commit a marital offense so that the other may obtain a divorce.

comity *(KOM·i·tee)* A doctrine stating that the courts of one jurisdiction will give effect to the laws and judicial decisions of another jurisdiction, not as a matter of obligation, but out of deference and respect.

Comments *(KAW·ments)* The official remarks that help a reader understand the focus of the Rules in the American Bar Association Model of Rules.

commerce clause *(KOM·erss)* A clause in Article I of the U.S. Constitution giving Congress the power to regulate commerce with foreign nations and among the different states.

common areas *(KOM·on AIR·ee·uz)* The part of a condominium or apartment building that is owned, as tenants in common, by all the unit owners.

common law *(KOM·on)* The case law used in England and the American Colonies before the American Revolution. Also, common law means judge-made law or appellate case decisions.

common law marriage *(KOM·on law MAR·ej)* A marriage without a formal ceremony or issuance of a legal license.

common law theory of mortgages *(KOM·on law THEE·ree ov MORE·ge·jes)* The legal theory that a mortgage is a conveyance of title, which becomes void on payment of the obligation. Also called *title theory of mortgages.*

common stock *(KOM·on stok)* Stock that has no preferences, but that gives the owner/shareholder the right to vote.

community property *(kom·YOON·i·tee PROP·er·tee)* Property (other than a gift or inheritance), acquired by a husband or wife during marriage, that belongs to both spouses equally.

commutation of sentence *(kom·yoo·TAY·shun ov SEN·tense)* The changing of a sentence to one that is less severe.

comparative fault *(kom·PAR·e·tiv fawlt)* Another term for comparative negligence.

comparative negligence *(kom·PAR·e·tiv NEG·li·jens)* The proportionate sharing between the plaintiff and the defendant of compensation for injuries, the division based on the relative negligence of the two.

compensatory damages *(kom·PEN·sa·tor·ee DAM·e·jez)* Damages that compensate the plaintiff for actual losses resulting from the breach.

competent *(KOM·peh·tent)* In a legal ethics context, the capability to adequately represent the client by possessing the underlying substantive and procedural legal expertise that is needed for the matter.

complaint *(kom·PLAYNT)* A formal document containing a short and plain statement of the claim, indicating that the plaintiff is entitled to relief and containing a demand for the relief sought.

compulsory arbitration *(kom·PUL·so·ree ar·be· TRAY·shun)* Arbitration that is required by agreement or by law. Also called *mandatory arbitration.*

computer fraud *(frawd)* Use of a computer to obtain money, property, or services by false pretenses.

computer fraud and abuse act *(frawd and a·byus)* The first federal legislation to respond to the increase of computer crime, amended seven times since its passage in 1986.

conciliation *(kon·sil·ee·AY·shun)* An informal process in which a neutral third person listens to both sides and makes suggestions for reaching a solution. Also called *mediation.*

conciliator *(kon·SIL·ee·ay·tor)* A neutral third person in a conciliation session who listens to both sides and makes suggestions for reaching a solution. Also called a *mediator.*

concurrent jurisdiction *(kon·KER·ent joo·res·DIK·shen)* The power of two or more courts to decide a particular case.

concurrent ownership *(kon·KER·ent OH·ner·ship)* Ownership by more than one person. Also called *co-ownership.*

concurrent sentences *(kon·KER·ent SEN·ten·sez)* Two or more sentences imposed on a defendant, to be served at the same time.

condition precedent *(kon·DISH·en pree·SEE·dent)* An event that must first occur before an agreement (or deed or will) becomes effective.

condition subsequent *(kon·DISH·en SUB·se·kwent)* A qualification that comes later.

condominium *(kon·de·MIN·ee·um)* A parcel of real property, portions of which are owned separately in fee simple by individual owners and the remainder of which is owned as tenants in common by all the unit owners.

condominium association *(kon·de·MIN·ee·um a·so·see·AY·shun)* A group of people consisting of condominium unit owners that manages and maintains a condominium.

condonation *(kon·do·NAY·shun)* The forgiveness of a matrimonial offense.

confession and avoidance *(kon·FESH·en and a·VOY·denss)* A defense that admits the plaintiff's allegations, but introduces another factor that avoids liability. Also called *affirmative defense.*

confidentiality agreement *(kon·fe·den·shee·AL·i·tee a·GREE·ment)* An agreement to refrain from disclosing trade secrets to others. Also called *nondisclosure agreement.*

confidential communication *(kon·fi·DEN·shul kom·yoo·ni·KAY·shun)* a conversation or writing that expresses personal or private information.

conflict of interest *(KON·flict of IN·ter est)* A situation in which a lawyer is torn between loalty between two or more clients, or loyalty between client and lawyer.

conforming goods *(kon·FORM·ing)* Goods that are in accordance with the obligations under the contract.

conjugal *(KON·je·gel)* Pertaining to the marriage relationship.

connivance *(ke·NY·venss)* The plaintiff's secret cooperation in the commission of a marital wrong—that is a common law defense to an action for divorce—committed by the defendant.

consanguinity *(kon·san·GWIN·i·tee)* Related by blood.

consecutive sentences *(kon·SEK·yoo·tiv SEN· ten·sez)* Two or more sentences imposed on a defendant to be served one after the other. Also called *cumulative sentences.*

consent decree *(kon· SENT de ·KREE)* A decree that is entered by consent of the parties, usually without admission of guilt or wrongdoing.

consequential damages *(kon·se·KWEN·shel DAM·e·jez)* Losses that flow not directly from a breach of contract, but from the consequences of it.

conservator *(kon·SER·ve·tor)* One who legally has the care and management of the property, but not the person, of someone who is incompetent.

consideration *(kon·sid·er·AY·shun)* An exchange of promises or benefits and detriments or obligations by the parties to an agreement.

consignee *(kon·sine·EE)* One to whom a consignment is made.

consignment *(kon·SINE·ment)* The process of delivering goods to a bailee, called a factor, who attempts to sell them.

consignor *(kon·sine·OR)* One who makes a consignment.

consortium *(kon·SORE·shum)* The fellowship between a husband and wife.

conspiracy *(kon·SPIR·a·see)* The getting together of two or more people to accomplish some criminal or unlawful act.

constructive eviction *(kon·STRUK·tiv e·VIK·shun)* Dispossession caused by the landlord's doing some act that deprives the tenant of the beneficial enjoyment of the demised premises.

constructively *(kon·STRUK·tiv·lee)* Made so by legal interpretation.

constructive possession *(kon·STRUK·tiv po·SESH·en)* Possession not actual, but assumed to exist. When something is under a person's control that person is in constructive possession.

constructive service *(kon·STRUK·tiv SER·viss)* A type of service in which the summons and complaint are left at the defendant's last and usual place of abode.

constructive trust *(kon·STRUK·tiv)* An implied trust that arises in favor of one who is defrauded when title to property is obtained by fraud.

contingency fee *(kon·TIN·jen·cee fee)* A percentage of the plaintiff's awarded damages or settlement amount. A contingency fee must be in writing and signed by the client.

contract *(KON·trakt)* Any agreement that is enforceable in a court of law. An agreement that has consideration is a contract.

contract implied in fact *(KON·trakt im·PLIDE)* A contract that arises from the conduct of the parties rather than from their express statements.

contract implied in law *(KON·trakt im·PLIDE)* A contract imposed by law to prevent unjust enrichment. Also called *quasi contract.*

contract to sell *(KON·trakt)* A contract under which title to goods is to pass at a future time.

contractual capacity *(kon·TRAK·chew·el ka·PA·si·tee)* The legal ability to be able to enter into a contract.

contributory negligence *(kon·TRIB·u·tor·ee NEG·li· jens)* Negligence on the part of the plaintiff that contributed to his or her injuries and is a proximate cause of them. In a contributory negligence jurisdiction, any proven negligence on the part of the plaintiff results in the plaintiff losing.

controlled substance *(kon·TROLED SUB·stanss)* A drug that is included in any of the five schedules established by the Federal Controlled Substances Act.

conversion *(kon·VER·zhun)* The wrongful exercise of dominion and control over the personal property in another's possession.

convey *(kon·VAY)* To transfer.

conveyance *(kon·VAY·enss)* A formal, written instrument by which title to real property is transferred from one person to another. Also called a *deed.*

conveyance in trust *(kon·VAY·enss)* A transfer of legal title to property by the settlor to a trustee to hold for the benefit of a beneficiary.

conveyancing *(kon·VAY·enss·ing)* Transferring title to real property.

convict *(KON·vict)* A person who is found guilty of a crime.

convicted *(kon·VICT·ed)* Found guilty of a crime.

cooperative apartment *(koh·OP·er·a·tiv a·PART·ment)* A dwelling building in which the occupants lease individual units and, at the same time, own shares of stock in the corporation that owns the building.

co-ownership *(koh-OH·ner·ship)* Ownership by more than one person. Also called *concurrent ownership.*

coparceners *(koh·PAR·se·ners)* Persons to whom an estate of inheritance descends jointly and by whom it is held as an entire estate (early English law).

co-partnership *(koh-PART·ner·ship)* An association of two or more persons to carry on as co-owners of a business for profit. Also called *partnership.*

copulate *(KOP·yoo·late)* to engage in sexual intercourse.

copulation *(kop·yoo·LA·shun)* Sexual intercourse.

copyright *(KOP·ee·rite)* The exclusive right given to an author, composer, artist, or photographer to publish and sell exclusively a creative work for the life of the author plus 70 years.

copyright infringement *(KOP·ee·rite in·FRINJ·ment)* The unauthorized use of copyrighted material.

co-respondent *(KOH-re·spond·ent)* The person charged with committing adultery with the defendant in a divorce action.

corporation *(kor·por·AY·shun)* A legal entity created under state law with the power to conduct its affairs as though it were a natural person. A corporation has a legal existence that is separate from the life of its owners.

corpus *(KOR·pus)* The body, principal sum, or capital of a trust. Also called *trust fund, trust principal, trust property,* and *trust res.*

corpus delicti *(KOR·pus de·LIK·tie)* A body on which a crime has been committed.

costs *(KOSTS)* Expenses associated with a legal matter, such as filing fees.

co-tenants *(koh-TEN·ents)* Two or more owners of real property.

counterclaim *(KOWN·ter·klame)* A claim that the defendant has against the plaintiff.

counteroffer *(KOWN·ter·off·er)* A response to an offer in which the terms of the original offer are changed.

court *(KORT)* A governmental unit organized to administer justice.

court of equity *(EK·wi·tee)* A court that administers justice according to the system of equity.

Court of Ordinary *(OR·di·ner·ee)* A name given, in some states, to the court that exercises the function of settling decedents' estates.

court of appeals *(a·PEELS)* A court that reviews the decisions of a lower court. Also called an *appellate court.*

covenant *(KOV·e·nent)* A promise or assurance.

covenant, conditions and restrictions (CC&R) Part of a deed used to regulate the appearance and use of a property that is part of a condominium or cooperative that are stricter that local ordinances or zoning laws.

covenant marriage *(KOV·e·nent MAR·ej)* A type of marriage in which the parties agree to go through counseling before the marriage and also during the marriage to resolve conflicts.

co-venture *(KOH-ven·cher)* A relationship in which two or more people combine their labor or property for a single business undertaking. Also called *joint enterprise, joint venture,* and *syndicate.*

cover *(KUV·er)* The right of a buyer, after breach by a seller, to purchase similar goods from someone else.

coverture *(KUV·er·cher)* Marriage.

creditors *(KRED·et·ers)* People to whom money is owed.

credit-shelter trust *(KRED·et-SHEL·ter)* A type of marital deduction trust that reduces the taxation of the second spouse to die by limiting the amount in that person's estate to a sum that is not taxable. Also called *A–B trust, bypass trust,* and *exemption equivalent trust.*

crime *(krym)* A wrong against society.

crime of moral turpitude *(MOR·el TER·pi·tood)* A crime that is base, vile, and depraved.

criminal complaint *(KRIM·i·nel kom·PLAYNT)* A written statement of the essential facts making up an offense charged in a criminal action.

criminal conversation *(KRIM·i·nel kon·ver·SAY·shun)* A tort action brought by a husband or wife against a third party who committed adultery with the husband's or wife's spouse.

criminal fraud *(KRIM·i·nel frawd)* Knowingly and deliberately obtaining the property of another by false pretenses with intent to defraud. Also called *larceny by false pretenses.*

cross claim *(kross klame)* A claim brought by one defendant against another defendant in the same suit.

cross complaint *(kross kom·PLAYNT)* A pleading used in California by a defendant to file a claim against another defendant, a third party, and the plaintiff in the same action.

cross-examination *(kross-eg·zam·in·AY·shun)* The examination of an opposing or hostile witness.

cross questions *(kross KWES·chens)* Questions asked by a deponent in response to questions asked at a deposition.

cruelty *(KROO·el·tee)* In a divorce action, personal violence by one spouse that endangers the life, limb, or health of the other spouse.

Crummey powers *(KRUM·ee)* Authority that gives trust beneficiaries the right to withdraw each year the money that is contributed to the trust that year.

culpable negligence *(KUL·pe·bel NEG·li·jens)* The intentional commission of an act that a reasonable person knows would cause injury to another. Also called *willful, wanton, and reckless conduct.*

cumulative sentences *(KYOOM·yoo·la·tiv SEN· tensses)* Two or more sentences imposed on a defendant to be served one after the other. Also called *consecutive sentences.*

cure *(kyoor)* To correct.

curtesy *(KUR·te·see)* At common law, the right of a widower, if issue of the marriage were born alive, to a life estate in all real property owned by his wife during coverture.

curtilage *(KUR·til·ej)* The enclosed space of ground and buildings immediately surrounding a dwelling house.

custody *(KUSS·te·dee)* The care and keeping of anything.

custody of children *(KUSS·te·dee)* The care, control, and maintenance of children.

cyber-bullying *(SI·ber·BULL·ee·ing)* Using the Internet to malign or threaten someone.

cybercrime *(SY·ber krym)* Criminal activity associated with a computer.

cyber-harrassment *(SI·ber·har·Ass·ment)* Using the Internet to repeatedly interfere with someone's life.

cyberlaw *(SY·ber law)* The area of law that involves computers and their related problems.

cyber-stalking *(STA WK·ing)* Using the Internet to put another person in fear for their or their loved one's safety or life.

cyber stalking Using a computer to communicate willful, malicious and repeated harassment and threats to a person with violence intended to place the person in fear or serious bodily injury. Some state interchange laws on cyber bullying and cyber harassment, which are related.

cybertort *(SY·ber·tort)* A tort associated with a computer.

cy pres doctrine *(sy pray DOK·trin)* A French term that means as near as possible. This term is used in gift or trust law when an intended gift or benefit fails because the named recipient doesn't exist and the court must determine who should next be given it.

damages *(DAM·e·jez)* Money which is intended to compensate the injured party for losses caused by the tortious act of the tortfeasor.

dangerous instrumentalities *(DAYN·jer·ess in· stroo·men·TAL· i·tees)* Hazardous items such as explosives and wild animals.

dangerous weapon *(DAYN·jer·ess WEP·en)* An item that is, from the way it is used, capable of causing death or serious bodily injury. Also called *deadly weapon.*

deadly weapon *(DED·lee WEP·en)* An item that is, from the way it is used, capable of causing death or serious bodily injury. Also called *dangerous weapon.*

debtor *(DET·er)* One who owes a debt to another.

debtor-in-possession *(DET·er-in-po·SESH·en)* Another name for a debtor in Chapter 11, 12, and 13 bankruptcy cases.

decedent *(de·SEE·dent)* A deceased person.

deceit *(dee·SEET)* A misrepresentation of a material, existing fact, knowingly made, that causes someone reasonably relying on it to suffer damages. Also called *fraud.*

declaration *(dek·la·RAY·shun)* At common law, a formal document containing a short and plain statement of the claim, indicating that the plaintiff is entitled to relief and containing a demand for the relief sought.

declaration of trust *(dek·la·RAY·shun)* A written declaration by a settlor that he or she is holding legal title to property as trustee for the benefit of another person.

decree *(de·KREE)* The decision of a court of equity.

deed A formal, written instrument by which title to real property is transferred from one person to another. Also called *conveyance.*

deed of release *(re·LEESS)* A deed releasing property from an encumbrance.

deed of trust An instrument used in some states that replaces a mortgage, by which the legal title to real property is placed in a trustee to secure the repayment of a debt.

deed-poll *(deed-pole)* A deed or lease in which only the party making the instrument executes it.

deed without covenants (*KOV·e·nents*) A deed to real property in which the grantor transfers only his or her interest, if any, in the property and gives no warranties of title. Also called *fiduciary deed* and *quitclaim deed.*

de facto corporation (*de FAK·toh kor·por·AY·shun*) A corporation that has a defect in its establishment, but that is recognized as a valid corporation unless set aside by the state.

defamation (*de·fa·MAY·shun*) The wrongful act of damaging another's character or reputation by the use of false statements made orally.

default (*de·FAWLT*) A failure to perform a legal duty.

default judgment (*de·FAWLT JUJ·ment*) A court decision entered against a party who has failed to respond to or defend a lawsuit.

defeasance clause (*de·FEE·zenss*) A clause in a mortgage providing that the mortgage deed shall be void on payment of the obligation.

defeasible estate (*de·FEEZ·i·bel es·TATE*) An estate that can be lost or defeated.

defendant (*de·FEN·dent*) A person against whom a legal action is brought.

defendant in error (*de·FEN·dent in ERR·er*) A party against whom an appeal is brought. Also called *appellee* and *respondent.*

defense (*de·FENSS*) Evidence or argument offered by a defendant to defeat a criminal charge or civil lawsuit.

deficiency judgment (*de·FISH·en·see JUJ·ment*) A judgment for the amount remaining due to the mortgagee after a foreclosure sale.

degree of kindred (*de·GREE ov KIN·dred*) The determination of the respective relationships between a decedent and his or her relatives, undertaken to measure who are most nearly related by blood.

de jure corporation (*de JOOR·ee kor·por·AY·shun*) A corporation that is established in strict compliance with the law.

del credere agent (*del KREH·de·ray AY·jent*) A factor who sells consigned goods on credit and who guarantees to the consignor that the buyer will pay for the goods.

delegation (*del·e·GA·shun*) The transfer of a duty by one person to another.

deliberate (*dee·LIB·e·rate*) To consider slowly and carefully.

demand for bill of particulars (*de·MAND for bill of par·TIK·yoo·lars*) A pleading calling for details of a claim or the separate items of an account.

demise (*de·MIZE*) To lease.

demonstrative legacy (*de·MON·stre·tiv LEG·a·see*) A bequest of a certain sum of money with a direction that it be paid out of a particular fund.

demurrer (*de·MER·er*) A pleading used by the defendant to attack the plaintiff's complaint by raising a point of law, such as the failure of the complaint to state a cause of action.

deponent (*de·PONE·ent*) One who gives testimony under oath. A person who signs an affidavit. Also called *affiant.*

deposition (*dep·e·ZISH·en*) The transcribed testimony of a witness, given under oath and in anticipation of an eventual trial, but not in open court.

deposition on oral examination (*eg·zam·in·AY·shun*) A deposition in which lawyers orally examine and cross-examine a witness.

deposition on written questions (*KWES·chens*) A deposition in which lawyers examine and cross-examine a witness who has received, in advance, written questions to be answered.

derivative action (*de·RIV·a·tiv AK·shun*) A suit by a stockholder to enforce a corporate cause of action.

descendants (*de·SEN·dents*) Those who are of the bloodstream (including adopted children) of a common ancestor.

descent (*de·SENT*) Succession to the ownership of real property by inheritance (early English law).

desertion (*des·ER·shun*) The voluntary separation of one spouse from the other, for the statutory period, without justification and with the intent of not returning.

design defect (*dee·ZINE DEE·fekt*) The theory that a product was negligently designed or could have been designed more safely.

design patent A patent that protects the way an article looks, which includes its shape or configuration, and lasts for 14 or 15 years, depending on the date of the patent.

destination contract (*des·te·NAY·shun KON·trakt*) A contract that requires the seller to deliver goods to a specific destination.

determinable fee (*de·TER·min·e·bel*) An estate in real property that is capable of coming to an end automatically because of the happening of some event. Also called *fee simple determinable.*

determine (*de·TER·min*) Coming to an end.

detriment (*DET·ri·ment*) The giving up of a legal right.

devise (*de·VIZE*) A gift of real property in a will.

devisee (*dev·iy·ZEE*) A person to whom real property is given by will.

devisor (*dev·iy·ZOR*) A person who gives real property by will.

digital signature (*DI·gi·tl SIG·na·cher*) an algorithmically created message that is unique for the recipient, allowing the recipient to respond electronically in a cryptographic way, so as to confirm that the actual recipient was the one "signing" online.

diligence (*DIL·uh·jents*) An important part of competence involving keeping a client reasonably informed about the status of his or her matter and responding to client requests for information.

direct evidence (*de·REKT EV·i·dens*) Evidence that directly relates to the fact in issue. Evidence that doesn't require the making of an inference based upon the facts presented, such as eyewitness testimony.

direct examination (*de·REKT eg·zam·in·AY·shun*) The examination of one's own witness.

directive to physicians (*de·REKT·iv to fi·ZI·shens*) A written expression of a person's wishes to be allowed to die a natural death and not be kept alive by heroic or artificial methods. Also called *health care declaration, living will,* and *medical directive.*

directors (*de·REK·ters*) People who are elected by stockholders or shareholders to manage a corporation.

disaffirm (*diss·a·FERM*) To get out of a voidable contract; repudiate. Also called *avoid.*

disbarment (*dis·BAR·ment*) Permanent loss of a law license, ordered by a court that oversees the practice of law.

discharge in bankruptcy (*DIS·charj in BANK·rupt·see*) A release of a debtor from all debts that were proved in a bankruptcy proceeding.

disciplinary commission (*dis·i·plin·AIR·eekom·i·shun*) A group of people empowered by its jurisdiction's higest court to investigate grievances against lawyers.

discovery (*diss·KUV·e·ree*) Methods that allow each party in litigation to obtain information from the other party and from witnesses about a case before going to court.

discovery sanction (*diss·KOV·er·ee SANK·shun*) Court-ordered penalties for failing to produce evidence.

discretion (*diss·KRE·shun*) The power that a judge has to make a decision based on his or her own judgment and conscience.

discretionary trust (*dis·KRE·shun·air·ee*) A trust that allows the trustee to decide, in the trustee's discretion, how much will be given to each beneficiary. Also called *spray trust* and *sprinkling trust.*

disinheritance (*dis·in·HAIR·uh·tents*) Purposely omitted from a will.

disinterested witness An attesting witness to a will who will not inherit property under the will.

dismissal (*diss·MISS·el*) An order disposing of an action without a trial of the issues.

dismissal without prejudice A dismissal in which the plaintiff is allowed to correct the error and bring another action on the same claim.

dismissal with prejudice (*PREJ·e·diss*) A dismissal in which the plaintiff is barred from bringing another action on the same claim.

dispositive clauses (*diss·POS·a·tiv*) The clauses in a will that state exactly what each beneficiary is to receive.

dispossessory warrant proceedings (*diss·po·SESS·o·ree WAR·ent pro·SEED·ings*) The legal action used by landlords to evict tenants. Also called *forcible entry and detainer, summary ejectment, summary process,* and *unlawful detainer.*

disseised (*di·SEEZD*) Dispossessed.

dissociation Under the Revised Uniform Partnership Act (RUPA), dissociation is the legal effect of a partner's ceasing to be associated in carrying on on the partnership business. Under the Uniform Partnership Act (UPA), the term "dissolution" is used instead, but according to the RUPA, dissociation does not automatically require partnership dissolution, winding up, and termination.

dissolution (*diss·uh·LOO·zhun*) An act or occurrence that requires the partnership to eventually terminate.

dissolution of marriage (*diss·o·LU·shun ov MAR·ej*) The act, by a court, of terminating a valid marriage. Also called *divorce.*

distribution (*diss·tre·BYOO·shun*) The apportionment and division of the personal property of an intestate among his or her heirs (early English law).

divested (*dy·VEST·ed*) Taken away.

diversity of citizenship (*dy·VER·sit·ee ov SIT·e·sen·ship*) A phrase used in connection with the jurisdiction of the federal courts.

divided custody (*de·VIE·ded KUS·te·dee*) Custody in which the child lives with each parent part of the year, the other parent usually having visitation rights, but not control of the child, during that period.

dividends (*DIV·i·denz*) Profits distributed to the stockholders of a corporation.

divorce (*de·VORSS*) The act, by a court, of terminating a valid marriage. Also called *dissolution of marriage.*

divorce from bed and board The discontinuance of cohabitation by the spouses. Also called *limited divorce* and *separation of spouses.*

DNA Abbreviation for deoxyribonucleic acid. The double strand of molecules that carries a cell's unique genetic code.

DNA sample Biological evidence of any nature that is utilized to conduct DNA analysis.

do not resuscitate order (DNR) A medical order written by a doctor, but at the wishes of the patient, instructing medical personnel that the patient is refusing CPR.

docket (*DOK·et*) A record of cases that are filed with the court.

docket number (*DOK·et NUM·ber*) A number assigned to each case by the clerk of the court.

doctrine of charitable immunity (*DOK·trin ov CHAR·i·ta·bel im·YOO·ni·tee*) A legal doctrine under which charitable institutions are immune from tort liability.

doctrine of respondeat superior (*res·PON·dee·at soo·PEER·e·or*) A legal doctrine under which an employer is responsible for the torts of its employees, that are committed within the scope of employment. Initially called the master servant rule.

doctrine of sovereign immunity (*SOV·er·in im·YOO·ni·tee*) A legal doctrine under which governmental bodies are immune from tort liability.

documentary evidence (*dok·u·MENT·ta·ree EV·i· denss*) Evidence consisting of such documents as written contracts, business records, correspondence, wills, and deeds.

Doe defendants (*de·FEN·dents*) The device used to refer to defendants whose names are unknown.

domestic asset protection trust (DAPT) A self-settled trust allowed in 16 states (as of 2017) that uses an independent trustee and which is designed to benefit the settlor or grantor with income but also protect those assets from the settlor's creditors.

domestic corporation (*do·MES·tik kor·por·A·shun*) A corporation organized in the state in which it is operating.

domestic violence (*do·MES·tik VY·o·lenss*) The abuse of a closely related person such as a present or former spouse or cohabitant.

domicile (*DOM·i·sile*) A person's principal place of abode; the place to which, whenever one is absent from it, one has the present intent of returning.

donee (*doh·NEE*) A person who receives a gift.

donor (*doh·NOR*) A person who gives a gift. A person who establishes a trust. Also called *grantor, settlor,* and *trustor.*

dormant partner (*DOR·ment PART·ner*) A partner who is not known to the public as a partner and who takes no active part in the business.

double jeopardy (*DUB·el JEP·er·dee*) The situation in which a defendant is tried twice for the same offense. Prohibited by the 5th Amendment to the U.S. Constitution.

double taxation (*DUB·el taks·AY·shun*) Taxes on a corporation's income and on the dividends earned by the corporation's stockholders.

dower (*DOW·er*) At common law, the right of a widow to a life estate in one-third of all real property owned by her husband during coverture.

drugs Chemical substances that have an effect on the body or mind.

drug trafficking (*TRAF·ik·ing*) The unauthorized manufacture or distribution of any controlled substance, or the possession of such a substance with the intention of manufacturing or distributing it illegally.

due process clause (*dew PRO·sess*) A clause in the U.S. Constitution's Fifth and Fourteenth Amendments requiring that no person shall be deprived of life, liberty, or property without fairness and justice.

dummy corporation (*DUM·mee kor·por·AY·shun*) A lawful corporation created to take title assets while safeguarding the corporation owner's identity and liability.

durable power of attorney (*DYOOR·e·bel POW·er ov a·TERN·ee*) A document authorizing another person to act on one's behalf, with language indicating that the authorization either is to survive one's incapacity or is to become effective when one becomes incapacitated.

duress *(dyoor·ESS)* The overcoming of a person's free will by the use of threat or physical harm.

duty of care *(DYOO·tee ov kare)* A legal obligation of carefulness or prudence toward those likely to be injured by one's conduct.

duty of confidentiality *(DEW·tee of kon·fi·den·she·AL·i·tee)* A rule requiring lawyers to protect his or her client information including statements made to the lawyer, documents given to the lawyer, and any information the lawyer learns about the client, whatever the source.

dwelling house *(DWEL·ing)* A house in which the occupier and family usually reside, including all outbuildings within the curtilage.

easement appurtenant *(EEZ·ment a·PER·ten·ent)* An easement that benefits a particular tract of land.

e-commerce *(ee-KOM·erss)* Abbreviation for electronic commerce. The buying and selling of goods and services, or the transfer of money, over the Internet.

e-contracts *(ee KON·traks)* Contracts entered into over the Internet, including licenses to use software.

e-discovery *(ee diss·KOV·er·ee)* Obtaining electronic communications or other information stored electronically for the purposes of trial preparation.

efficacy *(EF·i·ka·see)* Effectiveness.

ejectment *(e·JEKT·ment)* At common law, the legal action used by landlords to evict tenants.

elastic powers *(ee·LASS·tick pow·erz)* The power of Congress to make all laws necessary and proper to carry out its express powers.

elective share *(e·LEK·tiv)* A statutory sum given to a surviving spouse who disclaims the provisions made for him or her in a deceased spouse's will. Also called *forced share* or *statutory share.*

Electronically stored information (ESI) *(ee·lek·TRON·i·kel·lee stord in·fore·MAY·shun)* Information created, manipulated, communicated, and stored by computer.

eleemosynary corporation *(el·ee·MOS·en·er·ee kor·por·AY·shun)* A corporation that is created for charitable and benevolent purposes.

emancipated *(e·MAN·si·pay·ted)* Freed from parental control.

embezzlement *(em·BEZ·ul·ment)* The fraudulent appropriation of property by a person to whom it has been entrusted.

emotional distress *(e·MO·shun·el dis·TRESS)* Emotional suffering caused by the infliction of extreme and outrageous conduct by another.

employee *(em·PLOY·ee)* One who performs services under the direction and control of another.

employer *(em·PLOY·er)* One who employs the services of others in exchange for wages or salaries.

encumbrance *(en·KUM·brenss)* A claim that one has against the property of another. A lien, charge, or liability attached to and binding on real property.

enjoin *(en·JOYN)* To require a person to perform, or to abstain from performing, some act.

entrapment *(en·TRAP·ment)* A defense that may be used when a law enforcement induces a person to commit a crime that the person would not have otherwise committed.

equal protection clause *(EE·kwell pro·TEK·shen)* A clause in the U.S. Constitution's Fourteenth Amendment requiring similarly situated persons to receive similar treatment under the law.

equitable distribution laws *(EK·wit·a·bel dis·tre·BYOO·shun)* Laws that give courts the power to distribute property equitably between the parties upon divorce.

equitable theory of mortgages *(EK·wit·a·bel THEE·ree ov MORE·gejes)* The legal theory that a mortgage is not a conveyance of title, but merely a lien against the property. Also called *lien theory of mortgages.*

equitable title *(EK·wit·a·bel TY·tel)* The right to beneficial enjoyment. Also called *beneficial title.*

equity *(EK·wi·tee)* That which is just and fair.

equity of redemption *(EK·wi·tee ov re·DEMP·shun)* The right of a mortgagor to redeem the property at any time before the completion of a foreclosure proceeding by paying the amount of the debt, interest, and costs.

erosion *(e·RO·zhen)* The gradual eating away of the soil by the operation of currents or tides.

escheat *(es·CHEET)* The reversion of property to the state if the property owner dies without heirs.

e-signature *(ee-SIG·na·choor)* Abbreviation for electronic signature, a method of signing an electronic message that identifies the sender and signifies his or her approval of the message's content.

Esquire *(ES·kwyr)* A title following the name of an attorney, in place of the prefixes Mr., Mrs., Miss, or Ms. (abbreviated Esq.)

establishment clause *(es·TAB·lish·ment)* A clause in the U.S. Constitution that prohibits the government from establishing a state religion.

estate *(es·TATE)* Ownership interest.

estate in severalty A form of title to real estate where there is only one tenant/owner, without any other joint interest.

estate planning *(es·TATE PLAN·ing)* Arranging a person's assets in a way that maintains and protects the family most effectively both during the person's life and after the person's death.

estate pur autre vie *(per OH·tra vee)* An estate that a person holds during the life of another person.

estate tail male A freehold estate restricting ownership to men in the family line.

estate tail special *(SPESH·el)* A freehold estate restricting ownership to a husband and wife and the heirs of their two bodies.

estate tax *(es·TATE)* A tax imposed upon the estate of a deceased person.

ethics opinions *(e-thicks o-PIN-yuns)* formal answers (which have a similarity in style to appellate court opinions) to questions about the interpretation or application of the ethics rules.

euthanasia *(yooth·e·NAY·zha)* An active procedure to hasten the death of one who is terminally ill or in immense suffering.

eviction *(e·VIK·shun)* The act of depriving a person of the possession of real property either by reentry or by legal process.

exclusionary rule *(eks·KLOO·shun·a·ree)* A court-created doctrine holding that evidence obtained by an unconstitutional search or seizure cannot be used at the trial of a defendant.

exclusive jurisdiction *(eks·KLOO·siv joo·res·DIK·shen)* The power of one court only to hear a particular case, to the exclusion of all other courts.

exculpatory clause *(eks·KUL·pa·toh·ree)* A clause that is used in a contract allowing a party to the contract to avoid legal responsibility.

excusable homicide *(eks·KYOO·se·bel HOM·i·side)* The taking of a human life when an excuse exists.

execute *(EK·se·kyoot)* To complete, to make, to perform, or to do, such as sign a will. Also, the act of the state in committing capital punishment.

executed *(EK·se·kyoo·ted)* Carried out or performed.

executive branch *(ex·ECK·kew·tiv branch)* The branch of government headed by the President of the United States. It includes the cabinet, which are the executive departments of government appointed by the president.

executor *(eg·ZEK·yoo·tor)* A male nominated in a will of a decedent to carry out the terms of the will; a personal representative of an estate. Generally, this term is used whether the executor is male or female.

executor de son tort *(eg·ZEK·yoo·tor day sown tort)* A person who performs the duties of an executor without authority to do so.

executory *(eg·ZEK·yoo·tor·ee)* That which is yet to be executed or performed.

executrix *(eg·ZEK·yoo·triks)* A female nominated in a will of a decedent to carry out the terms of the will; a personal representative of an estate.

exemplary damages *(eg·ZEMP·le·ree DAM·e·jez)* Damages as a measure of punishment for the defendant's wrongful acts. Also called *punitive damages.*

exemption equivalent trust *(eg·ZEMP·shun)* A type of marital deduction trust that reduces the taxation of the second spouse to die by limiting the amount in that person's estate to a sum that is not taxable. Also called *A–B trust, bypass trust,* and *credit-shelter trust.*

exemptions *(eg·ZEMP·shuns)* Items of property that are excepted from bankruptcy proceedings and may be retained by the debtor.

exhibits *(eg·ZIB·its)* Tangible items that are introduced in evidence.

exordium clause *(eks·ORD·ee·um)* The introductory paragraph of a will. Also called *publication clause.*

ex parte *(eks PAR·tay)* On one side only.

ex parte communication *(ex PAR·tay kom·YOU·ni·kay·shun)* A lawyer communicating with a judge while the other party's lawyer is unaware of the commmunication.

ex parte foreign divorce *(eks·PAR·tay FOR·en de·VORSS)* A divorce that occurs when one spouse appears in a foreign jurisdiction, and the other spouse does not appear and fails to respond to the notice of divorce or service of process.

ex post facto *(eks post FAC·toh)* After the fact.

express authority *(eks·PRESS aw·THAW·ri·tee)* Authority that is given explicitly.

express contract *(eks·PRESS KON·trakt)* A contract in which the terms are stated or expressed by the parties.

express powers *(ex·PRESS pow·erz)* The specific stated powers of Congress in Article 1, Section 8 of the Constitution.

express warranty *(eks·PRESS WAR·en·tee)* A statement of fact or promise that goods have certain qualities.

extinction *(eks·TINK·shun)* The act of extinguishing or putting to an end.

extortion *(eks·TOR·shun)* The corrupt demanding or receiving by a person in office of a fee for services that should be performed gratuitously.

extradition *(ex·tre·DI·shun)* A process that permits the return of fugitives, to the state in which they are accused of having committed a crime, by the governor of the state to which they have fled.

fact finder *(fakt FINE·der)* The jury in a jury trial or the judge in a nonjury or bench trial.

factor *(FAK·ter)* A bailee to whom goods are consigned for sale.

failure of consideration *(FAYL·yer ov kon·sid· er·AY·shun)* A defense available when the consideration provided for in an agreement is not in fact given to the party being sued.

failure to warn *(FALE·yer to warn)* The theory that dangerous products were inadequately labeled or the danger inadequately communicated to the consumer or user.

fair-use doctrine *(DOK·trin)* A rule stating that the limited use of a copyrighted work for purposes such as criticism, comment, news reporting, teaching, scholarship, or research is not a copyright infringement.

false arrest *(a·REST)* The intentional confinement of a person without legal justification. Also called *false imprisonment.*

false imprisonment *(im·PRIS·on·ment)* The intentional confinement of a person without legal justification. Also called *false arrest.*

family farmer debt adjustment *(a·JUST·ment)* A method for family farmers to adjust their financial affairs while continuing to operate their farms. Also called Chapter 12 *bankruptcy.*

federalism *(FED·er·al·izm)* Established by the Constitution, this allows states to retain their individual governing powers, even though the federal government is given broad powers.

federal district courts *(FED·er·el DISS·trikt korts)* Also known as U.S. District Courts. The Courts that hear most federal cases before an appeal. Each state, territory, and the District of Columbia has at least one.

federal question *(FED·er·ul KWES·chen)* A matter that involves the U.S. Constitution, acts of Congress, or treaties.

fee The largest estate that one can own in land, giving the holder the absolute ownership and power of disposition during life, and descending to the owner's heirs at death. Also called *fee simple absolute* and *fee simple estate.*

fee simple absolute *(SIM·pel ab·so·LOOT)* The largest estate that one can own in land, giving the holder the absolute ownership and power of disposition during life, and descending to the owner's heirs at death. Also called *fee* and *fee simple estate.*

fee simple determinable *(de·TER·min·e·bel)* An estate in real property that is capable of coming to an end automatically because of the happening of some event. Also called *determinable fee.*

fee simple estate *(es·TATE)* The largest estate that one can own in land, giving the holder the absolute ownership and power of disposition during life, and descending to the owner's heirs at death. Also called *fee* and *fee simple absolute.*

fee tail estate *(es·TATE)* A freehold estate that restricts ownership of real property to a particular family blood line.

felon *(FEL·en)* A person who has committed a felony.

felonious homicide *(fe·LONE·ee·es HOM·i·side)* Homicide done with the intent to commit a felony.

felony *(FEL·en·ee)* A major crime, punishable by imprisonment in a state prison.

felony murder *(FEL·en·ee MER·der)* Murder committed while in the commission or attempted commission of a crime punishable with death or imprisonment for life.

feticide *(FET·e·side)* The killing of a fetus in the womb; abortion.

fiduciary *(fi·DOO·shee·air·ee)* A person in a position of trust, such as an executor, administrator, guardian, or trustee.

fiduciary capacity *(fi·DOO·shee·air·ee ka·PASS·e·tee)* A position of trust.

fiduciary deed *(fi·DOO·shee·air·ee)* A deed to real property in which the grantor transfers only his or her interest, if any, in the property and gives no warranties of title. Also called *deed without covenants* and *quitclaim deed.*

firm offer *(OFF·er)* A merchant's written promise to hold open an offer for the sale of goods.

first and final account *(a·KOWNT)* An accounting, if it is the only one, presented to the court in final settlement of a decedent's estate.

first-degree murder *(de·GREE MER·der)* Murder committed with premeditation malice aforethought, or with extreme atrocity or cruelty, or while in the commission of crimes like burglary, robbery, or rape. Definitions of first-degree murder vary jurisdictionally.

fixed-rate mortgage *(fiksd-rate MORE·gej)* A mortgage with an interest rate that does not change during the life of the mortgage.

fixture *(FIKS·cher)* Personal property that is physically attached to real property and becomes part of the real property.

flat fee One fee for legal work, not billed by the hour. A sum-certain cost of the lawyer's services not based on hourly rate and billable hours.

flexible-rate mortgage *(FLEKS·i·bel-rate MORE·gej)* A mortgage with an interest rate that fluctuates according to changes in an index to which it is connected. Also called *variable-rate mortgage.*

f.o.b. the place of destination *(des·te·NAY·shun)* Free on board (no delivery charges) to the place of destination.

f.o.b. the place of shipment *(SHIP·ment)* Free on board (no delivery charges) to the place of shipment.

forbearance *(for·BARE·enss)* Refraining from taking action.

forced heir *(forssd air)* A surviving spouse who elects to disclaim the provisions of a deceased spouse's will.

forced share A statutory sum given to a surviving spouse who disclaims the provisions made for him or her in a deceased spouse's will. Also called *elective share.*

forcible entry and detainer *(FORSS·i·bel EN·tree and de·TAYN·er)* The legal action used by landlords to evict tenants. Also called *dispossessory warrant proceedings, summary ejectment, summary process,* and *unlawful detainer.*

foreclose *(for·KLOZE)* To shut out, bar, or terminate.

foreign corporation *(FOR·en kor·por·AY·shun)* A corporation that is organized in a state other than that in which it is operating.

foreign divorce *(FOR·en de·VORSS)* A divorce in a state or country other than the one in which the party lives.

foreign jurisdiction *(FOR·en joo·res·DIK·shen)* A jurisdiction, such as another state or country, other than that in which a current litigation is taking place.

foreperson *(FORE·per·son)* The presiding member of a jury who speaks for the group.

foreseeable *(fore·SEE·e·bel)* Known in advance; anticipated; likely to occur.

forgery *(FOR·jer·ee)* The fraudulent making or altering of a writing whereby the rights of another might be prejudiced.

fornication *(for·ni·KAY·shun)* Sexual intercourse between two unmarried persons.

forum *(FOR·em)* The place of litigation.

forum non conveniens *(FOR·em non kon·VEEN·yenz)* Latin for a forum (location) that is not convenient. The right of a court to refuse to hear a case if it believes that justice would be better served if the trial were held in a different court.

franchise *(FRAN·chize)* An arrangement in which the owner of a trademark, trade name, or copyright licenses others, under special conditions or limitations, to use the trademark, trade name, or copyright in purveying goods or services.

franchisee *(fran·chize·EE)* A person to whom a franchise is given.

franchiser *(FRAN·chize·er)* A person who gives a franchise to another.

franchise disclosure document (FDD) A document required by the Federal Trade Commission to be given by franchisors to prospective franchisees at least 14 days prior to the prospective franchisee signing any franchise agreement or paying any money to the franchisor. The FDD has 23 various sections of franchise information, including franchise costs and fees, the number of franchises in existence, and the litigation history of the franchisor.

fratricide *(FRAT·re·side)* The killing of one's brother.

fraud *(frawd)* A misrepresentation of a material, existing fact, knowingly made, that causes someone reasonably relying on it to suffer damages. Also called *deceit.*

fraud in esse contractus *(ESS·ay kon·TRAKT·es)* Fraud as to the essential nature of the transaction.

fraud in the execution *(frawd in the ex·e·KEW·shun)* Fraud as to the essential nature of the transaction. Also called *fraud in esse contractus.*

fraud in the inducement *(in·DEWSS·ment)* Fraud that causes another to enter into a contract.

freedom of assembly *(FREE·dum ov a·SEM·blee)* A clause in the U.S. Constitution's First Amendment that guarantees to all persons the right to peaceably associate and assemble with others.

freedom of speech *(FREE·dum)* A clause in the U.S. Constitution's First Amendment that guarantees to all persons the right to speak, both orally and in writing, free from governmental interference or prohibition.

freedom of the press *(FREE·dum)* A clause in the U.S. Constitution's First Amendment that guarantees to all persons the right to publish and circulate their ideas, without governmental interference.

free exercise clause *(EKS·er·size)* A clause in the U.S. Constitution's First Amendment that guarantees to all persons the right to freely practice their religion.

freehold estate *(FREE·hold es·TATE)* An estate in which the holder owns the land for life or forever.

frivolous suits *(FRIV·uh·luss sutes)* A lawsuit meant to harass someone or one that has no basis in law or fact for bringing the claim or appeal.

fruit of the poisonous tree doctrine *(DOK·trin)* A court-created rule holding that evidence generated or derived from an illegal search or seizure cannot be used at the trial of a defendant.

full age *(ayj)* Adulthood.

full covenant and warranty deed *(KOV·e·nent and WAR·en·tee)* A deed containing warranties under which the grantor guarantees the property to be free from all encumbrances and to defend the title against the claims of all persons. Also called *general warranty deed.*

full faith and credit clause *(KRED·et)* A clause in the U.S. Constitution Sixth Article, requiring each state to recognize the laws and court decisions of every other state.

full warranty *(WAR·en·tee)* An express warranty given for consumer goods under which the seller must repair or replace, without cost to the buyer, defective goods or else refund the purchase price.

fungible goods *(FUN·ji·bel)* Goods such as grain or oil, of which any unit is the same as any like unit.

future goods *(FEW·cher)* Goods that are not yet in existence or under anyone's control.

garnishee *(gar·nish·EE)* A third party who holds money or property of a debtor that is subject to a garnishment action.

garnishment *(GAR·nish·ment)* A procedure for attaching a defendant's property that is in the hands of a third person.

gay marriage *(gay MA·rij)* The legal union of two same-sex partners; also called same-sex marriage.

general agent *(JEN·e·rel AY·jent)* An agent who is authorized to conduct all of a principal's activity in connection with a particular business.

general damages *(JEN·er·el DAM·e·jez)* Money meant to compensate the plaintiff for pain and suffering (physical discomfort and emotional trauma).

general legacy *(JEN·e·rel LEG·a·see)* A gift of money out of the general assets of the estate. Also called *general pecuniary legacy.*

general partner *(JEN·e·rel PART·ner)* A partner in a business organized as a partnership and who is personally liable for its debts and obligations.

general partnership *(JEN·e·rel PART·ner·ship)* A partnership in which the parties carry on a business for the joint benefit and profit of all partners.

general pecuniary legacy *(JEN·e·rel pee·KYOO·nee·er·ee LEG·a·see)* A gift of money out of the general assets of the estate. Also called *general legacy.*

general warranty deed *(JEN·e·rel WAR·en·tee)* A deed containing warranties under which the grantor guarantees the property to be free from all encumbrances and to defend the title against the claims of all persons. Also called *full covenant and warranty deed.*

generic term *(jen·ER·ik)* A term that means relating to or characteristic of a whole group.

genocide *(JEN·o·side)* The killing of a racial or political group.

gift causa mortis *(KAWS·ah MORE·tes)* A gift made in contemplation of impending death. Gifts causa mortis are automatically revoked if the donor doesn't die from that which was contemplated by the donative intent.

gifts made in contemplation of death *(kon·tem·PLAY· shun)* For federal estate tax law purposes, gifts made within three years of the date of death and which are subject to the federal estate tax. Also called *gifts causa mortis.*

gift tax A federal tax that is imposed (with exceptions) on gifts totaling more than $5.45 million during one's lifetime, as of 2016. One may give away $14,000 per year, per person without incurring any annual gift tax obligations.

good faith exception to the exclusionary rule *(ek·SEP·shun)* Evidence that is discovered by officers acting in good faith, but under the mistaken belief that a search was valid, and that can be used at the trial of a defendant.

goods Things that are movable.

Good Samaritan statutes *(sem·EHR·i·ten STAT·shoots)* Laws providing that physicians, nurses, and certain other medical personnel will not be liable for negligent acts that occur when they voluntarily, without a fee, render emergency care or treatment outside of the ordinary course of their practice.

government survey system *(GUV·ern·ment SER·vay SIS·tem)* A method of describing real property according to the property's relationship to intersecting lines running east and west (base lines) and lines running north and south (principal, or prime, meridians). Also called *rectangular survey system.*

graduated-payment mortgage *(GRAD·yoo·ay·ted-PAY·ment MORE·gej)* A mortgage under which payments increase gradually over the life of the loan.

grand jury *(JOOR·ee)* A jury consisting of not more than 23 people who listen to and see a prosecutor's evidence and decide whether or not to charge someone with the commission of a crime.

grand larceny *(LAR·sen·ee)* Larceny that is a felony or of a dollar amount that exceeds a threshold.

grantee *(gran·TEE)* A person to whom real property is transferred.

grantor *(gran·TOR)* A person who transfers real property to another. A person who establishes a trust. Also called *donor, settlor,* and *trustor.*

gratuitous bailment *(gra·TYOO·i·tes BAYL·ment)* A bailment for the sole benefit of either the bailor or the bailee, in which no consideration is given by one of the parties in exchange for the benefits bestowed by the other.

gratuitous guest *(gra·TYOO·i·tes)* One invited on the premises for nonbusiness purposes.

gravamen *(GRAH·ve·men)* The essential basis or gist of a complaint filed in a lawsuit.

grievance *(GREE·vance)* A written accusation against a lawyer and filed with the appropriate lawyer disicplinary commisison.

gross estate *(es·TATE)* All property that the decedent owned at death, including individually and jointly owned property, life insurance, living trusts, and gifts made in contemplation of death.

gross negligence *(NEG·li·jenss)* Extreme negligence.

guardian *(GAR·dee·en)* One who legally has the care and management of the person, property, or both of a minor or incompetent.

guardian ad litem *(GAR·dee·en ad LY·tem)* Guardian for the suit. A guardian appointed by a court to protect a minor who brings or defends a lawsuit.

guidelines *(guyd·lines)* Directed to lawyers to address how to ethically used their employees in support of the clients' needs.

guilty *(GILL·tee)* The state of having committed a crime.

habendum clause *(ha·BEN·dum)* The portion of a deed beginning with the words "To have and to hold," which defines the extent of the ownership of the property granted.

half-blood A relatives who has one parent in common with another relative, but not both.

health care declaration *(dek·la·RAY·shun)* A written expression of a person's wishes to be allowed to die a natural death and not be kept alive by heroic or artificial methods. Also called *directive to physicians, living will,* and *medical directive.*

health care proxy *(PROK·see)* A written statement authorizing an agent or surrogate to make medical treatment decisions for another in the event of the other's inability to do so.

heart balm statutes *(hart bahm STAT·shoots)* Laws passed in most states abolishing suits for loss of consortium, breach of promise to marry, and alienation of affections.

heir *(air)* A person who inherits property.

heirlooms *(AIR·looms)* Valued possessions with sentimental value passed down through generations within a family.

heirs at law *(airs)* People who would have inherited had a decedent died intestate.

hereditaments *(her·e·DIT·a·ments)* Things capable of being inherited, including not only lands and everything thereon, but also heirlooms.

high treason *(hy TREE·zun)* Acts against the king (under the English common law).

holdover tenant *(HOLD·o·ver TEN·ent)* A tenant who wrongfully remains in possession of the premises after a tenancy has expired. Also called *tenant at sufferance.*

holographic will *(hol·o·GRAF·ik)* A will written entirely in the hand of the testator and not signed by the required number of witnesses.

homestead *(HOME·sted)* Property that is beyond the reach of creditors' and others' claims as long as the family uses the property as a home.

Home Owner's Association (HOA) A non-profit organization for the purpose of marketing and managing a housing development.

homestead exemption *(HOME·sted eg·ZEMP·shun)* In bankruptcy, the exemption of one's residence up to a specific amount.

homestead exemption laws *(HOME·sted eg·ZEMP·shun lawz)* a bankruptcy law that grants the debtor a credit up to a certain amount in the value in their home.

homicide *(HOM·i·side)* The killing of a human being by a human being.

hot pursuit doctrine *(pur·SYOOT DOK·trin)* The principle that a search warrant is not needed when police pursue a fleeing suspect into a private area.

hourly billing *(OUW·er·lee BIL·ing)* A lawyer's hourly rate times the lawyer's billable hours.

House of Representatives *(howse ov rep·ree·ZEN·tah·tivz)* Part of the federal Congress that has 435 members who have two year terms.

humanitarian doctrine *(hew·man·i·TAYR·ee·en DOK·trin)* The doctrine which holds that a defendant who had the last clear chance to avoid injuring the plaintiff is liable even though the plaintiff was contributorily negligent. Also called the *last clear chance doctrine.*

hung jury *(JOOR·ee)* A deadlocked jury; one that cannot agree.

identified goods *(eye·DENT·i·fyd)* Goods that have been selected as the subject matter of a contract.

illegal profiling *(ill·EE·gul PRO·fyl·ing)* A law enforcement action, such as a detention or arrest, based solely on race, religion, national origin, ethnicity, gender, or sexual orientation.

illegitimate children *(il·e·JIT·i·met CHIL·dren)* Children born out of wedlock. Also called *bastards* and *nonmarital children.*

imminent danger *(IM·i·nent DANE·jer)* The situation that exists when an unlawful attack is about to happen.

immune *(im·YOON)* Exempt.

impaneled *(im·PAN·eld)* Listed as members of the jury.

impeach *(im·PEECH)* Call into question.

impediment *(im·PED·i·ment)* Disability or hindrance to the making of a contract.

implied authority *(im·PLIDE aw·THAW·ri·tee)* The power granted to an agent to perform incidental functions that are reasonably and customarily necessary to accomplish the overall purpose of the agency.

implied contract *(im·PLIDE KON·trakt)* A contract in which the terms are not stated or expressed by the parties.

implied trust *(im·PLIDE)* A trust that arises, by implication of law, from the conduct of the parties.

implied warranty *(im·PLIDE WAR·en·tee)* A warranty that is imposed by law rather than given voluntarily.

impossibility *(im·pos·i·BIL·i·tee)* A method of discharging one's obligations under a contract because it is impossible to perform, not merely difficult or costly.

impotency *(IM·pe·ten·see)* The incapacity of either party to consummate a marriage by sexual intercourse because of some physical infirmity or disarrangement.

impute *(im·PEWT)* To charge; to lay the responsibility or blame.

imputed liability *(im·PEW·ted ly·a·BIL·i·tee)* Vicarious responsibility for the torts committed by another person.

inadmissible *(in·ad·MISS·i·bel)* Cannot be received as evidence in court.

incarceration *(in·kar·ser·AY·shun)* Confinement.

incest *(IN·sest)* Sexual intercourse between people who are related, by consanguinity or affinity, in such a way that they cannot legally marry.

incidental beneficiary *(in·si·DEN·tal ben·uh·FISH·air·ee)* One who is indirectly benefited by a contract.

incidental damages *(in·si·DEN·tel DAM·e·jez)* Reasonable expenses that indirectly result from a breach of contract.

incompatibility *(in·kom·pat·e·BIL·i·tee)* Conflicts in personalities and dispositions that are so deep as to be irreconcilable and irremediable and that render it impossible for the parties to continue to live together in a normal marital relationship. Also called *irreconcilable differences* and *irretrievable breakdown.*

incorporation by reference *(in·kore·per·AY·shen by REF·e·renss)* Making a second document part of first document by referring to it in the first document and stating the intention of including it.

incorporators *(in·KOR·por·ay·tors)* People who organize a corporation by filing articles of organization with the state government.

indenture *(in·DEN·cher)* A deed or lease to which two or more persons are parties.

independent contractor *(in·de·PEN·dent KON·trak·ter)* One who performs services for others, but who is not under the others' control.

indictment *(in·DITE·ment)* A formal, written charge of a crime made by a grand jury.

indifferent *(in·DIF·rent)* Impartial, unbiased, and disinterested.

infancy *(IN·fen·see)* Under the age of majority.

infant *(IN·fent)* The legal name for a minor.

infanticide *(in·FANT·e·side)* The killing of an infant soon after birth.

information *(in·for·MA·shun)* A formal written charge of a crime made by a public official rather than by a grand jury.

informed consent *(in·FORMED kon·SENT)* Acknowledged awareness of the likely consequences for taking a course of action.

inheritance tax *(in·HER·i·tenss)* A tax imposed on a person who inherits from a decedent's estate.

injunction *(in·JUNK·shun)* An order of a court of equity to do or refrain from doing a particular act.

in pari delicto *(in PAH·ree de·LIK·toh)* In equal fault.

in personam action *(in per·SOH·nem AK·shun)* A lawsuit in which the court has jurisdiction over the person.

personam jurisdiction *(per·SOH·nem joo·res·DIK·shen)* Jurisdiction over the person.

in rem action *(in rem AK·shun)* A lawsuit that is directed against property rather than against a particular person.

insanity *(in·SAN·i·tee)* A defense available to mentally ill defendants who can prove that they did not know the nature and quality of their actions or did not appreciate the criminality of their conduct.

instrument A formal or written legal document, such as a deed or contract or will.

intangible personal property *(in·TAN·je·bel PER·son·al PROP·er·tee)* Property that is not perceptible to the senses and that cannot be touched.

intellectual property *(in·te·LEK·choo·el PROP· er·tee)* A wide variety of intangible property, whose creation is the product of human intelligence or creativity. Common intellectual property include patents, trademarks, and copyrights..

intended beneficiary *(in·TEN·ded ben·e·FISH·air·ee)* The third party of a contract made with the purpose of benefiting that party.

intent *(in·IENT)* Mental desire and will to act in a particular way, including wishing not to participate.

intentional infliction of emotional distress (IIED) *(in·TEN·shun·el in·FLIK·shun ov ee·MO·shun·el diss·TRESS)* A type of tort whereby the intentional conduct of a person results in extreme emotional suffering.

intentional torts *(in·TEN·shun·el)* Torts that are committed intentionally or knowingly. Also called *willful torts.*

interlocutory decree *(in·ter·LOK·ye·tore·ee de·KREE)* A provisional or temporary decision of a court.

interrogatories *(in·te·RAW·ga·tore·rees)* A form of discovery in a civil action in which parties are given a series of written questions to be answered under oath.

in terrorem clause *(in ter·RAW·rem)* A clause in a will that attempts to disinherit any legatee, devisee, or beneficiary who contests the provisions of the will. Also called *no-contest clause.*

interval ownership *(IN·ter·vel OH·ner·ship)* A fee simple ownership of a unit of real property in which the owner can exercise the right of possession for only an interval, such as a week or two, each year. Also called *time-sharing.*

inter vivos gift *(IN·ter VY·vose)* A legal term referring to a transfer or gift made during one's lifetime as opposed to a gift that takes effect at death.

inter vivos trust *(IN·ter VY·vose)* A trust that is created by the settlor when he or she is alive. Also called *living trust.*

intestacy *(in·TESS·te·see)* The state of having died without having made a valid will.

intestate *(in·TESS·tate)* The description of a person who dies having made no valid will.

intestate share *(in·TESS·tate)* An amount that is inherited when a decedent has died without a will.

intestate succession *(in·TESS·tate suk·SESH·en)* The act or process of an heir's becoming beneficially entitled to the property of one who has died without a will.

intoxication *(in·tox·i·KAY·shun)* A state in which a person is under the influence of drugs or alcohol—a defense that rarely works.

invasion of privacy *(in·VA·zhun ov PRY·ve·see)* A violation of the right of privacy.

inventory *(IN·ven·tor·ee)* A detailed list of articles of property in an estate, made by the executor or administrator thereof.

invitation to deal *(in·vi·TA·shun)* A request to an individual or to the public to make an offer. Also called *invitation to negotiate.*

invitation to negotiate *(ne·GO·shee·ate)* A request to an individual or to the public to make an offer. Also called *invitation to deal.*

involuntary bankruptcy *(in·VOL·en·ter·ee BANK·rupt·see)* A bankruptcy proceeding that is initiated by one or more creditors.

involuntary manslaughter *(in·VOL·en·ter·ee MAN·slaw·ter)* The unintentional killing of another while in the commission of an unlawful act or while in the commission of a reckless act.

irreconcilable differences *(ir·rek·en·SY·le·bel DIF·ren·sez)* Conflicts in personalities and dispositions that are so deep as to be irreconcilable and irremediable and that render it impossible for the parties to continue to live together in a normal marital relationship. Also called *incompatibility* and *irretrievable breakdown.*

irretrievable breakdown *(ir·ree·TREE·ve·bel BRAKE·down)* Conflicts in personalities and dispositions that are so deep as to be irreconcilable and irremediable and that render it impossible for the parties to continue to live together in a normal marital relationship. Also called *incompatibility* and *irreconcilable differences.*

irrevocable living trust *(ir·REV·e·ke·bel)* A trust that may not be rescinded or changed by the settlor at any time during his or her lifetime.

issue *(ISH·oo)* All people who have descended from a common ancestor.

joint custody *(joynt KUSS·te·dee)* Custody in which both parents share the responsibility and authority of child rearing.

joint enterprise *(joynt EN·ter·prize)* A relationship in which two or more people combine their labor or property for a single business undertaking. Also called *co-venture, joint venture,* and *syndicate.*

joint liability *(joynt ly·a·BIL·i·tee)* Liability under which all joint tortfeasors must be named as defendants in a lawsuit.

joint tenancy *(TEN·en·see)* The estate owned by joint tenants. Also called *joint tenancy with the right of survivorship.*

joint tenancy with the right of survivorship *(ser·VIVE·er·ship)* The estate owned by joint tenants. Also called *joint tenancy.*

joint tenants *(TEN·entz)* Two or more persons holding one and the same interest, accruing by one and the same conveyance, commencing at one and the same time, and held by one and the same undivided possession.

joint tortfeasors *(tort·FEE·zors)* Two or more people who participate in the commission of a tort.

joint venture *(joynt VEN·cher)* A relationship in which two or more people combine their labor or property for a single business undertaking. Also called *co-venture, joint enterprise,* and *syndicate.*

judgment *(JUJ·ment)* The decision of a court of law.

judgment nisi *(JUJ·ment NY·sie)* A provisional judgment that becomes final at the end of a stated period unless a valid reason is shown for not issuing it.

judgment notwithstanding the verdict *(VER·dikt)* A judgment a court renders in favor of one party notwithstanding a verdict in favor of the other party. Also called *judgment n.o.v.*

judgment n.o.v A judgment a court renders in favor of one party notwithstanding a verdict in favor of the other party (n.o.v. is the abbreviation for non obstante verdicto, which means notwithstanding a verdict).

judgment on the merits *(MER·its)* A court decision based on the evidence and facts introduced.

judgment on the pleadings *(PLEED·ings)* A judgment rendered without hearing evidence when the court determines that it is clear from the pleadings that one party is entitled to win the case.

judicial branch *(jew·DIH·sheel branch)* The U.S. Supreme Court, which has primarily appellate jurisdiction, but can be given original jurisdiction in certain legal matters. It is the highest court in the federal judicial system which makes federal law preeminent when federal and state law conflict.

judicial review *(jew·DIH·sheel ree·VEE·U)* The Supreme Court has the power to declare acts of Congress or acts of the executive branches unconstitutional.

junior mortgage *(JOO·nyer MORE·gej)* A mortgage subject to a prior mortgage.

jurisdiction *(joo·res·DIK·shen)* The power or authority that a court has to hear a case.

jurors *(JOOR·ors)* Members of a jury.

jury *(JOOR·ee)* A group of people selected according to law and sworn to determine the facts in a case.

jury charge *(JOOR·ee charj)* Instructions to a jury on matters of law.

jury panel *(JOOR·ee PAN·el)* The large group of people from which a jury is selected for a trial. Also called *array, jury pool,* and *venire.*

jury pool *(JOOR·ee pool)* The large group of people from which a jury is selected for a trial. Also called *array, jury panel,* and *venire.*

jury waived trial *(JOOR·ee waved tryl)* A trial without a jury. Also called *bench trial.*

justice *(JUSS·tis)* The title of an appellate court judge.

justiciable *(jus·TISH·e·bel)* Appropriate for court assessment.

justifiable homicide *(jus·ti·FY·a·bel HOM·i·side)* The taking of a human life when a lawful justification exists. A killing made in self-defense is a justifiable homicide.

kindred *(KIN·dred)* Blood relatives.

lack of consideration *(kon·sid·er·AY·shun)* A defense available to a party being sued for breach of contract when no consideration is contained in the agreement that is the subject of the suit.

landlord A person who owns real property and who rents it to another under a lease. Also called *lessor.*

lapsed devise *(lapsd de·VIZE)* A gift of real property in a will that fails because the devisee predeceased the testator.

lapsed legacy *(lapsd LEG·a·see)* A gift of personal property in a will that fails because the legatee predeceased the testator.

larceny *(LAR·sen·ee)* At common law, the wrongful taking and carrying away of personal property of another with the intent to steal.

larceny by false pretenses *(PRE·ten·sez)* Knowingly and deliberately obtaining the property of another by false pretenses with the intent to defraud. Also called *criminal fraud.*

last clear chance doctrine *(DOK·trin)* The doctrine which holds that a defendant who had the last clear chance to avoid injuring the plaintiff is liable even though the plaintiff was contributorily negligent. Also called *humanitarian doctrine.*

leading questions *(LEE·ding)* Questions that suggest to the witness the desired answer.

lease *(leess)* A contract granting the use of certain real property by its owner to another for a specified period in return for the payment of rent.

leasehold estate *(LEESS·hold es·TATE)* An estate that is less than a freehold estate. The interest that is conveyed by a lease.

legacy *(LEG·a·see)* A gift of personal property in a will.

legal assistant *(LEE·gl uh·SIS·tant)* A person who is trained to work in a legal office. It is often synonymous with paralegal, although some lawyers consider a legal assistant to be someone less trained or educated than a paralegal.

legal ethics *(LEE·gl e·thicks)* The do's and don'ts applied in the legal profession and formalized into ethics rules.

legal fees *(LEE·gl FEES)* Charges for a lawyer's time and efforts.

legal fiction *(LEE·gul FIK·shun)* An assumption, for purposes of justice, of a fact that does not exist.

legal issues *(LEE·gul ISH·oos)* Questions of law to be decided by the court in a lawsuit.

legal tender *(LEE·gul TEN·der)* Coin, paper, or other currency that is sufficient under law for the payment of debts.

legal title *(LEE·gul TY·tel)* Full, absolute ownership.

legatee *(leg·a·TEE)* A person who receives a gift of personal property under a will.

legator *(leg·a·TOR)* A person who makes a gift of personal property by a will.

legislative branch *(lej·uh·SLAY·tiv branch)* Federal Congress which makes federal laws.

lessee *(less·EE)* A person who has temporary possession of and an interest in real property of another under a lease. Also called *tenant.*

lesser included offense *(o·FENSS)* A crime that contains some, but not all, elements of a greater offense, making it impossible to commit the greater offense without also committing the lesser offense.

lessor *(less·OR)* A person who owns real property and who rents it to another under a lease. Also called *landlord.*

letters of administration *(ad·min·iss·TRAY·shun)* A certificate of appointment as administrator of an estate.

letters testamentary *(test·e·MEN·ter·ee)* A certificate of appointment as executor of a will.

levy on execution *(LEV·ee on ek·se·KYOO·shen)* To collect a sum of money by putting into effect the judgment of a court.

liability *(ly·a·BIL·i·tee)* Legal responsibility, obligation, or duty.

libel *(LIE·bel)* Defamation communicated by a writing, drawing, photograph, television program, or other means that can be considered "published." Also, the initial pleading in a divorce action.

libelant *(lie·bel·AHNT)* The plaintiff in a divorce action.

libelee *(lie·bel·EE)* The defendant in a divorce action.

license *(LY·sense)* A grant or permission to do a particular thing.

licensee *(ly·sen·SEE)* A person who has permission to do certain acts.

license suspension *(LYE·senz suh·SPEN·shun)* A lawyer not being able to practice law for a period of time.

lien *(leen)* A claim or charge on property for the payment of a debt.

lien theory of mortgages *(leen THEE·ree ov MORE·ge·jes)* The legal theory that a mortgage is not a conveyance of title, but merely a lien against the property. Also called *equitable theory of mortgages.*

life estate *(es·TATE)* An estate in real property that is limited in duration to either the life of the owner or the life of another person.

life tenant *(TEN·ent)* The owner of a life estate.

limited divorce *(LIM·i·ted de·VORSS)* The discontinuance of cohabitation by the spouses. Also called *divorce from bed and board* and *separation of spouses.*

limited liability company (LLC) *(LIM·i·ted ly·a·BIL·i·tee KUM·pe·nee)* A nonpartnership form of business organization that has the tax benefits of a partnership and the limited liability benefits of a corporation. Limited liability companies must be formed with the formalities required of corporations.

limited liability limited partnership (LLLP) The combination of a limited partnership and a limited liability partnership.

limited liability partnership (LLP) *(LIM·i·ted ly·a·BIL·i·tee PART·ner·ship)* A general partnership in which only the partnership, and not the individual partners, is liable for the tort liabilities of the partnership. Also called *registered limited liability partnership (RLLP)* and *registered partnership having limited liability (RPLL).*

limited partner *(LIM·i·ted PART·ner)* A partner who invests money or other property in the business, but who is not liable for the debts or obligations of the partnership.

limited partnership *(LIM·i·ted PART·ner·ship)* A partnership formed by two or more persons having as members one or more general partners and one or more limited partners.

limited warranty *(LIM·i·ted WAR·en·tee)* An express warranty given for consumer goods that is less than a full warranty.

limited warranty deed *(LIM·i·ted WAR·en·tee)* A deed containing warranties under which the grantor guarantees that the property is free from all encumbrances made during the time that he or she owned the property and agrees to defend the title only against claims through him or her. Also called *special warranty deed.*

lineal ascendants *(LIN·ee·el e·SEN·dents)* People who are in a direct line of ascent (upward) from the decedent—parents, grandparents, and great grandparents.

lineal descendants *(LIN·ee·el de·SEN·dents)* People who are in a direct line of descent (downward) from the decedent—children, grandchildren, and great grandchildren.

liquidate *(LIK·wi·date)* To turn into cash, accomplished by selling.

liquidated damages *(LIK·wi·day·ted DAM·e·jez)* Damages that are agreed on by the parties at the time of the execution of a contract, in the event of a subsequent breach.

liquidation *(lik·wi·DAY·shun)* A proceeding designed to liquidate a debtor's property, pay off creditors, and discharge the debtor from most debts. Also called *Chapter 7 bankruptcy* and *straight bankruptcy.*

lis pendens *(lis PEN·denz)* Pending suit.

litigants *(LIT·i·gants)* Parties to a lawsuit.

litigation *(lit·i·GAY·shun)* A suit at law.

living trust A trust that is created by the settlor when he or she is alive. Also called *inter vivos trust.*

living will A written expression of a person's wishes to be allowed to die a natural death and not be kept alive by heroic or artificial methods. Also called *directive to physicians, health care declaration,* and *medical directive.*

local action *(LO·kel AK·shun)* A lawsuit that can occur only in one place.

locus *(LOH·kus)* Place; locality.

locus sigilli *(LOH·kus se·JIL·i)* Place of the seal.

long-arm statutes *(STAT·shoots)* Statutes that allow one state to reach out and obtain personal jurisdiction over a person in another state.

loss of consortium *(kon·SORE·shum)* The destruction of fellowship between a husband and wife.

lost property Personal property that is accidentally separated from its owner. Finders of lost property own it, except with respect to the original owner who lost it.

mail fraud *(frawd)* Using the mail system to obtain money, property, or services by false pretenses.

maim *(maym)* To cripple or mutilate in any way.

maintenance *(MAIN·ten·ens)* The legal obligations of parents to contribute to the economic maintenance and education of their children. Also called *child support.*

majority *(ma·JAW·ri·tee)* Full age; adulthood.

mala in se *(MAL·ah in say)* Wrong in and of itself.

mala prohibita *(MAL·ah pro·HIB·i·ta)* Wrong because it is prohibited.

malefactor *(mal·e·FAK·ter)* A person found guilty of a crime.

malfeasance *(mal·FEE·zenss)* The doing of an act that ought not to be done at all.

malice aforethought *(MAL·iss e·FOR·thawt)* Evil intent; that state of mind which is reckless of law and of the legal rights of others.

malicious prosecution *(ma·LISH·us pros·e·KYOO·shun)* Prosecution begun in malice without probable cause.

malpractice *(mal·PRAK·tiss)* Professional misconduct; negligence of a professional.

managers *(MAN·a·jers)* People who are designated by the members of a limited liability company to manage the company.

mandatory arbitration *(MAN·da·tor·ee ar·be·TRAY·shun)* Arbitration that is required by agreement or by law. Also called *compulsory arbitration.*

mandatory sentence *(MAN·da·tor·ee SEN·tenss)* A fixed sentence that must be imposed with no room for discretion.

manslaughter *(MAN·slaw·ter)* The unlawful killing of one human being by another without malice aforethought. Is classified as either voluntary or involuntary manslaughter.

manufacturing defect *(man·yew·FAK·chur·ing DEE·fekt)* The theory that a product was negligently built or built with substandard materials.

marital deduction *(MAR·i·tal de·DUK·shun)* The amount that passes from a decedent to a surviving spouse and is not taxable under the federal estate tax law.

maritime *(MER·i·tym)* Pertaining to the sea.

marriage *(MAR·ej)* Historically, the laws of the federal government and most states, the union of one man and one woman. Has been expanded to include same sex marriage.

marital deduction trust *(MAR·i·tal de·DUK·shun)* A trust that is arranged to make maximum use of the marital deduction that is found in the federal estate tax law.

marriage banns *(MAR·ej)* Public notice of a marriage contract for a certain number of weeks before the wedding date. Also called *banns of matrimony.*

master *(MAS·ter)* An employer. A lawyer appointed by the court to hear testimony in a case and report back to the court as to his or her findings or conclusions.

master deed *(MAS·ter deed)* A deed to a condominium that describes the entire property that is owned by the condominium association.

material breach (*ma-TEER-ee-al breech*) When a major or essential part of the contract has not been performed.

matricide (*MAT·ri·side*) Killing one's mother.

mayhem (*MAY·hem*) At common law, violently depriving others of the use of such members (leg, arm, hand, foot, eye) as may render them less able to fight or defend himself or herself.

means testing (*meenz TEST·ing*) A comparison of one's income and expenses to a standard to determine whether a debtor meets eligibility requirements to be in Chapter 7 or Chapter 13 bankruptcy.

mediation (*mee·dee·AY·shun*) An informal dispute resolution process in which a neutral, third person listens to both sides' claims and arguments and makes suggestions for reaching a solution without having to go to trial.

mediator (*MEE·dee·ay·tor*) A neutral, third person in a mediation session who listens to both sides and makes suggestions for reaching a solution.

medical directive (*MED·i·kel de·REKT·iv*) A written expression of a person's wishes to be allowed to die a natural death and not be kept alive by heroic or artificial methods. Also called *directive to physicians, health care declaration,* and *living will.*

medical power of attorney (*MED·i·kel POW·er ov e·TERN·ee*) A written statement authorizing an agent or surrogate to make medical treatment decisions for another in the event of the other's inability to do so.

members (*MEM·bers*) Owners of a limited liability company.

memorandum (*mem·o·RAN·dum*) The writing that is necessary to satisfy the statute of frauds.

mens rea (*menz RAY·eh*) Criminal intent.

merchant (*MER·chent*) A person who sells goods of the kind sold in the ordinary course of business or who has knowledge or skills peculiar to those goods, or who relies on the expertise of a merchant when dealing in goods.

meridians (*mer·ID·ee·ens*) Lines running north and south in the United States government survey. Also called *prime meridians* and *principal meridians.*

metadata (*ME·te·da·te*) Data or other information on a computer which is about the structure of the computer or the contents of its files, and which is akin to an electronic fingerprint.

metes (*meets*) Distances between points.

metes and bounds A system of describing real property by its outer boundaries, with reference to courses, distances, and monuments.

minimum sentence (*MIN·i·mum SEN·tenss*) The smallest amount of time that a prisoner must serve before being released or placed on parole.

mini-trials (*tryls*) Informal trials run by private organizations established for the purpose of settling disputes out of court.

minor (*MY·ner*) A person under the age of majority; usually under 18.

Miranda warnings (*mer·AN·de*) The constitutional right given to people who are arrested to be told before being questioned that they have the right to remain silent, that any statements made by them may be used against them, that they have a right to have a lawyer present, and that a lawyer will be provided without cost if they cannot afford one. Comes from the 1966 U.S. Supreme Court case Miranda v. Arizona.

miscegenation (*mis·sej·e·NA·shun*) Marriage between people of different races.

misdemeanor (*mis·de·MEEN·er*) A minor crime; not a felony.

misfeasance (*mis·FEE·zenss*) The improper doing of an act.

mislaid property Personal property that is temporarily separated from its owner because of oversight or mistake. Finders or mislaid property own it, except with respect to the original owner who mislaid it.

misnomer (*mis·NO·mer*) Mistake in name.

misrepresentation (*mis·rep·rez·en·TAY·shun*) A false or deceptive statement or act.

mistrial (*MIS·tryl*) An invalid trial of no consequence.

mitigate (*MIT·i·gate*) Lessen; keep as low as possible.

Model Code of Professional Responsibility (*MAH·dl kode of pro·FEH·shun·al ree·SPON·si·bil·i·tee*) Rules for lawyer conduct created by the American Bar Association in 1969.

Model Penal Code (*MAH·dl PEE·nl kode*) Created by the American Law Institute, this serves as the template for many states' criminal codes, and breaks from the common law doctrine. For example, it makes an accessory liable only for those acts that were contemplated by the perpetrator, as opposed to those acts which were foreseeable from the plan.

Model Rules of Professional Conduct (*MAH·dl ROOLS of pro·Feh·shun·al KON·dukt*) First created by the American Bar Association in 1983 to replace its Model Code of Professional Responsibility, this is a collection of lawyer conduct rules.

moiety (*MOY·e·tee*) A part, portion, or fraction.

money laundering (*MUN·ee LAWN·der·ing*) A metaphor used to describe how money acquired through criminal activities is "washed" so that it can appear to have been earned legitimately.

monuments (*MON·yoo·ments*) Visible marks indicating boundaries.

mortgage (*MORE·gej*) A conveyance of real property for the purpose of securing a debt. Also called *mortgage deed.*

mortgage assignment (*MORE·gej e·SINE·ment*) The transfer of a mortgagee's interest in a mortgage to another person.

mortgage assumption (*MORE·gej e·SUMP·shun*) An agreement by a new owner of real property to pay the former owner's mortgage. Also called *mortgage take-over.*

mortgage deed (*MORE·gej*) A conveyance of real property for the purpose of securing a debt. Also called *mortgage.*

mortgage discharge (*MORE·gej DIS·charj*) A document stating that a mortgage debt is satisfied.

mortgagee (*more·gej·EE*) One who lends money and takes back a mortgage as security for the loan.

mortgagee's foreclosure sale (*more·gej·EEZ for·KLOH·zher*) A sale of real property that terminates all rights of the mortgagor in the property covered by the mortgage.

mortgage take-over (*MORE·gej*) An agreement by a new owner of real property to pay the former owner's mortgage. Also called *mortgage assumption.*

mortgagor (*more·gej·OR*) One who borrows money and gives a mortgage—that is, pledges property to the lender as security for the loan.

motion (*MOH·shun*) A written or oral request made to a court for certain action to be taken.

motion for a directed verdict (*de·REK·ted VER·dikt*) In a jury trial, a motion asking the court to find in favor of the moving party as a matter of law, without having the case go to the jury.

motion for a more definite statement (*DEF·e·net STATE·ment*) A motion by a party, when a pleading is vague, asking the court to order the other party to make a more definite statement.

motion for judgment on the pleadings (*JUJ·ment on the PLEED·ings*) A motion by either party for a judgment in that party's favor based solely on information contained in the pleadings.

motion for order compelling discovery (*com·PEL·ing diss·KUV·e·ree*) A motion asking the court to order the other party to produce certain writings, photographs, or other requested items.

motion for recusal (*re·KYOO·zel*) A request that a judge disqualify himself or herself from a case because of bias or prejudice.

motion for summary judgment (*MOH·shun for SUM·er·ee JUJ·ment*) A motion that may be made when all of the papers filed in a case show that there is no genuine issue of fact and that the party making the motion will win the case as a matter of law.

motion in limine (*MOH·shun in LIM·e·nee*) A pretrial motion asking the court to prohibit the introduction of prejudicial evidence by the other party.

motion to dismiss (*dis·MISS*) A motion made by the defendant asking the court to dismiss the case.

motion to quash the array (*MOH·shun to kwawsh the e·RAY*) A challenge to the entire jury because of some irregularity in the selection of the jury. Also called *challenge to the array*.

motion to strike A motion asking the court to order the other party to remove from a pleading any insufficient defense or any redundant, immaterial, impertinent, or scandalous matter.

Multistate Bar Exam (*mul·ty state bar x·am*) a 200-multiple choice exam covering seven subject areas, developed by the National Conference of Bar Examiners. The Multistate Bar Exam is part of the Uniform Bar Exam.

Multistate Performance Test (MPT) (*mul·ty state per·for·manse test*) a test developed by the National Conference of Bar Examiners to evaluate an examinee's fundamental lawyering skills, rather than measuring substantive legal knowledge.

murder (*MER·der*) The unlawful killing of a human being by another with malice aforethought.

mutual benefit bailment (*MYOO·choo·el BEN·e·fit BAYL·ment*) A bailment in which both the bailor and the bailee receive some benefit.

mutual mistake (*MYOO·choo·el mis·TAKE*) The situation that exists when both parties are mistaken about an important or material aspect of an agreement. Also called *bilateral mistake*.

mutuum (*MYOO·choo·um*) A loan of goods, on the agreement that the borrower may consume them, returning to the lender an equivalent in kind and quantity.

necessaries (*NESS·e·seh·reez*) Food, clothing, shelter, and medical care that are needed by a minor, but not supplied by a parent or guardian.

negligence (*NEG·li·jenss*) The failure to use that amount of care and skill that a reasonably prudent person would have used under the same circumstances and conditions.

negotiable instrument (*ne·GOH·shee·e·bel IN·stre·ment*) A written, unconditional order or promise to pay money, which can be transferred by the original receiver to others.

negotiation (*ne·go·shee·AY·shun*) A two-party process in which each side attempts to conclude a dispute by bargaining with the other until one side agrees to the other side's offer or settlement. Also, the act of transferring a negotiable instrument to another party.

next friend One acting for the benefit of an infant in bringing a legal action.

next of kin Those most nearly related by blood.

nighttime The time between one hour after sunset on one day and one hour before sunrise on the next day.

no-contest clause (*no-KON·test*) A clause in a will that attempts to disinherit any legatee, devisee, or beneficiary who contests the provisions of the will. Also called *in terrorem clause*.

no-fault divorce (*de·VORSE*) A dissolution of marriage without regard to fault.

nolo contendere (*NO·lo kon·TEN·de·ray*) A plea in which the defendant neither admits nor denies the charges.

nominal damages (*NOM·i·nel DAM·e·jez*) Damages in name only.

nominal partner (*NOM·i·nel PART·ner*) A partner in name only, who has no real interest in the partnership. Also called *ostensible partner*.

nonbillables (*non·BIL·uh·bls*) Overhead expenses (such as paper clips, rent, utilities) that cannot be charged to a lawyer's client.

nonbinding arbitration (*non·BIND·ing ar·be·TRAY·shun*) Arbitration in which the arbitrator's decision is simply a recommendation and need not be complied with.

nonconforming goods (*non·ken·FORM·ing*) Goods that are not the same as those called for under the contract.

nondisclosure agreement (*non·diss·KLOH·zher e·GREE·ment*) An agreement to refrain from disclosing trade secrets to others. Also called *confidentiality agreement*.

nonfeasance (*non·FEE·zenss*) The failure to do an act that ought to be done.

nonmarital children (*non·MAR·i·tel*) Children born out of wedlock. Also called *bastards* and *illegitimate children*.

non obstante verdicto (*non ob·STAN·tee ver·DIK·toh*) Abbreviated n.o.v. Notwithstanding a verdict.

nonsuit (*NON·soot*) The termination of an action that did not adjudicate issues on the merits.

notary public (*NOH·te·ree PUB·lik*) A person authorized by law to administer oaths, attest to and certify documents, take acknowledgments, and perform other official acts.

not-for-profit corporation (*not fore PRO·fit*) A corporation created for charitable and benevolent purposes.

novation (*noh·VAY·shun*) An agreement whereby an original party to a contract is replaced by a new party.

nudum pactum (*NOO·dum PAK·tum*) Barren promise with no consideration.

nuisance (*NYOO·senss*) The use of one's property in a way that causes annoyance, inconvenience, or discomfort to another.

nullity (*NUL·i·tee*) Nothing; as though it had not occurred.

nuncupative will (*NUN·kyoo·pay·tiv*) An oral will.

obscenity (*ob·SEN·i·tee*) Offensive or legally prohibitable material or conduct that shows or describes some kind of sexual activity and is designed to sexually arouse people.

offer (*OFF·er*) A proposal to enter into a contract made by an offeror.

offeree (*off·er·EE*) One to whom an offer is made.

offeror (*off·er·OR*) One who makes an offer.

one day–one trial jury system (*JOOR·ee SYS·tem*) A system designed to provide the courts with juries consisting of fair cross sections of the community and to reduce the burden of jury duty on certain classes of citizens.

opening statement *(OH·pen·ing STATE·ment)* An attorney's outline, to the jury (or to a judge in a bench trial), of the anticipated evidence to be shown.

operating agreement *(OP·er·ate·ing e·GREE· ment)* An agreement that sets forth the rights and obligations of the members and establishes the rules for operating a limited liability company.

option contract *(OP·shen KON·trakt)* A binding promise to hold an offer open.

order for relief *(re·LEEF)* The acceptance of a case by a bankruptcy court.

Ordinance *(OR·di·nense)* Law passed by a local or municipal legislative bodies, such as a city council.

ordinary negligence *(OR·di·ner·ee NEG·li·jens)* The lack of ordinary care.

original jurisdiction *(o·RIJ·i·nel joo·res·DIK·shen)* The authority to hear a case when it first goes to court.

Orphan's Court A name given, in some states, to the court that exercises the function of settling decedents' estates.

ostensible partner *(os·TEN·si·bel PART·ner)* A partner in name only, who has no real interest in the partnership. Also called *nominal partner.*

output contract *(OWT·put KON·trakt)* A contract to sell "all the goods a company manufactures" or "all the crops a farmer grows."

overrule *(o·ver·ROOL)* To annul, make void, or refuse to sustain.

pain and suffering *(SUF·er·ing)* Physical discomfort and emotional trauma.

paralegal *(pare·uh·LEE·gl)* A non-lawyer employee trained or educated to do substantive legal work under the supervision of employing attorneys. Sometimes, paralegal and legal assistant are used synonymously.

pardon *(PAR·den)* A setting aside of punishment altogether by a government official; an act by a governor or president absolving someone of their past or future conviction.

parole *(pa·ROLE)* A conditional release from prison; allows the person to serve the remainder of a sentence outside of prison under specific terms.

parole board A group of people authorized to grant parole. Also called *parole commission.*

parole commission *(ke·MISH·en)* A group of people authorized to grant parole. Also called *parole board.*

parolee *(pa·role·EE)* A person placed on parole.

parol evidence rule *(pa·ROLE EV·i·denss)* The rule that oral evidence of prior or contemporaneous negotiations between the parties is not admissible in court to alter, vary, or contradict the terms of a written agreement.

partial release of mortage *(PAR·shell re·LEESS)* A document stating that specified parcels of property are released from an encumbrance.

partially disclosed principal A principal on whose behalf an agent is transacting with a third party, where the third party is aware the agent is acting as an agent but does not know who the principal is.

partition *(par·TI·shun)* The division of land, held by joint tenants or tenants in common, into distinct portions so that they may hold them separately.

partnership *(PART·ner·ship)* An association of two or more persons to carry on as co-owners of a business for profit. Also called *co-partnership* or *general partnership.*

party to a suit *(PAR·tee)* A person or organization participating or having a direct interest in a legal proceeding.

patent *(PAT·ent)* A grant by the U.S. Government of the exclusive right to make, use, and sell an invention. Patent length depends on the type of patent.

patent infringement *(PAT·ent in·FRINJ·ment)* The unauthorized making, using, or selling of a patented invention during the term of the patent.

paternity proceeding *(pa·TERN·i·tee pro·SSEED·ing)* A court action to determine whether a person is the father of a child born out of wedlock. Also called *affiliation proceeding.*

patricide *(PAT·ri·side)* The killing of one's father.

pay on death (POD) account *(pay on death uh·COWNT)* A bank account in the name of the depositor as trustee for another person. While alive, the depositor can deposit money and withdraw from the account. Upon the depositor's death, the account belongs to the named beneficiary. Also known as a Totten trust and "poor man's trust" because it costs nothing to create and administer.

pecuniary gift *(pee·KYOO·nee·er·ee)* Gift of money in a will.

penal laws *(PEE·nel)* Laws that impose a penalty or punishment for a wrong against society.

pendente lite *(pen·DEN·tay LIE·tay)* Litigation pending.

per capita *(per KAP·i·ta)* Per head.

peremptory challenge *(per·EMP·ter·ee CHAL·enj)* The challenge of a juror, for which no reason need be given.

performance *(per·FORM·enss)* The discharging of a contract by doing that which one agreed to do under the terms of the contract.

periodic tenancy *(peer·ee·ODD·ik TEN·en·see)* An estate in real property that continues for successive periods until one of the parties terminates it by giving notice to the other party. Also called *tenancy from year to year.*

perjury *(PER·jer·ee)* The giving of false testimony under oath.

per se *(per say)* In and of itself; taken alone.

personal property *(PER·son·al PROP·er·tee)* Anything that is the subject of ownership other than real property. Also called *chattels* and *personalty.*

personal recognizance *(PER·son·al re·KOG·ni· zense)* A personal obligation by a person to return to stand trial.

personal representative *(PER·son·al rep·re· ZEN·ta·tiv)* The executor or administrator of a deceased person.

personal service *(PER·son·al SER·viss)* The personal delivery of a copy of the summons and complaint to the defendant.

personalty *(PER·sen·el·tee)* Anything that is the subject of ownership other than real property. Also called *chattels* and *personal property.*

per stirpes *(per STIR·peez)* By right of representation.

petition *(pe·TI·shun)* A written application for a court order.

petitioner *(pe·TI·shun·er)* One who presents a petition to a court.

petit jury *(PET·ee JOOR·ee)* The ordinary jury of 6 or 12 people; used for the trial of a civil or criminal action.

petit larceny *(PET·ee LAR·sen·ee)* Larceny that is a misdemeanor rather than a felony. Also called *petty larceny.*

petit treason *(PET·ee TREE·zan)* Acts against one's master or lord (under the English common law).

petty larceny *(PET·ee LAR·sen·ee)* Larceny that is a misdemeanor rather than a felony. Also called *petit larceny.*

physical custody *(FIZ·i·cul CUSS·te·dee)* The day-to-day care of a child, including his or her residence.

plaintiff *(PLAIN·tif)* A person who brings a legal action against another.

plain view doctrine *(DOK·trin)* The principle which asserts that search warrant is not needed for a police officer to seize items that are in plain view of where the police officer is lawfully situated.

plant patent A patent granted for the discovery or invention of an asexually reproducing plant, meaning, by other than the use of seeds. Plant patents last 20 years from the date the application is filed.

plat A map designating the size and shape of a specific land area. Also called *plat map* and *plot.*

plat book A book that is recorded at the registry of deeds, containing plat maps.

plat map A map designating the size and shape of a specific land area. Also called *plat* and *plot.*

plea bargaining *(plee BAR·gen·ing)* The working out of a mutually satisfactory disposition of a case by the prosecution and the defense, whereby the defendant pleads guilty to a lesser charge.

pleadings *(PLEED·ings)* The written statements of claims and defenses used by the parties in a lawsuit.

plenary jurisdiction *(PLEN·e·ree joo·res·DIK·shen)* Complete jurisdiction over both the parties and the subject matter of a lawsuit.

plot A map designating the size and shape of a specific land area. Also called *plat* and *plat map.*

pocket veto *(PAH·ket VEE·tow)* The president refusing to sign a piece of legislation.

polling the jury *(POLE·ing)* A procedure in which each individual juror is asked whether he or she agrees with the verdict given by the jury foreperson.

polygamy *(po·LIG·e·mee)* The state of having several wives or husbands at the same time.

pornography *(por·NAW·graf·ee)* Material or conduct that shows or describes some kind of sexual activity and is designed sexually arouse people.

possession *(po·SESH·en)* The detention and control of anything.

possibility of reverter *(pos·i·BIL·i·tee ov re·VERT·er)* An interest in property due to the possibility that an event will occur that will cause the property to revert to the grantor.

pour-over trust *(pore-OH·ver)* A provision in a will leaving a bequest or devise to the trustee of an existing living trust.

power of attorney *(POW·er ov a·TERN·ee)* A formal writing that authorizes an agent to act for a principal.

power of sale clause *(POW·er)* A clause in a mortgage allowing the mortgagee to hold a foreclosure sale without involving the court when a default in payment of the mortgage occurs.

precatory trust *(PREK·a·tore·ee)* An express trust that arises from the use of polite, noncommanding language by a testator in a will.

predecease *(pree·de·SEEZ)* To die before.

preferences *(PREF·er·en·sez)* Transfers made by a debtor to creditors before a bankruptcy proceeding, enabling the creditors to receive a greater percentage of their claim than they would have otherwise received.

preferred stock *(pre·FERD)* Stock that has a superior right to dividends, and to capital when the corporation is dissolved.

preliminary hearing *(pre·LIM·i·ner·ee HEER·ing)* A hearing before a judge to determine whether there is sufficient evidence to believe that the person has committed a crime. Also called *probable cause hearing.*

preliminary injunction *(pre·LIM·i·ner·ee in·JUNK·shun)* An injunction issued by a court before hearing the merits of a case.

premarital agreement *(pre·MAR·i·tel a·GREE·ment)* A contract made in contemplation of marriage between prospective spouses setting forth, among other points, the right that each spouse will have to property brought into the marriage as well as property distribution in the event of divorce. Also called *antenuptial agreement* and *prenuptial agreement.*

premeditated malice aforethought *(pre·MED·i·tay·ted MAL·iss a·FORE·thawt)* Thinking over, deliberating on, or weighing in the mind beforehand.

prenuptial agreement *(pre·NUP·shel a·GREE·ment)* A contract made in contemplation of marriage between prospective spouses setting forth, among other points, the right that each spouse will have to property brought into the marriage. Also called *antenuptial agreement* and *premarital agreement.*

preponderance of evidence *(pre·PON·der·enss ov EV·i·denss)* Evidence having the greater weight.

Prerogative Court *(pre·ROG·e·tiv)* A name given in some states to the court that exercises the function of settling decedents' estates.

pretermitted child *(pre·ter·MIT·ed)* A child who is omitted by a testator from a will.

pretrial hearing *(PREE·tryl HEER·ing)* A hearing before the judge prior to a trial, attended by the attorneys, for the purpose of speeding up the trial.

prima facie case *(PRY·mah FAY·shee)* Legally sufficient for proof unless rebutted or contradicted by other evidence.

prime meridians *(mer·ID·ee·ens)* Lines running north and south in the United States government survey. Also called *meridians* and *principal meridians.*

primogeniture *(pry·mo·JEN·e·cher)* The state of being the first born among several children of the same parents (early English law).

principal *(PRIN·se·pel)* One who authorizes another to act on one's behalf.

principal in the first degree *(de·GREE)* One who actually commits a felony.

principal in the second degree One who did not commit the crime, but was present, aiding and abetting another in the commission of a felony.

principal meridians *(PRIN·se·pel mer·ID·ee·ens)* Lines running north and south in the United States government survey. Also called *meridians* and *prime meridians.*

private nuisance *(PRY·vet NYOO·sens)* A nuisance that disturbs one neighbor only.

private reprimand *(PRYE·vit REH·pri·mand)* A sanction issued against an attorney for a grievance where the attorney's name is not included in the official censure.

privileges and immunities clause *(PRIV·i·leg·ez and im·YOO·ni·teez)* A clause in the U.S. Constitution requiring states to give out-of-state citizens the same rights as it gives its own citizens.

privity of contract *(PRIV·i·tee ov KON·trakt)* The relationship that exists between contracting parties.

probable cause *(PROB·a·bel kawz)* Reasonable belief, based on the then-available facts, that a crime has been committed or that evidence of criminality exists.

probable cause hearing *(PROB·a·bel kawz HEER·ing)* A hearing before a judge to determine whether there is sufficient evidence to believe that the person has committed a crime. Also called *preliminary hearing.*

probate *(PROH·bate)* To prove and have allowed by the court; usually, of a will.

Probate and Family Court A name given in some states to the court that exercises the function of settling decedents' estates.

proceeding *(pro·SEED·ing)* The name given in California for the procedure for obtaining a dissolution of marriage.

process *(PROSS·ess)* The means of compelling the defendant in an action to appear in court.

process server *(PROSS·ess SERV·er)* A person who carries out service of process.

pro-choice *(pro-choyss)* Favoring legislation that allows abortion.

product liability *(PROD·ukt ly·a·BIL·i·tee)* Liability of manufacturers and sellers of goods to compensate people for injuries suffered because of defects in the manufacturers' and sellers' products.

pro-life *(pro-life)* Favoring legislation that prohibits or greatly restricts abortion.

promisee *(prom·i·SEE)* One to whom a promise is made.

promisor *(prom·i·SOHR)* One who makes a promise.

promissory estoppel *(PROM·i·sore·ee ess·TOP·el)* A doctrine under which no consideration is necessary when someone makes a promise that induces another's action or forbearance, and injustice can be avoided only by enforcing the promise.

promissory note *(PROM·i·sore·ee)* A written promise by the borrower to pay a sum of money to the lender.

promoters *(pro·MOH·terz)* People who begin a corporation by obtaining investors and taking charge up to the time of the corporation's existence.

proof of claim A signed, written statement setting forth a creditor's claim together with the basis for it.

proponent *(pro·POH·nent)* One who proposes or argues in support of something, such as the allowance of a will.

proprietary lease *(pro·PRY·e·ter·ee)* A lease to an owner of the property.

prorated *(PROH·ray·ted)* Divided proportionately.

prosecute *(PROSS·e·kyoot)* To proceed against a person criminally.

pro se *(PRO-SAY)* A plaintiff representing himself in litigation without an attorney's help.

prosecution *(pross·e·KYOO·shun)* A criminal action. The party by whom criminal proceedings are started or conducted; the state.

prosecutor *(PROSS·e·kew·ter)* The person representing the jurisdiction in which the crime occurred, who brings charges against those the police have arrested.

proximate cause *(PROK·si·met kaws)* The dominant or moving cause.

proxy marriage *(PROK·see MAR·ej)* A ceremonial marriage in which one of the parties is absent, but is represented by an agent who stands in his or her place.

prudent *(PROO·dent)* Cautious.

prurient interest *(PROO·ree·ent IN·trest)* A shameful or morbid interest in sex.

public administrator *(PUB·lik ad·MIN· iss·tray·tor)* An official who administers the estate of a person who dies intestate when no relative, heir, or other person appears who is entitled to act as administrator.

publication clause *(pub·li·KAY·shun)* The introductory paragraph of a will. Also called *exordium clause.*

public domain *(PUB·lik doh·MAYN)* Owned by the public.

public nuisance *(PUB·lik NYOO·sens)* A nuisance that affects the community at large.

public policy *(PUB·lik POL·i·see)* Underlying, foundational principles that bind various peoples into a close-knit society.

public reprimand *(PUH·blik REH·pri·mand)* A sanction ussued against an attorney for a grievance where the attorney's name is listed on the official censure.

public trust *(PUB·lik)* A trust established for charitable purposes. Also called charitable trust.

puffing *(PUF·ing)* Statements made by sellers that are opinions and attempts to put their goods in the best light possible; not warranties.

punitive damages *(PYOON·i·tiv)* Damages as a measure of punishment for the defendant's wrongful or malicious acts. Also called *exemplary damages.*

qualified indorsement *(KWAH·li·fide in·DORSS·ment)* An indorsement that limits the liability of the indorser.

qualified terminable interest property (QTIP) trust *(KWAH·li·fide TERM·in·a·bel IN·trest PROP·er·tee)* A marital deduction trust that gives all trust income to a surviving spouse for life, payable at least annually, with the principal passing to someone else upon the spouse's death.

quasi *(KWAY·zy)* As if; almost as it were.

quasi contract *(KWAY·zy KON·trakt)* A contract imposed by law to prevent unjust enrichment. Also called *contract implied in law.*

quasi in rem action *(KWAY·zi in rem AK·shun)* A lawsuit in which the court has jurisdiction over the defendant's property, but not over the defendant's person.

questions of fact *(KWES·chens)* Questions about the activities that took place between the parties which caused them to go to court.

questions of law Questions relating to the application or interpretation of law

quid pro quo *(kwid proh kwoh)* Something for something; one thing in return for another.

quiet enjoyment *(KWY·et en·JOY·ment)* The right of a tenant to possess the rented property and to be undisturbed in that possession.

quitclaim deed *(KWIT·klame)* A deed to real property in which the grantor transfers only his or her interest, if any, in the property and gives no warranties of title. Also called *deed without covenants* and *fiduciary deed.*

racketeering *(rak·e·TEER·ing)* Activities of organized criminals who extort money from legitimate businesses.

range *(rainj)* A row of townships running north and south in the United States government survey.

rape At common law, the unlawful, forcible carnal knowledge by a man of a woman against her will or without her consent.

rape shield laws *(sheeld)* Laws passed to help prevent rape victims from having their sexual history be sought or used by the defense as a defense strategy at trial.

ratify *(RAT·i·fy)* Approve; confirm.

real evidence *(reel EV·i·denss)* Actual objects that have a bearing on the case, such as an item of clothing, a weapon found at the scene of the crime, a photograph, a chart, or a model.

real property *(reel PROP·er·tee)* The ground and anything permanently attached to it, including land, buildings, and growing trees; and the airspace above the ground.

reasonable care *(REE·zen·e·bel)* The degree of care that a reasonable person would have used under the circumstances then known.

reasonable doubt *(REE·zen·e·bel dowt)* Doubt based on reason. Evidence that is beyond a reasonable doubt is sufficient to warrant a finding of guilt in a criminal trial.

reasonable time *(REE·zen·e·bel)* A time, left to the discretion of the judge, that may be fairly allowed depending on the circumstances.

rebuttal *(re·BUT·el)* The introduction of evidence that will destroy the effect of the evidence introduced by the other side.

receiving stolen goods *(re·SEEV·ing STOH·len)* The buying, receiving, or aiding in the concealment of stolen or embezzled property, knowing it to have been stolen.

reconciliation *(rek·on·sil·ee·AY·shun)* The renewal of amicable relations.

record owner *(REK·erd)* The person who appears to be owner of the property according to the records at the registry of deeds.

recrimination *(re·krim·i·NAY·shun)* Conduct on the part of the plaintiff that constitutes a ground for divorce, which is a common law defense to an action for divorce.

recross questions *(RE·kross KWES·chens)* Further questions asked of a witness in response to redirect questions.

rectangular survey system *(rek·TANG·yoo·ler SER·vey SIS·tem)* A method of describing real property according to the property's relationship to intersecting lines running east and west (base lines) and lines running north and south (principal, or prime, meridians). Also called *government survey system.**

recuse *(re·KYOOZ)* Disqualify.

redeem *(re·DEEM)* Buy back.

redirect questions *(re·de·REKT KWESS·chenz)* Further questions asked by an examiner at a deposition in response to cross-examination questions.

refinance *(ree·FY·nanss)* To extinguish a debt obligation and replace it with new debt that has different terms, such as a different interest rate or amortization schedule.

registered limited liability partnership (RLLP) *(REJ·is·terd)* A general partnership in which only the partnership, and not the individual partners, is liable for the tort liabilities of the partnership. Also called *limited liability partnership (LLP)* and *registered partnership having limited liability (RPLL)*.

registered partnership having limited liability (RPLL) A general partnership in which only the partnership, and not the individual partners, is liable for the tort liabilities of the partnership. Also called *limited liability partnership (LLP)* and *registered limited liability partnership (RLLP)*.

rejection *(re·JEK·shun)* The refusal by an offeree of an offer.

relevant evidence *(REL·e·vent EV·i·denss)* Evidence tending to prove or disprove an alleged factual issue in dispute at trial

reliction *(re·LIK·shun)* The gradual recession of water, leaving land permanently uncovered.

remainder interest *(re·MANE·der IN·trest)* An interest that takes effect after another estate is ended.

remand *(re·MAND)* To send back.

rendition *(ren·DI·shun)* The return of fugitives to the state in which they are accused of having committed a crime by the governor of the state to which they have fled.

reorganization bankruptcy *(ree·or·ge·ni·ZAY·shun)* A method for businesses to reorganize their financial affairs, keep their assets, and remain in business. Also called Chapter 11 *bankruptcy.*

reply *(re·PLY)* The plaintiff's answer to the defendant's counterclaim.

republishing a will *(re·PUB·lish·ing)* Reestablishing a will that has been formerly revoked or improperly executed.

requirements contract *(re·KWIRE·ments KON·trakt)* A contract to buy "all the fuel (or other goods) needed for one year."

res *(rayz)* The property; the thing.

rescind *(ree·SIND)* To cancel.

rescission *(ree·SIZH·en)* Cancellation.

reservation *(rez·er·VAY·shun)* The act of keeping back.

residence *(REZ·e·denss)* A place where a person actually lives.

residuary clause *(re·ZID·joo·er·ee)* The clause in a will that disposes all of the testator's property not otherwise distributed by the will.

residuary estate *(re·ZID·joo·e·ree es·TATE)* The estate remaining after individual items have been given out by a will.

res ipsa loquitur *(rayz IP·sa LO·kwe·ter)* A legal doctrine from tort law meaning, the thing speaks for itself.

respondeat superior *(res·PON·dee·at ssoo·PEER·ee·or)* A rule of law that makes principals and employers responsible for the torts of their agents and servants committed within the scope of their authority or employment.

respondent *(re·SPON·dent)* One who is called on to answer a petition. A party against whom an appeal is brought. Also called *appellee* and *defendant in error.*

response *(re·SPONSS)* The written answer to a petition filed by a respondent.

restitution *(ress·ti·TEW·shun)* Restoration made to an injured person to his or her original position prior to a loss.

restraining order *(re·STRANE·ing)* An order forbidding a person from doing a particular act.

resulting trust *(re·ZULT·ing)* An implied trust that arises in favor of the payor when property is transferred to one person after having been paid for by another person.

retaliatory eviction *(re·TAL·ee·a·tore·ee e·VIK·shun)* The eviction of a tenant for reporting sanitary or building code violations to the authorities.

reverse *(re·VERSS)* Make void. Also called *set aside.*

reversionary interest *(re·VER·zhen·e·ree IN·trest)* A right to the future enjoyment of property that one originally owned.

revert *(re·VERT)* To go back.

reverse mortgage *(re·VERSS MORE·gej)* A mortgage in which a bank pays a homeowner the equity in the home in exchange for taking title to the home. A reverse mortgage is actually a loan, but not in the traditional sense.

revocable *(REV·e·ke·bel)* Capable of being revoked.

revocable living trust *(REV·e·ke·bel)* A trust that may be rescinded or changed by the settlor at any time during his or her lifetime.

revocation *(rev·o·KAY·shun)* The act of revoking; the taking back of an offer by an offeror before it has been accepted.

revoke *(re·VOKE)* To cancel or rescind.

RICO *(REE·coh)* Acronym for Racketeer Influenced and Corrupt Organizations Act of 1970, a federal statute designed to stop organized criminal activity from invading legitimate businesses, and providing strong sanctions and forfeiture provisions.

right of contribution *(kon·tri·BYOO·shun)* The right to share a loss among joint tortfeasors or other codefendants.

right of privacy *(PRY·ve·see)* The right to be left alone, the right to be free from uncalled-for publicity, and the right to live without unreasonable interference by the public in private matters.

right of redemption *(re·DEMP·shun)* The right to take property back. A statutory right to redeem the property even after a foreclosure sale.

right-to-die laws Laws allowing dying people to refuse extraordinary treatment to prolong life.

ripe for judgment *(JUJ·ment)* The stage of a trial at which everything has been completed except the court's decision.

ripeness doctrine *(RIPE·ness DOK·trin)* A principle under which the court will not hear a case unless there is an actual, present controversy for the court to decide.

risk of loss Responsibility in case of damage or destruction.

robbery *(ROB·e·ree)* The wrongful taking and carrying away of the personal property of another, from the other's person or personal custody, against his or her will, by threat of force or violence.

Rules *(roolz)* The American Bar Association (ABA) Model Rules for Professional Conduct.

rule against perpetuities *(per·pe·TYOO·i·teez)* The principle that no interest in property is good unless it must vest, if at all, not later than 21 years after some life in being, plus the gestation period, at the creation of the interest.

rules of civil procedure *(SIV·el pre·SEED·jer)* Regulations that govern the proceedings in civil cases.

rules of criminal procedure *(KRIM·i·nel pre·SSEED·jer)* Regulations that govern the proceedings in criminal cases.

Safe harbor provision *(safe HAR·ber pre·VI·zhun)* Protection of a party from discovery sanctions when the party cannot produce electronically stored information (ESI) because it was lost through the routine good-faith operation of an electronic information system.

sale The passing of title from the seller to the buyer for a price.

sale on approval *(e·PROOV·el)* The sale of goods that are for the buyer's use rather than for resale, and that may be returned even though they conform to the contract, and were the buyer doesn't bear the risk of loss or damage until the buyer accepts the goods.

sale or return *(re·TURN)* The sale of goods that are primarily for resale and that may be returned even though they conform to the contract, but where the buyer bears the risk of loss or damage to the goods.

same-sex marriage *(same sex MAR·ej)* The union of two same-sex partners; also called gay marriage.

satisfaction *(sat·iss·FAK·shun)* The testator's disposing of or giving to a beneficiary, while alive, that which was provided in a will, so as to make it impossible to carry out the will. Also called *advancement*.

scienter *(si·EN·ter)* Knowingly; consciously.

scope of employment *(skope ov em·PLOY·ment)* The zone in which employees operate, which is acknowledged to be broader than the employee's stated job description.

S corporation *(kor·por·AY·shun)* A corporation governed by Subchapter S of the Internal Revenue Code, in which the income of the corporation is taxed directly to the shareholders rather than to the corporation itself.

seal A mark, impression, the word "seal," or the letters L.S. placed on a written contract next to a party's signature.

search warrant *(WAHR·ent)* A written order of the court authorizing law enforcement officers to search for and seize certain property.

secondary meaning A trademark granted for a mark that isn't inherently distinctive but which, over time, has come to be so well known as associated with a company's products or services.

second-degree murder *(SEK·end-de·GREE MER·der)* Murder that is not found to be in the first degree.

second mortgage *(SEK·end MORE·gej)* A mortgage subject to a prior mortgage. Also called *junior mortgage*.

secret partner *(SEE·kret PART·ner)* A partner who takes an active part in the business, but is not known to the public as a partner.

section *(SEK·shun)* A square mile of land, containing 640 acres, in the United States government survey.

secured creditors *(se·KYOORD KRED·et·ers)* Creditors who hold mortgages and other liens.

security *(se·KYOOR·i·tee)* Assurance (usually in the form of a pledge or deposit) given by a debtor to a creditor to make sure that a debt is paid.

seisin *(SEE·zin)* Possession of a freehold.

seizure *(SEE·zhoor)* The action of the police taking evidence of criminality from a person or from his or her property.

selectpeople *(sel·EKT·pee·pel)* People elected to serve as the chief administrative authority of a town.

self-defense *(de·FENSS)* A valid excuse for the use of force in resisting attack, especially for killing an assailant.

self-proving affidavit *(a·fi·DAY·vit)* A clause in a will containing an affidavit that allows the will to be accepted by the court as valid without the testimony of witnesses.

self-proving will A will with a self-proving clause, allowing the will to be accepted as valid without the testimony of witnesses.

Senate *(SEN·it)* Part of the federal Congress which has 100 members who have six-year terms.

sentence *(SEN·tenss)* The judgment of the court imposing punishment when the defendant is found guilty in a criminal case.

separation of powers *(she·per·A·shun ov POW·ers)* The independent authority given by the U.S. Constitution to each of the three branches of government.

separation of spouses *(sep·a·RAY·shun ov SPOW·sez)* The discontinuance of cohabitation by the spouses. Also called *divorce from bed and board* and *limited divorce*.

sequester *(see·KWEST·er)* To set apart; isolate.

servant *(SER·vent)* One who performs services under the direction and control of another; an employee.

servicemark *(SER·viss·mark)* A term used to describe trademark protection for services.

service of process *(SER·viss ov PROSS·ess)* The delivering of summonses or other legal documents to the people who are required to receive them.

set aside *(a·SYD)* Make void. Also called *reverse*.

settlor *(SET·lor)* A person who establishes a trust. Also called *donor, grantor,* and *trustor.*

several *(SEV·er·el)* Separate, individual, and independent.

several liability *(SEV·er·el ly·a·BIL·i·tee)* Liability under which joint tortfeasors may be sued separately in a lawsuit.

severance of actions *(SEV·er·ense ov AK·shuns)* The separation of lawsuits or prosecutions involving multiple parties into separate, independent cases, resulting in separate, final judgments.

sexual assault *(SEKSS·yoo·el e·SALT)* Any unwanted sexual contact.

shareholders *(SHARE·hold·ers)* People who own shares in a corporation. Also called *stockholders.*

sheriff's sale *(SHER·ifss)* A sale of property at public auction conducted by a sheriff.

shipment contract *(SHIP·ment KON·trakt)* A contract under which the seller turns the goods over to a carrier for delivery to a buyer.

shop right A doctrine that gives an implied license or some ownership interest to the employers of those employees who invent patentable items in the course of their employment.

short sale *(short sale)* The sale of a home for a price lower than the loan balance; occurs only if the lender allows it.

shrinkwrap contract *(SHRINK-rap KON-trakt)* A contract for the sale of goods (often computer software), whose terms are inside the packaged product that has been shrinkwrapped, causing the buyer to accept the contract without being able to inspect it. These contracts are disfavored in the law.

signature clause *(SIG·na·cher)* The clause in a will that precedes the testator's signature. Also called *testimonium clause.*

silent partners *(SY·lent PART·nerz)* Partners who may be known to the public as partners, but who take no active part in the business.

simultaneous death *(sy·mul·TAY·nee·us)* The death of two or more people in such a way that it is impossible to determine who died before whom.

slander *(SLAN·der)* Defamation that is communicated by the spoken word.

slayer statutes *(SLAY·er STAT·shoots)* Laws enacted by legislatures, stating that murderers cannot inherit from their victims.

sodomy *(SOD·e·mee)* Oral or anal copulation. An act that some state statutes still describe as an "abominable and detestable crime against nature." Sodomy is a crime when it is included in sexual assault statutes.

solemnized *(SAW·lem·nized)* Performed in a ceremonial fashion with witnesses present.

sole proprietorship *(pro·PRY·e·ter·ship)* An unincorporated business that is owned by one person.

soliciting *(so·LIH·sih·ting)* The act of live-contact attempts to seek new legal clients.

sororicide *(so·ROR·i·side)* The killing of one's sister.

soundness of mind Sufficient mental ability to make a will.

special administrator *(SPESH·el ad·MIN· iss·tray·tor)* A person appointed by the court to handle the affairs of an estate for a limited time only to take care of urgent affairs.

special agent *(SPESH·el AY·jent)* An agent authorized to carry out a single transaction or to perform a specified act.

special damages *(SPE·shel DAM·e·jez)* Damages that are capable of exact dollar-amount calculations, such as the cost of hospital and medical treatment and any loss of wages.

special warranty deed *(SPESH·el WAR·en·tee)* A deed containing warranties under which the grantor guarantees that the property is free from all encumbrances made during the time that he or she owned the property and agrees to defend the title only against claims through him or her. Also called *limited warranty deed.*

specific legacy *(spe·SIF·ic LEG·a·see)* A gift by will of a particular article of personal property.

specific performance *(spe·SIF·ic per·FORM·enss)* An order by the court commanding a breaching party to do that which he or she agreed to do under the terms of the contract.

spendthrift *(SPEND·thrift)* One who spends money profusely and improvidently.

spendthrift trust A trust designed to provide a fund for the maintenance of a beneficiary and at the same time to secure it against the beneficiary's improvidence or incapacity.

sponge tax *(spunj taks)* A tax that soaks up money for the state that the estate is being given credit for in any event.

spousal support *(SPOWZ·el su·PORT)* An allowance made to a divorced spouse by a former spouse for support and maintenance. Also called *alimony.*

spray trust A trust that allows the trustee to decide, in the trustee's discretion, how much will be given to each beneficiary. Also called *discretionary trust* and *sprinkling trust.*

springing power *(SPRING·ing POW·er)* A power in a durable power of attorney that does not become effective until the person making it actually becomes incapacitated.

sprinkling trust *(SPRINK·ling)* A trust that allows the trustee to decide, in the trustee's discretion, how much will be given to each beneficiary. Also called *discretionary trust* and *spray trust.*

stalking *(STAW·king)* The willful, malicious, and repeated following, harassing, and threatening of another person, intended to place the person in fear of death or serious bodily injury.

standing to sue *(STAND·ing to SOO)* The condition that exists when a party has a tangible, legally protected interest at stake in a lawsuit.

statute *(STAT·shoot)* A law passed by a legislature.

statute of frauds *(STAT·shoot of frawdz)* The law that deems that certain contracts must be in writing (and signed) to be enforceable.

statute of limitations *(STAT·shoot ov lim·i·TAY·shunz)* A time limit, set by statute, within which suit must be commenced after the cause of action accrues.

statute of repose *(STAT·shoot ov re·POSE)* An absolute time limit for bringing a cause of action regardless of when the cause of action accrues.

statutory arson *(STAT·shoo·tore·ee AR·sen)* The burning of a building other than a dwelling house or the burning of one's own house to collect insurance.

statutory burglary *(STAT·shoo·tore·ee BUR·gler·ee)* Burglary that does not contain all of the elements of common law burglary.

statutory rape *(STAT·shoo·tore·ee)* Sexual intercourse with a child under the age set by state statute regardless of whether the child consented or not. Also called *unlawful sexual intercourse.*

stipulate *(STIP·yoo·late)* Agree.

stipulation *(stip·yoo·LA·shun)* An agreement between the parties to an action regulating any matter relative to the proceedings.

stock certificate *(ser·TIF·i·ket)* A document that evidences ownership of stock in a corporation.

stockholders *(STAWK·hold·erz)* People who own shares in a corporation. Also called *shareholders.*

stop and frisk rule A rule that allows police officers who believe that a person is acting suspiciously and could be armed to stop and frisk that person for weapons, without a search warrant.

straight bankruptcy *(strayt BANK·rupt·see)* A proceeding designed to liquidate a debtor's property, pay off creditors, and discharge the debtor from most debts. Also called *Chapter 7 bankruptcy* and *liquidation.*

strict liability *(strikt ly·a·BIL·i·tee)* Liability for an act that causes harm, without regard to fault or negligence. Also called *absolute liability.*

strict liability crime *(strikt ly-a-BIL-i-tee krime)* A crime that has no criminal intent element. It was created to protect the public from acts thought to be so dangerous as to be categorized as crimes, regardless of the intent of the actor.

sublease *(SUB·leess)* **(to sublet, v.)** A lease given by a lessee to a third person conveying the same interest for a shorter term than the period for which the lessee holds it. Also called *underlease.*

sublet To give a lease to a third person conveying the same interest for a shorter term than the period for which the lessee holds it.

subpoena *(suh·PEEN·uh)* An order commanding a person to appear and testify in a legal action. Also called *subpoena ad testificandum.*

subpoena ad testificandum *(suh·PEEN·a ad tes·te·fe·KAN· dem)* An order commanding a person to appear and testify in a legal action. Also called *subpoena.*

subpoena duces tecum *(suh·PEEN·a DOO·sess TEK·um)* An order commanding a person to appear and bring certain papers or other materials that are pertinent to a legal action.

subscribe *(sub·SKRIBE)* To sign below or at the end; to write underneath.

substantial performance *(sub·STAN·shel per·FORM·enss)* A doctrine allowing a contracting party to sue the other party for breach, even though slight omissions or deviations were made in the first party's own performance of the contract.

substituted service *(SUB·sti·tew·ted SER·viss)* A type of service in which the summons and complaint are delivered to the defendant's agent, mailed, or published in a newspaper.

successor personal representative *(suk·SESS·or PER·son·al rep·re·ZEN·ta·tiv)* A person appointed to succeed a previously appointed personal representative.

suicide *(SOO·i·side)* The deliberate taking of one's own life.

summarily *(sum·EHR·i·lee)* Quickly.

summary administration *(SUM·e·ree ad·min·iss·TRAY·shun)* An informal method used to settle estates that do not exceed $75,000.

summary ejectment *(SUM·e·ree e·JEKT·ment)* The legal action used by landlords to evict tenants. Also called *dispossessory warrant proceedings, forcible entry and detainer, summary process,* and *unlawful detainer.*

summary judgment *(SUM·er·ee JUJ·ment)* An immediate decision by the court, without going to trial, based on the papers filed by the parties.

summary proceeding *(SUM·e·ree pre·SEED·ing)* A short and simple trial.

summary process *(SUM·e·ree PROSS·ess)* The legal action used by landlords to evict tenants. Also called *dispossessory warrant proceedings, forcible entry and detainer, summary ejectment,* and *unlawful detainer.*

summation *(sum·AY·shun)* Final statement by an attorney summarizing the evidence that has been introduced. Also called *closing argument.*

summons *(SUM·enz)* A formal notice to the defendant that a lawsuit has begun and that the defendant must file an answer within the number of days set by state law or else lose the case by default.

supervening cause *(soo·per·VEEN·ing)* A new occurrence that became the proximate cause of the injury.

Supremacy Clause *(soo·PREM·i·see)* A clause in the U.S. Constitution making the U.S. Constitution and federal laws the supreme law of the land.

sureties *(SHOOR·e·tees)* People who stand behind the personal representative in the event that he or she fails to do the job.

surety *(SHOOR·e·tee)* One who undertakes to stand behind another—that is, to pay money or do any other act in the event that his or her principal fails to meet an obligation.

suretyship *(SHOOR-e-tee SHIP)* Promises to a creditor to pay someone else's debts.

surrogate *(SER·o·get)* A person authorized to act on behalf of another and subject to the other's control. Also called *agent.*

Surrogate's Court *(SER·o·gets)* A name given in some states to the court that exercises the function of settling decedents' estates.

suspended sentence *(suss·PEN·ded SEN·tenss)* A sentence that is given formally, but not actually served.

sustain *(sus·TANE)* To support.

syndicate *(SIN·de·ket)* A relationship in which two or more people combine their labor or property for a single business undertaking. Also called *co-venture, joint enterprise,* and *joint venture.*

tacking The addition of a previous occupants' possession to one's own possession in order to meet the statutory period for adverse possession.

talesmen and taleswomen *(TAYLZ·men and taylz·WO·men)* Bystanders or people from the county at large chosen by the court to act as jurors when there are not enough people left on the venire.

tangible personal property *(TAN·je·bel PER·son·al PROP·er·tee)* Property that has substance and that can be touched.

tax credit *(tax CREH·dit)* Prepaid income tax (such as that deducted from dividend payment) that can be offset against the total income tax payable by an entity.

temporary custody *(TEM·po·rare·ee KUSS·te·dee)* Custody of a child awarded to a parent on a temporary basis, pending the outcome of a divorce or separation action.

tenancy at will *(TEN·en·see)* An estate in real property for an indefinite period.

tenancy by the entirety *(TEN·en·see by the en·TY·re·tee)* A type of joint tenancy held by spouses that offers protection against attachment and that cannot be terminated by one spouse alone.

tenancy for years *(TEN·en·see)* An estate in real property for a definite, or fixed, period no matter how long or how short.

tenancy from year to year *(TEN·en·see)* An estate in real property that continues for successive periods until one of the parties terminates it by giving notice to the other party. Also called *periodic tenancy.*

tenancy in partnership *(TEN·en·see in PART·ner·ship)* Ownership in which each person has an interest in partnership property and is a co-owner of such property.

tenant *(TEN·ent)* A person who has temporary possession of and an interest in real property of another under a lease. Also called *lessee.*

tenant at sufferance *(TEN·ent at SUF·er·enss)* A tenant who wrongfully remains in possession of the premises after a tenancy has expired. Also called *holdover tenant.*

tenants in common *(TEN·entz in KOM·on)* Two or more persons holding an undivided interest in property, with each owner's interests going to his or her heirs on death rather than to the surviving co-owners.

tender of payment *(TEN·der)* To offer to the other party the money owed under a contract.

tender of performance *(per·FORM·ens)* To offer to do that which one has agreed to do under the terms of a contract.

tenements *(TEN·e·mentz)* Everything of a permanent nature that may be possessed and, in a more restrictive sense, houses or dwellings.

testament *(TESS·te·ment)* A legal instrument stating a person's wishes as to the disposition of personal property at death. A will.

testamentary capacity *(test·e·MEN·ter·ee ca·PASS·i·tee)* Sufficient mental ability to make a will.

testamentary disposition *(test·e·MEN·ter·ee diss·pe·ZI·shun)* A gift of property that is not to take effect until the one who makes the gift dies.

testamentary trust *(test·e·MEN·ter·ee)* A trust that is created by will and that comes into existence only on the death of the testator.

testate *(TES·tate)* The condition of a person having made a valid will.

testator *(TES·tay·tor)* A man who makes or has made a testament or will.

testatrix *(TES·tay·trix)* A woman who makes or has made a testament or will.

testimonial evidence *(tes·ti·MOH·nee·el EV·i·denss)* Oral testimony of witnesses made under oath in open court.

testimonium clause *(tess·ti·MOH·nee·um)* The clause in a will that immediately precedes the testator's signature. Also called *signature clause.*

third party *(PAR·tee)* In agency law, one who deals with an agent in making a contract with the agent's principal.

third-party beneficiary *(ben·e·FISH·ee·air·ee)* Someone for whose benefit a promise is made, but who is not a party to the contract.

threat of force *(thret ov forss)* Intimidation designed to put someone in fear that he or she will be the victim of violence; equivalent to force.

time is of the essence *(ESS·ens)* Time is critical.

time-sharing A fee simple ownership of a unit of real property in which the owner can exercise the right of possession for only an interval, such as a week or two, each year. Also called *interval ownership.*

title *(TY·tel)* Ownership.

title insurance An insurance policy sold by a title company that protects the purchaser against past problems or defects with the property's title.

title theory of mortgages *(TY·tel THEE·ree ov MORE·ge·jes)* The legal theory that a mortgage is a conveyance of title, which becomes void on payment of the obligation. Also called *common law theory of mortgages.*

toll *(tohl)* To bar, defeat, or take away.

tort A wrong against an individual.

tortfeasor *(tort·FEE·zor)* One who commits a tort.

tortious *(TOR·shus)* Wrongful; implying or involving tort.

tortious bailee *(TOR·shus bay·LEE)* A person who is wrongfully in possession of another's personal property.

Totten trust *(TOT·en)* A bank account in the name of the depositor as trustee for another person.

township *(TOUN·ship)* A six-square-mile portion of land in the United States government survey.

tract of land *(trakt)* A large piece of land.

trade fixture *(FIKS·cher)* Personal property, necessary to carry on a trade or business, that is physically attached to real property, but does not become part of the real property.

trademark *(TRADE·mark)* Any word, name, symbol, or device used by a business to identify goods and distinguish them from those manufactured or sold by others.

trademark dilution The unauthorized use of a trademark in a commercially similar way that reduces or is likely to reduce the public's perception of the trademark.

trade secret *(SEE·kret)* A plan, process, or device that is used in business and is known only to employees who need to know the secret to accomplish their work.

transitory action *(TRAN·zi·tore·ee AK·shun)* A lawsuit that may be brought in more than one place as long as the court in which it is heard has proper jurisdiction.

treason *(TREE·zun)* Levying war against the United States or giving aid and comfort to its enemies.

treble damages Generally, three times the actual damages amount. Certain statutes grant treble damages.

trespass *(TRESS·pass)* The intentional and unauthorized entry by a person onto the land of another.

trespass de bonis asportatis *(de BO·nis as·por·TAH·tis)* An action brought to recover damages from a person who has taken goods or property from its rightful owner.

trial docket *(tryl DOK·et)* The calendar of cases that are ready for trial. Also called *trial list*.

trial list *(tryl list)* The calendar of cases that are ready for trial. Also called *trial docket*.

trust A right of ownership to property held by one person for the benefit of another.

trust deed An instrument that creates a living trust. Also called *trust indenture*.

trustee *(trus·TEE)* A person who holds legal title to property in trust for another.

trustee in bankruptcy *(trus·TEE in BANK·rupt·see)* A person appointed by a bankruptcy court to hold the debtor's assets in trust for the benefit of creditors.

trustee process *(trus·TEE PROSS·ess)* A procedure for attaching the defendant's property that is in the hands of a third person.

trust fund The body, principal sum, or capital of a trust. Also called *corpus, trust property,* and *trust res*.

trust indenture *(in·DEN·cher)* An instrument that creates a living trust. Also called *trust deed*.

trustor *(trus·TOR)* A person who establishes a trust. Also called *donor, grantor,* and *settlor*.

trust principal *(PRIN·se·pel)* The body, principal sum, or capital of a trust. Also called *corpus, trust fund, trust property,* and *trust res*.

trust property *(PROP·er·tee)* The body, principal sum, or capital of a trust. Also called *corpus, trust fund, trust principal,* and *trust res*.

trust res *(reyz)* The body, principal sum, or capital of a trust. Also called *corpus, trust fund, trust principal,* and *trust property*.

ultra vires act *(UL·tra VY·rees)* A corporate act committed outside of the corporation's authority.

unconscionable *(un·KON·shun·e·bel)* An act or contract that is so harshly one-sided and unfair that the court's conscience is shocked.

underlease *(UN·der·leess)* A lease given by a lessee to a third person, conveying the same interest for a shorter term than the period for which the lessee holds it. Also called *sublease*.

undisclosed principal *(un·dis·KLOZED PRIN·se·pel)* A person or company on whose behalf an agent acts, but who is not revealed to the third party.

undue influence *(un·DEW IN·flew·enss)* The overcoming of a person's free will by misusing a position of trust and taking advantage of the other person who is relying on the trust relationship.

unenforceable contract *(un·en·FORSS·e·bel KON·trakt)* A contract that cannot be enforced for some legal reason.

Uniform Bar Exam (UBE) *(YOON-i·form bar x-am)* – An exam coordinated by the National Conference of Bar Examiners that includes the Multistate Bar Exam and uniformly tests knowledge and skills required to practice law and results in a portable score that can be transferred for admission to practice law in those jurisdictions that accept the UBE.

Uniform Commercial Code (UCC) *(YOON·i·form ke·MERSH·el kode)* A uniform code adopted in every state, that governs various commercial transactions.

Uniform Probate Code (UPC) *(YOON·i·form PROH·bate kode)* A uniform code attempting to standardize and modernize laws relating to the affairs of decedents, minors, and certain other people who need protection.

unilateral contract *(yoon·i·LAT·er·el KON·trakt)* A contract containing one promise in exchange for an act.

unilateral mistake *(yoon·i·LAT·er·el miss·TAKE)* A mistake made by only one party to a contract.

unintentional torts *(un·in·TEN·shun·al)* Torts that are committed accidentally and due to negligence.

unit deed *(YOON·it)* A deed to an individual condominium unit being transferred.

units *(YOON·its)* The individual portions of a condominium that are owned separately in fee simple by individual owners.

unity of interest *(YOON·i·tee ov IN·trest)* Equal interest in a property by all owners.

unity of possession *(YOON·i·tee ov po·SESH·en)* Equal rights to possession of the entire property by all owners.

unity of time *(YOON·i·tee)* The condition that exists when all owners of a property take title at the same time.

unity of title *(YOON·i·tee ov TY·tle)* The condition that exists when all owners of a property receive title from the same instrument.

unjust enrichment *(un·JUST en·RICH·ment)* The situation that occurs when one person retains money, property, or other benefit that in equity and justice belongs to another.

unlawful detainer *(de·TAYN·er)* The legal action used by landlords to evict tenants. Also called *dispossessory warrant proceedings, forcible entry and detainer, summary ejectment,* and *summary process*.

unlawful sexual intercourse *(un·LAW·ful SEKS·yoo·el IN·ter·korss)* Sexual intercourse with a child under the age set by state statute regardless of whether the child consented or not. Also called *statutory rape*.

unlimited liability *(un·LIM·i·ted ly·a·BIL·i·tee)* Liability that has no bounds.

U.S. Constitution *(you ess kon·stih· TWO·shun)* The written document created by America's founders at the constitutional convention of 1787 and which was ratified by the 13 states. It creates our federal system of government. The first governing document in world history that creates representative democracy.

U.S. Supreme Court *(you ess sue·PREEM)* The highest court in the federal judicial system and which is created by Article III of the U.S. Constitution.

usury *(YOO·zer·ee)* The charging of a greater amount of interest than is allowed by law.

uttering *(UT·er·ing)* Offering a forged, negotiable instrument to another person, knowing it to be forged and intending to defraud.

utility patent A patent granted for the invention of a new process or item of manufacture, and which lasts for 20 years from the date of the application filing.

uxoricide *(uks·OR·i·side)* The killing of one's wife.

vacate *(VAY·kate)* To annul.

valid *(VAL·id)* Good; having legal effect.

variable-rate mortgage *(VAR·ee·a·bel-rate MORE·gej)* A mortgage with an interest rate that fluctuates according to changes in an index to which it is connected. Also called *flexible-rate mortgage.*

variance *(VAYR·ee·enss)* An exception to a zoning regulation.

vendor *(VEN·der)* A person who transfers property or goods by sale.

vendee *(ven·DEE)* A purchaser or buyer of property or goods.

venire *(ven·EYE·ree)* The large group of people from whom a jury is selected for a trial. Also called *array, jury panel,* and *jury pool.*

venue *(VEN·yoo)* The place where the trial is held; the location from which jurors are summoned.

verbatim *(ver·BATE·im)* Word for word.

verdict *(VER·dikt)* The decision of a jury.

verdict contrary to law *(KON·trare·ee)* A verdict that is incorrect as a matter of law.

(ver·i·fi·KAY·shun) A written statement or declaration made under penalty of perjury, often placed at the end of a document (such as a pleading), that the underlying document is true.

vest To give an immediate, fixed right of present or future enjoyment.

vested *(VES·ted)* Fixed or absolute; not contingent.

veto *(VEE·tow)* Latin for "I forbid." The right of the President of the United States to strike down a piece of legislation.

viable *(VY·e·bel)* Having the appearance of being able to live.

vicarious liability *(vy·KEHR·ee·us)* Liability that is imputed to principals and employers because of the wrongdoings of their agents and employees.

victim's impact statement *(VIK·temz IM·pakt)* A statement to the court, at the time of sentencing, relative to the impact that the crime had on the victim or the victim's family.

void Not good; having no legal effect.

voidable *(VOID·e·bel)* Capable of being disaffirmed or voided.

voir dire *(vwar deer)* To speak the truth. The examination of jurors by the court to see that they stand indifferent.

voluntary administrator *(VOL·en·ter·ee ad·MIN·is·tray·tor)* A person who undertakes the informal administration of a small estate.

voluntary bankruptcy *(VOL·en·ter·ee BANK·rupt·see)* A bankruptcy proceeding that is initiated by the debtor.

voluntary manslaughter *(VOL·en·ter·ee MAN·slaw·ter)* The unlawful killing of another, without malice, when an intention to kill exists, but through violence that is the result of what is often termed "the heat of passion."

wage earner's plan *(wayj ER·ners)* A plan for the installment payments of outstanding debts under a Chapter 13 bankruptcy.

waive a spouse's will *(SPOW·sez)* To renounce or disclaim a spouse's will.

waiver *(wave-er)* voluntary relinquishment of a known privilege or right.

warrant *(WAHR·ent)* To give assurance.

warranty of fitness for a particular purpose *(WAHR·en·tee ov FIT·ness)* An implied warranty, given when a buyer relies on any seller's skill and judgment in selecting goods, that the goods will be fit for a particular purpose.

warranty of habitability *(WAR·en·tee ov hab·i·ta·BIL·i·tee)* An implied warranty by a landlord that the premises are fit for human habitation.

warranty of merchantability *(WAR·en·tee ov mer·chent·a·BIL·e·tee)* An implied warranty, given by merchants in all sales unless excluded, that goods are fit for the ordinary purpose for which such goods are used.

warranty of title *(WAR·en·tee ov TY·tel)* A guarantee that title is good, that the transfer is rightful, and that no unknown liens on the goods exist.

waste The abuse or destructive use of property that is in one's rightful possession.

white collar crime *(hwite KOL·er krime)* Types of crimes such as racketeering, mail fraud, wire fraud, and computer fraud. The term was coined in 1939 to refer to crimes committed by those with high social status and respect in the course of their employment.

will Originally, a legal instrument stating a person's wishes as to the disposition of real property at death, but now referring to both real and personal property.

will and testament *(TES·te·ment)* Under early English law, a legal instrument that disposed of both real and personal property at death.

will contest A suit over the allowance or disallowance of a will.

willful torts *(WIL·ful)* Torts that are committed intentionally. Also called *intentional torts.*

willful, wanton, and reckless conduct *(WIL·ful WON·ten REK·less KON·dukt)* The intentional commission of an act that a reasonable person knows would cause injury to another. Also called *culpable negligence.*

winding-up period *(WINE·ding-up PEER·ee·ed)* A period during which partnership assets are liquidated, debts are paid, an accounting is made, and any remaining assets are distributed among the partners.

wire fraud *(frawd)* Wire fraud is a federal and state crime involving using wire communications facilities in carrying out a scheme to defraud. Wire fraud is similar to mail fraud except that the instrumentality of the crime is the telephone or other electronic communication technology.

writ A written order of a court, returnable to the same, commanding the performance or nonperformance of an act.

writ of attachment *(a·TACH·ment)* A written order to the sheriff, commanding the sheriff to attach the real or personal property of the defendant.

writ of certiorari *(ser·sho·RARE·ee)* An order from a higher court to a lower court to deliver its records to the higher court for review.

writ of execution *(ek·se·KYOO·shen)* A written order to the sheriff, commanding the sheriff to enforce a judgment of the court.

writ of garnishment *(GAR·nish·ment)* A written order of a court ordering a garnishee not to give out money or property held for another, but to appear and answer the plaintiff's suit.

writ of venire facias *(ven·EYE·ree FAY·shes)* A written order to cities and towns to provide a designated number of jurors for the next sitting of the court.

wrongful death action *(RONG·ful deth AK·shun)* A suit brought by a decedent's personal representative for the benefit of the decedent's heirs, claiming that death was caused by the defendant's negligent or intentionally wrongful act.

wrongful death statutes *(RONG·ful deth STAT·shoots)* Legislative enactments that govern wrongful death actions.

year-and-a-day rule The rule requiring that a victim's death must have occurred within a year and a day after the attack occurred in order for a defendant to be convicted of homicide.

GLOSSARY OF LATIN TERMS AND PHRASES

a fortiori. with stronger reason; much more — ah for·she·OR·i

a posteriori. from the effect to the cause; from what comes after — ah po·steer·ee·OR·i

a prendre. to take; to seize. — ah PRAWN·dre

a priori. from the cause to the effect; from what comes before — ah pri·OR·i

ab initio. from the beginning — ab in·ish·ee·oh

actio criminalis. a criminal action — AK·shee·oh kri·mi·NAH·lis

actio damni injuria. an action for damages — AK·shee·oh DAM·ni in·JUR·ee·ah

actio ex delicto. an action arising out of fault — AK·shee·oh eks da·lik·toh

ad damnum. to the damage; money loss claimed by the plaintiff — ad DAHM·num

ad hoc. for one special purpose — ad HOK

ad infinitum. indefinitely; forever — ad in·fin·ITE·em

ad litem. for the suit — ad LY·tem

ad respondendum. to make answer — ad ree·spon·DEN·dem

additur. addition by a judge to the amount of damages awarded by a jury — AH·di·toor

amicus curiae. friend of the court — a·MEE·kes KYOOR·ee

animus furandi. intent to steal — AN·i·mus fer·AN·di

animus testandi. intent to make a will — AN·i·mus tes·TAN·di

anno Domini. (a.d.) in the year of our Lord — AN·oh DOM·eh·ni

ante. before — AN·tee

arguendo. in arguing — ar·gyoo·EN·doh

assumpsit. he promised — a·SUMP·sit

bona fide. in good faith — BONE·ah FIDE

caveat. beware — KA·vee·at

caveat emptor. let the buyer beware — KA·vee·at EMP·tor

caveat venditor. let the seller beware — KA·vee·at VEN·de·tor

certiorari. to be informed of; to be assured — ser·sho·RARE·ee

cestui que trust. beneficiary of a trust — SES·twee KAY

compos mentis. sound of mind — KOM·pes MEN·tis

consortium. fellowship of husband and wife — kon·SORE·shum

contra. against — KON·trah

coram. before; in the presence of — KOR·em

corpus delicti. body of the crime — KORE·pus de·LIK·tie

corpus juris. body of law — KORE·pus JOOR·ess

cum testamento annexo. with the will annexed — kum tes·ta·MENT·o an·EKS·o

damnum absque injuria. loss without injury in the legal sense — DAM·num AHB·skwee in·JOO·ree·ah

de facto. in fact; actually — dee FAK·toh

de jure. according to law; rightfully — dee JUR·ee

de minimus. of little importance — dee MIN·e·mes

de novo. anew, afresh, a second time — dee NOH·voh

dictum. unessential statement or remark in a court decision — DIK·tum

doli capax. capable of criminal intent; able to distinguish between right and wrong — DO·li KAY·paks

duces tecum. bring with you — DOO·sess TEK·um

ergo. therefore; hence — EHR·go

et al. abbreviation for et alii; and others — et AHL

et seq. abbreviation for et sequentia; and the following — et SEK

et ux. abbreviation for et uxor; and wife — et UKS

et vir. and husband — et VEER

ex contractu. out of a contract — eks kon·TRAK·too

ex delicto. out of a tort or wrong — eks de·LIK·toh

ex officio. by virtue of an office — eks oh·FISH·ee·oh

ex parte. apart from; one side only — eks·PAR·tay

ex post facto. after the fact — eks post FAK·toh

forum non conveniens. inconvenient court — for·em non kon·VEEN·yenz

gratis. without reward or consideration — GRAT·is

habeas corpus. you have the body — HAY·bee·ess KORE·pus

habendum. to have thus; clause in a deed that defines extent of ownership — ha·BEN·dum

ibid. abbreviation for ibedim; in the same place — IBid

id. abbreviation for idem; the same — id

in camera. in chambers; in private — in KAM·er·ah

in curia. in court — in KYOOR·ee·ah

in flagrante delicto. in glaring fault; a crime in full light — in flay·GRAN·tee de·LIK·toh

in initio. at the beginning — in i·NISH·ee·o

in litem. during the suit — in LY·tem

in loco. in the place of — in LOH·ko

in loco parentis. in the place of a parent — in LOH·ko pa·REN·tis

in pari delicto. in equal fault — in pah·ree de·LIK·toh

in personam. against or with reference to a person — in per·SOH·nem

in re. in the matter of; concerning — in RAY

in rem. against the thing — in REM

in toto. in the whole; in total — in TOH·toh

infra. below, beneath — IN·frah

injuria absque damno. wrong without damage — in·JUR·ee·ya abs·kwee DAM·no

inter alia. among other things — IN·ter AY·lee·ah

inter vivos. between the living — IN·ter VY·vose.

ipse dixit. he himself says it — IP·see DIK·sit

ipso facto. by the fact itself — IP·soh FAK·toh

juris. of right; of law — JOOR·is

jus habendi. right to have something — jes he·BEN·di

jus tertii. right of a third party — jes ter·SHEE·yi

lis pendens. pending suit — liss PEN·denz

locus sigilli. place of the seal — LOH·kus se·JIL·i

malum in se. wrong in itself — MAL·um in SEH

malum prohibita. wrong because it is prohibited — MAL·um pro·HIB·i·ta

mandamus. we command; order by a court commanding a public official to perform a duty — man·DAY·mus

mens rea. guilty mind — menz RAY·ah

modus operandi. manner of operation — MOH·dus op·er·AN·di

mortis causa. by reason of death — MORE·tis KAW·sa

n.b. abbreviation of nota bene; note well; observe

nil. contraction of nihil; nothing — nil

nisi. unless — NIE·sie

nolle prosequi. prosecution not pursued — NO·lee PROSS·e·kwi

nolo contendere. I will not contest the action — NO·lo kon·TEN·de·ree

non assumpsit. not undertaken or promised — non a·SUMP·sit

non compos mentis. not of sound mind; insane — non KOM·pes MEN·tiss

non obstante verdicto. notwithstanding the verdict — non ob·STAN·tay ver·DIK·toh

non sequitur. it does not follow — non SEK·wi·ter

nudum pactum. naked promise; bare agreement without consideration — NOO·dum PAK·tum

nul tort. no wrong has been done — nul TORT

nulla bona. no goods — null·a·BONE·ah

nunc pro tunc. now for then — nunk pro tunk

obiter dictum. words of a prior decision unnecessary for the decision of the case — OH·bih·ter DIK·tum

onus probandi. burden of proof — OH·nus pro·BAN·di

pendente lite. pending suit — pen·DEN·tay lie·tay

per annum. by the year — per AN·num

per capita. by the head — per KA·pi·tah

per curiam. by the court — KYOO·ree·am

per diem. by the day — per DEE·em

per quod. whereby — per KWOD

per se. by itself; taken alone — per SAY

per stirpes. by representation — per STER·peez

post mortem. after death — post MOR·tem

prima facie. at first sight; on the face of it — PRY·muh FAY·shee

pro bono publico. for the public good — pro BO·no POOB·lek·oh

pro forma. as a matter of form — pro FORM·ah

pro rata. proportionately — pro RAY·ta

pro se. for himself or herself — pro say

pro tanto. for as far as it goes — pro TAHN·tah

pro tempore (pro tem.). temporary; for the time being — pro TEM·po·re

quantum meruit. as much as he or she deserves — KWAN·tum MEHR·oo·it

quasi. as if; almost as it were — KWAY·zie

quasi in rem. as if against the thing — KWAY·zie in REM

quid pro quo. something for something; one thing for another — kwid proh KWOH

res. thing, object — reyz

res gestae. things that have been done — reyz JESS·tee

res ipsa loquitur. thing speaks for itself — res IP·sa LO·kwe·ter

res judicata. thing decided or judged (also res adjudicata) — res joo·di·KAY·ta

respondeat superior. let the superior answer — re·SPOND·ee·yat se·PEER·ee·or

retraxit. he or she has withdrawn — re·TRAK·sit

scienter. knowingly — si·EN·ter

scilicet. to wit; namely; that is to say — SIL·e·set

scintilla. spark — sin·TIL·ah

secundum. according to — se·KUN·dem

seriatim. separately; one by one — see·ree·AH·tem

sic. thus; in such a manner — sik

sigillum. seal — se·JIL·um

simplex obligato. single obligation — SIM·pleks ob·le·GAT·oh

sine qua non. without which, the thing cannot be — SI·nee kway NON

stare decisis. to stand by the decision — STAHR·ee de·SY·sis

sua sponte. of its own motion — SOO·ah SPON·tay

sub curia. under law — sub KURE·ee·ah

sub judice. under judicial consideration — sub JOO·de·say

sub silentio. under silence — sub se·LEN·shee·oh

subpoena. under penalty; a process to cause a witness to appear and give testimony — suh·PEEN·a

subpoena duces tecum. bring with you; a subpoena ordering a witness to produce a paper — suh·PEEN·a DOO·sess TEK·um

sui generis. one of a kind; unique — SOO·ee JEN·e·ris

sue juris. of one's own right; not under guardianship — SOO·ee JOOR·is

supersedeas. writ commanding a stay in the proceedings — soo·per·SEE·dee·es

supra. above; earlier — SOO·prah

ultra vires. beyond the powers — UL·tra VY·res

venire facias. order to the sheriff to bring people to court to serve as jurors — ven·EYE·ree FAY·she·as

versus. against — VER·ses

viz. abbreviation for videlicit; to make more specific that which has been previously stated — viz

volenti non fit injuria. volunteer suffers no wrong — voh·LEN·tie nonfit in·JOOR·ee·ah

INDEX